C000126650

Windows NT 4
Programming
from the Ground Up

About the Author ...

Herbert Schildt is the world's leading programming author. He is an authority on the C and C++ languages, a master Windows programmer, and an expert on Java. His programming books have sold nearly two million copies worldwide and have been translated into all major foreign languages. He is the author of numerous best-sellers, including *C: The Complete Reference*, *C++: The Complete Reference*, *C++ from the Ground Up*, *MFC Programming from the Ground Up*, *Windows 95 Programming in C and C++*, and many others. He is also co-author of the highly acclaimed *Java: The Complete Reference*.

Windows NT 4
Programming
from the Ground Up

Herbert Schildt

Osborne **McGraw-Hill**

Berkeley New York St. Louis San Francisco
Auckland Bogotá Hamburg London Madrid
Mexico City Milan Montreal New Delhi Panama City
Paris São Paulo Singapore Sydney
Tokyo Toronto

Osborne/**McGraw-Hill**
2600 Tenth Street
Berkeley, California 94710
U.S.A.

For information on translations or book distributors outside the U.S.A., or to arrange bulk purchase discounts for sales promotions, premiums, or fundraisers, please contact Osborne/**McGraw-Hill** at the above address.

Windows NT 4 Programming from the Ground Up

1234567890 DOC 9987

ISBN 0-07-882298-X

Publisher	**Copy Editor**
Brandon A. Nordin	Erik Van Eaton
Editor-in-Chief	**Proofreader**
Scott Rogers	Pat Mannion
Acquisitions Editor	**Indexer**
Wendy Rinaldi	Sheryl Schildt
Project Editor	**Computer Designer**
Cynthia Douglas	Peter F. Hancik
Editorial Assistant	**Illustrator**
Ann Sellers	Roberta Steele
Technical Editor	**Cover Design**
Raj Rajagopal	Timm F. Sinclair

Contents at a Glance

Table of Contents

Preface

Windows NT is a force to be regarded seriously. It defines the standard for high-end, 32-bit computing. It is also one of the most challenging programming environments you are likely to encounter. Of course, the rewards of meeting this challenge are significant.

Windows NT is a finely tuned, carefully thought-out piece of software. It is flexible yet powerful, and its ease of use masks sophisticated internals. Its stability and built-in security features make it the operating system favored by corporate users. Of course, many software developers use it for the same reasons.

This book teaches you how to write programs for the latest release of Windows NT: version 4. It starts with the basics, covers all of the essentials, and includes many advanced topics. If you have never written a Windows program before, then you will want to read this book in order, starting at Chapter 1. Resist the temptation to skip ahead, because each new chapter builds upon material presented earlier. If you have experience programming another version of Windows, such as Windows 3.1 for DOS, then you will be able to advance more quickly. However, you should still skim through the introductory chapters because, in some areas, Windows NT 4 differs significantly from other versions of Windows.

What Programming Background Is Required?

To use this book effectively, you must be an experienced C programmer, and knowledge of C++ is strongly recommended. C and C++ are *the* languages of Windows NT. If you feel that your C/C++ skills are a little weak, then take some time to fortify them. Programming for Windows NT relies heavily on such things as structures, unions, and pointers. If you are not comfortable with these items, you will have trouble learning to write Windows NT programs.

What Software Is Needed?

To compile the code in this book you will need a C++ compiler capable of producing programs for Windows NT 4. The compilers used to test the code in this book are Microsoft's Visual C++ 4.2 and Borland's C++ version 5.0.

The examples in this book are written in standard C/C++ and they can be compiled as either C or C++ programs. That is, you may use either the .C or the .CPP extension. Thus, whether you are ultimately going to be writing your application in C or C++, the code in this book is compatible.

When compiling the programs in this book, use the default compiler settings suggested for compiling Windows-based code. Also, do not select any class library support, such as MFC or OWL. Specifically, when using Microsoft Visual C++, select Application when creating a new project. For Borland C++, select Application for the target and make sure that no Frameworks are checked.

Watch for the In Depth Boxes

Scattered throughout this book you will find special "In Depth" boxes. In Depth boxes delve deeper into specific NT 4 programming topics. Often they explain options, enhancements, or alternative methods that can be applied to an example described in the book. They also serve as pointers to areas of NT programming that you will want to explore further on your own.

Source Code Free on the Web

The source code contained in this book is available free online at **http://www.osborne.com**.

For Further Study

Windows NT 4 Programming from the Ground Up is just one of the many programming books written by Herbert Schildt. Here are some others that you will find of interest.

To learn more about Windows programming, we recommend the following:

Schildt's Windows 95 Programming in C and C++

Schildt's Advanced Windows 95 Programming in C and C++

If you want to learn more about the C language, then the following titles will be of interest.

C: The Complete Reference

The Annotated ANSI C Standard

Teach Yourself C

To learn more about C++, you will find these books especially helpful.

C++: The Complete Reference

Teach Yourself C++

C++ from the Ground Up

Expert C++

Borland C++: The Complete Reference

If you are interested in Java, then you will want to read

Java: The Complete Reference

Co-authored by Herbert Schildt and Patrick Naughton

When you need solid answers, fast, turn to Herbert Schildt, the recognized authority on programming.

CHAPTER 1

Windows NT 4 Overview

Windows NT 4 is the latest version of Microsoft's high-end 32-bit operating system. This book teaches you how to write programs for it.

As a practical guide to Windows NT 4 programming, this book does not spend much time on NT's theoretical aspects, architecture, or design elements unless they relate directly to the creation of programs. That said, the first step in learning to program for Windows NT 4 is understanding in a general way how it operates, what design concepts it embodies, and how it manages your computer. Since many programming tasks involve porting from or to Windows NT 4, it is also important to know how Windows NT 4 differs from its predecessor, Windows NT 3.51, and how it relates to Windows 95 and Windows 3.1. For these reasons, this chapter presents a brief overview of the theory and operation of Windows NT 4.

Keep in mind that Windows NT 4 is a very large and sophisticated operating system. It cannot be fully described in any single volume. This book describes those aspects of Windows NT 4 that are common to all programs, used frequently, or are important innovations. That is, it covers those things all Windows NT 4 programmers must know. It also gives you a firm foundation on which to build your further study of this important operating environment.

NOTE: For a complete and well-written discussion of the theoretical aspects and underpinnings of Windows NT, I suggest Helen Custer's *Inside Windows NT* (Redmond, WA: Microsoft Press, 1993).

Windows NT Key Features

From the start, Windows NT was designed to be a portable operating system, able to span several diverse hardware platforms. It can be easily extended or enhanced as hardware evolves. It was also designed to be stable, resilient, and reliable. In short, it was engineered to remedy many of the failings found in previous operating systems, including Windows 3.1.

Perhaps the single most important characteristic of Windows NT is that it is a full-fledged, 32-bit operating system. Because of this, Windows NT left behind many of the quirks and problems associated with the older 16-bit systems. It also avoids the 16-bit/32-bit hybrid code found in Windows 95.

A primary design goal of Windows NT was compatibility with other PC-based operating systems and the programs designed to run under them. As a result, Windows NT was designed to allow downward compatibility with the large base of existing PC applications. Windows NT contains

1

emulators that allow it to automatically (and seamlessly) execute programs written for the following operating systems:

♦ Windows 3.1 (including 16-bit applications)

♦ DOS

♦ OS/2

♦ POSIX (Portable Operating System Interface based on UNIX)

Windows NT 4 is also able to run Windows 95 programs. Windows NT automatically creates the right environment for the type of program you run. For example, when you execute a DOS program, Windows NT automatically creates a 16-bit DOS virtual machine and windowed command prompt in which the program runs.

Another design consideration of Windows NT was security. Windows NT provides a secure environment that meets the DOD C2 security classification. This level of security provides for password-protected log on, resource access control and ownership, and an activity log that provides an audit tail of certain activities. Also, memory is cleared before reuse. Further, memory used by one program is protected from memory used by another. It is not possible for one program to "corrupt" another or to interrogate the contents of another program's variables.

One other important aspect of Windows NT is that it can run on computers with multiple CPUs. While this type of computer is not common at the time of this writing, it may be in the future.

Windows NT is Based on the Client/Server Model

Windows NT can effectively and efficiently operate your computer, provide compatibility with other operating systems, and allow for extensibility because its organization is based on the *client/server* model. As you may know, there are various ways to organize an operating system, including layered and client/server. The layered approach layers the operating system components in a top-down fashion. While Windows NT does incorporate layering, its architecture is primarily that of a client/server operating system. Before explaining how the client/server system works, two important terms, *user mode* and *kernel mode*, must be defined.

NOTE: In the context of this chapter, the terms *client* and *server* refer to parts of an operating system and not to a networked environment.

User and Kernel Modes

Most operating systems define two modes of execution. Application programs run in one mode, system code runs in the other. In short, the purpose of having two modes is to enforce the control of the operating system over the system. That is, this scheme prevents an application program from improperly accessing a system resource.

User mode is the non-privileged mode of execution used by applications.

When you write an application program, it executes in *user mode*. A user-mode process has restrictions on what actions it may perform. For example, in Windows NT, a user-mode program cannot directly interact with the hardware of the computer or even with the lower levels of the operating system. Instead, it interacts only with the operating system interface. In this way, an application program is both managed and prevented from inappropriately calling a low-level system routine or directly accessing a hardware resource. Therefore, user mode has access to the hardware and the low-level system services only through the kernel interface.

Kernel mode is the mode of execution used by the kernel and privileged subsystems.

By contrast, the operating system kernel runs in *kernel mode*. The kernel provides the low-level functionality of the operating system. It has access to all system services and to the hardware itself. Code running in kernel mode has full access to the machine and runs at the highest priority setting.

In a layered operating system, the entire operating system runs in kernel mode and application programs run in user mode. This means that all system services run in kernel mode.

Windows NT breaks from the layered model in the following way: it moves many of the operating system services out of the kernel. Therefore, the kernel for Windows NT is small. Further, the services moved out of the kernel now execute in user mode. By moving system services out of the kernel, it is possible to update, modify, or enhance a service without altering the operating system kernel. This makes Windows NT extensible and portable. It also makes it easy to emulate several different operating systems. Since the services are no longer running in kernel mode, but rather in user mode, they are called *servers*.

Understanding the Client/Server Model

Since Windows NT moves many of its system services out of kernel mode and transforms them into servers running in user mode, you might think that a Windows NT application program would be free to interact with these servers directly. This is not the case. Even though Windows NT servers run in user mode, they are still fully protected and isolated from application

A client/server operating system is based on message passing between applications (clients) and servers (which provide services) through the kernel.

programs. In fact, each server runs in its own address space. The way this protection is provided is the essence of the client/server model.

The client/server approach is based on the passing of messages between the application program and the servers it uses. The only way that an application program (i.e., the client) can access a system service (i.e., the server) is to pass a message to the kernel. The kernel then passes this message to the appropriate server, which processes the message and sends a response back to the kernel. The kernel then returns the information to the application program. Thus, an application program can never directly communicate with a server. All communication is routed through the kernel and any improper access is screened out. In this way, the operating system still retains complete control of the computer.

To help you better understand the client/server relationship, here is a simplified example: Assume an application program wants to open a file. To do this, the program sends a message to the kernel telling it to open the file. The kernel routes this message to the appropriate server. This server opens the file and obtains a handle to it. This handle is then sent to the kernel, which passes it back to the application program. This scheme is depicted in Figure 1-1. By using the client/server approach, it is possible to protect and control access to low-level system services while reducing the size of the kernel. Although Windows NT's actual implementation of this process is a bit more complex, it still operates essentially the same way.

Since services are moved out of the kernel and into servers, the kernel in a client/server-based operating system is usually quite small. In fact, it is sometimes called the *microkernel* for this reason.

The client/server model offers several advantages over the layered approach. First, it allows the various servers to be maintained and updated without altering the kernel. In essence, new servers can be "dropped-in" as needed without altering the low-level portions of the kernel. Second, by keeping the kernel small, it helps make the kernel portable. Finally, the client/server approach makes it easier to provide compatibility with other operating systems. To understand why, consider this: since the servers run in user mode and are not part of the kernel, the actual servers can be easily changed. Further, there may be multiple servers for the same services, each one emulating a different operating system. Thus, when a program designed for a different operating system is run, its requests for kernel services can be easily and automatically routed to the correct server. It is this approach that allows Windows NT to support OS/2 and POSIX programs.

One last point: Windows NT servers are also referred to as *protected subsystems*. This term reflects that fact that NT servers are separate processes.

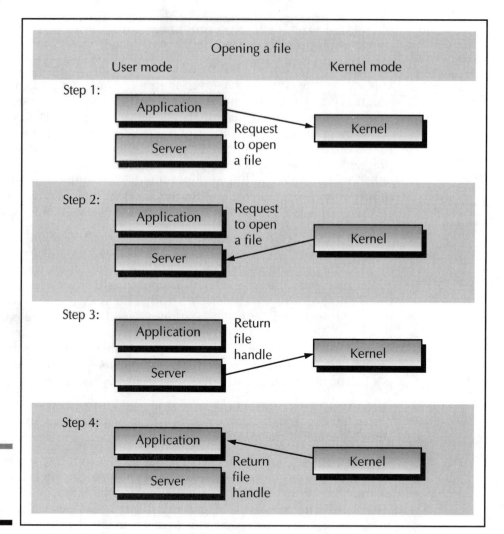

How the
client/server
model works
Figure 1-1.

The Windows NT Architecture

The architecture of Windows NT 4 is shown in Figure 1-2. As you can see,
it is constructed in accordance with the client/server model. Applications
supported by Windows NT and the protected subsystems run in user mode.
The subsystem labeled CSR is the *client/server runtime subsystem*. This is the
subsystem that handles 32-bit Windows programs. The OS/2 and POSIX
subsystems also utilize the CSR.

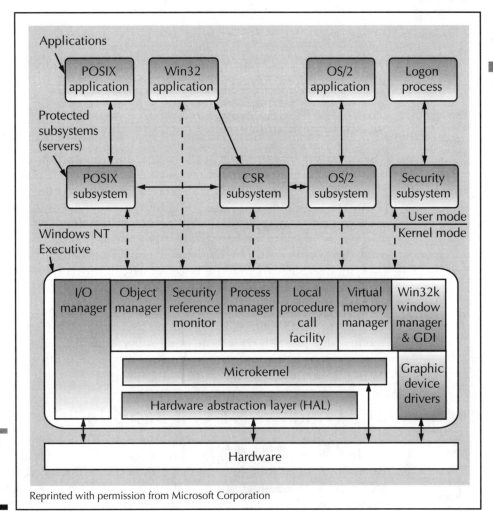

The Windows
NT 4
architecture
Figure 1-2.

Reprinted with permission from Microsoft Corporation

The Windows NT Executive

The part of
Windows NT
that runs in
kernel mode
is called the
Windows NT
Executive.

The part of Windows NT that runs in kernel mode is called the *Windows NT Executive*, or *NT Executive*, for short. It contains the following items:

◆ The process manager

◆ The object manager

◆ The hardware abstraction layer

◆ The I/O manager

◆ The virtual memory manager

◆ The security subsystem

◆ The local procedure call subsystem

◆ The Win32k executive

◆ The kernel itself (also called the microkernel)

The process manager manages the execution tasks and threads in the system. The object manager handles various system resources. The hardware abstraction layer (HAL) contains code that interfaces with the hardware itself. The local procedure call (LPC) subsystem manages the passing of messages between applications and servers as just described. I/O, security, and virtual memory are handled by their respective components. The Win32k executive is a new addition to the NT Executive that has been added by Windows NT 4. Its purpose is explained later. Finally, there is the kernel itself, which runs the lowest-level details associated with Windows NT, such as scheduling threads and handling interrupts.

Within the NT Executive, the hardware abstraction layer and the kernel are the foundation upon which the other subsystems are built. Thus, Windows NT utilizes a small amount of the layered model at its lowest level. Windows NT is not a pure client/server operating system.

The Windows NT Call-Based Interface

The API defines the programming interface to Windows NT.

Your application programs communicate with Windows NT through a *call-based interface*. The Windows NT call-based interface is an extensive set of system-defined functions that provide access to operating system features. Collectively, these functions are called the *Application Programming Interface*, or API. The API contains several hundred functions that your application program calls in order to communicate with Windows NT. These functions perform all necessary operating system-related activities, such as memory allocation, outputting to the screen, creating windows, and the like. There is a subset to the API called the GDI (Graphics Device Interface), which is the part of Windows that provides device-independent graphics support.

Win16 is the 16-bit API used by Windows 3.1.

Win32 is the 32-bit API used by Windows NT.

There are two basic flavors of the API in common use: Win16 and Win32. Win16 is the older, 16-bit version of the API. Win32 is the modern, 32-bit version. Win16 is used by Windows 3.1. Windows NT programs use Win32. For the most part, Win32 is a superset of Win16. Indeed, most of their functions are called by the same name and are used in the same way.

However, even though similar in spirit and purpose, the two APIs differ in two fundamental ways. First, Win32 supports 32-bit, flat addressing while Win16 supports only the 16-bit, segmented memory model. This difference has caused several API functions to be widened to accept 32-bit arguments and return 32-bit values. Also, a few API functions have had to be altered to accommodate the 32-bit architecture. Second, API functions have also been added to support thread-based multitasking, security, and the other enhanced Windows NT features. If you are new to Windows programming in general, then these changes will not affect you significantly. However, if you will be porting code from Windows 3.1 to Windows NT, then you will need to carefully examine the arguments you pass to each API function.

NOTE: The Win16 API is still available for use by Windows 3.1 applications running in a DOS environment. However, Windows NT programs must use the Win32 API.

Dynamic Link Libraries (DLLs)

The Win32 API functions are contained in *Dynamic Link Libraries*, or DLLs, which each program has access to when it is executed. The Win32 API functions are stored in a relocatable format within a DLL. During the compilation phase, when your program calls an API function, the linker does not add the code for that function to the executable version of your program. Instead, it adds loading instructions for that function, such as what DLL it resides in and its name. When your program is executed, the necessary API routines are also loaded by the Windows NT loader. In this way, each application program does not need to contain the actual API code while stored on disk. The code is added only when the program is loaded into memory for execution.

The Windows NT API is implemented in DLLs.

Dynamic linking has some very important benefits. First, since virtually all programs will use the API functions, DLLs prevent disk space from being wasted by the significant amount of duplicated object code that would be created if the API functions were actually added to each program's executable file on disk. Second, updates and enhancements to Windows NT can be accomplished by changing the dynamic link library routines. Existing application programs do not need to be recompiled. Third, using the dynamic link approach makes the emulation of other operating systems an easier task.

NT DLLs Are Different

A stub is a
small piece
of code that
transforms an
API call into
a message.

Although all versions of Windows use a DLL-based API to provide access to the operating system, they differ in what actually occurs when an API function is called. While this difference does not affect the way you write programs, it is something worth knowing. In other versions of Windows the DLL actually contains the API functions which are linked to an executable program when it is run. However, in Windows NT, the DLLs contain short pieces of code called *stubs*. Each stub transforms the application's function call into a message, which is then passed to the NT Executive. The NT Executive then passes this message to the appropriate server. After the server completes its necessary activities as requested by the message, the result is returned to the NT Executive, which then passes it back to the application program via the DLL stub. Although the mechanism differs substantially from other versions of Windows, it does not affect the way you program for Windows NT.

Understanding Processes and Threads

As you almost certainly know, Windows NT is a multitasking operating system. As such, it can run two or more programs concurrently. Of course, on systems with only one processor, the programs share the CPU and do not technically run simultaneously. However, Windows NT can be run on computers that have two or more CPUs. When this is the case, programs may actually execute simultaneously. Since you can't always know what type of computer your program will be executed on, it is best to assume that true, concurrent execution is always occurring.

A process is
essentially a
program that
is executing.

Windows NT supports two forms of multitasking: process based and thread based. A *process* is a program that is executing. Because Windows NT can multitask processes, it can run more than one program at a time. Thus, Windows NT supports the traditional, process-based multitasking with which you are probably familiar.

A thread is an
individual unit
of executable
code within
a process.

Windows NT's second form of multitasking is thread based. A *thread* is a dispatchable unit of executable code. The name comes from the concept of a "thread of execution." All processes have at least one thread. However, a Windows NT process may have several.

Since Windows NT multitasks threads and each process can have more than one thread, this means that it is possible for one process to have two or more pieces of itself executing simultaneously. Therefore, when working with Windows NT, it is possible to multitask both programs and pieces of a single program. You can take advantage of this to write very efficient programs.

File Systems

DOS and versions of Windows prior to NT support only the FAT file system. FAT stands for File Allocation Table. The FAT system is inherently limited because of its need to maintain compatibility with DOS. Windows NT supports the FAT file system, but it also includes the NTFS (NT File System) designed specifically for Windows NT. There are many advantages to using the NT File System, including security. However, most programs won't be affected by the file system being used.

One other point: Windows NT was initially designed to also support the HPFS (High-Performance File System), which was created for OS/2. However, HPFS has several disadvantages when compared with the NTFS and is not widely used. At the time of this writing, the HPFS is no longer supported by Windows NT 4. (But this situation is subject to change.)

New Features Added by Version 4

Windows NT 4 adds many new features to the NT environment. The single most important change is the use of the Windows 95-style user interface. The new interface is not only snappier and more visually appealing, but it also makes better use of the limited space available on the desktop. It also uses a slightly redesigned form of the window. Since much of the code associated with any Windows application deals with the user interface, this is an important upgrade.

Because of the new user interface, several new control elements, called *common controls*, have taken on increased importance. Common controls include such things as toolbars, tree views, wizards, progress bars, and tooltips. While the common controls were technically available prior to Windows NT 4, they were not extensively used. Today, this situation is different because the common controls are widely used by the various components and accessories that come with Windows NT 4. In order for your applications to have the modern look and feel of the new user interface, they must also employ the common controls. As you will see, several chapters of this book are devoted to them.

Windows NT 4 also adds a number of new utilities, such as the Internet Explorer and various other accessories. While these are important additions for the user of Windows NT, they don't affect how you will program for it.

An Architectural Difference Between NT 4 and Earlier Versions

Although it won't affect how you write programs, the architecture of Windows NT 4 differs slightly from earlier versions. This change is designed to improve performance. In previous versions of Windows, Win32 programs used the Win32 protected subsystem (i.e., server), which, among other things, handled window management and graphics. In Windows NT 4 the window and graphics-handling code (i.e., the GDI) have been moved into the Windows NT Executive. By moving the window and graphics-handling code to the NT Executive, application programs bypass a portion of the message-passing overhead associated with displaying information on the screen. As mentioned, this new subsystem is called the *Win32k executive*. Since less functionality is now contained in the Win32 subsystem, it has been renamed the CSR subsystem.

One final point: although some functionality has been moved out of user mode and into kernel mode, Windows NT is still a client/server-based operating system. It's just that precise placement of certain pieces of code has changed.

How Windows NT Differs from Windows 95

Frankly, programming for Windows NT 4 is very similar to programming for Windows 95. Both use the Win32 API library. Both use the new user interface. Both support thread-based multitasking. There are, however, two important differences. First, Windows 95 is not a full-fledged 32-bit system; Windows NT 4 is. Windows 95 contains some 16-bit code. However, for most intents and purposes, this difference has only a marginal effect on how you program. The second difference is security. Windows NT supports security, Windows 95 does not. While this won't make a difference for most simple programs, it may affect real applications. For example, Windows 95 programs never need to worry about whether a user has the proper security rights to access some object. In Windows NT, this can be a concern.

One other area of difference between Windows NT 4 and Windows 95 is that Windows 95 is not built on the client/server model. As such, it is less resilient and robust. (That is, it is easier to crash!) However, because Windows 95 bypasses the overhead associated with the client/sever approach, it will, on average, run applications faster than Windows NT 4. Although the performance improvements mentioned in the preceding section have narrowed the gap, it still exists (and probably always will). This is the price paid for stability and security.

At the time of this writing, Windows 95 does not support the NT File System. But this difference has little effect on how you write programs.

For the most part, a program written for Windows 95 runs fine under Windows NT and vice versa. However, there are some things to watch out for. Several are mentioned throughout the course of this book.

How Windows NT Differs from Windows 3.1

Although Windows 3.1 is a thing of the past, many readers will be familiar with it. Many will also be porting older Windows 3.1 code to Windows NT 4. For this reason, we will spend a little time describing the main differences between the two. As you can probably already guess, Windows NT 4 differs rather significantly from Windows 3.1 in many areas. But the good news is that you will still program for Windows NT 4 in much the same way that you did for Windows 3.1.

1

Several of the most important differences are described here.

32-Bit Versus 16-Bit Addressing

Perhaps the biggest difference between programming for Windows NT and programming for Windows 3.1 is that Windows 3.1 is a 16-bit operating system that is built on top of DOS. Windows NT is a full-fledged, stand-alone 32-bit operating system. Thus, Windows 3.1 uses the old Win16 API and Windows NT 4 uses the modern Win32 API. Fortunately, most of the API functions that the two have in common work in the same way, but Win32 supplies many more. It also supplies improvements to the API not found in Win16.

Windows NT 4 supports 32-bit addressing and uses virtual memory. Windows 3.1 uses a 16-bit segmented addressing mode. For many application programs these differences will have little effect. For others, the effect will be substantial. Frankly, while the transition may not be painless, you will find it much easier to program for the Windows NT 32-bit memory model.

Because Windows NT supports 32-bit addressing it makes sense that integers are also 32 bits long. This means that types **int** and **unsigned** will be 32 bits, not 16 bits long as is the case for Windows 3.1. If you want to use a 16-bit integer, it must be declared as **short**. (Portable **typedef** names are provided by Windows NT for these types.) If you will be porting code from the 16-bit environment, you will need to check your use of integers because they will automatically be expanded from 16 to 32 bits and side effects may result.

Another result of 32-bit addressing is that pointers no longer need to be declared as **near** or **far**. Any pointer can access any part of memory.

Multitasking

A second big difference between Windows 3.1 and Windows NT concerns the way multitasking is accomplished. Windows 3.1 uses a non-preemptive approach to task switching. This means that a Windows 3.1 task must

Preemptive
multitasking
gives each
task a slice
of CPU time.
Non-preemptive
multitasking
relies upon each
application
to relinquish
control of
the CPU.

manually return control to the scheduler in order for another task to run. In other words, a Windows program retains control of the CPU until it decides to give it up. Therefore, an ill-behaved program could monopolize the CPU. By contrast, Windows NT 4 uses preemptive, time-slice based tasking. In this scheme, tasks are automatically preempted by Windows NT 4 and the CPU is then assigned to the next task (if one exists). Preemptive multitasking is generally the superior method because it allows the operating system to fully control tasking and prevents one task from dominating the system. Most programmers view the move to preemptive multitasking as a step forward.

Another difference is that Windows 3.1 does not support thread-based multitasking. Windows 3.1 can only multitask processes (i.e., programs). When porting to Windows NT, you will want to watch for ways to apply multithreading to enhance the performance of your programs.

In addition to the two major changes just described, Windows NT differs from Windows 3.1 in some other, less dramatic ways, which are described next.

Multiple Input Queues

Input queues hold messages, such as those generated by a keypress or a mouse activation, until they can be sent to your program. In Windows 3.1, there is just one input queue for all tasks running in the system. However, Windows NT supplies each thread with its own input queue. The advantage to each thread having its own queue is that no one process can reduce system performance by responding to its messages slowly. Although multiple input queues are an important addition, this change has no direct impact on how you program for Windows NT.

Consoles

Windows NT supports a special type of window called a *console*. Windows 3.1 does not. A console window provides a standard text-based interface, command-prompt environment. However, aside from being text-based, a console window acts and can be manipulated like other windows.

Flat Addressing

Windows NT applications have available to them 4 gigabytes of virtual memory. Further, this address space is *flat*. Unlike Windows 3.1 or DOS, which use segmented memory, Windows NT treats memory as linear. Because this address space is virtualized, each application has access to as much memory as it could reasonably need. While the change to flat addressing is mostly transparent to the programmer, it does relieve much of the tedium and frustration of dealing with the old, segmented approach.

File Systems

Windows 3.1 only supports the FAT file system.

Changes to Messages and Parameter Types

Because Windows NT uses 32-bit addressing, some messages passed to a Windows NT program will be organized differently than they are when passed to a Windows 3.1 program. Also, the parameter types used to declare a window function have changed because of the move to 32-bit addressing.

Terminology

To avoid confusion, for the remainder of this book the following terms will be used. When discussing a feature of Windows NT in general, the term *Windows NT* is used. When a feature specific to version 4 is described, then *Windows NT 4* is used. When discussing all Windows environments generically or when the difference doesn't matter, the term *Windows* will be used.

Challenging but Rewarding

Now that the stage has been set, we are ready to begin writing programs. If you have never written any type of Windows program before, then the next few chapters will contain many unfamiliar concepts and require the use of several new programming techniques. Just be patient. Although a bit overwhelming at first, before long, writing programs for Windows NT 4 will be second nature. Even though Windows NT is a challenging environment, it is also a rewarding one. Once mastered, you will possess some of the most highly-demanded skills in the programming profession.

CHAPTER 2

Windows NT
Programming
Fundamentals

17

This chapter introduces Windows NT programming. It has two purposes. First, it discusses how a program must interact with Windows NT and what rules must be followed by every Windows NT application. Secondly, it develops an application skeleton that will be used as a basis for the other Windows NT programs developed in this book. As you will see, all Windows NT programs share several common traits. It is these shared attributes that will be contained in the application skeleton.

We will begin by explaining the two ways that you can write Windows NT programs.

Two Ways to Program for NT

There are two ways you can write programs for Windows NT. The first is to use the API functions defined by Win32. In this approach, your NT programs directly utilize the API and explicitly handle all of the details associated with a Windows NT program. This is the method used by this book.

The second way to program for Windows NT uses a special C++ class library, which encapsulates the API. By far the most popular Windows programming class library is MFC (Microsoft Foundation Classes). MFC, and other Windows class libraries, are powerful development tools that offer significant advantages in some situations. However, they are best employed after you have gained a firm foundation in Windows programming using the API. The reasons for this are simple.

First, there is a fundamental architecture that all Windows programs share. MFC masks many elements of this architecture. Knowledge of the Windows architecture is crucial to long-term programming success. For example, it makes debugging a Windows application easier. Second, using the API gives you detailed and complete control over how your program executes. Some types of low-level control are not possible using MFC. Third, all Windows NT programming environments support API-based programming; it is a portable skill. Fourth, the API can be programmed in C, which is a standardized language. MFC requires C++, which is (at the time of this writing) not yet standardized. Because many software shops require the use of a standardized language, it prevents their use of MFC. Finally, if you can program for Windows NT using the API, you can more easily learn to use MFC or any other class library. Simply put: You cannot be a top-notch, professional Windows NT programmer unless you know how to program using the API.

NOTE: If you are interested in MFC programming, I suggest my book *MFC Programming from the Ground Up* (Berkeley, CA, Osborne/McGraw-Hill, 1996). It contains a detailed description of MFC programming and includes coverage of the new user interface elements supported by Windows NT 4.

Windows NT Programming Perspective

2

At its most fundamental level, the goal of Windows NT (and Windows in general) is to enable a person who has basic familiarity with the system to sit down and run virtually any application without prior training. Toward this end, Windows provides a consistent interface to the user. In theory, if you can run one Windows-based program, you can run them all. Of course, in actuality, most useful programs will still require some sort of training in order to be used effectively, but at least this instruction can be restricted to *what* the program *does*, not *how* the user must *interact* with it. In fact, much of the code in a Windows application is there just to support the user interface.

It is important to understand that not every program that runs under Windows NT will automatically present the user with a Windows-style interface. Windows defines an environment that encourages consistency, but does not enforce it. For example, it is possible to write Windows programs that do not take advantage of the standard Windows interface elements. To create a Windows-style program, you must purposely do so using the techniques described in this book. Only those programs written to take advantage of Windows will look and feel like Windows programs. While you can override the basic Windows design philosophy, you had better have a good reason to do so, because your program will be violating one of the primary goals of Windows: a consistent user interface. In general, if you are writing application programs for Windows NT, they should conform to the standard Windows style guidelines and design practices.

Let's look at some of the essential elements that define the Windows NT application environment.

The Desktop Model

With few exceptions, the point of a window-based user interface is to provide on the screen the equivalent of a desktop. On a desk may be found several different pieces of paper, one on top of another, often with fragments of different pages visible beneath the top page. The equivalent of the desktop in Windows NT is the screen. The equivalents of pieces of paper are windows on the screen. On a desk you may move pieces of paper about, maybe switching which piece of paper is on top or how much of another is exposed to view. Windows NT allows the same type of operations on its windows. By selecting a window you can make it current, which means putting it on top of all other windows. You can enlarge or shrink a window, or move it about on the screen. In short, Windows lets you control the surface of the screen the way you control the surface of your desk. All conforming programs must allow these types of user interactions.

The Mouse

Like all preceding versions of Windows, Windows NT uses the mouse for almost all control, selection, and drawing operations. Of course, the keyboard may also be used, but Windows is optimized for the mouse. Thus, your programs must support the mouse as an input device wherever possible. Fortunately, most of the common tasks, such as menu selection, scroll bars, and the like, automatically utilize the mouse.

Icons, Bitmaps, and Graphics

Icons and bitmaps are graphical images.

Windows NT encourages the use of icons, bitmaps, and other types of graphics. The theory behind these items is found in the old adage: a picture is worth a thousand words. An icon is a small symbol that is used to represent some operation, resource, or program. A bitmap is a rectangular graphics image often used to simply convey information quickly to the user. However, bitmaps can also be used as menu elements. Windows NT supports a full range of graphics capabilities, including the ability to draw lines, rectangles, and circles. The proper use of these graphical elements is an important part of successful Windows programming.

Menus, Controls, and Dialog Boxes

A menu is a list from which the user may select an option.

Windows provides several standard items that allow user input. They are the menu, various types of controls, and the dialog box. Briefly, a menu displays options from which the user makes a selection. Since menus are standard elements in Windows programming, built-in menu-management functions are provided in the API. Your program does not need to handle all of the clerical overhead associated with menus by itself.

A control allows a specific type of user interaction.

A control is a special type of window that allows a specific type of user interaction. Examples are push buttons, scroll bars, edit windows, and check boxes. Like menus, the controls defined by Windows are nearly completely automated. Your program can use one without having to handle the details.

A dialog box is used when non-menu input is required.

A dialog box is a special window that allows more complex interaction with the application than that allowed by a menu. For example, your application might use a dialog box to input a filename. Dialog boxes are typically used to house controls. With few exceptions, non-menu input is accomplished via a dialog box.

The Components of a Window

Before moving on to specific aspects of Windows NT programming, a few important terms need to be defined. Figure 2-1 shows a standard window with each of its elements pointed out. Notice that the style of a window in NT 4 differs slightly from that provided by earlier versions. This is because Windows NT 4 uses the new "Windows 95-style" user interface.

All windows have a border that defines the limits of the window and is used to resize the window. At the top of the window are several items. On the far left is the system menu icon (also called the title bar icon). Clicking on this box causes the system menu to be displayed. To the right of the system menu box is the window's title. At the far right are the minimize, maximize, and close boxes. (Versions of Windows NT prior to 4 did not include a close box.) The client area is the part of the window in which your program activity takes place. Windows may also have horizontal and vertical scroll bars that are used to move text through the window.

How Windows NT and Your Program Interact

When you write a program for many operating systems, it is your program that initiates interaction with the operating system. For example, in a DOS

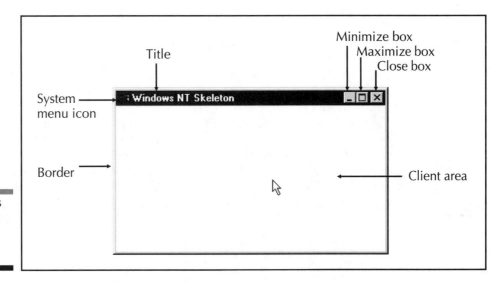

The elements of a standard window

Figure 2-1.

program, it is the program that requests such things as input and output. Put differently, programs written in the "traditional way" call the operating system. The operating system does not call your program. However, in a large measure, Windows NT works in the opposite way. It is Windows NT that calls your program. The process works like this: a program waits until it is sent a *message* by Windows NT. The message is passed to your program through a special function that is called by Windows NT. Once a message is received, your program is expected to take an appropriate action. While your program may call one or more Windows NT API functions when responding to a message, it is still Windows NT that initiates the activity. More than anything else, it is the message-based interaction with Windows NT that dictates the general form of all Windows NT programs.

Windows communicates with your program by sending it messages.

There are many different types of messages that Windows NT may send your program. For example, each time the mouse is clicked on a window belonging to your program, a mouse-clicked message will be sent. Another type of message is sent each time a window belonging to your program must be redrawn. Still another message is sent each time the user presses a key when your program is the focus of input. Keep one fact firmly in mind: as far as your program is concerned, messages arrive randomly. This is why Windows NT programs resemble interrupt-driven programs. You can't know what message will be next.

Some Windows NT Application Basics

Before developing the Windows NT application skeleton, some basic concepts common to all Windows NT programs need to be discussed.

WinMain( )

WinMain( ) is where a Windows program begins execution.

All Windows NT programs begin execution with a call to **WinMain( )**. (Windows programs do not have a **main( )** function.) **WinMain( )** has some special properties that differentiate it from other functions in your application. First, it must be compiled using the **WINAPI** calling convention. (You will also see **APIENTRY** used. Currently, they both mean the same thing.) By default, functions in your C or C++ programs use the C calling convention. However, it is possible to compile a function so that it uses a different calling convention. For example, a common alternative is to use the Pascal calling convention. For various technical reasons, the calling convention Windows NT uses to call **WinMain( )** is **WINAPI**. The return type of **WinMain( )** should be **int**.

PORTABILITY: In older Windows 3.1 programs, the calling convention used for **WinMain( )** was **PASCAL**. However, this should be changed to **WINAPI** when porting existing applications to Windows NT.

The Window Procedure

All Windows NT programs must contain a special function that is *not* called by your program, but is called by Windows NT. This function is generally called the *window procedure* or *window function*. It is through this function that Windows NT communicates with your program. The window function is called by Windows NT when it needs to pass a message to your program. The window function receives the message in its parameters. All window functions must be declared as returning type **LRESULT CALLBACK**. The type **LRESULT** is a **typdef** that (at the time of this writing) is another name for a long integer. The **CALLBACK** calling convention is used with those functions that will be called by Windows NT. In Windows terminology, any function that is called by Windows is referred to as a *callback* function.

2

A window procedure is a function called by Windows, not by your program.

PORTABILITY: Older Windows 3.1 code specifies a window function as **LONG FAR PASCAL**. You should change this to **LRESULT CALLBACK** when porting to NT 4.

In addition to receiving the messages sent by Windows NT, the window function must initiate any actions indicated by a message. Typically, a window function's body consists of a **switch** statement that links a specific response to each message that the program will respond to. Your program need not respond to every message that Windows NT will send. For messages that your program doesn't care about, you can let Windows NT provide default processing. Since there are hundreds of different messages that Windows NT can generate, it is common for most messages simply to be processed by Windows NT and not your program.

All messages are 32-bit integer values. Further, all messages are accompanied by any additional information that the message requires.

Window Classes

When your Windows NT program first begins execution, it will need to define and register a *window class*. (Here, the word *class* is not being used in its C++ sense. Rather, it means *style* or *type*.) When you register a window class, you are telling Windows NT about the form and function of the

A window class
defines the
style of a
window.

window. However, registering the window class does not cause a window to come into existence. To actually create a window requires additional steps.

The Message Loop

As explained earlier, Windows NT communicates with your program by sending it messages. All Windows NT applications must establish a *message loop* inside the **WinMain( )** function. This loop reads any pending message from the application's message queue and then dispatches that message back to Windows NT, which then calls your program's window function with that message as a parameter. This may seem to be an overly complex way of passing messages, but it is, nevertheless, the way all Windows programs must function. (Part of the reason for this is to return control to Windows NT so that the scheduler can allocate CPU time as it sees fit rather than waiting for your application's time slice to end.)

The message
loop retrieves
messages
from your
application's
message queue.

Windows Data Types

As you will soon see, Windows NT programs do not make extensive use of standard C/C++ data types, such as **int** or **char ***. Instead, all data types used by Windows NT have been **typdef**ed within the WINDOWS.H file and/or its subordinate files. This file is supplied by Microsoft (and any other company that makes a Windows NT C/C++ compiler) and must be included in all Windows NT programs. Some of the most common types are **HANDLE, HWND, UINT, BYTE, WORD, DWORD, LONG, BOOL**, **LPSTR**, and **LPCSTR**. **HANDLE** is a 32-bit integer that is used as a handle. As you will see, there are numerous handle types, but they are all the same size as **HANDLE**. A *handle* is simply a value that identifies some resource. For example, **HWND** is a 32-bit integer that is used as a window handle. Also, all handle types begin with an H. **BYTE** is an 8-bit unsigned character. **WORD** is a 16-bit unsigned short integer. **DWORD** is an unsigned long integer. **UINT** is an unsigned 32-bit integer. **LONG** is another name for **long**. **BOOL** is an integer. This type is used to indicate values that are either true or false. **LPSTR** is a pointer to a string and **LPCSTR** is a **const** pointer to a string.

In addition to the basic types described above, Windows NT defines several structures. The two that are needed by the skeleton program are **MSG** and **WNDCLASSEX**. The **MSG** structure holds a Windows NT message and **WNDCLASSEX** is a structure that defines a window class. These structures will be discussed later in this chapter.

PORTABILITY: **UINT** is a 32-bit unsigned integer when compiling Windows NT programs. It is a 16-bit unsigned integer if you compile your code for Windows 3.1. Remember this when porting applications to Windows NT.

A Windows NT Skeleton

Now that the necessary background information has been covered, it is time to develop a minimal Windows NT application. As stated, all Windows NT programs have certain things in common. In this section a skeleton is developed that provides these necessary features. In the world of Windows programming, application skeletons are commonly used because there is a substantial "price of admission" when creating a Windows program. Unlike DOS programs, for example, in which a minimal program is about 5 lines long, a minimal Windows program is approximately 50 lines long.

2

A minimal Windows NT program contains two functions: **WinMain( )** and the window function. The **WinMain( )** function must perform the following general steps:

1. Define a window class.
2. Register that class with Windows NT.
3. Create a window of that class.
4. Display the window.
5. Begin running the message loop.

The window function must respond to all relevant messages. Since the skeleton program does nothing but display its window, the only message that it must respond to is the one that tells the application that the user has terminated the program.

Before discussing the specifics, examine the following program, which is a minimal Windows NT skeleton. It creates a standard window that includes a title, a system menu, and the standard minimize, maximize, and close boxes. The window is, therefore, capable of being minimized, maximized, moved, resized, and closed.

```
/* A minimal Windows NT skeleton. */

#include <windows.h>
```

```
LRESULT CALLBACK WindowFunc(HWND, UINT, WPARAM, LPARAM);

char szWinName[] = "MyWin"; /* name of window class */

int WINAPI WinMain(HINSTANCE hThisInst, HINSTANCE hPrevInst,
                   LPSTR lpszArgs, int nWinMode)
{
  HWND hwnd;
  MSG msg;
  WNDCLASSEX wcl;

  /* Define a window class. */
  wcl.cbSize = sizeof(WNDCLASSEX);

  wcl.hInstance = hThisInst; /* handle to this instance */
  wcl.lpszClassName = szWinName; /* window class name */
  wcl.lpfnWndProc = WindowFunc; /* window function */
  wcl.style = 0; /* default style */

  wcl.hIcon = LoadIcon(NULL, IDI_APPLICATION); /* standard icon */
  wcl.hIconSm = LoadIcon(NULL, IDI_WINLOGO); /* small icon */
  wcl.hCursor = LoadCursor(NULL, IDC_ARROW); /* cursor style */

  wcl.lpszMenuName = NULL; /* no menu */
  wcl.cbClsExtra = 0; /* no extra */
  wcl.cbWndExtra = 0; /* information needed */

  /* Make the window background white. */
  wcl.hbrBackground = (HBRUSH) GetStockObject(WHITE_BRUSH);

  /* Register the window class. */
  if(!RegisterClassEx(&wcl)) return 0;

  /* Now that a window class has been registered, a window
     can be created. */
  hwnd = CreateWindow(
    szWinName, /* name of window class */
    "Windows NT Skeleton", /* title */
    WS_OVERLAPPEDWINDOW, /* window style - normal */
    CW_USEDEFAULT, /* X coordinate - let Windows decide */
    CW_USEDEFAULT, /* Y coordinate - let Windows decide */
    CW_USEDEFAULT, /* width - let Windows decide */
    CW_USEDEFAULT, /* height - let Windows decide */
    HWND_DESKTOP, /* no parent window */
    NULL,
    hThisInst, /* handle of this instance of the program */
    NULL /* no additional arguments */
  );
```

```
  /* Display the window. */
  ShowWindow(hwnd, nWinMode);
  UpdateWindow(hwnd);

  /* Create the message loop. */
  while(GetMessage(&msg, NULL, 0, 0))
  {
    TranslateMessage(&msg); /* allow use of keyboard */
    DispatchMessage(&msg); /* return control to Windows NT */
  }
  return msg.wParam;
}

/* This function is called by Windows NT and is passed
   messages from the message queue.
*/
LRESULT CALLBACK WindowFunc(HWND hwnd, UINT message,
                            WPARAM wParam, LPARAM lParam)
{
  switch(message) {
    case WM_DESTROY: /* terminate the program */
      PostQuitMessage(0);
      break;
    default:
      /* Let Windows NT process any messages not specified in
         the preceding switch statement. */
      return DefWindowProc(hwnd, message, wParam, lParam);
  }
  return 0;
}
```

2

Let's go through this program step by step.

First, all Windows NT programs must include the header file WINDOWS.H. As stated, this file (along with its support files) contains the API function prototypes and various types, macros, and definitions used by Windows NT. For example, the data types **HWND** and **WNDCLASSEX** are defined in WINDOWS.H (or its subordinate files).

The window function used by the program is called **WindowFunc( )**. It is declared as a callback function because this is the function that Windows NT calls to communicate with the program.

As stated, program execution begins with **WinMain( )**. **WinMain( )** is passed four parameters. **hThisInst** and **hPrevInst** are handles. **hThisInst** refers to the current instance of the program. Remember, Windows NT is a multitasking system, so it is possible that more than one instance of your program may be running at the same time. For Windows NT, **hPrevInst** will always be **NULL**. The **lpszArgs** parameter is a pointer to a string that holds any command line arguments specified when the application was begun. In Windows NT, the string contains the entire command line, including the name of the program itself. (In Windows 3.1 programs, the program name is not included.) The **nWinMode** parameter contains a value that determines how the window will be displayed when your program begins execution.

Inside the function, three variables are created. The **hwnd** variable will hold the handle to the program's window. The **msg** structure variable will hold window messages and the **wcl** structure variable will be used to define the window class.

PORTABILITY: As mentioned above, the **hPrevInst** parameter will always be **NULL** in a Windows NT program. In a Windows 3.1 program, **hPrevInst** would be nonzero if there were other instances of the program currently executing. This reflects a fundamental difference between Windows 3.1 and Windows NT. In Windows 3.1, multiple instances of a program share window classes and various other bits of data. Therefore, it is important for an application to know if another version of itself is running in the system. However, in Windows NT each process is isolated from the next and there is no automatic sharing of window classes and the like. The only reason that **hPrevInst** exists in Windows NT is for the sake of compatibility.

Defining the Window Class

The first two actions that **WinMain( )** takes are to define a window class and then register it. A window class is defined by filling in the fields defined by the **WNDCLASSEX** structure. Its fields are shown here.

```
UINT cbSize; /* size of the WNDCLASSEX structure */
UINT style; /* type of window */
WNDPROC lpfnWndProc; /* address to window func */
int cbClsExtra; /* extra class info */
int cbWndExtra; /* extra window info */
HINSTANCE hInstance; /* handle of this instance */
HICON hIcon; /* handle of standard icon */
HICON hIconSm; /* handle of small icon */
HCURSOR hCursor; /* handle of mouse cursor */
HBRUSH hbrBackground; /* background color */
LPCSTR lpszMenuName; /* name of main menu */
LPCSTR lpszClassName; /* name of window class */
```

As you can see by looking at the program, **cbSize** is assigned the size of the **WNDCLASSEX** structure. The **hInstance** member is assigned the current instance handle as specified by **hThisInst**. The name of the window class is pointed to by **lpszClassName**, which points to the string "MyWin" in this case. The address of the window function is assigned to **lpfnWndProc**. In the program, no default style is specified, no extra information is needed, and no main menu is specified. While most programs will contain a main menu, none is required by the skeleton. (Menus are described in Chapter 4.)

PORTABILITY: In Windows 3.1, each window class must be registered only once. Therefore, if another instance of the program is running, then the current instance must not define and register the window class. To avoid this possibility, the value of **hPrevInst** is tested. If it is nonzero, then the window class has already been registered by a previous instance. If not, then the window class is defined and registered. However, this test is not needed by Windows NT and is not included in any of the examples in this book. However, for downward compatibility with Windows 3.1, you may wish to include it and doing so causes no harm.

2

All Windows applications need to define a default shape for the mouse cursor and for the application's icons. An application can define its own custom version of these resources or it may use one of the built-in styles, as the skeleton does. In either case, handles to these resources must be assigned to the appropriate members of the **WNDCLASSEX** structure. To see how this is done, let's begin with icons.

Beginning with version 4, a Windows NT application has two icons associated with it: one standard size and one small. The small icon is used when the application is minimized and it is also the icon that is used for the system menu. The standard size icon (also frequently called the large icon) is displayed when you move or copy an application to the desktop. Standard icons are 32 × 32 bitmaps and small icons are 16 × 16 bitmaps. The style of each icon is loaded by the API function **LoadIcon( )**, whose prototype is shown here:

HICON LoadIcon(HINSTANCE *hInst*, LPCSTR *lpszName*);

This function returns a handle to an icon. Here, *hInst* specifies the handle of the module that contains the icon. The icon's name is specified in *lpszName*. However, to use one of the built-in icons, you must use **NULL** for the first parameter and specify one of the following macros for the second.

Icon Macro	Shape
IDI_APPLICATION	Default icon
IDI_ASTERISK	Information icon
IDI_EXCLAMATION	Exclamation point icon
IDI_HAND	Stop sign
IDI_QUESTION	Question mark icon
IDI_WINLOGO	Windows NT Logo

In the skeleton, **IDI_APPLICATION** is used for the standard icon and **IDI_WINLOGO** is used for the small icon.

To load the mouse cursor, use the API **LoadCursor( )** function. This function has the following prototype:

HCURSOR LoadCursor(HINSTANCE *hInst*, LPCSTR *lpszName*);

This function returns a handle to a cursor resource. Here, *hInst* specifies the handle of the module that contains the mouse cursor, and the name of the mouse cursor is specified in *lpszName*. However, to use one of the built in cursors, you must use **NULL** for the first parameter and specify one of the built-in cursors using its macro for the second parameter. Some of the most common built-in cursors are shown here.

Cursor Macro	Shape
IDC_ARROW	Default arrow pointer
IDC_CROSS	Cross hairs
IDC_IBEAM	Vertical I-beam
IDC_WAIT	Hourglass

The background color of the window created by the skeleton is specified as white and a handle to this *brush* is obtained using the API function **GetStockObject( ).** A brush is a resource that paints the screen using a predetermined size, color, and pattern. The function **GetStockObject( )** is used to obtain a handle to a number of standard display objects, including brushes, pens (which draw lines), and character fonts. It has this prototype:

HGDIOBJ GetStockObject(int *object*);

The function returns a handle to the object specified by *object*. (The type **HGDIOBJ** is a GDI handle.) Here are some of the built-in brushes available to your program:

Macro Name	Background Type
BLACK_BRUSH	Black
DKGRAY_BRUSH	Dark gray
HOLLOW_BRUSH	See through window
LTGRAY_BRUSH	Light gray
WHITE_BRUSH	White

You may use these macros as parameters to **GetStockObject( )** to obtain a brush.

Once the window class has been fully specified, it is registered with Windows NT using the API function **RegisterClassEx( )**, whose prototype is shown here.

ATOM RegisterClassEx(CONST WNDCLASSEX *lpWClass);

The function returns a value that identifies the window class. **ATOM** is a **typedef** that means **WORD**. Each window class is given a unique value. *lpWClass* must be the address of a **WNDCLASSEX** structure.

Moving Up to NT 4: Adding the Small Icon

Versions of Windows NT prior to 4 only supported the standard icon. The handle to this icon was stored in the **hIcon** member of a **WNDCLASS** structure. **WNDCLASS** is similar to **WNDCLASSEX** except that it does not contain the **cbSize** or **hIconSm** members. The **WNDCLASS** structure is registered using **RegisterClass( )**, not **RegisterClassEx( )**. When moving up to NT 4, you will want to add a small icon to all of your applications. If you don't, then the standard icon is automatically shrunk when the small icon is needed. While this may be OK in some situations, it will be unacceptable in others. Frankly, all Windows NT 4 programs should define both icons.

Remember, to add the small icon you must use **WNDCLASSEX** and **RegisterClassEx( )**, as shown in the skeleton.

Creating a Window

Once a window class has been defined and registered, your application can actually create a window of that class using the API function **CreateWindow( )**, whose prototype is shown here.

```
HWND CreateWindow(
        LPCSTR lpszClassName, /* name of window class */
        LPCSTR lpszWinName, /* title of window */
        DWORD dwStyle, /* type of window */
        int X, int Y, /* upper-left coordinates */
        int Width, int Height, /* dimensions of window */
        HWND hParent, /* handle of parent window */
        HMENU hMenu, /* handle of main menu */
        HINSTANCE hThisInst, /* handle of creator */
        LPVOID lpszAdditional /* pointer to additional info */
);
```

As you can see by looking at the skeleton program, many of the parameters to **CreateWindow( )** may be defaulted or specified as **NULL**. In fact, most often the *X*, *Y*, *Width*, and *Height* parameters will simply use the macro **CW_USEDEFAULT**, which tells Windows NT to select an appropriate size and location for the window. If the window has no parent, which is the case in the skeleton, then *hParent* can be specified as **HWND_DESKTOP**. (You may also use **NULL** for this parameter.) If the window does not contain a main menu or uses the main menu defined by the window class, then *hMenu* must be **NULL**. (The *hMenu* parameter has other uses, too.) Also, if no additional information is required, as is most often the case, then *lpszAdditional* is **NULL.** (The type **LPVOID** is **typedef**ed as **void ***. Historically, **LPVOID** stands for long pointer to **void**.)

The remaining four parameters must be explicitly set by your program. First, *lpszClassName* must point to the name of the window class. (This is the name you gave it when it was registered.) The title of the window is a string pointed to by *lpszWinName*. This can be a null string, but usually a window will be given a title. The style (or type) of window actually created is determined by the value of *dwStyle*. The macro **WS_OVERLAPPED-WINDOW** specifies a standard window that has a system menu, a border, and minimize, maximize, and close boxes. While this style of window is the most common, you can construct one to your own specifications. To accomplish this, simply OR together the various style macros that you want. Some other common styles are shown here.

Style Macros	Window Feature
WS_OVERLAPPED	Overlapped window with border
WS_MAXIMIZEBOX	Maximize box
WS_MINIMIZEBOX	Minimize box
WS_SYSMENU	System menu
WS_HSCROLL	Horizontal scroll bar
WS_VSCROLL	Vertical scroll bar

The *hThisInst* parameter must contain the current instance handle of the application.

The **CreateWindow( )** function returns the handle of the window it creates or **NULL** if the window cannot be created.

Once the window has been created, it is still not displayed on the screen. To cause the window to be displayed, call the **ShowWindow( )** API function. This function has the following prototype:

    BOOL ShowWindow(HWND *hwnd*, int *nHow*);

The handle of the window to display is specified in *hwnd*. The display mode is specified in *nHow*. The first time the window is displayed, you will want to pass **WinMain( )**'s **nWinMode** as the *nHow* parameter. Remember, the value of **nWinMode** determines how the window will be displayed when the program begins execution. Subsequent calls can display (or remove) the window as necessary. Some common values for *nHow* are shown here:

Display Macros	Effect
SW_HIDE	Removes the window
SW_MINIMIZE	Minimizes the window into an icon
SW_MAXIMIZE	Maximizes the window
SW_RESTORE	Returns a window to normal size

The **ShowWindow( )** function returns the previous display status of the window. If the window was displayed, then nonzero is returned. If the window was not displayed, zero is returned.

Although not technically necessary for the skeleton, a call to **UpdateWindow( )** is included because it is needed by virtually every Windows NT application that you will create. It essentially tells Windows NT to send a message to your application that the main window needs to be updated. (This message will be discussed in the next chapter.)

The Message Loop

The final part of the skeletal **WinMain( )** is the *message loop*. The message loop is a part of all Windows applications. Its purpose is to receive and process messages sent by Windows NT. When an application is running, it is continually being sent messages. These messages are stored in the application's message queue until they can be read and processed. Each time your application is ready to read another message, it must call the API function **GetMessage( )**, which has this prototype:

BOOL GetMessage(LPMSG *msg*, HWND *hwnd*, UINT *min*, UINT *max*);

The message will be received by the structure pointed to by *msg*. All Windows messages are of structure type **MSG**, shown here.

```
/* Message structure */
typedef struct tagMSG
{
  HWND hwnd; /* window that message is for */
  UINT message; /* message */
  WPARAM wParam; /* message-dependent info */
  LPARAM lParam; /* more message-dependent info */
  DWORD time; /* time message posted */
  POINT pt; /* X,Y location of mouse */
} MSG;
```

In **MSG**, the handle of the window for which the message is intended is contained in **hwnd**. The message itself is contained in **message**. Additional information relating to each message is passed in **wParam** and **lParam**. The type **WPARAM** is a **typedef** for **UINT** and **LPARAM** is a **typedef** for **LONG**.

PORTABILITY: The **message** field of **MSG** is 16 bits long in Windows 3.1, but it is widened to 32 bits for Windows NT. Also, the **wParam** field, which is 16 bits in Windows 3.1, has been widened to 32 bits in Windows NT. Be aware of these changes when porting code.

The time the message was sent (posted) is specified in milliseconds in the **time** field.

The **pt** member will contain the coordinates of the mouse when the message was sent. The coordinates are held in a **POINT** structure which is defined like this:

```
typedef struct tagPOINT {
  LONG x, y;
} POINT;
```

PORTABILITY: In Windows 3.1, the **x** and **y** in the **POINT** structure are declared as integers. In Windows NT, they are widened to **LONG**.

2

If there are no messages in the application's message queue, then a call to **GetMessage( )** will pass control back to Windows NT.

The *hwnd* parameter to **GetMessage( )** specifies for which window messages will be obtained. It is possible (even likely) that an application will contain several windows and you may only want to receive messages for a specific window. If you want to receive all messages directed at your application, this parameter must be **NULL**.

The remaining two parameters to **GetMessage( )** specify a range of messages that will be received. Generally, you want your application to receive all messages. To accomplish this, specify both *min* and *max* as 0, as the skeleton does.

GetMessage( ) returns zero when the user terminates the program, causing the message loop to terminate. Otherwise it returns nonzero.

Inside the message loop, two functions are called. The first is the API function **TranslateMessage( )**. This function translates virtual key codes generated by Windows NT into character messages. (Virtual keys are discussed later in this book.) Although it is not necessary for all applications, most call **TranslateMessage( )** because it is needed to allow full integration of the keyboard into your application program.

Once the message has been read and translated, it is dispatched back to Windows NT using the **DispatchMessage( )** API function. Windows NT then holds this message until it can pass it to the program's window function.

Once the message loop terminates, the **WinMain( )** function ends by returning the value of **msg.wParam** to Windows NT. This value contains the return code generated when your program terminates.

The Window Function

The second function in the application skeleton is its window function. In this case the function is called **WindowFunc( )**, but it could have any name you like. The window function is passed messages by Windows NT. The first four members of the **MSG** structure are its parameters. For the skeleton, the only parameter that is used is the message itself. However, in the next chapter you will learn more about the parameters to this function.

The skeleton's window function responds to only one message explicitly: **WM_DESTROY**. This message is sent when the user terminates the program. When this message is received, your program must execute a call to the API function **PostQuitMessage( )**. The argument to this function is an exit code that is returned in **msg.wParam** inside **WinMain( )**. Calling **PostQuitMessage( )** causes a **WM_QUIT** message to be sent to your application, which causes **GetMessage( )** to return false, thus stopping your program.

Any other messages received by **WindowFunc( )** are passed along to Windows NT, via a call to **DefWindowProc( )**, for default processing. This step is necessary because all messages must be dealt with in one fashion or another.

Definition File No Longer Needed

If you are familiar with Windows 3.1 programming, then you have used *definition files*. For Windows 3.1, all programs need to have a definition file associated with them. A definition file is simply a text file that specifies certain information and settings needed by your Windows 3.1 program. Because of the 32-bit architecture of Windows NT (and other improvements) definition files are not usually needed for Windows NT programs. If you are new to Windows programming in general and you don't know what a definition file is, the following discussion will give you a brief overview.

Definition files are not usually needed by Windows NT programs.

All definition files use the extension .DEF. For example, the definition file for the skeleton program could be called SKEL.DEF. Here is a definition file that you can use to provide downward compatibility to Windows 3.1:

```
DESCRIPTION 'Skeleton Program'
EXETYPE WINDOWS
CODE PRELOAD MOVEABLE DISCARDABLE
DATA PRELOAD MOVEABLE MULTIPLE
HEAPSIZE 8192
STACKSIZE 8192
EXPORTS WindowFunc
```

IN DEPTH

Positioning a Window

Although it is common for an application to allow Windows NT to choose a position and size for its window when the program begins execution, it is possible to explicitly specify these attributes. To do so, simply pass the coordinates of the window's upper left corner and its width and height to **CreateWindow( )**. For example, if you substitute the following call to **CreateWindow( )** into the skeleton, the window will be displayed in the upper left corner of the screen and will be 300 units wide and 100 units tall.

```
hwnd = CreateWindow(
  szWinName, /* name of window class */
  "Windows NT Skeleton", /* title */
  WS_OVERLAPPEDWINDOW, /* window style - normal */
  0, /* X coordinate */
  0, /* Y coordinate */
  300, /* width */
  100, /* height */
  HWND_DESKTOP, /* no parent window */
  NULL,
  hThisInst, /* handle of this instance of the program */
  NULL /* no additional arguments */
);
```

When determining the location and dimensions of a window, keep in mind that these are specified in *device units,* which are the physical units used by the device (in this case, pixels). This means that the coordinates and dimensions are relative to the screen. The coordinates of the upper left corner are 0, 0. As you will see later in this book, output to a window is generally specified in terms of *logical units*, which are mapped to a window according to the current mapping mode. However, since the position of a window is relative to the entire screen, it makes sense that **CreateWindow( )** would require physical units rather than logical ones.

This file specifies the name of the program and its description, both of which are optional. It also states that the executable file will be compatible with Windows (rather than DOS, for example). The **CODE** statement tells

Windows NT to load all of the program at startup (PRELOAD), that the code may be moved in memory (MOVEABLE), and that the code may be removed from memory and reloaded if (and when) necessary (DISCARDABLE). The file also states that your program's data must be loaded upon execution and may be moved about in memory. It also specifies that each instance of the program has its own data (MULTIPLE). Next, the size of the heap and stack allocated to the program are specified. Finally, the name of the window function is exported. Exporting allows Windows 3.1 to call the function.

REMEMBER: Definition files are almost never used when programming for Windows NT.

Naming Conventions

Before finishing this chapter, a short comment on naming functions and variables needs to be made. If you are new to Windows NT programming, several of the variable and parameter names in the skeleton program and its description probably seemed rather unusual. The reason for this is that they follow a set of naming conventions that was invented by Microsoft for Windows programming. For functions, the name consists of a verb followed by a noun. The first character of the verb and noun is capitalized. For the most part, this book will use this convention for function names.

For variable names, Microsoft chose to use a rather complex system of imbedding the data type into a variable's name. To accomplish this, a lowercase type prefix is added to the start of the variable's name. The name itself is begun with a capital letter. The type prefixes are shown in Table 2-1. Frankly, the use of type prefixes is controversial and is not universally supported. Many Windows programmers use this method, many do not. This method will be used by the Windows NT programs in this book when it seems reasonable to do so. However, you are free to use any naming convention you like.

Prefix	Data Type
b	Boolean (one byte)
c	character (one byte)
dw	long unsigned integer
f	16-bit bitfield (flags)
fn	function
h	handle
l	long integer
lp	long pointer
n	short integer
p	pointer
pt	long integer holding screen coordinates
w	short unsigned integer
sz	pointer to null-terminated string
lpsz	long pointer to null-terminated string
rgb	long integer holding RGB color values

Variable Type
Prefix
Characters
Table 2-1.

2

CHAPTER 3

Application Essentials: Messages and Basic I/O

Although the skeleton developed in Chapter 2 forms the framework for a Windows NT program, by itself it is useless. To be useful, a program must be capable of performing two fundamental operations. First, it must be able to respond to various messages sent by Windows NT. The processing of these messages is at the core of all Windows NT applications. Second, your program must provide some means of outputting information to the user. (That is, it must be able to display information on the screen.) Unlike programs that you may have written for other operating systems, outputting information to the user is a non-trivial task in Windows. In fact, managing output forms a large part of any Windows application. Without the ability to process messages and display information, no useful Windows program can be written. For this reason, message processing and the basic I/O operations are the subject of this chapter.

Message Boxes

A message box is a predefined window that displays simple output.

The easiest way to output information to the screen is to use a *message box*. As you will see, many of the examples in this book make use of message boxes. A message box is a simple window that displays a message to the user and waits for an acknowledgment. Unlike other types of windows that you must create, a message box is a system-defined window that you may use. In general, the purpose of a message box is to inform the user that some event has taken place. However, it is possible to construct a message box that allows the user to select from among a few basic alternatives as a response to the message. For example, one common form of message box allows a user to select Abort, Retry, or Ignore.

NOTE: In the term *message box*, the word *message* refers to human-readable text that is displayed on the screen. It does not refer to Windows NT messages which are sent to your program's window function. Although the terms sound similar, *message boxes* and *messages* are two entirely separate concepts.

To create a message box, use the **MessageBox( )** API function. Its prototype is shown here:

  int MessageBox(HWND *hwnd*, LPCSTR *lpText*, LPCSTR *lpCaption*, UINT *MBType*);

Here, *hwnd* is the handle to the parent window. The *lpText* parameter is a pointer to a string that will appear inside the message box. The string pointed to by *lpCaption* is used as the title for the box. The value of *MBType* determines the exact nature of the message box, including what type of buttons and icons will be present. Some of the most common values are shown in Table 3-1. These macros are defined by including WINDOWS.H. You can OR together two or more of these macros so long as they are not mutually exclusive.

MessageBox( ) returns the user's response to the box. The possible return values are shown here:

Button Pressed	Return Value
Abort	IDABORT
Retry	IDRETRY
Ignore	IDIGNORE
Cancel	IDCANCEL
No	IDNO
Yes	IDYES
OK	IDOK

3

Remember, depending upon the value of *MBType*, only certain buttons will be present. Quite often message boxes are simply used to display an item of information and the only response offered to the user is the OK button. In

Value	Effect
MB_ABORTRETRYIGNORE	Displays Abort, Retry, and Ignore push buttons.
MB_ICONEXCLAMATION	Displays Exclamation-point icon.
MB_ICONHAND	Displays a stop sign icon.
MB_ICONINFORMATION	Displays an information icon.
MB_ICONQUESTION	Displays a question mark icon.
MB_ICONSTOP	Same as MB_ICONHAND
MB_OK	Displays OK button.
MB_OKCANCEL	Displays OK and Cancel push buttons.
MB_RETRYCANCEL	Displays Retry and Cancel push buttons.
MB_YESNO	Displays Yes and No push buttons.
MB_YESNOCANCEL	Displays Yes, No, and Cancel push buttons.

Some Common Values for *MBType*
Table 3-1.

these cases, the return value of a message box is simply ignored by the program.

To display a message box, simply call the **MessageBox( )** function. Windows NT will display it at its first opportunity. **MessageBox( )** automatically creates a window and displays your message in it. For example, this call to **MessageBox( )**

```
i = MessageBox(hwnd, "This is Caption", "This is Title", MB_OKCANCEL);
```

produces the following message box.

Depending on which button the user presses, **i** will contain either **IDOK** or **IDCANCEL**.

Message boxes are typically used to notify the user that some event has occurred. However, because message boxes are so easy to use, they make excellent debugging tools when you need a simple way to output something to the screen. As you will see, examples in this book will use a message box whenever a simple means of displaying information is needed.

Now that we have a means of outputting information, we can move on to processing messages.

PORTABILITY: Message boxes in Windows NT have additional features and options that are not found under Windows 3.1 and that may be of interest if you are porting older code.

Understanding Windows NT Messages

As it relates to Windows NT, a message is a unique 32-bit integer value. Windows NT communicates with your program by sending it messages. Each message corresponds to some event. For example, there are messages to indicate that the user has pressed a key, that the mouse has moved, or that a window has been resized.

Although you could, in theory, refer to each message by its numeric value, in practice this is seldom done. Instead, there are macro names defined for all Windows NT messages. Typically, you will use the macro name, not the actual integer value, when referring to a message. The standard names for the messages are defined by including WINDOWS.H in your program. Here are some common Windows NT message macros:

WM_CHAR	WM_PAINT	WM_MOVE
WM_CLOSE	WM_LBUTTONUP	WM_LBUTTONDOWN
WM_COMMAND	WM_HSCROLL	WM_SIZE

Two other values accompany each message and contain information related to it. One of these values is of type **WPARAM**, the other is of type **LPARAM**. For Windows NT, both of these types translate into 32-bit integers. These values are commonly called **wParam** and **lParam**, respectively. The contents of **wParam** and **lParam** are determined by which message is received. They typically hold things like mouse coordinates; the value of a key press; or a system-related value, such as window size. As each message is discussed, the meaning of the values contained in **wParam**, and **lParam** will be described.

3

PORTABILITY: In Windows 3.1, **wParam** is a 16-bit value. It is a 32-bit value in Windows NT. As a result, some messages differ between Windows 3.1 and Windows NT. Such differences will be noted.

As mentioned in Chapter 2, the function that actually processes messages is your program's window function. As you should recall, this function is passed four parameters: the handle of the window that the message is for, the message itself, **wParam,** and **lParam**.

Sometimes two pieces of information are encoded into the two words that comprise the **wParam** or **lParam** parameters. To provide easy access to each value, Windows defines two macros called **LOWORD** and **HIWORD**. They return the low-order and high-order words of a long integer, respectively. They are used like this:

```
x = LOWORD(lParam);
x = HIWORD(lParam);
```

You will see these macros in use soon.

Windows NT defines a large number of messages. Although it is not possible to examine every message, this chapter discusses some of the most common ones. Other messages are described throughout the remainder of this book as the need arises.

Responding to a Keypress

One of the most common Windows NT messages is generated when a key is pressed. This message is called **WM_CHAR**. It is important to understand that your application never receives, per se, keystrokes directly from the keyboard. Instead, each time a key is pressed, a **WM_CHAR** message is sent to the active window (i.e., the one that currently has input focus). To see how this process works, this section extends the skeletal application developed in Chapter 2 so that it processes keystroke messages.

Each time **WM_CHAR** is sent, **wParam** contains the ASCII value of the key pressed. **LOWORD(lParam)** contains the number of times the key has been repeated as a result of the key being held down. The bits of **HIWORD(lParam)** are encoded as shown in Table 3-2.

For our purposes, the only value that is important at this time is **wParam**, since it holds the key that was pressed. However, notice how detailed the information is that Windows NT supplies about the state of the system. Of course, you are free to use as much or as little of this information as you like.

Bit	Meaning
15	Set if the key is being released; cleared if the key is being pressed.
14	Set if the key was pressed before the message was sent; cleared if it was not pressed.
13	Set if the ALT key is also being pressed; cleared if ALT is not pressed.
12	Used by Windows NT.
11	Used by Windows NT.
10	Used by Windows NT.
9	Used by Windows NT.
8	Set if the key pressed is an extended key provided by an enhanced keyboard; cleared otherwise.
7 - 0	Manufacturer-dependent key code (i.e., the scan code).

How **lParam** is encoded for keyboard data
Table 3-2.

To process a **WM_CHAR** message, you must add it to the **switch** statement inside your program's window function. For example, here is a program that processes a keystroke by displaying the character on the screen using a message box.

```c
/* Processing WM_CHAR messages. */

#include <windows.h>
#include <string.h>
#include <stdio.h>

LRESULT CALLBACK WindowFunc(HWND, UINT, WPARAM, LPARAM);

char szWinName[] = "MyWin"; /* name of window class */

char str[255] = ""; /* holds output string */

int WINAPI WinMain(HINSTANCE hThisInst, HINSTANCE hPrevInst,
                   LPSTR lpszArgs, int nWinMode)
{
  HWND hwnd;
  MSG msg;
  WNDCLASSEX wcl;

  /* Define a window class. */
  wcl.cbSize = sizeof(WNDCLASSEX);

  wcl.hInstance = hThisInst; /* handle to this instance */
  wcl.lpszClassName = szWinName; /* window class name */
  wcl.lpfnWndProc = WindowFunc; /* window function */
  wcl.style = 0; /* default style */

  wcl.hIcon = LoadIcon(NULL, IDI_APPLICATION); /* standard icon */
  wcl.hIconSm = LoadIcon(NULL, IDI_APPLICATION); /* small icon */
  wcl.hCursor = LoadCursor(NULL, IDC_ARROW); /* cursor style */

  wcl.lpszMenuName = NULL; /* no main menu */
  wcl.cbClsExtra = 0; /* no extra */
  wcl.cbWndExtra = 0; /* information needed */

  /* Make the window white. */
  wcl.hbrBackground = GetStockObject(WHITE_BRUSH);

  /* Register the window class. */
  if(!RegisterClassEx(&wcl)) return 0;
```

3

```
  /* Now that a window class has been registered, a window
     can be created. */
  hwnd = CreateWindow(
    szWinName, /* name of window class */
    "Processing WM_CHAR Messages", /* title */
    WS_OVERLAPPEDWINDOW, /* window style - normal */
    CW_USEDEFAULT, /* X coordinate - let Windows decide */
    CW_USEDEFAULT, /* Y coordinate - let Windows decide */
    CW_USEDEFAULT, /* width - let Windows decide */
    CW_USEDEFAULT, /* height - let Windows decide */
    HWND_DESKTOP, /* no parent window */
    NULL,
    hThisInst, /* handle of this instance of the program */
    NULL /* no additional arguments */
  );

  /* Display the window. */
  ShowWindow(hwnd, nWinMode);
  UpdateWindow(hwnd);

  /* Create the message loop. */
  while(GetMessage(&msg, NULL, 0, 0))
  {
    TranslateMessage(&msg); /* allow use of keyboard */
    DispatchMessage(&msg); /* return control to Windows NT */
  }
  return msg.wParam;
}

/* This function is called by Windows NT and is passed
   messages from the message queue.
*/

LRESULT CALLBACK WindowFunc(HWND hwnd, UINT message,
                            WPARAM wParam, LPARAM lParam)
{
  switch(message) {
    case WM_CHAR: /* process keystroke */
      sprintf(str, "Character is %c", (char) wParam);
      MessageBox(hwnd, str, "WM_CHAR Received", MB_OK);
      break;
    case WM_DESTROY: /* terminate the program */
      PostQuitMessage(0);
      break;
    default:
      /* Let Windows NT process any messages not specified in
         the preceding switch statement. */
      return DefWindowProc(hwnd, message, wParam, lParam);
```

```
      }
      return 0;
}
```

Sample output produced by this program is shown in Figure 3-1. In the program, look carefully at these lines of code from **WindowFunc( )**:

```
case WM_CHAR: /* process keystroke */
  sprintf(str, "Character is %c", (char) wParam);
  MessageBox(hwnd, str, "WM_CHAR Received", MB_OK);
  break;
```

As you can see, the **WM_CHAR** message has been added to the **case** statement. When you run the program, each time you press a key, a **WM_CHAR** message is generated and sent to **WindowFunc( )**. Inside the **WM_CHAR** case, the character received in **wParam** is converted into a string using **sprintf( )** and then displayed using a message box.

A Closer Look at Keyboard Messages

While **WM_CHAR** is probably the most commonly handled keyboard message, it is not the only one. In fact, **WM_CHAR** is actually a synthetic message that is constructed by the **TranslateMessage( )** function inside your program's message loop. At the lowest level, Windows NT generates two messages each time you press a key. When a key is pressed, a **WM_KEYDOWN** message is sent. When the key is released, a **WM_KEYUP** message is posted. If possible, a **WM_KEYDOWN** message is translated into a **WM_CHAR** message by **TranslateMessage( )**. Thus, unless you include **TranslateMessage( )** in your message loop, your program will not receive **WM_CHAR** messages. To prove this to yourself, try commenting out the call to **TranslateMessage( )** in the preceding program. After doing so, it will no longer respond to your keypresses.

3

Sample output
from the
WM_CHAR
program
Figure 3-1.

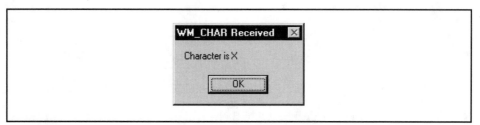

The reason you will seldom use **WM_KEYDOWN** or **WM_KEYUP** for character input is that the information they contain is in a raw format. For example, the value in **wParam** contains the *virtual key code*, not the key's ASCII value. Part of what **TranslateMessage( )** does is transform the virtual key codes into ASCII characters, taking into account the state of the shift key, etc. Also, **TranslateMessage( )** also automatically handles auto-repeat.

Virtual keys are device-independent key mappings.

A virtual key is a device-independent key code. As you may know, there are keys on nearly all computer keyboards that do not correspond to the ASCII character set. The arrow keys and the function keys are examples. Each key that can be generated has been assigned a value, which is its virtual key code. All of the virtual key codes are defined as macros in the header file WINUSER.H (which is automatically included in your program when you include WINDOWS.H). The codes begin with **VK_**. Here are some examples.

Virtual Key Code	Corresponding Key
VK_DOWN	Down arrow
VK_LEFT	Left arrow
VK_RIGHT	Right arrow
VK_UP	Up arrow
VK_SHIFT	SHIFT
VK_CONTROL	CTRL
VK_ESCAPE	ESC
VK_F1 through VK_F24	Function keys
VK_HOME	HOME
VK_END	END
VK_INSERT	INSERT
VK_DELETE	DELETE
VK_PRIOR	PAGE UP
VK_NEXT	PAGE DN
VK_A through VK_Z	The letters of the alphabet
VK_0 through VK_9	The digits 0 through 9

For keys that have ASCII equivalents, **TranslateMessage( )** converts the virtual key code into its ASCII code and sends it in a **WM_CHAR** message.

Of course, the non-ASCII keys are not converted. This means that if your program wants to handle non-ASCII keypresses it must use **WM_KEYDOWN** or **WM_KEYUP** (or both).

Here is an enhanced version of the preceding program that handles both **WM_KEYDOWN** and **WM_CHAR** messages. The handler for **WM_KEYDOWN** reports if the key is an arrow, shift, or control key. Sample output is shown in Figure 3-2.

```
/* Processing WM_KEYDOWN and WM_CHAR messages. */

#include <windows.h>
#include <string.h>
#include <stdio.h>

LRESULT CALLBACK WindowFunc(HWND, UINT, WPARAM, LPARAM);

char szWinName[] = "MyWin"; /* name of window class */

char str[255] = ""; /* holds output string */

int WINAPI WinMain(HINSTANCE hThisInst, HINSTANCE hPrevInst,
                   LPSTR lpszArgs, int nWinMode)
{
  HWND hwnd;
  MSG msg;
  WNDCLASSEX wcl;

  /* Define a window class. */
  wcl.cbSize = sizeof(WNDCLASSEX);

  wcl.hInstance = hThisInst; /* handle to this instance */
  wcl.lpszClassName = szWinName; /* window class name */
  wcl.lpfnWndProc = WindowFunc; /* window function */
  wcl.style = 0; /* default style */

  wcl.hIcon = LoadIcon(NULL, IDI_APPLICATION); /* standard icon */
  wcl.hIconSm = LoadIcon(NULL, IDI_APPLICATION); /* small icon */
  wcl.hCursor = LoadCursor(NULL, IDC_ARROW); /* cursor style */

  wcl.lpszMenuName = NULL; /* no main menu */
  wcl.cbClsExtra = 0; /* no extra */
  wcl.cbWndExtra = 0; /* information needed */

  /* Make the window white. */
  wcl.hbrBackground = GetStockObject(WHITE_BRUSH);

  /* Register the window class. */
```

3

```
  if(!RegisterClassEx(&wcl)) return 0;

  /* Now that a window class has been registered, a window
     can be created. */
  hwnd = CreateWindow(
    szWinName, /* name of window class */
    "Processing WM_CHAR and WM_KEYDOWN Messages",
    WS_OVERLAPPEDWINDOW, /* window style - normal */
    CW_USEDEFAULT, /* X coordinate - let Windows decide */
    CW_USEDEFAULT, /* Y coordinate - let Windows decide */
    CW_USEDEFAULT, /* width - let Windows decide */
    CW_USEDEFAULT, /* height - let Windows decide */
    HWND_DESKTOP, /* no parent window */
    NULL,
    hThisInst, /* handle of this instance of the program */
    NULL /* no additional arguments */
  );

  /* Display the window. */
  ShowWindow(hwnd, nWinMode);
  UpdateWindow(hwnd);

  /* Create the message loop. */
  while(GetMessage(&msg, NULL, 0, 0))
  {
    TranslateMessage(&msg); /* allow use of keyboard */
    DispatchMessage(&msg); /* return control to Windows NT */
  }
  return msg.wParam;
}

/* This function is called by Windows NT and is passed
   messages from the message queue.
*/

LRESULT CALLBACK WindowFunc(HWND hwnd, UINT message,
                            WPARAM wParam, LPARAM lParam)
{
  switch(message) {
    case WM_CHAR: /* process character */
      sprintf(str, "Character is %c", (char) wParam);
      MessageBox(hwnd, str, "WM_CHAR Received", MB_OK);
      break;
    case WM_KEYDOWN: /* process raw keystroke */
      switch((char)wParam) {
        case VK_UP:
          strcpy(str, "Up Arrow");
          break;
```

```
                    case VK_DOWN:
                      strcpy(str, "Down Arrow");
                      break;
                    case VK_LEFT:
                      strcpy(str, "Left Arrow");
                      break;
                    case VK_RIGHT:
                      strcpy(str, "Right Arrow");
                      break;
                    case VK_SHIFT:
                      strcpy(str, "Shift");
                      break;
                    case VK_CONTROL:
                      strcpy(str, "Control");
                      break;
                    default:
                      strcpy(str, "Other Key");
                  }
                  MessageBox(hwnd, str, "WM_KEYDOWN Received", MB_OK);
                  break;
                case WM_DESTROY: /* terminate the program */
                  PostQuitMessage(0);
                  break;
                default:
                  /* Let Windows NT process any messages not specified in
                     the preceding switch statement. */
                  return DefWindowProc(hwnd, message, wParam, lParam);
              }
              return 0;
            }
```

When you try this program notice one important point: when you press a
standard ASCII key, such as X, the program will receive two messages: one
will be **WM_CHAR** and the other will be **WM_KEYDOWN**. The reason for
this is easy to understand. Each time you press a key, a **WM_KEYDOWN**
message is generated. (That is, all keystrokes generate a key down message.)
If the key is an ASCII key, it is transformed into a **WM_CHAR** message by
TranslateMessage( ).

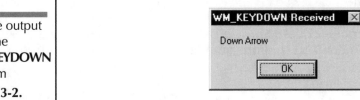

Sample output
from the
WM_KEYDOWN
program
Figure 3-2.

More Keyboard Messages

In addition to **WM_KEYDOWN** and **WM_KEYUP**, other keyboard messages are shown here.

Keyboard Message	Explanation
WM_SYSKEYDOWN	Raw keyboard message when a system key is pressed. **wParam** contains virtual key code.
WM_SYSKEYUP	Raw keyboard message when a system key is released. **wParam** contains virtual key code.
WM_DEADCHAR	Message generated by **TranslateMessage( )** when a key has no translation into the current environment. **wParam** contains character code.
WM_SYSCHAR	Message generated by **TranslateMessage( )** when a system key is pressed. **wParam** contains character code.
WM_SYSDEADCHAR	Message generated by **TranslateMessage( )** when a system key has no translation into the current environment. **wParam** contains character code.

A system key is generated by holding down the ALT key, as in ALT-F, for example. For all keyboard messages, the value of **lParam** is encoded as shown in Table 3-2.

For most applications, you will include **TranslateMessage( )** in your message loop and process messages for **WM_CHAR**. The other messages are available for those few programs that have specialized keyboard needs. Although the low-level control of keyboard input may have been essential in other programming environments in which you have worked, it is seldom necessary in Windows. The main reason for this is that Windows contains several controls, such as edit boxes and list controls, that automate the handling of keyboard input.

Outputting Text to a Window

Although the message box is the easiest means of displaying information, it is obviously not suitable for all situations. There is another way for your program to output information: it can write directly to the client area of its window. Windows NT supports both text and graphics output. In this section, you will learn the basics of text output. Graphics output is reserved for later in this book.

The first thing to understand about outputting text to a window is that you cannot use the standard C or C++ I/O system. The reason for this is that the standard C/C++ I/O functions and operators direct their output to standard output. However, in a Windows program, output is directed to a window. To see how text can be written to a window, let's begin with an example that outputs each character that you type to the program's window, instead of using a message box. Here is a version of **WindowFunc( )** that does this.

```
LRESULT CALLBACK WindowFunc(HWND hwnd, UINT message,
                            WPARAM wParam, LPARAM lParam)
{
  HDC hdc;
  static unsigned j=0;

  switch(message) {
    case WM_CHAR: /* process keystroke */
      hdc = GetDC(hwnd); /* get device context */
      sprintf(str, "%c", (char) wParam); /* stringize character */
      TextOut(hdc, j*10, 0, str, strlen(str)); /* output char */
      j++; /* try commenting-out this line */
      ReleaseDC(hwnd, hdc); /* release device context */
      break;
    case WM_DESTROY: /* terminate the program */
      PostQuitMessage(0);
      break;
    default:
      /* Let Windows NT process any messages not specified in
         the preceding switch statement. */
      return DefWindowProc(hwnd, message, wParam, lParam);
  }
  return 0;
}
```

Look carefully at the code inside the **WM_CHAR** case. It simply echoes each character that you type to the program's window. Compared to using the standard C/C++ I/O functions or operators, this code probably seems overly complex. The reason for this is that Windows must establish a link between your program and the screen. This link is called a *device context* (DC) and it is acquired by calling **GetDC( )**. For now, don't worry about the precise definition of a device context. It will be discussed in the next section.

However, once you obtain a device context, you may write to the window. At the end of the process, the device context is released using **ReleaseDC( )**. Your program *must* release the device context when it is done with it. Although the number of device contexts is limited only by the size of free memory, the number is still finite. If your program doesn't release the DC, eventually, the available DCs will be exhausted and a subsequent call to **GetDC( )** will fail. Both **GetDC( )** and **ReleaseDC( )** are API functions. Their prototypes are shown here:

    HDC GetDC(HWND *hwnd*);
    int ReleaseDC(HWND *hwnd*, HDC *hdc*);

GetDC( ) returns a device context associated with the window whose handle is specified by *hwnd*. The type **HDC** specifies a handle to a device context. If a device context cannot be obtained, the function returns **NULL**.

PORTABILITY: In Windows 3.1, there are only five device contexts available. In Windows NT, the number is limited only by the amount of free memory. Be aware of this difference if you will be porting NT programs into a 16-bit environment.

ReleaseDC( ) returns true if the device context was released, false otherwise. The *hwnd* parameter is the handle of the window for which the device context is released. The *hdc* parameter is the handle of device context obtained through the call to **GetDC( )**.

The function that actually outputs the character is the API function **TextOut( )**. Its prototype is shown here:

    BOOL TextOut(HDC *DC*, int *x*, int *y*, LPCSTR *lpstr*, int *nlength*);

The **TextOut( )** function outputs the string pointed to by *lpstr* at the window coordinates specified by *x, y*. (By default, these coordinates are in terms of pixels.) The length of the string is specified in *nlength*. The **TextOut( )** function returns nonzero if successful, zero otherwise.

In the **WindowFunc( )**, each time a **WM_CHAR** message is received, the character that is typed by the user is converted, using **sprintf( )**, into a string that is one character long, and then displayed in the window using **TextOut( )**. The first character is displayed at location 0, 0. Remember, in a window the upper left corner of the client area is location 0, 0. Window coordinates are always relative to the window, not the screen. Therefore, the first character is displayed in the upper left corner no matter where the window is physically located on the screen. The reason for the variable **j** is to allow each character to be displayed to the right of the preceding character. That is, the second character is displayed at 10, 0, the third at 20, 0, and so on. Windows does not support any concept of a text cursor which is automatically advanced. Instead, you must explicitly specify where each **TextOut( )** string will be written. Also, **TextOut( )** does not advance to the next line when a newline character is encountered, nor does it expand tabs. You must perform all these activities yourself.

Before moving on, you might want to try one simple experiment: comment out the line of code that increments **j.** This will cause all characters to be displayed at location 0, 0. Next, run the program and try typing several characters. Specifically, try typing a **W** followed by an **i.** Because Windows is a graphics-based system, characters are of different sizes and the overwriting of one character by another does not necessarily cause all of the previous character to be erased. For example, when you type a **W** followed by an **i**, part of the **W** will still be displayed. The fact that characters are proportional also explains why the spacing between characters that you type is not even.

3

Understand that the method used in this program to output text to a window is quite crude. In fact, no real Windows NT application would use this approach. Later in this book, you will learn how to manage text output in a more sophisticated fashion.

No Windows NT API function will allow output beyond the borders of a window. Output will automatically be clipped to prevent the boundaries from being crossed. To confirm this for yourself, try typing characters past the border of the window. As you will see, once the right edge of the window has been reached, no further characters are displayed.

At first you might think that using **TextOut( )** to output a single character is an inefficient application of the function. The fact is that Windows NT (and Windows in general) does not contain a function that simply outputs a character. Instead, Windows NT performs much of its user interaction through dialog boxes, menus, toolbars, etc. For this reason it contains only a few functions that output text to the client area. Further, you will generally construct output in advance and then use **TextOut( )** to simply move that output to the screen.

Here is the entire program that echoes keystrokes to the window. Figure 3-3 shows sample output.

```
/* Displaying text using TextOut(). */

#include <windows.h>
#include <string.h>
```

```c
#include <stdio.h>

LRESULT CALLBACK WindowFunc(HWND, UINT, WPARAM, LPARAM);

char szWinName[] = "MyWin"; /* name of window class */

char str[255] = ""; /* holds output string */

int WINAPI WinMain(HINSTANCE hThisInst, HINSTANCE hPrevInst,
                   LPSTR lpszArgs, int nWinMode)
{
  HWND hwnd;
  MSG msg;
  WNDCLASSEX wcl;

  /* Define a window class. */
  wcl.cbSize = sizeof(WNDCLASSEX);

  wcl.hInstance = hThisInst; /* handle to this instance */
  wcl.lpszClassName = szWinName; /* window class name */
  wcl.lpfnWndProc = WindowFunc; /* window function */
  wcl.style = 0; /* default style */

  wcl.hIcon = LoadIcon(NULL, IDI_APPLICATION); /* standard icon */
  wcl.hIconSm = LoadIcon(NULL, IDI_APPLICATION); /* small icon */
  wcl.hCursor = LoadCursor(NULL, IDC_ARROW); /* cursor style */

  wcl.lpszMenuName = NULL; /* no main menu */
  wcl.cbClsExtra = 0; /* no extra */
  wcl.cbWndExtra = 0; /* information needed */

  /* Make the window white. */
  wcl.hbrBackground = GetStockObject(WHITE_BRUSH);

  /* Register the window class. */
  if(!RegisterClassEx(&wcl)) return 0;

  /* Now that a window class has been registered, a window
     can be created. */
  hwnd = CreateWindow(
    szWinName, /* name of window class */
    "Display WM_CHAR Messages Using TextOut", /* title */
    WS_OVERLAPPEDWINDOW, /* window style - normal */
    CW_USEDEFAULT, /* X coordinate - let Windows decide */
    CW_USEDEFAULT, /* Y coordinate - let Windows decide */
    CW_USEDEFAULT, /* width - let Windows decide */
    CW_USEDEFAULT, /* height - let Windows decide */
```

```
      HWND_DESKTOP, /* no parent window */
      NULL,
      hThisInst, /* handle of this instance of the program */
      NULL /* no additional arguments */
    );

    /* Display the window. */
    ShowWindow(hwnd, nWinMode);
    UpdateWindow(hwnd);

    /* Create the message loop. */
    while(GetMessage(&msg, NULL, 0, 0))
    {
      TranslateMessage(&msg); /* allow use of keyboard */
      DispatchMessage(&msg); /* return control to Windows NT */
    }
    return msg.wParam;
}

/* This function is called by Windows NT and is passed
   messages from the message queue.
*/

LRESULT CALLBACK WindowFunc(HWND hwnd, UINT message,
                            WPARAM wParam, LPARAM lParam)
{
  HDC hdc;
  static unsigned j=0;

  switch(message) {
    case WM_CHAR: /* process keystroke */
      hdc = GetDC(hwnd); /* get device context */
      sprintf(str, "%c", (char) wParam); /* stringize character */
      TextOut(hdc, j*10, 0, str, strlen(str)); /* output char */
      j++; /* try commenting-out this line */
      ReleaseDC(hwnd, hdc); /* release device context */
      break;
    case WM_DESTROY: /* terminate the program */
      PostQuitMessage(0);
      break;
    default:
      /* Let Windows NT process any messages not specified in
         the preceding switch statement. */
      return DefWindowProc(hwnd, message, wParam, lParam);
  }
  return 0;
}
```

3

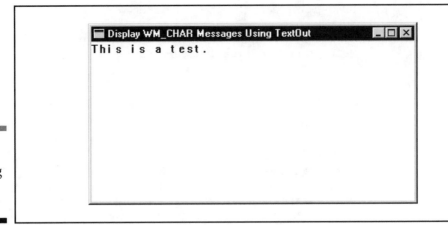

Sample
window
produced using
TextOut( )
Figure 3-3.

Device Contexts

The program in the previous section had to obtain a device context prior to outputting to the window. Also, that device context had to be released prior to the termination of that function. It is now time to understand what a device context is. A device context is a structure that describes the display environment of a window, including its device driver and various display parameters, such as the current type font. As you will see later in this book, you have substantial control over the display environment of a window.

A device context is a structure that describes a window's output environment.

Before your application can output information to the client area of the window a device context must be obtained. Until this is done, there is no linkage between your program and the window relative to output. Since **TextOut( )** and other output functions require a handle to a device context, this is a self-enforcing rule.

Processing the WM_PAINT Message

One of the most important messages that your program will receive is **WM_PAINT**. This message is sent when your program needs to restore the contents of its window. To understand why this is important, run the program from the previous section and enter a few characters. Next, minimize and then restore the window. As you will see, the characters that you typed are not displayed after the window is restored. Also, if the window is overwritten by another window and then redisplayed, the characters are not redisplayed. The reason for this is simple: in general, Windows does not keep a record of what a window contains. Instead, it is your program's job to maintain the contents of a window. To help your program accomplish this, each time the contents of a window must be redisplayed, your program will be sent a **WM_PAINT** message. (This message will also be sent when your window is first displayed.) Each time your program receives this message it must redisplay the contents of the window.

Before explaining how to respond to a **WM_PAINT** message it might be useful to explain why Windows does not automatically rewrite your window. The answer is short and to the point:. In many situations, it is easier for your program, which has intimate knowledge of the contents of the window, to rewrite it than it would be for Windows to do so. While the merits of this approach have been much debated by programmers, you should simply accept it, because it is unlikely to change.

The first step to processing a **WM_PAINT** message is to add it to the **switch** statement inside the window function. For example, here is one way to add a **WM_PAINT** case to the previous program:.

```
case WM_PAINT: /* process a repaint request */
  hdc = BeginPaint(hwnd, &paintstruct); /* get DC */
  TextOut(hdc, 0, 0, str, strlen(str));
  EndPaint(hwnd, &paintstruct); /* release DC */
  break;
```

Let's look at this closely. First, notice that a device context is obtained using a call to **BeginPaint( )** instead of **GetDC( )**. For various reasons, when you process a **WM_PAINT** message, you must obtain a device context using **BeginPaint( )**, which has this prototype:

HDC BeginPaint(HWND *hwnd*, PAINTSTRUCT *lpPS*);

BeginPaint( ) returns a device context if successful or **NULL** on failure. Here, *hwnd* is the handle of the window for which the device context is being obtained. The second parameter is a pointer to a structure of type **PAINTSTRUCT**. On return, the structure pointed to by *lpPS* will contain information that your program can use to repaint the window. **PAINTSTRUCT** is defined like this:

```
typedef struct tagPAINTSTRUCT {
  HDC hdc; /* handle to device context */
  BOOL fErase; /* true if background must be erased */
  RECT rcPaint; /* coordinates of region to redraw */
  BOOL fRestore;  /* reserved */
  BOOL fIncUpdate; /* reserved */
  BYTE rgbReserved[32]; /* reserved */
} PAINTSTRUCT;
```

3

Here, **hdc** will contain the device context of the window that needs to be repainted. This DC is also returned by the call to **BeginPaint( ). fErase** will be nonzero if the background of the window needs to be erased. However, as long as you specified a background brush when you created the window, you can ignore the **fErase** member. Windows NT will erase the window for you.

The type **RECT** is a structure that specifies the upper left and lower right coordinates of a rectangular region. This structure is shown here:

```
typedef tagRECT {
  LONG left, top; /* upper left */
  LONG right, bottom; /* lower right */
} RECT;
```

In **PAINTSTRUCT**, the **rcPaint** element contains the coordinates of the region of the window that needs to be repainted. For now, you will not need to use the contents of **rcPaint** because you can assume that the entire window must be repainted. However, real programs that you write will probably need to utilize this information.

Once the device context has been obtained, output can be written to the window. After the window has been repainted, you must release the device context using a call to **EndPaint( )**, which has this prototype:

BOOL EndPaint(HWND *hwnd*, CONST PAINTSTRUCT **lpPS*);

EndPaint( ) returns nonzero. (It cannot fail.) Here, *hwnd* is the handle of the window that was repainted. The second parameter is a pointer to the **PAINTSTRUCT** structure used in the call to **BeginPaint( )**.

It is critical to understand that a device context obtained using **BeginPaint( )** must be released only through a call to **EndPaint( )**. Further, **BeginPaint( )** must only be used when a **WM_PAINT** message is being processed.

Here is the full program that now processes **WM_PAINT** messages.

```
/* Process WM_PAINT Messages */

#include <windows.h>
#include <string.h>
#include <stdio.h>

LRESULT CALLBACK WindowFunc(HWND, UINT, WPARAM, LPARAM);

char szWinName[] = "MyWin"; /* name of window class */
```

```c
char str[255] = "Sample Output"; /* holds output string */

int WINAPI WinMain(HINSTANCE hThisInst, HINSTANCE hPrevInst,
                   LPSTR lpszArgs, int nWinMode)
{
  HWND hwnd;
  MSG msg;
  WNDCLASSEX wcl;

  /* Define a window class. */
  wcl.cbSize = sizeof(WNDCLASSEX);

  wcl.hInstance = hThisInst; /* handle to this instance */
  wcl.lpszClassName = szWinName; /* window class name */
  wcl.lpfnWndProc = WindowFunc; /* window function */
  wcl.style = 0; /* default style */

  wcl.hIcon = LoadIcon(NULL, IDI_APPLICATION); /* standard icon */
  wcl.hIconSm = LoadIcon(NULL, IDI_APPLICATION); /* small icon */
  wcl.hCursor = LoadCursor(NULL, IDC_ARROW); /* cursor style */

  wcl.lpszMenuName = NULL; /* no main menu */
  wcl.cbClsExtra = 0; /* no extra */
  wcl.cbWndExtra = 0; /* information needed */

  /* Make the window white. */
  wcl.hbrBackground = GetStockObject(WHITE_BRUSH);

  /* Register the window class. */
  if(!RegisterClassEx(&wcl)) return 0;

  /* Now that a window class has been registered, a window
     can be created. */
  hwnd = CreateWindow(
    szWinName, /* name of window class */
    "Process WM_PAINT Messages", /* title */
    WS_OVERLAPPEDWINDOW, /* window style - normal */
    CW_USEDEFAULT, /* X coordinate - let Windows decide */
    CW_USEDEFAULT, /* Y coordinate - let Windows decide */
    CW_USEDEFAULT, /* width - let Windows decide */
    CW_USEDEFAULT, /* height - let Windows decide */
    HWND_DESKTOP, /* no parent window */
    NULL,
    hThisInst, /* handle of this instance of the program */
    NULL /* no additional arguments */
  );
```

```
/* Display the window. */
ShowWindow(hwnd, nWinMode);
UpdateWindow(hwnd);

/* Create the message loop. */
while(GetMessage(&msg, NULL, 0, 0))
{
  TranslateMessage(&msg); /* allow use of keyboard */
  DispatchMessage(&msg); /* return control to Windows NT */
}
return msg.wParam;
}

/* This function is called by Windows NT and is passed
   messages from the message queue.
*/

LRESULT CALLBACK WindowFunc(HWND hwnd, UINT message,
                            WPARAM wParam, LPARAM lParam)
{
  HDC hdc;
  static unsigned j=0;
  PAINTSTRUCT paintstruct;

  switch(message) {
    case WM_CHAR: /* process keystroke */
      hdc = GetDC(hwnd); /* get device context */
      sprintf(str, "%c", (char) wParam); /* stringize character */
      TextOut(hdc, j*10, 0, str, strlen(str)); /* output char */
      j++; /* try commenting-out this line */
      ReleaseDC(hwnd, hdc); /* release device context */
      break;
    case WM_PAINT: /* process a repaint request */
      hdc = BeginPaint(hwnd, &paintstruct); /* get DC */
      TextOut(hdc, 0, 0, str, strlen(str));
      EndPaint(hwnd, &paintstruct); /* release DC */
      break;
    case WM_DESTROY: /* terminate the program */
      PostQuitMessage(0);
      break;
    default:
      /* Let Windows NT process any messages not specified in
         the preceding switch statement. */
      return DefWindowProc(hwnd, message, wParam, lParam);
  }
  return 0;
}
```

Before continuing, enter, compile, and run this program. Try typing a few characters and then minimizing and restoring the window. As you will see, each time the window is redisplayed, the last character you typed is automatically redrawn. The reason that only the last character is redisplayed is because **str** only contains the last character that you typed. You might find it fun to alter the program so that it adds each character to a string and then redisplays that string each time a **WM_PAINT** message is received. (You will see one way to do this in the next example.) Notice that the global array **str** is initialized to **Sample Output** and that this is displayed when the program begins execution. The reason for this is that when a window is created, a **WM_PAINT** message is automatically generated.

While the handling of the **WM_PAINT** message in this program is quite simple, it must be emphasized that most real-world applications will be more complex because most windows contain considerably more output. Since it is your program's responsibility to restore the window if it is resized or overwritten, you must always provide some mechanism to accomplish this. In real-world programs, this is usually accomplished one of three ways. First, your program can regenerate the output by computational means. This is most feasible when no user input is used. Second, in some instances, you can keep a record of events and replay the events when the window needs to be redrawn. Finally, your program can maintain a virtual window that you copy to the window each time it must be redrawn. This is the most general method. (The implementation of this approach is described later in this book.) Which approach is best depends completely upon the application. Most of the examples in this book won't bother to redraw the window because doing so typically involves substantial additional code which often just muddies the point of an example. However, your programs will need to restore their windows in order to be conforming Windows NT applications.

Generating a WM_PAINT Message

It is possible for your program to cause a **WM_PAINT** message to be generated. At first, you might wonder why your program would need to generate a **WM_PAINT** message since it seems that it can repaint its window whenever it wants. However, this is a false assumption. Remember, updating a window is a costly process in terms of time. Because Windows is a multitasking system that might be running other programs that are also demanding CPU time, your program should simply tell Windows that it wants to output information, but let Windows decide when it is best to actually perform that output. This allows Windows to better manage the system and efficiently allocate CPU time to all the tasks in the system. Using this approach, your program holds all output until a **WM_PAINT** message is received.

In the previous example, the **WM_PAINT** message was received only when the window was resized or uncovered. However, if all output is held until a **WM_PAINT** message is received, then to achieve interactive I/O, there must be some way to tell Windows that it needs to send a **WM_PAINT** message to your window whenever output is pending. As expected, Windows NT includes such a feature. Thus, when your program has information to output, it simply requests that a **WM_PAINT** message be sent when Windows is ready to do so.

To cause Windows to send a **WM_PAINT** message, your program will call the **InvalidateRect( )** API function. Its prototype is shown here:

BOOL InvalidateRect(HWND *hwnd*, CONST RECT **lpRect*, BOOL *bErase*);

Here, *hwnd* is the handle of the window to which you want to send the **WM_PAINT** message. The **RECT** structure pointed to by *lpRect* specifies the coordinates within the window that must be redrawn. If this value is **NULL** then the entire window will be specified. If *bErase* is true, then the background will be erased. If it is zero, then the background is left unchanged. The function returns nonzero if successful; it returns zero otherwise. (In general, this function will always succeed.)

When **InvalidateRect( )** is called, it tells Windows that the window is invalid and must be redrawn. This, in turn, causes Windows to send a **WM_PAINT** message to the program's window function.

Here is a reworked version of the previous program that routes all output through the **WM_PAINT** message. The code that responds to a **WM_CHAR** message stores each character and then calls **InvalidateRect( )**. In this version of the program, notice that inside the **WM_CHAR** case, each character you type is added to the string **str.** Thus, each time the window is repainted, the entire string containing all the characters you typed is output, not just the last character, as was the case with the preceding program.

```
/* A Windows skeleton that routes output through
   the WM_PAINT message. */

#include <windows.h>
#include <string.h>
#include <stdio.h>

LRESULT CALLBACK WindowFunc(HWND, UINT, WPARAM, LPARAM);

char szWinName[] = "MyWin"; /* name of window class */
```

```c
char str[255] = ""; /* holds output string */

int WINAPI WinMain(HINSTANCE hThisInst, HINSTANCE hPrevInst,
                   LPSTR lpszArgs, int nWinMode)
{
  HWND hwnd;
  MSG msg;
  WNDCLASSEX wcl;

  /* Define a window class. */
  wcl.cbSize = sizeof(WNDCLASSEX);

  wcl.hInstance = hThisInst; /* handle to this instance */
  wcl.lpszClassName = szWinName; /* window class name */
  wcl.lpfnWndProc = WindowFunc; /* window function */
  wcl.style = 0; /* default style */

  wcl.hIcon = LoadIcon(NULL, IDI_APPLICATION); /* standard icon */
  wcl.hIconSm = LoadIcon(NULL, IDI_APPLICATION); /* small icon */
  wcl.hCursor = LoadCursor(NULL, IDC_ARROW); /* cursor style */

  wcl.lpszMenuName = NULL; /* no main menu */
  wcl.cbClsExtra = 0; /* no extra */
  wcl.cbWndExtra = 0; /* information needed */

  /* Make the window white. */
  wcl.hbrBackground = GetStockObject(WHITE_BRUSH);

  /* Register the window class. */
  if(!RegisterClassEx(&wcl)) return 0;

  /* Now that a window class has been registered, a window
     can be created. */
  hwnd = CreateWindow(
    szWinName, /* name of window class */
    "Routing Output Through WM_PAINT", /* title */
    WS_OVERLAPPEDWINDOW, /* window style - normal */
    CW_USEDEFAULT, /* X coordinate - let Windows decide */
    CW_USEDEFAULT, /* Y coordinate - let Windows decide */
    CW_USEDEFAULT, /* width - let Windows decide */
    CW_USEDEFAULT, /* height - let Windows decide */
    HWND_DESKTOP, /* no parent window */
    NULL,
    hThisInst, /* handle of this instance of the program */
    NULL /* no additional arguments */
  );

  /* Display the window. */
```

3

```
  ShowWindow(hwnd, nWinMode);
  UpdateWindow(hwnd);

  /* Create the message loop. */
  while(GetMessage(&msg, NULL, 0, 0))
  {
    TranslateMessage(&msg); /* allow use of keyboard */
    DispatchMessage(&msg); /* return control to Windows NT */
  }
  return msg.wParam;
}


/* This function is called by Windows NT and is passed
   messages from the message queue.
*/


LRESULT CALLBACK WindowFunc(HWND hwnd, UINT message,
                            WPARAM wParam, LPARAM lParam)
{
  HDC hdc;
  PAINTSTRUCT paintstruct;
  char temp[2];

  switch(message) {
    case WM_CHAR: /* process keystroke */
      hdc = GetDC(hwnd); /* get device context */
      sprintf(temp, "%c", (char) wParam); /* stringize character */
      strcat(str, temp); /* add character to string */
      InvalidateRect(hwnd, NULL, 1); /* paint the screen */
      break;
    case WM_PAINT: /* process a repaint request */
      hdc = BeginPaint(hwnd, &paintstruct); /* get DC */
      TextOut(hdc, 0, 0, str, strlen(str)); /* output char */
      EndPaint(hwnd, &paintstruct); /* release DC */
      break;
    case WM_DESTROY: /* terminate the program */
      PostQuitMessage(0);
      break;
    default:
      /* Let Windows NT process any messages not specified in
         the preceding switch statement. */
      return DefWindowProc(hwnd, message, wParam, lParam);
  }
  return 0;
}
```

Many Windows applications route all (or most) output to the client area through **WM_PAINT**, for the reasons already stated. However, there is nothing wrong with outputting text or graphics as needed. Which method you use will depend on the exact nature of each situation.

IN DEPTH

Generating a Message

As you know, **InvalidateRect( )** is used to generate a **WM_PAINT** message. However, this raises a larger question: How does a program generate a message, in general? You will be happy to learn that the answer to this question is quite easy. Simply use another API function: **SendMessage( )**. Using **SendMessage( )** you can send a message to any window you want. Its prototype is shown here:

LRESULT SendMessage(HWND *hwnd*, UINT *message*, WPARAM *wParam*, LPARAM *lParam*);

Here, *hwnd* is the handle of the window to which the message will be sent. The message to send is specified in *message*. Any additional information associated with the message is passed in *wParam* and *lParam*. **SendMessage( )** returns a response related to the message.

SendMessage( ) is used frequently when working with Windows NT's control elements — especially its common controls. You will see examples of this usage later in this book. However, it can be used any time you want to send a message to a window. For example, the following version of **WindowFunc( )** uses **SendMessage( )** to generate a stream of **WM_CHAR** messages whenever the user presses CTRL-A.

```
LRESULT CALLBACK WindowFunc(HWND hwnd, UINT message,
                                WPARAM wParam, LPARAM lParam)
{
  HDC hdc;
  unsigned i;
  static unsigned j=0;
  char s[] = "Hello There";

  switch(message) {
    case WM_CHAR: /* process keystroke */
      hdc = GetDC(hwnd); /* get device context */

      /* print Hello There if user presses Ctrl-A */
      if((char)wParam == (char) 1) for(i=0; s[i]; i++)
```

```
        SendMessage(hwnd, WM_CHAR, (WPARAM) s[i], (LPARAM) 0);
      else {
        sprintf(str, "%c", (char) wParam); /* stringize
                                                character */
        TextOut(hdc, j*10, 0, str, strlen(str)); /* output
                                                    char */
        j++;
      }

      ReleaseDC(hwnd, hdc); /* release device context */
      break;
    case WM_DESTROY: /* terminate the program */
      PostQuitMessage(0);
      break;
    default:
      /* Let Windows NT process any messages not specified in
         the preceding switch statement. */
      return DefWindowProc(hwnd, message, wParam, lParam);
  }
  return 0;
}
```

If you substitute this version of **WindowFunc( )** into one of the
preceding programs, then each time you press CTRL-A, the string "Hello
There" will be sent as a series of **WM_CHAR** messages to your program.
You could use this basic concept to provide a keyboard macro capability
in programs that you write.

One other point: Since the information contained in **lParam** is not used
by the program when a **WM_CHAR** message is processed, this parameter is
simply specified as zero inside the call to **SendMessage( )**. However, in
other contexts you may need to generate the appropriate values for this
information.

Responding to Mouse Messages

Since Windows is, to a great extent, a mouse-based operating system, all
Windows NT programs should respond to mouse input. Because the mouse
is so important, there are several different types of mouse messages. The ones
discussed in this chapter are:

WM_LBUTTONDOWN	WM_LBUTTONUP	WM_LBUTTONDBLCLK
WM_RBUTTONDOWN	WM_RBUTTONUP	WM_RBUTTONDBLCLK

While most computers use a two-button mouse, Windows NT is capable of handling a mouse with up to three buttons. These buttons are called the left, middle, and right. For the rest of this chapter we will only be concerned with the left and right buttons.

Let's begin with the two most common mouse messages, **WM_LBUTTONDOWN** and **WM_RBUTTONDOWN**. They are generated when the left button and right button are pressed, respectively.

When either a **WM_LBUTTONDOWN** or a **WM_RBUTTONDOWN** message is received, the mouse's current X, Y location is specified in **LOWORD(lParam)** and **HIWORD(lParam)**, respectively. The value of **wParam** contains various pieces of status information, which are described in the next section.

The following program responds to mouse messages. Each time you press a mouse button when the program's window contains the mouse cursor, a message will be displayed at the current location of the mouse pointer. Figure 3-4 shows sample output from this program.

```
/* Process Mouse Messages. */

#include <windows.h>
#include <string.h>
#include <stdio.h>

LRESULT CALLBACK WindowFunc(HWND, UINT, WPARAM, LPARAM);

char szWinName[] = "MyWin"; /* name of window class */

char str[255] = ""; /* holds output string */

int WINAPI WinMain(HINSTANCE hThisInst, HINSTANCE hPrevInst,
                   LPSTR lpszArgs, int nWinMode)
{
  HWND hwnd;
  MSG msg;
  WNDCLASSEX wcl;

  /* Define a window class. */
  wcl.cbSize = sizeof(WNDCLASSEX);

  wcl.hInstance = hThisInst; /* handle to this instance */
```

```
wcl.lpszClassName = szWinName; /* window class name */
wcl.lpfnWndProc = WindowFunc; /* window function */
wcl.style = 0; /* default style */

wcl.hIcon = LoadIcon(NULL, IDI_APPLICATION); /* standard icon */
wcl.hIconSm = LoadIcon(NULL, IDI_WINLOGO); /* small icon */
wcl.hCursor = LoadCursor(NULL, IDC_ARROW); /* cursor style */

wcl.lpszMenuName = NULL; /* no main menu */
wcl.cbClsExtra = 0; /* no extra */
wcl.cbWndExtra = 0; /* information needed */

/* Make the window white. */
wcl.hbrBackground = GetStockObject(WHITE_BRUSH);

/* Register the window class. */
if(!RegisterClassEx(&wcl)) return 0;

/* Now that a window class has been registered, a window
   can be created. */
hwnd = CreateWindow(
  szWinName, /* name of window class */
  "Processing Mouse Messages", /* title */
  WS_OVERLAPPEDWINDOW, /* window style - normal */
  CW_USEDEFAULT, /* X coordinate - let Windows decide */
  CW_USEDEFAULT, /* Y coordinate - let Windows decide */
  CW_USEDEFAULT, /* width - let Windows decide */
  CW_USEDEFAULT, /* height - let Windows decide */
  HWND_DESKTOP, /* no parent window */
  NULL,
  hThisInst, /* handle of this instance of the program */
  NULL /* no additional arguments */
);

/* Display the window. */
ShowWindow(hwnd, nWinMode);
UpdateWindow(hwnd);

/* Create the message loop. */
while(GetMessage(&msg, NULL, 0, 0))
{
  TranslateMessage(&msg); /* allow use of keyboard */
```

```
        DispatchMessage(&msg); /* return control to Windows NT */
  }
  return msg.wParam;
}

/* This function is called by Windows NT and is passed
   messages from the message queue.
*/

LRESULT CALLBACK WindowFunc(HWND hwnd, UINT message,
                            WPARAM wParam, LPARAM lParam)
{
  HDC hdc;

  switch(message) {
    case WM_RBUTTONDOWN: /* process right button */
      hdc = GetDC(hwnd); /* get DC */
      sprintf(str, "Right button is down at %d, %d",
              LOWORD(lParam), HIWORD(lParam));
      TextOut(hdc, LOWORD(lParam), HIWORD(lParam),
              str, strlen(str));
      ReleaseDC(hwnd, hdc); /* Release DC */
      break;
    case WM_LBUTTONDOWN: /* process left button */
      hdc = GetDC(hwnd); /* get DC */
      sprintf(str, "Left button is down at %d, %d",
              LOWORD(lParam), HIWORD(lParam));
      TextOut(hdc, LOWORD(lParam), HIWORD(lParam),
              str, strlen(str));
      ReleaseDC(hwnd, hdc); /* Release DC */
      break;
    case WM_DESTROY: /* terminate the program */
      PostQuitMessage(0);
      break;
    default:
       /* Let Windows NT process any messages not specified in
          the preceding switch statement. */
       return DefWindowProc(hwnd, message, wParam, lParam);
  }
  return 0;
}
```

3

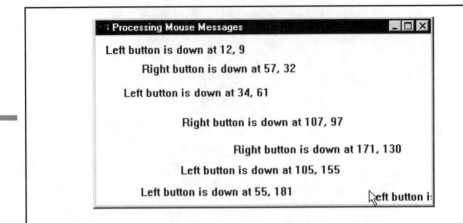

Sample
output from
the Mouse
Messages
program
Figure 3-4.

A Closer Look at Mouse Messages

For all of the mouse messages described in this chapter, the meaning of
lParam and **wParam** is the same. As described earlier, the value of
lParam contains the coordinates of the mouse when the message was
generated. The value of **wParam** supplies information about the state
of the mouse and keyboard. It may contain any combination of the
following values:

MK_CONTROL
MK_SHIFT
MK_MBUTTON
MK_RBUTTON
MK_LBUTTON

If the control key is pressed when a mouse button is pressed, then **wParam**
will contain **MK_CONTROL**. If the shift key is pressed when a mouse
button is pressed, then **wParam** will contain **MK_SHIFT**. If the right
button is down when the left button is pressed, then **wParam** will contain
MK_RBUTTON. If the left button is down when the right button is pressed,
then **wParam** will contain **MK_LBUTTON.** If the middle button (if it
exists) is down when one of the other buttons is pressed, then **wParam** will
contain **MK_MBUTTON**. Before moving on, you might want to try
experimenting with these messages.

Using Button Up Messages

When a mouse button is clicked, your program actually receives
two messages. The first is a button down message, such as

WM_LBUTTONDOWN, when the button is pressed. The second is a button up message, when the button is released. The button up messages for the left and right buttons are called **WM_LBUTTONUP** and **WM_RBUTTONUP**. For some applications, when selecting an item, it is better to process button-up, rather than button-down messages. This gives the user a chance to change his or her mind after the mouse button has been pressed.

Responding to a Double-Click

While it is easy to respond to a single-click, handling double-clicks requires a bit more work. First, you must enable your program to receive double-click messages. By default, double-click messages are not sent to your program. Second, you will need to add message response code for the double-click message to which you want to respond.

To allow your program to receive double-click messages, you will need to specify **CS_DBLCLKS** in the **style** member of the **WNDCLASSEX** structure prior to registering the window class. That is, you must use a line of code like that shown here:

```
wcl.style = CS_DBLCLKS; /* allow double-clicks */
```

After you have enabled double-clicks, your program can receive these double-click messages: **WM_LBUTTONDBLCLK** and **WM_RBUTTONDBLCLK.** The contents of the **lParam** and **wParam** parameters are the same as for the other mouse messages.

As you know, a double-click is two presses of a mouse button in quick succession. You can obtain and/or set the time interval within which two presses of a mouse button must occur in order for a double-click message to be generated. To obtain the double-click interval, use the API function **GetDoubleClickTime( ),** whose prototype is shown here:

UINT GetDoubleClickTime(void);

This function returns the interval of time (specified in milliseconds). To set the double-click interval, use **SetDoubleClickTime( )**. Its prototype is shown here:

BOOL SetDoubleClickTime(UINT *interval*);

Here, *interval* specifies the number of milliseconds within which two presses of a mouse button must occur in order for a double-click to be generated. If you specify zero, then the default double-click time is used. (The default

3

interval is approximately half a second.) The function returns nonzero if successful and zero on failure.

The following program responds to double-click messages. It also demonstrates the use of **GetDoubleClickTime( )** and **SetDoubleClickTime( )**. Each time you press the up arrow key, the double-click interval is increased. Each time you press the down arrow, the interval is decreased. Each time you double-click either the right or left mouse button, a message box that reports the current double-click interval is displayed. Since the double-click interval is a system-wide setting, changes to it will affect all other programs in the system. For this reason, when the program begins, it saves the current double-click interval. When the program ends, the original interval is restored. In general, if your program changes a system-wide setting, it should be restored before the program ends. Sample output is shown in Figure 3-5.

```
/* Respond to double clicks and control
   the double-click interval. */

#include <windows.h>
#include <string.h>
#include <stdio.h>

LRESULT CALLBACK WindowFunc(HWND, UINT, WPARAM, LPARAM);

char szWinName[] = "MyWin"; /* name of window class */

char str[255] = ""; /* holds output string */

UINT OrgDblClkTime; /* holds original double-click interval. */

int WINAPI WinMain(HINSTANCE hThisInst, HINSTANCE hPrevInst,
                   LPSTR lpszArgs, int nWinMode)
{
  HWND hwnd;
  MSG msg;
  WNDCLASSEX wcl;

  /* Define a window class. */
  wcl.cbSize = sizeof(WNDCLASSEX);

  wcl.hInstance = hThisInst; /* handle to this instance */
  wcl.lpszClassName = szWinName; /* window class name */
  wcl.lpfnWndProc = WindowFunc; /* window function */

  wcl.style = CS_DBLCLKS; /* enable double clicks */
```

```
wcl.hIcon = LoadIcon(NULL, IDI_APPLICATION); /* standard icon */
wcl.hIconSm = LoadIcon(NULL, IDI_WINLOGO); /* small icon */
wcl.hCursor = LoadCursor(NULL, IDC_ARROW); /* cursor style */

wcl.lpszMenuName = NULL; /* no main menu */
wcl.cbClsExtra = 0; /* no extra */
wcl.cbWndExtra = 0; /* information needed */

/* Make the window white. */
wcl.hbrBackground = GetStockObject(WHITE_BRUSH);

/* Register the window class. */
if(!RegisterClassEx(&wcl)) return 0;

/* Now that a window class has been registered, a window
   can be created. */
hwnd = CreateWindow(
  szWinName, /* name of window class */
  "Processing Double-Clicks", /* title */
  WS_OVERLAPPEDWINDOW, /* window style - normal */
  CW_USEDEFAULT, /* X coordinate - let Windows decide */
  CW_USEDEFAULT, /* Y coordinate - let Windows decide */
  CW_USEDEFAULT, /* width - let Windows decide */
  CW_USEDEFAULT, /* height - let Windows decide */
  HWND_DESKTOP, /* no parent window */
  NULL,
  hThisInst, /* handle of this instance of the program */
  NULL /* no additional arguments */
);

/* save original double-click time interval */
OrgDblClkTime = GetDoubleClickTime();

/* Display the window. */
ShowWindow(hwnd, nWinMode);
UpdateWindow(hwnd);

/* Create the message loop. */
while(GetMessage(&msg, NULL, 0, 0))
{
  TranslateMessage(&msg); /* allow use of keyboard */
  DispatchMessage(&msg); /* return control to Windows NT */
}
return msg.wParam;
}

LRESULT CALLBACK WindowFunc(HWND hwnd, UINT message,
                            WPARAM wParam, LPARAM lParam)
```

```
{
  HDC hdc;
  UINT interval;

  switch(message) {
    case WM_KEYDOWN:
      if((char)wParam == VK_UP) { /* increase interval */
        interval = GetDoubleClickTime();
        interval += 100;
        SetDoubleClickTime(interval);
      }
      if((char)wParam == VK_DOWN) { /* decrease interval */
        interval = GetDoubleClickTime();
        interval -= 100;
        if(interval < 0) interval = 0;
        SetDoubleClickTime(interval);
      }
      sprintf(str, "New interval is %u milliseconds",
              interval);
      MessageBox(hwnd, str, "Setting Double-Click Interval",
              MB_OK);
      break;
    case WM_RBUTTONDOWN: /* process right button */
      hdc = GetDC(hwnd); /* get DC */
      sprintf(str, "Right button is down at %d, %d",
              LOWORD(lParam), HIWORD(lParam));
      TextOut(hdc, LOWORD(lParam), HIWORD(lParam),
              str, strlen(str));
      ReleaseDC(hwnd, hdc); /* Release DC */
      break;
    case WM_LBUTTONDOWN: /* process left button */
      hdc = GetDC(hwnd); /* get DC */
      sprintf(str, "Left button is down at %d, %d",
              LOWORD(lParam), HIWORD(lParam));
      TextOut(hdc, LOWORD(lParam), HIWORD(lParam),
              str, strlen(str));
      ReleaseDC(hwnd, hdc); /* Release DC */
      break;
    case WM_LBUTTONDBLCLK: /* process left button double-click */
      interval = GetDoubleClickTime();
      sprintf(str, "Left Button\nInterval is %u milliseconds", interval);
      MessageBox(hwnd, str, "Double Click", MB_OK);
      break;
    case WM_RBUTTONDBLCLK: /* process right button double-click */
      interval = GetDoubleClickTime();
      sprintf(str, "Right Button\nInterval is %u milliseconds", interval);
      MessageBox(hwnd, str, "Double Click", MB_OK);
      break;
```

```
      case WM_DESTROY: /* terminate the program */
        SetDoubleClickTime(OrgDblClkTime); /* restore interval */
        PostQuitMessage(0);
        break;
      default:
        /* Let Windows NT process any messages not specified in
           the preceding switch statement. */
        return DefWindowProc(hwnd, message, wParam, lParam);
  }
  return 0;
}
```

More Messages

As mentioned at the start, Windows NT generates many more messages than the ones described in this chapter. Others are described, as needed, throughout the rest of this book. Even so, you will still want to study messages on your own. The Windows NT message environment is both rich and varied.

3

Sample
output from
the
Double-Click
program
Figure 3-5.

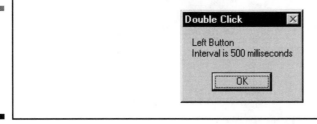

CHAPTER 4

Introducing Menus

This chapter begins our exploration of Windows NT's user interface components. If you are learning to program Windows for the first time, it is important to understand that your application will most often communicate with the user through one or more predefined interface components. There are several different types of these supported by Windows NT. This chapter introduces the most fundamental: the menu. Virtually any program you write will use one. As you will see, the basic style of the menu is predefined. You need only supply the specific information that relates to your application. Because of their importance, Windows NT provides extensive support for menus and the topic of menus is a large one. This chapter describes the fundamentals. Later, the advanced features are covered.

This chapter also introduces the resource. A resource is, essentially, an object defined outside your program but used by your program. Icons, cursors, menus, and bitmaps are common resources. Resources are a crucial part of nearly all Windows applications.

Menus Basics

The most common element of control within a Windows program is the menu. Windows NT supports three general types:

♦   The menu bar (or main menu)

♦   Pop-up submenus

♦   Floating, stand-alone pop-up menus

The menu bar is an application's top-level menu.

A pop-up submenu drops down from the main menu.

A floating pop-up menu is a free-standing menu.

In a Windows application, the menu bar is displayed across the top of the window. This is frequently called the main menu. The menu bar is your application's top-level menu. Submenus descend from the menu bar and are displayed as pop-up menus. (You should be accustomed to this approach because it is used by virtually all Windows programs.) Floating pop-up menus are free-standing pop-up menus which are typically activated by pressing the right mouse button. In this chapter, we will explore the first two types: the menu bar and pop-up submenus. Floating menus are described in a later chapter.

It is actually quite easy to add a menu bar to your program's main window. To do so involves just these three steps:

1.   Define the form of the menu in a resource file.

2.   Load the menu when your program creates its main window.

3.   Process menu selections.

In the remainder of this chapter, you will see how to implement these steps.

Since the first step is to define a menu in a resource file, it is necessary to explain resources and resource files.

Resources

A resource is an object used by your program, but defined outside of it. A menu is one type of resource.

Resources are contained within a resource file, which uses the .RC extension.

Windows defines several common types of objects as *resources*. As mentioned at the beginning of this chapter, resources are, essentially, objects that are used by your program, but are defined outside your program. A menu is one type of resource. A resource is created separately from your program, but is added to the .EXE file when your program is linked. Resources are contained in *resource files*, which have the extension .RC. For small projects, the name of the resource file is often the same as that of your program's .EXE file. For example, if your program is called PROG.EXE, then its resource file will typically be called PROG.RC. Of course, you can call a resource file by any name you please as long as it has the .RC extension.

Depending on the resource, some are text-based and you create them using a standard text editor. Text resources are typically defined within the resource file. Others, such as icons, are most easily generated using a resource editor, but they still must be referred to in the .RC file that is associated with your application. The example resource files in this chapter are simply text files because menus are text-based resources.

4

Resource files do not contain C or C++ statements. Instead, resource files consist of special resource statements. In the course of this chapter, the resource commands needed to support menus are discussed. Others are described as needed throughout this book.

Compiling .RC files

Resource files are not used directly by your program. Instead, they must be converted into a linkable format. Once you have created a .RC file, you compile it into a .RES file using a *resource compiler*. (Often, the resource compiler is called RC.EXE, but this varies.) Exactly how you compile a resource file will depend on what compiler you are using. Also, some integrated development environments handle this phase for you. For example, both Microsoft Visual C++ and Borland C++ compile and incorporate resource files automatically. In any event, the output of the resource compiler will be a .RES file and it is this file that is linked with your program to build the final Windows NT application.

Creating a Simple Menu

Menus are defined within a resource file by using the **MENU** resource statement. All menu definitions have this general form:

MenuName MENU [*options*]
{
 menu items
}

Here, *MenuName* is the name of the menu. (It may also be an integer value identifying the menu, but all examples in this book will use the name when referring to the menu.) The keyword **MENU** tells the resource compiler that a menu is being created. There are only a few options that apply to Windows NT programs. They are shown here:

Option	Meaning
DISCARDABLE	Menu may be removed from memory when no longer needed.
CHARACTERISTICS *info*	Application-specific information, which is specified as a LONG value in *info*.
LANGUAGE *lang, sub-lang*	The language used by the resource is specified by *lang* and *sub-lang*. This is used by internationalized menus. The valid language identifiers are found in the header file WINNT.H.
VERSION *ver*	Application-defined version number is specified in *ver*.

Most simple applications do not require the use of any options and simply use the default settings.

PORTABILITY: Windows 3.1 defines several additional options such as PRELOAD, that may be applied to a MENU statement, but they have no effect for Windows NT programs. When porting code, you can eliminate these obsolete options.

There are two types of items that can be used to define the menu: **MENUITEM**s and **POPUP**s. A **MENUITEM** specifies a final selection. A **POPUP** specifies a pop-up submenu, which may contain other

MENUITEMs or **POPUP**s. The general form of these two statements is shown here:

MENUITEM "*ItemName*", *MenuID* [, *Options*]
POPUP "*PopupName*" [, *Options*]

Here, *ItemName* is the name of the menu selection, such as "Help" or "Save". *MenuID* is a unique integer associated with a menu item that will be sent to your application when a selection is made. Typically, these values are defined as macros inside a header file that is included in both your application code and its resource file. *PopupName* is the name of the pop-up menu. For both cases, the values for *Options* (defined by including WINDOWS.H) are shown in Table 4-1.

Here is a simple menu that will be used by subsequent example programs. You should enter it at this time. Call the file MENU.RC.

```
; Sample menu resource file.
#include "menu.h"

MyMenu MENU
{
  POPUP "&File"
  {
    MENUITEM "&Open", IDM_OPEN
    MENUITEM "&Close", IDM_CLOSE
    MENUITEM "&Exit", IDM_EXIT
  }
  POPUP "&Options"
  {
    MENUITEM "&Colors", IDM_COLORS
    POPUP "&Priority"
    {
      MENUITEM "&Low", IDM_LOW
      MENUITEM "&High", IDM_HIGH
    }
    MENUITEM "&Fonts", IDM_FONT
    MENUITEM "&Resolution", IDM_RESOLUTION
  }
  MENUITEM "&Help", IDM_HELP
}
```

This menu, called **MyMenu**, contains three top-level menu bar options: File, Options, and Help. The File and Options entries contain pop-up submenus. The Priority option activates a pop-up submenu of its own. Notice that options that activate submenus do not have menu ID values associated with

Option	Meaning
CHECKED	A check mark is displayed next to the name. (Not applicable to top-level menus.)
GRAYED	The name is shown in gray and may not be selected.
HELP	May be associated with a help selection. Applies to MENUITEMs only.
INACTIVE	The option may not be selected.
MENUBARBREAK	For menu bar, causes the item to be put on a new line. For pop-up menus, causes the item to be put in a different column. In this case, the item is separated using a bar.
MENUBREAK	Same as MENUBARBREAK except that no separator bar is used.
SEPARATOR	Creates an empty menu item that acts as a separator. Applies to MENUITEMs only.

The
MENUITEM
and **POPUP**
Options
Table 4-1.

them. Only actual menu items have ID numbers. In this menu, all menu ID values are specified as macros beginning with **IDM**. (These macros are defined in the header file MENU.H.) The names you give these values are arbitrary.

An **&** in an item's name causes the key that it precedes to become the shortcut key associated with that option. That is, once that menu is active, pressing that key causes that menu item to be selected. It doesn't have to be the first key in the name, but it should be unless a conflict with another name exists.

NOTE: You can embed comments into a resource file on a line-by-line basis by beginning them with a semicolon, as the first line of the resource file shows. You may also use C and C++ style comments.

The MENU.H header file, which is included in MENU.RC, contains the macro definitions of the menu ID values. It is shown here. Enter it at this time.

```
#define IDM_OPEN      100
#define IDM_CLOSE     101
```

```
#define IDM_EXIT          102
#define IDM_COLORS        103
#define IDM_LOW           104
#define IDM_HIGH          105
#define IDM_FONT          106
#define IDM_RESOLUTION    107
#define IDM_HELP          108
```

This file defines the menu ID values that will be returned when the various menu items are selected. This file will also be included in the program that uses the menu. Remember, the actual names and values you give the menu items are arbitrary, but each value must be unique. The valid range for ID values is 0 through 65,565.

Including a Menu in Your Program

Once you have created a menu, the easiest way to include that menu in a program is by specifying its name when you create the window's class. Specifically, you assign **lpszMenuName** a pointer to a string that contains the name of the menu. For example, to use the menu **MyMenu**, you would use this line when defining the window's class:

```
wcl.lpszMenuName = "MyMenu"; /* main menu */
```

Now **MyMenu** is the default main menu for all windows of its class. This means that all windows of this type will have the menu defined by **MyMenu**. (As you will see, you can override this class menu, if you like.)

Responding to Menu Selections

Each time the user makes a menu selection, your program's window function is sent a **WM_COMMAND** command message. When that message is received, the value of **LOWORD(wParam)** contains the menu item's ID value. That is, **LOWORD(wParam)** contains the value you associated with the item when you defined the menu in its .RC file. Since **WM_COMMAND** is sent whenever a menu item is selected and the value associated with that item is contained in **LOWORD(wParam)**, you will need to use a nested **switch** statement to determine which item was selected. For example, this fragment responds to a selection made from **MyMenu**:

```
switch(message) {
  case WM_COMMAND:
    switch(LOWORD(wParam)) {
      case IDM_OPEN: MessageBox(hwnd, "Open File", "Open", MB_OK);
```

```
      break;
    case IDM_CLOSE: MessageBox(hwnd, "Close File", "Close", MB_OK);
      break;
    case IDM_EXIT:
      response = MessageBox(hwnd, "Quit the Program?",
                                 "Exit", MB_YESNO);
      if(response == IDYES) PostQuitMessage(0);
      break;
    case IDM_COLORS: MessageBox(hwnd, "Set Colors", "Colors", MB_OK);
      break;
    case IDM_LOW: MessageBox(hwnd, "Low", "Priority", MB_OK);
      break;
    case IDM_HIGH: MessageBox(hwnd, "High", "Priority", MB_OK);
      break;
    case IDM_RESOLUTION: MessageBox(hwnd, "Resolution Options",
                                    "Resolution", MB_OK);
      break;
    case IDM_FONT: MessageBox(hwnd, "Font Options", "Fonts", MB_OK);
      break;
    case IDM_HELP: MessageBox(hwnd, "No Help", "Help", MB_OK);
      break;
  }
  break;
```

For the sake of illustration, the response to each selection simply displays an acknowledgment of that selection on the screen. Of course, in a real application, the response to menu selections will perform the specified operations.

A Sample Menu Program

Here is a program that demonstrates the previously defined menu. Sample output from the program is shown in Figure 4-1.

```
/* Demonstrate menus. */

#include <windows.h>
#include <string.h>
#include <stdio.h>
#include "menu.h"

LRESULT CALLBACK WindowFunc(HWND, UINT, WPARAM, LPARAM);
```

```
char szWinName[] = "MyWin"; /* name of window class */
int WINAPI WinMain(HINSTANCE hThisInst, HINSTANCE hPrevInst,
                   LPSTR lpszArgs, int nWinMode)
{
  HWND hwnd;
  MSG msg;
  WNDCLASSEX wcl;

  /* Define a window class. */
  wcl.cbSize = sizeof(WNDCLASSEX);

  wcl.hInstance = hThisInst; /* handle to this instance */
  wcl.lpszClassName = szWinName; /* window class name */
  wcl.lpfnWndProc = WindowFunc; /* window function */
  wcl.style = 0; /* default style */

  wcl.hIcon = LoadIcon(NULL, IDI_APPLICATION); /* standard icon */
  wcl.hIconSm = LoadIcon(NULL, IDI_WINLOGO); /* small icon */

  wcl.hCursor = LoadCursor(NULL, IDC_ARROW); /* cursor style */

  /* specify name of menu resource */
  wcl.lpszMenuName = "MyMenu"; /* main menu */

  wcl.cbClsExtra = 0; /* no extra */
  wcl.cbWndExtra = 0; /* information needed */

  /* Make the window white. */
  wcl.hbrBackground = GetStockObject(WHITE_BRUSH);

  /* Register the window class. */
  if(!RegisterClassEx(&wcl)) return 0;

  /* Now that a window class has been registered, a window
     can be created. */
  hwnd = CreateWindow(
    szWinName, /* name of window class */
    "Introducing Menus", /* title */
    WS_OVERLAPPEDWINDOW, /* window style - normal */
    CW_USEDEFAULT, /* X coordinate - let Windows decide */
    CW_USEDEFAULT, /* Y coordinate - let Windows decide */
    CW_USEDEFAULT, /* width - let Windows decide */
    CW_USEDEFAULT, /* height - let Windows decide */
    HWND_DESKTOP, /* no parent window */
    NULL,
```

```
      hThisInst, /* handle of this instance of the program */
      NULL /* no additional arguments */
    );

    /* Display the window. */
    ShowWindow(hwnd, nWinMode);
    UpdateWindow(hwnd);

    /* Create the message loop. */
    while(GetMessage(&msg, NULL, 0, 0))
    {
      TranslateMessage(&msg); /* allow use of keyboard */
      DispatchMessage(&msg); /* return control to Windows NT */
    }
    return msg.wParam;
}

/* This function is called by Windows NT and is passed
   messages from the message queue.
*/
LRESULT CALLBACK WindowFunc(HWND hwnd, UINT message,
                            WPARAM wParam, LPARAM lParam)
{
  int response;

  switch(message) {
    case WM_COMMAND:
      switch(LOWORD(wParam)) {
        case IDM_OPEN: MessageBox(hwnd, "Open File", "Open", MB_OK);
          break;
        case IDM_CLOSE: MessageBox(hwnd, "Close File", "Close", MB_OK);
          break;
        case IDM_EXIT:
          response = MessageBox(hwnd, "Quit the Program?",
                                "Exit", MB_YESNO);
          if(response == IDYES) PostQuitMessage(0);
          break;
        case IDM_COLORS: MessageBox(hwnd, "Set Colors", "Colors", MB_OK);
          break;
        case IDM_LOW: MessageBox(hwnd, "Low", "Priority", MB_OK);
          break;
```

```
          case IDM_HIGH: MessageBox(hwnd, "High", "Priority", MB_OK);
            break;
          case IDM_RESOLUTION: MessageBox(hwnd, "Resolution Options",
                                          "Resolution", MB_OK);
            break;
          case IDM_FONT: MessageBox(hwnd, "Font Options", "Fonts", MB_OK);
            break;
          case IDM_HELP: MessageBox(hwnd, "No Help", "Help", MB_OK);
            break;
      }
      break;
    case WM_DESTROY: /* terminate the program */
      PostQuitMessage(0);
      break;
    default:
      /* Let Windows NT process any messages not specified in
         the preceding switch statement. */
      return DefWindowProc(hwnd, message, wParam, lParam);
  }
  return 0;
}
```

4

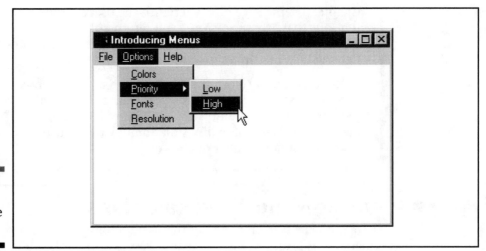

Sample output
from the
Menu example
Figure 4-1.

IN DEPTH

Using MessageBox( ) Responses

In the example menu program, when the user selects Exit, the following code sequence is executed:

```
case IDM_EXIT:
  response = MessageBox(hwnd, "Quit the Program?",
                        "Exit", MB_YESNO);
  if(response == IDYES) PostQuitMessage(0);
  break;
```

The message box displayed by this fragment is shown here:

As you can see, it contains two buttons: Yes and No. As discussed in Chapter 3, a message box will return the user's response. In this case, it means that **MessageBox( )** will return either **IDYES** or **IDNO**. If the user's response is **IDYES**, then the program terminates. Otherwise, it continues execution.

This is an example of a situation in which a message box is used to allow the user to select between two courses of action. As you begin to write your own Windows NT programs, keep in mind that the message box is useful in any situation in which the user must choose between a small number of choices.

Adding Menu Accelerator Keys

There is one feature of Windows that is commonly used in conjunction with a menu. This feature is the accelerator key. *Accelerator keys* are special keystrokes that you define which, when pressed, automatically select a menu option even though the menu in which that option resides is not displayed. Put differently, you can select an item directly by pressing an accelerator key, bypassing the menu entirely. The term *accelerator key* is an accurate description because pressing one is generally a faster way to select a menu item than first activating its menu and then selecting the item.

An accelerator key allows you to select a menu item using the keyboard, bypassing the menus themselves.

To define accelerator keys relative to a menu, you must add an accelerator key table to your resource file. An accelerator table has this general form:

TableName ACCELERATORS [*accel-options*]
{
 Key1, MenuID1 [, *type*] [*options*]
 Key2, MenuID2 [, *type*] [*options*]
 Key3, MenuID3 [, *type*] [*options*]
 .
 .
 .
 KeyN, MenuIDN [, *type*] [*options*]
}

Here, *TableName* is the name of the accelerator table. An **ACCELERATORS** statement can have the same options as those described for MENU. If needed, they are specified by *accel-options*. However, most applications simply use the default settings.

Inside the accelerator table, *Key* is the keystroke that selects the item and *MenuID* is the ID value associated with the desired item. The *type* specifies whether the key is a standard key (the default) or a virtual key. The *options* may be one of the following macros: **NOINVERT, ALT, SHIFT,** and **CONTROL**. **NOINVERT** prevents the selected menu item from being highlighted when its accelerator key is pressed. **ALT** specifies an ALT key. **SHIFT** specifies a SHIFT key. **CONTROL** specifies a CTRL key.

The value of *Key* will be either a quoted character, an ASCII integer value corresponding to a key, or a virtual key code. If a quoted character is used, then it is assumed to be an ASCII character. If it is an integer value, then you must tell the resource compiler explicitly that this is an ASCII character by specifying *type* as **ASCII**. If it is a virtual key, then *type* must be **VIRTKEY**.

If the key is an uppercase quoted character then its corresponding menu item will be selected if it is pressed while holding down the SHIFT key. If it is a lowercase character, then its menu item will be selected if the key is pressed by itself. If the key is specified as a lowercase character and **ALT** is specified as an option, then pressing ALT and the character will select the item. (If the key is uppercase and **ALT** is specified, then you must press SHIFT and ALT to select the item.) Finally, if you want the user to press CTRL and the character to select an item, precede the key with a ^.

As explained in Chapter 3, a virtual key is a system-independent code for a variety of keys. To use a virtual key as an accelerator, simply specify its macro for the *key* and specify **VIRTKEY** for its *type*. You may also specify **ALT**, **SHIFT**, or **CONTROL** to achieve the desired key combination.

4

Here are some examples:

```
"A", IDM_x           ; select by pressing Shift-A
"a", IDM_x           ; select by pressing a
"^a", IDM_x          ; select by pressing Ctrl-a
"a", IDM_x, ALT      ; select by pressing Alt-a
VK_F2, IDM_x         ; select by pressing F2
VK_F2, IDM_x, SHIFT  ; select by pressing Shift-F2
```

Here is the MENU.RC resource file that also contains accelerator key definitions for **MyMenu**.

```
; Sample menu resource file and accelerators.
#include <windows.h>
#include "menu.h"

MyMenu MENU
{
  POPUP "&File"
  {
    MENUITEM "&Open\tF2", IDM_OPEN
    MENUITEM "&Close\tF3", IDM_CLOSE
    MENUITEM "&Exit\tCtrl-X", IDM_EXIT
  }
  POPUP "&Options"
  {
    MENUITEM "&Colors\tCtrl-C", IDM_COLORS
    POPUP "&Priority"
    {
      MENUITEM "&Low\tF4", IDM_LOW
      MENUITEM "&High\tF5", IDM_HIGH
    }
    MENUITEM "&Fonts\tCtrl-F", IDM_FONT
    MENUITEM "&Resolution\tCtrl-R", IDM_RESOLUTION
  }
  MENUITEM "&Help", IDM_HELP
}


; Define menu accelerators
MyMenu ACCELERATORS
{
  VK_F2, IDM_OPEN, VIRTKEY
  VK_F3, IDM_CLOSE, VIRTKEY
  "^X", IDM_EXIT
  "^C", IDM_COLORS
  VK_F4, IDM_LOW, VIRTKEY
  VK_F5, IDM_HIGH, VIRTKEY
```

```
  "^F", IDM_FONT
  "^R", IDM_RESOLUTION
  VK_F1, IDM_HELP, VIRTKEY
}
```

Notice that the menu definition has been enhanced to display which accelerator key selects which option. Each item is separated from its accelerator key using a tab. The header file WINDOWS.H is included because it defines the virtual key macros.

Loading the Accelerator Table

Even though the accelerators are contained in the same resource file as the menu, they must be loaded separately using another API function called **LoadAccelerators( )**, whose prototype is shown here:

HACCEL LoadAccelerators(HINSTANCE *ThisInst*, LPCSTR *Name*);

where *ThisInst* is the instance handle of the application and *Name* is the name of the accelerator table. The function returns a handle to the accelerator table or **NULL** if the table cannot be loaded.

4

You must call **LoadAccelerators( )** soon after the window is created. For example, this shows how to load the **MyMenu** accelerator table:

```
HACCEL hAccel;

hAccel = LoadAccelerators(hThisInst, "MyMenu");
```

The value of **hAccel** will be used later to help process accelerator keys.

Translating Accelerator Keys

Although the **LoadAccelerators( )** function loads the accelerator table, your program still cannot process accelerator keys until you add another API function to the message loop. This function is called **TranslateAccelerator( )** and its prototype is shown here:

int TranslateAccelerator(HWND *hwnd*, HACCEL *hAccel*, LPMSG *lpMess*);

Here, *hwnd* is the handle of the window for which accelerator keys will be translated. *hAccel* is the handle to the accelerator table that will be used. This is the handle returned by **LoadAccelerators( )**. Finally, *lpMess* is a pointer to the message. The **TranslateAccelerator( )** function returns true if an accelerator key was pressed and false otherwise.

TranslateAccelerator( ) translates an accelerator keystroke into its corresponding **WM_COMMAND** message and sends that message to the window. In this message, the value of **LOWORD(wParam)** will contain the ID associated with the accelerator key. Thus, to your program, the **WM_COMMAND** message will appear to have been generated by a menu selection.

Since **TranslateAccelerator( )** sends a **WM_COMMAND** message whenever an accelerator key is pressed, your program must not execute **TranslateMessage( )** or **DispatchMessage( )** when such a translation takes place. When using **TranslateAccelerator( )**, your message loop should look like this:

```
while(GetMessage(&msg, NULL, 0, 0))
{
  if(!TranslateAccelerator(hwnd, hAccel, &msg)) {
    TranslateMessage(&msg); /* allow use of keyboard */
    DispatchMessage(&msg); /* return control to Windows */
  }
}
```

Trying Accelerator Keys

To try using accelerators, substitute the following version of **WinMain( )** into the preceding application and add the accelerator table to your resource file.

```
/* Process accelerator keys. */

#include <windows.h>
#include <string.h>
#include <stdio.h>
#include "menu.h"

LRESULT CALLBACK WindowFunc(HWND, UINT, WPARAM, LPARAM);

char szWinName[] = "MyWin"; /* name of window class */

int WINAPI WinMain(HINSTANCE hThisInst, HINSTANCE hPrevInst,
                   LPSTR lpszArgs, int nWinMode)
{
  HWND hwnd;
  MSG msg;
  WNDCLASSEX wcl;
  HACCEL hAccel;

  /* Define a window class. */
  wcl.cbSize = sizeof(WNDCLASSEX);
```

```
wcl.hInstance = hThisInst; /* handle to this instance */
wcl.lpszClassName = szWinName; /* window class name */
wcl.lpfnWndProc = WindowFunc; /* window function */
wcl.style = 0; /* default style */

wcl.hIcon = LoadIcon(NULL, IDI_APPLICATION); /* standard icon */
wcl.hIconSm = LoadIcon(NULL, IDI_WINLOGO); /* small icon */

wcl.hCursor = LoadCursor(NULL, IDC_ARROW); /* cursor style */

/* specify name of menu resource */
wcl.lpszMenuName = "MyMenu"; /* main menu */

wcl.cbClsExtra = 0; /* no extra */
wcl.cbWndExtra = 0; /* information needed */

/* Make the window white. */
wcl.hbrBackground = GetStockObject(WHITE_BRUSH);

/* Register the window class. */
if(!RegisterClassEx(&wcl)) return 0;

/* Now that a window class has been registered, a window
   can be created. */
hwnd = CreateWindow(
  szWinName, /* name of window class */
  "Adding Accelerator Keys", /* title */
  WS_OVERLAPPEDWINDOW, /* window style - normal */
  CW_USEDEFAULT, /* X coordinate - let Windows decide */
  CW_USEDEFAULT, /* Y coordinate - let Windows decide */
  CW_USEDEFAULT, /* width - let Windows decide */
  CW_USEDEFAULT, /* height - let Windows decide */
  HWND_DESKTOP, /* no parent window */
  NULL,
  hThisInst, /* handle of this instance of the program */
  NULL /* no additional arguments */
);

/* load the keyboard accelerators */
hAccel = LoadAccelerators(hThisInst, "MyMenu");

/* Display the window. */
ShowWindow(hwnd, nWinMode);
UpdateWindow(hwnd);

/* Create the message loop. */
while(GetMessage(&msg, NULL, 0, 0))
{
```

4

```
    if(!TranslateAccelerator(hwnd, hAccel, &msg)) {
      TranslateMessage(&msg); /* allow use of keyboard */
      DispatchMessage(&msg); /* return control to Windows NT */
    }
  }
  return msg.wParam;
}
```

IN DEPTH

A Closer Look at WM_COMMAND

As you know, each time you make a menu selection or press an accelerator key, a **WM_COMMAND** message is sent and the value in **LOWORD(wParam)** contains the ID of the menu item selected or the accelerator key pressed. However, using only the value in **LOWORD(wParam)** it is not possible to determine which event occurred. In most situations, it doesn't matter whether the user actually made a menu selection or just pressed an accelerator key. But in those situations in which it does, you can find out because Windows provides this information in the high-order word of **wParam**. If the value in **HIWORD(wParam)** is 0, then the user has made a menu selection. If this value is 1, then the user pressed an accelerator key. For example, try substituting the following fragment into the menu program. It reports whether the Open option was selected using the menu or by pressing an accelerator key.

```
case IDM_OPEN:
  if(HIWORD(wParam))
    MessageBox(hwnd, "Open File via Accelerator", "Open",
               MB_OK);
  else
    MessageBox(hwnd, "Open File via Menu Selection",
               "Open", MB_OK);
  break;
```

The value of **lParam** for **WM_COMMAND** messages generated by menu selections or accelerator keys is unused and always contains **NULL**.

As you will see in the next chapter, a **WM_COMMAND** is also generated when the user interacts with various types of controls. In this case, the meanings of **lParam** and **wParam** are somewhat different. For example, the value of **lParam** will contain the handle of the control.

Non-Menu Accelerator Keys

Although keyboard accelerators are most commonly used to provide a fast means of selecting menu items, they are not limited to this role. For example, you can define an accelerator key for which there is no corresponding menu item. You might use such a key to activate a keyboard macro or to initiate some frequently used option. To define a non-menu accelerator key, simply add it to the accelerator table, assigning it a unique ID value.

As an example, let's add a non-menu accelerator key to the menu program. The key will be CTRL-T and each time it is pressed, the current time and date are displayed in a message box. The standard ANSI C time and date functions are used to obtain the current time and date. To begin, change the key table so that it looks like this:

```
MyMenu ACCELERATORS
{
  VK_F2, IDM_OPEN, VIRTKEY
  VK_F3, IDM_CLOSE, VIRTKEY
  "^X", IDM_EXIT
  "^C", IDM_COLORS
  VK_F4, IDM_LOW, VIRTKEY
  VK_F5, IDM_HIGH, VIRTKEY
  "^R", IDM_RESOLUTION
  "^F", IDM_FONT
  VK_F1, IDM_HELP, VIRTKEY
  "^T", IDM_TIME
}
```

Next, add this line to MENU.H:

```
#define IDM_TIME   500
```

Finally, substitute this version of **WindowFunc( )** into the menu program. You will also need to include the TIME.H header file.

```
LRESULT CALLBACK WindowFunc(HWND hwnd, UINT message,
                            WPARAM wParam, LPARAM lParam)
{
  int response;
  struct tm *tod;
  time_t t;
  char str[80];

  switch(message) {
    case WM_COMMAND:
```

4

```
      switch(LOWORD(wParam)) {
        case IDM_OPEN: MessageBox(hwnd, "Open File", "Open", MB_OK);
          break;
        case IDM_CLOSE: MessageBox(hwnd, "Close File", "Close", MB_OK);
          break;
        case IDM_EXIT:
          response = MessageBox(hwnd, "Quit the Program?",
                                "Exit", MB_YESNO);
          if(response == IDYES) PostQuitMessage(0);
          break;
        case IDM_COLORS: MessageBox(hwnd, "Set Colors", "Colors", MB_OK);
          break;
        case IDM_LOW: MessageBox(hwnd, "Low", "Priority", MB_OK);
          break;
        case IDM_HIGH: MessageBox(hwnd, "High", "Priority", MB_OK);
          break;
        case IDM_RESOLUTION: MessageBox(hwnd, "Resolution Options",
                                        "Resolution", MB_OK);
          break;
        case IDM_FONT: MessageBox(hwnd, "Font Options", "Fonts", MB_OK);
          break;
        case IDM_TIME: /* show time */
          t = time(NULL);
          tod = localtime(&t);
          strcpy(str, asctime(tod));
          str[strlen(str)-1] = '\0'; /* remove /r/n */
          MessageBox(hwnd, str, "Time and Date", MB_OK);
          break;
        case IDM_HELP: MessageBox(hwnd, "No Help", "Help", MB_OK);
          break;
      }
      break;
    case WM_DESTROY: /* terminate the program */
      PostQuitMessage(0);
      break;
    default:
      /* Let Windows NT process any messages not specified in
         the preceding switch statement. */
      return DefWindowProc(hwnd, message, wParam, lParam);
  }
  return 0;
}
```

When you run this program, each time you press CTRL-T, you will see a message box similar to the following:

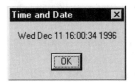

Overriding the Class Menu

In the preceding programs, the main menu has been specified in the
lpszMenuName member of the **WNDCLASSEX** structure. As mentioned,
this specifies a class menu that will be used by all windows that are created
of its class. This is the way most main menus are specified for simple
applications. However, there is another way to specify a main menu that
uses the **CreateWindow( )** function. As you may recall from Chapter 2,
CreateWindow( ) is defined like this:

```
HWND CreateWindow(
  LPCSTR lpClassName, /* name of window class */
  LPCSTR lpWinName, /* title of window */
  DWORD dwStyle, /* type of window */
  int X, int Y, /* upper-left coordinates */
  int Width, int Height, /* dimensions of window */
  HWND hParent, /* handle of parent window */
  HMENU hMenu, /* handle of main menu */
  HINSTANCE hThisInst, /* handle of creator */
  LPVOID lpszAdditional /* pointer to additional info */
);
```

Notice the *hMenu* parameter. It can be used to specify a main menu for the
window being created. In the preceding programs, this parameter has been
specified as **NULL**. When *hMenu* is **NULL**, the class menu is used. However,
if it contains the handle to a menu, then that menu will be used as the main
menu for the window being created. In this case, the menu specified by
hMenu overrides the class menu. Although simple applications, such as those
shown in this book, do not need to override the class menu, there can be
times when this is beneficial. For example, you might want to define a
generic window class which your application will tailor to specific needs.

To specify a main menu using **CreateWindow( )**, you need a handle to the
menu. The easiest way to obtain one is by calling the **LoadMenu( )** API
function, shown here:

4

HMENU LoadMenu(HINSTANCE *hInst*, LPCSTR *lpName*);

Here, *hInst* is the instance handle of your application. A pointer to the name of the menu is passed in *lpName*. **LoadMenu( )** returns a handle to the menu if successful or **NULL** on failure. Once you have obtained a handle to a menu, it can be used as the *hMenu* parameter to **CreateWindow( )**.

When you load a menu using **LoadMenu( )** you are creating an object that allocates memory. This memory must be released before your program ends. If the menu is linked to a window, then this is done automatically. However, when it is not, then you must free it explicitly. This is accomplished using the **DestroyMenu( )** API function. Its prototype is shown here:

BOOL DestroyMenu(HMENU *hMenu*);

Here, *hMenu* is the handle of the menu being destroyed. The function returns nonzero if successful and zero on failure. As stated, you will not need to use **DestroyMenu( )** if the menu you load is linked to a window.

An Example that Overrides the Class Menu

To illustrate how the class menu can be overridden, let's modify the preceding menu program. To do so, add a second menu, called **PlaceHolder**, to the MENU.RC file, as shown here.

```
; Define two menus.
#include <windows.h>
#include "menu.h"

; Placeholder class menu.
PlaceHolder MENU
{
  POPUP "&File"
  {
    MENUITEM "&Exit\tCtrl-X", IDM_EXIT
  }
  MENUITEM "&Help", IDM_HELP
}

; Menu used by CreateWindow.
MyMenu MENU
{
  POPUP "&File"
  {
    MENUITEM "&Open\tF2", IDM_OPEN
    MENUITEM "&Close\tF3", IDM_CLOSE
```

```
      MENUITEM "&Exit\tCtrl-X", IDM_EXIT
    }
    POPUP "&Options"
    {
      MENUITEM "&Colors\tCtrl-C", IDM_COLORS
      POPUP "&Priority"
      {
        MENUITEM "&Low\tF4", IDM_LOW
        MENUITEM "&High\tF5", IDM_HIGH
      }
      MENUITEM "&Font\tCtrl-F", IDM_FONT
      MENUITEM "&Resolution\tCtrl-R", IDM_RESOLUTION
    }
    MENUITEM "&Help", IDM_HELP
}

; Define menu accelerators
MyMenu ACCELERATORS
{
  VK_F2, IDM_OPEN, VIRTKEY
  VK_F3, IDM_CLOSE, VIRTKEY
  "^X", IDM_EXIT
  "^C", IDM_COLORS
  VK_F4, IDM_LOW, VIRTKEY
  VK_F5, IDM_HIGH, VIRTKEY
  "^F", IDM_FONT
  "^R", IDM_RESOLUTION
  VK_F1, IDM_HELP, VIRTKEY
  "^T", IDM_TIME
}
```

4

The **PlaceHolder** menu will be used as the class menu. That is, it will be assigned to the **lpszMenuName** member of **WNDCLASSEX**. **MyMenu** will be loaded separately and its handle will be used in the *hMenu* parameter of **CreateWindow( )**. Thus, **MyMenu** will override **PlaceHolder**.

The contents of MENU.H are shown here. They are unchanged from the original version except for the addition of **IDM_TIME**, from the previous section.

```
#define IDM_OPEN        100
#define IDM_CLOSE       101
#define IDM_EXIT        102
#define IDM_COLORS      103
#define IDM_LOW         104
#define IDM_HIGH        105
#define IDM_FONT        106
```

```
#define IDM_RESOLUTION    107
#define IDM_HELP          108
#define IDM_TIME          500
```

Here is the complete program that overrides the class menu. This program incorporates all of the features discussed in this chapter. Since we have made so many changes to the menu program throughout the course of this chapter, the entire program is shown here for your convenience.

```c
/* Overriding the class menu. */

#include <windows.h>
#include <string.h>
#include <stdio.h>
#include <time.h>
#include "menu.h"

LRESULT CALLBACK WindowFunc(HWND, UINT, WPARAM, LPARAM);

char szWinName[] = "MyWin"; /* name of window class */

int WINAPI WinMain(HINSTANCE hThisInst, HINSTANCE hPrevInst,
                   LPSTR lpszArgs, int nWinMode)
{
  HWND hwnd;
  MSG msg;
  WNDCLASSEX wcl;
  HACCEL hAccel;
  HMENU hmenu;

  /* Define a window class. */
  wcl.cbSize = sizeof(WNDCLASSEX);

  wcl.hInstance = hThisInst; /* handle to this instance */
  wcl.lpszClassName = szWinName; /* window class name */
  wcl.lpfnWndProc = WindowFunc; /* window function */
  wcl.style = 0; /* default style */

  wcl.hIcon = LoadIcon(NULL, IDI_APPLICATION); /* standard icon */
  wcl.hIconSm = LoadIcon(NULL, IDI_WINLOGO); /* small icon */

  wcl.hCursor = LoadCursor(NULL, IDC_ARROW); /* cursor style */

  /* specify name of menu resource -- this will be overridden */
  wcl.lpszMenuName = "PlaceHolder"; /* class menu */

  wcl.cbClsExtra = 0; /* no extra */
```

```
      wcl.cbWndExtra = 0; /* information needed */

      /* Make the window white. */
      wcl.hbrBackground = GetStockObject(WHITE_BRUSH);

      /* Register the window class. */
      if(!RegisterClassEx(&wcl)) return 0;

      /* load main menu manually */
      hmenu = LoadMenu(hThisInst, "MyMenu");

      /* Now that a window class has been registered, a window
         can be created. */
      hwnd = CreateWindow(
        szWinName, /* name of window class */
        "Using an Alternative Menu", /* title */
        WS_OVERLAPPEDWINDOW, /* window style - normal */
        CW_USEDEFAULT, /* X coordinate - let Windows decide */
        CW_USEDEFAULT, /* Y coordinate - let Windows decide */
        CW_USEDEFAULT, /* width - let Windows decide */
        CW_USEDEFAULT, /* height - let Windows decide */
        HWND_DESKTOP, /* no parent window */
        hmenu, /* specify alternative main menu */
        hThisInst, /* handle of this instance of the program */
        NULL /* no additional arguments */
      );

      /* load the keyboard accelerators */
      hAccel = LoadAccelerators(hThisInst, "MyMenu");

      /* Display the window. */
      ShowWindow(hwnd, nWinMode);
      UpdateWindow(hwnd);

      /* Create the message loop. */
      while(GetMessage(&msg, NULL, 0, 0))
      {
        if(!TranslateAccelerator(hwnd, hAccel, &msg)) {
          TranslateMessage(&msg); /* allow use of keyboard */
          DispatchMessage(&msg); /* return control to Windows NT */
        }
      }
      return msg.wParam;
    }

    /* This function is called by Windows NT and is passed
       messages from the message queue.
    */
```

4

```
LRESULT CALLBACK WindowFunc(HWND hwnd, UINT message,
                             WPARAM wParam, LPARAM lParam)
{
  int response;
  struct tm *tod;
  time_t t;
  char str[80];

  switch(message) {
    case WM_COMMAND:
      switch(LOWORD(wParam)) {
        case IDM_OPEN: MessageBox(hwnd, "Open File", "Open", MB_OK);
          break;
        case IDM_CLOSE: MessageBox(hwnd, "Close File", "Close", MB_OK);
          break;
        case IDM_EXIT:
          response = MessageBox(hwnd, "Quit the Program?",
                                "Exit", MB_YESNO);
          if(response == IDYES) PostQuitMessage(0);
          break;
        case IDM_COLORS: MessageBox(hwnd, "Set Colors", "Colors", MB_OK);
          break;
        case IDM_LOW: MessageBox(hwnd, "Low", "Priority", MB_OK);
          break;
        case IDM_HIGH: MessageBox(hwnd, "High", "Priority", MB_OK);
          break;
        case IDM_RESOLUTION: MessageBox(hwnd, "Resolution Options",
                                        "Resolution", MB_OK);
          break;
        case IDM_FONT: MessageBox(hwnd, "Font Options", "Fonts", MB_OK);
          break;
        case IDM_TIME: /* show time */
          t = time(NULL);
          tod = localtime(&t);
          strcpy(str, asctime(tod));
          str[strlen(str)-1] = '\0'; /* remove /r/n */
          MessageBox(hwnd, str, "Time and Date", MB_OK);
          break;
        case IDM_HELP: MessageBox(hwnd, "No Help", "Help", MB_OK);
          break;
      }
      break;
    case WM_DESTROY: /* terminate the program */
      PostQuitMessage(0);
      break;
    default:
```

```
        /* Let Windows NT process any messages not specified in
           the preceding switch statement. */
        return DefWindowProc(hwnd, message, wParam, lParam);
  }
  return 0;
}
```

Pay special attention to the code inside **WinMain( )**. It creates a window
class that specifies **PlaceHolder** as its class menu. However, before a
window is actually created, **MyMenu** is loaded and its handle is used in the
call to **CreateWindow( )**. This causes the class menu to be overridden and
MyMenu to be displayed. You might want to experiment with this program
a little. For example, since the class menu is being overridden, there is no
reason to specify one at all. To prove this, assign **lpszMenuName** the value
NULL. The operation of the program is unaffected.

In this example, both **MyMenu** and **PlaceHolder** contain menus that can
be processed by the same window function. That is, they both use the same
set of menu IDs. (Of course, **PlaceHolder** only contains two selections.)
This allows either menu to work in the preceding program. Although you are
not restricted in the form or structure of an overriding menu, you must
always make sure that whatever menu you use, your window function
contains the proper code to respond to it.

4

REMEMBER: It is usually easier to specify the main menu using
WNDCLASSEX rather than **CreateWindow( )**. This is the approach used
by the rest of the programs in this book.

One last point: since **MyMenu** is linked to the window created by
CreateWindow( ), it is destroyed automatically when the program
terminates. There is no need to call **DestroyMenu( )**.

More Menus to Come

The menus discussed in this chapter form the backbone of the Windows NT
menu system. However, once you have learned more about Windows NT
programming in general, we will return to the topic of menus. As you
will see, there are several exciting features to these foundational
input components.

CHAPTER 5

Dialog Boxes

Although menus are an important part of nearly every Windows NT application, they cannot be used to handle all types of user responses. For example, it would be difficult to use a menu to input the time or date. To handle all types of input, Windows provides the *dialog box*. A dialog box is a special type of window that provides a flexible means by which the user can interact with your application. In general, dialog boxes allow the user to select or enter information that would be difficult or impossible to enter using a menu. In this chapter, you will learn how to create and manage a dialog box.

Also discussed in this chapter are three of Windows' standard controls. Within a dialog box, interaction with the user is performed through a control. In a sense, a dialog box is simply a container that holds various control elements.

As a means of illustrating the dialog box and several controls, a very simple database application will be developed. The database contains the titles of several books along with the names of their authors, publishers, and copyright dates. The dialog box created in this chapter will allow you to select a title and obtain information about it. While the database example is, necessarily, quite simple, it will give you the flavor of how a real application can effectively use a dialog box.

Dialog Boxes Use Controls

By itself, a dialog box does nothing. Instead, it is the controls within the dialog box that interact with the user. Technically, the dialog box is simply a management device. Formally stated, a *control* is a special type of input or output window. A control is owned by its parent window, which, for the examples presented in this chapter, is the dialog box. Windows NT supports several standard controls, including push buttons, check boxes, radio buttons, list boxes, edit boxes, combo boxes, scroll bars, and static controls. (Windows NT also supports several enhanced controls called *common controls,* which are discussed later in this book.) In the course of explaining how to use dialog boxes, the examples in this chapter illustrate three of these controls: the push button, the list box, and the edit box. In the next chapter, other controls will be examined.

A control is a special window that provides for input or output.

A push button is a control that the user "pushes on" to activate some response. You have already been using push buttons in message boxes. For example, the OK button that we have been using in most message boxes is a push button.

A list box displays a list of items from which the user selects one (or more). List boxes are commonly used to display things such as file names.

An edit box allows the user to enter a string. Edit boxes provide all necessary text editing features. Therefore, to input a string, your program simply displays an edit box and waits until the user has finished typing in the string. Typically, a combo box is a combination of a list box and an edit box.

It is important to understand that controls both generate messages (when accessed by the user) and receive messages (from your application). A message generated by a control indicates what type of interaction the user has had with the control. A message sent to the control is essentially an instruction to which the control must respond. You will see examples of this type of message-passing later in this chapter.

Modal vs. Modeless Dialog Boxes

A modal dialog box must be closed before its owner window can be reactivated.

There are two types of dialog boxes: *modal* and *modeless*. The most common dialog boxes are modal. A modal dialog box demands a response from the user before the program will continue. When a modal dialog box is active, the user cannot refocus input to another part of the application without first closing the dialog box. More precisely, the *owner window* of a modal dialog box is deactivated until the dialog box is closed. (The owner window is usually the one that activates the dialog box.)

A modeless dialog box allows its owner window to remain active.

A modeless dialog box does not prevent other parts of the program from being used. That is, it does not need to be closed before input can be refocused to another part of the program. The owner window of a modeless dialog box remains active. In essence, modeless dialog boxes are more independent than modal ones.

5

We will examine modal dialog boxes first, since they are the most common. A modeless dialog box example concludes this chapter.

Receiving Dialog Box Messages

A dialog box is a type of window. Events that occur within it are sent to your program using the same message-passing mechanism that the main window uses. However, dialog box messages are not sent to your program's main window function. Instead, each dialog box that you define will need its own window function, which is generally called a *dialog function or dialog procedure*. This function must have this prototype. (Of course, the name of the function may be anything that you like.)

```
BOOL CALLBACK DFunc(HWND hdwnd, UINT message, WPARAM wParam,
                    LPARAM lParam);
```

As you can see, a dialog function receives the same parameters as your program's main window function. However, it differs from the main window function in that it returns a true or false result. Like your program's main window function, the dialog box window function will receive many messages. If it processes a message, then it must return true. If it does not respond to a message, it must return false.

Dialog box messages are handled by a dialog procedure.

In general, each control within a dialog box will be given its own resource ID. Each time that control is accessed by the user, a **WM_COMMAND** message will be sent to the dialog function, indicating the ID of the control and the type of action the user has taken. The function will then decode the message and take appropriate actions. This process parallels the way messages are decoded by your program's main window function.

PORTABILITY: As mentioned in Chapter 4, Windows 3.1 organizes the *lParam* and *wParam* components of a **WM_COMMAND** differently than does Windows NT.

Activating a Dialog Box

To activate a modal dialog box (that is, to cause it to be displayed) you must call the **DialogBox( )** API function, whose prototype is shown here:

> int DialogBox(HINSTANCE *hThisInst*, LPCSTR *lpName*, HWND *hwnd*, DLGPROC *lpDFunc*);

Here, *hThisInst* is a handle to the current application that is passed to your program in the instance parameter to **WinMain( )**. The name of the dialog box as defined in the resource file is pointed to by *lpName*. The handle to the window that owns the dialog box is passed in *hwnd*. (This is typically the handle of the window that calls **DialogBox( )**.) The *lpDFunc* parameter contains a pointer to the dialog function described in the preceding section. If **DialogBox( )** fails, it returns –1. Otherwise, the return value is that specified by **EndDialog( )**, discussed next.

PORTABILITY : In Windows 3.1, the *lpDFunc* parameter to **DialogBox( )** is a pointer to a *procedure-instance*, which is a short piece of code that links the dialog function with the data segment that the program is currently using. A procedure-instance is obtained using the **MakeProcInstance( )** API function. However, this does not apply to Windows NT. The *lpDFunc* parameter is a pointer to the dialog function itself. You should remove calls to **MakeProcInstance( )** if you are converting older, Win16 code.

Deactivating a Dialog Box

To deactivate (that is, destroy and remove from the screen) a modal dialog box, use **EndDialog( )**. It has this prototype:

BOOL EndDialog(HWND *hdwnd*, int *nStatus*);

Here, *hdwnd* is the handle to the dialog box and *nStatus* is a status code returned by the **DialogBox( )** function. (The value of *nStatus* may be ignored, if it is not relevant to your program.) This function returns nonzero if successful and zero otherwise. (In normal situations, the function is successful.)

Creating a Simple Dialog Box

To illustrate the basic dialog box concepts, we will begin with a simple dialog box. This dialog box will contain four push buttons called Author, Publisher, Copyright, and Cancel. When either the Author, Publisher, or Copyright button is pressed, it will activate a message box indicating the choice selected. (Later these push buttons will be used to obtain information from the database. For now, the message boxes are simply placeholders.) The dialog box will be removed from the screen when the Cancel button is pressed.

The Dialog Box Resource File

5

A dialog box is another resource that is contained in your program's resource file. Before developing a program that uses a dialog box, you will need a resource file that specifies one. Although it is possible to specify the contents of a dialog box using a text editor and enter its specifications as you do when creating a menu, this is seldom done. Instead, most programmers use a dialog editor. The main reason for this is that dialog box definitions involve the positioning of the various controls inside the dialog box, which is best done interactively. However, since the complete .RC files for the examples in this chapter are supplied in their text form, you should simply enter them as text. Just remember that when creating your own dialog boxes, you will want to use a dialog editor.

Dialog boxes are defined within your program's resource file using the **DIALOG** statement. Its general form is shown here:

Dialog-name DIALOG [DISCARDABLE] *X, Y, Width, Height*
Features
{
  Dialog-items
}

The *Dialog-name* is the name of the dialog box. The box's upper left corner will be at *X, Y* and the box will have the dimensions specified by *Width* and *Height*. If the box may be removed from memory when not in use, then specify it as **DISCARDABLE**. One or more optional features of the dialog box may be specified. As you will see, two of these are the caption and the style of the box. The *Dialog-items* are the controls that comprise the dialog box.

The following resource file defines the dialog box that will be used by the first example program. It includes a menu that is used to activate the dialog box, the menu accelerator keys, and then the dialog box itself. You should enter it into your computer at this time, calling it DIALOG.RC.

```
; Sample dialog box and menu resource file.
#include <windows.h>
#include "dialog.h"

MyMenu MENU
{
  POPUP "&Dialog"
  {
    MENUITEM "&Dialog\tF2", IDM_DIALOG
    MENUITEM "&Exit\tF3", IDM_EXIT
  }
  MENUITEM "&Help", IDM_HELP
}


MyMenu ACCELERATORS
{
  VK_F2, IDM_DIALOG, VIRTKEY
  VK_F3, IDM_EXIT, VIRTKEY
  VK_F1, IDM_HELP, VIRTKEY
}

MyDB DIALOG 10, 10, 210, 110
CAPTION "Books Dialog Box"
STYLE DS_MODALFRAME | WS_POPUP | WS_CAPTION | WS_SYSMENU
{
  DEFPUSHBUTTON "Author", IDD_AUTHOR, 11, 10, 36, 14,
            WS_CHILD | WS_VISIBLE | WS_TABSTOP
  PUSHBUTTON "Publisher", IDD_PUBLISHER, 11, 34, 36, 14,
            WS_CHILD | WS_VISIBLE | WS_TABSTOP
  PUSHBUTTON "Copyright", IDD_COPYRIGHT, 11, 58, 36, 14,
            WS_CHILD | WS_VISIBLE | WS_TABSTOP
  PUSHBUTTON "Cancel", IDCANCEL, 11, 82, 36, 16,
            WS_CHILD | WS_VISIBLE | WS_TABSTOP
}
```

This defines a dialog box called **MyDB** that has its upper left corner at location 10, 10. Its width is 210 and its height is 110. The string after **CAPTION** becomes the title of the dialog box. The **STYLE** statement determines what type of dialog box is created. Some common style values, including those used in this chapter, are shown in Table 5-1. You can OR together the values that are appropriate for the style of dialog box that you desire. These style values may also be used by other controls.

Within the **MyDB** definition are defined four push buttons. The first is the default push button. This button is automatically highlighted when the dialog box is first displayed. The general form of a push button declaration is shown here:

PUSHBUTTON "*string*", *PBID*, *X*, *Y*, *Width*, *Height* [, *Style*]

Here, *string* is the text that will be shown inside the push button. *PBID* is the value associated with the push button. It is this value that is returned to your program when this button is pushed. The button's upper left corner will be at *X, Y* and the button will have the dimensions specified by *Width* and *Height*. *Style* determines the exact nature of the push button. To define a default push button use the **DEFPUSHBUTTON** statement. It has the same parameters as the regular push buttons.

Value	Meaning
DS_MODALFRAME	Dialog box has a modal frame. This style can be used with either modal or modeless dialog boxes.
WS_BORDER	Include a border.
WS_CAPTION	Include title bar.
WS_CHILD	Create as child window.
WS_POPUP	Create as pop-up window.
WS_MAXIMIZEBOX	Include maximize box.
WS_MINIMIZEBOX	Include minimize box.
WS_SYSMENU	Include system menu.
WS_TABSTOP	Control may be tabbed to.
WS_VISIBLE	Box is visible when activated.

Some Common Dialog Box Style Options

Table 5-1.

The header file DIALOG.H, which is also used by the example program, is shown here:

```
#define IDM_DIALOG    100
#define IDM_EXIT      101
#define IDM_HELP      102

#define IDD_AUTHOR    200
#define IDD_PUBLISHER 201
#define IDD_COPYRIGHT 202
```

Enter this file now.

The Dialog Box Window Function

As stated earlier, events that occur within a dialog box are passed to the window function associated with that dialog box and not to your program's main window function. The following dialog box window function responds to the events that occur within the **MyDB** dialog box.

```
/* A simple dialog function. */
BOOL CALLBACK DialogFunc(HWND hdwnd, UINT message,
                         WPARAM wParam, LPARAM lParam)
{
  switch(message) {
    case WM_COMMAND:
      switch(LOWORD(wParam)) {
        case IDCANCEL:
          EndDialog(hdwnd, 0);
          return 1;
        case IDD_COPYRIGHT:
          MessageBox(hdwnd, "Copyright", "Copyright", MB_OK);
          return 1;
        case IDD_AUTHOR:
          MessageBox(hdwnd, "Author", "Author", MB_OK);
          return 1;
        case IDD_PUBLISHER:
          MessageBox(hdwnd, "Publisher", "Publisher", MB_OK);
          return 1;
      }
  }
  return 0;
}
```

Each time a control within the dialog box is accessed, a **WM_COMMAND** message is sent to **DialogFunc( )**, and **LOWORD(wParam)** contains the ID of the control affected.

DialogFunc( ) processes the four messages that can be generated by the box. If the user presses **Cancel**, then **IDCANCEL** is sent, causing the dialog box to be closed using a call to the API function **EndDialog( )**. (**IDCANCEL** is a standard ID defined by including WINDOWS.H.) Pressing either of the other three buttons causes a message box to be displayed that confirms the selection. As mentioned, these buttons will be used by later examples to display information from the database.

A First Dialog Box Sample Program

Here is the entire dialog box example. When the program begins execution, only the top-level menu is displayed on the menu bar. By selecting **Dialog**, the user causes the dialog box to be displayed. Once the dialog box is displayed, selecting a push button causes the appropriate response. A sample screen is shown in Figure 5-1. Notice that the books database is included in this program, but is not used. It will be used by subsequent examples.

```
/* Demonstrate a modal dialog box. */

#include <windows.h>
#include <string.h>
```

5

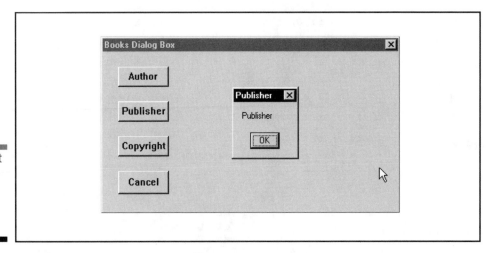

Sample output
from the first
dialog box
program
Figure 5-1.

```
#include <stdio.h>
#include "dialog.h"

#define NUMBOOKS 7

LRESULT CALLBACK WindowFunc(HWND, UINT, WPARAM, LPARAM);
BOOL CALLBACK DialogFunc(HWND, UINT, WPARAM, LPARAM);

char szWinName[] = "MyWin"; /* name of window class */

HINSTANCE hInst;

/* books database */
struct booksTag {
  char title[40];
  unsigned copyright;
  char author[40];
  char publisher[40];
} books[NUMBOOKS] = {
  { "C: The Complete Reference", 1995,
    "Herbert Schildt", "Osborne/McGraw-Hill" },
  { "MFC Programming from the Ground Up", 1996,
    "Herbert Schildt", "Osborne/McGraw-Hill" },
  { "Java: The Complete Reference", 1997,
    "Naughton and Schildt", "Osborne/McGraw-Hill" },
  { "Design and Evolution of C++", 1994,
    "Bjarne Stroustrup", "Addison-Wesley" },
  { "Inside OLE", 1995,
    "Kraig Brockschmidt", "Microsoft Press" },
  { "HTML Sourcebook", 1996,
    "Ian S. Graham", "John Wiley & Sons" },
  { "Standard C++ Library", 1995,
    "P. J. Plauger", "Prentice-Hall" }
};

int WINAPI WinMain(HINSTANCE hThisInst, HINSTANCE hPrevInst,
                   LPSTR lpszArgs, int nWinMode)
{
  HWND hwnd;
  MSG msg;
  WNDCLASSEX wcl;
  HANDLE hAccel;

  /* Define a window class. */
  wcl.cbSize = sizeof(WNDCLASSEX);

  wcl.hInstance = hThisInst; /* handle to this instance */
  wcl.lpszClassName = szWinName; /* window class name */
```

```
wcl.lpfnWndProc = WindowFunc; /* window function */
wcl.style = 0; /* default style */

wcl.hIcon = LoadIcon(NULL, IDI_APPLICATION); /* standard icon */
wcl.hIconSm = LoadIcon(NULL, IDI_WINLOGO); /* small icon */
wcl.hCursor = LoadCursor(NULL, IDC_ARROW); /* cursor style */

/* specify name of menu resource. */
wcl.lpszMenuName = "MyMenu"; /* main menu */

wcl.cbClsExtra = 0; /* no extra */
wcl.cbWndExtra = 0; /* information needed */

/* Make the window white. */
wcl.hbrBackground = GetStockObject(WHITE_BRUSH);

/* Register the window class. */
if(!RegisterClassEx(&wcl)) return 0;

/* Now that a window class has been registered, a window
   can be created. */
hwnd = CreateWindow(
  szWinName, /* name of window class */
  "Demonstrate Dialog Boxes", /* title */
  WS_OVERLAPPEDWINDOW, /* window style - normal */
  CW_USEDEFAULT, /* X coordinate - let Windows decide */
  CW_USEDEFAULT, /* Y coordinate - let Windows decide */
  CW_USEDEFAULT, /* width - let Windows decide */
  CW_USEDEFAULT, /* height - let Windows decide */
  HWND_DESKTOP, /* no parent window */
  NULL, /* no override of class menu */
  hThisInst, /* handle of this instance of the program */
  NULL /* no additional arguments */
);

hInst = hThisInst; /* save the current instance handle */

/* load accelerators */
hAccel = LoadAccelerators(hThisInst, "MyMenu");

/* Display the window. */
ShowWindow(hwnd, nWinMode);
UpdateWindow(hwnd);

/* Create the message loop. */
while(GetMessage(&msg, NULL, 0, 0))
{
```

5

```
      if(!TranslateAccelerator(hwnd, hAccel, &msg)) {
        TranslateMessage(&msg); /* translate keyboard messages */
        DispatchMessage(&msg); /* return control to Windows NT */
      }
    }
    return msg.wParam;
}


/* This function is called by Windows NT and is passed
   messages from the message queue.
*/
LRESULT CALLBACK WindowFunc(HWND hwnd, UINT message,
                                WPARAM wParam, LPARAM lParam)
{
  int response;

  switch(message) {
    case WM_COMMAND:
      switch(LOWORD(wParam)) {
        case IDM_DIALOG:
          DialogBox(hInst, "MyDB", hwnd, (DLGPROC) DialogFunc);
          break;
        case IDM_EXIT:
          response = MessageBox(hwnd, "Quit the Program?",
                                  "Exit", MB_YESNO);
          if(response == IDYES) PostQuitMessage(0);
          break;
        case IDM_HELP:
          MessageBox(hwnd, "No Help", "Help", MB_OK);
          break;
      }
      break;
    case WM_DESTROY: /* terminate the program */
      PostQuitMessage(0);
      break;
    default:
      /* Let Windows NT process any messages not specified in
         the preceding switch statement. */
      return DefWindowProc(hwnd, message, wParam, lParam);
  }
  return 0;
}

/* A simple dialog function. */
BOOL CALLBACK DialogFunc(HWND hdwnd, UINT message,
                            WPARAM wParam, LPARAM lParam)
```

```
{
  switch(message) {
    case WM_COMMAND:
      switch(LOWORD(wParam)) {
        case IDCANCEL:
          EndDialog(hdwnd, 0);
          return 1;
        case IDD_COPYRIGHT:
          MessageBox(hdwnd, "Copyright", "Copyright", MB_OK);
          return 1;
        case IDD_AUTHOR:
          MessageBox(hdwnd, "Author", "Author", MB_OK);
          return 1;
        case IDD_PUBLISHER:
          MessageBox(hdwnd, "Publisher", "Publisher", MB_OK);
          return 1;
      }
  }
  return 0;
}
```

Notice the global variable **hInst**. This variable is assigned a copy of the
current instance handle passed to **WinMain( )**. The reason for this variable
is that the dialog box needs access to the current instance handle. However,
the dialog box is not created in **WinMain( )**. Instead, it is created in
WindowFunc( ). Therefore, a copy of the instance parameter must be
made so that it can be accessible outside of **WinMain( )**.

5

Adding a List Box

To continue exploring dialog boxes, let's add another control to the dialog
box defined in the previous program. One of the most common controls
after the push button is the list box. We will use the list box to display a list
of the titles in the database and allow the user to select the one in which he
or she is interested. The **LISTBOX** statement has this general form:

LISTBOX *LBID*, *X*, *Y*, *Width*, *Height* [, *Style*]

Here, *LBID* is the value that identifies the list box. The box's upper left
corner will be at *X*, *Y* and the box will have the dimensions specified by
Width and *Height*. *Style* determines the exact nature of the list box.

To add a list box, you must change the dialog box definition in DIALOG.RC.
First, add this list box description to the dialog box definition:

```
LISTBOX IDD_LB1, 60, 5, 140, 33, LBS_NOTIFY | WS_VISIBLE |
          WS_BORDER | WS_VSCROLL | WS_TABSTOP
```

Second, add this push button to the dialog box definition:

```
PUSHBUTTON "Select Book", IDD_SELECT, 103, 41, 54, 14,
          WS_CHILD | WS_VISIBLE | WS_TABSTOP
```

After these changes, your dialog box definition should now look like this:

```
MyDB DIALOG 10, 10, 210, 110
CAPTION "Books Dialog Box"
STYLE DS_MODALFRAME | WS_POPUP | WS_CAPTION | WS_SYSMENU
{
  DEFPUSHBUTTON "Author", IDD_AUTHOR, 11, 10, 36, 14,
            WS_CHILD | WS_VISIBLE | WS_TABSTOP
  PUSHBUTTON "Publisher", IDD_PUBLISHER, 11, 34, 36, 14,
            WS_CHILD | WS_VISIBLE | WS_TABSTOP
  PUSHBUTTON "Copyright", IDD_COPYRIGHT, 11, 58, 36, 14,
            WS_CHILD | WS_VISIBLE | WS_TABSTOP
  PUSHBUTTON "Cancel", IDCANCEL, 11, 82, 36, 16,
            WS_CHILD | WS_VISIBLE | WS_TABSTOP
  LISTBOX IDD_LB1, 60, 5, 140, 33, LBS_NOTIFY | WS_VISIBLE |
            WS_BORDER | WS_VSCROLL | WS_TABSTOP
  PUSHBUTTON "Select Book", IDD_SELECT, 103, 41, 54, 14,
            WS_CHILD | WS_VISIBLE | WS_TABSTOP
}
```

You will also need to add these macros to DIALOG.H:

```
#define IDD_LB1      203
#define IDD_SELECT   204
```

IDD_LB1 identifies the list box specified in the dialog box definition in the resource file. **IDD_SELECT** is the ID value of the Select Book push button.

List Box Basics

When using a list box, you must perform two basic operations. First, you must initialize the list box when the dialog box is first displayed. This consists of sending the list box the list that it will display. (By default, the list box will be empty.) Second, once the list box has been initialized, your program will need to respond to the user selecting an item from the list.

List boxes generate various types of *notification messages*. A notification message describes what type of control event has occurred. (Several of the

standard controls generate notification messages.) For the list box used in
the following example, the only notification message we will use is
LBN_DBLCLK. This message is sent when the user has double-clicked on an
entry in the list. This message is contained in **HIWORD(wParam)** each
time a **WM_COMMAND** is generated for the list box. (The list box must
have the **LBS_NOTIFY** style flag included in its definition in order to
generate **LBN_DBLCLK** messages.) Once a selection has been made, you
will need to query the list box to find out which item has been selected.

A list box is a control that receives messages as well as generating them. You
can send a list box several different messages. To send a message to the list
box (or any other control) use the **SendDlgItemMessage( )** API function.
Its prototype is shown here:

LONG SendDlgItemMessage(HWND *hdwnd*, int *ID*, UINT *IDMsg*,
WPARAM *wParam*, LPARAM *lParam*);

SendDlgItemMessage( ) sends the message specified by *IDMsg* to the
control (within the dialog box) whose ID is specified by *ID*. The handle of
the dialog box is specified in *hdwnd*. Any additional information required by
the message is specified in *wParam* and *lParam*. The additional information,
if any, varies from message to message. If there is no additional information
to pass to a control, the *wParam* and the *lParam* arguments should be zero.
The value returned by **SendDlgItemMessage( )** contains the information
requested by *IDMsg*.

Here are a few of the most common messages that you can send to a list box.

5

Macro	Purpose
LB_ADDSTRING	Adds a string (selection) to the list box.
LB_GETCURSEL	Requests the index of the selected item.
LB_SETCURSEL	Selects an item.
LB_FINDSTRING	Finds a matching entry.
LB_SELECTSTRING	Finds a matching entry and selects it.
LB_GETTEXT	Obtains the text associated with an item.

Let's take a closer look at these messages.

LB_ADDSTRING adds a string to the list box. That is, the specified string
becomes another selection within the box. The string must be pointed to
by *lParam*. (*wParam* is unused by this message.) The value returned by the

list box is the index of the string in the list. If an error occurs, **LB_ERR** is returned.

The **LB_GETCURSEL** message causes the list box to return the index of the currently selected item. All list box indexes begin with zero. Both *lParam* and *wParam* are unused. If an error occurs, **LB_ERR** is returned. If no item is currently selected, then an error results.

You can set the current selection inside a list box using the **LB_SETCURSEL** command. For this message, *wParam* specifies the index of the item to select. *lParam* is not used. On error, **LB_ERR** is returned.

You can find an item in the list that matches a specified prefix using **LB_FINDSTRING**. That is, **LB_FINDSTRING** attempts to match a partial string with an entry in the list box. *wParam* specifies the index at which point the search begins and *lParam* points to the string that will be matched. If a match is found, the index of the matching item is returned. Otherwise, **LB_ERR** is returned. **LB_FINDSTRING** does not select the item within the list box.

If you want to find a matching item and select it, use **LB_SELECTSTRING**. It takes the same parameters as **LB_FINDSTRING** but also selects the matching item.

You can obtain the text associated with an item in a list box using **LB_GETTEXT**. In this case, *wParam* specifies the index of the item and *lParam* points to the character array that will receive the null terminated string associated with that index. The length of the string is returned if successful. **LB_ERR** is returned on failure.

Initializing the List Box

As mentioned, when a list box is created, it is empty. This means that you will need to initialize it each time the dialog box that contains it is displayed. This is easy to accomplish because each time a dialog box is activated, its window function is sent a **WM_INITDIALOG** message. Therefore, you will need to add this case to the outer **switch** statement in **DialogFunc( )**.

```
case WM_INITDIALOG: /* initialize list box */
  for(i=0; i<NUMBOOKS; i++)
    SendDlgItemMessage(hdwnd, IDD_LB1,
                LB_ADDSTRING, 0, (LPARAM)books[i].title);
   /* select first item */
  SendDlgItemMessage(hdwnd, IDD_LB1, LB_SETCURSEL, 0, 0);

  return 1;
```

This code loads the list box with the titles of books as defined in the **books** array. Each string is added to the list box by calling **SendDlgItemMessage( )** with the **LB_ADDSTRING** message. The string to add is pointed to by the *lParam* parameter. (The type cast to **LPARAM** is necessary in this case to convert a pointer into a unsigned integer.) In this example, each string is added to the list box in the order it is sent. (However, depending on how you construct the list box, it is possible to have the items displayed in alphabetical order.) If the number of items you send to a list box exceeds what it can display in its window, vertical scroll bars will be added automatically.

This code also selects the first item in the list box. When a list box is first created, no item is selected. While this might be desirable under certain circumstances, it is not in this case. Most often, you will want to automatically select the first item in a list box as a convenience to the user.

REMEMBER: **WM_INITDIALOG** is sent to a dialog box each time it is activated. You should perform all initializations required by the dialog box when this message is received.

Processing a Selection

5

After the list box has been initialized, it is ready for use. There are essentially two ways a user makes a selection from a list box. First, the user may double-click on an item. This causes a **WM_COMMAND** message to be passed to the dialog box's window function. In this case, **LOWORD(wParam)** contains the ID associated with the list box and **HIWORD(wParam)** contains the **LBN_DBLCLK** notification message. Double-clicking causes your program to be immediately aware of the user's selection. The other way to use a list box is to simply highlight a selection (either by single-clicking or by using the array keys to move the highlight). The list box remembers the selection and waits until your program requests it. Both methods will be demonstrated in the example program.

Once an item has been selected in a list box, you determine which item was chosen by sending the **LB_GETCURSEL** message to the list box. The list box then returns the index of the selected item. Remember, if this message is sent before an item has been selected, the list box returns **LB_ERR**. (This is one reason that it is a good idea to select a list box item when it is initialized.)

To process a list box selection, add these cases to the inner switch inside
DialogFunc( ). You will also need to declare a long integer called **i** and a
character array called **str** inside **DialogFunc( )**. Your dialog box will now
look like that shown in Figure 5-2. Each time a selection is made because of a
double-click or when the user presses the "Select Book" push button, the
currently selected book has its information displayed.

```
case IDD_LB1: /* process a list box LBN_DBLCLK */
  /* see if user made a selection */
  if(HIWORD(wParam)==LBN_DBLCLK) {
    i = SendDlgItemMessage(hdwnd, IDD_LB1,
            LB_GETCURSEL, 0, 0);  /* get index */
    sprintf(str, "%s\n%s\n%s, %u",
            books[i].title, books[i].author,
            books[i].publisher, books[i].copyright);

    MessageBox(hdwnd, str, "Selection Made", MB_OK);

    /* get string associated with that index */
    SendDlgItemMessage(hdwnd, IDD_LB1, LB_GETTEXT,
        i, (LPARAM) str);
  }
  return 1;
case IDD_SELECT: /* Select Book button has been pressed */
  i = SendDlgItemMessage(hdwnd, IDD_LB1,
          LB_GETCURSEL, 0, 0);  /* get index */
  sprintf(str, "%s\n%s\n%s, %u",
          books[i].title, books[i].author,
          books[i].publisher, books[i].copyright);

  MessageBox(hdwnd, str, "Selection Made", MB_OK);

  /* get string associated with that index */
  SendDlgItemMessage(hdwnd, IDD_LB1, LB_GETTEXT,
      i, (LPARAM) str);
  return 1;
```

Notice the code under the **IDD_LB1** case. Since the list box can generate
several different types of notification messages, it is necessary to examine the
high-order word of **wParam** to determine if the user double-clicked on an
item. That is, just because the control generates a notification message does
not mean it is a double-click message. (You will want to explore the other list
box notification messages on your own.)

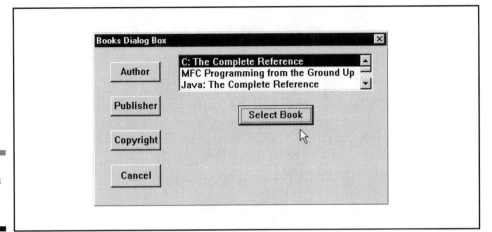

A dialog box
that contains a
list box
Figure 5-2.

Adding an Edit Box

In this section we will add an edit control to the dialog box. Edit boxes are particularly useful because they allow users to enter a string of their own choosing. The edit box in this example will be used to allow the user to enter the title (or part of a title) of a book. If the title is in the list, then it will be selected and information about the book can be obtained. Although the addition of an edit box enhances our simple database application, it also serves another purpose. It will illustrate how two controls can work together. **5**

Before you can use an edit box, you must define one in your resource file. For this example, change **MyDB** so that it looks like this:

```
MyDB DIALOG 10, 10, 210, 110
CAPTION "Books Dialog Box"
STYLE DS_MODALFRAME | WS_POPUP | WS_CAPTION | WS_SYSMENU
{
  DEFPUSHBUTTON "Author", IDD_AUTHOR, 11, 10, 36, 14,
             WS_CHILD | WS_VISIBLE | WS_TABSTOP
  PUSHBUTTON "Publisher", IDD_PUBLISHER, 11, 34, 36, 14,
             WS_CHILD | WS_VISIBLE | WS_TABSTOP
  PUSHBUTTON "Copyright", IDD_COPYRIGHT, 11, 58, 36, 14,
             WS_CHILD | WS_VISIBLE | WS_TABSTOP
  PUSHBUTTON "Cancel", IDCANCEL, 11, 82, 36, 16,
             WS_CHILD | WS_VISIBLE | WS_TABSTOP
  LISTBOX IDD_LB1, 60, 5, 140, 33, LBS_NOTIFY | WS_VISIBLE |
             WS_BORDER | WS_VSCROLL | WS_TABSTOP
  PUSHBUTTON "Select Book", IDD_SELECT, 103, 41, 54, 14,
             WS_CHILD | WS_VISIBLE | WS_TABSTOP
```

```
   EDITTEXT IDD_EB1, 65, 73, 130, 12, ES_LEFT | WS_VISIBLE |
            WS_BORDER | ES_AUTOHSCROLL | WS_TABSTOP
   PUSHBUTTON "Title Search", IDD_DONE, 107, 91, 46, 14,
            WS_CHILD | WS_VISIBLE | WS_TABSTOP
}
```

This version adds a push button called Title Search which will be used to tell the program that you entered the title of a book into the edit box. It also adds the edit box itself. The ID for the edit box is **IDD_EB1**. This definition causes a standard edit box to be created.

The **EDITTEXT** statement has this general form:

> EDITTEXT *EDID*, *X*, *Y*, *Width*, *Height* [,*Style*]

Here, *EDID* is the value that identifies the edit box. The box's upper left corner will be at *X, Y* and its dimensions are specified by *Width* and *Height*. *Style* determines the exact nature of the list box.

You must also add these macro definitions to DIALOG.H:

```
#define IDD_EB1      205
#define IDD_DONE     206
```

Edit boxes recognize many messages and generate several of their own. However, for the purposes of this example, there is no need for the program to respond to any messages. As you will see, edit boxes perform the editing function on their own, independently. No program interaction is required. Your program simply decides when it wants to obtain the current contents of the edit box.

To obtain the current contents of the edit box, use the API function **GetDlgItemText( )**. It has this prototype:

> UINT GetDlgItemText(HWND *hdwnd*, int *ID*, LPSTR *lpstr*, int *Max*);

This function causes the edit box to copy the current contents of the box to the string pointed to by *lpstr*. The handle of the dialog box is specified by *hdwnd*. The ID of the edit box is specified by *ID*. The maximum number of characters to copy is specified by *Max*. The function returns the length of the string.

Although not required by all applications, it is possible to initialize the contents of an edit box using the **SetDlgItemText( )** function. Its prototype is shown here:

> BOOL SetDlgItemText(HWND *hdwnd*, int *ID*, LPSTR *lpstr*);

This function sets the contents of the edit box to the string pointed to by *lpstr*. The handle of the dialog box is specified by *hdwnd*. The ID of the edit box is specified by *ID*. The function returns nonzero if successful or zero on failure.

To add an edit box to the sample program, add this case statement to the inner **switch** of the **DialogFunc( )** function. Each time the Title Search button is pressed, the list box is searched for a title that matches the string that is currently in the edit box. If a match is found, then that title is selected in the list box. Remember that you only need to enter the first few characters of the title. The list box will automatically attempt to match them with a title.

```
case IDD_DONE: /* Title Search button pressed */
  /* get current contents of edit box */
  GetDlgItemText(hdwnd, IDD_EB1, str, 80);

  /* find a matching string in the list box */
  i = SendDlgItemMessage(hdwnd, IDD_LB1, LB_FINDSTRING,
        0, (LPARAM) str);

  if(i != LB_ERR) { /* if match is found */
    /* select the matching title in list box */
    SendDlgItemMessage(hdwnd, IDD_LB1, LB_SETCURSEL, i, 0);

    /* get string associated with that index */
    SendDlgItemMessage(hdwnd, IDD_LB1, LB_GETTEXT,
        i, (LPARAM) str);

    /* update text in edit box */
    SetDlgItemText(hdwnd, IDD_EB1, str);
  }
  else
    MessageBox(hdwnd, str, "No Title Matching", MB_OK);
  return 1;
```

5

This code obtains the current contents of the edit box and looks for a match with the strings inside the list box. If it finds one, it selects the matching item in the list box and then copies the string from the list box back into the edit box. In this way, the two controls work together, complementing each other. As you become a more experienced Windows NT programmer, you will find that there are often instances in which two or more controls can work together.

You will also need to add this line of code to the **INITDIALOG** case. It causes the edit box to be initialized each time the dialog box is activated.

```
/* initialize the edit box */
SetDlgItemText(hdwnd, IDD_EB1, books[0].title);
```

In addition to these changes, the code that processes the list box will be enhanced so that it automatically copies the name of the book selected in the list box into the edit box. These changes are reflected in the full program listing that follows. You should have no trouble understanding them.

The Entire Modal Dialog Box Program

The entire modal dialog box sample program that includes push buttons, a list box, and an edit box, is shown here. Notice that the code associated with the push buttons now displays information about the title currently selected in the list box.

```
/* A complete modal dialog box example. */

#include <windows.h>
#include <string.h>
#include <stdio.h>
#include "dialog.h"

#define NUMBOOKS 7

LRESULT CALLBACK WindowFunc(HWND, UINT, WPARAM, LPARAM);
BOOL CALLBACK DialogFunc(HWND, UINT, WPARAM, LPARAM);

char szWinName[] = "MyWin"; /* name of window class */

HINSTANCE hInst;

/* books database */
struct booksTag {
  char title[40];
  unsigned copyright;
  char author[40];
  char publisher[40];
} books[NUMBOOKS] = {
  { "C: The Complete Reference", 1995,
    "Herbert Schildt", "Osborne/McGraw-Hill" },
  { "MFC Programming from the Ground Up", 1996,
    "Herbert Schildt", "Osborne/McGraw-Hill" },
  { "Java: The Complete Reference", 1997,
    "Naughton and Schildt", "Osborne/McGraw-Hill" },
  { "Design and Evolution of C++", 1994,
    "Bjarne Stroustrup", "Addison-Wesley" },
  { "Inside OLE", 1995,
```

```
          "Kraig Brockschmidt", "Microsoft Press" },
        { "HTML Sourcebook", 1996,
          "Ian S. Graham", "John Wiley & Sons" },
        { "Standard C++ Library", 1995,
          "P. J. Plauger", "Prentice-Hall" }
      };


int WINAPI WinMain(HINSTANCE hThisInst, HINSTANCE hPrevInst,
                   LPSTR lpszArgs, int nWinMode)
{
  HWND hwnd;
  MSG msg;
  WNDCLASSEX wcl;
  HANDLE hAccel;

  /* Define a window class. */
  wcl.cbSize = sizeof(WNDCLASSEX);

  wcl.hInstance = hThisInst; /* handle to this instance */
  wcl.lpszClassName = szWinName; /* window class name */
  wcl.lpfnWndProc = WindowFunc; /* window function */
  wcl.style = 0; /* default style */

  wcl.hIcon = LoadIcon(NULL, IDI_APPLICATION); /* standard icon */
  wcl.hIconSm = LoadIcon(NULL, IDI_WINLOGO); /* small icon */
  wcl.hCursor = LoadCursor(NULL, IDC_ARROW); /* cursor style */

  /* specify name of menu resource */
  wcl.lpszMenuName = "MyMenu"; /* main menu */

  wcl.cbClsExtra = 0; /* no extra */
  wcl.cbWndExtra = 0; /* information needed */

  /* Make the window white. */
  wcl.hbrBackground = GetStockObject(WHITE_BRUSH);

  /* Register the window class. */
  if(!RegisterClassEx(&wcl)) return 0;

  /* Now that a window class has been registered, a window
     can be created. */
  hwnd = CreateWindow(
    szWinName, /* name of window class */
    "Demonstrate Dialog Boxes", /* title */
    WS_OVERLAPPEDWINDOW, /* window style - normal */
    CW_USEDEFAULT, /* X coordinate - let Windows decide */
    CW_USEDEFAULT, /* Y coordinate - let Windows decide */
```

```
      CW_USEDEFAULT, /* width - let Windows decide */
      CW_USEDEFAULT, /* height - let Windows decide */
      HWND_DESKTOP, /* no parent window */
      NULL, /* no override of class menu */
      hThisInst, /* handle of this instance of the program */
      NULL /* no additional arguments */
    );

    hInst = hThisInst; /* save the current instance handle */

    /* load accelerators */
    hAccel = LoadAccelerators(hThisInst, "MyMenu");

    /* Display the window. */
    ShowWindow(hwnd, nWinMode);
    UpdateWindow(hwnd);

    /* Create the message loop. */
    while(GetMessage(&msg, NULL, 0, 0))
    {
      if(!TranslateAccelerator(hwnd, hAccel, &msg)) {
        TranslateMessage(&msg); /* translate keyboard messages */
        DispatchMessage(&msg); /* return control to Windows NT */
      }
    }
    return msg.wParam;
}

/* This function is called by Windows NT and is passed
   messages from the message queue.
*/
LRESULT CALLBACK WindowFunc(HWND hwnd, UINT message,
                                WPARAM wParam, LPARAM lParam)
{
  int response;

  switch(message) {
    case WM_COMMAND:
      switch(LOWORD(wParam)) {
        case IDM_DIALOG:
          DialogBox(hInst, "MyDB", hwnd, (DLGPROC) DialogFunc);
          break;
        case IDM_EXIT:
          response = MessageBox(hwnd, "Quit the Program?",
                                "Exit", MB_YESNO);
          if(response == IDYES) PostQuitMessage(0);
          break;
        case IDM_HELP:
```

```
                    MessageBox(hwnd, "No Help", "Help", MB_OK);
                    break;
              }
              break;
         case WM_DESTROY: /* terminate the program */
           PostQuitMessage(0);
           break;
         default:
           /* Let Windows NT process any messages not specified in
              the preceding switch statement. */
           return DefWindowProc(hwnd, message, wParam, lParam);
      }
   return 0;
}


/* A simple dialog function. */
BOOL CALLBACK DialogFunc(HWND hdwnd, UINT message,
                         WPARAM wParam, LPARAM lParam)
{
   long i;
   char str[255];

   switch(message) {
     case WM_COMMAND:
       switch(LOWORD(wParam)) {
         case IDCANCEL:
           EndDialog(hdwnd, 0);
           return 1;
         case IDD_COPYRIGHT:
           i = SendDlgItemMessage(hdwnd, IDD_LB1,
                  LB_GETCURSEL, 0, 0);  /* get index */
           sprintf(str, "%u", books[i].copyright);
           MessageBox(hdwnd, str, "Copyright", MB_OK);
           return 1;
         case IDD_AUTHOR:
           i = SendDlgItemMessage(hdwnd, IDD_LB1,
                  LB_GETCURSEL, 0, 0);  /* get index */
           sprintf(str, "%s", books[i].author);
           MessageBox(hdwnd, str, "Author", MB_OK);
           return 1;
         case IDD_PUBLISHER:
           i = SendDlgItemMessage(hdwnd, IDD_LB1,
                  LB_GETCURSEL, 0, 0);  /* get index */
           sprintf(str, "%s", books[i].publisher);
           MessageBox(hdwnd, str, "Publisher", MB_OK);
           return 1;
         case IDD_DONE: /* Title Search button pressed */
           /* get current contents of edit box */
```

```
          GetDlgItemText(hdwnd, IDD_EB1, str, 80);

          /* find a matching string in the list box */
          i = SendDlgItemMessage(hdwnd, IDD_LB1, LB_FINDSTRING,
                  0, (LPARAM) str);

          if(i != LB_ERR) { /* if match is found */
            /* select the matching title in list box */
            SendDlgItemMessage(hdwnd, IDD_LB1, LB_SETCURSEL, i, 0);

            /* get string associated with that index */
            SendDlgItemMessage(hdwnd, IDD_LB1, LB_GETTEXT,
                i, (LPARAM) str);

            /* update text in edit box */
            SetDlgItemText(hdwnd, IDD_EB1, str);
          }
          else
            MessageBox(hdwnd, str, "No Title Matching", MB_OK);
          return 1;
        case IDD_LB1: /* process a list box LBN_DBLCLK */
          /* see  if user made a selection */
          if(HIWORD(wParam)==LBN_DBLCLK) {
            i = SendDlgItemMessage(hdwnd, IDD_LB1,
                    LB_GETCURSEL, 0, 0);  /* get index */
            sprintf(str, "%s\n%s\n%s, %u",
                    books[i].title, books[i].author,
                    books[i].publisher, books[i].copyright);

            MessageBox(hdwnd, str, "Selection Made", MB_OK);

            /* get string associated with that index */
            SendDlgItemMessage(hdwnd, IDD_LB1, LB_GETTEXT,
                i, (LPARAM) str);

            /* update edit box */
            SetDlgItemText(hdwnd, IDD_EB1, str);
          }
          return 1;
        case IDD_SELECT: /* Select Book button has been pressed */
          i = SendDlgItemMessage(hdwnd, IDD_LB1,
                  LB_GETCURSEL, 0, 0);  /* get index */
          sprintf(str, "%s\n%s\n%s, %u",
                  books[i].title, books[i].author,
                  books[i].publisher, books[i].copyright);

          MessageBox(hdwnd, str, "Selection Made", MB_OK);
```

```
                    /* get string associated with that index */
                    SendDlgItemMessage(hdwnd, IDD_LB1, LB_GETTEXT,
                        i, (LPARAM) str);

                    /* update edit box */
                    SetDlgItemText(hdwnd, IDD_EB1, str);
                    return 1;
            }
            break;
        case WM_INITDIALOG: /* initialize list box */
            for(i=0; i<NUMBOOKS; i++)
                SendDlgItemMessage(hdwnd, IDD_LB1,
                            LB_ADDSTRING, 0, (LPARAM)books[i].title);

            /* select first item */
            SendDlgItemMessage(hdwnd, IDD_LB1, LB_SETCURSEL, 0, 0);

            /* initialize the edit box */
            SetDlgItemText(hdwnd, IDD_EB1, books[0].title);

            return 1;
    }
    return 0;
}
```

Figure 5-3 shows sample output created by the complete modal dialog box program.

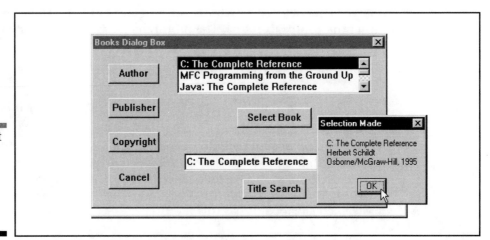

Sample output produced by the complete modal dialog box program

Figure 5-3.

5

Using a Modeless Dialog Box

To conclude this chapter, the modal dialog box used by the preceding program will be converted into a modeless dialog box. As you will see, using a modeless dialog box requires a little more work. The main reason for this is that a modeless dialog box is more independent than a modal dialog box. Specifically, the rest of your program is still active when a modeless dialog box is displayed. Also, both it and your application's window function continue to receive messages. Thus, some additional overhead is required in your application's message loop to accommodate the modeless dialog box.

To create a modeless dialog box, you do not use **DialogBox( )**. Instead, you must use the **CreateDialog( )** API function. Its prototype is shown here:

HWND CreateDialog(HINSTANCE *hThisInst*, LPCSTR *lpName*,
               HWND *hwnd*, DLGPROC *lpDFunc*);

Here, *hThisInst* is a handle to the current application that is passed to your program in the instance parameter to **WinMain( )**. The name of the dialog box as defined in the resource file is pointed to by *lpName*. The handle to the owner of the dialog box is passed in *hwnd*. (This is typically the handle to the window that calls **CreateDialog( )**.) The *lpDFunc* parameter contains a pointer to the dialog function. The dialog function is of the same type as that used for a modal dialog box. **CreateDialog( )** returns a handle to the dialog box. If the dialog box cannot be created, **NULL** is returned.

Unlike a modal dialog box, a modeless dialog box is not automatically visible, so you may need to call **ShowWindow( )** to cause it to be displayed after it has been created. However, if you add **WS_VISIBLE** to the dialog box's definition in its resource file, then it will be visible automatically.

To close a modeless dialog box your program must call **DestroyWindow( )** rather than **EndDialog( )**. The prototype for **DestroyWindow( )** is shown here:

BOOL DestroyWindow(HWND *hwnd*);

Here, *hwnd* is the handle to the window (in this case, dialog box) being closed. The function returns nonzero if successful and zero on failure.

Since your application's window function will continue receiving messages while a modeless dialog box is active, you must make a change to your program's message loop. Specifically, you must add a call to **IsDialogMessage( )**. This function routes dialog box messages to your modeless dialog box. It has this prototype:

BOOL IsDialogMessage(HWND *hdwnd*, LPMSG *msg*);

IN DEPTH

Disabling a Control

Sometimes you will have a control that is not applicable to all situations. When a control is not applicable it can be (and should be) disabled. A control that is disabled is displayed in gray and may not be selected. To disable a control, use the **EnableWindow( )** API function, shown here:

BOOL EnableWindow(HWND *hCntl*, BOOL *How*);

Here, *hCntl* specifies the handle of the window to be affected. (Remember, controls are simply specialized windows.) If *How* is nonzero, then the control is enabled. That is, it is activated. If *How* is zero, the control is disabled. The function returns nonzero if the control was already disabled. It returns zero if the control was previously enabled.

To obtain the handle of a control, use the **GetDlgItem( )** API function. It is shown here:

HWND GetDlgItem(HWND *hDwnd*, int *ID*);

Here, *hDwnd* is the handle of the dialog box that owns the control. The control ID is passed in *ID*. This is the value that you associate with the control in its resource file. The function returns the handle of the specified control or **NULL** on failure.

To see how you can use these functions to disable a control, the following fragment disables the Author push button. In this example **hwpb** is a handle of type **HWND**.

```
hwpb = GetDlgItem(hdwnd, IDD_AUTHOR); /* get handle of button */
EnableWindow(hwpb, 0); /* disable it */
```

On your own, you might want to try disabling and enabling the other controls used by the examples in this and later chapters.

5

Here, *hdwnd* is the handle of the modeless dialog box and *msg* is the message obtained from **GetMessage( )** within your program's message loop. The function returns nonzero if the message is for the dialog box. It returns zero otherwise. If the message is for the dialog box, then it is automatically passed to the dialog box function. Therefore, to process modeless dialog box messages, your program's message loop must look something like this:

```
while(GetMessage(&msg, NULL, 0, 0))
  {
    if(!IsDialogMessage(hDlg, &msg)) {
      /* not dialog box message */
      if(!TranslateAccelerator(hwnd, hAccel, &msg)) {
        TranslateMessage(&msg); /* translate keyboard message */
        DispatchMessage(&msg); /* return control to Windows */
      }
    }
  }
```

As you can see, the message is processed by the rest of the message loop only if it is not a dialog box message.

Creating a Modeless Dialog Box

To convert the modal dialog box shown in the preceding example into a modeless one, surprisingly few changes are needed. The first change that you need to make is to the dialog box definition in the DIALOG.RC resource file. Since a modeless dialog box is not automatically visible, add **WS_VISIBLE** to the dialog box definition. Also, although not technically necessary, you can remove the **DS_MODALFRAME** style, if you like. Since we have made several changes to DIALOG.RC since the start of the chapter, its final form is shown here after making these adjustments.

```
; Sample dialog box and menu resource file.
#include <windows.h>
#include "dialog.h"

MyMenu MENU
{
  POPUP "&Dialog"
  {
    MENUITEM "&Dialog\tF2", IDM_DIALOG
    MENUITEM "&Exit\tF3", IDM_EXIT
  }
  MENUITEM "&Help", IDM_HELP
}

MyMenu ACCELERATORS
{
  VK_F2, IDM_DIALOG, VIRTKEY
  VK_F3, IDM_EXIT, VIRTKEY
  VK_F1, IDM_HELP, VIRTKEY
}
```

```
MyDB DIALOG 10, 10, 210, 110
CAPTION "Books Dialog Box"
STYLE WS_POPUP | WS_CAPTION | WS_SYSMENU | WS_VISIBLE
{
  DEFPUSHBUTTON "Author", IDD_AUTHOR, 11, 10, 36, 14,
            WS_CHILD | WS_VISIBLE | WS_TABSTOP
  PUSHBUTTON "Publisher", IDD_PUBLISHER, 11, 34, 36, 14,
            WS_CHILD | WS_VISIBLE | WS_TABSTOP
  PUSHBUTTON "Copyright", IDD_COPYRIGHT, 11, 58, 36, 14,
            WS_CHILD | WS_VISIBLE | WS_TABSTOP
  PUSHBUTTON "Cancel", IDCANCEL, 11, 82, 36, 16,
            WS_CHILD | WS_VISIBLE | WS_TABSTOP
  LISTBOX IDD_LB1, 60, 5, 140, 33, LBS_NOTIFY | WS_VISIBLE |
          WS_BORDER | WS_VSCROLL | WS_TABSTOP
  PUSHBUTTON "Select Book", IDD_SELECT, 103, 41, 54, 14,
            WS_CHILD | WS_VISIBLE | WS_TABSTOP
  EDITTEXT IDD_EB1, 65, 73, 130, 12, ES_LEFT | WS_VISIBLE |
            WS_BORDER | ES_AUTOHSCROLL | WS_TABSTOP
  PUSHBUTTON "Title Search", IDD_DONE, 107, 91, 46, 14,
            WS_CHILD | WS_VISIBLE | WS_TABSTOP
}
```

Next, you must make the following changes to the program:

1. Create a global handle called **hDlg.**
2. Add **IsDialogMessage( )** to the message loop.
3. Create the dialog box using **CreateDialog( )** rather than **DialogBox( ).**
4. Close the dialog box using **DestroyWindow( )** instead of **EndDialog( ).**

The entire listing (which incorporates these changes) for the modeless dialog box example is shown here. Sample output from this program is shown in Figure 5-4. (You should try this program on your own to fully understand the difference between modal and modeless dialog boxes.)

```
/* A modeless dialog box example. */

#include <windows.h>
#include <string.h>
#include <stdio.h>
#include "dialog.h"

#define NUMBOOKS 7
```

5

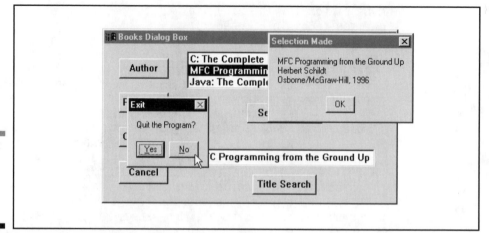

Sample output
using the
modeless
dialog box
Figure 5-4.

```
LRESULT CALLBACK WindowFunc(HWND, UINT, WPARAM, LPARAM);
BOOL CALLBACK DialogFunc(HWND, UINT, WPARAM, LPARAM);

char szWinName[] = "MyWin"; /* name of window class */

HINSTANCE hInst;

HWND hDlg = 0; /* dialog box handle */

/* books database */
struct booksTag {
  char title[40];
  unsigned copyright;
  char author[40];
  char publisher[40];
} books[NUMBOOKS] = {
  { "C: The Complete Reference", 1995,
    "Herbert Schildt", "Osborne/McGraw-Hill" },
  { "MFC Programming from the Ground Up", 1996,
    "Herbert Schildt", "Osborne/McGraw-Hill" },
  { "Java: The Complete Reference", 1997,
    "Naughton and Schildt", "Osborne/McGraw-Hill" },
  { "Design and Evolution of C++", 1994,
    "Bjarne Stroustrup", "Addison-Wesley" },
  { "Inside OLE", 1995,
    "Kraig Brockschmidt", "Microsoft Press" },
  { "HTML Sourcebook", 1996,
    "Ian S. Graham", "John Wiley & Sons" },
  { "Standard C++ Library", 1995,
    "P. J. Plauger", "Prentice-Hall" }
};
```

```
int WINAPI WinMain(HINSTANCE hThisInst, HINSTANCE hPrevInst,
                   LPSTR lpszArgs, int nWinMode)
{
  HWND hwnd;
  MSG msg;
  WNDCLASSEX wcl;
  HANDLE hAccel;

  /* Define a window class. */
  wcl.cbSize = sizeof(WNDCLASSEX);

  wcl.hInstance = hThisInst; /* handle to this instance */
  wcl.lpszClassName = szWinName; /* window class name */
  wcl.lpfnWndProc = WindowFunc; /* window function */
  wcl.style = 0; /* default style */

  wcl.hIcon = LoadIcon(NULL, IDI_APPLICATION); /* standard icon */
  wcl.hIconSm = LoadIcon(NULL, IDI_WINLOGO); /* small icon */
  wcl.hCursor = LoadCursor(NULL, IDC_ARROW); /* cursor style */

  /* specify name of menu resource */
  wcl.lpszMenuName = "MyMenu"; /* main menu */

  wcl.cbClsExtra = 0; /* no extra */
  wcl.cbWndExtra = 0; /* information needed */

  /* Make the window white. */
  wcl.hbrBackground = GetStockObject(WHITE_BRUSH);

  /* Register the window class. */
  if(!RegisterClassEx(&wcl)) return 0;

  /* Now that a window class has been registered, a window
     can be created. */
  hwnd = CreateWindow(
    szWinName, /* name of window class */
    "Demonstrate A Modeless Dialog Box", /* title */
    WS_OVERLAPPEDWINDOW, /* window style - normal */
    CW_USEDEFAULT, /* X coordinate - let Windows decide */
    CW_USEDEFAULT, /* Y coordinate - let Windows decide */
    CW_USEDEFAULT, /* width - let Windows decide */
    CW_USEDEFAULT, /* height - let Windows decide */
    HWND_DESKTOP, /* no parent window */
    NULL, /* no override of class menu */
    hThisInst, /* handle of this instance of the program */
    NULL /* no additional arguments */
```

5

```
      );

      hInst = hThisInst; /* save the current instance handle */

      /* load accelerators */
      hAccel = LoadAccelerators(hThisInst, "MyMenu");

      /* Display the window. */
      ShowWindow(hwnd, nWinMode);
      UpdateWindow(hwnd);

      /* Create the message loop. */
      while(GetMessage(&msg, NULL, 0, 0))
      {
        if(!IsDialogMessage(hDlg, &msg)) {
          /* is not a dialog message */
          if(!TranslateAccelerator(hwnd, hAccel, &msg)) {
            TranslateMessage(&msg); /* translate keyboard messages */
            DispatchMessage(&msg); /* return control to Windows NT */
          }
        }
      }
      return msg.wParam;
}

/* This function is called by Windows NT and is passed
   messages from the message queue.
*/
LRESULT CALLBACK WindowFunc(HWND hwnd, UINT message,
                             WPARAM wParam, LPARAM lParam)
{
  int response;

  switch(message) {
    case WM_COMMAND:
      switch(LOWORD(wParam)) {
        case IDM_DIALOG:
          hDlg = CreateDialog(hInst, "MyDB", hwnd,
                     (DLGPROC) DialogFunc);
          break;
        case IDM_EXIT:
          response = MessageBox(hwnd, "Quit the Program?",
                          "Exit", MB_YESNO);
          if(response == IDYES) PostQuitMessage(0);
          break;
        case IDM_HELP:
          MessageBox(hwnd, "No Help", "Help", MB_OK);
          break;
```

```
        }
        break;
      case WM_DESTROY: /* terminate the program */
        PostQuitMessage(0);
        break;
      default:
        /* Let Windows NT process any messages not specified in
           the preceding switch statement. */
        return DefWindowProc(hwnd, message, wParam, lParam);
    }
    return 0;
}

/* A simple dialog function. */
BOOL CALLBACK DialogFunc(HWND hdwnd, UINT message,
                         WPARAM wParam, LPARAM lParam)
{
  long i;
  char str[255];

  switch(message) {
    case WM_COMMAND:
      switch(LOWORD(wParam)) {
        case IDCANCEL:
          DestroyWindow(hdwnd);
          return 1;
        case IDD_COPYRIGHT:
          i = SendDlgItemMessage(hdwnd, IDD_LB1,
                  LB_GETCURSEL, 0, 0);  /* get index */
          sprintf(str, "%u", books[i].copyright);
          MessageBox(hdwnd, str, "Copyright", MB_OK);
          return 1;
        case IDD_AUTHOR:
          i = SendDlgItemMessage(hdwnd, IDD_LB1,
                  LB_GETCURSEL, 0, 0);  /* get index */
          sprintf(str, "%s", books[i].author);
          MessageBox(hdwnd, str, "Author", MB_OK);
          return 1;
        case IDD_PUBLISHER:
          i = SendDlgItemMessage(hdwnd, IDD_LB1,
                  LB_GETCURSEL, 0, 0);  /* get index */
          sprintf(str, "%s", books[i].publisher);
          MessageBox(hdwnd, str, "Publisher", MB_OK);
          return 1;
        case IDD_DONE: /* Title Search button pressed */
          /* get current contents of edit box */
          GetDlgItemText(hdwnd, IDD_EB1, str, 80);
```

```
            /* find a matching string in the list box */
            i = SendDlgItemMessage(hdwnd, IDD_LB1, LB_FINDSTRING,
                   0, (LPARAM) str);

            if(i != LB_ERR) { /* if match is found */
              /* select the matching title in list box */
              SendDlgItemMessage(hdwnd, IDD_LB1, LB_SETCURSEL, i, 0);

              /* get string associated with that index */
              SendDlgItemMessage(hdwnd, IDD_LB1, LB_GETTEXT,
                  i, (LPARAM) str);

              /* update text in edit box */
              SetDlgItemText(hdwnd, IDD_EB1, str);
            }
            else
              MessageBox(hdwnd, str, "No Title Matching", MB_OK);
            return 1;
      case IDD_LB1: /* process a list box LBN_DBLCLK */
            /* see  if user made a selection */
            if(HIWORD(wParam)==LBN_DBLCLK) {
              i = SendDlgItemMessage(hdwnd, IDD_LB1,
                     LB_GETCURSEL, 0, 0);  /* get index */
              sprintf(str, "%s\n%s\n%s, %u",
                     books[i].title, books[i].author,
                     books[i].publisher, books[i].copyright);

              MessageBox(hdwnd, str, "Selection Made", MB_OK);

              /* get string associated with that index */
              SendDlgItemMessage(hdwnd, IDD_LB1, LB_GETTEXT,
                  i, (LPARAM) str);

              /* update edit box */
              SetDlgItemText(hdwnd, IDD_EB1, str);
            }
            return 1;
      case IDD_SELECT: /* Select Book button has been pressed */
            i = SendDlgItemMessage(hdwnd, IDD_LB1,
                   LB_GETCURSEL, 0, 0);  /* get index */
            sprintf(str, "%s\n%s\n%s, %u",
                   books[i].title, books[i].author,
                   books[i].publisher, books[i].copyright);

            MessageBox(hdwnd, str, "Selection Made", MB_OK);

            /* get string associated with that index */
            SendDlgItemMessage(hdwnd, IDD_LB1, LB_GETTEXT,
```

```
                        i, (LPARAM) str);

          /* update edit box */
          SetDlgItemText(hdwnd, IDD_EB1, str);
          return 1;
      }
      break;
    case WM_INITDIALOG: /* initialize list box */
      for(i=0; i<NUMBOOKS; i++)
        SendDlgItemMessage(hdwnd, IDD_LB1,
                  LB_ADDSTRING, 0, (LPARAM)books[i].title);

      /* select first item */
      SendDlgItemMessage(hdwnd, IDD_LB1, LB_SETCURSEL, 0, 0);

      /* initialize the edit box */
      SetDlgItemText(hdwnd, IDD_EB1, books[0].title);

      return 1;
  }
  return 0;
}
```

CHAPTER 6

More Controls

Controls were introduced in the preceding chapter, when dialog boxes were first discussed. This chapter continues the topic by examining three more of Windows NT's standard controls: scroll bars, check boxes, and radio buttons. As you will see, many of the techniques that you learned when using controls in Chapter 5 will apply to the controls described here.

This chapter begins with a discussion of the scroll bar and illustrates its use in a short example program. Although scroll bars offer a bit more of a programming challenge than do the other standard controls, they are still quite easy to use. Next, check boxes and radio buttons are discussed. To illustrate the practical use of scroll bars, check boxes, and radio buttons, a simple countdown timer application is developed. You could use such a program as a darkroom timer, for example. In the process of developing the countdown timer, Windows NT timer interrupts and the **WM_TIMER** message are explored. The chapter concludes with a look at Windows static controls.

Scroll Bars

Standard scroll bars are attached to a window.

A scroll bar control is a free-standing scroll bar.

To add standard scroll bars to a window, specify the WS_VSCROLL and/or WS_HSCROLL styles.

The scroll bar is one of Windows NT's most important controls. Scroll bars exist in two forms. The first type of scroll bar is an integral part of a normal window or dialog box. These are called *standard scroll bars*. The other type of scroll bar exists separately as a control and is called a *scroll bar control*. Both types of scroll bars are managed in much the same way.

Activating the Standard Scroll Bars

For a window to include standard scroll bars, you must explicitly request it. For windows created using **CreateWindow( )**, such as your application's main window, you do this by including the styles **WS_VSCROLL** and/or **WS_HSCROLL** in the style parameter. In the case of a dialog box, you include the **WS_VSCROLL** and/or **WS_HSCROLL** styles in the dialog box's definition inside its resource file. As expected, the **WS_VSCROLL** causes a standard vertical scroll bar to be included and **WS_HSCROLL** activates a horizontal scroll bar. After you have added these styles, the window will automatically display the standard vertical and horizontal scroll bars.

Receiving Scroll Bar Messages

Unlike other controls, a scroll bar control does not generate a **WM_COMMAND** message. Instead, scroll bars send either a **WM_VSCROLL** or a **WM_HSCROLL** message when either a vertical or horizontal scroll bar is accessed, respectively. The value of the low-order word of **wParam** contains a code that describes the activity. For the standard window scroll bars, **lParam** is zero. However, if a scroll bar control generates the message, then **lParam** contains its handle.

As mentioned, the value in **LOWORD(wParam)** specifies what type of scroll bar action has taken place. Here are some common scroll bar values:

SB_LINEUP	SB_LINERIGHT
SB_LINEDOWN	SB_PAGELEFT
SB_PAGEUP	SB_PAGERIGHT
SB_PAGEDOWN	SB_THUMBPOSITION
SB_LINELEFT	SB_THUMBTRACK

For vertical scroll bars, each time the user moves the scroll bar up one position, **SB_LINEUP** is sent. Each time the scroll bar is moved down one position, **SB_LINEDOWN** is sent. **SB_PAGEUP** and **SB_PAGEDOWN** are sent when the scroll bar is moved up or down one page.

For horizontal scroll bars, each time the user moves the scroll bar left one position, **SB_LINELEFT** is sent. Each time the scroll bar is moved right one position, **SB_LINERIGHT** is sent. **SB_PAGELEFT** and **SB_PAGERIGHT** are sent when the scroll bar is moved left or right one page.

For both types of scroll bars, the **SB_THUMBPOSITION** value is sent after the slider box (thumb) of the scroll bar has been dragged to a new position. The **SB_THUMBTRACK** message is also sent when the thumb is dragged to a new position. However, it is sent each time the thumb passes over a new position. This allows you to "track" the movement of the thumb before it is released. When **SB_THUMBPOSITION** or **SB_THUMBTRACK** is received, the high-order word of **wParam** contains the current slider box position.

PORTABILITY: In Windows 3.1, the organization of **lParam** and **wParam** differs from their equivalents in Windows NT. Specifically, the handle of the scroll bar is in the high-order word of **lParam**. The position of the slider box is in the low-order word of **lParam**. The nature of the scroll bar action is in **wParam**. Because of these differences, you must rewrite all scroll bar message-handling code when porting from Windows 3.1 to NT.

6

SetScrollInfo( ) and GetScrollInfo( )

Scroll bars are, for the most part, manually managed controls. This means that in addition to responding to scroll bar messages, your program will also need to update various attributes associated with a scroll bar. For example, your program must update the position of the slider box manually. Windows NT contains two functions that help you manage scroll bars.

The first is **SetScrollInfo( )**, which is used to set various attributes associated with a scroll bar. Its prototype is shown here:

int SetScrollInfo(HWND *hwnd*, int *which*, LPSCROLLINFO *lpSI*,
                   BOOL *repaint*);

Here, *hwnd* is the handle that identifies the scroll bar. For window scroll bars, this is the handle of the window that owns the scroll bar. For scroll bar controls, this is the handle of the scroll bar itself. The value of *which* determines which scroll bar is affected. If you are setting the attributes of the vertical window scroll bar, then this parameter must be **SB_VERT**. If you are setting the attributes of the horizontal window scroll bar, this value must be **SB_HORZ**. However, to set a scroll bar control, this value must be **SB_CTL** and *hwnd* must be the handle of the control. The attributes are set according to the information pointed to by *lpSI* (discussed shortly). If *repaint* is true, then the scroll bar is redrawn. If false, the bar is not redisplayed. The function returns the position of the slider box.

To obtain the attributes associated with a scroll bar, use **GetScrollInfo( )**, shown here:

BOOL GetScrollInfo(HWND *hwnd*, int *which*, LPSCROLLINFO *lpSI*);

The *hwnd* and *which* parameters are the same as those just described for **SetScrollInfo( )**. The information obtained by **GetScrollInfo( )** is put into the structure pointed to by *lpSI*. The function returns nonzero if successful and zero on failure.

The *lpSI* parameter of both functions points to a structure of type **SCROLLINFO**, which is defined like this:

```
typedef struct tagSCROLLINFO
{
  UINT cbSize; /* size of SCROLLINFO */
  UINT fMask; /* Operation performed */
  int nMin; /* minimum range */
  int nMax; /* maximum range */
  UINT nPage; /* Page value */
  int nPos; /* slider box position */
  int nTrackPos; /* current tracking position */
} SCROLLINFO;
```

Here, **cbSize** must contain the size of the **SCROLLINFO** structure. The value or values contained in **fMask** determine which of the remaining members are meaningful. Specifically, when used in a call to **SetScrollInfo( )**, the value in **fMask** specifies which scroll bar values will be updated. When used with **GetScrollInfo( )**, the value in **fMask** determines which settings will be obtained. **fMask** must be one or more of these values. (To combine values, simply OR them together.)

SIF_ALL	Same as SIF_PAGE	SIF_POS	SIF_RANGE	SIF_TRACKPOS.
SIF_DISABLENOSCROLL	Scroll bar is disabled rather than removed if its range is set to zero.
SIF_PAGE	**nPage** contains valid information.
SIF_POS	**nPos** contains valid information.
SIF_RANGE	**nMin** and **nMax** contain valid information.
SIF_TRACKPOS	**nTrackPos** contains valid information.

nPage contains the current page setting for proportional scroll bars. **nPos** contains the position of the slider box. **nMin** and **nMax** contain the minimum and maximum range of the scroll bar. **nTrackPos** contains the current tracking position. The tracking position is the current position of the slider box while it is being dragged by the user. This value cannot be set.

PORTABILITY: Windows 3.1 programs use the API functions **SetScrollRange( )** and **SetScrollPos( )** to manage scroll bars. Although these functions are still supported under Win32, their use is not recommended and you should upgrade them to calls to **SetScrollInfo( )** when porting older programs.

Working with Scroll Bars

6

As stated, scroll bars are manually managed controls. This means that your program will need to update the position of the slider box within the scroll bar each time it is moved. To do this you will need to assign **nPos** the value of the new position, assign **fMask** the value **SIF_POS**, and then call **SetScrollInfo( )**. For example, to update the slider box for the vertical scroll bar, your program will need to execute a sequence like the following:

```
SCROLLINFO si;
/* ... */
si.cbSize = sizeof(SCROLLINFO);
si.fMask = SIF_POS;
si.nPos = newposition;
SetScrollInfo(hwnd, SB_VERT, &si, 1);
```

The range of the scroll bar determines how many positions there are between one end and the other. By default, window scroll bars have a range of 0 to 100. However, you can set their range to meet the needs of your program. Control scroll bars have a default range of 0 to 0, which means that the range needs to be set before the scroll bar control can be used. (A scroll bar that has a zero range is inactive.)

A Sample Scroll Bar Program

The following program demonstrates both vertical and horizontal standard scroll bars. The scroll bar program requires the following resource file:

```
; Demonstrate scroll bars.
#include "scroll.h"
#include <windows.h>

MyMenu MENU
{
  POPUP "&Dialog"
  {
    MENUITEM "&Scroll Bars\tF2", IDM_DIALOG
    MENUITEM "&Exit\tF3", IDM_EXIT
  }
  MENUITEM "&Help", IDM_HELP
}

MyMenu ACCELERATORS
{
  VK_F2, IDM_DIALOG, VIRTKEY
  VK_F3, IDM_EXIT, VIRTKEY
  VK_F1, IDM_HELP, VIRTKEY
}

MyDB DIALOG 18, 18, 142, 92
CAPTION "Using Scroll Bars"
STYLE DS_MODALFRAME | WS_POPUP | WS_CAPTION | WS_SYSMENU
      | WS_VSCROLL | WS_HSCROLL
{
}
```

As you can see, the dialog box definition is empty. The scroll bars are added automatically because of the **WS_VSCROLL** and **WS_HSCROLL** style specifications.

You will also need to create this header file, called SCROLL.H:

```
#define IDM_DIALOG    100
#define IDM_EXIT      101
#define IDM_HELP      102
```

The entire scroll bar demonstration program is shown here. The vertical scroll bar responds to the **SB_LINEUP**, **SB_LINEDOWN**, **SB_PAGEUP**, **SB_PAGEDOWN**, **SB_THUMBPOSITION**, and **SB_THUMBTRACK** messages by moving the slider box appropriately. It also displays the current position of the thumb. The position will change as you move the slider. The horizontal scroll bar only responds to **SB_LINELEFT** and **SB_LINERIGHT**. Its thumb position is also displayed. (On your own, you might try adding the necessary code to make the horizontal scroll bar respond to other messages.) Notice that the range of both the horizontal and vertical scroll bar is set when the dialog box receives a **WM_INITDIALOG** message. You might want to try changing the range of the scroll bars and observing the results. Sample output from the program is shown in Figure 6-1.

One other point: notice that the thumb position of each scroll bar is displayed by outputting text into the client area of the dialog box using **TextOut( )**. Although a dialog box performs a special purpose, it is still a window with the same basic characteristics as the main window.

```
/* Demonstrate Standard Scroll Bars */

#include <windows.h>
#include <string.h>
#include <stdio.h>
#include "scroll.h"

#define VERTRANGEMAX 200
#define HORZRANGEMAX  50

LRESULT CALLBACK WindowFunc(HWND, UINT, WPARAM, LPARAM);
BOOL CALLBACK DialogFunc(HWND, UINT, WPARAM, LPARAM);

char szWinName[] = "MyWin"; /* name of window class */

HINSTANCE hInst;

int WINAPI WinMain(HINSTANCE hThisInst, HINSTANCE hPrevInst,
                   LPSTR lpszArgs, int nWinMode)
{
```

```
HWND hwnd;
MSG msg;
WNDCLASSEX wcl;
HANDLE hAccel;

/* Define a window class. */
wcl.cbSize = sizeof(WNDCLASSEX);

wcl.hInstance = hThisInst; /* handle to this instance */
wcl.lpszClassName = szWinName; /* window class name */
wcl.lpfnWndProc = WindowFunc; /* window function */
wcl.style = 0; /* default style */

wcl.hIcon = LoadIcon(NULL, IDI_APPLICATION); /* standard icon */
wcl.hIconSm = LoadIcon(NULL, IDI_WINLOGO); /* small icon */
wcl.hCursor = LoadCursor(NULL, IDC_ARROW); /* cursor style */

/* specify name of menu resource */
wcl.lpszMenuName = "MyMenu"; /* main menu */

wcl.cbClsExtra = 0; /* no extra */
wcl.cbWndExtra = 0; /* information needed */

/* Make the window white. */
wcl.hbrBackground = GetStockObject(WHITE_BRUSH);

/* Register the window class. */
if(!RegisterClassEx(&wcl)) return 0;

/* Now that a window class has been registered, a window
   can be created. */
hwnd = CreateWindow(
  szWinName, /* name of window class */
  "Managing Scroll Bars", /* title */
  WS_OVERLAPPEDWINDOW, /* window style - normal */
  CW_USEDEFAULT, /* X coordinate - let Windows decide */
  CW_USEDEFAULT, /* Y coordinate - let Windows decide */
  CW_USEDEFAULT, /* width - let Windows decide */
  CW_USEDEFAULT, /* height - let Windows decide */
  HWND_DESKTOP, /* no parent window */
  NULL, /* no override of class menu */
  hThisInst, /* handle of this instance of the program */
  NULL /* no additional arguments */
);

hInst = hThisInst; /* save the current instance handle */

/* load accelerators */
hAccel = LoadAccelerators(hThisInst, "MyMenu");
```

```
        /* Display the window. */
        ShowWindow(hwnd, nWinMode);
        UpdateWindow(hwnd);

        /* Create the message loop. */
        while(GetMessage(&msg, NULL, 0, 0))
        {
          if(!TranslateAccelerator(hwnd, hAccel, &msg)) {
            TranslateMessage(&msg); /* translate keyboard messages */
            DispatchMessage(&msg); /* return control to Windows NT */
          }
        }
        return msg.wParam;
}


/* This function is called by Windows NT and is passed
   messages from the message queue.
*/
LRESULT CALLBACK WindowFunc(HWND hwnd, UINT message,
                                  WPARAM wParam, LPARAM lParam)
{
  int response;

  switch(message) {
    case WM_COMMAND:
      switch(LOWORD(wParam)) {
        case IDM_DIALOG:
          DialogBox(hInst, "MyDB", hwnd, (DLGPROC) DialogFunc);
          break;
        case IDM_EXIT:
          response = MessageBox(hwnd, "Quit the Program?",
                                  "Exit", MB_YESNO);
          if(response == IDYES) PostQuitMessage(0);
          break;
        case IDM_HELP:
          MessageBox(hwnd, "Try the Scroll Bar", "Help", MB_OK);
          break;
      }
      break;
    case WM_DESTROY: /* terminate the program */
      PostQuitMessage(0);
      break;
    default:
      /* Let Windows NT process any messages not specified in
         the preceding switch statement. */
      return DefWindowProc(hwnd, message, wParam, lParam);
  }
  return 0;
}
```

6

```
/* Dialog function */
BOOL CALLBACK DialogFunc(HWND hdwnd, UINT message,
                         WPARAM wParam, LPARAM lParam)
{
  char str[80];
  static int vpos = 0; /* vertical slider box position */
  static int hpos = 0; /* horizontal slider box position */
  static SCROLLINFO si; /* scroll bar info structure */

  HDC hdc;
  PAINTSTRUCT paintstruct;

  switch(message) {
    case WM_COMMAND:
  switch(LOWORD(wParam)) {
        case IDCANCEL:
          EndDialog(hdwnd, 0);
          return 1;
      }
      break;
    case WM_INITDIALOG:
      si.cbSize = sizeof(SCROLLINFO);
      si.fMask = SIF_RANGE;
      si.nMin = 0; si.nMax = VERTRANGEMAX;
      SetScrollInfo(hdwnd, SB_VERT, &si, 1);
      si.nMax = HORZRANGEMAX;
      SetScrollInfo(hdwnd, SB_HORZ, &si, 1);
      vpos = hpos = 0;
      return 1;
    case WM_PAINT:
      hdc = BeginPaint(hdwnd, &paintstruct);
      sprintf(str, "Vertical: %d", vpos);
      TextOut(hdc, 1, 1, str, strlen(str));
      sprintf(str, "Horizontal: %d", hpos);
      TextOut(hdc, 1, 30, str, strlen(str));
      EndPaint(hdwnd, &paintstruct);
      return 1;
    case WM_VSCROLL:
      switch(LOWORD(wParam)) {
        case SB_LINEDOWN:
          vpos++;
          if(vpos>VERTRANGEMAX) vpos = VERTRANGEMAX;
          break;
        case SB_LINEUP:
          vpos--;
          if(vpos<0) vpos = 0;
          break;
```

```
              case SB_THUMBPOSITION:
                vpos = HIWORD(wParam); /* get current position */
                break;
              case SB_THUMBTRACK:
                vpos = HIWORD(wParam); /* get current position */
                break;
              case SB_PAGEDOWN:
                vpos += 5;
                if(vpos>VERTRANGEMAX) vpos = VERTRANGEMAX;
                break;
              case SB_PAGEUP:
                vpos -= 5;
                if(vpos<0) vpos = 0;
            }
            /* update vertical bar position */
            si.fMask = SIF_POS;
            si.nPos = vpos;
            SetScrollInfo(hdwnd, SB_VERT, &si, 1);
            hdc = GetDC(hdwnd);
            sprintf(str, "Vertical: %d    ", vpos);
            TextOut(hdc, 1, 1, str, strlen(str));
            ReleaseDC(hdwnd, hdc);
            return 1;
        case WM_HSCROLL:
          switch(LOWORD(wParam)) {
              /* Try adding the other event handling code
                 for the horizontal scroll bar, here. */
              case SB_LINERIGHT:
                hpos++;
                if(hpos>HORZRANGEMAX) hpos = HORZRANGEMAX;
                break;
              case SB_LINELEFT:
                hpos--;
                if(hpos<0) hpos = 0;
            }
            /* update horizontal bar position */
            si.fMask = SIF_POS;
            si.nPos = hpos;
            SetScrollInfo(hdwnd, SB_HORZ, &si, 1);
            hdc = GetDC(hdwnd);
            sprintf(str, "Horizontal: %d    ", hpos);
            TextOut(hdc, 1, 30, str, strlen(str));
            ReleaseDC(hdwnd, hdc);
            return 1;
      }
      return 0;
    }
```

6

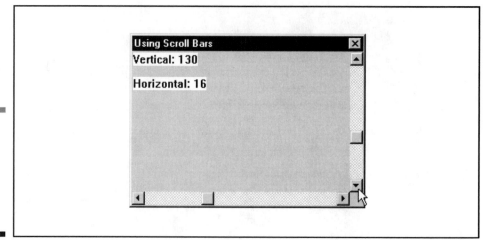

Sample
output from
the standard
scroll bar
demonstration
program
Figure 6-1.

Using a Scroll Bar Control

When a control scroll bar generates a message, its handle is passed in lParam.

A scroll bar control is a stand-alone scroll bar; it is not attached to a window. Scroll bar controls are handled much like standard scroll bars, but two important differences exist. First, the range of a scroll bar control must be set because it has a default range of zero. Thus, it is initially inactive. This differs from standard scroll bars, whose default range is 0 to 100.

The second difference has to do with the meaning of **lParam** when a scroll bar message is received. Recall that all scroll bars — standard or control — generate a **WM_HSCROLL** or a **WM_VSCROLL** message, depending upon whether the scroll bar is horizontal or vertical. When these messages a generated by a standard scroll bar, **lParam** is always zero. However, when they are generated by a scroll bar control, the handle of the control is passed in **lParam**. In windows that contain both standard and control scroll bars, you will need to make use of this fact to determine which scroll bar generated the message.

Creating a Scroll Bar Control

To create a scroll bar control in a dialog box, use the **SCROLLBAR** statement, which has this general form:

SCROLLBAR *SBID, X, Y, Width, Height* [, *Style*]

Here, *SBID* is the value associated with the scroll bar. The scroll bar's upper left corner will be at *X, Y* and the scroll bar will have the dimensions specified by *Width* and *Height*. *Style* determines the exact nature of the scroll bar. Its default style is **SBS_HORZ**, which creates a horizontal scroll bar. For a vertical scroll bar, specify the **SBS_VERT** style. If you want the scroll bar to be able to receive keyboard focus, include the **WS_TABSTOP** style.

Demonstrating a Scroll Bar Control

To demonstrate a control scroll bar, one will be added to the preceding program. First, change the dialog box definition as shown here. This version adds a vertical scroll bar control.

```
MyDB DIALOG 18, 18, 142, 92
CAPTION "Adding a Control Scroll Bar"
STYLE DS_MODALFRAME | WS_POPUP | WS_CAPTION | WS_SYSMENU
      | WS_VSCROLL | WS_HSCROLL
{
  SCROLLBAR ID_SB1, 110, 10, 10, 70, SBS_VERT | WS_TABSTOP
}
```

Then, add this line to SCROLL.H:

```
#define ID_SB1 200
```

Next, you will need to add the code that handles the control scroll bar. This code must distinguish between the standard scroll bars and the scroll bar control, since both generate **WM_VSCROLL** messages. To do this, just remember that a scroll bar control passes its handle in **lParam**. For standard scroll bars, **lParam** is zero. For example, here is the **SB_LINEDOWN** case that distinguishes between the standard scroll bar and the control scroll bar.

```
case SB_LINEDOWN:
  if((HWND)lParam==GetDlgItem(hdwnd, ID_SB1)) {
    /* is control scroll bar */
    cntlpos++;
    if(cntlpos>VERTRANGEMAX) cntlpos = VERTRANGEMAX;
  }
  else {
    /* is window scroll bar */
    vpos++;
    if(vpos>VERTRANGEMAX) vpos = VERTRANGEMAX;
  }
  break;
```

6

Here, the handle in **lParam** is compared with the handle of the scroll bar control, as obtained using **GetDlgItem( )**. If the handles are the same, then the message was generated by the scroll bar control. If not, then the message came from the standard scroll bar.

As mentioned in Chapter 5, the **GetDlgItem( )** API function obtains the handle of a control. Its prototype is:

HWND GetDlgItem(HWND *hDwnd*, int *ID*);

Here, *hDwnd* is the handle of the dialog box that owns the control. The control ID is passed in *ID*. This is the value you associate with the control in its resource file. The function returns the handle of the specified control or **NULL** on failure.

Here is the entire program that includes the vertical scroll bar control. It is the same as the preceding program except for the following additions: First, **DialogFunc( )** defines the static variable **cntlpos**, which holds the position of the control scroll bar. Second, the control scroll bar is initialized inside **WM_INITDIALOG**. Third, all the handlers that process **WM_VSCROLL** messages determine whether the message came from the standard scroll bar or the control scroll bar. Finally, code has been added to display the current position of the control scroll bar.

Sample output is shown in Figure 6-2. On your own, try adding a horizontal control scroll bar.

```
/* Demonstrate a Control Scroll Bar */

#include <windows.h>
#include <string.h>
#include <stdio.h>
#include "scroll.h"

#define VERTRANGEMAX 200
#define HORZRANGEMAX   50

LRESULT CALLBACK WindowFunc(HWND, UINT, WPARAM, LPARAM);
BOOL CALLBACK DialogFunc(HWND, UINT, WPARAM, LPARAM);

char szWinName[] = "MyWin"; /* name of window class */

HINSTANCE hInst;

int WINAPI WinMain(HINSTANCE hThisInst, HINSTANCE hPrevInst,
                   LPSTR lpszArgs, int nWinMode)
{
  HWND hwnd;
  MSG msg;
```

```
WNDCLASSEX wcl;
HANDLE hAccel;

/* Define a window class. */
wcl.cbSize = sizeof(WNDCLASSEX);

wcl.hInstance = hThisInst; /* handle to this instance */
wcl.lpszClassName = szWinName; /* window class name */
wcl.lpfnWndProc = WindowFunc; /* window function */
wcl.style = 0; /* default style */

wcl.hIcon = LoadIcon(NULL, IDI_APPLICATION); /* standard icon */
wcl.hIconSm = LoadIcon(NULL, IDI_WINLOGO); /* small icon */
wcl.hCursor = LoadCursor(NULL, IDC_ARROW); /* cursor style */

/* specify name of menu resource */
wcl.lpszMenuName = "MyMenu"; /* main menu */

wcl.cbClsExtra = 0; /* no extra */
wcl.cbWndExtra = 0; /* information needed */

/* Make the window white. */
wcl.hbrBackground = GetStockObject(WHITE_BRUSH);

/* Register the window class. */
if(!RegisterClassEx(&wcl)) return 0;

/* Now that a window class has been registered, a window
   can be created. */
hwnd = CreateWindow(
  szWinName, /* name of window class */
  "Managing Scroll Bars", /* title */
  WS_OVERLAPPEDWINDOW, /* window style - normal */
  CW_USEDEFAULT, /* X coordinate - let Windows decide */
  CW_USEDEFAULT, /* Y coordinate - let Windows decide */
  CW_USEDEFAULT, /* width - let Windows decide */
  CW_USEDEFAULT, /* height - let Windows decide */
  HWND_DESKTOP, /* no parent window */
  NULL, /* no override of class menu */
  hThisInst, /* handle of this instance of the program */
  NULL /* no additional arguments */
);

hInst = hThisInst; /* save the current instance handle */

/* load accelerators */
hAccel = LoadAccelerators(hThisInst, "MyMenu");
```

6

```
  /* Display the window. */
  ShowWindow(hwnd, nWinMode);
  UpdateWindow(hwnd);

  /* Create the message loop. */
  while(GetMessage(&msg, NULL, 0, 0))
  {
    if(!TranslateAccelerator(hwnd, hAccel, &msg)) {
      TranslateMessage(&msg); /* translate keyboard messages */
      DispatchMessage(&msg); /* return control to Windows NT */
    }
  }
  return msg.wParam;
}


/* This function is called by Windows NT and is passed
   messages from the message queue.
*/
LRESULT CALLBACK WindowFunc(HWND hwnd, UINT message,
                            WPARAM wParam, LPARAM lParam)
{
  int response;

  switch(message) {
    case WM_COMMAND:
      switch(LOWORD(wParam)) {
        case IDM_DIALOG:
          DialogBox(hInst, "MyDB", hwnd, (DLGPROC) DialogFunc);
          break;
        case IDM_EXIT:
          response = MessageBox(hwnd, "Quit the Program?",
                                "Exit", MB_YESNO);
          if(response == IDYES) PostQuitMessage(0);
          break;
        case IDM_HELP:
          MessageBox(hwnd, "Try the Scroll Bar", "Help", MB_OK);
          break;
      }
      break;
    case WM_DESTROY: /* terminate the program */
      PostQuitMessage(0);
      break;
    default:
      /* Let Windows NT process any messages not specified in
         the preceding switch statement. */
      return DefWindowProc(hwnd, message, wParam, lParam);
  }
  return 0;
```

```
  }

/* Dialog function */
BOOL CALLBACK DialogFunc(HWND hdwnd, UINT message,
                         WPARAM wParam, LPARAM lParam)
{
  char str[80];
  static int vpos = 0; /* vertical slider box position */
  static int hpos = 0; /* horizontal slider box position */
  static int cntlpos = 0; /* control slider box position */
  static SCROLLINFO si; /* scroll bar info structure */

  HDC hdc;
  PAINTSTRUCT paintstruct;

  switch(message) {
    case WM_COMMAND:
      switch(LOWORD(wParam)) {
        case IDCANCEL:
          EndDialog(hdwnd, 0);
          return 1;
      }
      break;
    case WM_INITDIALOG:
      si.cbSize = sizeof(SCROLLINFO);
      si.fMask = SIF_RANGE;
      si.nMin = 0; si.nMax = VERTRANGEMAX;

      /* set range of standard vertical scroll bar */
      SetScrollInfo(hdwnd, SB_VERT, &si, 1);

      /* set range of scroll bar control */
      SetScrollInfo(GetDlgItem(hdwnd, ID_SB1), SB_CTL, &si, 1);

      si.nMax = HORZRANGEMAX;
      /* set range of standard horizontal scroll bar */
      SetScrollInfo(hdwnd, SB_HORZ, &si, 1);

      vpos = hpos = cntlpos = 0;
      return 1;
    case WM_PAINT:
      hdc = BeginPaint(hdwnd, &paintstruct);
      sprintf(str, "Vertical: %d", vpos);
      TextOut(hdc, 1, 1, str, strlen(str));
      sprintf(str, "Horizontal: %d", hpos);
      TextOut(hdc, 1, 30, str, strlen(str));
      sprintf(str, "Scroll Bar Control: %d   ", cntlpos);
      TextOut(hdc, 1, 60, str, strlen(str));
```

6

```
        EndPaint(hdwnd, &paintstruct);
        return 1;
    case WM_VSCROLL:
      /* Now we must now determine whether the control
         scroll bar or the standard scroll bar generated
         the message. */
      switch(LOWORD(wParam)) {
        case SB_LINEDOWN:
          if((HWND)lParam==GetDlgItem(hdwnd, ID_SB1)) {
            /* is control scroll bar */
            cntlpos++;
            if(cntlpos>VERTRANGEMAX) cntlpos = VERTRANGEMAX;
          }
          else {
            /* is window scroll bar */
            vpos++;
            if(vpos>VERTRANGEMAX) vpos = VERTRANGEMAX;
          }
          break;
        case SB_LINEUP:
          if((HWND)lParam==GetDlgItem(hdwnd, ID_SB1)) {
            /* is control scroll bar */
            cntlpos--;
            if(cntlpos<0) cntlpos = 0;
          }
          else {
            /* is window scroll bar */
            vpos--;
            if(vpos<0) vpos = 0;
          }
          break;
        case SB_THUMBPOSITION:
          if((HWND)lParam==GetDlgItem(hdwnd, ID_SB1)) {
            /* is control scroll bar */
            cntlpos = HIWORD(wParam); /* get current position */
          }
          else {
            /* is window scroll bar */
            vpos = HIWORD(wParam); /* get current position */
          }
          break;
        case SB_THUMBTRACK:
          if((HWND)lParam==GetDlgItem(hdwnd, ID_SB1)) {
            /* is control scroll bar */
            cntlpos = HIWORD(wParam); /* get current position */
          }
          else {
            /* is window scroll bar */
```

```
        vpos = HIWORD(wParam); /* get current position */
      }
    break;
    case SB_PAGEDOWN:
      if((HWND)lParam==GetDlgItem(hdwnd, ID_SB1)) {
        /* is control scroll bar */
        cntlpos += 5;
        if(cntlpos>VERTRANGEMAX) cntlpos = VERTRANGEMAX;
      }
      else {
        /* is window scroll bar */
        vpos += 5;
        if(vpos>VERTRANGEMAX) vpos = VERTRANGEMAX;
      }
    break;
    case SB_PAGEUP:
      if((HWND)lParam==GetDlgItem(hdwnd, ID_SB1)) {
        /* is control scroll bar */
        cntlpos -= 5;
        if(cntlpos<0) cntlpos = 0;
      }
      else {
        /* is window scroll bar */
        vpos -= 5;
        if(vpos<0) vpos = 0;
      }
    break;
  }

  if((HWND)lParam==GetDlgItem(hdwnd, ID_SB1)) {
    /* update control scroll bar position */
    si.fMask = SIF_POS;
    si.nPos = cntlpos;
    SetScrollInfo((HWND)lParam, SB_CTL, &si, 1);
    hdc = GetDC(hdwnd);
    sprintf(str, "Scroll Bar Control: %d   ", cntlpos);
    TextOut(hdc, 1, 60, str, strlen(str));
    ReleaseDC(hdwnd, hdc);
  }
  else {
    /* update standard scroll bar position */
    si.fMask = SIF_POS;
    si.nPos = vpos;
    SetScrollInfo(hdwnd, SB_VERT, &si, 1);
    hdc = GetDC(hdwnd);
    sprintf(str, "Vertical: %d   ", vpos);
    TextOut(hdc, 1, 1, str, strlen(str));
    ReleaseDC(hdwnd, hdc);
```

6

```
      }
      return 1;
   case WM_HSCROLL:
     switch(LOWORD(wParam)) {
        /* Try adding the other event handling code
           for the horizontal scroll bar, here. */
        case SB_LINERIGHT:
          hpos++;
          if(hpos>HORZRANGEMAX) hpos = HORZRANGEMAX;
          break;
        case SB_LINELEFT:
          hpos--;
          if(hpos<0) hpos = 0;
      }
      /* update horizontal scroll bar position */
      si.fMask = SIF_POS;
      si.nPos = hpos;
      SetScrollInfo(hdwnd, SB_HORZ, &si, 1);
      hdc = GetDC(hdwnd);
      sprintf(str, "Horizontal: %d   ", hpos);
      TextOut(hdc, 1, 30, str, strlen(str));
      ReleaseDC(hdwnd, hdc);
      return 1;
  }
  return 0;
}
```

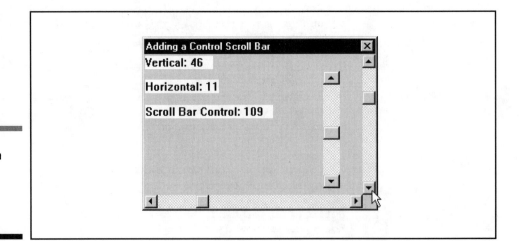

Sample
output from
the control
scroll bar
program
Figure 6-2.

Check Boxes

A *check box* is a control that is used to turn on or off an option. It consists of a small rectangle which can either contain a check mark or not. A check box has associated with it a label that describes what option the box represents. If the box contains a check mark, the box is said to be *checked* and the option is selected. If the box is empty, the option will be deselected.

A check box is a control that is typically part of a dialog box and is generally defined within the dialog box's definition in your program's resource file. To add a check box to a dialog box definition, use either the **CHECKBOX** or **AUTOCHECKBOX** command, which have these general forms:

CHECKBOX "*string*", *CBID*, *X*, *Y*, *Width*, *Height* [, *Style*]
AUTOCHECKBOX "*string*", *CBID*, *X*, *Y*, *Width*, *Height* [, *Style*]

Here, *string* is the text that will be shown alongside the check box. *CBID* is the value associated with the check box. The box's upper left corner will be at *X*, *Y* and the box plus its associated text will have the dimensions specified by *Width* and *Height*. *Style* determines the exact nature of the check box. If no explicit style is specified, then the check box defaults to displaying the *string* on the right and allowing the box to be tabbed to. When a check box is first created, it is unchecked.

As you know from using Windows NT, check boxes are toggles. Each time you select a check box, its state changes from checked to unchecked, and vice versa. However, this is not necessarily accomplished automatically. When you use the **CHECKBOX** resource command, you are creating a *manual check box*, which your program must manage by checking and unchecking the box each time it is selected. (That is, a manual check box must be manually toggled by your program.) However, you can have Windows NT perform this housekeeping function for you if you create an *automatic check box* using **AUTOCHECKBOX**. When you use an automatic check box, Windows NT automatically toggles its state (between checked and not checked) each time it is selected. Since most applications do not need to manually manage a check box, we will be using only **AUTOCHECKBOX** in the examples that follow.

6

PORTABILITY: The resource compiler for Windows 3.1 does not support **AUTOCHECKBOX**. You will want to watch for opportunities to use **AUTOCHECKBOX** when converting from Windows 3.1.

Obtaining the State of a Check Box

A check box is either checked or unchecked. You can determine the status of a check box by sending it the message **BM_GETCHECK** using the **SendDlgItemMessage( )** API function. (**SendDlgItemMessage( )** is described in Chapter 5.) When sending this message, both *wParam* and *lParam* are zero. The check box returns **BST_CHECKED** (1) if the box is checked and **BST_UNCHECKED** (0) otherwise.

Checking a Check Box

A check box can be checked by your program. To do this, send the check box a **BM_SETCHECK** message using **SendDlgItemMessage( ).** In this case, *wParam* determines whether the check box will be checked or cleared. If *wParam* is **BST_CHECKED**, the check box is checked. If it is **BST_UNCHECKED**, the box is cleared. In both cases, *lParam* is zero.

As mentioned, manual check boxes will need to be manually checked or cleared by your program each time they are toggled by the user. However, when using an automatic check box your program will need to explicitly check or clear a check box during program initialization only. When you use an automatic check box, the state of the box will be changed automatically each time it is selected.

Check boxes are cleared (that is, unchecked) each time the dialog box that contains them is activated. If you want the check boxes to reflect their previous state, then you must initialize them. The easiest way to do this is to send them the appropriate **BM_SETCHECK** messages when the dialog box is created. Remember, each time a dialog box is activated, it is sent a **WM_INITDIALOG** message. When this message is received, you can set the state of the check boxes (and anything else) inside the dialog box.

Check Box Messages

Each time the user clicks on the check box or selects the check box and then presses the space bar, a **WM_COMMAND** message is sent to the dialog function and the low-order word of **wParam** contains the identifier associated with that check box. If you are using a manual check box, then you will want to respond to this command by changing the state of the box.

The 3-State Check Box

Windows NT provides an interesting variation of the check box called the *3-state check box*. This check box has three possible states: checked, cleared, or grayed. (When the control is grayed, it is disabled.) Like its relative, the 3-state check box can be implemented as either an automatic or manually managed control using the **AUTO3STATE** and **STATE3** resource commands, respectively. Their general forms are shown here:

> STATE3 "*string*", *ID*, *X*, *Y*, *Width*, *Height* [, *Style*]
> AUTO3STATE "*string*", *ID*, *X*, *Y*, *Width*, *Height* [, *Style*]

Here, *string* is the text that will be shown alongside the check box. *ID* is the value associated with the check box. The box's upper left corner will be at *X, Y* and the box plus its associated text will have the dimensions specified by *Width* and *Height*. *Style* determines the exact nature of the check box. If no explicit style is specified, then the check box defaults to displaying the *string* on the right and allowing the box to be tabbed to. When a 3-state check box is first created, it is unchecked.

In response to a **BM_GETCHECK** message, 3-state check boxes return **BST_UNCHECKED** if unchecked, **BST_CHECKED** if checked, and **BST_INDETERMINATE** if grayed. Correspondingly, when setting a 3-state check box using **BM_SETCHECK**, use **BST_UNCHECKED** to clear it, **BST_CHECKED** to check it, and **BST_INDETERMINATE** to gray it.

6

Radio Buttons

The next control that we will examine is the *radio button*. Radio buttons are used to present mutually exclusive options. A radio button consists of a label and a small circular button. If the button is empty, then the option is not selected. If the button is filled, then the option is selected. Windows NT supports two types of radio buttons: manual and automatic. The manual

Radio buttons get their name from the fact that their operation resembles that of the selector buttons of a car radio. Only one station can be tuned in at a time.

radio button (like the manual check box) requires that you perform all management functions. The automatic radio button performs the management functions for you. Because automatic radio buttons are used almost exclusively, they are the only ones examined here.

Like other controls, automatic radio buttons are defined in your program's resource file, within a dialog definition. To create an automatic radio button, use **AUTORADIOBUTTON**, which has this general form:

> AUTORADIOBUTTON *"string"*, *RBID*, *X*, *Y*, *Width*, *Height* [, *Style*]

Here, *string* is the text that will be shown alongside the button. *RBID* is the value associated with the radio button. The button's upper left corner will be at *X,Y* and the button plus its associated text will have the dimensions specified by *Width* and *Height*. *Style* determines the exact nature of the radio button. If no explicit style is specified, then the button defaults to displaying the *string* on the right and allowing the button to be tabbed to. By default, a radio button is unchecked.

PORTABILITY: The resource compiler for the Windows 3.1 does not support **AUTORADIOBUTTON**. You will want to watch for opportunities to use **AUTORADIOBUTTON** when converting from Windows 3.1.

As stated, radio buttons are generally used to create groups of mutually exclusive options. When you use automatic radio buttons to create such a group, then Windows NT automatically manages the buttons in a mutually exclusive manner. That is, each time the user selects one button, the previously selected button is turned off. Also, it is not possible for the user to select more than one button at any one time.

A radio button (even an automatic one) may be set to a known state by your program by sending it the **BM_SETCHECK** message using the **SendDlgItemMessage( )** function. The value of *wParam* determines whether the button will be checked or cleared. If *wParam* is **BST_CHECKED**, then the button will be checked. If it is **BST_UNCHECKED**, the box will be cleared. By default, a radio button is unchecked.

NOTE: It is possible to manually set more than one button or to clear all buttons using **SendDlgItemMessage( )**. However, normal Windows style dictates that radio buttons be used in a mutually exclusive fashion, with one (and only one) option selected. It is strongly suggested that you do not violate this rule.

You can obtain the status of a radio button by sending it the **BM_GETCHECK** message. The button returns **BST_CHECKED** if the button is selected and **BST_UNCHECKED** if it is not.

Demonstrating Check Boxes, Radio Buttons, and Scroll Bars

In this section a simple but useful program is developed that demonstrates check boxes, radio buttons, and scroll bars. The program implements a countdown timer. Using the timer, you can set the number of seconds that you want to delay. The program will then wait that number of seconds and notify you when the time is up. The countdown timer uses a scroll bar to set the delay period. It uses check boxes and radio buttons to set various options, such as whether the program will beep when the end of the time has been reached. However, before we can develop the program, you will need to learn about another feature of Windows NT: timers. The countdown program will use one of Windows NT's built-in timers to monitor the passage of time. As you will see, using a timer is straightforward. Also, as you begin to write your own applications, you will find that timers are useful in a variety of programming situations.

Generating Timer Messages

Windows NT provides timers which your program can use.

Using Windows NT, it is possible to establish a timer that will interrupt your program at periodic intervals. Each time the timer goes off, Windows NT sends a **WM_TIMER** message to your program. Using a timer is a good way to "wake up your program" every so often. This is particularly useful when your program is running as a background task.

To start a timer, use the **SetTimer( )** API function, whose prototype is shown here:

    UINT SetTimer(HWND *hwnd*, UINT *ID*, UINT *wLength*,
                  TIMERPROC *lpTFunc*);

Here, *hwnd* is the handle of the window that uses the timer. Generally, this window will be either your program's main window or a dialog box window. The value of *ID* specifies a value that will be associated with this timer. (More than one timer can be active.) The value of *wLength* specifies the length of the period, in milliseconds. That is, *wLength* specifies how much time there is between interrupts. The function pointed to by *lpTFunc* is the timer function that will be called when the timer goes off. However, if the value of *lpTFunc* is **NULL**, then the window function associated with the window specified by *hwnd* will be called each time the timer goes off and

6

there is no need to specify a separate timer function. In this case, when the timer goes off, a **WM_TIMER** message is put into your program's message queue and processed like any other message. This is the approach used by the example that follows. The **SetTimer( )** function returns *ID* if successful. If the timer cannot be allocated, zero is returned.

If you wish to define a separate timer function, it must be a callback function that has the following prototype (of course, the name of the function may be different):

VOID CALLBACK TFunc(HWND *hwnd*, UINT *msg*, UINT *TimerID*,

DWORD Sys*Time*);

Here, *hwnd* will contain the handle of the timer window, *msg* will contain the message **WM_TIMER**, *TimerID* will contain the ID of the timer that went off, and *SysTime* will contain the current system time.

Once a timer has been started, it continues to interrupt your program until you either terminate the application or your program executes a call to the **KillTimer( )** API function, whose prototype is shown here:

BOOL KillTimer(HWND *hwnd*, UINT *ID*);

Here, *hwnd* is the window that contains the timer and *ID* is the value that identifies that particular timer. The function returns nonzero if successful and zero on failure.

Each time a **WM_TIMER** message is generated, the value of **wParam** contains the ID of the timer and **lParam** contains the address of the timer callback function (if it is specified). For the example that follows, **lParam** will be **NULL**.

The Countdown Timer Resource and Header Files

The countdown timer uses the following resource file:

```
; Demonstrate scroll bars, check boxes, and radio buttons.
#include "cd.h"
#include <windows.h>

MyMenu MENU
{
  POPUP "&Dialog"
  {
    MENUITEM "&Timer\tF2", IDM_DIALOG
    MENUITEM "&Exit\tF3", IDM_EXIT
```

```
   }
   MENUITEM "&Help", IDM_HELP
}

MyMenu ACCELERATORS
{
  VK_F2, IDM_DIALOG, VIRTKEY
  VK_F3, IDM_EXIT, VIRTKEY
  VK_F1, IDM_HELP, VIRTKEY
}

MyDB DIALOG 18, 18, 152, 92
CAPTION "A Countdown Timer"
STYLE DS_MODALFRAME | WS_POPUP | WS_CAPTION | WS_SYSMENU
      | WS_VSCROLL
{
  PUSHBUTTON "Start", IDD_START, 10, 60, 30, 14,
             WS_CHILD | WS_VISIBLE | WS_TABSTOP
  PUSHBUTTON "Cancel", IDCANCEL, 60, 60, 30, 14,
             WS_CHILD | WS_VISIBLE | WS_TABSTOP
  AUTOCHECKBOX "Show Countdown", IDD_CB1, 1, 20, 70, 10
  AUTOCHECKBOX "Beep At End", IDD_CB2, 1, 30, 50, 10
  AUTORADIOBUTTON "Minimize", IDD_RB1, 80, 20, 50, 10
  AUTORADIOBUTTON "Maximize", IDD_RB2, 80, 30, 50, 10
  AUTORADIOBUTTON "As-Is", IDD_RB3, 80, 40, 50, 10
}
```

The header file required by the timer program is shown here. Call this file CD.H.

```
#define IDM_DIALOG    100
#define IDM_EXIT      101
#define IDM_HELP      102

#define IDD_START     300
#define IDD_TIMER     301

#define IDD_CB1       400
#define IDD_CB2       401
#define IDD_RB1       402
#define IDD_RB2       403
#define IDD_RB3       404
```

The Countdown Timer Program

The entire countdown timer program is shown here. Sample output from this program is shown in Figure 6-3.

```
/* A Countdown Timer */

#include <windows.h>
#include <string.h>
#include <stdio.h>
#include "cd.h"

#define VERTRANGEMAX 200

LRESULT CALLBACK WindowFunc(HWND, UINT, WPARAM, LPARAM);
BOOL CALLBACK DialogFunc(HWND, UINT, WPARAM, LPARAM);

char szWinName[] = "MyWin"; /* name of window class */

HINSTANCE hInst;

HWND hwnd;

int WINAPI WinMain(HINSTANCE hThisInst, HINSTANCE hPrevInst,
                   LPSTR lpszArgs, int nWinMode)
{
  MSG msg;
  WNDCLASSEX wcl;
  HANDLE hAccel;

  /* Define a window class. */
  wcl.cbSize = sizeof(WNDCLASSEX);

  wcl.hInstance = hThisInst; /* handle to this instance */
  wcl.lpszClassName = szWinName; /* window class name */
  wcl.lpfnWndProc = WindowFunc; /* window function */
  wcl.style = 0; /* default style */

  wcl.hIcon = LoadIcon(NULL, IDI_APPLICATION); /* standard icon */
  wcl.hIconSm = LoadIcon(NULL, IDI_WINLOGO); /* small icon */
  wcl.hCursor = LoadCursor(NULL, IDC_ARROW); /* cursor style */

  /* specify name of menu resource */
  wcl.lpszMenuName = "MyMenu"; /* main menu */

  wcl.cbClsExtra = 0; /* no extra */
  wcl.cbWndExtra = 0; /* information needed */

  /* Make the window white. */
  wcl.hbrBackground = GetStockObject(WHITE_BRUSH);
```

```
    /* Register the window class. */
    if(!RegisterClassEx(&wcl)) return 0;

    /* Now that a window class has been registered, a window
       can be created. */
    hwnd = CreateWindow(
      szWinName, /* name of window class */
      "Demonstrating Controls", /* title */
      WS_OVERLAPPEDWINDOW, /* window style - normal */
      CW_USEDEFAULT, /* X coordinate - let Windows decide */
      CW_USEDEFAULT, /* Y coordinate - let Windows decide */
      CW_USEDEFAULT, /* width - let Windows decide */
      CW_USEDEFAULT, /* height - let Windows decide */
      HWND_DESKTOP, /* no parent window */
      NULL, /* no override of class menu */
      hThisInst, /* handle of this instance of the program */
      NULL /* no additional arguments */
    );

    hInst = hThisInst; /* save the current instance handle */

    /* load accelerators */
    hAccel = LoadAccelerators(hThisInst, "MyMenu");

    /* Display the window. */
    ShowWindow(hwnd, nWinMode);
    UpdateWindow(hwnd);

    /* Create the message loop. */
    while(GetMessage(&msg, NULL, 0, 0))
    {
      if(!TranslateAccelerator(hwnd, hAccel, &msg)) {
        TranslateMessage(&msg); /* translate keyboard messages */
        DispatchMessage(&msg); /* return control to Windows NT */
      }
    }
    return msg.wParam;
}

/* This function is called by Windows NT and is passed
   messages from the message queue.
*/
LRESULT CALLBACK WindowFunc(HWND hwnd, UINT message,
                            WPARAM wParam, LPARAM lParam)
{
  int response;
```

6

```
      switch(message) {
        case WM_COMMAND:
          switch(LOWORD(wParam)) {
            case IDM_DIALOG:
              DialogBox(hInst, "MyDB", hwnd, (DLGPROC) DialogFunc);
              break;
            case IDM_EXIT:
              response = MessageBox(hwnd, "Quit the Program?",
                                    "Exit", MB_YESNO);
              if(response == IDYES) PostQuitMessage(0);
              break;
            case IDM_HELP:
              MessageBox(hwnd, "Try the Timer", "Help", MB_OK);
              break;
          }
          break;
        case WM_DESTROY: /* terminate the program */
          PostQuitMessage(0);
          break;
        default:
          /* Let Windows NT process any messages not specified in
             the preceding switch statement. */
          return DefWindowProc(hwnd, message, wParam, lParam);
      }
      return 0;
}

/* Dialog function */
BOOL CALLBACK DialogFunc(HWND hdwnd, UINT message,
                         WPARAM wParam, LPARAM lParam)
{
  char str[80];
  static int vpos = 0; /* vertical slider box position */
  static SCROLLINFO si; /* scroll bar info structure */

  HDC hdc;
  PAINTSTRUCT paintstruct;

  static int t;

  switch(message) {
    case WM_COMMAND:
      switch(LOWORD(wParam)) {
        case IDCANCEL:
          EndDialog(hdwnd, 0);
          return 1;
        case IDD_START: /* start the timer */
          SetTimer(hdwnd, IDD_TIMER, 1000, NULL);
          t = vpos;
```

```
        if(SendDlgItemMessage(hdwnd,
               IDD_RB1, BM_GETCHECK, 0, 0) == BST_CHECKED)
          ShowWindow(hwnd, SW_MINIMIZE);
        else
        if(SendDlgItemMessage(hdwnd,
               IDD_RB2, BM_GETCHECK, 0, 0) == BST_CHECKED)
          ShowWindow(hwnd, SW_MAXIMIZE);
        return 1;
    }
    break;
  case WM_TIMER: /* timer went off */
    if(t==0) {
      KillTimer(hdwnd, IDD_TIMER);
      if(SendDlgItemMessage(hdwnd,
             IDD_CB2, BM_GETCHECK, 0, 0) == BST_CHECKED)
        MessageBeep(MB_OK);
      MessageBox(hdwnd, "Timer Went Off", "Timer", MB_OK);
      ShowWindow(hwnd, SW_RESTORE);
      return 1;
    }
    t--;

    /* see if countdown is to be displayed */
    if(SendDlgItemMessage(hdwnd,
           IDD_CB1, BM_GETCHECK, 0, 0) == BST_CHECKED) {
      hdc = GetDC(hdwnd);
      sprintf(str, "Counting: %d   ", t);
      TextOut(hdc, 1, 1, str, strlen(str));
      ReleaseDC(hdwnd, hdc);
    }
    return 1;
  case WM_INITDIALOG:
    si.cbSize = sizeof(SCROLLINFO);
    si.fMask = SIF_RANGE;
    si.nMin = 0; si.nMax = VERTRANGEMAX;
    SetScrollInfo(hdwnd, SB_VERT, &si, 1);
    /* check the As-Is radio button */
    SendDlgItemMessage(hdwnd, IDD_RB3, BM_SETCHECK, BST_CHECKED, 0);
    return 1;
  case WM_PAINT:
    hdc = BeginPaint(hdwnd, &paintstruct);
    sprintf(str, "Interval: %d", vpos);
    TextOut(hdc, 1, 1, str, strlen(str));
    EndPaint(hdwnd, &paintstruct);
    return 1;
  case WM_VSCROLL:
    switch(LOWORD(wParam)) {
      case SB_LINEDOWN:
```

6

```
            vpos++;
            if(vpos>VERTRANGEMAX) vpos = VERTRANGEMAX;
            break;
          case SB_LINEUP:
            vpos--;
            if(vpos<0) vpos = 0;
            break;
          case SB_THUMBPOSITION:
            vpos = HIWORD(wParam); /* get current position */
            break;
          case SB_THUMBTRACK:
            vpos = HIWORD(wParam); /* get current position */
            break;
          case SB_PAGEDOWN:
            vpos += 5;
            if(vpos>VERTRANGEMAX) vpos = VERTRANGEMAX;
            break;
          case SB_PAGEUP:
            vpos -= 5;
            if(vpos<0) vpos = 0;
        }
        si.fMask = SIF_POS;
        si.nPos = vpos;
        SetScrollInfo(hdwnd, SB_VERT, &si, 1);
        hdc = GetDC(hdwnd);
        sprintf(str, "Interval: %d   ", vpos);
        TextOut(hdc, 1, 1, str, strlen(str));
        ReleaseDC(hdwnd, hdc);
        return 1;
    }
```

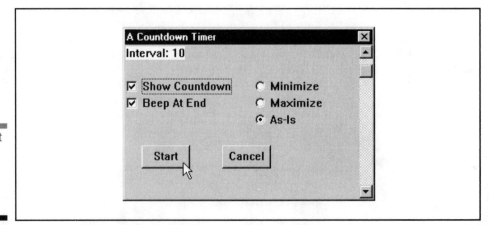

Sample output
from the
countdown
timer program
Figure 6-3.

```
   return 0;
}
```

A Closer Look at the Countdown Program

To better understand how each control in the countdown program operates, let's take a closer look at it now. As you can see, the vertical scroll bar is used to set the delay. It uses much of the same code that was described earlier in this chapter when scroll bars were examined and no further explanation is needed. However, the code that manages the check boxes and radio buttons deserves detailed attention.

As mentioned, by default no radio button is checked when they are first created. Thus, the program must manually select one each time the dialog box is activated. In this example, each time a **WM_INITDIALOG** message is received, the As-Is radio button (**IDD_RB3**) is checked using this statement.

```
SendDlgItemMessage(hdwnd, IDD_RB3, BM_SETCHECK, BST_CHECKED, 0);
```

To start the timer, the user presses the Start button. This causes the following code to execute:

```
case IDD_START: /* start the timer */
  SetTimer(hdwnd, IDD_TIMER, 1000, NULL);
  t = vpos;
  if(SendDlgItemMessage(hdwnd,
        IDD_RB1, BM_GETCHECK, 0, 0) == BST_CHECKED)
    ShowWindow(hwnd, SW_MINIMIZE);
  else
  if(SendDlgItemMessage(hdwnd,
        IDD_RB2, BM_GETCHECK, 0, 0) == BST_CHECKED)
    ShowWindow(hwnd, SW_MAXIMIZE);
  return 1;
```

6

Here, the timer is set to go off once every second (1,000 milliseconds). The value of the counter variable **t** is set to the value determined by the position of the vertical scroll bar. If the Minimize radio button is checked, the program windows are minimized. If the Maximize button is checked, the program windows are maximized. Otherwise, the program windows are left unchanged. Notice that the main window handle, **hwnd**, rather than the dialog box handle, **hdwnd**, is used in the call to **ShowWindow( )**. To minimize or maximize the program, the main window handle—not the handle of the dialog box—must be used. Also, notice that **hwnd** is a global variable in this program. This allows it to be used inside **DialogFunc( )**.

Each time a **WM_TIMER** message is received, the following code executes:

```
case WM_TIMER: /* timer went off */
  if(t==0) {
    KillTimer(hdwnd, IDD_TIMER);
    if(SendDlgItemMessage(hdwnd,
            IDD_CB2, BM_GETCHECK, 0, 0) == BST_CHECKED)
      MessageBeep(MB_OK);
    MessageBox(hdwnd, "Timer Went Off", "Timer", MB_OK);
    ShowWindow(hwnd, SW_RESTORE);
    return 1;
  }
  t--;

  /* see if countdown is to be displayed */
  if(SendDlgItemMessage(hdwnd,
          IDD_CB1, BM_GETCHECK, 0, 0) == BST_CHECKED) {
    hdc = GetDC(hdwnd);
    sprintf(str, "Counting: %d    ", t);
    TextOut(hdc, 1, 1, str, strlen(str));
    ReleaseDC(hdwnd, hdc);
  }
  return 1;
```

If the countdown has reached zero, the timer is killed, a message box informing the user that the specified time has elapsed is displayed, and the window is restored to its former size, if necessary. If the Beep At End button is checked, then the computer's speaker is beeped using a call to the API function **MessageBeep( )**. If there is still time remaining, then the counter variable **t** is decremented. If the Show Countdown button is checked, then the time remaining in the countdown is displayed.

MessageBeep( ) is a function you will probably find useful in other programs that you write. Its prototype is shown here:

  BOOL MessageBeep(UINT *sound*);

Here, *sound* specifies the type of sound that you want to make. It can be –1, which produces a standard beep, or one of these built in values:

MB_ICONASTERISK	MB_ICONEXCLAMATION	MB_ICONHAND
MB_ICONQUESTION	MB_OK	

MB_OK also produces a standard beep. **MessageBeep( )** returns nonzero if successful or zero on failure.

As you can see by looking at the program, since automatic check boxes and radio buttons are mostly managed by Windows NT, there is surprisingly little code within the countdown program that actually deals with these two controls. In fact, the ease of use of check boxes and radio buttons helps make them two of the most commonly used control elements.

Static Controls

Static controls do not generate or receive messages.

Although none of the standard controls are difficult to use, there is no question that the static controls are the easiest. The reason for this is simple: a *static control* is one that neither receives nor generates any messages. In short, the term static control is just a formal way of describing something that is simply displayed in a dialog box. Static controls include **CTEXT**, **RTEXT**, and **LTEXT**, which are static text controls; and **GROUPBOX**, which is used to visually group other controls.

The **CTEXT** control outputs a string that is centered within a predefined area. **LTEXT** displays the string left justified. **RTEXT** outputs the string right justified. The general forms for these controls are shown here:

CTEXT "*text*", *ID, X, Y, Width, Height* [, *Style*]
RTEXT "*text*", *ID, X, Y, Width, Height* [, *Style*]
LTEXT "*text*", *ID, X, Y, Width, Height* [, *Style*]

Here, *text* is the text that will be displayed. *ID* is the value associated with the text. The text will be shown in a box whose upper left corner will be at *X, Y* and whose dimensions are specified by *Width* and *Height*. *Style* determines the exact nature of the text box. Understand that the box itself is *not* displayed. The box simply defines the space that the text is allowed to occupy.

The static text controls provide a convenient means of outputting text to a dialog box. Frequently, static text is used to label other dialog box controls or to provide simple directions to the user. You will want to experiment with the static text controls on your own.

6

A group box is simply a box the surrounds other dialog elements and is generally used to visually group other items. The box may contain a title. The general form for **GROUPBOX** is shown here:

GROUPBOX "*title*", *ID, X, Y, Width, Height* [, *Style*]

Here, *title* is the title to the box. *ID* is the value associated with the box. The upper left corner will be at *X,Y* and its dimensions are specified by *Width* and *Height*. *Style* determines the exact nature of the group box. Generally, the default setting is sufficient.

To see the effect of a group box, add the following definition to the resource file you created for the countdown program.

```
GROUPBOX "Display As", 1, 72, 10, 60, 46
```

After you have added the group box, the dialog box will look like that shown in Figure 6-4. Remember that although a group box makes the dialog box look different, its function has not been changed.

IN DEPTH

Stand Alone Controls

Although controls are most often used within a dialog box, they may also be free-standing within the client area of the main window. To create a free-standing control, simply use the **CreateWindow( )** function, specifying the name of the control class and the style of control that you desire. The standard control class names are shown here:

> BUTTON
> COMBOBOX
> EDIT
> LISTBOX
> SCROLLBAR
> STATIC

Each of these classes has several style macros associated with it that can be used to customize the control. However, it is beyond the scope of this book to describe them. A list of these style macros can be found by examining WINDOWS.H (and its support files) or by referring to an API reference guide.

The following code creates a free-standing scroll bar and push button.

```
hsbwnd = CreateWindow(
  "SCROLLBAR", /* name of scroll bar class */
  "", /* no title */
  SBS_HORZ | WS_CHILD | WS_VISIBLE, /* horizontal scroll bar */
  10, 10, /* position */
  120, 20, /* dimensions */
```

```
      hwnd, /* parent window */
      NULL, /* no control ID needed for scroll bar */
      hThisInst, /* handle of this instance of the program */
      NULL /* no additional arguments */
    );

    hpbwnd = CreateWindow(
      "BUTTON", /* name of pushbutton class */
      "Push Button", /* text inside button */
      BS_PUSHBUTTON | WS_CHILD | WS_VISIBLE, /* pushbutton */
      10, 60, /* position */
      90, 30, /* dimensions */
      hwnd, /* parent window */
      (HWND) 500, /* control ID */
      hThisInst, /* handle of this instance of the program */
      NULL /* no additional arguments */
    );
```

As the push button shows, when required, the ID associated with
a free-standing control is specified in the ninth parameter to
CreateWindow( ). As you should recall, this is the parameter that
we used to specify the handle of a menu that overrides the class menu.
However, when creating a control, you use this parameter to specify
the control's ID.

When a free-standing control generates a message, it is sent to the
parent window. You will need to add code to handle these messages
within the parent's window function.

6

The countdown
dialog box
that includes
a group box
static control

Figure 6-4.

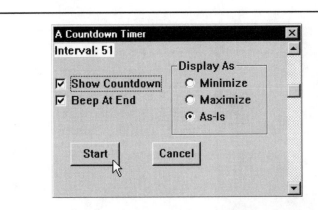

CHAPTER 7

Working with Bitmaps and Solving the Repaint Problem

A *bitmap* is a display object that contains a rectangular graphical image. The term comes from the fact that a bitmap contains a set of bits which defines the image. Since Windows is a graphics-based operating system, it makes sense that you can include graphical images as resources in your applications. However, bitmaps have broader application than simply providing support for graphical resources. As you will see, bitmaps underlie many of the features that comprise the Windows graphical user interface. They can also help solve one of the must fundamental programming problems facing the Windows programmer: repainting a window. Once you gain mastery over the bitmap you are well on your way to taking charge of many other aspects of Windows.

In addition to bitmaps proper, there are two specialized types: the icon and the cursor. As you know, an icon represents some resource or object. The cursor indicates the current mouse position. So far, we have only been using built-in icons and cursors. Here you will learn to create your own, custom versions of these items.

Two Types of Bitmaps

There are two general types of bitmaps supported by Windows NT: device-dependent and device-independent. Device-dependent bitmaps (DDB) are designed for use with a specific device. Device-independent bitmaps (DIB) are not tied to a specific device. Device-dependent bitmaps were initially the only type available in Windows. However, all versions of Windows since 3.0 have included device-independent bitmaps, too.

A device-dependent bitmap (DDB) is tied to a specific device.

A device-independent bitmap (DIB) works with different types of devices.

DIBs are most valuable when you are creating a bitmap that will be used in environments other than the one in which it was created. For example, if you want to distribute a bitmap, a device-independent bitmap is the best way to do this. However, DDBs are still commonly used when a program needs to create a bitmap for its own, internal use. In fact, this is the main reason that DDBs remain widely used. Also, Win32 provides various functions that allow you to convert between DDBs and DIBs, should you need to.

The organization of a DDB differs from that of a DIB. However, for the purposes of this chapter, the differences are not important. In fact, the binary format of a bitmap is seldom significant from the application's perspective because Windows provides high-level API functions that manage bitmaps—you will seldom need to "get your hands dirty" with their internals.

For the purposes of this chapter, we will be using device-dependent bitmaps because we will be focusing on bitmaps used by the program that creates them.

Two Ways to Obtain a Bitmap

A bitmap can be obtained two different ways: it may be specified as a resource or it may be created dynamically, by your program. A bitmap resource is a graphical image that is defined outside your program, but specified in the program's resource file. A dynamic bitmap is created by your program during its execution. Each type is discussed in this chapter, beginning with the bitmap resource.

Using a Bitmap Resource

In general, to use a bitmap resource you must follow these three steps:

1. The bitmap must be specified within your program's resource file.
2. The bitmap must be loaded by your program.
3. The bitmap must be selected into a device context.

This section describes the procedures necessary to accomplish these steps.

Creating a Bitmap Resource

Bitmap resources are not like the resources described in the preceding chapters, such as menus, dialog boxes, and controls. These resources are defined using textual statements in a resource file. Bitmaps are graphical images that must reside in special, bitmap files. However, the bitmap file must still be referred to in your program's resource file.

A bitmap resource is typically created using an *image editor*. An image editor will usually be supplied with your compiler. It displays an enlarged view of your bitmap. This allows you easily to construct or alter the image. For example, a custom bitmap is displayed inside the Microsoft Visual C++ image editor in Figure 7-1.

Except for specialized bitmaps, such as icons and cursors, the size of a bitmap is arbitrary and under your control. Within reason, you can create bitmaps as large or as small as you like. To try the example that follows, your bitmap must be 256 × 128 pixels. Call your bitmap file BP.BMP. If you want your program to produce the results shown in the figures in this chapter, then make your bitmap look like the one shown in Figure 7-1. After you have defined your bitmap, create a resource file called BP.RC that contains this line.

7

```
MyBP BITMAP BP.BMP
```

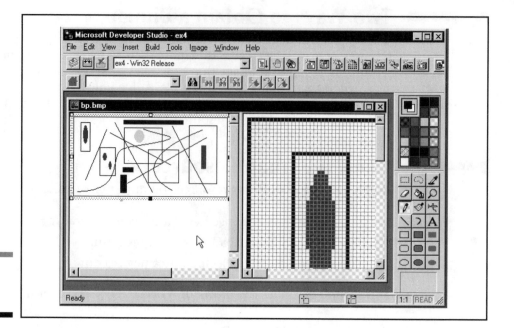

An image
editor

Figure 7-1.

As you can guess, the **BITMAP** statement defines a bitmap resource called
MyBP that is contained in the file BP.BMP. The general form of the
BITMAP statement is:

BitmapName BITMAP *Filename*

Here, *BitmapName* is the name that identifies the bitmap. This name is used
by your program to refer to the bitmap. *Filename* is the name of the file that
contains the bitmap.

Displaying a Bitmap

Once you have created a bitmap and included it in your application's
resource file, you may display it whenever you want in the client area of a
window. However, displaying a bitmap requires a little work on your part.
The following discussion explains the proper procedure.

Before you can use your bitmap, you must load it and store its handle. This
can be done inside **WinMain( )** or when your application's main window
receives a **WM_CREATE** message. A **WM_CREATE** message is sent to a
window when it is first created, but before it is visible. **WM_CREATE** is a
good place to perform any initializations that relate to (and are subordinate
to) a window. Since the bitmap resource will be displayed within the client
area of the main window, it makes sense to load the bitmap when the

window receives the **WM_CREATE** message. This is the approach that will be used in this chapter.

To load the bitmap, use the **LoadBitmap( )** API function, whose prototype is shown here:

HBITMAP LoadBitmap(HINSTANCE *hThisInst*, LPCSTR *lpszName*);

The current instance is specified in *hThisInst* and a pointer to the name of the bitmap as specified in the resource file is passed in *lpszName*. The function returns the handle to the bitmap, or **NULL** if an error occurs. For example:

```
HBITMAP hbit; /* handle of bitmap */
/* ... */
hbit = LoadBitmap(hInst, "MyBP"); /* load bitmap */
```

This fragment loads a bitmap called **MyBP** and stores a handle to it in **hbit**.

When it comes time to display the bitmap, your program must follow these four steps:

1. Obtain the device context so that your program can output to the window.
2. Obtain an equivalent memory device context that will hold the bitmap until it is displayed. (A bitmap is held in memory until it is copied to your window.)
3. Select the bitmap into the memory device context.
4. Copy the bitmap from the memory device context to the window device context. This causes the bitmap to be displayed.

To see how the preceding four steps can be implemented, consider the following fragment. It causes a bitmap to be displayed at two different locations each time a **WM_PAINT** message is received.

```
HDC hdc, memdc;
PAINTSTRUCT ps;

/* ... */

case WM_PAINT:
  hdc = BeginPaint(hwnd, &ps); /* get device context */

  memdc = CreateCompatibleDC(hdc); /* create compatible DC */
  SelectObject(memdc, hbit); /* select bitmap */
```

7

```
BitBlt(hdc, 10, 10, 256, 128,
       memdc, 0, 0, SRCCOPY); /* display image */
BitBlt(hdc, 300, 100, 256, 128,
       memdc, 0, 0, SRCCOPY); /* display image */

EndPaint(hwnd, &ps); /* release DC */
DeleteDC(memdc); /* free the memory context */
break;
```

Let's examine this code, step by step.

First, two device context handles are declared. **hdc** will hold the current window device context as obtained by **BeginPaint( )**. The other, called **memdc**, will hold the device context of the memory that stores the bitmap until it is drawn in the window.

Within the **WM_PAINT** case, the window device context is obtained. This is necessary because the bitmap will be displayed in the client area of the window and no output can occur until your program is granted a device context. Next, a memory context is created that will hold the bitmap. This memory device context must be compatible with the window device context. The compatible memory device context is created using the **CreateCompatibleDC( )** API function. Its prototype is shown here:

HDC CreateCompatibleDC(HDC *hdc*);

This function returns a handle to a region of memory that is compatible with the device context of the window, specified by *hdc*. This memory will be used to construct an image before it is actually displayed. The function returns **NULL** if an error occurs.

Next, the bitmap must be selected into the memory device context using the **SelectObject( )** API function. Its prototype is shown here:

HGDIOBJ SelectObject(HDC *hdc*, HGDIOBJ *hObject*);

A bitmap must be selected into a memory device context before it can be displayed.

Here, *hdc* specifies the device context and *hObject* is the handle of the object being selected into that context. The function returns the handle of the previously selected object (if one exists), allowing it to be reselected later, if desired.

To actually display the bitmap, use the **BitBlt( )** API function. This function copies a bitmap from one device context to another. Its prototype is shown here:

BOOL BitBlt(HDC *hDest*, int *X*, int *Y*, int *Width*, int *Height*, HDC *hSource*, int *SourceX*, int *SourceY*, DWORD *dwHow*);

Here, *hDest* is the handle of the target device context, and *X* and *Y* are the upper left coordinates at which point the bitmap will be drawn. The width and height of the destination region are specified in *Width* and *Height*. The *hSource* parameter contains the handle of the source device context, which in this case will be the memory context obtained using **CreateCompatibleDC( )**. The *SourceX* and *SourceY* parameters specify the upper left coordinates within the bitmap at which the copy operation will begin. To begin copying at the upper-left corner of the bitmap, these values must be zero. The value of *dwHow* determines how the bit-by-bit contents of the bitmap will be drawn on the screen. Some of the most common values are shown here:

Macro	Effect
DSTINVERT	Inverts the bits in the destination bitmap.
SRCAND	ANDs bitmap with current destination.
SRCCOPY	Copies bitmap as is, overwriting any preexisting output.
SRCPAINT	ORs bitmap with current destination.
SRCINVERT	XORs bitmap with current destination.

BitBlt( ) returns nonzero if successful and zero on failure.

In the example, each call to **BitBlt( )** displays the entire bitmap by copying it to the client area of the window.

After the bitmap is displayed, both device contexts are released. In this case, **EndPaint( )** is called to release the device context obtained by calling **BeginPaint( )**. To release the memory device context obtained using **CreateCompatibleDC( )**, you must use **DeleteDC( )**, which takes as its parameter the handle of the device context to release. You cannot use **ReleaseDC( )** for this purpose. (Only a device context obtained through a call to **GetDC( )** can be released using a call to **ReleaseDC( )**.)

Deleting a Bitmap

A bitmap is a resource that must be removed before your application ends. To do this, your program must call **DeleteObject( )** when the bitmap is no longer needed or when a **WM_DESTROY** message is received. **DeleteObject( )** has this prototype:

    BOOL DeleteObject(HGDIOBJ *hObj*);

Here, *hObj* is the handle to the object being deleted. The function returns nonzero if successful and zero on failure.

The Complete Bitmap Example Program

Here is the complete bitmap program. Sample output is shown in Figure 7-2.

```c
/*  Display a bitmap. */

#include <windows.h>
#include <string.h>
#include <stdio.h>

LRESULT CALLBACK WindowFunc(HWND, UINT, WPARAM, LPARAM);

char szWinName[] = "MyWin"; /* name of window class */

HBITMAP hbit; /* handle of bitmap */
HINSTANCE hInst; /* handle to this instance */

int WINAPI WinMain(HINSTANCE hThisInst, HINSTANCE hPrevInst,
                   LPSTR lpszArgs, int nWinMode)
{
  HWND hwnd;
  MSG msg;
  WNDCLASSEX wcl;

  /* Define a window class. */
  wcl.cbSize = sizeof(WNDCLASSEX);

  wcl.hInstance = hThisInst; /* handle to this instance */
  wcl.lpszClassName = szWinName; /* window class name */
  wcl.lpfnWndProc = WindowFunc; /* window function */
  wcl.style = 0; /* default style */

  wcl.hIcon = LoadIcon(NULL, IDI_APPLICATION); /* standard icon */
  wcl.hIconSm = LoadIcon(NULL, IDI_APPLICATION); /* small icon */
  wcl.hCursor = LoadCursor(NULL, IDC_ARROW); /*cursor style */

  wcl.lpszMenuName = NULL; /* no main menu */

  wcl.cbClsExtra = 0; /* no extra */
  wcl.cbWndExtra = 0; /* information needed */

  /* Make the window white. */
  wcl.hbrBackground = GetStockObject(WHITE_BRUSH);

  /* Register the window class. */
  if(!RegisterClassEx(&wcl)) return 0;
```

```
   hInst = hThisInst; /* save instance handle */

   /* Now that a window class has been registered, a window
      can be created. */
   hwnd = CreateWindow(
     szWinName, /* name of window class */
     "Displaying a Bitmap", /* title */
     WS_OVERLAPPEDWINDOW, /* window style - normal */
     CW_USEDEFAULT, /* X coordinate - let Windows decide */
     CW_USEDEFAULT, /* Y coordinate - let Windows decide */
     CW_USEDEFAULT, /* width - let Windows decide */
     CW_USEDEFAULT, /* height - let Windows decide */
     HWND_DESKTOP, /* no parent window */
     NULL, /* no override of class menu */
     hThisInst, /* handle of this instance of the program */
     NULL /* no additional arguments */
   );

   /* Display the window. */
   ShowWindow(hwnd, nWinMode);
   UpdateWindow(hwnd);

   /* Create the message loop. */
   while(GetMessage(&msg, NULL, 0, 0))
   {
     TranslateMessage(&msg); /* translate keyboard messages */
     DispatchMessage(&msg); /* return control to Windows NT */
   }
   return msg.wParam;
}

/* This function is called by Windows NT and is passed
   messages from the message queue.
*/
LRESULT CALLBACK WindowFunc(HWND hwnd, UINT message,
                            WPARAM wParam, LPARAM lParam)
{
  HDC hdc, memdc;
  PAINTSTRUCT ps;

  switch(message) {
    case WM_CREATE:
      /* load the bitmap */
      hbit = LoadBitmap(hInst, "MyBP"); /* load bitmap */
      break;
    case WM_PAINT:
      hdc = BeginPaint(hwnd, &ps); /* get device context */
```

7

```
      memdc = CreateCompatibleDC(hdc); /* create compatible DC */
      SelectObject(memdc, hbit); /* select bitmap */

      BitBlt(hdc, 10, 10, 256, 128,
             memdc, 0, 0, SRCCOPY); /* display image */
      BitBlt(hdc, 300, 100, 256, 128,
             memdc, 0, 0, SRCCOPY); /* display image */

      EndPaint(hwnd, &ps); /* release DC */
      DeleteDC(memdc); /* free the memory context */
      break;
    case WM_DESTROY: /* terminate the program */
      DeleteObject(hbit); /* remove the bitmap */
      PostQuitMessage(0);
      break;
    default:
      /* Let Windows NT process any messages not specified in
         the preceding switch statement. */
      return DefWindowProc(hwnd, message, wParam, lParam);
  }
  return 0;
}
```

You might want to experiment with the bitmap program before continuing.
For example, try using different copy options with **BitBlt( )**. Also, try
bitmaps of differing sizes.

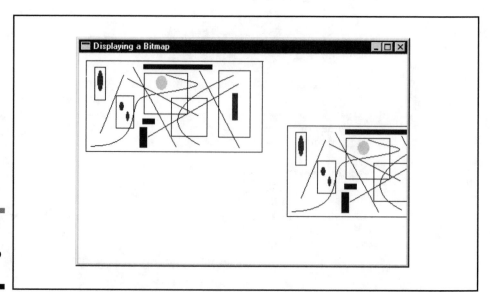

Sample output
using the
custom bitmap

Figure 7-2.

XORing an Image to a Window

As explained, **BltBlt( )** can copy the bitmap contained in one device context into another device context a number of different ways. For example, if you specify **SRCPAINT**, the image is ORed with the destination. Using **SRCAND** causes the bitmap to be ANDed with the destination. Perhaps the most interesting way to copy the contents of one DC to another uses **SRCINVERT**. This method XORs the source with the destination. There are two reasons this is particularly valuable.

First, XORing an image onto a window guarantees that the image will be visible. It doesn't matter what color or colors the source image or the destination uses; an XORed image is always visible. Second, XORing an image to the same destination twice removes the image and restores the destination to its original condition. As you might guess, XORing is an efficient way to temporarily display and then remove an image from a window without disturbing its original contents.

To see the effects of XORing an image to a window, insert the following cases into **WindowFunc( )** in the first bitmap program.

```
case WM_LBUTTONDOWN:
  hdc = GetDC(hwnd);

  memdc = CreateCompatibleDC(hdc); /* create compatible DC */
  SelectObject(memdc, hbit); /* select bitmap */

  /* XOR image onto the window */
  BitBlt(hdc, LOWORD(lParam), HIWORD(lParam), 256, 128,
         memdc, 0, 0, SRCINVERT);
  ReleaseDC(hwnd, hdc);
  DeleteDC(memdc);
  break;
case WM_LBUTTONUP:
  hdc = GetDC(hwnd);

  memdc = CreateCompatibleDC(hdc); /* create compatible DC */
  SelectObject(memdc, hbit); /* select bitmap */

  /* XOR image onto the window a second time */
  BitBlt(hdc, LOWORD(lParam), HIWORD(lParam), 256, 128,
         memdc, 0, 0, SRCINVERT);
```

7

```
ReleaseDC(hwnd, hdc);
DeleteDC(memdc);
break;
```

The code works like this: Each time the left mouse button is pressed, the bitmap is XORed to the window starting at the location of the mouse pointer. This causes an inverted image of the bitmap to be displayed. When the left mouse pointer is released, the image is XORed a second time, causing the bitmap to be removed and the previous contents to be restored. Be careful not to move the mouse while you are holding down the left button. If you do, then the second XOR copy will not take place directly over the top of the first and the original contents of the window will not be restored.

Creating a Bitmap Dynamically

In addition to using bitmap resources, your program can create bitmaps dynamically. As you know, the size and content of a bitmap resource are predefined. This is not the case for bitmaps created during the execution of your program. The easiest way to create a bitmap is to call the **CreateCompatibleBitmap( )** API function. It creates a bitmap that is compatible with a specified device context. This device-dependent bitmap can be used by any device context that is compatible with the device context for which it was created. The function's prototype is shown here:

HBITMAP CreateCompatibleBitmap(HDC *hdc*, int *width*, int *height*);

Here, *hdc* is the handle for the device with which the bitmap will be compatible. The dimensions of the bitmap are specified in *width* and *height*. These values are in pixels. The function returns a handle to the compatible bitmap or **NULL** on failure. The bitmap will initially be empty.

Using a Dynamically Created Bitmap

The ability to create bitmaps as needed allows you to perform several types of useful operations. For example, you can use a dynamically created bitmap to construct some type of image during run time. Or, you can use one to temporarily store an image (or part of an image) that is contained in a larger bitmap. One of the most interesting uses of a dynamically constructed bitmap is to store a copy of the information contained in the client area of a window.

To demonstrate the use of a dynamically created bitmap, a short program is developed that allows you to move a region of the screen from one part of a window to another. The program works like this: Each time you press the left mouse button, a 100×100 region of the window that has its upper left corner at the current mouse position is copied into a bitmap. Each time you press the right mouse button, the bitmap is copied to the window at the current location of the mouse. Thus, using this program, you can move pieces of the main window around within the client area.

The entire dynamic bitmap program is shown here. Sample output is shown in Figure 7-3.

```c
/* This program creates a bitmap dynamically and uses it
   to copy portions of the client area of its main window. */

#include <windows.h>
#include <string.h>
#include <stdio.h>

LRESULT CALLBACK WindowFunc(HWND, UINT, WPARAM, LPARAM);

char szWinName[] = "MyWin"; /* name of window class */

HINSTANCE hInst; /* handle to this instance */
HBITMAP hdynbit; /* handle to dynamically created bitmap */

int WINAPI WinMain(HINSTANCE hThisInst, HINSTANCE hPrevInst,
                   LPSTR lpszArgs, int nWinMode)
{
  HWND hwnd;
  MSG msg;
  WNDCLASSEX wcl;

  /* Define a window class. */
  wcl.cbSize = sizeof(WNDCLASSEX);

  wcl.hInstance = hThisInst; /* handle to this instance */
  wcl.lpszClassName = szWinName; /* window class name */
  wcl.lpfnWndProc = WindowFunc; /* window function */
  wcl.style = 0; /* default style */

  wcl.hIcon = LoadIcon(NULL, IDI_APPLICATION); /* standard icon */
  wcl.hIconSm = LoadIcon(NULL, IDI_APPLICATION); /* small icon */
  wcl.hCursor = LoadCursor(NULL, IDC_ARROW); /*cursor style */

  wcl.lpszMenuName = NULL; /* no main menu */
```

```
  wcl.cbClsExtra = 0; /* no extra */
  wcl.cbWndExtra = 0; /* information needed */

  /* Make the window white. */
  wcl.hbrBackground = GetStockObject(WHITE_BRUSH);

  /* Register the window class. */
  if(!RegisterClassEx(&wcl)) return 0;

  hInst = hThisInst; /* save instance handle */

  /* Now that a window class has been registered, a window
     can be created. */
  hwnd = CreateWindow(
    szWinName, /* name of window class */
    "Using Dynamic Bitmaps", /* title */
    WS_OVERLAPPEDWINDOW, /* window style - normal */
    CW_USEDEFAULT, /* X coordinate - let Windows decide */
    CW_USEDEFAULT, /* Y coordinate - let Windows decide */
    CW_USEDEFAULT, /* width - let Windows decide */
    CW_USEDEFAULT, /* height - let Windows decide */
    HWND_DESKTOP, /* no parent window */
    NULL, /* no override of class menu */
    hThisInst, /* handle of this instance of the program */
    NULL /* no additional arguments */
  );

  /* Display the window. */
  ShowWindow(hwnd, nWinMode);
  UpdateWindow(hwnd);

  /* Create the message loop. */
  while(GetMessage(&msg, NULL, 0, 0))
  {
    TranslateMessage(&msg); /* translate keyboard messages */
    DispatchMessage(&msg); /* return control to Windows NT */
  }
  return msg.wParam;
}

/* This function is called by Windows NT and is passed
   messages from the message queue.
*/
LRESULT CALLBACK WindowFunc(HWND hwnd, UINT message,
                            WPARAM wParam, LPARAM lParam)
{
  HDC hdc, memdc;
  PAINTSTRUCT ps;
```

```
int i;
char str[80] = "Using a dynamic bitmap.";
char instructions[] =  "Click left button at source, "
                       "right button at destination.";

switch(message) {
  case WM_CREATE:
    /* dynamically create a bitmap */
    hdc = GetDC(hwnd);
    hdynbit = CreateCompatibleBitmap(hdc, 100, 100);
    ReleaseDC(hwnd, hdc);
    break;
  case WM_LBUTTONDOWN: /* copy region of window to bitmap */
    hdc = GetDC(hwnd);

    memdc = CreateCompatibleDC(hdc); /* create compatible DC */

   /* select dynamic bitmap into memory DC */
    SelectObject(memdc, hdynbit);

    /* copy region into dynamic bitmap */
    BitBlt(memdc, 0, 0, 100, 100,
          hdc, LOWORD(lParam), HIWORD(lParam), SRCCOPY);

    ReleaseDC(hwnd, hdc);
    DeleteDC(memdc);
    break;
  case WM_RBUTTONDOWN: /* copy bitmap to window */
    hdc = GetDC(hwnd);

    memdc = CreateCompatibleDC(hdc); /* create compatible DC */

    /* select dynamic bitmap into memory DC */
    SelectObject(memdc, hdynbit);

    /* copy dynamic bitmap to window */
    BitBlt(hdc, LOWORD(lParam), HIWORD(lParam), 100, 100,
          memdc, 0, 0, SRCCOPY);

    ReleaseDC(hwnd, hdc);
    DeleteDC(memdc);
    break;
  case WM_PAINT:
    hdc = BeginPaint(hwnd, &ps); /* get device context */

    TextOut(hdc, 1, 0, instructions, strlen(instructions));

    for(i=1; i<10; i++)
      TextOut(hdc, 1, i*20, str, strlen(str));
```

```
        EndPaint(hwnd, &ps); /* release DC */
        break;
      case WM_DESTROY: /* terminate the program */
        DeleteObject(hdynbit); /* remove the bitmap */
        PostQuitMessage(0);
        break;
      default:
        /* Let Windows NT process any messages not specified in
           the preceding switch statement. */
        return DefWindowProc(hwnd, message, wParam, lParam);
  }
  return 0;
}
```

When the program first begins execution, the main window receives a
WM_CREATE message and a bitmap is created that is compatible with the
device context used by the main window. The handle to this bitmap is saved
in **hdynbit**, which is a global variable. Each time the left mouse button is
pressed, a compatible memory DC is created, the bitmap is selected into that
device context, and a 100 x 100 rectangular region of the window is copied
into the bitmap. Each time the right mouse button is pressed, a similar
sequence occurs, but the source and targets are reversed. This causes the
current contents of the bitmap to be copied to the window.

As you can undoubtedly imagine, the ability to create bitmaps dynamically
has several important uses. Perhaps the most important is described in the
following section.

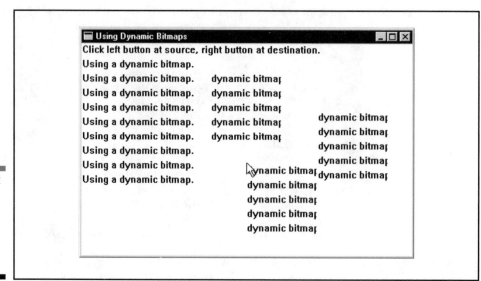

Sample output
from the
dynamic
bitmap
program

Figure 7-3.

Solving the Repaint Problem

Now that you know the basic operations involved with using bitmaps, you can use that knowledge to solve one of the most fundamental problems encountered when writing a Windows NT program: restoring the contents of a window when a **WM_PAINT** message is received. In Windows NT (and all version of Windows) it is the application's responsibility to redraw the contents of the client area of a window each time a **WM_PAINT** message is received. In general, a window needs to be redrawn each time it is uncovered. That is, when you run a program, display something in the client area of a window, and then overlay the window with another, your output is lost. Thus, when the window is uncovered, its contents will need to be repainted. As you will see, the techniques used to display a bitmap form the basis by which you can solve the repaint problem.

Let's start by reviewing the three basic methods that you can use to repaint a window. First, you can regenerate the output if that output is created by some computational method. Second, you can store a record of display events and "replay" those events. Third, you can maintain a virtual window and simply copy the contents of the virtual window to the physical window each time a **WM_PAINT** message is received. The most general of these is, of course, the third and this is the method that will be developed here.

A virtual window is a memory device context combined with a bitmap that is compatible with the physical device context used by your program.

Here is how output will be accomplished using a virtual window. First, a memory device context and bitmap (i.e., the virtual window) are created that are compatible with the physical device context used by your application. Thus, a virtual window is simply a compatible bitmap that has the same characteristics as your program's actual window. Once you have created a virtual window, all output intended for the client area of the main window must also be written to the virtual window. This causes the virtual window to contain a complete and current copy of whatever you output to the physical window. Each time a **WM_PAINT** message is received, the contents of the virtual window are copied into the actual window, restoring its contents. Therefore, a window that has been covered and then uncovered will be redrawn automatically when it receives the **WM_PAINT** message.

7

Some Additional API Functions

To implement a virtual window requires the use of several API functions. Five have been discussed already. These are **CreateCompatibleBitmap( )**, **CreateCompatibleDC( )**, **SelectObject( )**, **GetStockObject( )**, and **BitBlt( )**. We will also be using **PatBlt( )** and **GetSystemMetrics( )**, which are described here.

PatBlt( )

The **PatBlt( )** function fills a rectangle with the color and pattern of the currently selected *brush*. A brush is an object that specifies how a window (or region) will be filled. Filling an area using a brush is also commonly referred to as *painting* the region. **PatBlt( )** has this prototype:

    BOOL PatBlt(HDC *hdc*, int *X*, int *Y*, int *width*, int *height*, DWORD *dwHow*);

Here, *hdc* is the handle of the device context. The coordinates *X* and *Y* specify the upper left corner of the region to be filled. The width and height of the region are specified in *width* and *height*. The value passed in *dwHow* determines how the brush will be applied. It must be one of these macros:

Macro	Meaning
BLACKNESS	Region is black (brush is ignored).
WHITENESS	Region is white (brush is ignored).
PATCOPY	Brush is copied to region.
PATINVERT	Brush is ORed to region.
DSTINVERT	Region is inverted (brush is ignored).

Therefore, if you wish to apply the current brush unaltered, you would select **PATCOPY** for the value of *dwHow*. The function returns nonzero if successful, zero otherwise.

Obtaining the System Metrics

To create a virtual window requires that we know how big to make the bitmap that will be used as the virtual window. One way to do this is to obtain the size, in pixels, of the screen and use its dimensions for the bitmap. To obtain the size of the screen, and other information, use the **GetSystemMetrics( )** API function, whose prototype is shown here:

    int GetSystemMetrics(int *what*);

Here, *what* will be a value that specifies the value that you want to obtain. **GetSystemMetrics( )** can obtain many different values. The values for screen coordinates are returned in pixel units. Here are the macros for some common values:

Value	Metric Obtained
SM_CXFULLSCREEN	Width of maximized client area.
SM_CYFULLSCREEN	Height of maximized client area.
SM_CXICON	Width of standard icon.
SM_CYICON	Height of standard icon.
SM_CXSMICON	Width of small icon.
SM_CYSMICON	Height of small icon.
SM_CXSCREEN	Width of entire screen.
SM_CYSCREEN	Height of entire screen.

We will be using the values associated with **SM_CXSCREEN** and **SM_CYSCREEN** as the dimensions of the virtual window.

Creating and Using a Virtual Window

Let's begin by restating the procedure that will be implemented. To create an easy and convenient means of restoring a window after a **WM_PAINT** message has been received, a virtual window will be maintained. All output intended for the client area will be written to both the virtual window and the physical window. This means that the virtual window will always contain a complete copy of whatever has been output to the physical window. Each time a repaint request is received, the contents of the virtual window are copied into the window that is physically on the screen. This causes the contents of the physical window to be restored. Now, let's implement this approach.

The first step you must follow to create a virtual window is to obtain a memory device context that is compatible with the current physical device context. This will be done only once, when the window is first created. This compatible device context will stay in existence the entire time the program is executing. Here is the code that performs this function:

```
case WM_CREATE:
  /* get screen coordinates */
  maxX = GetSystemMetrics(SM_CXSCREEN);
  maxY = GetSystemMetrics(SM_CYSCREEN);
```

7

```
/* make a compatible memory image */
hdc = GetDC(hwnd);
memdc = CreateCompatibleDC(hdc);
hbit = CreateCompatibleBitmap(hdc, maxX, maxY);
SelectObject(memdc, hbit);
hbrush = GetStockObject(WHITE_BRUSH);
SelectObject(memdc, hbrush);
PatBlt(memdc, 0, 0, maxX, maxY, PATCOPY);
ReleaseDC(hwnd, hdc);
break;
```

Let's examine this code closely. First, the dimensions of the screen are obtained. They will be used to create a compatible bitmap. Then, the current device context is obtained. Next, a compatible device context is created in memory, using **CreateCompatibleDC( )**. The handle to this device context is stored in **memdc**, which is a global variable. Then, a compatible bitmap is created. This establishes a one-to-one mapping between the virtual window and the physical window. The dimensions of the bitmap are those of the maximum screen size. This ensures that the bitmap will always be large enough to fully restore the window no matter how large the physical window is. (Actually, slightly smaller values could be used, since the borders aren't repainted, but this minor improvement is left to you, as an exercise.) The handle to the bitmap is stored in the global variable **hbit**. It is also selected into the memory device context. Next, a stock white brush is obtained and its handle is stored in the global variable **hbrush**. This brush is selected into the memory device context and then **PatBlt( )** paints the entire virtual window using the brush. Thus, the virtual window will have a white background, which matches the background of the physical window in the example program that follows. (Remember, these colors are under your control. The colors used here are arbitrary.) Finally, the physical device context is released. However, the memory device context stays in existence until the program ends.

Once the virtual window has been created, you must make sure that a complete copy of all output is also written to the virtual window. Each time a **WM_PAINT** message is received, you will use the contents of the virtual window to restore the contents of the physical window. You will do this in much the same way that you copied a bitmapped image to the window in the preceding section: by using the **BitBlt( )** function.

The Entire Virtual Window Demonstration Program

Here is the complete program that demonstrates using a virtual window to solve the repaint problem. Sample output is shown in Figure 7-4. The program responds to **WM_CHAR** messages by outputting each character to both the virtual window and the physical window. (That is, it echoes the characters you type to both the physical window and the virtual window.) When a **WM_PAINT** message is received, the contents of the virtual window are used to restore the physical window.

```c
/* Repaint using a virtual window. */

#include <windows.h>
#include <string.h>
#include <stdio.h>

LRESULT CALLBACK WindowFunc(HWND, UINT, WPARAM, LPARAM);

char szWinName[] = "MyWin"; /* name of window class */

char str[255]; /* holds output strings */

int X=0, Y=0; /* current output location */
int maxX, maxY; /* screen dimensions */

HDC memdc; /* store the virtual device handle */
HBITMAP hbit; /* store the virtual bitmap */
HBRUSH hbrush; /* store the brush handle */

int WINAPI WinMain(HINSTANCE hThisInst, HINSTANCE hPrevInst,
                   LPSTR lpszArgs, int nWinMode)
{
  HWND hwnd;
  MSG msg;
  WNDCLASSEX wcl;

  /* Define a window class. */
  wcl.cbSize = sizeof(WNDCLASSEX);

  wcl.hInstance = hThisInst; /* handle to this instance */
  wcl.lpszClassName = szWinName; /* window class name */
  wcl.lpfnWndProc = WindowFunc; /* window function */
  wcl.style = 0; /* default style */

  wcl.hIcon = LoadIcon(NULL, IDI_APPLICATION); /* standard icon */
  wcl.hIconSm = LoadIcon(NULL, IDI_APPLICATION); /* small icon */
  wcl.hCursor = LoadCursor(NULL, IDC_ARROW); /* cursor style */

  wcl.lpszMenuName = NULL; /* no main menu */

  wcl.cbClsExtra = 0; /* no extra */
  wcl.cbWndExtra = 0; /* information needed */
```

7

```
/* Make the window white. */
wcl.hbrBackground = GetStockObject(WHITE_BRUSH);

/* Register the window class. */
if(!RegisterClassEx(&wcl)) return 0;

/* Now that a window class has been registered, a window
   can be created. */
hwnd = CreateWindow(
  szWinName, /* name of window class */
  "Using a Virtual Window", /* title */
  WS_OVERLAPPEDWINDOW, /* window style - normal */
  CW_USEDEFAULT, /* X coordinate - let Windows decide */
  CW_USEDEFAULT, /* Y coordinate - let Windows decide */
  CW_USEDEFAULT, /* width - let Windows decide */
  CW_USEDEFAULT, /* height - let Windows decide */
  HWND_DESKTOP, /* no parent window */
  NULL, /* no override of class menu */
  hThisInst, /* handle of this instance of the program */
  NULL /* no additional arguments */
);

/* Display the window. */
ShowWindow(hwnd, nWinMode);
UpdateWindow(hwnd);

/* Create the message loop. */
while(GetMessage(&msg, NULL, 0, 0))
{
  TranslateMessage(&msg); /* translate keyboard messages */
  DispatchMessage(&msg); /* return control to Windows NT */
}
return msg.wParam;
}

/* This function is called by Windows NT and is passed
   messages from the message queue.
*/
LRESULT CALLBACK WindowFunc(HWND hwnd, UINT message,
                            WPARAM wParam, LPARAM lParam)
{
  HDC hdc;
  PAINTSTRUCT ps;

  switch(message) {
    case WM_CREATE:
      /* get screen coordinates */
      maxX = GetSystemMetrics(SM_CXSCREEN);
      maxY = GetSystemMetrics(SM_CYSCREEN);
```

```
      /* make a compatible memory image */
      hdc = GetDC(hwnd);
      memdc = CreateCompatibleDC(hdc);
      hbit = CreateCompatibleBitmap(hdc, maxX, maxY);
      SelectObject(memdc, hbit);
      hbrush = GetStockObject(WHITE_BRUSH);
      SelectObject(memdc, hbrush);
      PatBlt(memdc, 0, 0, maxX, maxY, PATCOPY);
      ReleaseDC(hwnd, hdc);
      break;
    case WM_CHAR:
      hdc = GetDC(hwnd);
      sprintf(str, "%c", (char) wParam); /* stringize character */

      /* a "primitive" carriage return, linefeed sequence */
      if((char)wParam == '\r') {
        Y += 14; /* advance to next line */
        X = 0; /* reset to start of line */
      }
      else {
        TextOut(memdc, X, Y, str, strlen(str)); /* output to memory */
        TextOut(hdc, X, Y, str, strlen(str)); /* output to window */
        X += 10;
      }
      ReleaseDC(hwnd, hdc);
      break;
    case WM_PAINT: /* process a repaint request */
      hdc = BeginPaint(hwnd, &ps); /* get DC */

      /* copy memory image onto screen */
      BitBlt(hdc, 0, 0, maxX, maxY, memdc, 0, 0, SRCCOPY);
      EndPaint(hwnd, &ps); /* release DC */
      break;
    case WM_DESTROY: /* terminate the program */
      DeleteDC(memdc); /* delete the memory device */
      DeleteObject(hbit); /* remove the bitmap */
      PostQuitMessage(0);
      break;
    default:
      /* Let Windows NT process any messages not specified in
         the preceding switch statement. */
      return DefWindowProc(hwnd, message, wParam, lParam);
  }
  return 0;
}
```

7

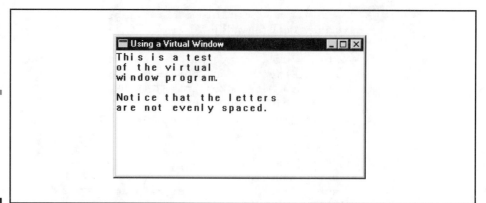

Sample output
from the
virtual
window
program
Figure 7-4.

Let's look at this program in detail. First, examine the code associated with the **WM_CHAR** message. It is shown here for your convenience:

```
case WM_CHAR:
  hdc = GetDC(hwnd);
  sprintf(str, "%c", (char) wParam); /* stringize character */

  /* a "primitive" carriage return, linefeed sequence */
  if((char)wParam == '\r') {
    Y += 14; /* advance to next line */
    X = 0; /* reset to start of line */
  }
  else {
    TextOut(memdc, X, Y, str, strlen(str)); /* output to memory */
    TextOut(hdc, X, Y, str, strlen(str)); /* output to window */
    X += 10;
  }
  ReleaseDC(hwnd, hdc);
  break;
```

The variables **X** and **Y** are two global integers that are used to maintain the coordinates at which the next character will be displayed. They are initially zero. Each time a character is typed, it is "stringized" and output to both the physical window and the virtual window. Thus, a complete copy of each keystroke is maintained in the virtual window.

As you can see, **X** is advanced by 10 for each character typed and **Y** is increased by 14 to advance to the next line each time ENTER is pressed. This method of determining the proper X, Y location is a crude, temporary measure. In the next chapter, you will learn the proper way to manage text output.

Each time a **WM_PAINT** message is received, the contents of the virtual device are copied into the physical device. This is accomplished by the following code.

```
case WM_PAINT: /* process a repaint request */
  hdc = BeginPaint(hwnd, &ps); /* get DC */

  /* copy memory image onto screen */
  BitBlt(hdc, 0, 0, maxX, maxY, memdc, 0, 0, SRCCOPY);
  EndPaint(hwnd, &ps); /* release DC */
  break;
```

The **BitBlt( )** function copies the image from **memdc** into **hdc**. Remember, the parameter **SRCCOPY** simply means to copy the image as-is without alteration directly from the source to the target. Because all output has been stored in **memdc**, this statement causes the window to be restored. You should try this by entering some characters, covering, and then uncovering the window. As you will see, the characters that you typed are redisplayed.

There is a variation on the virtual window mechanism that you might find useful in some situations. Instead of outputting information twice, once to the physical window and once to the virtual window, your program can simply write all information to the virtual window and then call **InvalidateRect( )** to cause the information to be displayed. (Remember, **InvalidateRect( )** generates a **WM_PAINT** message.) If you try this approach in the example program, you will find that the window seems to "flash" each time you press a key because the entire window is being updated with each keypress. This makes this approach inappropriate for this example. However, for programs that perform infrequent output, such an approach may make sense.

Improving Repaint Efficiency

The virtual window method just described shows the general technique for using a virtual window to handle repaint requests. However, it is possible to make a rather significant improvement to the preceding program. As the program is written, it suffers from two inefficiencies. First, the entire virtual window is copied to the physical window no matter how large (or small) the physical window actually is. Since the virtual window is the size of the entire screen, this approach is clearly inefficient. Because output is automatically clipped, no harm is caused by this approach. It just wastes CPU time.

The second problem is that no matter how much of the physical window actually needs to be repainted, the entire window is repainted each time a

7

WM_PAINT message arrives. This is the way most beginning Windows programmers handle a repaint request. It is, of course, not the best way. The trouble is that often only a corner of a window actually needs to be restored. It is important to understand that restoring a window is expensive in terms of time. The larger the window, the longer it takes to restore it. Repainting parts of a window that don't need it wastes time and can make your application look sluggish.

Both of these inefficiencies are rooted in the fact that the preceding program paints more of the window that it needs to. The solution is to change the program so that it only repaints those portions of the window that actually need to be restored. Using this approach, repaints take less time and your application has a much snappier feel. Frankly, optimizing window repainting is one of the most important performance improvements that you can make to your program.

Fortunately, Windows NT automatically provides the information we need in order to implement a more efficient repaint handler. This information is obtained when the **BeginPaint( )** function is called. To begin, let's review the information obtained by **BeginPaint( )**.

A Closer Look at BeginPaint( )

As you learned in Chapter 3, when a **WM_PAINT** message is processed, you must call **BeginPaint( )** to obtain a device context. In addition to acquiring a device context, **BeginPaint( )** also obtains information about the display state of the window. We will use this information to optimize repainting.

Recall the prototype for **BeginPaint( )**, shown here:

HDC BeginPaint(HWND *hwnd*, PAINTSTRUCT **lpPS*);

BeginPaint( ) returns a device context if successful or **NULL** on failure. Here, *hwnd* is the handle of the window for which the device context is being obtained. The second parameter is a pointer to a structure of type **PAINTSTRUCT**. The structure pointed to by *lpPS* will contain information that your program can use to repaint the window. **PAINTSTRUCT** is defined like this:

```
typedef struct tagPAINTSTRUCT {
  HDC hdc; /* handle to device context */
  BOOL fErase; /* true if background must be erased */
  RECT rcPaint; /* coordinates of region to redraw */
  BOOL fRestore;  /* reserved */
  BOOL fIncUpdate; /* reserved */
  BYTE rgbReserved[32]; /* reserved */
} PAINTSTRUCT;
```

The field that is of particular interest to us is **rcPaint**. This element contains the coordinates of the region of the window that needs to be repainted. We can take advantage of this information to reduce the time needed to restore a window.

Reducing Virtual Window Repaint Time

The key to decreasing the time it takes to restore a window when a **WM_PAINT** message is received is to only restore the portion of the window defined by **rcPaint**. This is easy to accomplish when using a virtual window. Simply copy the same region from the virtual window to the physical window. Since the two device contexts are identical, so are their coordinate systems. The coordinates that are contained in **rcPaint** can be used for both the physical window and the virtual window. For example, here is one way to respond to **WM_PAINT**:

```
case WM_PAINT: /* an improved response to a repaint request */
  hdc = BeginPaint(hwnd, &ps); /* get DC */

  /* copy a portion of the virtual window */
  BitBlt(hdc, ps.rcPaint.left, ps.rcPaint.top,
         ps.rcPaint.right-ps.rcPaint.left, /* width */
         ps.rcPaint.bottom-ps.rcPaint.top, /* height */
         memdc,
         ps.rcPaint.left, ps.rcPaint.top,
         SRCCOPY);

  EndPaint(hwnd, &ps); /* release DC */
  break;
```

To see the effectiveness of this version, substitute it into the program from the preceding section. Because this version only copies the rectangle defined by **rcPaint**, no time is wasted copying information that has not been overwritten or that is outside the current boundaries of the window.

Notice how easy it is to optimize the repainting of a window when using the virtual window method. Almost no additional programming effort is required. The virtual window method of repainting is an elegant solution to many repaint-related operations.

7

As an experiment, you can see the coordinates associated with each **WM_PAINT** message by putting this code directly after the call to **BeginPaint( )**:

```
sprintf(str, "top, left: %d %d\nBotton, right: %d %d",
        ps.rcPaint.top, ps.rcPaint.left,
        ps.rcPaint.bottom, ps.rcPaint.right);
MessageBox(hwnd, str, "coordinates", MB_OK);
```

Here, **str** is a character array. When you run the program, try overlaying two or more different portions of its window. You will see a separate message for each portion that you uncover.

For most of the examples in this book, efficient repaints are not needed. In fact, most programs won't even bother repainting the client area because the extra code will simply clutter the point of the example. However, in real programs that you write, the efficient handling of **WM_PAINT** is a crucial performance issue.

Creating a Custom Icon and Cursor

To conclude this chapter we will examine the creation and use of custom icons and cursors. As you know, all Windows NT applications first create a window class, which defines the attributes of the window, including the shape of the application's icon and mouse cursor. The handles to the icons and the mouse cursor are stored in the **hIcon, hIconSm**, and **hCursor** fields of the **WNDCLASSEX** structure. So far, we have been using the built-in icons and cursors supplied by Windows NT. However, it is possible to define your own.

Defining Icons and Cursors

To use a custom icon and mouse cursor, you must first define their images, using an image editor. Remember, you will need to make both a small and a standard-size icon. Actually, icons come in three sizes: small, standard, and large. The small icon is 16×16, the standard icon is 32×32, and the large icon is 48×48. However, the large icon is seldom used. In fact, most programmers mean the 32×32 icon when they use the term "large icon". All three sizes of icons are defined within a single icon file. Of course, you don't need to define the large icon. If one is ever needed, Windows will automatically enlarge the standard icon. All cursors are the same size, 32×32.

PORTABILITY: Windows 3.1 defines only the standard icon. You will want to add others when porting to Windows NT.

For the examples that follow, you should call the file that holds your icons ICON.ICO. Be sure to create both the 32 × 32 and the 16 × 16 icons. (The 48 × 48 icon is not needed.) Call the file that holds your cursor CURSOR.CUR. Figure 7-5 shows the icons and cursor used by the example in this chapter.

Once you have defined the icon and cursor images, you will need to add an **ICON** and a **CURSOR** statement to your program's resource file. These statements have these general forms:

> *IconName* ICON *filename*
> *CursorName* CURSOR *filename*

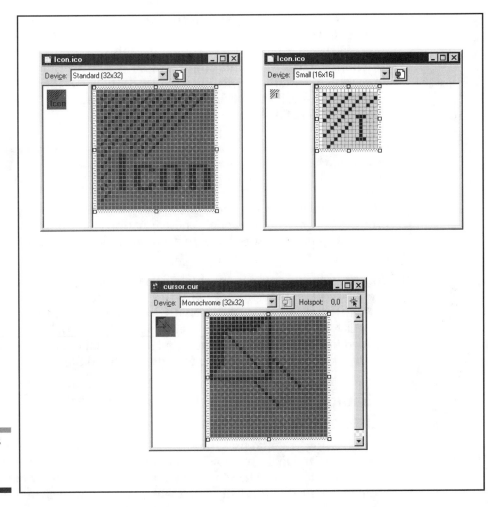

Custom icons
and cursor
Figure 7-5.

7

Here, *IconName* is the name that identifies the icon and *CursorName* is the name that identifies the cursor. These names are used by your program to refer to the icon and cursor. The *filename* specifies the file that holds the custom icon or cursor.

For the example program, you will need a resource file that contains the following statements:

```
MyCursor CURSOR CURSOR.CUR
MyIcon ICON ICON.ICO
```

Loading Your Icons and Cursor

To use your custom icons and cursor, you must load them and assign their handles to the appropriate fields in the **WNDCLASSEX** structure before the window class is registered. To accomplish this you must use the API functions **LoadIcon( )** and **LoadCursor( )**, which you learned about in Chapter 2. For example, the following loads the icons identified as **MyIcon** and the cursor called **MyCursor** and stores their handles in the appropriate fields of **WNDCLASSEX**.

```
wcl.hIcon = LoadIcon(hThisInst, "MyIcon"); /* standard icon */
wcl.hIconSm = NULL; /* use small icon in MyIcon */
wcl.hCursor = LoadCursor(hThisInst, "MyCursor"); /* load cursor */
```

Here, **hThisInst** is the handle of the current instance of the program. In the previous programs in this book, these functions have been used to load default icons and cursors. Here, they will be used to load your custom icons and cursor.

You are probably wondering why **hIconSm** is assigned **NULL**. As you should recall, in previous programs the handle of the small icon is assigned to the **hIconSm** field of the **WNDCLASSEX** structure. However, if this value is **NULL**, then the program automatically uses the 16×16 pixel icon defined in the file that holds the standard icon. Of course, you are free to specify a different icon resource for this icon, if you like.

A Sample Program that Demonstrates a Custom Icon and Cursor

The following program uses the custom icons and cursor. The small icon is displayed in the main window's system menu box and in the program's entry in the task bar. The standard icon is displayed when you move your program to the desktop. The cursor will be used when the mouse pointer is over the window. That is, the shape of the mouse cursor will automatically change to the one defined by your program when the mouse moves over the program's window. It will automatically revert to its default shape when it moves off the program's window.

Remember, before you try to compile this program, you must define the custom icons and cursor using an image editor and then add these resources to the resource file associated with the program.

```c
/* Demonstrate custom icons and mouse cursor. */

#include <windows.h>
#include <string.h>
#include <stdio.h>

LRESULT CALLBACK WindowFunc(HWND, UINT, WPARAM, LPARAM);

char szWinName[] = "MyWin"; /* name of window class */

int WINAPI WinMain(HINSTANCE hThisInst, HINSTANCE hPrevInst,
                   LPSTR lpszArgs, int nWinMode)
{
  HWND hwnd;
  MSG msg;
  WNDCLASSEX wcl;

  /* Define a window class. */
  wcl.cbSize = sizeof(WNDCLASSEX);

  wcl.hInstance = hThisInst; /* handle to this instance */
  wcl.lpszClassName = szWinName; /* window class name */
  wcl.lpfnWndProc = WindowFunc; /* window function */
  wcl.style = 0; /* default style */

  wcl.hIcon = LoadIcon(hThisInst, "MyIcon"); /* standard icon */
  wcl.hIconSm = NULL; /* use small icon in MyIcon */
  wcl.hCursor = LoadCursor(hThisInst, "MyCursor"); /* load cursor */

  wcl.lpszMenuName = NULL; /* no main menu */

  wcl.cbClsExtra = 0; /* no extra */
  wcl.cbWndExtra = 0; /* information needed */

  /* Make the window white. */
  wcl.hbrBackground = GetStockObject(WHITE_BRUSH);

  /* Register the window class. */
  if(!RegisterClassEx(&wcl)) return 0;
```

7

```
/* Now that a window class has been registered, a window
   can be created. */
hwnd = CreateWindow(
  szWinName, /* name of window class */
  "Custom Icons and Cursor", /* title */
  WS_OVERLAPPEDWINDOW, /* window style - normal */
  CW_USEDEFAULT, /* X coordinate - let Windows decide */
  CW_USEDEFAULT, /* Y coordinate - let Windows decide */
  CW_USEDEFAULT, /* width - let Windows decide */
  CW_USEDEFAULT, /* height - let Windows decide */
  HWND_DESKTOP, /* no parent window */
  NULL, /* no override of class menu */
  hThisInst, /* handle of this instance of the program */
  NULL /* no additional arguments */
);

/* Display the window. */
ShowWindow(hwnd, nWinMode);
UpdateWindow(hwnd);

/* Create the message loop. */
while(GetMessage(&msg, NULL, 0, 0))
{
  TranslateMessage(&msg); /* translate keyboard messages */
  DispatchMessage(&msg); /* return control to Windows NT */
}
return msg.wParam;
}

/* This function is called by Windows NT and is passed
   messages from the message queue.
*/
LRESULT CALLBACK WindowFunc(HWND hwnd, UINT message,
                           WPARAM wParam, LPARAM lParam)
{
  switch(message) {
    case WM_DESTROY: /* terminate the program */
      PostQuitMessage(0);
      break;
    default:
      /* Let Windows NT process any messages not specified in
         the preceding switch statement. */
      return DefWindowProc(hwnd, message, wParam, lParam);
  }
  return 0;
}
```

The small custom icon is shown here:

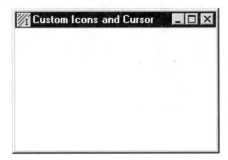

Of course, your custom icon may look different. The custom mouse cursor will appear when you move the mouse over the window. (Try this before continuing.)

One last point about custom icons: When you create custom icons for your application, you will usually want all sizes of icons to display the same general image since it is this image that is associated with your program.

CHAPTER 8

Working with Text

Windows NT provides extensive, detailed, and sophisticated support for displaying text in the client area of a window. In the preceding chapters we have been performing only the most rudimentary text output. For example, we have been using an arbitrary and fixed spacing between lines and characters. This approach is inherently inadequate because Windows NT uses proportional character fonts and adjustable font sizes. In this chapter you will learn the correct way to properly manage text output.

As with most other aspects of the Windows NT environment, you, the programmer, have nearly unlimited control over the way text is displayed, including its size, weight, and typeface. You can fine tune a type font to your choosing and can change fonts whenever you desire. You can even change the orientation of a line of text so that it displays diagonally or vertically, rather than horizontally. Of course, this high level of control comes at a price: the management overhead incurred by your program for text output is much greater than you might otherwise expect. But the results are definitely worth the added effort.

This chapter begins with a discussion of the window coordinate system and how text is mapped to it. Next, several text and window API functions that help you control and manage text output to the client area of a window are described. Then, a sample program is developed that illustrates how to apply these functions and how to properly manage the spacing of text output within the client area. The chapter concludes by examining Windows support for text fonts.

Window Coordinates

Window coordinates are specified in logical units, which by default are equal to pixels.

As you know, **TextOut( )** is one of Windows' text output functions. It displays a string at the specified coordinates, which are always relative to the window. Therefore, where a window is positioned on the screen has no effect upon the coordinates passed to **TextOut( )**. By default, the upper-left corner of the client area of the window is location 0, 0. The X value increases to the right and the Y value increases downward.

So far, we have been using window coordinates for **TextOut( )** without any specific mention of what those coordinates actually refer to. Now is the time to clarify a few details. First, the coordinates that are specified in **TextOut( )** are *logical coordinates*. That is, the units used by **TextOut( )** (and other window display functions, including the graphics functions described in the next chapter) are *logical units*. Windows maps these logical units onto pixels when output is actually displayed. The reason that we haven't had to worry about this distinction is that, by default, logical units are the same as pixels.

It is important to understand, however, that different mapping modes can be selected in which this convenient default will not be the case.

Setting the Text and Background Color

By default, when you output text to a window using **TextOut( )**, it is shown as black text against the current background. However, you can set both the color of the text and the background color using the API functions **SetTextColor( )** and **SetBkColor( )**, whose prototypes are shown here.

COLORREF SetTextColor(HDC *hdc*, COLORREF *color*);
COLORREF SetBkColor(HDC *hdc*, COLORREF *color*);

The **SetTextColor( )** function sets the current text color of the device associated with *hdc* to that specified by *color* (or the closest color that the display device is capable of displaying). The **SetBkColor( )** function sets the current text background color to that specified by *color* (or the nearest possible). For both functions, the previous color setting is returned. If an error occurs, the value **CLR_INVALID** is returned.

The color is specified as a value of type **COLORREF**, which is a 32-bit integer. Windows NT allows colors to be specified in three different ways. First, and by far most common, is as an RGB (red, green, blue) value. In an RGB value, the relative intensities of the three colors are combined to produce the actual color. The second way a color can be specified is as an index into a logical palette. The third is as an RGB value relative to a palette. In this chapter, only the first way will be discussed.

COLORREF
defines a color.

A long integer value that holds an RGB color is passed to either **SetTextColor( )** or **SetBkColor( )** using the following encoding:

Byte	Color
byte 0 (low-order byte)	red
byte 1	green
byte 2	blue
byte 3 (high-order byte)	must be zero

Each color in an RGB value is in the range 0 through 255, with 0 being the lowest intensity and 255 being the brightest intensity.

8

Although you are free to manually construct a **COLORREF** value, Windows defines the macro **RGB( )** that does this for you. It has this general form:

COLORREF RGB(int *red*, int *green*, int *blue*);

Here, *red, green,* and *blue* must be values in the range 0 through 255. Therefore, to create magenta, use **RGB(255, 0, 255)**. To create white, use **RGB(255, 255, 255)**. To create black use **RGB(0, 0, 0)**. To create other colors, you combine the three basic colors in varying intensities. For example, this creates a light aqua: **RGB(0, 100, 100)**. You can experiment to determine which colors are best for your application.

Setting the Background Display Mode

You can control the way the background is affected when text is displayed on the screen by using the **SetBkMode( )** API function, whose prototype is shown here:

int SetBkMode(HDC *hdc*, int *mode*);

The handle of the device context affected is specified by *hdc*. The background mode is specified in *mode* and must be one of these two macros: **OPAQUE** or **TRANSPARENT**. The function returns the previous setting or 0 if an error occurs.

If *mode* is **OPAQUE**, then each time text is output, the background is changed to that of the current background color. If *mode* is **TRANSPARENT**, the background is not altered. In this case, any effects of a call to **SetBkColor( )** are ignored. By default, the background mode is **OPAQUE**.

Obtaining the Text Metrics

As you know, characters are not all the same dimension. That is, in Windows, most text fonts are proportional. Therefore, the character "i" is not as wide as a character "w". Also, the height of each character and length of descenders vary between fonts. The amount of space between horizontal lines is also changeable. That these (and other) attributes are variable would not be of too much consequence except for the fact that Windows demands that you, the programmer, manually manage virtually all text output.

Windows provides only a few functions that output text to the client area of a window. The main one is **TextOut( )**, which we have been using. As you know, this function does only one thing: it displays a string at a specified location. It will not format output or even automatically perform a carriage return/linefeed sequence, for example. Instead, these operations are completely your job.

The fact that the size of each font may be different (and that fonts may be changed while your program is executing) implies that there must be some way to determine the dimensions and various other attributes of the currently selected font. For example, in order to write one line of text after another implies that you have some way of knowing how tall the font is and how many pixels are between lines. The API function that obtains information about the current font is called **GetTextMetrics( )**, and it has this prototype:

BOOL GetTextMetrics(HDC *hdc*, LPTEXTMETRIC *lpTAttrib*);

Here, *hdc* is the handle of the device context, which is generally obtained using **GetDC( )** or **BeginPaint( )**, and *lpTAttrib* is a pointer to a structure of type **TEXTMETRIC**, which will, upon return, contain the text metrics for the currently selected font. The **TEXTMETRIC** structure is defined as shown here.

```
typedef struct tagTEXTMETRIC
{
  LONG tmHeight; /* total height of font */
  LONG tmAscent; /* height above base line */
  LONG tmDescent; /* length of descenders */
  LONG tmInternalLeading; /* space above characters */
  LONG tmExternalLeading; /* blank space between rows */
  LONG tmAveCharWidth; /* average width */
  LONG tmMaxCharWidth; /* maximum width */
  LONG tmWeight; /* weight */
  LONG tmOverhang; /* extra width added to special fonts */
  LONG tmDigitizedAspectX; /* horizontal aspect */
  LONG tmDigitizedAspectY; /* vertical aspect */
  BYTE tmFirstChar; /* first character in font */
  BYTE tmLastChar; /* last character in font */
  BYTE tmDefaultChar; /* default character */
  BYTE tmBreakChar; /* character used to break words */
  BYTE tmItalic; /* non-zero if italic */
  BYTE tmUnderlined; /* non-zero if underlined */
  BYTE tmStruckOut; /* non-zero if struck out */
  BYTE tmPitchAndFamily; /* pitch and family of font */
  BYTE tmCharSet; /* character set identifier */
} TEXTMERIC;
```

8

While most of the values obtained by this function will not be used in this chapter, two are very important because they are needed to compute the vertical distance between lines of text. The distance between lines is required if you want to output more than one line of text to a window. Unlike a console-based application in which there is only one font and its size is fixed, there may be several Windows fonts and they may vary in size. Specifically, each font defines the height of its characters and its row spacing. This means that it is not possible to know in advance the proper vertical (Y) distance between one line of text and the next. To determine where the next line of text will begin, you must call **GetTextMetrics( )** to acquire two values: **tmHeight** and **tmExternalLeading**. These contain the character height and the amount of blank space that should be left between lines. By adding together these two values, you obtain the total number of vertical units between the start of one line of text and the start of the next.

The vertical distance between lines of text is tmHeight plus tmExternal-Leading.

REMEMBER: The value **tmExternalLeading** contains, in essence, the number of vertical units that should be left blank between lines of text. This value is separate from the height of the font. Thus, both values are needed to compute the total height of a line of text.

NEWTEXTMETRIC and NEWTEXTMETRICEX

There is an enhanced version of **TEXTMETRIC**, called **NEWTEXTMETRIC,** that is exactly the same as **TEXTMETRIC** except that it adds four fields at the end. These fields provide support for TrueType fonts. (TrueType fonts provide superior scalability features.) The new fields in **NEWTEXTMETRIC** are shown here.

```
DWORD ntmFlags; /* indicates style of font */
UINT ntmSizeEM; /* size of an em */
UINT ntmCellHeight; /* font height */
UINT ntmAvgWidth; /* average character width */
```

An extension to **NEWTEXTMETRIC**, called **NEWTEXTMETRICEX**, has recently been added to Win32. It is defined like this:

```
typedef struct tagNEWTEXTMETRICEX
{
  NEWTEXTMETRIC ntmTm;
  FONTSIGNATURE ntmFontSig; /* font signature */
} NEWTEXTMETRICEX;
```

As you can see, it includes all of **NEWTEXTMETRIC** and adds the structure **FONTSIGNATURE**, which contains information relating to Unicode and code pages.

For the purposes of this chapter, none of these fields added by **NEWTEXTMETRIC** or **NEWTEXTMETRICEX** are needed. However, they may be of value to applications that you create. You should consult an API reference manual for details.

Computing the Length of a String

Remember, Windows does not automatically maintain a text cursor or keep track of your current output location. This means that if you wish to display one string after another on the same line, you will need to remember where the previous output left off. This implies that you must have some way of knowing the length of a string in logical units. Because characters in most fonts are not the same size, it is not possible to know the length of a string, in logical units, simply by knowing how many characters it contains. That is, the result returned by **strlen( )** is not meaningful to managing output to a window because characters are of differing widths. To solve this problem, Windows NT includes the API function **GetTextExtentPoint32( )**, whose prototype is shown here:

BOOL GetTextExtentPoint32(HDC *hdc*, LPCSTR *lpszString*, int *len*,
LPSIZE *lpSize*);

Here, *hdc* is the handle of the output device. The string whose length you want is pointed to by *lpszString*. The number of characters in the string is specified in *len*. The width and height of the string, in logical units, are returned in the **SIZE** structure pointed to by *lpSize*. The **SIZE** structure is defined as shown here.

```
typedef struct tagSIZE {
  LONG cx; /* width */
  LONG cy; /* height */
} SIZE;
```

8

Upon return from a call to **GetTextExtentPoint32( )**, the **cx** field will contain the length of the string. This value can be used to determine the location of the end point of the string when displayed. To display another string on the same line, continue on from where the previous output left off.

GetTextExtentPoint32( ) returns nonzero if successful and zero on failure.

PORTABILITY: **GetTextExtentPoint32( )** replaces the Win16 function **GetTextExtent( )** used by Windows 3.1 programs.

A Short Text Demonstration

The following program demonstrates text output and the text-based functions just described. It displays several lines of text within the client area of the main window each time a **WM_PAINT** message is received.

```c
/* Managing Text Output */

#include <windows.h>
#include <string.h>
#include <stdio.h>

LRESULT CALLBACK WindowFunc(HWND, UINT, WPARAM, LPARAM);

char szWinName[] = "MyWin"; /* name of window class */

char str[255]; /* holds output strings */
int X=0, Y=0; /* current output location */

int WINAPI WinMain(HINSTANCE hThisInst, HINSTANCE hPrevInst,
                   LPSTR lpszArgs, int nWinMode)
{
  HWND hwnd;
  MSG msg;
  WNDCLASSEX wcl;

  /* Define a window class. */
  wcl.hInstance = hThisInst; /* handle to this instance */
  wcl.lpszClassName = szWinName; /* window class name */
  wcl.lpfnWndProc = WindowFunc; /* window function */
  wcl.style = 0; /* default style */

  wcl.cbSize = sizeof(WNDCLASSEX);
```

```
wcl.hIcon = LoadIcon(NULL, IDI_APPLICATION); /* standard icon */
wcl.hIconSm = LoadIcon(NULL, IDI_APPLICATION); /* small icon */
wcl.hCursor = LoadCursor(NULL, IDC_ARROW); /* cursor style */

wcl.lpszMenuName = NULL; /* no main menu */

wcl.cbClsExtra = 0; /* no extra */
wcl.cbWndExtra = 0; /* information needed */

/* Make the window white. */
wcl.hbrBackground = GetStockObject(WHITE_BRUSH);

/* Register the window class. */
if(!RegisterClassEx(&wcl)) return 0;

/* Now that a window class has been registered, a window
   can be created. */
hwnd = CreateWindow(
  szWinName, /* name of window class */
  "Managing Text Output", /* title */
  WS_OVERLAPPEDWINDOW, /* window style - normal */
  CW_USEDEFAULT, /* X coordinate - let Windows decide */
  CW_USEDEFAULT, /* Y coordinate - let Windows decide */
  CW_USEDEFAULT, /* width - let Windows decide */
  CW_USEDEFAULT, /* height - let Windows decide */
  HWND_DESKTOP, /* no handle of parent window */
  NULL, /* no override of class menu */
  hThisInst, /* handle of this instance of the program */
  NULL /* no additional arguments */
);

/* Display the window. */
ShowWindow(hwnd, nWinMode);
UpdateWindow(hwnd);

/* Create the message loop. */
while(GetMessage(&msg, NULL, 0, 0))
{
  TranslateMessage(&msg); /* translate keyboard messages */
  DispatchMessage(&msg); /* return control to Windows NT */
}
return msg.wParam;
}

/* This function is called by Windows NT and is passed
   messages from the message queue. */
```

8

```c
*/
LRESULT CALLBACK WindowFunc(HWND hwnd, UINT message,
                            WPARAM wParam, LPARAM lParam)
{
  HDC hdc;
  TEXTMETRIC tm;
  SIZE size;
  PAINTSTRUCT paintstruct;

  switch(message) {
    case WM_PAINT:
      hdc = BeginPaint(hwnd, &paintstruct);

      /* get text metrics */
      GetTextMetrics(hdc, &tm);

      X = Y = 0;

      sprintf(str, "This is on the first line.");
      TextOut(hdc, X, Y, str, strlen(str));
      Y = Y + tm.tmHeight + tm.tmExternalLeading; /* next line */

      strcpy(str, "This is on the second line. ");
      TextOut(hdc, X, Y, str, strlen(str));
      Y = Y + tm.tmHeight + tm.tmExternalLeading; /* next line */

      strcpy(str, "This is on the third line. ");
      TextOut(hdc, X, Y, str, strlen(str));

      /* compute length of a string */
      GetTextExtentPoint32(hdc, str, strlen(str), &size);
      sprintf(str, "The preceding sentence is %ld units long",
              size.cx);
      X = size.cx; /* advance to end of previous string */
      TextOut(hdc, X, Y, str, strlen(str));
      Y = Y + tm.tmHeight + tm.tmExternalLeading; /* next line */
      X = 0; /* return to start of line */

      sprintf(str, "The space between lines is %ld pixels.",
              tm.tmExternalLeading+tm.tmHeight);
      TextOut(hdc, X, Y, str, strlen(str));
      Y = Y + tm.tmHeight + tm.tmExternalLeading; /* next line */

      sprintf(str, "Average character width is %ld pixels",
              tm.tmAveCharWidth);
      TextOut(hdc, X, Y, str, strlen(str));
      Y = Y + tm.tmHeight + tm.tmExternalLeading; /* next line */
```

```
                    /* set text color to red */
                    SetTextColor(hdc, RGB(255, 0, 0));
                    /* set background color to blue */
                    SetBkColor(hdc, RGB(0, 0, 255));

                    sprintf(str, "This line is red on blue background.");
                    TextOut(hdc, X, Y, str, strlen(str));
                    Y = Y + tm.tmHeight + tm.tmExternalLeading; /* next line */

                    /* switch to transparent mode */
                    SetBkMode(hdc, TRANSPARENT);
                    sprintf(str, "This line is red. The background is unchanged.");
                    TextOut(hdc, X, Y, str, strlen(str));

                    EndPaint(hwnd, &paintstruct);
                    break;
                  case WM_DESTROY: /* terminate the program */
                    PostQuitMessage(0);
                    break;
                  default:
                    /* Let Windows NT process any messages not specified in
                       the preceding switch statement. */
                    return DefWindowProc(hwnd, message, wParam, lParam);
                }
                return 0;
}
```

Sample output is shown in Figure 8-1. Let's take a closer look at this program. The program declares two global variables called **X** and **Y** and initializes both to 0. These variables contain the current window location at which text will be displayed. They are updated by the program after each output sequence.

The interesting part of this program is mostly contained within the **WM_PAINT** message. Each time a **WM_PAINT** message is received, a device context is obtained and the text metrics are acquired. Next, the first line of text is output. Notice that it is constructed using **sprintf( )** and then actually output using **TextOut( )**. As you know from earlier in this book, neither **TextOut( )** nor any other API function performs text formatting, so it is up to you, the programmer, to construct your output first and then display it using **TextOut( )**. After the string is displayed, the **Y** coordinate is advanced to the next line by adding the font height to the distance between rows.

The program continues by next outputting the lines "This is on the second line." and "This is on the third line.", each on its own line. Then, the length

8

of the third line is computed using a call to **GetTextExtentPoint32( )**.
This value is then used to advance the **X** coordinate to the end of the
previous line before the next line is printed. Notice that here, the **Y**
coordinate is unchanged. This causes the next string to be displayed
immediately after the previous one, but still on the same line. Before
continuing, the program advances **Y** to the next line and resets **X** to 0,
which is the leftmost coordinate. This causes subsequent output to be started
once again at the beginning of the next line.

Next, some information about the currently selected character font is
displayed. Then, the background color is set to blue, the text color is set to
red, and a line of text is displayed. Finally, the background mode is set to
transparent and a line of text is displayed. In this case, the blue background
color is ignored.

Working with Fonts

Windows in general, and Windows NT, specifically, gives you nearly
complete control over the user interface. As such, it has a rich and varied set
of text-based features that you can take advantage of. One such feature is its
collection of various type fonts. By taking control of the type fonts used by
your application, you can create a unique and distinctive look that sets your
program apart from the crowd. Using Windows NT, you have several built-in
type fonts to choose from. You can also create custom fonts. Both of these
topics are discussed here. We will begin by defining a few terms.

Fonts, Families, Typefaces, and Styles

In the most general sense, a *font* describes a set of characters and features
common to those characters. As you almost certainly know, there are many
different kinds of type fonts in common use. For example, Courier and

Times Roman are two of the most popular. A font defines four attributes: a character set, a typeface, a style, and a size. Let's look at each.

♦ Windows NT supports various *character sets*. The one that we will be using is the standard Windows character set. This set is based upon the ANSI character set and each character is 8 bits. This makes the Windows character set suitable for most Western languages. Other character sets supported by Windows are Unicode, OEM (Original Equipment Manufacturer), and symbol (a set of symbolic characters used for representing mathematical expressions). Custom character sets are also allowed.

♦ A *typeface* defines the precise shape and design of the characters within a font. Thus, the typeface determines the unique visual characteristics of a font.

♦ In general, the *style* of a font determines whether a font is displayed normally, in bold, or in italics. In Windows, you have fine-grained control over the weight (thickness) of a font, so there are actually several gradients of font thickness.

♦ Type *size* is measured in *points*, which are 1/72 of an inch.

Windows organizes fonts into five *families*, which share basic attributes. These families are Decorative, Modern, Roman, Script, and Swiss. Decorative fonts are specialty fonts. Modern fonts are nonproportional. The Roman family is proportional and includes serifs. (*Serifs* are short lines found at the end points of characters.) Members of the Script family appear somewhat like handwriting. The Swiss family is proportional and *sans serif* (that is, does not have serifs).

In proportional fonts, the width of each character, or *pitch*, may differ. These are also called *variable-pitch* fonts. In nonproportional fonts, the width of each character is the same. These are called *fixed-pitch* or *monospaced* fonts.

Raster, Vector, and TrueType Fonts

Windows NT supports three ways in which a font can be stored and displayed: raster, vector, and TrueType. *Raster* fonts store bitmaps for each character, or *glyph*, in the font. This makes them easy to display, but they scale poorly. Raster fonts are most often used on display monitors and bitmapped printers. *Vector* fonts store the end points to the line segments that make up each glyph. These segments are then drawn to display each character. Vector fonts are best when used on plotters. *TrueType* fonts store information about the lines and arcs that make up each glyph, as well as instructions on how to draw the character. This approach gives TrueType fonts excellent scalability. They are also the most faithfully translated from

8

screen to printer. For this reason, TrueType fonts are quite popular for desktop publishing applications.

Using Built-In Fonts

Windows NT's built-in fonts are stock objects that are selected using **GetStockObject( )**. At the time of this writing, Windows NT supports six built-in fonts. The macros associated with these fonts are shown here.

Font	Description
ANSI_FIXED_FONT	Fixed-pitch font
ANSI_VAR_FONT	Variable-pitch font
DEVICE_DEFAULT_FONT	Default device font
OEM_FIXED_FONT	OEM defined font
SYSTEM_FONT	Font used by Windows NT
SYSTEM_FIXED_FONT	Font used by older versions of Windows

The system fonts are those character fonts used by Windows for things like menus and dialog boxes. Older versions of Windows used a fixed-pitch system font, but beginning with Windows 3.0, a variable font is used. Windows NT also uses the variable font.

Selecting and using a built-in font is easy. To do so, your program must first create a font handle, which is of type **HFONT**. Next, it must load the desired font, using **GetStockObject( )**, which returns a handle to the font. To switch to the font, select the font using **SelectObject( )** with the new font as a parameter. **SelectObject( )** will return a handle to the old font, which you may want to save so that you can switch back to it after you are done using the other font.

The following program demonstrates changing fonts. It uses the virtual window technology developed in Chapter 7 to handle repainting.

```
/* Demonstrate built-in fonts. */

#include <windows.h>
#include <string.h>
#include <stdio.h>
#include "text.h"
```

```
LRESULT CALLBACK WindowFunc(HWND, UINT, WPARAM, LPARAM);

char szWinName[] = "MyWin"; /* name of window class */

char str[255]; /* holds output strings */

int X=0, Y=0; /* current output location */
int maxX, maxY; /* screen dimensions */

HDC memdc; /* store the virtual device handle */
HBITMAP hbit; /* store the virtual bitmap */
HBRUSH hbrush; /* store the brush handle */
HFONT holdf, hnewf; /* store the font handles */

int WINAPI WinMain(HINSTANCE hThisInst, HINSTANCE hPrevInst,
                   LPSTR lpszArgs, int nWinMode)
{
  HWND hwnd;
  MSG msg;
  WNDCLASSEX wcl;
  HANDLE hAccel;

  /* Define a window class. */
  wcl.cbSize = sizeof(WNDCLASSEX);

  wcl.hInstance = hThisInst; /* handle to this instance */
  wcl.lpszClassName = szWinName; /* window class name */
  wcl.lpfnWndProc = WindowFunc; /* window function */
  wcl.style = 0; /* default style */

  wcl.hIcon = LoadIcon(NULL, IDI_APPLICATION); /* standard icon */
  wcl.hIconSm = LoadIcon(NULL, IDI_APPLICATION); /* small icon */
  wcl.hCursor = LoadCursor(NULL, IDC_ARROW); /* cursor style */

  /* specify name of menu resource */
  wcl.lpszMenuName = "FontMenu"; /* main menu */

  wcl.cbClsExtra = 0; /* no extra */
  wcl.cbWndExtra = 0; /* information needed */

  /* Make the window white. */
  wcl.hbrBackground = GetStockObject(WHITE_BRUSH);

  /* Register the window class. */
  if(!RegisterClassEx(&wcl)) return 0;
```

8

```
/* Now that a window class has been registered, a window
   can be created. */
hwnd = CreateWindow(
  szWinName, /* name of window class */
  "Using Built-in Fonts", /* title */
  WS_OVERLAPPEDWINDOW, /* window style - normal */
  CW_USEDEFAULT, /* X coordinate - let Windows decide */
  CW_USEDEFAULT, /* Y coordinate - let Windows decide */
  CW_USEDEFAULT, /* width - let Windows decide */
  CW_USEDEFAULT, /* height - let Windows decide */
  HWND_DESKTOP, /* no parent window */
  NULL, /* no override of class menu */
  hThisInst, /* handle of this instance of the program */
  NULL /* no additional arguments */
);

/* load accelerators */
hAccel = LoadAccelerators(hThisInst, "FontMenu");

/* Display the window. */
ShowWindow(hwnd, nWinMode);
UpdateWindow(hwnd);

/* Create the message loop. */
while(GetMessage(&msg, NULL, 0, 0))
{
  if(!TranslateAccelerator(hwnd, hAccel, &msg)) {
    TranslateMessage(&msg); /* translate keyboard messages */
    DispatchMessage(&msg); /* return control to Windows NT */
  }
}
return msg.wParam;
}


/* This function is called by Windows NT and is passed
   messages from the message queue.
*/
LRESULT CALLBACK WindowFunc(HWND hwnd, UINT message,
                            WPARAM wParam, LPARAM lParam)
{
  HDC hdc;
  PAINTSTRUCT paintstruct;
  static TEXTMETRIC tm;
  SIZE size;
  static fontswitch = 0;
  int response;
```

```
switch(message) {
  case WM_CREATE:
    /* get screen coordinates */
    maxX = GetSystemMetrics(SM_CXSCREEN);
    maxY = GetSystemMetrics(SM_CYSCREEN);

    /* create a virtual window */
    hdc = GetDC(hwnd);
    memdc = CreateCompatibleDC(hdc);
    hbit = CreateCompatibleBitmap(hdc, maxX, maxY);
    SelectObject(memdc, hbit);
    hbrush = GetStockObject(WHITE_BRUSH);
    SelectObject(memdc, hbrush);
    PatBlt(memdc, 0, 0, maxX, maxY, PATCOPY);

    /* get new font */
    hnewf = GetStockObject(ANSI_VAR_FONT);

    ReleaseDC(hwnd, hdc);
    break;
  case WM_COMMAND:
    switch(LOWORD(wParam)) {
      case IDM_SHOW:
        /* set text color to black and mode to transparent */
        SetTextColor(memdc, RGB(0, 0, 0));
        SetBkMode(memdc, TRANSPARENT);

        /* get text metrics */
        GetTextMetrics(memdc, &tm);

        sprintf(str, "The font is %ld pixels high.", tm.tmHeight);
        TextOut(memdc, X, Y, str, strlen(str));
        Y = Y + tm.tmHeight + tm.tmExternalLeading; /* next line */

        strcpy(str, "This is on the next line. ");
        TextOut(memdc, X, Y, str, strlen(str));

        /* compute length of a string */
        GetTextExtentPoint32(memdc, str, strlen(str), &size);
        sprintf(str, "Previous string is %ld units long", size.cx);
        X = size.cx; /* advance to end of previous string */
        TextOut(memdc, X, Y, str, strlen(str));
        Y = Y + tm.tmHeight + tm.tmExternalLeading; /* next line */
        X = 0; /* reset X */
```

8

```
        sprintf(str, "Screen dimensions: %d %d", maxX, maxY);
        TextOut(memdc, X, Y, str, strlen(str));
        Y = Y + tm.tmHeight + tm.tmExternalLeading; /* next line */
        InvalidateRect(hwnd, NULL, 1);
        break;
      case IDM_RESET:
        X = Y = 0;
        /* erase by repainting background */
        PatBlt(memdc, 0, 0, maxX, maxY, PATCOPY);

        InvalidateRect(hwnd, NULL, 1);
        break;
      case IDM_FONT:
        if(!fontswitch) {   /* switch to new font */
          holdf = SelectObject(memdc, hnewf);
          fontswitch = 1;
        }
        else { /* switch to old font */
          SelectObject(memdc, holdf);
          fontswitch = 0;
        }
        break;
      case IDM_EXIT:
        response = MessageBox(hwnd, "Quit the Program?",
                              "Exit", MB_YESNO);
        if(response == IDYES) PostQuitMessage(0);
        break;
      case IDM_HELP:
        MessageBox(hwnd, "F2: Display\nF3: Change Font\nF4: Reset",
                   "Font Fun", MB_OK);
        break;
    }
    break;
  case WM_PAINT: /* process a repaint request */
    hdc = BeginPaint(hwnd, &paintstruct); /* get DC */

    /* copy virtual window onto screen */
    BitBlt(hdc, 0, 0, maxX, maxY, memdc, 0, 0, SRCCOPY);

    EndPaint(hwnd, &paintstruct); /* release DC */
    break;
  case WM_DESTROY: /* terminate the program */
    DeleteDC(memdc);
    PostQuitMessage(0);
    break;
  default:
    /* Let Windows NT process any messages not specified in
```

```
        the preceding switch statement. */
        return DefWindowProc(hwnd, message, wParam, lParam);
  }
  return 0;
}
```

The resource file used by the program is shown here:

```
#include <windows.h>
#include "text.h"

FontMenu MENU
{
  POPUP "&Fonts" {
    MENUITEM "&Display\tF2", IDM_SHOW
    MENUITEM "Change &Font\tF3", IDM_FONT
    MENUITEM "&Reset\tF4", IDM_RESET
    MENUITEM "E&xit\tF5", IDM_EXIT
  }
  MENUITEM "&Help", IDM_HELP
}


FontMenu ACCELERATORS
{
  VK_F2, IDM_SHOW, VIRTKEY
  VK_F3, IDM_FONT, VIRTKEY
  VK_F4, IDM_RESET, VIRTKEY
  VK_F5, IDM_EXIT, VIRTKEY
  VK_F1, IDM_HELP, VIRTKEY
}
```

The TEXT.H header file is shown here:

```
#define IDM_SHOW    100
#define IDM_FONT    101
#define IDM_RESET   102
#define IDM_EXIT    103
#define IDM_HELP    104
```

Sample output produced by this program is shown in Figure 8-2.

The program works like this: Each time you select Display, text is output using the currently selected font. Each time you select Change Font, the currently selected font is toggled between the ANSI variable font and the default font. You can clear the window by selecting Reset. Notice that this option simply resets the X and Y coordinates to zero and then calls **PatBlt()** using **PATCOPY** to overpaint the background of the virtual window.

8

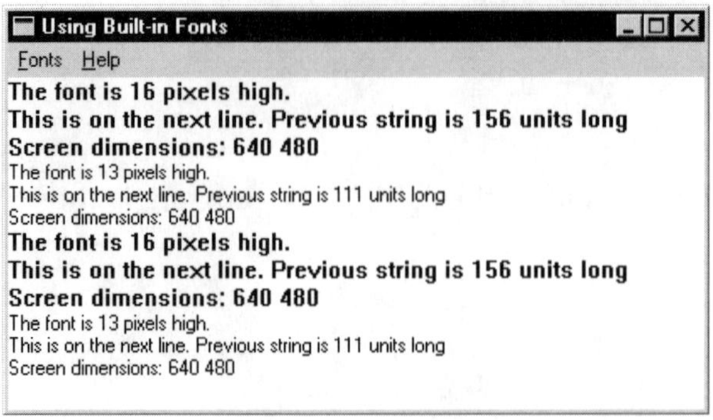

Sample output from the built-in font program
Figure 8-2.

Unicode

As you probably know, the character sets associated with Western languages, such as English or German, can be represented by the ANSI character set. ANSI uses an 8-bit character and is, therefore, capable of holding no more than 256 individual characters. (The ANSI character set is a superset of the 7-bit ASCII characters.) The trouble is that several Eastern languages, such as Chinese, require more than 256 characters. To handle these languages, the Unicode character set was created. Unicode characters are 16 bits long, which means that they can represent very large character sets (up to 16,536). To provide for compatibility, the first 256 characters in Unicode are the same as those defined by the ANSI character set.

Windows NT provides full support for Unicode to allow for the creation of internationalized versions of Windows NT programs. Several Win32 API functions provide a means of translating into and out of Unicode. For example, **ToUnicode( )** converts a virtual key into its Unicode equivalent. Also, Windows NT provides generic character data types that will automatically map to either Unicode or ANSI, depending upon how you compile your program.

While it is beyond the scope of this book to discuss the creation of internationalized applications, it is something that you will probably need to look into if you will be creating code for the world market.

Creating Custom Fonts

Although it may sound complex, it is actually very easy to create a custom font. There are two major advantages to doing this. First, a custom font gives your application a unique look that will set it apart. Second, creating your own font lets you control precisely what occurs when text is output. Before beginning, it is important to understand that you will not be defining a new typeface. Instead, you will be tailoring an existing typeface so that it meets your specifications. (That is, you don't need to define the shape of each character in the font that you create.)

To create your own font, use the **CreateFont( )** API function, whose prototype is shown here:

```
HFONT CreateFont(int Height, int Width, int Escapement,
                 int Orientation, int Weight,
                 DWORD Ital, DWORD Underline,
                 DWORD StrikeThru, DWORD Charset,
                 DWORD Precision, DWORD ClipPrecision,
                 DWORD Quality, DWORD PitchFam,
                 LPCSTR TypefaceName);
```

The height of the font is passed in *Height*. If *Height* is zero, a default size is used. The width of the font is specified in *Width*. If *Width* is zero, Windows chooses an appropriate value based upon the current aspect ratio. Both *Height* and *Width* are in terms of logical units.

Text can be output at any angle within the window. The angle at which it is displayed is determined by the *Escapement* parameter. For normal, horizontal text, this value should be 0. Otherwise, it specifies the number of 1/10-degree increments through which the text should be rotated in a counterclockwise direction. For example, a value of 900 causes the text to be rotated 90 degrees, causing output to be vertical.

The angle of each individual character can also be specified using the *Orientation* parameter. It too uses 1/10-degree increments to specify the angle of each character relative to horizontal in a counterclockwise direction.

The escapement specifies the angle of a line of text. Orientation specifies the angle of a character itself.

NOTE: By default, both the *Escapement* and *Orientation* parameters of **CreateFont( )** must be the same. However, if you set the graphics mode to **GM_ADVANCED**, these two parameters may differ. You will see how to set the graphics mode in Chapter 9.

8

Weight specifies the preferred weight of the font in the range of 0 to 1000. A value of 0 specifies the default weight. To specify a normal weight, use 400.

For bold, use 700. You can also use any of the following macros to specify the font weight.

FW_DONTCARE	FW_MEDIUM
FW_THIN	FW_SEMIBOLD
FW_EXTRALIGHT	FW_BOLD
FW_LIGHT	FW_EXTRABOLD
FW_NORMAL	FW_HEAVY

To create an italic font, specify *Ital* as nonzero. Otherwise, this parameter should be zero. To create an underlined font, specify *Underline* as nonzero. Otherwise, this parameter should be zero. To create a strike-through font, specify *StrikeThru* as nonzero. Otherwise, this parameter should be zero.

Charset indicates which character set is desired. The example that follows uses **ANSI_CHARSET**. *Precision* specifies the preferred output precision. This determines just how closely the output must match the requested font's characteristics. The example in this chapter uses **OUT_DEFAULT_PRECIS**. *ClipPrecision* specifies the preferred clipping precision, which determines how each character that extends beyond the clipping region is to be "clipped." The value used by the example in this chapter is **CLIP_DEFAULT_PRECIS**. (For other valid values for *Charset, Precision,* and *ClipPrecision*, consult an API reference manual.)

Quality determines how closely the logical font will be matched with the actual physical fonts provided for the requested output device. It can be one of these values:

DEFAULT_QUALITY
DRAFT_QUALITY
PROOF_QUALITY

PitchFam specifies the pitch and family of the font. You have three pitch choices:

DEFAULT_PITCH
FIXED_PITCH
VARIABLE_PITCH

There are six possible font families:

FF_DECORATIVE   FF_ROMAN
FF_DONTCARE   FF_SCRIPT
FF_MODERN   FF_SWISS

The **FF_DONTCARE** family is used when you don't care what font family is used. The font family is meaningful only if the typeface you specify is not available on the system. To create the value for *PitchFam*, OR together one pitch value and one font family value.

A pointer to the name of the typeface is passed in *TypefaceName*. This name cannot be longer than 32 characters. The font you specify must be installed in your system. Alternatively, you can specify **NULL** for this parameter, and Windows NT will automatically select a font that is compatible with the characteristics that you specify in the other parameters. (You will see how to obtain a list of available fonts later in this chapter.)

If successful, **CreateFont( )** returns a handle to the font. On failure, **NULL** is returned. Fonts created using **CreateFont( )** must be deleted before your program ends. To delete a font, call **DeleteObject( )**.

Here is a program that demonstrates two custom fonts. The first is based upon the Courier New font, the second upon Century Gothic. Each time you choose the Change Font menu item, a new font is selected and displayed. This program uses the same resource and header files as the program in the preceding section. Sample output is shown in Figure 8-3.

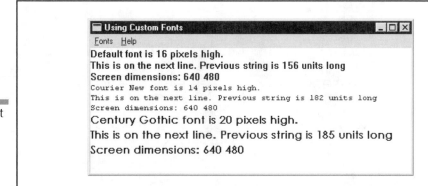

Sample output from the custom font program

Figure 8-3.

8

```
/* Create a custom font. */

#include <windows.h>
#include <string.h>
#include <stdio.h>
#include "text.h"

LRESULT CALLBACK WindowFunc(HWND, UINT, WPARAM, LPARAM);

char szWinName[] = "MyWin"; /* name of window class */

char str[255]; /* holds output strings */
char fname[40] = "Default"; /* name of font */

int X=0, Y=0; /* current output location */
int maxX, maxY; /* screen dimensions */

HDC memdc; /* store the virtual device handle */
HBITMAP hbit; /* store the virtual bitmap */
HBRUSH hbrush; /* store the brush handle */
HFONT holdf, hnewf1, hnewf2; /* store the font handles */

int WINAPI WinMain(HINSTANCE hThisInst, HINSTANCE hPrevInst,
                   LPSTR lpszArgs, int nWinMode)
{
  HWND hwnd;
  MSG msg;
  WNDCLASSEX wcl;
  HANDLE hAccel;

  /* Define a window class. */
  wcl.cbSize = sizeof(WNDCLASSEX);

  /* Define a window class. */
  wcl.hInstance = hThisInst; /* handle to this instance */
  wcl.lpszClassName = szWinName; /* window class name */
  wcl.lpfnWndProc = WindowFunc; /* window function */
  wcl.style = 0; /* default style */

  wcl.hIcon = LoadIcon(NULL, IDI_APPLICATION); /* standard icon */
  wcl.hIconSm = LoadIcon(NULL, IDI_APPLICATION); /* small icon */
  wcl.hCursor = LoadCursor(NULL, IDC_ARROW); /* cursor style */

  /* specify name of menu resource */
  wcl.lpszMenuName = "FontMenu"; /* main menu */

  wcl.cbClsExtra = 0; /* no extra */
  wcl.cbWndExtra = 0; /* information needed */
```

```
/* Make the window white. */
wcl.hbrBackground = GetStockObject(WHITE_BRUSH);

/* Register the window class. */
if(!RegisterClassEx(&wcl)) return 0;

/* Now that a window class has been registered, a window
   can be created. */
hwnd = CreateWindow(
  szWinName, /* name of window class */
  "Using Custom Fonts", /* title */
  WS_OVERLAPPEDWINDOW, /* window style - normal */
  CW_USEDEFAULT, /* X coordinate - let Windows decide */
  CW_USEDEFAULT, /* Y coordinate - let Windows decide */
  CW_USEDEFAULT, /* width - let Windows decide */
  CW_USEDEFAULT, /* height - let Windows decide */
  HWND_DESKTOP, /* no parent window */
  NULL, /* no override of class menu */
  hThisInst, /* handle of this instance of the program */
  NULL /* no additional arguments */
);

/* load accelerators */
hAccel = LoadAccelerators(hThisInst, "FontMenu");

/* Display the window. */
ShowWindow(hwnd, nWinMode);
UpdateWindow(hwnd);

/* Create the message loop. */
while(GetMessage(&msg, NULL, 0, 0))
{
  if(!TranslateAccelerator(hwnd, hAccel, &msg)) {
    TranslateMessage(&msg); /* translate keyboard messages */
    DispatchMessage(&msg); /* return control to Windows NT */
  }
}
return msg.wParam;
}

/* This function is called by Windows NT and is passed
   messages from the message queue.
*/
LRESULT CALLBACK WindowFunc(HWND hwnd, UINT message,
                            WPARAM wParam, LPARAM lParam)
{
  HDC hdc;
  PAINTSTRUCT paintstruct;
```

8

```
static TEXTMETRIC tm;
SIZE size;
static fontswitch = 0;
int response;

switch(message) {
  case WM_CREATE:
    /* get screen coordinates */
    maxX = GetSystemMetrics(SM_CXSCREEN);
    maxY = GetSystemMetrics(SM_CYSCREEN);

    /* create a virtual window */
    hdc = GetDC(hwnd);
    memdc = CreateCompatibleDC(hdc);
    hbit = CreateCompatibleBitmap(hdc, maxX, maxY);
    SelectObject(memdc, hbit);
    hbrush = GetStockObject(WHITE_BRUSH);
    SelectObject(memdc, hbrush);
    PatBlt(memdc, 0, 0, maxX, maxY, PATCOPY);

    /* create new fonts */
    hnewf1 = CreateFont(14, 0, 0, 0, FW_NORMAL,
                        0, 0, 0, ANSI_CHARSET,
                        OUT_DEFAULT_PRECIS,
                        CLIP_DEFAULT_PRECIS,
                        DEFAULT_QUALITY,
                        DEFAULT_PITCH | FF_DONTCARE,
                        "Courier New");
    hnewf2 = CreateFont(20, 0, 0, 0, FW_SEMIBOLD,
                        0, 0, 0, ANSI_CHARSET,
                        OUT_DEFAULT_PRECIS,
                        CLIP_DEFAULT_PRECIS,
                        DEFAULT_QUALITY,
                        DEFAULT_PITCH | FF_DONTCARE,
                        "Century Gothic");
    ReleaseDC(hwnd, hdc);
    break;
  case WM_COMMAND:
    switch(LOWORD(wParam)) {
      case IDM_SHOW:
        /* set text to black and mode to transparent */
        SetTextColor(memdc, RGB(0, 0, 0));
        SetBkMode(memdc, TRANSPARENT);

        /* get text metrics */
        GetTextMetrics(memdc, &tm);
```

```
          sprintf(str, "%s font is %ld pixels high.",
                  fname, tm.tmHeight);
      TextOut(memdc, X, Y, str, strlen(str));
      Y = Y + tm.tmHeight + tm.tmExternalLeading; /* next line */

          strcpy(str, "This is on the next line. ");
      TextOut(memdc, X, Y, str, strlen(str));

          /* compute length of a string */
      GetTextExtentPoint32(memdc, str, strlen(str), &size);
      sprintf(str, "Previous string is %ld units long", size.cx);
      X = size.cx; /* advance to end of previous string */
      TextOut(memdc, X, Y, str, strlen(str));
      Y = Y + tm.tmHeight + tm.tmExternalLeading; /* next line */
      X = 0; /* reset X */


          sprintf(str, "Screen dimensions: %d %d", maxX, maxY);
      TextOut(memdc, X, Y, str, strlen(str));
      Y = Y + tm.tmHeight + tm.tmExternalLeading; /* next line */

      InvalidateRect(hwnd, NULL, 1);
      break;
    case IDM_RESET:
      X = Y = 0;
      /* erase by repainting background */
      PatBlt(memdc, 0, 0, maxX, maxY, PATCOPY);
      InvalidateRect(hwnd, NULL, 1);
      break;
    case IDM_FONT:
      switch(fontswitch) {
        case 0: /* switch to new font1 */
          holdf = SelectObject(memdc, hnewf1);
          fontswitch = 1;
         strcpy(fname, "Courier New");
          break;
        case 1: /* switch to new font2 */
          SelectObject(memdc, hnewf2);
          fontswitch = 2;
          strcpy(fname, "Century Gothic");
          break;
        default: /* switch to old font */
          SelectObject(memdc, holdf);
```

8

```
              fontswitch = 0;
              strcpy(fname, "Default");
          }
        break;
      case IDM_EXIT:
        response = MessageBox(hwnd, "Quit the Program?",
                             "Exit", MB_YESNO);
        if(response == IDYES) PostQuitMessage(0);
        break;
      case IDM_HELP:
        MessageBox(hwnd, "F2: Display\nF3: Change Font\nF4: Reset",
                   "Custom Fonts", MB_OK);
        break;
    }
    break;
  case WM_PAINT: /* process a repaint request */
    hdc = BeginPaint(hwnd, &paintstruct); /* get DC */

    /* copy virtual window onto screen */
    BitBlt(hdc, 0, 0, maxX, maxY, memdc, 0, 0, SRCCOPY);

    EndPaint(hwnd, &paintstruct); /* release DC */
    break;
  case WM_DESTROY: /* terminate the program */
    DeleteDC(memdc);
    DeleteObject(hnewf1);
    DeleteObject(hnewf2);
    PostQuitMessage(0);
    break;
  default:
    /* Let Windows NT process any messages not specified in
    the preceding switch statement. */
    return DefWindowProc(hwnd, message, wParam, lParam);
  }
  return 0;
}
```

Using CreateFontIndirect( )

There is an alternative to **CreateFont( )** that you will find useful in some situations. It is called **CreateFontIndirect( )**, and it creates a font based upon the information contained in a **LOGFONT** structure. Its prototype is shown here:

HFONT CreateFontIndirect(CONST LOGFONT *lpFont);

The function returns a handle to the font that best matches the information supplied in the structure pointed to by *lpFont*. It returns **NULL** on failure. You must delete the font handle, using **DeleteObject( )**, before your program ends.

The **LOGFONT** structure encapsulates logical information about a font. It is defined like this:

```
typedef struct tagLOGFONT
{
  LONG lfHeight; /* height of font */
  LONG lfWidth; /* width of font */
  LONG lfEscapement; /* angle of text */
  LONG lfOrientation; /* angle of character */
  LONG lfWeight; /* darkness */
  BYTE lfItalic; /* 1 if ital */
  BYTE lfUnderline; /* 1 if underline */
  BYTE lfStrikeOut; /* 1 if strike-through */
  BYTE lfCharSet; /* character set */
  BYTE lfOutPrecision; /* output precision */
  BYTE lfClipPrecision; /* clipping precision  */
  BYTE lfQuality; /* display quality */
  BYTE lfPitchAndFamily; /* pitch and family */
  CHAR lfFaceName[LF_FACESIZE]; /* name */
} LOGFONT;
```

The fields in **LOGFONT** have the same meaning and use the same values as the parameters to **CreateFont( )**, described earlier. For example, here is the call to **CreateFontIndirect( )** that creates the same Century Gothic font that was created by calling **CreateFont( )** in the preceding program.

```
LOGFONT lf;

lf.lfHeight = 20;
lf.lfWidth = 0;
lf.lfEscapement = 0;
lf.lfOrientation = 0;
lf.lfWeight = FW_SEMIBOLD;
lf.lfItalic = 0;
lf.lfUnderline = 0;
lf.lfStrikeOut = 0;
lf.lfCharSet = ANSI_CHARSET;
lf.lfOutPrecision = OUT_DEFAULT_PRECIS;
lf.lfClipPrecision = CLIP_DEFAULT_PRECIS;
lf.lfQuality = DEFAULT_QUALITY;
lf.lfPitchAndFamily = DEFAULT_PITCH | FF_DONTCARE;
strcpy(lf.lfFaceName, "Century Gothic");
hnewf2 = CreateFontIndirect(&lf);
```

8

While there is no particular benefit in this situation to using **CreateFontIndirect( )** over **CreateFont( )**, there are times when there will be. For example, when you obtain information about existing fonts, each font's description is stored in a **LOGFONT** structure. The contents of this structure can be used in a call to **CreateFontIndirect( )** to create the font.

Rotating Text

One of the most exciting features of Windows NT's font system is that you may easily rotate and orient the characters relative to the X axis. This allows you to display text in ways other than horizontally on the screen. To change the angle of text output, specify the desired angle in the *Escapement* and *Orientation* parameters when creating a font using **CreateFont( )**. Recall that these angles are specified in tenths of a degree from horizontal, with counterclockwise being the positive direction. Escapement determines the angle of a line of text, and orientation determines the angle of each individual character. For now, both of these angles must be the same. This is usually what you want anyway because it means that the orientation of each individual character is aligned in agreement with the rotated base line.

The following program modifies the Courier and Gothic fonts created by the preceding program so that they print at 45-degree angles. The Courier text is printed sloping up because it is given a positive escapement and orientation. The Gothic text is displayed sloping down because it is given a negative escapement and orientation. Sample output is shown in Figure 8-4.

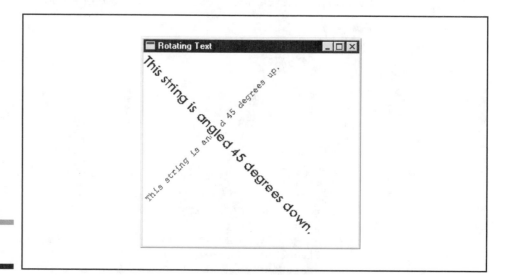

Rotating text

Figure 8-4.

```
/* Rotating Text. */

#include <windows.h>
#include <string.h>
#include <stdio.h>

LRESULT CALLBACK WindowFunc(HWND, UINT, WPARAM, LPARAM);

char szWinName[] = "MyWin"; /* name of window class */

char str[255]; /* holds output strings */

HFONT hnewf1, hnewf2; /* store the font handles */

int WINAPI WinMain(HINSTANCE hThisInst, HINSTANCE hPrevInst,
                   LPSTR lpszArgs, int nWinMode)
{
  HWND hwnd;
  MSG msg;
  WNDCLASSEX wcl;

  /* Define a window class. */
  wcl.cbSize = sizeof(WNDCLASSEX);

  /* Define a window class. */
  wcl.hInstance = hThisInst; /* handle to this instance */
  wcl.lpszClassName = szWinName; /* window class name */
  wcl.lpfnWndProc = WindowFunc; /* window function */
  wcl.style = 0; /* default style */

  wcl.hIcon = LoadIcon(NULL, IDI_APPLICATION); /* standard icon */
  wcl.hIconSm = LoadIcon(NULL, IDI_APPLICATION); /* small icon */
  wcl.hCursor = LoadCursor(NULL, IDC_ARROW); /* cursor style */

  /* specify name of menu resource */
  wcl.lpszMenuName = NULL; /* no main menu */

  wcl.cbClsExtra = 0; /* no extra */
  wcl.cbWndExtra = 0; /* information needed */

  /* Make the window white. */
  wcl.hbrBackground = GetStockObject(WHITE_BRUSH);

  /* Register the window class. */
  if(!RegisterClassEx(&wcl)) return 0;

  /* Now that a window class has been registered, a window
     can be created. */
```

8

```
hwnd = CreateWindow(
  szWinName, /* name of window class */
  "Rotating Text", /* title */
  WS_OVERLAPPEDWINDOW, /* window style - normal */
  CW_USEDEFAULT, /* X coordinate - let Windows decide */
  CW_USEDEFAULT, /* Y coordinate - let Windows decide */
  CW_USEDEFAULT, /* width - let Windows decide */
  CW_USEDEFAULT, /* height - let Windows decide */
  HWND_DESKTOP, /* no parent window */
  NULL, /* no override of class menu */
  hThisInst, /* handle of this instance of the program */
  NULL /* no additional arguments */
);

/* Display the window. */
ShowWindow(hwnd, nWinMode);
UpdateWindow(hwnd);

/* Create the message loop. */
while(GetMessage(&msg, NULL, 0, 0))
{
  TranslateMessage(&msg); /* translate keyboard messages */
  DispatchMessage(&msg); /* return control to Windows NT */
}
return msg.wParam;
}


/* This function is called by Windows NT and is passed
   messages from the message queue.
*/
LRESULT CALLBACK WindowFunc(HWND hwnd, UINT message,
                            WPARAM wParam, LPARAM lParam)
{
  HDC hdc;
  PAINTSTRUCT ps;

  switch(message) {
    case WM_CREATE:
      /* This font is angled 45 degrees up */
      hnewf1 = CreateFont(14, 0, 450, 450, FW_NORMAL,
                          0, 0, 0, ANSI_CHARSET,
                          OUT_DEFAULT_PRECIS,
                          CLIP_DEFAULT_PRECIS,
                          DEFAULT_QUALITY,
                          DEFAULT_PITCH | FF_DONTCARE,
                          "Courier New");
```

```
                /* This font is angled 45 degrees down */
                hnewf2 = CreateFont(20, 0, -450, -450, FW_SEMIBOLD,
                                    0, 0, 0, ANSI_CHARSET,
                                    OUT_DEFAULT_PRECIS,
                                    CLIP_DEFAULT_PRECIS,
                                    DEFAULT_QUALITY,
                                    DEFAULT_PITCH | FF_DONTCARE,
                                    "Century Gothic");
                break;
            case WM_PAINT: /* process a repaint request */
                hdc = BeginPaint(hwnd, &ps); /* get DC */

                SelectObject(hdc, hnewf1);

                strcpy(str, "This string is angled 45 degrees up.");
                TextOut(hdc, 0, 200, str, strlen(str));

                SelectObject(hdc, hnewf2);
                strcpy(str, "This string is angled 45 degrees down.");
                TextOut(hdc, 10, 0, str, strlen(str));

                EndPaint(hwnd, &ps); /* release DC */
                break;
            case WM_DESTROY: /* terminate the program */
                DeleteObject(hnewf1);
                DeleteObject(hnewf2);
                PostQuitMessage(0);
                break;
            default:
                /* Let Windows NT process any messages not specified in
                the preceding switch statement. */
                return DefWindowProc(hwnd, message, wParam, lParam);
    }
    return 0;
}
```

Enumerating Fonts

The preceding programs have assumed that the desired fonts were available when creating fonts. However, it is usually not a good idea to assume anything when programming for Windows. For example, it is possible to add fonts to or to remove fonts from a system. Fortunately, there is a relatively easy way to determine what fonts are available for use.

To enumerate the available fonts, you will use the **EnumFontFamiliesEx( )** API function, shown here.

8

```
int EnumFontFamiliesEx(HDC hdc, LPLOGFONT lpFontInfo,
                       FONTENUMPROC EnumFunc,
                       LPARAM lParam, DWORD NotUsed);
```

Here, *hdc* is the device context from which the fonts are being obtained. Different device contexts may support different fonts. Various characteristics that define the type of fonts you want enumerated are passed in the **LOGFONT** structure pointed to by *lpFontInfo*. (**LOGFONT** was described earlier in this chapter.) *EnumFunc* is a pointer to a callback function that will be called once for each font enumerated. You can use *lParam* to pass any application-dependent information to the callback function pointed to by *EnumProc*. *NotUsed* is unused and must be zero. The function returns the last value returned by *EnumProc*.

Before calling **EnumFontFamiliesEx( )**, you must initialize three fields in the **LOGFONT** structure pointed to by *lpFontInfo*: **lfCharSet**, **lfPitchAndFamily**, and **lfFaceName**. To enumerate only fonts with a particular character set, specify the name of that set in **lfCharSet**. To enumerate fonts with any type of character set, use **DEFAULT_CHARSET**. To enumerate all fonts of a particular typeface, specify the name of the typeface in **lfFaceName**. To enumerate a representative font for all typefaces, initialize this member using the null string. Finally, for most applications, **lfPitchAndFamily** must be set to zero. (For Hebrew or Arabic, set this field to **MONO_FONT**.)

Each time Windows NT enumerates a font, it calls the function pointed to by *EnumFunc*. This function processes each enumerated font and then returns nonzero if it wishes to process another font or zero to stop. This function must have this general form:

```
int CALLBACK EnumFunc(ENUMLOGFONTEX *lpLFInfo,
                      NEWTEXTMETRICEX *lpTMInfo,
                      int type, LPARAM lParam);
```

Here, *lpLFInfo* is a pointer to an **ENUMLOGFONTEX** structure that contains logical information about the enumerated font. *lpTMInfo* is a pointer to a **NEWTEXTMETRICEX** structure that contains physical information about the font. Non-TrueType fonts receive a pointer to a **TEXTMETRIC** structure, instead. The value of *type* indicates the font type. It can be one of the following:

```
RASTER_FONTTYPE
TRUETYPE_FONTTYPE
DEVICE_FONTTYPE
```

lParam receives the value passed by *lParam* in **EnumFontFamiliesEx( )**.

PORTABILITY: Windows 3.1 does not support **EnumFontFamiliesEx( )**. Windows 3.1 programs use either **EnumFonts( )** or **EnumFontFamilies( )**. You will want to upgrade these when porting to Windows NT. Windows 95 does not support **NEWTEXTMETRICEX.**

The **ENUMLOGFONTEX** structure is defined as shown here.

```
typedef struct tagENUMLOGFONTEX
{
  LOGFONT elfLogFont;
  BYTE elfFullName[LF_FULLFACESIZE]; /* full name of font */
  BYTE elfStyle[LF_FACESIZE]; /* style of font */
  BYTE elfScript[LF_FACESIZE]; /* script used by font */
} ENUMLOGFONTEX;
```

elfLogFont is a **LOGFONT** structure that contains most of the logical font information. The information used in this structure could be used in a call to **CreateFont( )** or **CreateFontIndirect( )**. The full name of the font is contained in **elfFullName**. The style (bold, italics, and so on) is contained in **elfStyle**. The name of the script is found in **elfScript**.

Moving Up to NT 4: EnumFontFamiliesEx( )

Versions of Windows NT prior to 4.0 did not support **EnumFontFamiliesEx( )** or the **ENUMLOGFONTEX** structure. Since these items supply more information about the available fonts, you should upgrade older NT programs. In general, support for fonts continues to improve and expand in Windows NT. You will want to review the Win32 API for any additional support for fonts.

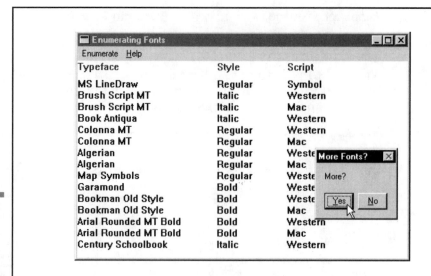

Sample output
from the font
enumeration
program
Figure 8-5.

A Font Enumeration Program

The following program shows how to enumerate fonts two different ways. First, when you select Available Fonts from the Enumerate menu, you obtain representative fonts for all of the supported typefaces. By choosing Selected Typeface, you will obtain all fonts for the typeface that you specify. Sample output is shown in Figure 8-5.

```
/* Enumerating Fonts */

#include <windows.h>
#include <string.h>
#include <stdio.h>
#include "font.h"

LRESULT CALLBACK WindowFunc(HWND, UINT, WPARAM, LPARAM);
int CALLBACK FontFunc(ENUMLOGFONTEX *lpLF,
                      NEWTEXTMETRICEX *lpTM,
                      int type, LPARAM lParam);
BOOL CALLBACK FontDialog(HWND hdwnd, UINT message,
                      WPARAM wParam, LPARAM lParam);

char szWinName[] = "MyWin"; /* name of window class */

char str[255]; /* holds output strings */
char fontstr[255]; /* holds user-entered font name */
```

```
int X=0, Y=0; /* current output location */
int maxX, maxY; /* screen dimensions */

int linespacing; /* spacing between lines */

HDC memdc; /* store the virtual device handle */
HBITMAP hbit; /* store the virtual bitmap */
HBRUSH hbrush; /* store the brush handle */

HINSTANCE hInst;

int WINAPI WinMain(HINSTANCE hThisInst, HINSTANCE hPrevInst,
                   LPSTR lpszArgs, int nWinMode)
{
  HWND hwnd;
  MSG msg;
  WNDCLASSEX wcl;
  HANDLE hAccel;

  /* Define a window class. */
  wcl.cbSize = sizeof(WNDCLASSEX);

  /* Define a window class. */
  wcl.hInstance = hThisInst; /* handle to this instance */
  wcl.lpszClassName = szWinName; /* window class name */
  wcl.lpfnWndProc = WindowFunc; /* window function */
  wcl.style = 0; /* default style */

  wcl.hIcon = LoadIcon(NULL, IDI_APPLICATION); /* standard icon */
  wcl.hIconSm = LoadIcon(NULL, IDI_APPLICATION); /* small icon */
  wcl.hCursor = LoadCursor(NULL, IDC_ARROW); /* cursor style */

  /* specify name of menu resource */
  wcl.lpszMenuName = "FontEnumMenu"; /* main menu */

  wcl.cbClsExtra = 0; /* no extra */
  wcl.cbWndExtra = 0; /* information needed */

  /* Make the window white. */
  wcl.hbrBackground = GetStockObject(WHITE_BRUSH);

  /* Register the window class. */
  if(!RegisterClassEx(&wcl)) return 0;

  /* Now that a window class has been registered, a window
     can be created. */
  hwnd = CreateWindow(
    szWinName, /* name of window class */
```

8

```
    "Enumerating Fonts", /* title */
    WS_OVERLAPPEDWINDOW, /* window style - normal */
    CW_USEDEFAULT, /* X coordinate - let Windows decide */
    CW_USEDEFAULT, /* Y coordinate - let Windows decide */
    CW_USEDEFAULT, /* width - let Windows decide */
    CW_USEDEFAULT, /* height - let Windows decide */
    HWND_DESKTOP, /* no parent window */
    NULL, /* no override of class menu */
    hThisInst, /* handle of this instance of the program */
    NULL /* no additional arguments */
  );

  hInst = hThisInst;

  /* load accelerators */
  hAccel = LoadAccelerators(hThisInst, "FontEnumMenu");

  /* Display the window. */
  ShowWindow(hwnd, nWinMode);
  UpdateWindow(hwnd);

  /* Create the message loop. */
  while(GetMessage(&msg, NULL, 0, 0))
  {
    if(!TranslateAccelerator(hwnd, hAccel, &msg)) {
      TranslateMessage(&msg); /* translate keyboard messages */
      DispatchMessage(&msg); /* return control to Windows NT */
    }
  }
  return msg.wParam;
}


/* This function is called by Windows NT and is passed
   messages from the message queue.
*/
LRESULT CALLBACK WindowFunc(HWND hwnd, UINT message,
                            WPARAM wParam, LPARAM lParam)
{
  HDC hdc;
  static TEXTMETRIC tm;
  PAINTSTRUCT ps;
  LOGFONT lf;
  int result;
  int response;

  switch(message) {
    case WM_CREATE:
      /* get screen coordinates */
```

```
    maxX = GetSystemMetrics(SM_CXSCREEN);
    maxY = GetSystemMetrics(SM_CYSCREEN);

    /* create a virtual window */
    hdc = GetDC(hwnd);
    memdc = CreateCompatibleDC(hdc);
    hbit = CreateCompatibleBitmap(hdc, maxX, maxY);
    SelectObject(memdc, hbit);
    hbrush = GetStockObject(WHITE_BRUSH);
    SelectObject(memdc, hbrush);
    PatBlt(memdc, 0, 0, maxX, maxY, PATCOPY);

    /* get text metrics */
    GetTextMetrics(memdc, &tm);
    /* compute linespacing */
    linespacing = tm.tmHeight + tm.tmExternalLeading;

    /* display header in bright red/orange */
    SetTextColor(memdc, RGB(255, 100, 0));
    TextOut(memdc, X, 0, "Typeface", strlen("Typeface"));
    TextOut(memdc, X+200, 0, "Style", strlen("Style"));
    TextOut(memdc, X+300, 0, "Script", strlen("Script"));
    SetTextColor(memdc, RGB(0, 0, 0));

    ReleaseDC(hwnd, hdc);
    break;
case WM_COMMAND:
    switch(LOWORD(wParam)) {
      case IDM_FONTS: /* display fonts */
        Y = linespacing + linespacing/2;
        PatBlt(memdc, 0, linespacing, maxX, maxY, PATCOPY);

        lf.lfCharSet = DEFAULT_CHARSET;
        strcpy(lf.lfFaceName, "");
        lf.lfPitchAndFamily = 0;

        /* enumerate fonts */
        hdc = GetDC(hwnd);
        EnumFontFamiliesEx(hdc, &lf,
            (FONTENUMPROC) FontFunc, (LPARAM)hwnd, 0);
        ReleaseDC(hwnd, hdc);

        break;
      case IDM_TYPEFACE: /* display selected typeface */
        /* get name of font */
        result = DialogBox(hInst, "FontDB", hwnd,
                           (DLGPROC) FontDialog);
```

8

```
        if(!result) break; /* user cancelled */

        Y = linespacing + linespacing/2;
        PatBlt(memdc, 0, linespacing, maxX, maxY, PATCOPY);

        lf.lfCharSet = DEFAULT_CHARSET;
        strcpy(lf.lfFaceName, fontstr);
        lf.lfPitchAndFamily = 0;

        /* enumerate all styles for given font */
        hdc = GetDC(hwnd);
        EnumFontFamiliesEx(hdc, &lf,
            (FONTENUMPROC) FontFunc, (LPARAM) hwnd, 0);
        ReleaseDC(hwnd, hdc);

        break;
      case IDM_EXIT:
        response = MessageBox(hwnd, "Quit the Program?",
                            "Exit", MB_YESNO);
        if(response == IDYES) PostQuitMessage(0);
        break;
      case IDM_HELP:
        MessageBox(hwnd, "F2: Show Fonts\nF3: Show Typeface\n"
                        "F3: Exit", "Show Fonts", MB_OK);
        break;
    }
    break;
  case WM_PAINT: /* process a repaint request */
    hdc = BeginPaint(hwnd, &ps); /* get DC */

    /* copy virtual window onto the screen */
    BitBlt(hdc, 0, 0, maxX, maxY, memdc, 0, 0, SRCCOPY);
    EndPaint(hwnd, &ps); /* release DC */
    break;
  case WM_DESTROY: /* terminate the program */
    DeleteDC(memdc);
    PostQuitMessage(0);
    break;
  default:
    /* Let Windows NT process any messages not specified in
    the preceding switch statement. */
    return DefWindowProc(hwnd, message, wParam, lParam);
  }
  return 0;
}


/* Enumerate Fonts */
int CALLBACK FontFunc(ENUMLOGFONTEX *lpLF,
```

```
                    NEWTEXTMETRICEX *lpTM,
                    int type, LPARAM lParam)
{
   int response;
   RECT rect;

   /* display font info */
   TextOut(memdc, X, Y, lpLF->elfLogFont.lfFaceName,
           strlen(lpLF->elfLogFont.lfFaceName)); /* font name */
   TextOut(memdc, X+200, Y, (char *)lpLF->elfStyle,
           strlen((char *)lpLF->elfStyle)); /* style */
   TextOut(memdc, X+300, Y, (char *)lpLF->elfScript,
           strlen((char *)lpLF->elfScript)); /* script style */


   Y += linespacing;

   InvalidateRect((HWND)lParam, NULL, 0);

   /* get current dimensions of the client area */
   GetClientRect((HWND)lParam, &rect);

   /* pause at bottom of window */
   if( (Y + linespacing) >= rect.bottom) {
     Y = linespacing + linespacing/2; /* reset to top */
     response = MessageBox((HWND)lParam, "More?",
                           "More Fonts?", MB_YESNO);
     if(response == IDNO) return 0;
     PatBlt(memdc, 0, linespacing, maxX, maxY, PATCOPY);
   }

   return 1;
}

/* Enumerate font dialog box */
BOOL CALLBACK FontDialog(HWND hdwnd, UINT message,
                         WPARAM wParam, LPARAM lParam)
{
   switch(message) {
     case WM_COMMAND:
       switch(LOWORD(wParam)) {
         case IDCANCEL:
           EndDialog(hdwnd, 0);
           return 1;
         case IDD_ENUM:
           /* get typeface name */
           GetDlgItemText(hdwnd, IDD_EB1, fontstr, 80);
           EndDialog(hdwnd, 1);
```

8

```
            return 1;
      }
      break;
  }
  return 0;
}
```

This program uses the following resource file.

```
#include <windows.h>
#include "font.h"

FontEnumMenu MENU
{
  POPUP "Enumerate" {
    MENUITEM "Available &Fonts\tF2", IDM_FONTS
    MENUITEM "Selected &Typeface\tF3", IDM_TYPEFACE
    MENUITEM "E&xit\tF4", IDM_EXIT
  }
  MENUITEM "&Help", IDM_HELP
}


FontEnumMenu ACCELERATORS
{
  VK_F2, IDM_FONTS, VIRTKEY
  VK_F3, IDM_TYPEFACE, VIRTKEY
  VK_F4, IDM_EXIT, VIRTKEY
  VK_F1, IDM_HELP, VIRTKEY
}


FontDB DIALOG 10, 10, 100, 60
CAPTION "Enumerate Typeface"
STYLE WS_POPUP | WS_CAPTION | WS_SYSMENU | WS_VISIBLE
{
  CTEXT "Enter Typeface", 300, 10, 10, 80, 12
  EDITTEXT IDD_EB1, 10, 20, 80, 12, ES_LEFT |
          WS_VISIBLE | WS_BORDER | ES_AUTOHSCROLL |
          WS_TABSTOP
  DEFPUSHBUTTON "Enumerate" IDD_ENUM, 30, 40, 40, 14,
          WS_CHILD | WS_VISIBLE | WS_TABSTOP
}
```

The FONT.H header file is shown here:

```
#define IDM_FONTS      100
#define IDM_TYPEFACE   101
#define IDM_EXIT       102
#define IDM_HELP       103

#define IDD_EB1        200
#define IDD_ENUM       201
```

Let's take a closer look at this program. When you select Available Fonts, **EnumFontFamiliesEx( )** is called with **lf.lfFaceName** containing a null string. This causes a representative font from each typeface supported by the system to be returned. When you choose Selected Typeface, you activate a small dialog box in which you can enter the name of the desired typeface. This string is then used for the **lf.lfFaceName** field. This causes all fonts of only that typeface to be enumerated.

The callback function **FontFunc( )** receives each enumerated font and displays it. For simplicity, the function displays a window full of fonts and then pops up a message box, asking if you want to see more. If you do, the next window's worth is shown. To determine the current size of the window, **FontFunc( )** calls **GetClientRect( )**. **GetClientRect( )** has this prototype:

BOOL GetClientRect(HWND *hwnd*, LPRECT *lpDim*);

Here, *hwnd* is the handle of the window in question and *lpDim* is a pointer to a **RECT** structure that will receive the current coordinates of the client area of the window. (The **RECT** structure was described in Chapter 3.) The function returns nonzero if successful and zero on failure. This function is useful whenever you need to know the current size of the client area of a window. In this program, the value in **rect.bottom** is used to determine whether there is sufficient room to display another line of text within the current height of the window.

Here is a challenge that you might find interesting: Each time a font is enumerated, its logical settings are returned in a **LOGFONT** structure. Use this structure to create a font, using **CreateFontIndirect( )**, to actually create each font that is enumerated and then display a string in that font. This makes an easy way to see what fonts are available for your use.

Remember, Windows NT support for fonts and text is quite rich. You will want to explore this area on your own. In the next chapter, we will continue exploring window output by working with graphics.

8

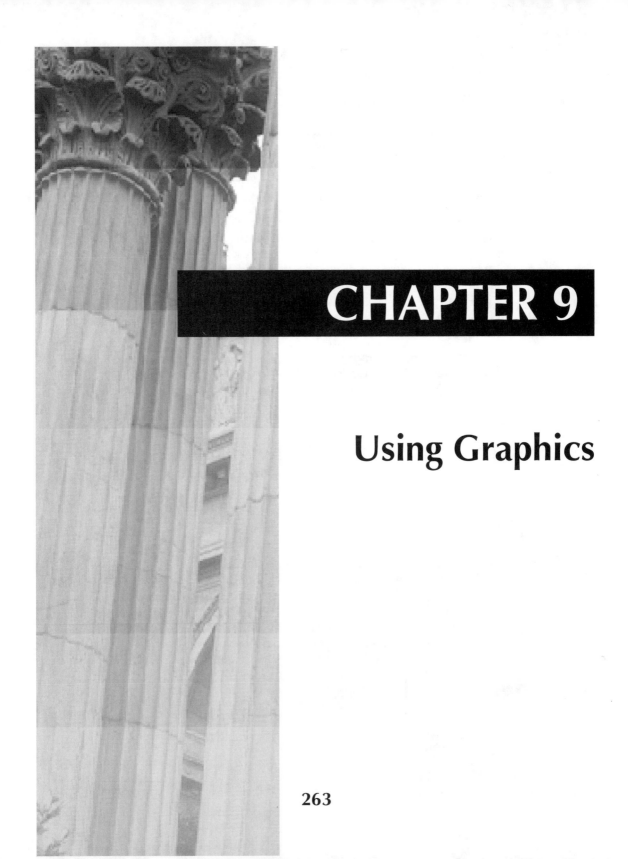

CHAPTER 9

Using Graphics

Windows NT supports a wide array of graphics-oriented API functions. For example, earlier in this book, you learned about bitmapped graphics. In this chapter, you will learn about the graphics functions that allow you to draw in a window. Since Windows is a graphical operating system, graphics are an important part of nearly every major Windows application. As you will see, graphics are easy to handle within a Windows program because they are fully integrated into the overall landscape of the Windows environment.

While it is not possible to examine all of the graphics-related functions supported by Windows NT, this chapter describes the most important, including those used to draw a point, a line, a rectangle, and an ellipse. It also explains how to change the way graphics output is written to a window. Keep in mind that the discussion of graphics and related topics in this chapter only scratches the surface. The Windows NT graphics system is quite powerful and you will want to explore it further on your own.

To demonstrate the graphics functions and techniques, a simple version of the standard Paint accessory is developed. As you will see, because of the power of the Windows NT graphics subsystem, surprisingly little code is required for this program.

The Graphics Coordinate System

The graphics coordinate system is the same as that used by the text-based functions. This means that, by default, the upper-left corner is location 0, 0 and that logical units are equivalent to pixels. However, the coordinate system and the mapping of logical units to pixels is under your control and may be changed.

Windows NT (and Windows in general) maintains a *current position* that is used and updated by certain graphics functions. When your program begins, the current location is set to 0, 0. Keep in mind that the location of the current position is completely invisible. That is, no graphics "cursor" is displayed. Instead, the current position is simply the next place in the window at which certain graphics functions will begin.

Pens and Brushes

The Windows graphics system is based on two important objects: pens and brushes. By default, closed graphics shapes, such as rectangles and ellipses, are filled using the currently selected brush. Pens are resources that draw

Pens draw lines
and brushes
fill areas.

the lines and curves specified by the various graphics functions that are described next. The default pen is black and one pixel thick, but you can alter these attributes.

Until now, we have only been working with stock objects, such as the stock white brush that has been used to paint the client area of a window. In this chapter you will learn how to create custom brushes and pens.

Setting a Pixel

You can set the color of any specific pixel using the API function **SetPixel( )**, whose prototype is shown here:

COLORREF SetPixel(HDC *hdc*, int *X*, int *Y*, COLORREF *color*);

Here, *hdc* is the handle to the desired device context. The coordinates of the point to set are specified by *X, Y*, and the color is specified in *color*. (The **COLORREF** data type is described in Chapter 8.) The function returns the original color of the pixel, or –1 if an error occurs or if the location specified is outside the window.

Drawing a Line

To draw a line, use the **LineTo( )** function. This function draws a line using the currently selected pen. Its prototype is shown here:

BOOL LineTo(HDC *hdc*, int *X*, int *Y*);

The handle of the device context in which to draw the line is specified by *hdc*. The line is drawn from the current graphics position to the coordinates specified by *X, Y*. The current position is then changed to *X, Y*. The function returns nonzero if successful (i.e., the line is drawn) and zero on failure.

Some programmers are surprised by the fact that **LineTo( )** uses the current position as its starting location and then sets the current position to the end point of the line that is drawn (instead of leaving it unchanged). However, there is a good reason for this. Many times, when displaying lines, one line will begin at the end of the previous line. When this is the case, **LineTo( )** operates very efficiently by avoiding the additional overhead caused by passing an extra set of coordinates. When this is not the case, you can set the current location to any position you like using the **MoveToEx( )** function, described next, prior to calling **LineTo( )**.

Setting the Current Location

To set the current position, use the **MoveToEx( )** function, whose prototype is shown here:

BOOL MoveToEx(HDC *hdc*, int *X*, int *Y*, LPPOINT *lpCoord*);

The handle to the device context is specified in *hdc*. The coordinates of the new current position are specified by *X, Y*. The previous current position is returned in the **POINT** structure pointed to by *lpCoord*. **POINT** is defined like this:

```
typedef struct tagPOINT {
  LONG x;
  LONG y;
} POINT;
```

However, if you use **NULL** for the *lpCoord* parameter, then **MoveToEx( )** does not return the previous current position.

MoveToEx( ) returns nonzero if successful and zero on failure.

Drawing an Arc

You can draw an elliptical arc (a portion of an ellipse) in the current pen color using the **Arc( )** function. Its prototype is shown here:

BOOL Arc(HDC *hdc*, int *upX*, int *upY*, int *lowX*, int *lowY*,
         int *startX*, int *startY*, int *endX*, int *endY*);

Here, *hdc* is the handle of the device context in which the arc will be drawn. The arc is defined by two objects. First, the arc is a portion of an ellipse that is bounded by the rectangle whose upper-left corner is at *upX, upY* and whose lower right corner is at *lowX, lowY*. The portion of the ellipse that is actually drawn (i.e., the arc) starts at the intersection of a line from the center of the rectangle through the point specified by *startX, startY* and ends at the intersection of a line from the center of the rectangle through the point *endX, endY*. By default, the arc is drawn counterclockwise starting from *startX, startY*. You can set the drawing direction using the **SetArcDirection( )** API function. Figure 9-1 illustrates how **Arc( )** works.

Arc( ) returns nonzero if successful and zero on failure.

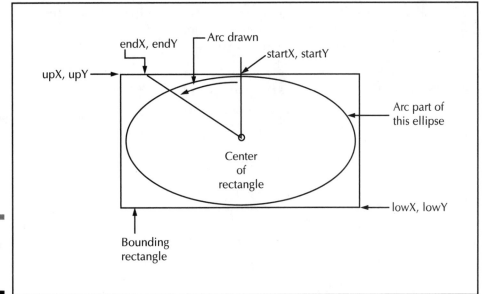

How the
Arc( ) function
operates
Figure 9-1.

Displaying Rectangles

You can display a rectangle in the current pen color using the **Rectangle( )**
function, whose prototype is shown here.

BOOL Rectangle(HDC *hdc*, int *upX*, int *upY*, int *lowX*, int *lowY*);

As usual, *hdc* is the handle of the device context. The upper left corner of the
rectangle is specified by *upX, upY* and the lower right corner is specified by
lowX, lowY. The function returns nonzero if successful and zero if an error
occurs. The rectangle is automatically filled using the current brush.

You can display a rounded rectangle using the **RoundRect( )** function.
A rounded rectangle has its corners rounded slightly. The prototype for
RoundRect( ) is shown here:

BOOL RoundRect(HDC *hdc*, int *upX*, int *upY*, int *lowX*, int *lowY*,
                int *curveX*, int *curveY*);

The first five parameters are the same as for **Rectangle( )**. How the corners
are curved is determined by the values of *curveX* and *curveY*, which define

the width and the height of the ellipse that describes the curve. The function returns nonzero if successful and zero if a failure occurs. The rounded rectangle is automatically filled using the current brush.

Drawing Ellipses and Pie Slices

To draw an ellipse or a circle in the current pen color, use the **Ellipse( )** function, whose prototype is shown here

BOOL Ellipse(HDC *hdc*, int *upX*, int *upY*, int *lowX*, int *lowY*);

Here, *hdc* is the handle of the device content in which the ellipse will be drawn. The ellipse is defined by specifying its bounding rectangle. The upper left corner of the rectangle is specified by *upX,upY* and the lower right corner is specified by *lowX,lowY*. To draw a circle, specify a square.

The function returns nonzero if successful and zero if a failure occurs. The ellipse is filled using the current brush.

Related to the ellipse is the pie slice. A pie slice is an object that includes an arc and lines from each end point of the arc to the center. To draw a pie slice use the **Pie( )** function, whose prototype is shown here:

BOOL Pie(HDC hdc, int *upX*, int *upY*, int *lowX*, int *lowY*,
      int *startX*, int *startY*, int *endX*, int *endY*);

Here, *hdc* is the handle of the device context in which the pie slice will be drawn. The arc of the slice is defined by two objects. First, the arc is a portion of an ellipse that is bounded by the rectangle whose upper left corner is at *upX, upY* and whose lower right corner is at *lowX, lowY*. The portion of the ellipse that is actually drawn (i.e., the arc of the slice) starts at the intersection of a line from the center of the rectangle through the point specified by *startX, startY* and ends at the the intersection of a line from the center of the rectangle through the point *endX, endY*. By default, the arc is drawn in a counterclockwise direction. The endpoints are then connected to the center to form the pie slice.

The slice is drawn in the current pen color and filled using the current brush. The **Pie( )** function returns nonzero if successful and zero if an error occurs.

Working with Pens

Graphics objects are drawn using the currently selected pen. By default, this is a black pen that is one pixel wide. There are three stock pens: black, white, and null. A handle to each of these can be obtained using **GetStockObject( )**, discussed earlier in this book. The macros for these stock pens are **BLACK_PEN**, **WHITE_PEN**, and **NULL_PEN**, respectively. Pen handles are of type **HPEN**.

Frankly, the stock pens are quite limited and usually you will want to define your own pens for your application. This is accomplished using the function **CreatePen( )**, whose prototype is shown here:

HPEN CreatePen(int *style*, int *width*, COLORREF *color*);

The *style* parameter determines what type of pen is created. It must be one of these values:

Macro	Pen Style
PS_DASH	Dashed
PS_DASHDOT	Dash-dot
PS_DASHDOTDOT	Dash-dot-dot
PS_DOT	Dotted
PS_INSIDEFRAME	Solid pen that is within a bounded region
PS_NULL	None
PS_SOLID	Solid line

The dotted and/or dashed styles may only be applied to pens that are one unit thick. The **PS_INSIDEFRAME** pen is a solid pen that will be completely within the dimensions of any object that is drawn, even when that pen is more than one unit thick. For example, if a pen with **PS_INSIDEFRAME** style and width greater than one is used to draw a rectangle, then the outside of the line will be within the coordinates of the rectangle. (When a wide pen of a different style is used, the line may be partially outside the dimensions of the object.)

The thickness of a pen is specified by *width*, which is in logical units. The color of the pen is specified by *color*, which is a **COLORREF** value.

CreatePen( ) returns a handle to the pen if successful or **NULL** on failure.

Once a pen has been created, it is selected into a device context using **SelectObject( )**. For example, the following fragment creates a red pen and then selects it for use.

```
HPEN hRedpen;
hRedpen = CreatePen(PS_SOLID, 1, RGB(255,0,0));
SelectObject(dc, hRedpen);
```

You must delete any custom pens you create by calling **DeleteObject( )** before your program terminates.

Creating Custom Brushes

As is the case with the stock pens, the stock brushes provided by Windows NT are also quite limited. Often you will want to create your own brushes. Custom brushes are created in a way similar to custom pens. There are various styles of brushes. The most common custom brush is a *solid brush*. A solid brush is created using the **CreateSolidBrush( )** API function, whose prototype is shown here:

HBRUSH CreateSolidBrush(COLORREF *color*);

The color of the brush is specified in *color* and a handle to the brush is returned. **NULL** is returned on failure.

Once a custom brush has been created, it is selected into the device context using **SelectObject( )**. For example, the following fragment creates a green brush and then selects it for use.

```
HBRUSH hGreenbrush

hGreenbrush = CreateSolidBrush(RGB(0, 255 ,0));
SelectObject(dc, hGreenbrush);
```

In addition to solid brushes, there are two other types of brushes that you can create: a pattern brush and a hatch brush. A pattern brush fills areas with a bitmapped image. A hatch brush uses some form of hatchwork design. These brushes are created using **CreatePatternBrush( )** and **CreateHatchBrush( )**, respectively. The prototypes for these functions are shown here:

HBRUSH CreatePatternBrush(HBITMAP *hBMap*);
HBRUSH CreateHatchBrush(int *Style*, COLORREF *color*);

For **CreatePatternBrush( )**, *hBMap* is the handle of the bitmap whose pattern will be used as the brush. That is, the specified bitmap will be used to fill areas and paint backgrounds. The function returns a handle to the brush or **NULL** on error.

NOTE: To create a brush using a device-independent bitmap, use **CreateDIBPatternBrushPt( )**.

Brushes created using **CreateHatchBrush( )** have a hatched appearance. The exact nature of the hatching is determined by the value of *Style*, which must be one of those shown here:

Style	Hatching
HS_BDIAGONAL	Angled downward
HS_CROSS	Horizontal and vertical
HS_DIAGCROSS	Angled crosshatch
HS_FDIAGONAL	Angled upward
HS_HORIZONTAL	Horizontal
HS_VERTICAL	Vertical

The color of the brush is determined by the **COLORREF** value specified in *color*. It returns a handle to the brush or **NULL** on failure.

Deleting Custom Pens and Brushes

You must delete custom pens and brushes before your program terminates. You do this using the **DeleteObject( )** API function. Remember, you cannot (and must not) delete stock objects. Also, the object being deleted must not be currently selected into any device context.

Setting the Output Mode

Whenever your program outputs graphics to a window, how that output is actually copied to the window is determined by the output mode in effect at the time. By default, information is copied as-is to the window, overwriting any previous contents. However, other output modes can be used. For example, output can be ANDed, ORed, or XORed with the current contents of the window. To specify the output mode, use the **SetROP2( )** function. Its prototype is shown here:

        int SetROP2(HDC *hdc*, int *Mode*);

Here, *hdc* is the handle of the device context being affected and *Mode* specifies the new drawing mode. **SetROP2( )** returns the previous drawing mode or 0 on failure. *Mode* must be one of the values shown in Table 9-1.

Macro	Drawing Mode
R2_BLACK	Result is black.
R2_COPYPEN	Output is copied to the window, overwriting current contents.
R2_MASKPEN	Output is ANDed with the current screen color.
R2_MASKNOTPEN	Inverse of output is ANDed with the current screen color.
R2_MASKPENNOT	Output is ANDed with the inverse of the current screen color.
R2_MERGEPEN	Output is ORed with the current screen color.
R2_MERGENOTPEN	Inverse of output is ORed with the current screen color.
R2_MERGEPENNOT	Output is ORed with the inverse of the current screen color.
R2_NOP	No effect.
R2_NOT	Result is the inverse of the current screen color.

Values for
Mode for
SetROP2( )
Table 9-1.

Macro	Drawing Mode
R2_NOTCOPYPEN	Inverse of the output color is copied to the window.
R2_NOTMASKPEN	Resulting color is the inverse of R2_MASKPEN.
R2_NOTMERGEPEN	Resulting color is the inverse of R2_MERGEPEN.
R2_NOTXORPEN	Resulting color is the inverse of R2_XORPEN.
R2_WHITE	Result is white.
R2_XORPEN	Output is exclusive-ORed with the current screen color.

Values for
Mode for
SetROP2( )
(*continued*)
Table 9-1.

The **R2_XORPEN** mode is especially useful because it allows output to be temporarily written to the screen without losing the information that is already on the screen. The reason for this has to do with a special property of the XOR operation. Consider the following: When one value, called A, is XORed with another, called B, it produces a result which, when XORed with B a second time, produces the original value, A. Thus, if you XOR output to the screen and then XOR the same output to the screen a second time, the original contents of the screen will be restored. This means that you can XOR output to the screen to display something temporarily and then simply XOR it to the screen again to restore the screen's original contents. This technique was discussed briefly in Chapter 7 as it related to the displaying of bitmaps. As you will see in the graphics demonstration program that follows, it can be applied to all types of output.

One final point: The ROP in the name of the function stands for Raster OPerations. This function applies only to raster devices, such as monitors.

A Graphics Demonstration

The following program demonstrates several of the graphics functions just discussed. It implements a simplified version of the standard Paint accessory. The program uses the virtual window technique developed in Chapter 7 to allow the window to be properly restored when a **WM_PAINT** message is received.

```
/* A Simple Paint Program */

#include <windows.h>
#include <string.h>
```

```c
#include <stdio.h>
#include "graph.h"

LRESULT CALLBACK WindowFunc(HWND, UINT, WPARAM, LPARAM);

char szWinName[] = "MyWin"; /* name of window class */

char str[255]; /* holds output strings */
int maxX, maxY; /* screen dimensions */

HDC memdc; /* handle of memory DC */
HBITMAP hbit; /* handle of compatible bitmap */
HBRUSH hCurrentbrush, hOldbrush; /* handles of brushes */
HBRUSH hRedbrush, hGreenbrush, hBluebrush, hNullbrush;

/* create pens */
HPEN hOldpen; /* handle of old pen */
HPEN hCurrentpen; /* currently selected pen */
HPEN hRedpen, hGreenpen, hBluepen, hBlackpen;

int X=0, Y=0;
int pendown = 0;
int endpoints = 0;
int StartX=0, StartY=0, EndX=0, EndY=0;
int Mode;

int WINAPI WinMain(HINSTANCE hThisInst, HINSTANCE hPrevInst,
                   LPSTR lpszArgs, int nWinMode)
{
  HWND hwnd;
  MSG msg;
  WNDCLASSEX wcl;
  HANDLE hAccel;

  /* Define a window class. */
  wcl.cbSize = sizeof(WNDCLASSEX);

  wcl.hInstance = hThisInst; /* handle to this instance */
  wcl.lpszClassName = szWinName; /* window class name */
  wcl.lpfnWndProc = WindowFunc; /* window function */
  wcl.style = 0; /* default style */

  wcl.hIcon = LoadIcon(NULL, IDI_APPLICATION); /* standard icon */
  wcl.hIconSm = LoadIcon(NULL, IDI_APPLICATION); /* small icon */

  wcl.hCursor = LoadCursor(NULL, IDC_ARROW); /* cursor style */
```

```c
/* specify name of menu resource */
wcl.lpszMenuName = "GraphMenu"; /* main menu */

wcl.cbClsExtra = 0; /* no extra */
wcl.cbWndExtra = 0; /* information needed */

/* Make the window white. */
wcl.hbrBackground = GetStockObject(WHITE_BRUSH);

/* Register the window class. */
if(!RegisterClassEx(&wcl)) return 0;

/* Now that a window class has been registered, a window
   can be created. */
hwnd = CreateWindow(
  szWinName, /* name of window class */
  "A Simple Paint Program", /* title */
  WS_OVERLAPPEDWINDOW, /* window style - normal */
  CW_USEDEFAULT, /* X coordinate - let Windows decide */
  CW_USEDEFAULT, /* Y coordinate - let Windows decide */
  CW_USEDEFAULT, /* width - let Windows decide */
  CW_USEDEFAULT, /* height - let Windows decide */
  HWND_DESKTOP, /* no parent window */
  NULL, /* no override of class menu */
  hThisInst, /* handle of this instance of the program */
  NULL /* no additional arguments */
);

/* load accelerators */
hAccel = LoadAccelerators(hThisInst, "GraphMenu");

/* Display the window. */
ShowWindow(hwnd, nWinMode);
UpdateWindow(hwnd);

/* Create the message loop. */
while(GetMessage(&msg, NULL, 0, 0))
{
  if(!TranslateAccelerator(hwnd, hAccel, &msg)) {
    TranslateMessage(&msg); /* translate keyboard messages */
    DispatchMessage(&msg); /* return control to Windows NT */
  }
}
return msg.wParam;
}
```

```
/* This function is called by Windows NT and is passed
   messages from the message queue.
*/
LRESULT CALLBACK WindowFunc(HWND hwnd, UINT message,
                             WPARAM wParam, LPARAM lParam)
{
  HDC hdc;
  PAINTSTRUCT paintstruct;
  int response;

  switch(message) {
    case WM_CREATE:
      /* get screen coordinates */
      maxX = GetSystemMetrics(SM_CXSCREEN);
      maxY = GetSystemMetrics(SM_CYSCREEN);

      /* create virtual window */
      hdc = GetDC(hwnd);
      memdc = CreateCompatibleDC(hdc);
      hbit = CreateCompatibleBitmap(hdc, maxX, maxY);
      SelectObject(memdc, hbit);
      hCurrentbrush = GetStockObject(WHITE_BRUSH);
      SelectObject(memdc, hCurrentbrush);
      PatBlt(memdc, 0, 0, maxX, maxY, PATCOPY);

      /* create pens */
      hRedpen = CreatePen(PS_SOLID, 1, RGB(255,0,0));
      hGreenpen = CreatePen(PS_SOLID, 1, RGB(0,255,0));
      hBluepen = CreatePen(PS_SOLID, 1, RGB(0,0,255));

      /* create brushes */
      hRedbrush = CreateSolidBrush(RGB(255,0,0));
      hGreenbrush = CreateSolidBrush(RGB(0,255,0));
      hBluebrush = CreateSolidBrush(RGB(0,0,255));
      hNullbrush = GetStockObject(HOLLOW_BRUSH);

      /* save default pen */
      hBlackpen = hOldpen = SelectObject(memdc, hRedpen);
      hCurrentpen = hOldpen;
      SelectObject(memdc, hOldpen);

      ReleaseDC(hwnd, hdc);
      break;
    case WM_RBUTTONDOWN: /* start defining a region */
      endpoints = 1;
      X = StartX = LOWORD(lParam);
      Y = StartY = HIWORD(lParam);
      break;
```

```
case WM_RBUTTONUP: /* stop defining a region */
  endpoints = 0;
  EndX = LOWORD(lParam);
  EndY = HIWORD(lParam);
  break;
case WM_LBUTTONDOWN: /* start drawing */
  pendown = 1;
  X = LOWORD(lParam);
  Y = HIWORD(lParam);
  break;
case WM_LBUTTONUP: /* stop drawing */
  pendown = 0;
  break;
case WM_MOUSEMOVE:
  if(pendown) { /* draw */
    hdc = GetDC(hwnd);
    SelectObject(memdc, hCurrentpen);
    SelectObject(hdc, hCurrentpen);
    MoveToEx(memdc, X, Y, NULL);
    MoveToEx(hdc, X, Y, NULL);
    X = LOWORD(lParam);
    Y = HIWORD(lParam);
    LineTo(memdc, X, Y);
    LineTo(hdc, X, Y);
    MoveToEx(memdc, X, Y, NULL);
    MoveToEx(hdc, X, Y, NULL);
    ReleaseDC(hwnd, hdc);
  }
  if(endpoints) { /* display region boundaries */
    hdc = GetDC(hwnd);

    /* select "shadow" pen */
    hOldpen = SelectObject(hdc, hRedpen);

    /* change display mode to XOR */
    Mode = SetROP2(hdc, R2_XORPEN);

    /* display, but don't fill */
    hOldbrush =
        SelectObject(hdc, GetStockObject(HOLLOW_BRUSH));

    /* erase old shadow rectangle */
    Rectangle(hdc, StartX, StartY, X, Y);

    X = LOWORD(lParam);
    Y = HIWORD(lParam);

    /* display new shadow rectangle */
```

```
        Rectangle(hdc, StartX, StartY, X, Y);

      /* restore default brush */
      SelectObject(hdc, hOldbrush);
      SelectObject(hdc, hOldpen);
      SetROP2(hdc, Mode);
      ReleaseDC(hwnd, hdc);
    }
    break;
  case WM_COMMAND:
    switch(LOWORD(wParam)) {
      case IDM_LINE:
        /* select current pen */
        SelectObject(memdc, hCurrentpen);

        /* draw the line */
        MoveToEx(memdc, StartX, StartY, NULL);
        LineTo(memdc, EndX, EndY);

        InvalidateRect(hwnd, NULL, 1);
        break;
      case IDM_RECTANGLE:
        /* select fill brush and pen */
        SelectObject(memdc, hCurrentbrush);
        SelectObject(memdc, hCurrentpen);

        /* draw rectangle */
        Rectangle(memdc, StartX, StartY, EndX, EndY);

        InvalidateRect(hwnd, NULL, 1);
        break;
      case IDM_ELLIPSE:
        /* select fill brush and pen */
        SelectObject(memdc, hCurrentbrush);
        SelectObject(memdc, hCurrentpen);

        /* draw ellipse */
        Ellipse(memdc,  StartX, StartY, EndX, EndY);

        InvalidateRect(hwnd, NULL, 1);
        break;
      case IDM_RED:
        hCurrentpen = hRedpen;
        break;
      case IDM_BLUE:
        hCurrentpen = hBluepen;
        break;
      case IDM_GREEN:
```

```
          hCurrentpen = hGreenpen;
          break;
      case IDM_BLACK:
        hCurrentpen = hBlackpen;
        break;
      case IDM_REDFILL:
        hCurrentbrush = hRedbrush;
        break;
      case IDM_BLUEFILL:
        hCurrentbrush = hBluebrush;
        break;
      case IDM_GREENFILL:
        hCurrentbrush = hGreenbrush;
        break;
      case IDM_WHITEFILL:
        hCurrentbrush = hOldbrush;
        break;
      case IDM_NULLFILL:
        hCurrentbrush = hNullbrush;
        break;
      case IDM_RESET:
        /* reset current position to 0,0 */
        MoveToEx(memdc, 0, 0, NULL);

        /* erase by repainting background */
        SelectObject(memdc, hOldbrush);
        PatBlt(memdc, 0, 0, maxX, maxY, PATCOPY);

        InvalidateRect(hwnd, NULL, 1);
        break;
      case IDM_EXIT:
        response = MessageBox(hwnd, "Quit the Program?",
                              "Exit", MB_YESNO);
        if(response == IDYES) PostQuitMessage(0);
        break;
      case IDM_HELP:
        MessageBox(hwnd, "F2: Line\nF3: Rectangle\n"
                   "F4: Ellipse\nF5: Reset",
                   "Paint Hot Keys", MB_OK);
        break;
    }
    break;
  case WM_PAINT: /* process a repaint request */
    hdc = BeginPaint(hwnd, &paintstruct); /* get DC */

    /* copy virtual window onto screen */
    BitBlt(hdc, 0, 0, maxX, maxY, memdc, 0, 0, SRCCOPY);
```

```
      EndPaint(hwnd, &paintstruct); /* release DC */
      break;
   case WM_DESTROY: /* terminate the program */
      DeleteObject(hRedpen); /* delete pens */
      DeleteObject(hGreenpen);
      DeleteObject(hBluepen);
      DeleteObject(hBlackpen);

      DeleteObject(hRedbrush); /* delete brushes */
      DeleteObject(hGreenbrush);
      DeleteObject(hBluebrush);

      DeleteDC(memdc);
      PostQuitMessage(0);
      break;
   default:
     /* Let Windows NT process any messages not specified in
        the preceding switch statement. */
      return DefWindowProc(hwnd, message, wParam, lParam);
  }
  return 0;
}
```

This program requires the resource file shown here:

```
#include <windows.h>
#include "graph1.h"

GraphMenu MENU
{
  POPUP "&Shapes"
  {
    MENUITEM "&Line\tF2", IDM_LINE
    MENUITEM "&Rectangle\tF3", IDM_RECTANGLE
    MENUITEM "&Ellipse\tF4", IDM_ELLIPSE
    MENUITEM "E&xit\tF10", IDM_EXIT
  }
  POPUP "&Options"
  {
    POPUP "&Pen Color"
    {
      MENUITEM "&Red", IDM_RED
      MENUITEM "&Blue", IDM_BLUE
      MENUITEM "&Green", IDM_GREEN
      MENUITEM "Bl&ack", IDM_BLACK
    }
    POPUP "&Fill Color"
    {
```

```
      MENUITEM "&Red",  IDM_REDFILL
      MENUITEM "&Blue",  IDM_BLUEFILL
      MENUITEM "&Green",  IDM_GREENFILL
      MENUITEM "&White",  IDM_WHITEFILL
      MENUITEM "&Null",  IDM_NULLFILL
    }
    MENUITEM "&Reset\tF5",  IDM_RESET
  }
    MENUITEM "&Help",  IDM_HELP
}

GraphMenu ACCELERATORS
{
  VK_F1,  IDM_HELP,  VIRTKEY
  VK_F2,  IDM_LINE,  VIRTKEY
  VK_F3,  IDM_RECTANGLE,  VIRTKEY
  VK_F4,  IDM_ELLIPSE,  VIRTKEY
  VK_F5,  IDM_RESET,  VIRTKEY
  VK_F10,  IDM_EXIT,  VIRTKEY
}
```

It also requires the header file GRAPH.H shown here:

```
#define IDM_LINE        100
#define IDM_RECTANGLE 101
#define IDM_ELLIPSE     102
#define IDM_RED         103
#define IDM_GREEN       104
#define IDM_BLUE        105
#define IDM_BLACK       106
#define IDM_REDFILL     107
#define IDM_GREENFILL 108
#define IDM_BLUEFILL    109
#define IDM_WHITEFILL 110
#define IDM_NULLFILL    111
#define IDM_RESET       112
#define IDM_HELP        113
#define IDM_EXIT        114
```

Sample output is shown in Figure 9-2.

The paint program works like this. Free-style lines can be drawn using the mouse. To draw, press and hold the left button. The right button is used to define a region. To do this, move the mouse pointer to the first corner, press and hold the right mouse button, and then move the mouse pointer to the opposite corner. Release the right button when you reach the desired location. When defining a region, a "shadow" rectangle will appear that

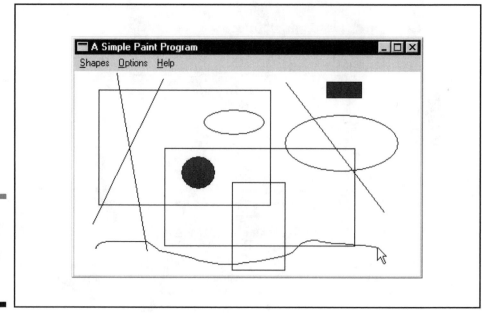

Sample
output from
the graphics
demonstration
program
Figure 9-2.

outlines the region as you define it. Once a region has been defined, you can
then draw a line, a rectangle, or an ellipse within that region. These options
are selected from the Shapes menu. Using the Options menu, you can select
a new pen color, a new brush color, or erase and reset the window. Most of
the code in the paint program should be easy to understand. However, let's
take a look a few of the more interesting sections.

IN DEPTH

Drawing Irregular Polygons

In addition to the basic graphical elements, such as lines, ellipses, and
rectangles, Windows NT allows you to define and draw irregular
objects. One such object is the polygon. Relative to Windows NT, a
polygon consists of three or more sides which enclose an area. To draw
a polygon, use the **Polygon( )** function shown here.

BOOL Polygon(HDC *hdc*, CONST POINT **vertices*, int *num*);

Here, *hdc* identifies the device context. An array containing the
coordinates of the endpoints of the polygon is pointed to by *vertices*

and the number of vertices is passed in *num*. The function returns nonzero if successful and zero on failure. The polygon is drawn using the currently selected pen and is filled using the currently elected brush. The **Polygon( )** function automatically draws a line from the last point to the first point in the *vertices* array, thus ensuring that the figure is enclosed. **Polygon( )** does not use or modify the current position.

To try **Polygon( )**, add this global declaration to the example paint program:

```
POINT polygon[5] = {
   10, 10,
   10, 40,
   40, 70,
   40, 90,
   10, 10};
```

Next, add this line to the **IDD_LINE** case:

```
Polygon(memdc, polygon, 5);
```

Now, each time you select the Line option, the five-sided polygon will also be displayed.

Here are some other API functions that draw complex objects that you might find of interest: **Polyline( )**, **PolylineTo( )**, **PolyPolyline( )**, **PolyPolygon( )**, **PolyBezier( )** and **PolyBezierTo( )**.

A Closer Look at the Paint Program

When the program first begins execution, the following objects are created: the virtual window bitmap, all pens needed by the program, and all brushes needed by the program. The pens and brushes are destroyed when the program terminates.

The variable **pendown** is set to 1 when the left mouse button is pressed. Otherwise, it is 0. The variable **endpoints** is set to 1 when a region is being defined (by pressing the right mouse button). Otherwise it is 0. These variables are used to determine the precise meaning of a **WM_MOUSEMOVE** message.

Perhaps the most involved part of the program is contained within the **WM_MOUSEMOVE** case, shown here. Let's go through it carefully.

```
case WM_MOUSEMOVE:
  if(pendown) { /* draw */
    hdc = GetDC(hwnd);
    SelectObject(memdc, hCurrentpen);
    SelectObject(hdc, hCurrentpen);
    MoveToEx(memdc, X, Y, NULL);
    MoveToEx(hdc, X, Y, NULL);
    X = LOWORD(lParam);
    Y = HIWORD(lParam);
    LineTo(memdc, X, Y);
    LineTo(hdc, X, Y);
    MoveToEx(memdc, X, Y, NULL);
    MoveToEx(hdc, X, Y, NULL);
    ReleaseDC(hwnd, hdc);
  }
  if(endpoints) { /* display region boundaries */
    hdc = GetDC(hwnd);

    /* select "shadow" pen */
    hOldpen = SelectObject(hdc, hRedpen);

    /* change display mode to XOR */
    Mode = SetROP2(hdc, R2_XORPEN);

    /* display, but don't fill */
    hOldbrush =
        SelectObject(hdc, GetStockObject(HOLLOW_BRUSH));

    /* erase old shadow rectangle */
    Rectangle(hdc, StartX, StartY, X, Y);

    X = LOWORD(lParam);
    Y = HIWORD(lParam);

    /* display new shadow rectangle */
    Rectangle(hdc, StartX, StartY, X, Y);

    /* restore default brush */
    SelectObject(hdc, hOldbrush);
    SelectObject(hdc, hOldpen);
    SetROP2(hdc, Mode);
    ReleaseDC(hwnd, hdc);
  }
  break;
```

A **WM_MOUSEMOVE** message is sent each time the mouse is moved. The X coordinate of the mouse is passed in the low-order word of **lParam** and the Y coordinate is passed in the high-order word of **lParam**.

If **pendown** is true, then the user is drawing a line. In this situation, each time the mouse is moved, the current pen is selected into both the window device context (**hdc**) and the virtual window device context (**memdc**). Next, a line is drawn (in both contexts) connecting the previous location of the mouse with the new location. This ensures that a smooth, unbroken line is displayed as you move the mouse. (As an experiment, try using **SetPixel( )**, rather than **LineTo( )** and observe the results. As you will see, a **WM_MOUSEMOVE** message is not generated for every pixel in the mouse's path, causing a disjointed line.) After each line is drawn, the current location is updated to the current mouse position.

If **endpoints** is true, then the mouse is being used to define a rectangular region. The first endpoint is set when the **WM_RBUTTONDOWN** message is received. The second endpoint is set when the **WM_RBUTTONUP** message is received. These messages also contain the X, Y coordinates of the mouse in **LOWORD(lParam)** and **HIWORD(lParam)**, respectively. As the mouse is moved, a "shadow" rectangle is displayed that shows the current extents of the region. This rectangle is XORed onto the window. The reason for this is that the outcome of two XORs is the original value. Therefore, using the **X2_XORPEN** drawing mode, one call to **Rectangle( )** displays the shadow rectangle; a second call erases it. This makes it easy to display the shadow rectangle without disrupting the current contents of the window.

Before moving on, make sure that you understand all of the graphics operations contained in the paint program. The next section will build upon them.

Using World Transforms

While all versions of Windows can perform the type of graphics operations found in the preceding paint program, Windows NT offers the programmer an exciting and powerful extension not supported by other versions of Windows: *world transforms*. Using a world transform it is possible to perform a number of transformations that change the way output is mapped to a window. These transformations include rotation, translation, scaling, shearing, and reflection. Using Windows NT, you can easily perform sophisticated graphical manipulations of the type found in a typical CAD (Computer-Aided Design) environment. For example, you can rotate or enlarge an image.

PORTABILITY: World transforms are not supported by Windows 3.1 or Windows 95.

Windows NT handles world transformations by mapping one coordinate space on to another. Therefore, we will begin by describing Windows NT's coordinate spaces.

Coordinate Spaces

A world transform changes the way output is mapped to a window.

Windows NT defines three coordinate spaces. The first is called the *world space*. This coordinate space is used to perform world transformations. The second is called *page space*. This is the logical coordinate space used by your program. The third is *device space*, which uses physical coordinates. Device space is mapped onto the physical device itself. Sometimes the physical device is referred to as the fourth coordinate space.

Windows NT defines three coordinates spaces: world, page, and device. The physical output device defines a fourth.

As you know, output coordinates are specified in logical units (which are pixels, by default, but may differ). These units are mapped to the physical device one coordinate space at a time. When world transforms are not in effect, output is mapped beginning at page space. When using world transforms, output mapping begins at world space. At each coordinate space transition, the contents of the previous space are mapped onto the next space. For example, the mapping from page space to device space converts logical units into physical ones. When using world transforms, the mapping from world space to page space performs the transformation that you have specified.

SetWorldTransform( )

World transforms are specified by calling **SetWorldTransform( )**. Its prototype is shown here:

BOOL SetWorldTransform(HDC *hdc*, CONST XFORM **lpTransform*);

Here, *hdc* is the handle of the device context that you wish to transform. The specific transformation is specified in the structure pointed to by *lpTransform*. The function returns nonzero if successful and zero on failure. After **SetWorldTransform( )** has been called, the transformation that you specify will be in effect.

The type of transform is specified in a structure of type **XFORM**, which is defined like this:

```
typedef struct   tagXFORM
{
  FLOAT eM11;
  FLOAT eM12;
  FLOAT eM21;
```

```
    FLOAT eM22;
    FLOAT eDx;
    FLOAT eDy;
} XFORM;
```

The exact transformation that takes place is determined by the values you place in the matrix defined by **XFORM**. Let's see how each type of transformation can be achieved.

To translate output (i.e., to offset the origin) the X offset is specified in **eDx** and the Y offset is specified in **eDy**. This is the simplest transformation that you can specify. It causes output to be shifted. It can also be combined with the other transforms.

To rotate output through an angle *theta*, the values of **eM11**, **eM12**, **eM21**, and **eM22** must be as shown here:

Field	Meaning
eM11	cosine of theta
eM12	sine of theta
eM21	–sine of theta
eM22	cosine of theta

To scale output, put the X scaling factor in **eM11** and the Y scaling factor in **eM22**. **eM12** and **eM21** are not used (and should be zero).

To shear output, put the X shear factor in **eM12** and the Y shear factor in **eM21**. **eM11** and **eM22** are unused (and should be zero).

To reflect output along the X axis, put –1 in **eM11** and 1 into **eM22**. To reflect along the Y axis, put –1 in **eM22** and 1 into **eM11**. To reflect along both axes, put –1 into both **eM11** and **eM22**. **eM12** and **eM21** are unused (and should be zero).

Although there is nothing difficult about initializing the **XFORM** structure to achieve a desired transformation, the various ways the fields to **XFORM** are used makes it seem more complicated than it is. The best way to understand the effects of each transformation is to try each one experimentally.

PORTABILITY: **SetWorldTransform( )** is not supported by Windows 3.1 or Windows 95.

Setting the Graphics Mode

In order for **SetWorldTransform( )** to have effect, you must have first
enabled Windows NT's advanced graphics mode. To do this use the
SetGraphicsMode( ) function, shown here:

int SetGraphicsMode(HDC *hdc*, int *GraphMode*);

Here, *hdc* is the device context being affected and *GraphMode* determines the
graphics mode. It must be either **GM_COMPATIBLE** or **GM_ADVANCED**.
The function returns the previous mode or zero on failure.

By default, the graphics mode is **GM_COMPATIBLE**. This is the mode used
by Windows 95 and Windows 3.1. To use **SetWorldTransform( )**, you
must set the mode to **GM_ADVANCED**.

PORTABILITY: **SetGraphicsMode( )** is not supported by Windows
3.1. Windows 95 does not support the **GM_ADVANCED** mode.

Adding Rotation to the Paint Program

To illustrate **SetWorldTransform( )**, the paint program has been enhanced
so that you can rotate the images that you create. Each time you press the
left arrow key, the image currently in view is rotated counterclockwise 30
degrees. Pressing the right arrow key rotates the image clockwise 30 degrees.
In each case, the image is rotated about the center of the current client area.
The program is shown here. Sample output is shown in Figure 9-3.

```
/* Using SetWorldTransform() to rotate images. */

#include <windows.h>
#include <string.h>
#include <stdio.h>
#include "graph1.h"
#include <math.h>

LRESULT CALLBACK WindowFunc(HWND, UINT, WPARAM, LPARAM);

char szWinName[] = "MyWin"; /* name of window class */

char str[255]; /* holds output strings */
int maxX, maxY; /* screen dimensions */

HDC memdc; /* handle of memory DC */
```

```
HBITMAP hbit; /* handle of compatible bitmap */
HBRUSH hCurrentbrush, hOldbrush; /* handles of brushes */
HBRUSH hRedbrush, hGreenbrush, hBluebrush, hNullbrush;

/* create pens */
HPEN hOldpen; /* handle of old pen */
HPEN hCurrentpen; /* currently selected pen */
HPEN hRedpen, hGreenpen, hBluepen, hBlackpen;

int X=0, Y=0;
int pendown = 0;
int endpoints = 0;
int StartX=0, StartY=0, EndX=0, EndY=0;
int Mode;

int theta = 0; /* angle of rotation */

int WINAPI WinMain(HINSTANCE hThisInst, HINSTANCE hPrevInst,
                   LPSTR lpszArgs, int nWinMode)
{
  HWND hwnd;
  MSG msg;
  WNDCLASSEX wcl;
  HANDLE hAccel;

  /* Define a window class. */
  wcl.cbSize = sizeof(WNDCLASSEX);

  wcl.hInstance = hThisInst; /* handle to this instance */
  wcl.lpszClassName = szWinName; /* window class name */
  wcl.lpfnWndProc = WindowFunc; /* window function */
  wcl.style = 0; /* default style */

  wcl.hIcon = LoadIcon(NULL, IDI_APPLICATION); /* standard icon */
  wcl.hIconSm = LoadIcon(NULL, IDI_APPLICATION); /* small icon */

  wcl.hCursor = LoadCursor(NULL, IDC_ARROW); /* cursor style */

  /* specify name of menu resource */
  wcl.lpszMenuName = "GraphMenu"; /* main menu */

  wcl.cbClsExtra = 0; /* no extra */
  wcl.cbWndExtra = 0; /* information needed */

  /* Make the window white. */
  wcl.hbrBackground = GetStockObject(WHITE_BRUSH);

  /* Register the window class. */
```

```
  if(!RegisterClassEx(&wcl)) return 0;

  /* Now that a window class has been registered, a window
     can be created. */
  hwnd = CreateWindow(
    szWinName, /* name of window class */
    "Paint With Rotation", /* title */
    WS_OVERLAPPEDWINDOW, /* window style - normal */
    CW_USEDEFAULT, /* X coordinate - let Windows decide */
    CW_USEDEFAULT, /* Y coordinate - let Windows decide */
    CW_USEDEFAULT, /* width - let Windows decide */
    CW_USEDEFAULT, /* height - let Windows decide */
    HWND_DESKTOP, /* no parent window */
    NULL, /* no override.of class menu */
    hThisInst, /* handle of this instance of the program */
    NULL /* no additional arguments */
  );

  /* load accelerators */
  hAccel = LoadAccelerators(hThisInst, "GraphMenu");

  /* Display the window. */
  ShowWindow(hwnd, nWinMode);
  UpdateWindow(hwnd);

  /* Create the message loop. */
  while(GetMessage(&msg, NULL, 0, 0))
  {
    if(!TranslateAccelerator(hwnd, hAccel, &msg)) {
      TranslateMessage(&msg); /* translate keyboard messages */
      DispatchMessage(&msg); /* return control to Windows NT */
    }
  }
  return msg.wParam;
}

/* This function is called by Windows NT and is passed
   messages from the message queue.
*/
LRESULT CALLBACK WindowFunc(HWND hwnd, UINT message,
                            WPARAM wParam, LPARAM lParam)
{
  HDC hdc;
  PAINTSTRUCT paintstruct;
  int response;
  RECT rect;
  XFORM tf; /* transformation matrix */
```

```
switch(message) {
  case WM_CREATE:
    /* get screen coordinates */
    maxX = GetSystemMetrics(SM_CXSCREEN);
    maxY = GetSystemMetrics(SM_CYSCREEN);

    /* create virtual window */
    hdc = GetDC(hwnd);
    memdc = CreateCompatibleDC(hdc);
    hbit = CreateCompatibleBitmap(hdc, maxX, maxY);
    SelectObject(memdc, hbit);
    hCurrentbrush = GetStockObject(WHITE_BRUSH);
    SelectObject(memdc, hCurrentbrush);
    PatBlt(memdc, 0, 0, maxX, maxY, PATCOPY);

    /* create pens */
    hRedpen = CreatePen(PS_SOLID, 1, RGB(255,0,0));
    hGreenpen = CreatePen(PS_SOLID, 1, RGB(0,255,0));
    hBluepen = CreatePen(PS_SOLID, 1, RGB(0,0,255));

    /* create brushes */
    hRedbrush = CreateSolidBrush(RGB(255,0,0));
    hGreenbrush = CreateSolidBrush(RGB(0,255,0));
    hBluebrush = CreateSolidBrush(RGB(0,0,255));
    hNullbrush = GetStockObject(HOLLOW_BRUSH);

    /* save default pen */
    hBlackpen = hOldpen = SelectObject(memdc, hRedpen);
    hCurrentpen = hOldpen;
    SelectObject(memdc, hOldpen);

    ReleaseDC(hwnd, hdc);
    break;
  case WM_KEYDOWN: /* rotate image */
    switch((char) wParam) {
      case VK_LEFT: /* counterclockwise */
        theta -= 30;
        InvalidateRect(hwnd, NULL, 1);
        break;
      case VK_RIGHT: /* clockwise */
        theta += 30;
        InvalidateRect(hwnd, NULL, 1);
        break;
    }
    break;
  case WM_RBUTTONDOWN: /* start defining a region */
    if(theta) { /* restore view */
      theta = 0;
```

```
      InvalidateRect(hwnd, NULL, 1);
    }
    endpoints = 1;
    X = StartX = LOWORD(lParam);
    Y = StartY = HIWORD(lParam);
    break;
  case WM_RBUTTONUP: /* stop defining a region */
    endpoints = 0;
    EndX = LOWORD(lParam);
    EndY = HIWORD(lParam);
    break;
  case WM_LBUTTONDOWN: /* start drawing */
    if(theta) { /* restore view */
      theta = 0;
      InvalidateRect(hwnd, NULL, 1);
    }
    pendown = 1;
    X = LOWORD(lParam);
    Y = HIWORD(lParam);
    break;
  case WM_LBUTTONUP: /* stop drawing */
    pendown = 0;
    break;
  case WM_MOUSEMOVE:
    if(pendown) { /* draw */
      hdc = GetDC(hwnd);
      SelectObject(memdc, hCurrentpen);
      SelectObject(hdc, hCurrentpen);
      MoveToEx(memdc, X, Y, NULL);
      MoveToEx(hdc, X, Y, NULL);
      X = LOWORD(lParam);
      Y = HIWORD(lParam);
      LineTo(memdc, X, Y);
      LineTo(hdc, X, Y);
      MoveToEx(memdc, X, Y, NULL);
      MoveToEx(hdc, X, Y, NULL);
      ReleaseDC(hwnd, hdc);
    }
    if(endpoints) { /* display region boundaries */
      hdc = GetDC(hwnd);

      /* select "shadow" pen */
      hOldpen = SelectObject(hdc, hRedpen);

      /* change display mode to XOR */
      Mode = SetROP2(hdc, R2_XORPEN);

      /* display, but don't fill */
```

```
        hOldbrush =
            SelectObject(hdc, GetStockObject(HOLLOW_BRUSH));

        /* erase old shadow rectangle */
        Rectangle(hdc, StartX, StartY, X, Y);

        X = LOWORD(lParam);
        Y = HIWORD(lParam);

        /* display new shadow rectangle */
        Rectangle(hdc, StartX, StartY, X, Y);

        /* restore default brush */
        SelectObject(hdc, hOldbrush);
        SelectObject(hdc, hOldpen);
        SetROP2(hdc, Mode);
        ReleaseDC(hwnd, hdc);
      }
    break;
  case WM_COMMAND:
    switch(LOWORD(wParam)) {
      case IDM_ROTATERESET:
        theta = 0;
        InvalidateRect(hwnd, NULL, 1);
        break;
      case IDM_LINE:
        /* select current pen */
        SelectObject(memdc, hCurrentpen);

        /* draw the line */
        MoveToEx(memdc, StartX, StartY, NULL);
        LineTo(memdc, EndX, EndY);

        InvalidateRect(hwnd, NULL, 1);
        break;
      case IDM_RECTANGLE:
        /* select fill brush and pen */
        SelectObject(memdc, hCurrentbrush);
        SelectObject(memdc, hCurrentpen);

        /* draw rectangle */
        Rectangle(memdc, StartX, StartY, EndX, EndY);

        InvalidateRect(hwnd, NULL, 1);
        break;
      case IDM_ELLIPSE:
        /* select fill brush and pen */
        SelectObject(memdc, hCurrentbrush);
```

```
        SelectObject(memdc, hCurrentpen);

        /* draw ellipse */
        Ellipse(memdc,  StartX, StartY, EndX, EndY);

        InvalidateRect(hwnd, NULL, 1);
        break;
      case IDM_RED:
        hCurrentpen = hRedpen;
        break;
      case IDM_BLUE:
        hCurrentpen = hBluepen;
        break;
      case IDM_GREEN:
        hCurrentpen = hGreenpen;
        break;
      case IDM_BLACK:
        hCurrentpen = hBlackpen;
        break;
      case IDM_REDFILL:
        hCurrentbrush = hRedbrush;
        break;
      case IDM_BLUEFILL:
        hCurrentbrush = hBluebrush;
        break;
      case IDM_GREENFILL:
        hCurrentbrush = hGreenbrush;
        break;
      case IDM_WHITEFILL:
        hCurrentbrush = hOldbrush;
        break;
      case IDM_NULLFILL:
        hCurrentbrush = hNullbrush;
        break;
      case IDM_RESET:
        /* reset current position to 0,0 */
        MoveToEx(memdc, 0, 0, NULL);

        /* erase by repainting background */
        SelectObject(memdc, hOldbrush);
        PatBlt(memdc, 0, 0, maxX, maxY, PATCOPY);

        theta = 0;

        InvalidateRect(hwnd, NULL, 1);
        break;
      case IDM_EXIT:
        response = MessageBox(hwnd, "Quit the Program?",
```

```
                                      "Exit", MB_YESNO);
          if(response == IDYES) PostQuitMessage(0);
          break;
        case IDM_HELP:
          MessageBox(hwnd, "F2: Line\nF3: Rectangle\n"
                      "F4: Ellipse\nF5: Rotation Reset\n"
                      "F6: Reset\n",
                      "Paint and Rotate", MB_OK);
          break;
      }
      break;
    case WM_PAINT: /* process a repaint request */
      hdc = BeginPaint(hwnd, &paintstruct); /* get DC */

      /* use Windows NT's advanced graphics mode */
      SetGraphicsMode(hdc, GM_ADVANCED);


      /* get current dimensions of client area */
      GetClientRect(hwnd, &rect);

      /* rotate image */
      tf.eM11 = (float) cos(theta * 3.1416/180);
      tf.eM12 = (float) sin(theta * 3.1416/180);
      tf.eM21 = (float) -sin(theta * 3.1416/180);
      tf.eM22 = (float) cos(theta * 3.1416/180);
      tf.eDx = (float) rect.right/2;
      tf.eDy = (float) rect.bottom/2;
      SetWorldTransform(hdc, &tf); /* set transform */

      /* copy virtual window onto screen */
      BitBlt(hdc, -rect.right/2, -rect.bottom/2,
             rect.right, rect.bottom, memdc, 0, 0, SRCCOPY);

      EndPaint(hwnd, &paintstruct); /* release DC */
      break;
    case WM_DESTROY: /* terminate the program */
      DeleteObject(hRedpen); /* delete pens */
      DeleteObject(hGreenpen);
      DeleteObject(hBluepen);
      DeleteObject(hBlackpen);

      DeleteObject(hRedbrush); /* delete brushes */
      DeleteObject(hGreenbrush);
      DeleteObject(hBluebrush);

      DeleteDC(memdc);
      PostQuitMessage(0);
```

```
      break;
    default:
      /* Let Windows NT process any messages not specified in
         the preceding switch statement. */
      return DefWindowProc(hwnd, message, wParam, lParam);
  }
  return 0;
}
```

The program uses this resource file:

```
#include <windows.h>
#include "graph1.h"

GraphMenu MENU
{
  POPUP "&Shapes"
  {
    MENUITEM "&Line\tF2", IDM_LINE
    MENUITEM "&Rectangle\tF3", IDM_RECTANGLE
    MENUITEM "&Ellipse\tF4", IDM_ELLIPSE
    MENUITEM "E&xit\tF10", IDM_EXIT
  }
  POPUP "&Options"
  {
    POPUP "&Pen Color"
    {
      MENUITEM "&Red", IDM_RED
      MENUITEM "&Blue", IDM_BLUE
      MENUITEM "&Green", IDM_GREEN
      MENUITEM "Bl&ack", IDM_BLACK
    }
    POPUP "&Fill Color"
    {
      MENUITEM "&Red", IDM_REDFILL
      MENUITEM "&Blue", IDM_BLUEFILL
      MENUITEM "&Green", IDM_GREENFILL
      MENUITEM "&White", IDM_WHITEFILL
      MENUITEM "&Null", IDM_NULLFILL
    }
    MENUITEM "Ro&tation Reset\tF5", IDM_ROTATERESET
    MENUITEM "&Reset\tF6", IDM_RESET
  }
    MENUITEM "&Help", IDM_HELP
}
```

```
GraphMenu ACCELERATORS
{
  VK_F1,  IDM_HELP, VIRTKEY
  VK_F2,  IDM_LINE, VIRTKEY
  VK_F3,  IDM_RECTANGLE, VIRTKEY
  VK_F4,  IDM_ELLIPSE, VIRTKEY
  VK_F5,  IDM_ROTATERESET, VIRTKEY
  VK_F6,  IDM_RESET, VIRTKEY
  VK_F10, IDM_EXIT, VIRTKEY
}
```

You must add this line to GRAPH.H:

```
#define IDM_ROTATERESET    200
```

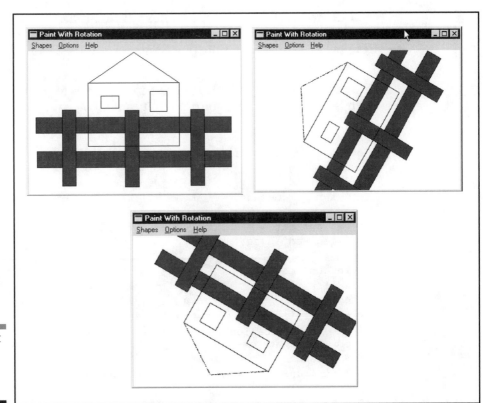

Sample output
that shows
rotation

Figure 9-3.

A Closer Look at the Rotation Mechanism

To handle the rotation of images, the paint program adds the following items:

1. The global variable **theta**, which holds the current angle of rotation, in degrees.
2. The local variable **tf** which holds the current transformation matrix.
3. Handlers for the left and right arrow keys, which increase or decrease **theta** by 30 degrees each time one is pressed.
4. The call to **SetWorldTransform( )** inside the handler for **WM_PAINT**.
5. The Rotation Reset menu option.

Here is how they work.

The value of **theta** determines the angle of rotation that will be applied to the image when it is copied from the virtual window device context (**memdc**) to the physical device context (**hdc**) inside **WM_PAINT**. The handlers for **VK_LEFT** and **VK_RIGHT** simply increase or decrease **theta** by 30 degrees each time one is pressed and then cause the window to be repainted.

The actual rotation of the image occurs inside the **WM_PAINT** handler, which is shown here. Let's go through it carefully.

```
case WM_PAINT: /* process a repaint request */
  hdc = BeginPaint(hwnd, &paintstruct); /* get DC */

  /* use Windows NT's advanced graphics mode */
  SetGraphicsMode(hdc, GM_ADVANCED);

  /* get current dimensions of client area */
  GetClientRect(hwnd, &rect);

  /* rotate image */
  tf.eM11 = (float) cos(theta * 3.1416/180);
  tf.eM12 = (float) sin(theta * 3.1416/180);
  tf.eM21 = (float) -sin(theta * 3.1416/180);
  tf.eM22 = (float) cos(theta * 3.1416/180);
  tf.eDx = (float) rect.right/2;
  tf.eDy = (float) rect.bottom/2;
  SetWorldTransform(hdc, &tf); /* set transform */

  /* copy virtual window onto screen */
  BitBlt(hdc, -rect.right/2, -rect.bottom/2,
```

```
                  rect.right, rect.bottom, memdc, 0, 0, SRCCOPY);

          EndPaint(hwnd, &paintstruct); /* release DC */
          break;
```

Each time a **WM_PAINT** message is received, the device context is obtained and set to advanced graphics mode, the current dimensions of the client area are retrieved, and the transformation matrix is initialized for rotation through the angle contained in **theta**. As you might recall, the standard C/C++ sine and cosine functions require that their arguments be in radians, so the expressions used as parameters to these functions simply convert the degrees in **theta** into their equivalent number of radians. When **theta** is 0 (its initial value), then no rotation occurs.

Notice that the transformation matrix sets **eDx** and **eDy** to **rect.right/2** and **rect.bottom/2**, respectively. Remember, all transformations occur relative to the origin, which for a window is, by default, the upper-left corner. By translating the origin one half of the length and width of the client area, we are effectively moving it to the center of the window. This causes the rotation to occur around the center of the window.

After **SetWorldTransform( )** is called, the specified transformation is activated and subsequent output is modified accordingly. Thus, when **BitBlt( )** is called inside the **WM_PAINT** handler to copy the contents of the virtual window onto the physical window, the rotation is automatically applied. Look closely at the call to **BitBlt( )**. Notice that the upper-left corner starts at **–rect.right/2** and **–rect.bottom/2**—not at 0, 0. The reason for this is that the transformation moves the origin down and right by half the size of the window. We must compensate for this when copying the virtual window.

To return the image to its initial, unrotated perspective, select Rotation Reset from the Options menu. This simply sets **theta** equal to 0 and then repaints the window. This sequence is also executed when you press either the left or right mouse button.

Things to Try

On your own, try implementing the following enhancements to the paint program: Allow the user to select between standard rectangles and rounded rectangles. Allow the user to draw an arc. Add an option that lets the user erase a portion of the window. Allow the user to select different line thicknesses. Implement the various other transformations supported by **SetWorldTransform( )**. (An easy one to try first is scaling.) Finally, add an "Undo" option that undoes the previous drawing command.

Mapping Modes and Viewports

Before concluding, we will examine two more aspects of Windows NT's graphics system: mapping modes and viewports. As you know, the text and graphics API functions operate on logical units. These logical units are then translated by Windows into physical units (i.e., pixels) when an object is displayed. The ratio of logical units to physical units is determined by the current *mapping mode*. That is, the mapping mode determines how page space units are mapped to the device space. (The mapping mode has nothing directly to do with the various transformations described in the previous section.) The mapping mode also affects the position of the origin.

In addition to changing the mapping mode, you can also set two other attributes that affect the translation of logical to physical units. First, you can define the length and width of a window in terms of logical units that you select. Second, for certain mapping modes you can set the physical extents of the viewport. The *viewport* is a rectangular region defined within the device space. The dimensions of the viewport help determine the ratio of logical units to physical units. Output is mapped so that it fits within the viewport's boundaries. For most mapping modes, the size of the viewport is predetermined and cannot be altered. But there are two mapping modes in which the size of the viewport is under your control. You can also set the origin of the viewport.

Setting the Mapping Mode

By default, logical units are the same as pixels. Thus, the default ratio of logical units to pixels is one-to-one. However, you can change this ratio by changing the mapping mode. To set the current mapping mode use **SetMapMode( )**. It has this prototype:

    int SetMapMode(HDC *hdc*, int *mode*);

The handle to the device context is specified by *hdc*. *mode* specifies the new mapping mode and it can be any one of the following constants:

Mapping Mode	Meaning
MM_ANISOTROPIC	Maps logical units to programmer-defined units with arbitrarily scaled axes.
MM_HIENGLISH	Maps each logical unit to 0.001 inch.
MM_HIMETRIC	Maps each logical unit to 0.01 millimeter.

Mapping Mode	Meaning
MM_ISOTROPIC	Maps logical units to programmer-defined units with equally scaled axes. (This establishes a one-to-one aspect ratio.)
MM_LOMETRIC	Maps each logical unit to 0.1 millimeter.
MM_LOENGLISH	Maps each logical unit to 0.01 inch.
MM_TEXT	Maps each logical unit to one device pixel.
MM_TWIPS	Maps each logical unit to one twentieth of a printer's point, or approximately 1/1440 inch.

For **MM_TEXT**, positive X values move right and positive Y values move down. For **MM_ANISOTROPIC** and **MM_ISOTROPIC**, the positive direction of the X and Y coordinates are user definable. For the remaining modes, positive X values move right and positive Y values move up as in the normal, Cartesian coordinate plane.

SetMapMode( ) returns the previous mapping mode or zero if an error occurs. The default mapping mode is **MM_TEXT**.

There are several reasons why you might want to change the current mapping mode. First, if you want your program's output to be displayed in physical units, then you can select one of the real-world modes, such as **MM_LOMETRIC**. Second, you might want to define units for your program that best fit the nature of what you are displaying. Third, you might want to change the scale of what is displayed. (That is, you might want to enlarge or shrink the size of what is output.) Finally, you may want to establish a one-to-one aspect ratio between the X and Y axis. When this is done, each X unit represents the same physical distance as each Y unit.

Defining Window Extents

If you select either the **MM_ISOTROPIC** or **MM_ANISOTROPIC** mapping mode, then you must define the size of the window in terms of logical units. (Since **MM_ISOTROPIC** and **MM_ANISOTROPIC** operate on programmer-defined units, the limits are technically undefined until you define them.) To define the X and Y extents of a window, use the **SetWindowExtEx( )** function, shown here:

```
BOOL SetWindowExtEx(HDC hdc, int Xextent,
                    int Yextent, LPSIZE lpOldSize);
```

The handle of the device context is specified in *hdc*. *Xextent* and *Yextent* specify the new horizontal and vertical extents measured in logical units. The previous window extents are copied into the **SIZE** structure pointed to by *lpOldSize*. However, if *lpOldSize* is **NULL**, then the previous extents are ignored. The function returns nonzero if successful, and zero on failure. **SetWindowExtEx( )** only has effect when the mapping mode is **MM_ANISOTROPIC** or **MM_ISOTROPIC**.

Keep in mind that when you change the logical dimensions of a window, you are not changing the physical size of the window on the screen. You are simply defining the size of the window in terms of logical units that you choose. (Or, more precisely, you are defining the relationship between the logical units used by the window and the physical units (pixels) used by the device.) For example, the same window could be given logical dimensions of 100×100 or 50×75. The only difference is the ratio of logical units to pixels when an image is displayed.

PORTABILITY: **SetWindowExtEx( )** replaces the older **SetWindowExt( )** function.

Defining a Viewport

As mentioned, a viewport is a region within the device space that determines how logical units are mapped to the physical device. The viewport dimensions define the physical part of the ratio used to convert logical units into pixels. (The window extents define the logical part.) For most mapping modes, the size of the viewport is fixed and cannot be altered by your program. However, for **MM_ISOTROPIC** and **MM_ANISOTROPIC**, the size of the viewport can be defined. This means that in these mapping modes, the ratio of logical units to pixels is under your control.

A viewport is defined using the **SetViewportExtEx( )** function. Its prototype is shown here:

    BOOL SetViewportExtEx(HDC *hdc*, int *Xextent*, int *Yextent*,
                          LPSIZE *lpOldSize*);

The handle of the device context is specified in *hdc*. *Xextent* and *Yextent* specify the new horizontal and vertical viewport extents, in pixels. The function returns nonzero if successful and zero on failure. The previous viewport extents are returned in the **SIZE** structure pointed to by *lpOldSize*. However, if *lpOldSize* is **NULL**, then the previous extents are ignored.

REMEMBER: **SetViewportExtEx( )** only has effect when the mapping mode is **MM_ANISOTROPIC** or **MM_ISOTROPIC**.

A viewport may be any size you desire. That is, it may encompass the entire window, be larger than the window, or be simply one part of the window.

Output is automatically mapped from page space (logical units) to the viewport (pixels) and scaled accordingly. Therefore, by changing the X and Y extents of the viewport, you are changing the ratio of logical units to pixels. This, in effect, changes the size of anything displayed within it. Thus, if you make the viewport extents larger, the contents of the viewport will get larger. Conversely, if you make the extents smaller, the contents of the viewport will shrink. This fact can be used as a means of enlarging or shrinking an image.

PORTABILITY: **SetViewportExtEx( )** replaces the older **SetViewportExt( )** function.

Setting the Viewport Origin

By default, the origin of the viewport is at 0, 0 within the window. However, you can change this using **SetViewportOrgEx( )**, shown here:

BOOL SetViewportOrgEx(HDC *hdc*, int *X*, int *Y*, LPPOINT *lpOldOrg*);

The handle of the device context is passed in *hdc*. The new origin, specified in pixels, for the viewport is passed in *X*, *Y*. The previous origin is returned in the **POINT** structure pointed to by *lpOldOrg*. If this parameter is **NULL**, the previous origin is ignored. The function returns nonzero if successful and zero on failure.

Changing the origin of the viewport changes where images are drawn in the window.

PORTABILITY: **SetViewportOrgEx( )** replaces the older **SetViewportOrg( )** function.

A Viewport and Mapping Mode Demonstration Program

The following program demonstrates mapping modes and viewports. Its operation is quite simple. Inside the **WM_PAINT** handler, the mapping mode is set to **MM_ANISOTROPIC**, the window extents are set to 200 × 200, the viewport extents are set to the values contained in **Xext** and **Yext**, and the viewport origin is set to the location specified by **Xorg** and **Yorg**. Next, some graphical objects are drawn. Each time you press the left mouse button, the origin is moved. Each time you press the right mouse button, the viewport's size is increased. Moving the origin translates the images within the window. Increasing the size of the viewport has the effect of enlarging the images. Sample output is shown in Figure 9-4. You may want to experiment with this program a little, just to make sure that you understand what is taking place.

```c
/* Demonstrate Mapping Modes and Viewports */

#include <windows.h>
#include <string.h>
#include <stdio.h>

LRESULT CALLBACK WindowFunc(HWND, UINT, WPARAM, LPARAM);

char szWinName[] = "MyWin"; /* name of window class */

/* viewport extents and origin */
int Xext=50, Yext=50;
int Xorg=0, Yorg=0;

int WINAPI WinMain(HINSTANCE hThisInst, HINSTANCE hPrevInst,
                   LPSTR lpszArgs, int nWinMode)
{
  HWND hwnd;
  MSG msg;
  WNDCLASSEX wcl;

  /* Define a window class. */
  wcl.cbSize = sizeof(WNDCLASSEX);

  wcl.hInstance = hThisInst; /* handle to this instance */
  wcl.lpszClassName = szWinName; /* window class name */
  wcl.lpfnWndProc = WindowFunc; /* window function */
  wcl.style = 0; /* default style */

  wcl.hIcon = LoadIcon(NULL, IDI_APPLICATION); /* standard icon */
  wcl.hIconSm = LoadIcon(NULL, IDI_APPLICATION); /* small icon */
```

```
    wcl.hCursor = LoadCursor(NULL, IDC_ARROW); /* cursor style */

    wcl.lpszMenuName = NULL;  /* no main menu */

    wcl.cbClsExtra = 0; /* no extra */
    wcl.cbWndExtra = 0; /* information needed */

    /* Make the window white. */
    wcl.hbrBackground = GetStockObject(WHITE_BRUSH);

    /* Register the window class. */
    if(!RegisterClassEx(&wcl)) return 0;

    /* Now that a window class has been registered, a window
       can be created. */
    hwnd = CreateWindow(
      szWinName, /* name of window class */
      "Mapping Modes and Viewports", /* title */
      WS_OVERLAPPEDWINDOW, /* window style - normal */
      CW_USEDEFAULT, /* X coordinate - let Windows decide */
      CW_USEDEFAULT, /* Y coordinate - let Windows decide */
      CW_USEDEFAULT, /* width - let Windows decide */
      CW_USEDEFAULT, /* height - let Windows decide */
      HWND_DESKTOP, /* no parent window */
      NULL, /* no override of class menu */
      hThisInst, /* handle of this instance of the program */
      NULL /* no additional arguments */
    );

    /* Display the window. */
    ShowWindow(hwnd, nWinMode);
    UpdateWindow(hwnd);

    /* Create the message loop. */
    while(GetMessage(&msg, NULL, 0, 0))
    {
        TranslateMessage(&msg); /* translate keyboard messages */
        DispatchMessage(&msg); /* return control to Windows NT */
    }
    return msg.wParam;
}

/* This function is called by Windows NT and is passed
   messages from the message queue.
*/
LRESULT CALLBACK WindowFunc(HWND hwnd, UINT message,
                            WPARAM wParam, LPARAM lParam)
{
  HDC hdc;
  PAINTSTRUCT paintstruct;
```

```
char str[80];

switch(message) {
  case WM_RBUTTONDOWN: /* increase size of viewport */
    Xext += 10;
    Yext += 10;
    InvalidateRect(hwnd, NULL, 1);
    break;
  case WM_LBUTTONDOWN: /* move origin */
    Xorg += 10;
    Yorg += 10;
    InvalidateRect(hwnd, NULL, 1);
    break;
  case WM_PAINT:
    hdc = BeginPaint(hwnd, &paintstruct); /* get DC */

    sprintf(str, "Viewport extents: %d %d, origin: %d %d",
            Xext, Yext, Xorg, Yorg);
    TextOut(hdc, 50, 0, str, strlen(str));

    /* set mapping mode */
    SetMapMode(hdc, MM_ANISOTROPIC);

    /* set window and viewport extents */
    SetWindowExtEx(hdc, 200, 200, NULL);
    SetViewportExtEx(hdc, Xext, Yext, NULL);

    /* set viewport origin */
    SetViewportOrgEx(hdc, Xorg, Yorg, NULL);

    /* draw some objects */
    LineTo(hdc, 50, 50);
    Rectangle(hdc, 20, 20, 80, 80);
    Ellipse(hdc, 40, 50, 100, 120);

    EndPaint(hwnd, &paintstruct); /* release DC */
    break;
  case WM_DESTROY: /* terminate the program */
    PostQuitMessage(0);
    break;
  default:
   /* Let Windows NT process any messages not specified in
      the preceding switch statement. */
    return DefWindowProc(hwnd, message, wParam, lParam);
}
return 0;
}
```

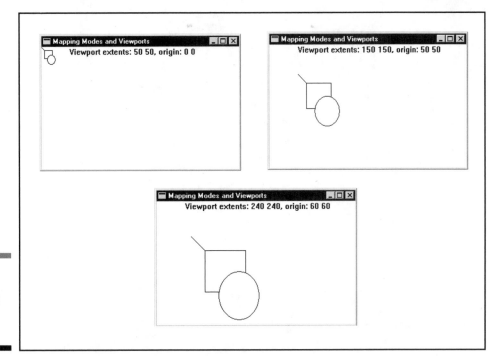

Sample
output from
the viewports
program
Figure 9-4.

Experiment with the GDI

Some of the concepts in this chapter, such as coordinate spaces, world transforms, viewports, and mapping modes, are not intuitive. The best way to become comfortable with these features, and the GDI in general, is to write a number of short programs that exercise various options. An afternoon experimenting with viewports, world transforms, and the like is time well spent.

CHAPTER 10

Introducing Common Controls and Common Dialog Boxes

309

This chapter begins our look at some of the most exciting features of Windows NT 4: common controls. All versions of Windows NT support the standard controls, such as push buttons, scroll bars, and check boxes. But, the common controls are a recent addition to Windows NT. They are sophisticated, high-powered components that expand the types of user interactions that your program may have. They also add excitement and "freshness" to your application and greatly enhance its interface. Without a doubt, the use of the common controls is the easiest way to give your application the modern, NT 4 look that users will expect. The common controls are so important to successful Windows NT 4 programming that we will be spending several chapters on them.

This chapter also introduces two of Windows' common dialog boxes. Unlike the common controls, which are quite new, the common dialog boxes have been available for some time (although some have looked different). Common dialog boxes are simply predefined dialog boxes that your program is free to use. The advantage of using common dialog boxes is twofold. First, they provide a standard interface for frequently used input tasks. Second, they simplify some rather tedious input requirements. In general, common dialog boxes are substantially easier to use than the common controls, and there are fewer of them, so we won't be spending as much time on them.

This chapter begins with an overview of the common controls. It then discusses one of the most important: the toolbar. The common dialogs are described at the end.

The Common Controls

The common controls supported by Windows NT 4 are:

Control	Description
Animation Control	Displays an AVI file.
Drag List Box	A list box that allows items to be dragged.
Header Control	A column heading.
Hot Key Control	Supports user-created hot keys.
Image List	A list of graphical images.

Control	Description
List View Control	A list of icons and labels.
Progress Bar	A visual gauge used to indicate the degree to which a task is completed.
Property Sheet	A properties dialog box.
Rich Edit Control	A sophisticated edit box.
Status Window	A bar that displays information related to an application.
Tab Control	A tab-based menu. (This control looks like the tabs on file folders.)
Toolbar	A graphics-based menu.
Tooltip	Small pop-up text boxes typically used to describe toolbar buttons.
Trackbar	A slider-based control. (Similar in concept to a scroll bar, but looks like a fader control on a stereo.)
Tree View Control	A tree-structured display.
Up/Down (Spin) Control	Up and down arrows. Called a spin control when linked with an edit box.

Common controls are sophisticated components available in Windows NT 4 and Windows 95.

These controls are called *common controls* because they represent an extended set of controls that will be used by many applications. You have certainly encountered several (if not all) of these controls if you have been using Windows NT 4 for very long. While it won't be possible to discuss all of the common controls in this book, we will look at several of the most important and representative.

PORTABILITY: All of the common controls are available in Windows 95. None are available for Windows 3.1. (A few of the common controls are supported by Windows 3.1 if you are using the Microsoft Foundation Classes, but they are not part of Win16.)

Moving Up to NT 4: Common Controls

The common controls described in this and subsequent chapters were not available for use in versions of Windows NT prior to 3.51. Further, even though they were included in NT 3.51, few applications took advantage of them. With the advent of NT 4, which includes the new user interface, the common controls have come into their own. When upgrading existing applications to NT 4, you will want to watch for opportunities to convert either standard controls or custom controls into common controls. Part of the reason for providing support for the common controls is to allow rich, flexible, but consistent user interface components to be used by applications. It is a good idea to take advantage of them.

Including and Initializing the Common Controls

Before you can use the common controls, you must include the standard header file COMMCTRL.H in your program. You must also make sure that the common controls library is linked into your program. For Microsoft Visual C++, the common controls library is called COMCTL32.LIB. This library is not automatically included, so you will need to add it to your project's linker options. To do this, select Settings under the Build main menu option, then find the Link tab; finally, add COMCTL32.LIB to the list of library modules. Borland C++ links the appropriate library automatically. For other compilers, consult your user manual.

Applications that use one or more common controls must call **InitCommonControls( )** prior to using the first common control. **InitCommonControls( )** ensures that the common controls dynamic link library (DLL) is loaded and that the common controls subsystem is initialized. The prototype for **InitCommonControls( )** is shown here:

```
void InitCommonControls(void);
```

A good place to call **InitCommonControls( )** is after your main window class has been registered.

Common Controls Are Windows

All of the common controls are child windows. They will be created using one of three methods: by calling **CreateWindow( )**, by calling

CreateWindowEx( ), or by calling a control-specific API function. (The **CreateWindowEx( )** function allows extended style attributes to be specified.) Because the common controls are windows, they can be managed in more or less the same way you manage other windows used by your program.

Many common controls send your program either **WM_COMMAND** or **WM_NOTIFY** messages when they are accessed by the user. Your program sends a control a message using the **SendMessage( )** API function, whose prototype is shown here:

LRESULT SendMessage(HWND *hwnd*, UINT *Msg*, WPARAM *wParam*,
        LPARAM *lParam*);

Here, *hwnd* is the handle of the control, *Msg* is the message you want to send to the control, and *wParam* and *lParam* contain any additional information associated with the message. The function returns the control's response, if any.

Using a Toolbar

One of the most important common controls is the toolbar because it can speed up menu selection when you are using a mouse. A *toolbar* is, essentially, a graphical menu. In the toolbar, menu items are represented by icons, which form graphical buttons. Often, a toolbar is used in conjunction with a standard menu. As such, it provides an alternative means of making a menu selection. In a sense, a toolbar is a menu accelerator for the mouse.

To create a toolbar, use the **CreateToolbarEx( )** function, which is shown here:

HWND CreateToolbarEx(HWND *hwnd*, DWORD *dwStyle*, UINT *ID*,
        int *NumBitmaps*, HINSTANCE *hInst*,
        UINT *BmpID*, LPCTBBUTTON *Buttons*,
        int *NumButtons*,
        int *ButtonWidth*, int *ButtonHeight*,
        int *BmpWidth*, int *BmpHeight*,
        UINT *Size*);

Here, *hwnd* is the handle of the parent window that owns the toolbar.

The style of the toolbar is passed in *dwStyle*. The toolbar style must include **WS_CHILD**. It can also include other standard styles, such as

WS_BORDER or **WS_VISIBLE**. There are two toolbar-specific styles that are commonly used. The first is **TBSTYLE_TOOLTIPS**. This style allows tooltips to be used. The second is **TBSTYLE_WRAPABLE**. This allows a long toolbar to be wrapped to the next line.

The identifier associated with the toolbar is passed in *ID*. The identifier of the bitmap resource that forms the toolbar is passed in *BmpID*. This bitmap contains all of the images displayed within the individual toolbar buttons. The number of individual bitmap images contained in the bitmap specified by *BmpID* is passed in *NumBitmaps*. The instance handle of the application is passed in *hInst*. If you prefer, you can pass the handle to a bitmap in *BmpID* instead of its resource ID. In this case, you must specify *hInst* as **NULL**.

Information about each button is passed in an array of **TBBUTTON** structures pointed to by *Buttons*. The number of buttons in the toolbar is specified in *NumButtons*. The width and height of the buttons are passed in *ButtonWidth* and *ButtonHeight*. The width and height of the images within each button are passed in *BmpWidth* and *BmpHeight*. These dimensions are specified in terms of pixels. If *ButtonWidth* and *ButtonHeight* are zero, then appropriate button dimensions that fit the bitmap size are supplied automatically. The size of the **TBBUTTON** structure is passed in *Size*.

The function returns a handle to the toolbar window. It returns **NULL** on failure.

Each button has a **TBBUTTON** structure associated with it that defines its various characteristics. The **TBBUTTON** structure is shown here:

```
typedef struct _TBBUTTON {
  int iBitmap;
  int idCommand;
  BYTE fsState;
  BYTE fsStyle;
  DWORD dwData;
  int iString;
} TBBUTTON;
```

The index of the bitmap image associated with the button is contained in **iBitmap**. The buttons begin their indexing at zero and are displayed left to right.

The ID associated with the button is stored in **idCommand**. Each time the button is pressed, a **WM_COMMAND** message will be generated and sent to the parent window. The value of **idCommand** will be contained in the low-order word of **wParam**.

The initial state of the button is stored in **fsState**. It can be one (or more) of the following values:

State	Meaning
TBSTATE_CHECKED	Button is pressed.
TBSTATE_ENABLE	Button may be pressed.
TBSTATE_HIDDEN	Button is hidden and inactive.
TBSTATE_INDETERMINATE	Button is gray and inactive.
TBSTATE_PRESSED	Button is pressed.
TBSTATE_WRAP	Following buttons are on new line.

The style of the button is contained in **fsStyle**. It can be any valid combination of the following values:

Style	Meaning
TBSTYLE_BUTTON	Standard button.
TBSTYLE_CHECK	Button toggles between checked and unchecked each time it is pressed.
TBSTYLE_CHECKGROUP	A check button that is part of a mutually exclusive group.
TBSTYLE_GROUP	A standard button that is part of a mutually exclusive group.
TBSTYLE_SEP	Separates buttons (**idCommand** must be zero when this style is used).

Notice the **TBSTYLE_SEP** style. This style is used to provide a gap between buttons on the toolbar. This allows you to visually group buttons into clusters.

The **dwData** field contains user-defined data. The **iString** field is the index of an optional string associated with the button. These fields should be zero if they are unused.

In their default configuration, toolbars are fully automated controls and require virtually no management by your program in order to use them. However, you can manually manage a toolbar if you like by sending it explicit control messages. These messages are sent to the toolbar using **SendMessage( )**. Three common toolbar messages are shown here. (You will want to explore the other toolbar messages on your own.)

Message	Meaning
TB_CHECKBUTTON	Presses or clears a toolbar button. *wParam* must contain the ID of the button. *lParam* must be nonzero to press or zero to clear.
TB_ENABLEBUTTON	Enables or disables a toolbar button. *wParam* must contain the ID of the button. *lParam* must be nonzero to enable or zero to disable.
TB_HIDEBUTTON	Hides or shows a toolbar button. *wParam* must contain the ID of the button. *lParam* must be nonzero to hide or zero to show.

Toolbars can also generate notification messages that inform your program about various activities related to the toolbar. For simple toolbars, you won't need to worry about these messages. (The notification messages all begin with **TBN_** and you can find information on them by examining the COMMCTRL.H header file or your API library reference.)

Adding Tooltips

As you have probably already seen when using Windows NT 4, some toolbars automatically pop up small text windows after the mouse pointer has paused for about one second over a toolbar button. These small text windows are called *tooltips*. Although not technically required, tooltips should be included with most toolbars because users will expect to see them. They also add polish to your application.

Tooltips are small text messages that appear when the mouse pauses over a control.

To add tooltips to a toolbar, you must first include the **TBSTYLE_TOOLTIPS** style when you create the toolbar. This enables the toolbar to send a **WM_NOTIFY** message when the mouse pointer lingers over a button for more than about one second. In general, **WM_NOTIFY** messages are generated by controls when some event occurs. In the case of tooltips, one is sent when the tooltip text needs to be displayed. When this occurs, **lParam** will point to a **TOOLTIPTEXT** structure, which is defined like this:

```
typedef struct {
  NMHDR hdr;
  LPSTR lpszText;
  char szText[80];
  HINSTANCE hinst;
  UINT uFlags;
} TOOLTIPTEXT;
```

The first member of **TOOLTIPTEXT** is an **NMHDR** structure, which is defined like this:

```
typedef struct tagNMHDR
{
  HWND  hwndFrom; /* handle of control */
  UINT  idFrom; /* control ID */
  UINT  code; /* notification code */
} NMHDR;
```

If a tooltip is being requested, then **code** will contain **TTN_NEEDTEXT** and **idFrom** will contain the ID of the button for which the tip is needed. Since other controls can generate **WM_NOTIFY** messages and toolbars can generate other types of notification messages, you will need to check these fields to determine precisely what event has occurred.

There are three ways to supply the required tooltip. You must either copy the tooltip text into the **szText** array of **TOOLTIPTEXT**, point **lpszText** to the text, or supply the resource ID of a string resource. When using a string resource, the string ID is assigned to **lpszText** and **hinst** must be the handle of the instance that contains the string resource (which is usually the instance handle of your program). By far the easiest way is to simply point **lpszText** to a string supplied by your program. For example, the following case responds to tooltip requests for the toolbar example program shown later.

```
case WM_NOTIFY: /* respond to tooltip request */
  TTtext = (LPTOOLTIPTEXT) lParam;
  if(TTtext->hdr.code == TTN_NEEDTEXT)
    switch(TTtext->hdr.idFrom) {
      case IDM_OPEN: TTtext->lpszText = "Open File";
        break;
      case IDM_UPPER: TTtext->lpszText = "Uppercase";
        break;
      case IDM_LOWER: TTtext->lpszText = "Lowercase";
        break;
      case IDM_SAVE: TTtext->lpszText = "Save File";
        break;
      case IDM_HELP: TTtext->lpszText = "Help";
        break;
    }
  break;
```

Once the tooltip text has been sent and control passes back to Windows, the tooltip will automatically be displayed. Your program need perform no further action. As you can see, tooltips are largely automated and easy to add to your application.

The **uFlags** field of **TOOLTIPTEXT** specifies whether the **idFrom** field in **hdr** contains an ID or a handle. If **uFlags** contains **TTF_IDISHWND**, then **idFrom** contains the handle of the control that requires the tooltip text. If it does not, then **idFrom** specifies the ID of the control. For tooltips for toolbars, **idFrom** will always specify an ID and you will not need to check the contents of **uFlags**.

Creating a Toolbar Bitmap

Before you can use a toolbar, you must create the bitmaps that form the graphics images inside each button. To do this, you must use an image editor. (The process is similar to that which you used when working with bitmaps in Chapter 7.) However, there is one important point to remember: there is only one bitmap associated with the toolbar and this bitmap must contain *all* of the button images. Thus, if your toolbar will have six buttons, then the bitmap associated with your toolbar must define six images. For example, if your toolbar images are each 16×16 bits and your toolbar has six buttons, then your toolbar bitmap will have to be 96 (6 times 16) bits long by 16 bits high.

For the toolbar example presented in this chapter, you will need five images. Each image must be 16×16 bits. This means that you will need to create a bitmap that is 80×16. Figure 10-1 shows how the toolbar bitmap used by the sample programs in this chapter looks inside the image editor. Store your bitmap in a file called TOOLBAR.BMP.

A Toolbar Sample Program

The following program demonstrates a toolbar. It implements a very simple set of text file utilities. The program can do the following operations:

♦ Load and display a file
♦ Convert a file to uppercase
♦ Convert a file to lowercase
♦ Save the file

Once the file has been loaded, it is displayed within the client area. A vertical scroll bar is included that allows you to scroll through the file. The toolbar duplicates the menu options and includes tooltips.

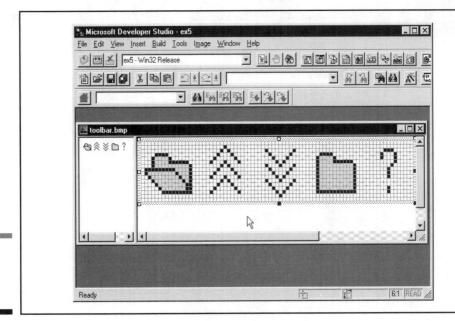

The toolbar
bitmap while
being edited
Figure 10-1.

When loading or saving a file, the program uses two common dialog boxes
to obtain the name of the file that you wish to use. These are the standard
Open and Save As dialog boxes. They are activated by calling the
GetOpenFileName( ) and **GetSaveFileName( )** API functions. The
operations of these functions are described later in this chapter.

The toolbar program is shown here:

```
/* Demonstrate a toolbar with tooltips.

   This program provides a small set
   of file utilities.

*/

#include <windows.h>
#include <commctrl.h>
#include <string.h>
#include <stdio.h>
#include <ctype.h>
#include "tb.h"

#define NUMBUTTONS 6
#define MAXSIZE 25000
```

```c
LRESULT CALLBACK WindowFunc(HWND, UINT, WPARAM, LPARAM);

void InitToolbar(); /* initialize the tool bar */

void display(int startY, HDC hdc); /* display file */

char szWinName[] = "MyWin"; /* name of window class */

TBBUTTON tbButtons[NUMBUTTONS];

HWND tbwnd; /* toolbar handle */

FILE *fp; /* file pointer */
char buf[MAXSIZE];   /* buffer to hold the file */

TEXTMETRIC tm;
SIZE size;

int SBPos = 0; /* scroll bar position */
int X = 5, Y = 32; /* scroll coordinates */
int NumLines = 0;
int ToolBarActive = 1;

HWND hwnd;

int WINAPI WinMain(HINSTANCE hThisInst, HINSTANCE hPrevInst,
                   LPSTR lpszArgs, int nWinMode)
{
  MSG msg;
  WNDCLASSEX wcl;
  HANDLE hAccel;

  /* Define a window class. */
  wcl.cbSize = sizeof(WNDCLASSEX);

  wcl.hInstance = hThisInst; /* handle to this instance */
  wcl.lpszClassName = szWinName; /* window class name */
  wcl.lpfnWndProc = WindowFunc; /* window function */
  wcl.style = 0; /* default style */

  wcl.hIcon = LoadIcon(NULL, IDI_APPLICATION);
  wcl.hIconSm = LoadIcon(NULL, IDI_APPLICATION);
  wcl.hCursor = LoadCursor(NULL, IDC_ARROW);

  /* specify name of menu resource */
  wcl.lpszMenuName = "ShowFileMenu"; /* main menu */
```

```
wcl.cbClsExtra = 0; /* no extra */
wcl.cbWndExtra = 0; /* information needed */

/* Make the window white. */
wcl.hbrBackground = GetStockObject(WHITE_BRUSH);

/* Register the window class. */
if(!RegisterClassEx(&wcl)) return 0;

/* Now that a window class has been registered, a window
   can be created. */
hwnd = CreateWindow(
  szWinName, /* name of window class */
  "Using a Toolbar", /* title */
  WS_OVERLAPPEDWINDOW | WS_VSCROLL, /* window style */
  CW_USEDEFAULT, /* X coordinate - let Windows decide */
  CW_USEDEFAULT, /* Y coordinate - let Windows decide */
  CW_USEDEFAULT, /* width - let Windows decide */
  CW_USEDEFAULT, /* height - let Windows decide */
  HWND_DESKTOP, /* no parent window */
  NULL, /* no override of class menu */
  hThisInst, /* handle of this instance of the program */
  NULL /* no additional arguments */
);

/* load accelerators */
hAccel = LoadAccelerators(hThisInst, "ShowFileMenu");

InitToolbar(); /* initialize the toolbar */

InitCommonControls(); /* activate the common controls */

tbwnd = CreateToolbarEx(hwnd,
                   WS_VISIBLE | WS_CHILD |
                   WS_BORDER | TBSTYLE_TOOLTIPS,
                   IDM_TOOLBAR,
                   NUMBUTTONS,
                   hThisInst,
                   IDTB_BMP,
                   tbButtons,
                   NUMBUTTONS,
                   0, 0, 16, 16,
                   sizeof(TBBUTTON));

/* Display the window. */
ShowWindow(hwnd, nWinMode);
UpdateWindow(hwnd);
```

```
  /* Create the message loop. */
  while(GetMessage(&msg, NULL, 0, 0))
  {
    if(!TranslateAccelerator(hwnd, hAccel, &msg)) {
      TranslateMessage(&msg); /* translate keyboard messages */
      DispatchMessage(&msg); /* return control to Windows NT */
    }
  }
  return msg.wParam;
}

/* This function is called by Windows NT and is passed
   messages from the message queue.
*/
LRESULT CALLBACK WindowFunc(HWND hwnd, UINT message,
                            WPARAM wParam, LPARAM lParam)
{
  HDC hdc;
  PAINTSTRUCT paintstruct;
  int i, response;
  SCROLLINFO si;
  OPENFILENAME fname;
  char filename[64]; /* file name */
  static char fn[256]; /* full path name */
  char filefilter[] = "C\0*.C\0C++\0*.CPP\0\0\0";

  LPTOOLTIPTEXT TTtext;
  RECT rect;

  switch(message) {
    case WM_CREATE:
      /* retrieve and save the text metrics */
      hdc = GetDC(hwnd);
      GetTextMetrics(hdc, &tm);
      ReleaseDC(hwnd, hdc);
      break;
    case WM_NOTIFY: /* respond to tooltip request */
      TTtext = (LPTOOLTIPTEXT) lParam;
      if(TTtext->hdr.code == TTN_NEEDTEXT)
        switch(TTtext->hdr.idFrom) {
          case IDM_OPEN: TTtext->lpszText = "Open File";
            break;
          case IDM_UPPER: TTtext->lpszText = "Uppercase";
            break;
          case IDM_LOWER: TTtext->lpszText = "Lowercase";
            break;
          case IDM_SAVE: TTtext->lpszText = "Save File";
            break;
```

```
              case IDM_HELP: TTtext->lpszText = "Help";
                break;
          }
        break;
      case WM_VSCROLL:
        switch(LOWORD(wParam)) {
          case SB_LINEDOWN:
            SBPos++;
            if(SBPos>NumLines) SBPos = NumLines;
            si.cbSize = sizeof(SCROLLINFO);
            si.fMask = SIF_POS;
            si.nPos = SBPos;
            SetScrollInfo(hwnd, SB_VERT, &si, 1);
            InvalidateRect(hwnd, NULL, 1);
            break;
          case SB_LINEUP:
            SBPos--;
            if(SBPos<0) SBPos = 0;
            si.cbSize = sizeof(SCROLLINFO);
            si.fMask = SIF_POS;
            si.nPos = SBPos;
            SetScrollInfo(hwnd, SB_VERT, &si, 1);
            InvalidateRect(hwnd, NULL, 1);
            break;
          case SB_PAGEDOWN:
            /* advance by the amount of lines that will fit
               within the current window */
            GetClientRect(hwnd, &rect);

            /* compensate for toolbar */
            if(ToolBarActive) rect.bottom -= 32;

            /* compute number of lines to advance */
            SBPos += rect.bottom /
                    (tm.tmHeight+tm.tmExternalLeading);

            if(SBPos>NumLines) SBPos = NumLines;
            si.cbSize = sizeof(SCROLLINFO);
            si.fMask = SIF_POS;
            si.nPos = SBPos;
            SetScrollInfo(hwnd, SB_VERT, &si, 1);
            InvalidateRect(hwnd, NULL, 1);
            break;
          case SB_PAGEUP:
            /* backup by the amount of lines that will fit
               within the current window */
            GetClientRect(hwnd, &rect);
```

```
        /* compensate for toolbar */
        if(ToolBarActive) rect.bottom -= 32;

        /* compute number of lines to backup */
        SBPos -= rect.bottom /
                (tm.tmHeight+tm.tmExternalLeading);

        if(SBPos<0) SBPos = 0;
        si.cbSize = sizeof(SCROLLINFO);
        si.fMask = SIF_POS;
        si.nPos = SBPos;
        SetScrollInfo(hwnd, SB_VERT, &si, 1);
        InvalidateRect(hwnd, NULL, 1);
        break;
      case SB_THUMBTRACK:
        SBPos = HIWORD(wParam); /* get curent position */
        if(SBPos<0) SBPos = 0;
        si.cbSize = sizeof(SCROLLINFO);
        si.fMask = SIF_POS;
        si.nPos = SBPos;
        SetScrollInfo(hwnd, SB_VERT, &si, 1);
        InvalidateRect(hwnd, NULL, 1);
        break;
    }
    break;
  case WM_COMMAND:
    switch(LOWORD(wParam)) {
      case IDM_OPEN:
        /* initialize the OPENFILENAME struct */
        memset(&fname, 0, sizeof(OPENFILENAME));
        fname.lStructSize = sizeof(OPENFILENAME);
        fname.hwndOwner = hwnd;
        fname.lpstrFilter = filefilter;
        fname.nFilterIndex = 1;
        fname.lpstrFile = fn;
        fname.nMaxFile = sizeof(fn);
        fname.lpstrFileTitle = filename;
        fname.nMaxFileTitle = sizeof(filename)-1;
        fname.Flags = OFN_FILEMUSTEXIST | OFN_HIDEREADONLY;

        if(!GetOpenFileName(&fname)) /* get the file name */
          break;

        if((fp=fopen(fn, "r"))==NULL) {
          MessageBox(hwnd, fn, "Cannot Open File", MB_OK);
          break;
        }
```

```
for(i=0; !feof(fp) && (i < MAXSIZE-1); i++) {
  fread(&buf[i], sizeof (char), 1, fp);
}
buf[i] = '\0';
fclose(fp);

/* count the number of lines */
for(NumLines=0, i=0; buf[i]; i++)
  if(buf[i] == '\n') NumLines++;

/* set scrollbar range to number of lines */
si.cbSize = sizeof(SCROLLINFO);
si.fMask = SIF_RANGE | SIF_POS;
si.nMin = 0; si.nMax = NumLines;
si.nPos = 0;
SetScrollInfo(hwnd, SB_VERT, &si, 1);

SBPos = 0;

if(ToolBarActive) Y = 32;
else Y = 0;

InvalidateRect(hwnd, NULL, 1);
break;
case IDM_UPPER: /* uppercase file */
  for(i=0; buf[i]; i++) buf[i] = toupper(buf[i]);
  InvalidateRect(hwnd, NULL, 1);
  break;
case IDM_LOWER: /* lowercase file */
  for(i=0; buf[i]; i++) buf[i] = tolower(buf[i]);
  InvalidateRect(hwnd, NULL, 1);
  break;
case IDM_SAVE:
  /* initialize the OPENFILENAME struct */
  memset(&fname, 0, sizeof(OPENFILENAME));
  fname.lStructSize = sizeof(OPENFILENAME);
  fname.hwndOwner = hwnd;
  fname.lpstrFilter = filefilter;
  fname.nFilterIndex = 1;
  fname.lpstrFile = fn;
  fname.nMaxFile = sizeof(fn);
  fname.lpstrFileTitle = filename;
  fname.nMaxFileTitle = sizeof(filename)-1;
  fname.Flags = OFN_HIDEREADONLY;

  if(!GetSaveFileName(&fname)) /* get the file name */
    break;
```

```
    if((fp=fopen(fn, "w"))==NULL) {
      MessageBox(hwnd, fn, "Cannot Open File", MB_OK);
      break;
    }

    for(i=0; buf[i]; i++) {
      fwrite(&buf[i], sizeof (char), 1, fp);
    }

    fclose(fp);
    InvalidateRect(hwnd, NULL, 1);
    break;
  case IDM_SHOW: /* show toolbar */
    ToolBarActive = 1;
    Y = 32; /* advance past toolbar */
    ShowWindow(tbwnd, SW_RESTORE);
    InvalidateRect(hwnd, NULL, 1);
    break;
  case IDM_HIDE: /* hide toolbar */
    ToolBarActive = 0;
    Y = 0;
    ShowWindow(tbwnd, SW_HIDE);
    InvalidateRect(hwnd, NULL, 1);
    break;
  case IDM_HELP:
    /* show help button as pressed */
    SendMessage(tbwnd, TB_CHECKBUTTON,
                (LPARAM) IDM_HELP, (WPARAM) 1);

    MessageBox(hwnd, "F2: Open\nF3: Uppercase\n"
               "F4: Lowercase\nF5: Save\n"
               "F6: Show Toolbar\n"
               "F7: Hide Toolbar\nF10: Exit",
               "File Utilities", MB_OK);

    /* reset the help button */
    SendMessage(tbwnd, TB_CHECKBUTTON,
                (LPARAM) IDM_HELP, (WPARAM) 0);
    break;
  case IDM_EXIT:
    response = MessageBox(hwnd, "Quit the Program?",
                          "Exit", MB_YESNO);
    if(response == IDYES) PostQuitMessage(0);
    break;
  }
  break;
case WM_PAINT: /* process a repaint request */
  hdc = BeginPaint(hwnd, &paintstruct); /* get DC */
```

```
          display(SBPos, hdc);
          EndPaint(hwnd, &paintstruct); /* release DC */
          break;
      case WM_DESTROY: /* terminate the program */
        PostQuitMessage(0);
        break;
      default:
        /* Let Windows NT process any messages not specified in
           the preceding switch statement. */
        return DefWindowProc(hwnd, message, wParam, lParam);
  }
  return 0;
}

/* Initialize the toolbar structures. */
void InitToolbar()
{
  tbButtons[0].iBitmap = 0;
  tbButtons[0].idCommand = IDM_OPEN;
  tbButtons[0].fsState = TBSTATE_ENABLED;
  tbButtons[0].fsStyle = TBSTYLE_BUTTON;
  tbButtons[0].dwData = 0L;
  tbButtons[0].iString = 0;

  tbButtons[1].iBitmap = 1;
  tbButtons[1].idCommand = IDM_UPPER;
  tbButtons[1].fsState = TBSTATE_ENABLED;
  tbButtons[1].fsStyle = TBSTYLE_BUTTON;
  tbButtons[1].dwData = 0L;
  tbButtons[1].iString = 0;

  tbButtons[2].iBitmap = 2;
  tbButtons[2].idCommand = IDM_LOWER;
  tbButtons[2].fsState = TBSTATE_ENABLED;
  tbButtons[2].fsStyle = TBSTYLE_BUTTON;
  tbButtons[2].dwData = 0L;
  tbButtons[2].iString = 0;

  tbButtons[3].iBitmap = 3;
  tbButtons[3].idCommand = IDM_SAVE;
  tbButtons[3].fsState = TBSTATE_ENABLED;
  tbButtons[3].fsStyle = TBSTYLE_BUTTON;
  tbButtons[3].dwData = 0L;
  tbButtons[3].iString = 0;

  /* button separator */
  tbButtons[4].iBitmap = 0;
  tbButtons[4].idCommand = 0;
```

```
  tbButtons[4].fsState = TBSTATE_ENABLED;
  tbButtons[4].fsStyle = TBSTYLE_SEP;
  tbButtons[4].dwData = 0L;
  tbButtons[4].iString = 0;

  tbButtons[5].iBitmap = 4;
  tbButtons[5].idCommand = IDM_HELP;
  tbButtons[5].fsState = TBSTATE_ENABLED;
  tbButtons[5].fsStyle = TBSTYLE_BUTTON;
  tbButtons[5].dwData = 0L;
  tbButtons[5].iString = 0;
}

/* Display the file. */
void display(int startline, HDC hdc)
{
  register int i, j;
  int linelim;
  int lines;
  char line[256];
  RECT rect;
  int tempY;

  GetClientRect(hwnd, &rect); /* get size of window */

  /* compute number of lines to display */
  lines = rect.bottom /
          (tm.tmHeight+tm.tmExternalLeading);

  /* find first line */
  for(i=0; startline && buf[i]; i++)
    if(buf[i] == '\n')  startline--;

  tempY = Y;

  /* erase old contents */
  PatBlt(hdc, X, Y, rect.right, rect.bottom, PATCOPY);

  /* display file */
  for(linelim=lines; linelim && buf[i]; i++) {
    for(j=0; j<256 && buf[i] && buf[i]!='\n'; j++, i++)
      line[j] = buf[i];

    if(!buf[i]) break;

    TextOut(hdc, X, Y, line, j);
```

```
            /* go to next line */
            Y = Y + tm.tmHeight + tm.tmExternalLeading;
            linelim--;
         }
         Y = tempY;
      }
```

This program requires the following resource file:

```
#include <windows.h>
#include "tb.h"

IDTB_BMP BITMAP toolbar.bmp

ShowFileMenu MENU
{
  POPUP "&File"
  {
    MENUITEM "&Open\tF2", IDM_OPEN
    MENUITEM "&Uppercase\tF3", IDM_UPPER
    MENUITEM "&Lowercase\tF4", IDM_LOWER
    MENUITEM "&Save\tF5", IDM_SAVE
    MENUITEM "&Exit\tF10", IDM_EXIT
  }
  POPUP "&Options"
  {
    MENUITEM "&Show Toolbar\tF6", IDM_SHOW
    MENUITEM "&Hide Toolbar\tF7", IDM_HIDE
  }
  MENUITEM "&Help", IDM_HELP
}

ShowFileMenu ACCELERATORS
{
  VK_F2, IDM_OPEN, VIRTKEY
  VK_F3, IDM_UPPER, VIRTKEY
  VK_F4, IDM_LOWER, VIRTKEY
  VK_F5, IDM_SAVE, VIRTKEY
  VK_F6, IDM_SHOW, VIRTKEY
  VK_F7, IDM_HIDE, VIRTKEY
  VK_F10, IDM_EXIT, VIRTKEY
  VK_F1, IDM_HELP, VIRTKEY
}
```

TheTB.H header file is shown here:

```
#define IDM_OPEN      100
#define IDM_UPPER     101
#define IDM_LOWER     102
#define IDM_SHOW      103
#define IDM_HIDE      104
#define IDM_SAVE      105
#define IDM_HELP      106
#define IDM_EXIT      107

#define IDM_TOOLBAR   200

#define IDTB_BMP      300
```

Sample output from the toolbar program is shown in Figure 10-2.

A Closer Look at the Toolbar Program

The toolbar program implements a very simple set of file operations. It works like this: When you select the Open option (either from the menu or the toolbar), a file is opened and its contents are read into the **buf** array. The

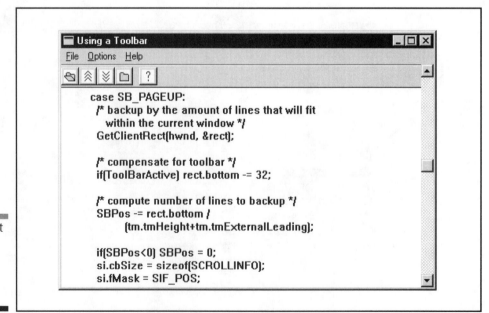

Sample output from the toolbar program

Figure 10-2.

size of **buf** is arbitrary and may be changed if you like. A window's worth of this buffer is displayed each time a **WM_PAINT** message is received, using the **display( )** function. The code within **display( )** should be familiar because it uses the same techniques as those described in Chapter 8 to output text to the window. By selecting Uppercase, you convert the contents of the buffer to uppercase. By selecting Lowercase, the buffer is converted to lowercase. You can save the contents of the buffer by selecting Save. Each of these operations can be initiated using the menu or the toolbar.

The toolbar information is held in the **tbButtons** array. This array is initialized in **InitToolBar( )**. Notice that the fifth structure is simply a button separator. In **WinMain( )**, the **InitCommonControls( )** function is called. Next, the toolbar is created and a handle to it is assigned to **tbwnd**.

Each button in the toolbar corresponds to a menu entry in the main menu. Specifically, each of the buttons (other than the separator) is associated with a menu ID. When a button is pressed, its associated ID will be sent to the program as part of a **WM_COMMAND** message, just as if a menu item had been selected. In fact, the same **case** statement handles both toolbar button presses and menu selections.

Since a toolbar is a window, it may be displayed or hidden like any other window using the **ShowWindow( )** function. To hide the window, select Hide Toolbar in the Options menu. To redisplay the toolbar, select Show Toolbar. Since the toolbar overlays part of the client area of the main window, you should always allow the user to remove the toolbar if it is not needed. As the program illustrates, this is very easy to do.

Notice the code inside the **IDM_HELP** case. When Help is selected (either through the main menu or by pressing the help button) the Help toolbar button is manually pressed by sending it a **TB_CHECKBUTTON** message. After the user closes the Help message box, the button is manually released. Thus, the Help button remains pressed while the Help message box is displayed. This is an example of how a toolbar can be manually managed by your program when necessary.

The file can be scrolled in the window using the vertical scroll bar. The operation of the scroll bar was described in Chapter 6. The function **display( )** actually displays the file. It only outputs sufficient text to fill the window as it is currently sized. (This is more efficient than outputting a screen full of information and letting Windows clip it.) The current size of the window is obtained by calling **GetClientRect( )**, described in Chapter 8, which returns the current window coordinates in a **RECT** structure. In this case, it is used to determine how much of the file can be displayed.

IN DEPTH

Passing Along WM_SIZE Messages

Try the following experiment with the toolbar program: Execute the program and then increase its horizontal size. As you will see, the toolbar is *not* automatically expanded to the new size. The reason for this is that a toolbar is a child window of the program's main window. Therefore, it does not automatically receive resize messages. Instead, if you want a child window (in this case, a toolbar) to receive resize messages, you must pass that message along to it. For example, to do this in the toolbar program, add the following case to **WindowFunc( )**.

```
case WM_SIZE:
  /* pass resize message along to toolbar */
  SendMessage(tbwnd, WM_SIZE, wParam, lParam);
  break;
```

After adding this code, when you expand the main window, the toolbar will automatically be resized appropriately.

In general, each time your main window is resized, it receives a **WM_SIZE** message. In **LOWORD(lParam)** is the new width of the window. The new height of the window is in **HIWORD(lParam)**. The value in **wParam** will be one of those shown here:

wParam	Meaning
SIZE_RESTORED	Window resized.
SIZE_MAXIMIZED	Window maximized.
SIZE_MINIMIZED	Window minimized.
SIZE_MAXHIDE	Another window has been maximized.
SIZE_MAXSHOW	Another window has been restored.

As a general rule, if your program contains a child window, your main window function will need to pass appropriate sizing messages along to the child window.

Introducing the Common Dialogs

10

In the toolbar example, the name of the file to open or to save to is obtained using the functions **GetOpenFileName( )** and **GetSaveFileName( )**, respectively. These functions activate built-in common dialog boxes, called Open and Save As, which obtain the name of a file. Open and Save As are two specific examples of a general class of built-in dialog boxes called *common dialog boxes*. Common dialog boxes are system-defined dialog boxes that your application may use to perform various common input tasks, such as obtaining a file name, choosing a font, or setting a color. Unlike the common controls, which are relatively new, the common dialog boxes are also available in earlier versions of Windows, such as Windows 3.1.

Common dialog boxes are predefined dialog boxes that perform commonly needed input tasks.

A common dialog box is activated by calling an API function. (This differs from the common controls, which are windows that must be created.) The common dialog boxes supported by Windows NT are shown here:

Function	Dialog Box Activated
ChooseColor( )	Activates the Color dialog. This allows the user to choose a color or create a custom color.
ChooseFont( )	Activates the Font dialog. This allows the user to select a font.
FindText( )	Activates the Find dialog, which supports text searches.
GetFileTitle( )	Extracts a file name (i.e., file title) from a full path and drive specification.
GetOpenFileName( )	Activates the Open dialog. This allows the user to select a file to open.
GetSaveFileName( )	Activates the Save As dialog. This allows the user to select a file into which information will be saved.
PageSetupDlg( )	Activates the Page Setup dialog, which is used to specify the format of a printed page.
PrintDlg( )	Activates the Print dialog, which is used to print a document.
ReplaceText( )	Activates the Replace dialog, which supports text replacements.

In this chapter you will learn about the Open and the Save As dialog boxes. In Chapter 18 you will see how to use the Print common dialog box. After understanding how to employ these common dialog boxes, the others are easy to master on your own.

While there is no technical reason why you cannot create your own dialog boxes to handle the types of input managed by the common dialogs, generally you should not. Instead, the common dialogs should be used by your program whenever one of the operations that they can perform is required. The reason for this is easy to understand: it is what the users of your programs have come to expect. Frankly, the common dialogs provide easy-to-use solutions to several fairly complex input situations. It is fortunate that they are built into Windows NT.

GetOpenFileName( ) and GetSaveFileName( )

The Open dialog box is used to input the name of a file to be opened. It allows a user to select a file name either by typing it or selecting it from a list. The user may also change directories or drives. The Open dialog box is activated by calling the **GetOpenFileName( )** API function. When called, it displays a dialog box similar to that shown here:

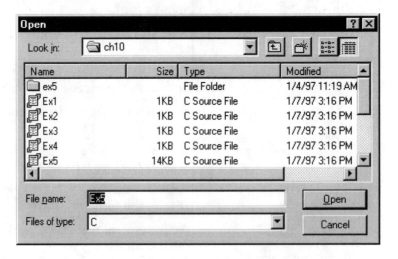

The Save As dialog box allows the user to select a file into which output will be written. The Save As dialog box looks like this:

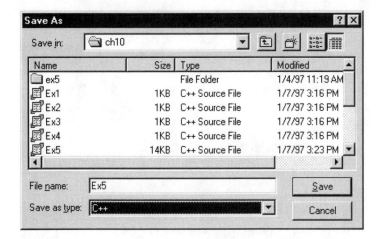

The **GetOpenFileName( )** and **GetSaveFileName( )** functions have these prototypes:

BOOL GetOpenFileName(LPOPENFILENAME *lpBuf*);
BOOL GetSaveFileName(LPOPENFILENAME *lpBuf*);

Here, *lpBuf* is a pointer to a structure of type **OPENFILENAME**. These functions return nonzero if a valid file name is specified by the user and zero otherwise.

The **OPENFILENAME** structure pointed to by *lpBuf* must be initialized prior to calling either function. Upon return, the file name specified by the user, and several other pieces of information, will be contained in that structure. The **OPENFILENAME** structure is defined like this:

```
typedef struct tagOFN
{
  DWORD lStructSize;
  HWND hwndOwner;
  HINSTANCE hInstance;
  LPCSTR lpstrFilter;
  LPSTR lpstrCustomFilter;
  DWORD nMaxCustFilter;
  DWORD nFilterIndex;
  LPSTR lpstrFile;
  DWORD nMaxFile;
```

```
    LPSTR lpstrFileTitle;
    DWORD nMaxFileTitle;
    LPCSTR lpstrInitialDir;
    LPCSTR lpstrTitle;
    DWORD Flags;
    WORD nFileOffset;
    WORD nFileExtension;
    LPCSTR lpstrDefExt;
    LPARAM lCustData;
    LPOFNHOOKPROC lpfnHook;
    LPCSTR  lpTemplateName;
} OPENFILENAME;
```

Each element of **OPENFILENAME** is described here:

lStructSize must contain the size of the **OPENFILENAME** structure.
hwndOwner must contain the handle of the window that owns the
dialog box. If **Flags** contains either **OFN_ENABLETEMPLATE** or
OFN_ENABLETEMPLATEHANDLE, then **hInstance** specifies a handle
that defines an alternative dialog box template. Otherwise, **hInstance** is
not used.

lpstrFilter must point to an array that contains pairs of strings that define
a file name filter. The pairs of strings must be organized like this:
"description""mask", where the description identifies the type of files
matched by the mask. For example, "C Files""C.*" specifies the description *C
Files* and the mask *C.**. The last two strings in the array must be null in order
to terminate the list. The names of the filters are displayed in a drop-down
list from which the user may choose. If this element is **NULL**, then no file
name filter is used.

lpstrCustomFilter points to a static array that will be used to store a file
filter entered by the user. This array must initially contain a description and
file filter using the format just described. However, after the user selects a file
name, the new filter is copied into the array. If **lpstrCustomFilter** is
NULL, then this element is ignored. The array must be 40 characters (or
more) long.

nMaxCustFilter specifies the size of the array pointed to by
lpstrCustomFilter. This value is needed only if **lpstrCustomFilter** is
not **NULL**.

nFilterIndex specifies which pair of strings pointed to by **lpstrFilter** will
provide the initial file filter and description when the dialog box is first
displayed. The value 1 corresponds to the first pair. The second pair is
specified by the value 2, and so on. This value is ignored if **lpstrFilter** is
NULL. If **nFilterIndex** is zero, the strings pointed to by
lpstrCustomFilter are used.

lpstrFile points to an array that will receive the complete file, path, and drive of the file name selected by the user. The array may contain an initial file name that will be used to initialize the file name edit box or it may point to a null string.

nMaxFile specifies the size of the array pointed to by **lpstrFile**. The array should be at least 256 bytes long so as to accommodate the longest possible file name.

lpstrFileTitle points to an array that receives the file name (without path or drive information) of the file selected by the user. If the file name by itself if not needed, this field may be **NULL**.

nMaxFileTitle specifies the size of the array pointed to by **lpstrFileTitle**.

lpstrInitialDir points to an array that contains the directory that will first be used when the dialog box is activated. If **lpstrInitialDir** is **NULL**, then the current directory is used.

lpstrTitle points to a string that will be used as the title for the dialog box. The default title is used if **lpstrTitle** is **NULL**. For the **GetOpenFileName( )** function, the default title is "Open"; for **GetSaveFileName( )**, the default title is "Save As".

The **Flags** element is used to set various options inside the dialog box. Both **GetOpenFilename( )** and **GetSaveFilename( )** support numerous options. Several of the most commonly used are shown here. You can OR together two or more flags if necessary.

Flags	Effect
OFN_ENABLEHOOK	Allows the function pointed to by **lpfnHook** to be used.
OFN_ENABLETEMPLATE	Allows alternative dialog box template to be used. In this case, **hInstance** specifies the instance handle of the module that contains the dialog box specified by **lpTemplateName**.
OFN_ENABLETEMPLATEHANDLE	Allows alternative dialog box template to be used. In this case, **hInstance** is the handle to a region of memory that contains the dialog box template.
OFN_FILEMUSTEXIST	User may only specify existent files.

Flags	Effect
OFN_HIDEREADONLY	Causes the read-only check box to be suppressed.
OFN_NOCHANGEDIR	Current directory remains unchanged by user selection.
OFN_OVERWRITEPROMPT	Causes a confirmation window to be displayed if the user selects a file that already exists.
OFN_PATHMUSTEXIST	User may only specify existent paths.

The **nFileOffset** element receives the index of the start of the file name within the string returned in the array pointed to by **lpstrFile**. (Remember, this array will contain drive and path information in addition to the file name.)

nFileExtension receives the index of the file extension within the string returned in the array pointed to by **lpstrFile**.

lpstrDefExt points to an array that contains a default extension that is appended to the file name entered by the user when no extension is included. (The extension should be specified without a leading period.)

lCustData contains data that is passed to the optional function pointed to by **lpfnHook**.

lpfnHook is a pointer to a function that preempts and processes messages intended for the dialog box. This element is used only if **Flags** contains the value **OFN_ENABLEHOOK**.

lpTemplateName points to the name of an alternative dialog box template. **hInstance** must be the handle to the module that contains the dialog box resource. **lpTemplateName** is ignored unless **Flags** contains the value **OFN_ENABLETEMPLATE**.

Notice how the **OPENFILENAME** structure (**fname**) is initialized within the toolbar program. Since many of the elements of the structure must be set to **NULL** if not used, it is common practice to first zero the entire structure using **memset( )**, as is done in the program. After **fname** has been zeroed, the essential elements are set. Pay special attention to how the array **filefilter** is initialized. Remember, the array pointed to by **lpstrFilter** must contain pairs of strings.

In the toolbar program, once a file name has been obtained, it is used to open the file. Notice that in this case, the entire drive, path, and file name contained in **fn** and pointed to by **lpstrFile** are used. If you wanted to restrict files to the current directory, then the contents of **filename** (pointed to by **lpstrFileTitle**) could have been used.

You might want to try experimenting with **GetOpenFileName( )** and **GetSaveFileName( )** on your own, trying different options. For example, try using a custom file filter. These are two important built-in dialog boxes that nearly all applications will need to use.

A Short Word on Using Files in a Windows NT Program

Before concluding this chapter, a short comment on using files in a Windows NT program is in order. Files are easily used by a Windows NT program. Because any C/C++ compiler that can create a Windows NT program will supply Windows NT-compatible file functions, such as **fopen( )** or **fclose( ),** you can generally use those functions to perform file I/O without any further worry. This is the approach used by the toolbar demo program. However, if you wish, you may use API functions defined by Win32, such as **CreateFile( )**, **ReadFile( )**, and **WriteFile( )**.

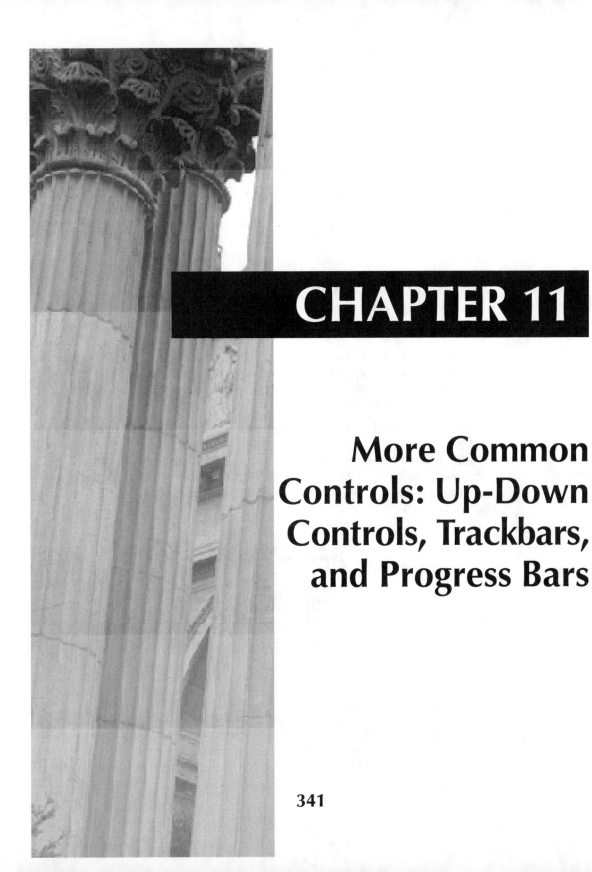

CHAPTER 11

More Common Controls: Up-Down Controls, Trackbars, and Progress Bars

This chapter explores three more of Windows NT 4's common controls: the up-down control, the trackbar, and the progress bar. These controls are particularly important for several reasons: They are visually appealing, are easily incorporated into any new application, and offer a convenient means of enhancing an existing program when it is ported to Windows NT.

This chapter begins by presenting an overview of these controls. It concludes by demonstrating their use in an enhanced version of the countdown timer program developed in Chapter 6. As you will see, the addition of the new controls improves the interface to this application.

Up-Down Controls

An up-down control is essentially a compressed scroll bar. That is, it consists of the arrows found on the ends of a scroll bar, but there is no bar between them. As you may have seen while using various Windows NT applications, some scroll bars are so small that the bar is essentially pointless. Also, some situations don't lend themselves to the concept of the bar, but benefit from the use of the up and down arrows. To accommodate these situations, the up-down control was invented.

An up-down control is essentially a scroll bar control without the bar.

An up-down control may be employed two different ways. First, it may be used more or less like a stand-alone scroll bar. Second, it can be used in conjunction with another control, called its *buddy window*. The most common buddy window is an edit box. When this is the case, a *spin control* (or *spinner*) is created. Here is the way these two controls appear. (The spin control is on the right.)

A spin control is a combination of an up-down control and an edit box.

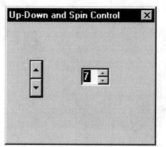

When using a spin control, almost all of the overhead required to manage the control is provided automatically by Windows NT. This makes the spin control easy to add to your application. The method of creating and managing both a stand-alone up-down control and a spin control is discussed here.

Creating an Up-Down Control

To create an up-down control, use the **CreateUpDownControl( )** function, shown here:

HWND CreateUpDownControl(DWORD *Style*, int *X*, int *Y*,
        int *Width*, int *Height*, HWND *hParent*,
        int *ID*, HINSTANCE *hInst*,
        HWND *hBuddy*, int *Max*, int *Min*, int *StartPos*);

Here, *Style* specifies the style of the up-down control. This parameter must include the standard styles **WS_CHILD**, **WS_VISIBLE**, and **WS_BORDER**. It may also include one or more of the up-down styles shown in Table 11-1.

The location of the upper-left corner of the up-down control is passed in *X* and *Y*. The width and height of the control is specified in *Width* and *Height*.

The handle of the parent window is passed in *hParent*. The ID associated with the up-down control is specified in *ID*. The instance handle of the

11

Style	Meaning
UDS_ALIGNLEFT	Aligns up-down control to the left of its buddy window.
UDS_ALIGNRIGHT	Aligns up-down control to the right of its buddy window.
UDS_ARROWKEYS	Enables arrows keys. (That is, arrow keys may be used to move the control.)
TBS_AUTOBUDDY	Buddy window is previous window in z-order.
UDS_HORZ	Up-down control is horizontal. Up-down controls are vertical by default.
UDS_NOTHOUSANDS	Commas not used in large values when displayed in buddy window. (Applies to spin controls only.)
UDS_SETBUDDYINT	Automatically sets the text within the buddy window when the control position is changed. This allows the buddy window to show the current position of the up-down control.
UDS_WRAP	Position of up-down control will "wrap around" when moved past an end.

The Up-Down
Control Styles
Table 11-1.

application is passed in *hInst*. The handle of the buddy window is passed in *hBuddy*. If there is no buddy window, then this parameter must be **NULL**.

The range of the control is passed in *Max* and *Min*. If *Max* is less than *Min*, then the control runs backward. The initial position of the control (which must be within the specified range) is passed in *StartPos*. This value determines the control's initial value. It is important to understand that an up-down control maintains an internal counter that is incremented or decremented each time one of the arrows is pressed. This internal value will always be within the range specified when the control is created.

The function returns a handle to the control. It returns **NULL** on failure.

Receiving Up-Down Control Messages

When one of the arrows of an up-down control is pressed, it sends either a **WM_VSCROLL** or a **WM_HSCROLL** message to its parent window, depending on whether the up-down control is vertical (the default) or horizontal. The handle of the up-down control will be in *lParam*. Since there may be more than one control that generates **WM_VSCROLL** or **WM_HSCROLL** messages, you will need to check this handle to determine if it is that of the up-down control. The new value of the up-down control will be in **HIWORD(wParam)**.

Sending Up-Down Control Messages

Up-down controls respond to a variety of messages. Several commonly used ones are shown in Table 11-2. For example, to obtain the value of the control (i.e., its position), send the control a **UDM_GETPOS** message. The current position of the control is returned. To set the position of an up-down control use the **UDM_SETPOS** message. You send the control messages using **SendMessage( )**.

Creating a Spin Control

While there is nothing wrong whatsoever with creating and using a stand-alone up-down control, the up-down control is most commonly linked with an edit box. As mentioned, this combination is called a spin control. Because the spin control is such a common use of an up-down control, Windows NT provides special support for it. In fact, a spin control is a completely automated control—your program incurs virtually no management overhead itself.

To create a spin control, you must specify an edit control as a buddy window to an up-down control. After you have done this, each time the up-down

Message	Meaning
UDM_GETBUDDY	Obtains handle of buddy window. The handle is returned. *wParam* is 0. *lParam* is 0.
UDM_GETPOS	Obtains the current position. The current position is in the low-order word of the return value. *wParam* is 0. *lParam* is 0.
UDM_GETRANGE	Obtains the current range. The maximum value is in the low-order word of the return value and the minimum value is in the high-order word of the return value. *wParam* is 0. *lParam* is 0.
UDM_SETBUDDY	Specifies a new buddy window. The handle of the old buddy window is returned. *wParam* is the handle of new buddy window. *lParam* is 0.
UDM_SETPOS	Sets the current position. *wParam* is 0. *lParam* is new current position.
UDM_SETRANGE	Sets the current range. *wParam* is 0. *lParam* is the range. Its low-order word contains maximum, high-order word contains minimum.

Common
Up-Down
Messages
Table 11-2.

control is changed, its new position is automatically displayed in the edit box. Further, if you manually change the value in the edit box, the up-down control is automatically set to reflect that value. Typically, you will define the edit box within your program's resource file. You will see an example of a spin control later in this chapter.

Using a Trackbar

One of the most visually appealing of the common controls is the trackbar (sometimes called a *slider control*). A trackbar resembles a slide control found on various types of electronic equipment, such as stereos. It consists of a pointer that moves within a track. Although it looks quite different from a scroll bar, a trackbar is handled in much the same way by your program. Trackbars are particularly useful when your program is emulating a real device. For example, if your program is controlling a graphic equalizer, then trackbars are an excellent choice for representing and setting the frequency curve. Here is a sample trackbar:

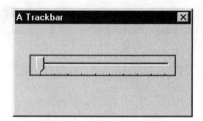

To create a trackbar, use either **CreateWindow( )** or **CreateWindowEx( )**. **CreateWindowEx( )** allows some extended style specifications. For the trackbar example in this chapter, we won't need to use any extended styles, but you may find them useful in your own applications. The window class of a trackbar is **TRACKBAR_CLASS**.

Trackbar Styles

When creating the trackbar, you can specify various style options. The most common ones are shown in Table 11-3. You will almost always want to include **TBS_AUTOTICKS** because this style causes small "tick" marks to be automatically shown on the bar. The tick marks provide a scale for the bar.

Sending Trackbar Messages

Like the other common controls we have examined, you send a trackbar a message using the **SendMessage( )** function. Common trackbar messages are shown in Table 11-4. Two messages that you will almost always need to

Style	Effect
TBS_AUTOTICKS	Automatically adds tick marks to the trackbar.
TBS_HORZ	Trackbar is horizontal. (This is the default.)
TBS_VERT	Trackbar is vertical.
TBS_BOTTOM	Tick marks on bottom of bar. (This is the default for horizontal trackbars.)
TBS_TOP	Tick marks on top of bar.
TBS_LEFT	Tick marks on left of bar.
TBS_RIGHT	Tick marks on right of bar. (This is the default for vertical trackbars.)
TBS_BOTH	Tick marks on both sides of bar.

Common
Trackbar Style
Options
Table 11-3.

Message	Meaning
TBM_GETPOS	Obtains the current position. *wParam* is 0. *lParam* is 0.
TBM_GETRANGEMAX	Gets the maximum trackbar range. *wParam* is 0. *lParam* is 0.
TBM_GETRANGEMIN	Gets the minimum trackbar range. *wParam* is 0. *lParam* is 0.
TBM_SETPOS	Sets the current position. *wParam* is nonzero to redraw the trackbar and zero otherwise. *lParam* contains the new position.
TBM_SETRANGE	Sets the trackbar range. *wParam* is nonzero to redraw trackbar and zero otherwise. *lParam* contains the range. The minimum value is in the low-order word. The maximum value is in the high-order word.
TBM_SETRANGEMAX	Sets the maximum range. *wParam* is nonzero to redraw trackbar and zero otherwise. *lParam* contains the maximum range value.
TBM_SETRANGEMIN	Sets the minimum range. *wParam* is nonzero to redraw trackbar and zero otherwise. *lParam* contains the minimum range value.

Common
Trackbar
Messages
Table 11-4.

send to a track bar are **TBM_SETRANGE** and **TBM_SETPOS**. These set the range of the trackbar and establish its initial position, respectively. These items cannot be set when the trackbar is created.

Processing Trackbar Notification Messages

When a trackbar is accessed, it generates either a **WM_HSCROLL** or a **WM_VSCROLL** scroll message, depending upon whether the trackbar is horizontal or vertical. A value describing the nature of the activity is passed in the low-order word of *wParam*. This value is referred to as a notification message. The handle of the trackbar that generated the message is in *lParam*. Common trackbar notification messages are shown in Table 11-5.

Trackbars are fully automated. For example, the trackbar will move itself when its position is changed by the user. Your program does not need to do this manually.

Message	Meaning
TB_BOTTOM	END key is pressed. Slider is moved to minimum value.
TB_ENDTRACK	End of trackbar activity.
TB_LINEDOWN	Right arrow or down arrow key pressed.
TB_LINEUP	Left arrow or up arrow key pressed.
TB_PAGEDOWN	Pagedown key pressed or mouse click before slider.
TB_PAGEUP	Pageup key pressed or mouse click after slider.
TB_THUMBPOSITION	Slider moved using the mouse.
TB_THUMBTRACK	Slider dragged using the mouse.
TB_TOP	HOME key pressed. Slider is moved to maximum value.

Common Trackbar Notification Messages
Table 11-5.

NOTE: When a **WM_VSCROLL** or **WM_HSCROLL** message is received from a trackbar, the value in **HIWORD(wParam)** should contain the current position of the bar. However, at the time of this writing, this is not always the case. To obtain the current trackbar position, you should always send a **TBM_GETPOS** message.

Using a Progress Bar

A progress bar indicates the degree to which a task has been completed.

A progress bar is a small, horizontal window that depicts the degree of completion of a task. As the task proceeds, the bar is filled from left to right. When the bar is filled, the task is finished. The progress bar is one of the simplest of the common controls and you have almost certainly seen one in action. Progress bars are created using either **CreateWindow( )** or **CreateWindowEx( )** by specifying the **PROGRESS_CLASS** window class.

Your program sends a progress bar a message using the **SendMessage( )** function. Progress bars do not generate messages. Generally, you will send messages to set a progress bar's range and to increment its progress. Here are a few of the most common progress bar messages.

Message	Meaning
PBM_SETPOS	Sets the progress bar's position. The old position is returned. *wParam* contains the new position. *lParam* is 0.
PBM_SETRANGE	Sets the progress bar's range. The old range is returned with the maximum in the high-order word and the minimum in the low-order word. *wParam* is 0. *lParam* contains the range. The maximum value is in the high-order word. The minimum value is in the low-order word.
PBM_SETSTEP	Sets the increment (or step) value. The old increment is returned. *wParam* contains the new increment. *lParam* is 0.
PBM_STEPIT	Advances the bar's progress by the step value. *wParam* is 0. *lParam* is 0.

By default, a progress bar has the range 0 through 100. However, you can set it to any value between 0 and 65,535. Typically, you will advance the bar by sending it a **PBM_STEPIT** message. This causes the bar's current position to advance by a predetermined increment called a *step*. By default, the step increment is 10, but it may be any value you like. As you increment the bar's position, more of the bar is filled. Since a progress bar is used to display the degree of completion of a long task, the task should end when the bar is fully filled.

Demonstrating a Spin Control, Trackbar, and Progress Bar

The following program demonstrates a spin control, a trackbar, and a progress bar by modifying the countdown timer program first developed in Chapter 6. Specifically, it uses the spin control to set the number of seconds to delay. It uses the trackbar to set the number of beeps that will be sounded when the timer goes off. A progress bar displays how far the countdown has advanced. The enhanced countdown timer program is shown here.

```
/* Add a spin control, trackbar, and progress bar to
   the countdown timer. */
```

```
#include <windows.h>
#include <commctrl.h>
#include <string.h>
#include <stdio.h>
#include "timer.h"

#define BEEPMAX 10
#define MAXTIME 99

LRESULT CALLBACK WindowFunc(HWND, UINT, WPARAM, LPARAM);
BOOL CALLBACK DialogFunc(HWND, UINT, WPARAM, LPARAM);

char szWinName[] = "MyWin"; /* name of window class */

HINSTANCE hInst;

HWND hwnd;

int WINAPI WinMain(HINSTANCE hThisInst, HINSTANCE hPrevInst,
                   LPSTR lpszArgs, int nWinMode)
{
  MSG msg;
  WNDCLASSEX wcl;
  HANDLE hAccel;

  /* Define a window class. */
  wcl.cbSize = sizeof(WNDCLASSEX);

  wcl.hInstance = hThisInst; /* handle to this instance */
  wcl.lpszClassName = szWinName; /* window class name */
  wcl.lpfnWndProc = WindowFunc; /* window function */
  wcl.style = 0; /* default style */

  wcl.hIcon = LoadIcon(NULL, IDI_APPLICATION);
  wcl.hIconSm = LoadIcon(NULL, IDI_APPLICATION);

  wcl.hCursor = LoadCursor(NULL, IDC_ARROW);

  /* specify name of menu resource */
  wcl.lpszMenuName = "TimerMenu"; /* main menu */

  wcl.cbClsExtra = 0; /* no extra */
  wcl.cbWndExtra = 0; /* information needed */

  /* Make the window white. */
  wcl.hbrBackground = GetStockObject(WHITE_BRUSH);

  /* Register the window class. */
  if(!RegisterClassEx(&wcl)) return 0;
```

```
/* Now that a window class has been registered, a window
   can be created. */
hwnd = CreateWindow(
  szWinName, /* name of window class */
  "Spin Controls, Trackbars, and Progess Bars", /* title */
  WS_OVERLAPPEDWINDOW, /* window style - normal */
  CW_USEDEFAULT, /* X coordinate - let Windows decide */
  CW_USEDEFAULT, /* Y coordinate - let Windows decide */
  CW_USEDEFAULT, /* width - let Windows decide */
  CW_USEDEFAULT, /* height - let Windows decide */
  HWND_DESKTOP, /* no parent window */
  NULL, /* no override of class menu */
  hThisInst, /* handle of this instance of the program */
  NULL /* no additional arguments */
);

hInst = hThisInst; /* save the current instance handle */

/* load accelerators */
hAccel = LoadAccelerators(hThisInst, "TimerMenu");

InitCommonControls(); /* activate the common controls */

/* Display the window. */
ShowWindow(hwnd, nWinMode);
UpdateWindow(hwnd);

/* Create the message loop. */
while(GetMessage(&msg, NULL, 0, 0))
{
  if(!TranslateAccelerator(hwnd, hAccel, &msg)) {
    TranslateMessage(&msg); /* translate keyboard messages */
    DispatchMessage(&msg); /* return control to Windows NT */
  }
}
return msg.wParam;
}

/* This function is called by Windows NT and is passed
   messages from the message queue.
*/
LRESULT CALLBACK WindowFunc(HWND hwnd, UINT message,
                            WPARAM wParam, LPARAM lParam)
{
  int response;

  switch(message) {
    case WM_COMMAND:
```

```
      switch(LOWORD(wParam)) {
        case IDM_DIALOG:
          DialogBox(hInst, "MYDB", hwnd, (DLGPROC) DialogFunc);
          break;
        case IDM_EXIT:
          response = MessageBox(hwnd, "Quit the Program?",
                                "Exit", MB_YESNO);
          if(response == IDYES) PostQuitMessage(0);
          break;
        case IDM_HELP:
          MessageBox(hwnd, "Try the Timer", "Help", MB_OK);
          break;
      }
      break;
    case WM_DESTROY: /* terminate the program */
      PostQuitMessage(0);
      break;
    default:
      /* Let Windows NT process any messages not specified in
         the preceding switch statement. */
      return DefWindowProc(hwnd, message, wParam, lParam);
  }
  return 0;
}

/* Timer Dialog function */
BOOL CALLBACK DialogFunc(HWND hdwnd, UINT message,
                          WPARAM wParam, LPARAM lParam)
{
  char str[80];

  HDC hdc;
  PAINTSTRUCT paintstruct;
  static int t;
  int i;

  static long udpos = 1;
  static long trackpos = 1;
  static HWND hEboxWnd;
  static HWND hTrackWnd;
  static HWND udWnd;
  static HWND hProgWnd;
  int low=1, high=BEEPMAX;


  switch(message) {
    case WM_INITDIALOG:
      hEboxWnd = GetDlgItem(hdwnd, IDD_EB1);
```

```
            udWnd = CreateUpDownControl(
                        WS_CHILD | WS_BORDER | WS_VISIBLE |
                        UDS_SETBUDDYINT | UDS_ALIGNRIGHT,
                        10, 10, 50, 50,
                        hdwnd,
                        IDD_UPDOWN,
                        hInst,
                        hEboxWnd,
                        MAXTIME, 1, udpos);

    /* create a track bar */
    hTrackWnd = CreateWindow(TRACKBAR_CLASS,
                    "",
                    WS_CHILD | WS_VISIBLE | WS_TABSTOP |
                    TBS_AUTOTICKS | WS_BORDER,
                    2, 50,
                    200, 28,
                    hdwnd,
                    NULL,
                    hInst,
                    NULL
    );
    SendMessage(hTrackWnd, TBM_SETRANGE,
                    1, MAKELONG(low, high));
    SendMessage(hTrackWnd, TBM_SETPOS,
                    1, trackpos);

    /* create progress bar */
    hProgWnd = CreateWindow(PROGRESS_CLASS,
                    "",
                    WS_CHILD | WS_VISIBLE | WS_BORDER,
                    2, 84,
                    240, 12,
                    hdwnd,
                    NULL,
                    hInst,
                    NULL);

    /* set step increment to 1 */
    SendMessage(hProgWnd, PBM_SETSTEP, 1, 0);

    /* check the As-Is radio button */
    SendDlgItemMessage(hdwnd, IDD_RB3, BM_SETCHECK, 1, 0);

    /* set number of beeps box */
    SetDlgItemInt(hdwnd, IDD_EB2, trackpos, 1);
    return 1;
```

```
case WM_VSCROLL: /* beep at each 10-second mark */
  if(udWnd==(HWND)lParam) /* if spin control */
    if(!(HIWORD(wParam) % 10)) MessageBeep(MB_OK);
  return 1;
case WM_HSCROLL: /* track bar was activated */
  if(hTrackWnd != (HWND)lParam) break; /* not track bar */

  switch(LOWORD(wParam)) {
    case TB_TOP:
    case TB_BOTTOM:         /* For this example */
    case TB_LINEUP:         /* all messages will be */
    case TB_LINEDOWN:       /* processed in the same */
    case TB_THUMBPOSITION: /* way. */
    case TB_THUMBTRACK:
    case TB_PAGEUP:
    case TB_PAGEDOWN:
      trackpos = SendMessage(hTrackWnd, TBM_GETPOS,
                    0, 0);
      SetDlgItemInt(hdwnd, IDD_EB2, trackpos, 1);
      return 1;
  }
  break;
case WM_COMMAND:
  switch(LOWORD(wParam)) {
    case IDCANCEL:
      KillTimer(hdwnd, IDD_TIMER);
      EndDialog(hdwnd, 0);
      return 1;
    case IDD_EB2:
      /* Update trackbar if user enters number
         of beeps into the Beeps edit box. */
      trackpos = GetDlgItemInt(hdwnd, IDD_EB2, NULL, 1);
      SendMessage(hTrackWnd, TBM_SETPOS, 1, trackpos);
      return 1;
    case IDD_START: /* start the timer */
      SetTimer(hdwnd, IDD_TIMER, 1000, NULL);

      /* get number of seconds to delay */
      t = udpos = SendMessage(udWnd, UDM_GETPOS, 0, 0);

      /* initialize progress bar */
      SendMessage(hProgWnd, PBM_SETRANGE, 0,
                MAKELONG(0, udpos));
      SendMessage(hProgWnd, PBM_SETPOS, 0, 0);

      if(SendDlgItemMessage(hdwnd,
              IDD_RB1, BM_GETCHECK, 0, 0))
        ShowWindow(hwnd, SW_MINIMIZE);
```

```
          else
          if(SendDlgItemMessage(hdwnd,
                     IDD_RB2, BM_GETCHECK, 0, 0))
             ShowWindow(hwnd, SW_MAXIMIZE);
          return 1;
     }
     break;
  case WM_TIMER: /* timer went off */
    if(t==0) {
       KillTimer(hdwnd, IDD_TIMER);
       if(SendDlgItemMessage(hdwnd,
                     IDD_CB2, BM_GETCHECK, 0, 0)) {

          /* beep and move track bar with each beep */
          for(i=trackpos ; i; i--) {
            SendMessage(hTrackWnd, TBM_SETPOS, 1, i);
            MessageBeep(MB_OK);
            Sleep(250);
          }

          /* reset track bar after countdown */
          SendMessage(hTrackWnd, TBM_SETPOS, 1, trackpos);
       }

       MessageBox(hdwnd, "Timer Went Off", "Timer", MB_OK);
       SetDlgItemInt(hdwnd, IDD_EB1, udpos, 1);
       ShowWindow(hwnd, SW_RESTORE);
       return 1;
    }
    t--;

    /* advance progress bar */
    SendMessage(hProgWnd, PBM_STEPIT, 0, 0);

    /* see if countdown is to be displayed */
    if(SendDlgItemMessage(hdwnd,
                  IDD_CB1, BM_GETCHECK, 0, 0)) {
       SetDlgItemInt(hdwnd, IDD_EB1, t, 1);
    }
    return 1;
  case WM_PAINT:
    hdc = BeginPaint(hdwnd, &paintstruct);
    SetBkMode(hdc, TRANSPARENT);
    sprintf(str, "Seconds");
    TextOut(hdc, 44, 6, str, strlen(str));
    sprintf(str, "Beeps");
    TextOut(hdc, 186, 6, str, strlen(str));
    sprintf(str, "Set Number of Beeps");
```

```
        TextOut(hdc, 30, 32, str, strlen(str));
        EndPaint(hdwnd, &paintstruct);
        return 1;
    }
    return 0;
}
```

This program uses the following resource file. The edit box identified as
IDD_EB1 is linked to the up-down control to form the spin control.

```
; Demonstrate a Spin Control and a Trackbar
#include <windows.h>
#include "timer.h"
TimerMenu MENU
{
  POPUP "&Options"
  {
    MENUITEM "&Timer\tF2", IDM_DIALOG
    MENUITEM "&Exit\tF3", IDM_EXIT
  }
  MENUITEM "&Help", IDM_HELP
}


TimerMenu ACCELERATORS
{
  VK_F2, IDM_DIALOG, VIRTKEY
  VK_F3, IDM_EXIT, VIRTKEY
  VK_F1, IDM_HELP, VIRTKEY
}


MYDB DIALOG 18, 18, 144, 100
CAPTION "A Countdown Timer"
STYLE DS_MODALFRAME | WS_POPUP | WS_CAPTION | WS_SYSMENU
{
  PUSHBUTTON "Start", IDD_START, 30, 80, 30, 14,
            WS_CHILD | WS_VISIBLE | WS_TABSTOP
  PUSHBUTTON "Cancel", IDCANCEL, 70, 80, 30, 14,
            WS_CHILD | WS_VISIBLE | WS_TABSTOP
  EDITTEXT IDD_EB1, 1, 1, 20, 12, ES_LEFT | WS_CHILD |
          WS_VISIBLE | WS_BORDER
  EDITTEXT IDD_EB2, 80, 1, 12, 12, ES_LEFT | WS_CHILD |
          WS_VISIBLE | WS_BORDER
  AUTOCHECKBOX "Show Countdown", IDD_CB1, 1, 48, 70, 10
  AUTOCHECKBOX "Beep At End", IDD_CB2, 1, 58, 50, 10
  AUTORADIOBUTTON "Minimize", IDD_RB1, 80, 48, 50, 10
  AUTORADIOBUTTON "Maximize", IDD_RB2, 80, 58, 50, 10
  AUTORADIOBUTTON "As-Is", IDD_RB3, 80, 68, 50, 10
}
```

The header file TIMER.H is shown here.

```
#define IDM_DIALOG    100
#define IDM_EXIT      101
#define IDM_HELP      102

#define IDD_START     300
#define IDD_TIMER     301

#define IDD_CB1       400
#define IDD_CB2       401
#define IDD_RB1       402
#define IDD_RB2       403
#define IDD_RB3       404

#define IDD_EB1       500
#define IDD_EB2       501

#define IDD_UPDOWN    602
```

Sample output from the program is shown in Figure 11-1. When the timer is started (by pressing Start), the currently specified delay is retrieved from the spin control. If the Show Countdown option is checked, then the time remaining is updated in the spin control once per second. When the end of the time period has been reached, the specified number of beeps is sounded (if the Beep At End option was selected). Also, the trackbar is moved leftward one position each time a beep sounds. Let's take a closer look at the enhanced countdown program now.

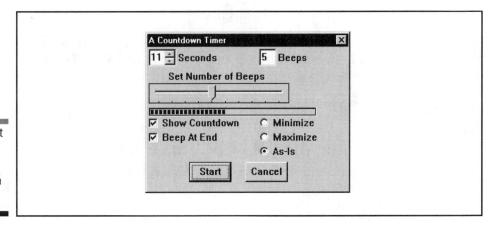

Sample output from the enhanced timer program
Figure 11-1.

The Sleep( ) Function

In the countdown program, the **Sleep( )** function provides a slight delay between beeps when the timer goes off. If a short delay does not separate each beep, then only one long, continuous sound is heard instead of the individual beeps that are desired. In the past, such a delay was generally achieved through the use of some sort of software-based delay loop, such as

```
for(x=0; x<100000; x++) ; /* a simple delay loop */
```

However, such software methods are problematic because of two main reasons. First, software delay loops are imprecise. Specifically, the length of the delay is affected by the speed of the CPU. On a fast computer, the delay will be shorter. On a slow computer, the delay will be longer. Further, even with equivalent CPU speeds, different compilers will use different machine instructions when compiling the preceding loop. This could lead to differences in the length of the delay. The second reason software delay loops can cause problems is that they are CPU intensive. That is, even though they do nothing, they are using CPU time that could be allocated to other processes running in your system. To prevent inconsistent delays and CPU intensive code, your Windows NT programs should use the **Sleep( )** function to provide a delay.

The **Sleep( )** function suspends the execution of the thread that calls it for a specified number of milliseconds. (For single-threaded programs, this means that the entire program is suspended.) Its prototype is shown here:

VOID Sleep(DWORD *delay*);

Here, *delay* specifies the number of milliseconds that the calling thread will suspend. While your program is asleep, CPU time is allocated to other processes running in the system.

Creating the Spin Control, Trackbar, and Progress Bar

The spin control, trackbar, and progress bar are created each time **DialogFunc( )** receives a **WM_INITDIALOG** message, using the code shown here:

```
case WM_INITDIALOG:
  hEboxWnd = GetDlgItem(hdwnd, IDD_EB1);
  udWnd = CreateUpDownControl(
              WS_CHILD | WS_BORDER | WS_VISIBLE |
              UDS_SETBUDDYINT | UDS_ALIGNRIGHT,
              10, 10, 50, 50,
              hdwnd,
              IDD_UPDOWN,
              hInst,
              hEboxWnd,
              MAXTIME, 1, udpos);

  /* create a track bar */
  hTrackWnd = CreateWindow(TRACKBAR_CLASS,
              "",
              WS_CHILD | WS_VISIBLE | WS_TABSTOP |
              TBS_AUTOTICKS | WS_BORDER,
              2, 50,
              200, 28,
              hdwnd,
              NULL,
              hInst,
              NULL
  );
  SendMessage(hTrackWnd, TBM_SETRANGE,
              1, MAKELONG(low, high));
  SendMessage(hTrackWnd, TBM_SETPOS,
              1, trackpos);

  /* create progress bar */
  hProgWnd = CreateWindow(PROGRESS_CLASS,
              "",
              WS_CHILD | WS_VISIBLE | WS_BORDER,
              2, 84,
              240, 12,
              hdwnd,
              NULL,
              hInst,
              NULL);

  /* set step increment to 1 */
  SendMessage(hProgWnd, PBM_SETSTEP, 1, 0);

  /* check the As-Is radio button */
  SendDlgItemMessage(hdwnd, IDD_RB3, BM_SETCHECK, 1, 0);

  /* set number of beeps box */
  SetDlgItemInt(hdwnd, IDD_EB2, trackpos, 1);
  return 1;
```

Look first at the call to **CreateUpDownControl( )**. This creates a spin control that is at location 10, 10 within the dialog box. The control is 50 pixels wide and 50 pixels tall. Because the control is a child window of the dialog box, the dialog box's handle (**hdwnd**) is passed as the parent handle. The ID of the up-down control is **IDD_UPDOWN**. **hInst** is the instance handle of the program. The buddy window is specified by **hEboxWnd**. This is the handle of the edit box that will be linked to the up-down control. The range of the up-down control is one to **MAXTIME** and the initial position is one.

Since the edit box that is part of the spin control is defined in the resource file, the program must call **GetDlgItem( )** to obtain its handle. (**GetDlgItem( )** was described in Chapter 5.) Once the handle of the dialog box has been obtained, it is passed as the buddy window to the **CreateUpDownControl( )** function. After the up-down control has been created with an edit box as its buddy window, the two controls are automatically linked together, forming the spin control.

Next, examine how the trackbar is created. It is located at 2, 50 and is 200 pixels long by 28 pixels high. The handle of the trackbar is stored in **hTrackWnd**. After the trackbar is created, its range is set to one through **BEEPMAX**. Its initial position is set at one. Notice that the range is set using the macro **MAKELONG( )**. This macro assembles two integers into a long integer. It has this prototype:

DWORD MAKELONG(WORD *low*, WORD *high*);

The low-order part of the double word value is specified in *low* and the high-order portion is specified in *high*. **MAKELONG( )** is quite useful when you need to encode two word values into a long integer.

Finally, the progress bar is created. It is located beneath the trackbar. Its step increment is set to one. The progress bar will be updated each time the timer goes off, showing the current state of the countdown.

Managing the Spin Control

Each time the spin control is accessed, a **WM_VSCROLL** message is sent to the dialog box. The handle of the up-down control is contained in **lParam**. This handle is tested against that returned by **CreateUpDownControl( )** to confirm that it is the up-down control that generated the message. While there is only one control in this example, real-world applications may have several controls capable of generating a **WM_VSCROLL** message, so you should always confirm which control has been accessed. The new position of the spin control is contained in **HIWORD(wParam)**. If this value is a multiple of ten, then a beep is sounded. That is, as the user increases (or decreases) the timing interval, a beep is sounded as each multiple of ten is passed. This can be useful when setting a large delay period.

Since a spin control is completely automated, there is no need to perform any other actions when the **WM_VSCROLL** message is received. Except for sounding the beep at each ten-second interval, there is no need to handle **WM_VSCROLL** messages, at all. In fact, most programs that use spin controls don't interact with the control until its current setting is required.

Inside the **IDD_START** handler, the current value of the spin control is obtained by sending a **UDM_GETPOS** message. When this message is received, the spin control returns the value shown in its buddy window. Remember, the value in the edit box always reflects the current value of the spin control. This is true even if the user changes this value manually by entering a new number.

Managing the Trackbar

Whenever the trackbar is moved, a **WM_HSCROLL** message is received and processed by the following code:

```
case WM_HSCROLL: /* track bar was activated */
  if(hTrackWnd != (HWND)lParam) break; /* not track bar */

  switch(LOWORD(wParam)) {
    case TB_TOP:
    case TB_BOTTOM:         /* For this example */
    case TB_LINEUP:         /* all messages will be */
    case TB_LINEDOWN:       /* processed in the same */
    case TB_THUMBPOSITION:  /* way. */
    case TB_THUMBTRACK:
    case TB_PAGEUP:
    case TB_PAGEDOWN:
      trackpos = SendMessage(hTrackWnd, TBM_GETPOS,
                       0, 0);
      SetDlgItemInt(hdwnd, IDD_EB2, trackpos, 1);
      return 1;
  }
  break;
```

When the user moves the slider within the trackbar, the trackbar's position is automatically updated—your program does not have to do this itself. After the trackbar has been moved, the program obtains its new value and then uses this value to update the edit box that displays the number of beeps.

The current value of the trackbar is displayed inside the Beeps edit box using **SetDlgItemInt( )**. This function displays an integer inside an edit box. It has the following prototype:

BOOL SetDlgItemInt(HWND *hDialog*, int *ID*, UINT *value*, BOOL *signed*);

The handle of the dialog box that contains the edit control is passed in *hDialog*. The ID of the dialog box is passed in *ID*. The value to put into the edit box is passed in *value*. If *signed* is a nonzero value, then negative values are allowed. Otherwise, an unsigned value is assumed. The function returns nonzero if successful and zero on failure.

The user many also manually set the number of beeps using the Beeps edit box. When this done, the trackbar is automatically adjusted to reflect the value entered by the user, using the sequence shown here:

```
case IDD_EB2:
  /* Update trackbar if user enters number
     of beeps into the Beeps edit box. */
  trackpos = GetDlgItemInt(hdwnd, IDD_EB2, NULL, 1);
  SendMessage(hTrackWnd, TBM_SETPOS, 1, trackpos);
  return 1;
```

Notice that the value inside the edit box is retrieved by calling **GetDlgItemInt( )**. This function returns the integer equivalent of the string currently inside the box. For example, if the box contains the string 102, then **GetDlgItemInt( )** will return the value 102. For obvious reasons, this function only applies to edit boxes that contain numeric values. The prototype for **GetDlgItemInt( )** is shown here:

UINT GetDlgItemInt(HWND *hDialog*, int *ID*, BOOL **error*, BOOL *signed*);

The handle of the dialog box that contains the edit control is passed in *hDialog*. The ID of the dialog box is passed in *ID*. If the edit box does not contain a valid numeric string, zero is returned. However, zero is also a valid value. For this reason, the success or failure of the function is returned in the variable pointed to by *error*. After the call, the variable pointed to by *error* will be nonzero if the return value is valid. It will be zero if an error occurred. If you don't care about errors, you can use **NULL** for this parameter. If *signed* is a nonzero value, then a signed value will be returned by **GetDlgItemInt( )**. Otherwise, an unsigned value is returned.

In this example, the trackbar may be moved using either the mouse or the keyboard. In fact, the reason that so many **TB_** messages are included is to support the keyboard interface. You might want to try taking some of these messages out and observing the results.

Managing the Progress Bar

11

The progress bar shows how far the countdown has advanced. To accurately reflect the progress of the countdown, the range of the bar must be initialized so that its maximum value is equal to the number of seconds in the countdown. The bar's initial position must be set to zero. This is done inside the **IDD_START** case, which is executed when the user presses the Start button, using the code sequence shown here:

```
/* initialize progress bar */
SendMessage(hProgWnd, PBM_SETRANGE, 0,
          MAKELONG(0, udpos));
SendMessage(hProgWnd, PBM_SETPOS, 0, 0);
```

Here, **udpos** contains the number of seconds specified in the spin control.

Each time the timer goes off, the bar is updated by the following statement.

```
/* advance progress bar */
SendMessage(hProgWnd, PBM_STEPIT, 0, 0);
```

This causes the bar to be advanced one step position.

Large Reward, Little Effort

As you have seen, incorporating an up-down control, trackbar, or progress bar into your application requires very little effort. Yet the reward is quite large. If you compare the look and feel of the original countdown program in Chapter 6 with the enhanced version just shown, it is obvious which has the more appealing interface. These are three controls that you will definitely want to use when updating older Windows NT 3.51 applications.

Getting the User's Attention

Sometimes your program may receive a message that requires action on the part of the user. For example, a clock program may notify a user that a certain time has been reached, a file transfer program may notify the user that an error has occurred, or a numeric analysis program may report a floating-point overflow. Whatever the reason, there can be instances in which you want to get the user's attention. To help accomplish this, Windows NT contains a useful function: **FlashWindow( )**. **FlashWindow( )** flashes a window's title bar (or icon if the window is minimized). Its prototype is shown here:

    BOOL FlashWindow(HWND *hwnd*, BOOL *How*);

Here, the handle of the window to be flashed is specified in *hwnd*. If *How* is nonzero, then the window is flashed. If *How* is zero, the window is returned to its original state prior to flashing. Each call to **FlashWindow( )** only flashes the window once, so you will most likely want to call **FlashWindow( )** several times, using a loop. **FlashWindow( )** returns nonzero if the title bar was highlighted prior to the first call and zero if it was not.

To try **FlashWindow( )**, substitute the following code into the countdown program inside the **WM_TIMER** handler. If you have selected Beep at End, then when the timer goes off the window will also flash.

```
/* flash window, and move track bar with each beep */
for(i=trackpos ; i; i--) {
  SendMessage(hTrackWnd, TBM_SETPOS, 1, i);
  MessageBeep(MB_OK);
  FlashWindow(hdwnd, 1);
  Sleep(250);
  FlashWindow(hdwnd, 1);
}
```

You might want to experiment with different delay periods, watching the differences they have on the flashing effect.

CHAPTER 12

Status Windows, Tab Controls, and the Tree-Views

365

Τhis chapter continues our look at the Windows NT common controls. We will examine the status window, the tab control, and the tree-view control.

Using a Status Window

A status
window or bar is
a small
horizontal
window that is
located at the
bottom of its
parent. It is
typically used
to display
status
information.

Frequently an application will need to keep the user apprised of the status of certain program variables, attributes, or parameters. In the past, each program had to define its own way of accomplishing this. However, Windows NT includes a standard control for this purpose, called the *status window* or *status bar*. A status window is a bar that (typically) is displayed along the bottom of a window. It is used to display information related to the program.

As you will see, status bars are easy to implement. If you make a status bar a standard feature of each application you write, then you will be providing status information in a consistent and easily recognizable manner.

Creating a Status Window

To create a status window, you can use **CreateStatusWindow( )**, shown here:

HWND CreateStatusWindow(LONG *WinStyle*, LPCSTR *lpszFirstPart*,
                        HWND *hParent*, UINT *ID*);

Here, *WinStyle* specifies the style of the status bar. It must include **WS_CHILD**. It is also usually created using the **WS_VISIBLE** style, so that it is automatically displayed. A status window can consist of two or more partitions in which text is displayed. A pointer to the string that will be displayed in the first part of the status bar is passed in *lpszFirstPart*. This parameter can be null if this text will be set later. The handle of the parent window is passed in *hParent* and the ID of the status bar is passed in *ID*. The handle to the status bar is returned. **NULL** is returned on failure.

Notice that you don't pass the dimensions or location of the status window when it is created. The reason for this is that it is automatically sized to fit its parent window and positioned along the bottom of the parent window. If you want to display the status bar at the top of the parent window, include the **CCS_TOP** style in the *WinStyle* parameter.

NOTE: You can also create a status bar by using either **CreateWindow( )** or **CreateWindowEx( )** and specifying the window class **STATUSCLASSNAME**. But **CreateStatusWindow( )** is easier.

A status window is generally divided into two or more parts. (However, a single-part status window is perfectly acceptable.) Once the parts have been established, you may write text to each part individually. Each part is referred to by its index. (The first part has an index value of 0.) As just described, you can set the text in the first part when the status bar is created.

Status Window Messages

A status window does not generate messages. However, your program will send the status bar messages using the standard **SendMessage( )** function. Common status window messages are shown in Table 12-1.

12

Message	Meaning
SB_GETPARTS	Obtains the X coordinate of the right edge of the parts in a status bar. The number of parts in the status bar is returned. (Zero is returned on failure.) *wParam* specifies the number of parts to obtain. *lParam* is a pointer to an integer array that will receive the X coordinate of the right edge of each part. The array must be at least as large as the number of parts requested. If an edge is bounded by the border of the window, its X coordinate will be –1.
SB_GETTEXT	Obtains the text from the specified part. The low-order word of the return value contains the number of characters in the text. The high-order word contains a value that describes how the text is displayed. If it is 0, the text appears beneath the level of the window. If it is **SBT_POPOUT**, the text appears above the level of the window. If it is **SBT_NOBORDERS**, the text is displayed without a border. If it is **SBT_RTLREADING**, the text is displayed right to left. *wParam* specifies the index of the desired part. *lParam* points to a character array that will receive the text. (Make sure that this array is large enough to hold the text contained in the part.)

Commonly Used Status Bar Messages

Table 12-1.

Message	Meaning
SB_SETPARTS	Specifies the number of parts in a status bar. It returns nonzero if successful and zero on failure. *wParam* specifies the number of parts. *lParam* is a pointer to an array of integers that contains the X coordinate of the right edge of each part. A value of –1 specifies the right boundary of the parent window.
SB_SETTEXT	Outputs text to a part. It returns nonzero if successful and zero on failure. *wParam* specifies the index of the part that will receive the text ORed to a value that determines how the text will be displayed. If the display value is zero, then the text appears beneath the level of the window. (This is the default.) If the display value is **SBT_POPOUT**, the text appears above the level of the window. If it is **SBT_NOBORDERS**, the text is displayed without a border. If the display value is **SBT_OWNERDRAW** the parent window displays the text. If it is **SBT_RTLREADING**, the text is displayed right to left. *lParam* is a pointer to the string to be displayed.

Commonly
Used Status
Bar Messages
(continued)
Table 12-1.

Almost all applications will send **SB_SETPARTS**, which sets the number of parts to the status bar, and **SB_SETTEXT**, which writes text to a part. The general procedure when creating a status bar is shown here:

1. Create the status window.
2. Set the number of parts by sending an **SB_SETPARTS** message.
3. Set the text in each part by sending an **SB_SETTEXT** message.

Once a status bar has been initialized, you can update each part as needed by sending an **SB_SETTEXT** message.

Using a Status Bar

The following program uses a status bar to report the settings within a dialog box. The dialog box contains a spin control, three check boxes, and two radio buttons. The status bar shows the current setting of each control. Sample output from the program is shown in Figure 12-1.

```
/* Demonstrate a status bar. */

#include <windows.h>
```

```
#include <commctrl.h>
#include <stdio.h>
#include "status.h"

#define NUMPARTS 5

LRESULT CALLBACK WindowFunc(HWND, UINT, WPARAM, LPARAM);
BOOL CALLBACK DialogFunc(HWND, UINT, WPARAM, LPARAM);
void InitStatus(HWND hwnd);

char szWinName[] = "MyWin"; /* name of window class */

HINSTANCE hInst;
HWND hwnd;
HWND hStatusWnd;

int parts[NUMPARTS];

int WINAPI WinMain(HINSTANCE hThisInst, HINSTANCE hPrevInst,
                   LPSTR lpszArgs, int nWinMode)
{
  MSG msg;
  WNDCLASSEX wcl;
  HANDLE hAccel;

  /* Define a window class. */
  wcl.cbSize = sizeof(WNDCLASSEX);

  /* Define a window class. */
  wcl.hInstance = hThisInst; /* handle to this instance */
  wcl.lpszClassName = szWinName; /* window class name */
  wcl.lpfnWndProc = WindowFunc; /* window function */
  wcl.style = 0; /* default style */

  wcl.hIcon = LoadIcon(NULL, IDI_APPLICATION);
  wcl.hIconSm = LoadIcon(NULL, IDI_APPLICATION);

  wcl.hCursor = LoadCursor(NULL, IDC_ARROW);

  /* specify name of menu resource */
  wcl.lpszMenuName = "StatusMenu"; /* main menu */

  wcl.cbClsExtra = 0; /* no extra */
  wcl.cbWndExtra = 0; /* information needed */

  /* Make the window white. */
  wcl.hbrBackground = GetStockObject(WHITE_BRUSH);
```

```
/* Register the window class. */
if(!RegisterClassEx(&wcl)) return 0;

/* Now that a window class has been registered, a window
   can be created. */
hwnd = CreateWindow(
  szWinName, /* name of window class */
  "Using a Status Bar", /* title */
  WS_OVERLAPPEDWINDOW, /* window style - normal */
  CW_USEDEFAULT, /* X coordinate - let Windows decide */
  CW_USEDEFAULT, /* Y coordinate - let Windows decide */
  CW_USEDEFAULT, /* width - let Windows decide */
  CW_USEDEFAULT, /* height - let Windows decide */
  HWND_DESKTOP, /* no parent window */
  NULL, /* no override of class menu */
  hThisInst, /* handle of this instance of the program */
  NULL /* no additional arguments */
);

InitCommonControls();

hInst = hThisInst; /* save the current instance handle */

/* load accelerators */
hAccel = LoadAccelerators(hThisInst, "StatusMenu");

/* Display the window. */
ShowWindow(hwnd, nWinMode);
UpdateWindow(hwnd);

/* Create the message loop. */
while(GetMessage(&msg, NULL, 0, 0))
{
  if(!TranslateAccelerator(hwnd, hAccel, &msg)) {
    TranslateMessage(&msg); /* translate keyboard messages */
    DispatchMessage(&msg); /* return control to Windows NT */
  }
}
return msg.wParam;
}

/* This function is called by Windows NT and is passed
   messages from the message queue.
*/
LRESULT CALLBACK WindowFunc(HWND hwnd, UINT message,
                            WPARAM wParam, LPARAM lParam)
{
  int response;
```

```
switch(message) {
  case WM_COMMAND:
    switch(LOWORD(wParam)) {
      case IDM_DIALOG:
        DialogBox(hInst, "StatusDB", hwnd, (DLGPROC) DialogFunc);
        break;
      case IDM_EXIT:
        response = MessageBox(hwnd, "Quit the Program?",
                                   "Exit", MB_YESNO);
        if(response == IDYES) PostQuitMessage(0);
        break;
      case IDM_HELP:
        MessageBox(hwnd, "Try the Dialog Box",
                   "Help", MB_OK);
        break;
    }
    break;
  case WM_DESTROY: /* terminate the program */
    PostQuitMessage(0);
    break;
  default:
    /* Let Windows NT process any messages not specified in
       the preceding switch statement. */
    return DefWindowProc(hwnd, message, wParam, lParam);
  }
  return 0;
}

/* Status bar demo dialog function. */
BOOL CALLBACK DialogFunc(HWND hdwnd, UINT message,
                         WPARAM wParam, LPARAM lParam)
{
  static long udpos = 0;
  static char str[80];
  static HWND hEboxWnd;
  static HWND udWnd;
  static statusCB1, statusCB2;
  static statusRB1;
  int low=0, high=10;

  switch(message) {
    case WM_INITDIALOG:
      InitStatus(hdwnd); /* initialize the status bar */

      hEboxWnd = GetDlgItem(hdwnd, ID_EB1);
      udWnd = CreateUpDownControl(
```

```
                           WS_CHILD | WS_BORDER | WS_VISIBLE |
                           UDS_SETBUDDYINT | UDS_ALIGNRIGHT,
                           10, 10, 50, 50,
                           hdwnd,
                           ID_UPDOWN,
                           hInst,
                           hEboxWnd,
                           high, low, high/2);

    /* Initialize radio buttons */
    SendDlgItemMessage(hdwnd, ID_RB2, BM_SETCHECK,
                       BST_CHECKED, 0);
    return 1;
  case WM_VSCROLL: /* process up-down control */
    if(udWnd==(HWND)lParam) {
      udpos = GetDlgItemInt(hdwnd, ID_EB1, NULL, 1);
      sprintf(str, "Power: %d", udpos);
      SendMessage(hStatusWnd, SB_SETTEXT,
                  (WPARAM) 0, (LPARAM) str);
    }
    return 1;
  case WM_COMMAND:
    switch(LOWORD(wParam)) {
      case ID_CB1: /* process Optimize checkbox */
        statusCB1 = SendDlgItemMessage(hdwnd, ID_CB1,
                    BM_GETCHECK, 0, 0);
        if(statusCB1) sprintf(str, "Optimize: Yes");
        else sprintf(str, "Optimize: No");
        SendMessage(hStatusWnd, SB_SETTEXT,
                    (WPARAM) 1, (LPARAM) str);
        return 1;
      case ID_CB2: /* process Debug checkbox */
        statusCB2 = SendDlgItemMessage(hdwnd, ID_CB2,
                    BM_GETCHECK, 0, 0);
        if(statusCB2) sprintf(str, "Debug: Yes");
        else sprintf(str, "Debug: No");
        SendMessage(hStatusWnd, SB_SETTEXT,
                    (WPARAM) 2, (LPARAM) str);
        return 1;
      case ID_CB3: /* process Win16 checkbox */
        statusCB2 = SendDlgItemMessage(hdwnd, ID_CB3,
                    BM_GETCHECK, 0, 0);
        if(statusCB2) sprintf(str, "Win16: Yes");
        else sprintf(str, "Win16: No");
        SendMessage(hStatusWnd, SB_SETTEXT,
                    (WPARAM) 3, (LPARAM) str);
        return 1;
```

```
        case ID_RB1: /* process radio buttons */
        case ID_RB2:
          statusRB1 = SendDlgItemMessage(hdwnd, ID_RB1,
                    BM_GETCHECK, 0, 0);
          if(statusRB1) sprintf(str, "Using C");
          else sprintf(str, "Using C++");
          SendMessage(hStatusWnd, SB_SETTEXT,
                    (WPARAM) 4, (LPARAM) str);
          return 1;
        case ID_RESET: /* reset options */
          SendMessage(udWnd, UDM_SETPOS, 0, (LPARAM) high /2);
          SendMessage(hStatusWnd, SB_SETTEXT, (WPARAM) 0,
              (LPARAM) "Power: 5");
          SendDlgItemMessage(hdwnd, ID_CB1,
                    BM_SETCHECK, 0, 0);
          SendDlgItemMessage(hdwnd, ID_CB2,
                    BM_SETCHECK, 0, 0);
          SendDlgItemMessage(hdwnd, ID_CB3,
                    BM_SETCHECK, 0, 0);
          SendMessage(hStatusWnd, SB_SETTEXT, (WPARAM) 1,
              (LPARAM) "Optimize: No");
          SendMessage(hStatusWnd, SB_SETTEXT, (WPARAM) 2,
              (LPARAM) "Debug: No");
          SendMessage(hStatusWnd, SB_SETTEXT, (WPARAM) 3,
              (LPARAM) "Win16: No");
          SendMessage(hStatusWnd, SB_SETTEXT, (WPARAM) 4,
              (LPARAM) "Using C++");
          return 1;
        case IDCANCEL:
        case IDOK:
          EndDialog(hdwnd, 0);
          return 1;
      }
  }
  return 0;
}

/* Initialize the status bar. */
void InitStatus(HWND hwnd)
{
  RECT WinDim;
  int i;

  GetClientRect(hwnd, &WinDim);

  for(i=1; i<=NUMPARTS; i++)
    parts[i-1] = WinDim.right/NUMPARTS * i;
```

```
/* Create a status bar */
hStatusWnd = CreateStatusWindow(
            WS_CHILD | WS_VISIBLE,
            "Power: 5", hwnd,
            ID_STATUSWIN);

SendMessage(hStatusWnd, SB_SETPARTS,
            (WPARAM) NUMPARTS, (LPARAM) parts);

SendMessage(hStatusWnd, SB_SETTEXT, (WPARAM) 1,
            (LPARAM) "Optimize: No");
SendMessage(hStatusWnd, SB_SETTEXT, (WPARAM) 2,
            (LPARAM) "Debug: No");
SendMessage(hStatusWnd, SB_SETTEXT, (WPARAM) 3,
            (LPARAM) "Win16: No");
SendMessage(hStatusWnd, SB_SETTEXT, (WPARAM) 4,
            (LPARAM) "Using C++");
}
```

The status bar program requires the following resource file:

```
#include <windows.h>
#include "status.h"

StatusMenu MENU
{
  POPUP "&Options" {
    MENUITEM "&Dialog\tF2", IDM_DIALOG
    MENUITEM "E&xit\tF10", IDM_EXIT
  }
  MENUITEM "&Help", IDM_HELP
}


StatusMenu ACCELERATORS
{
  VK_F2, IDM_DIALOG, VIRTKEY
  VK_F10, IDM_EXIT, VIRTKEY
  VK_F1, IDM_HELP, VIRTKEY
}

StatusDB DIALOG 18, 18, 180, 92
CAPTION "Demonstrate a Status Bar"
STYLE DS_MODALFRAME | WS_POPUP | WS_CAPTION | WS_SYSMENU
{
  PUSHBUTTON "Reset", ID_RESET, 112, 40, 37, 14,
            WS_CHILD | WS_VISIBLE | WS_TABSTOP
  PUSHBUTTON "OK", IDOK, 112, 60, 37, 14,
            WS_CHILD | WS_VISIBLE | WS_TABSTOP
```

```
EDITTEXT ID_EB1, 10, 10, 20, 12, ES_LEFT | WS_CHILD |
        WS_VISIBLE | WS_BORDER
LTEXT "Power Factor", ID_STEXT1, 36, 12, 50, 12
AUTOCHECKBOX "Optimize", ID_CB1, 10, 35, 48, 12
AUTOCHECKBOX "Debug Info", ID_CB2, 10, 50, 48, 12
AUTOCHECKBOX "Win16 Compatible", ID_CB3, 10, 65, 70, 12
AUTORADIOBUTTON "C", ID_RB1, 112, 8, 20, 12
AUTORADIOBUTTON "C++", ID_RB2, 112, 20, 28, 12
LTEXT "Language", ID_STEXT2, 140, 14, 40, 12
}
```

The header file STATUS.H is shown here:

```
#define IDM_DIALOG    100
#define IDM_EXIT      101
#define IDM_HELP      102
#define ID_UPDOWN     103
#define ID_EB1        104
#define ID_EB2        105
#define ID_CB1        106
#define ID_CB2        107
#define ID_CB3        108
#define ID_RB1        109
#define ID_RB2        110
#define ID_RESET      111

#define ID_STATUSWIN 200

#define ID_STEXT1     300
#define ID_STEXT2     301
```

12

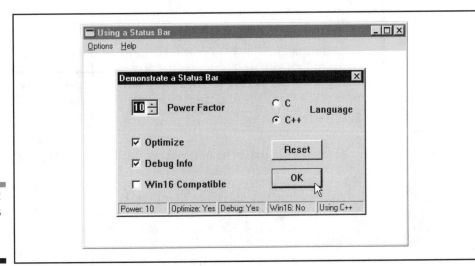

Sample output
from the status
bar program
Figure 12-1.

In the program, the function **InitStatus( )** creates and initializes the status window. First, the dimensions of the dialog box are obtained using **GetClientRect( )**. The width of the window is divided by **NUMPARTS** (which is defined as 5) to determine the right endpoints for the status bar parts and these values are put into the **parts** array. Remember, the end point of each part—not the width of each part—must be passed to the status window. Next, the status window is created. Then, its partitions are set. Finally, the initial text to each part is set. (The text for the first part is passed in **CreateStatusWindow( )**.)

Within **DialogFunc( )**, the text within the status bar is updated each time a control is changed. This is accomplished by sending an **SB_SETTEXT** message to the part of the bar associated with the control that has changed its state. One last point: the text written to a status bar part will be automatically truncated to fit within that part. Text will not spill over into the next part.

IN DEPTH

Resizing a Status Bar

Although a status bar will initially size itself to fit its parent window, it will not automatically change its size when the parent window does. Recall that a window receives a **WM_SIZE** message after its size has been changed. To allow a child status window to be resized with its parent, you must pass the **WM_SIZE** message received by the parent window to the status window using the **SendMessage( )** function. (This process is similar to that used to resize a toolbar, as described in Chapter 10.)

For example, to allow the status window in the preceding example to be automatically resized when the size of its parent dialog box is changed, add this case to **DialogFunc( )**. It passes along the **WM_SIZE** message and then resets the dimensions of the status bar partitions.

```
case WM_SIZE:
  SendMessage(hStatusWnd, WM_SIZE, wParam, lParam);
  GetClientRect(hdwnd, &WinDim);
  for(i=1; i<=NUMPARTS; i++)
    parts[i-1] = WinDim.right/NUMPARTS * i;
  SendMessage(hStatusWnd, SB_SETPARTS,
              (WPARAM) NUMPARTS, (LPARAM) parts);
  return 1;
```

You must also add

```
RECT WinDim;
int i;
```

to **DialogFunc( )**. Finally, in order for the dialog box to be capable of being resized, it must be created with the **WS_SIZEBOX** style also included.

Once you have made these modifications, execute the status bar program and then try resizing the status dialog box. As you will see, the status bar is automatically resized, too. For example, here is the dialog box after it has been lengthened.

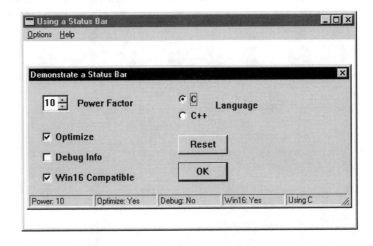

Introducing Tab Controls

A tab control creates a window that looks like a set of file folders.

One of the more visually interesting common controls is the tab control. A tab control emulates the tabs on a set of file folders. Each time a tab is selected, its associated folder comes to the surface. While tab controls are easy to use, programming for them is a bit complicated. In this section, tab control basics are introduced. In the next section, additional tab control features are discussed.

Creating a Tab Control

To create a tab control, you use either **CreateWindow( )** or **CreateWindowEx( )**, specifying the window class **WC_TABCONTROL**. Typically, a tab control will be child window. It is also usually created using the **WS_VISIBLE** style, so that it is automatically displayed. For example, the following creates a tab control:

```
hTabWnd = CreateWindow(
            WC_TABCONTROL,
            "",
            WS_VISIBLE | WS_TABSTOP | WS_CHILD,
            0, 0, 100, 100,
            hwnd, /* handle of parent */
            NULL,
            hInst, /* instance handle */
            NULL
        );
```

Once created, a tab control can be sent messages by your application or generate messages when it is accessed.

After a tab control has been created, it is empty. Before it can be used, you must insert tabs into it. Each tab is defined by a **TC_ITEM** structure, which is shown here:

```
typedef struct _TC_ITEM
{
  UINT mask;
  UINT lpReserved1;
  UINT lpReserved2;
  LPSTR pszText;
  int cchTextMax;
  int iImage;
  LPARAM lParam;
} TC_ITEM;
```

In this structure, the value contained in **mask** determines whether the **pszText**, **iImage**, or **lParam** members of the structure contain valid data. **mask** can contain one or more of the following values:

Value in Mask	Meaning
TCIF_ALL	**pszText**, **iImage**, and **lParam** contain data.
TCIF_IMAGE	**iImage** contains data.
TCIF_PARAM	**lParam** contains data.
TCIF_TEXT	**pszText** contains data.

mask may also contain the value **TCIF_RTLREADING**, which means that the text should be displayed right to left.

When a tab is being set, **pszText** points to the string that will be displayed within the tab. When information about a tab is being obtained, **pszText** must point to an array that will receive the text. In this case, the value of **cchTextMax** specifies the size of the array pointed to by **pszText**.

If there is an image list associated with the tab control, then **iImage** will contain the index of the image for the specified tab. If there is no image list associated with the tab control, **iImage** should be –1. We won't be using images in the tab control examples shown in this chapter, but you might find them useful for your applications.

lParam contains application-defined data.

Sending Tab Control Messages

You can send a tab control several different types of messages using the **SendMessage( )** function. Several commonly used tab control messages are shown in Table 12-2. As an alternative to using **SendMessage( )**, special macros were created that simplify the process of sending messages to tab controls. The tab control macros corresponding to the messages in Table 12-2 are shown here. In all cases, *hTabWnd* is the handle of the tab control.

VOID TabCtrl_AdjustRect(HWND *hTabWnd*, BOOL *operation*,
                    RECT **lpRect*);

BOOL TabCtrl_DeleteAllItems(HWND *hTabWnd*);

BOOL TabCtrl_DeleteItem(HWND *hTabWnd*, int *index*);

int TabCtrl_GetCurSel(HWND *hTabWnd*);

BOOL TabCtrl_GetItem(HWND *hTabWnd*, int *index*, TC_ITEM **lpitem*);

int TabCtrl_GetItemCount(HWND *hTabWnd*);

int TabCtrl_InsertItem(HWND *hTabWnd*, int *index*,
                 CONST TC_ITEM **lpitem*);

int TabCtrl_SetCurSel(HWND *hTabWnd*, int *index*);

BOOL TabCtrl_SetItem(HWND *hTabWnd*, int *index*, TC_ITEM **lpitem*);

In general, the macros are easier to use than the equivalent calls to **SendMessage( )**.

When a tab control is created, it has no tabs. Therefore, your program will always send at least one **TCM_INSERTITEM** message to it. Although neither of the examples in this chapter requires its use, one message that

Message	Meaning
TCM_ADJUSTRECT	Translates between the dimensions of the tab control's display area and its window. *wParam* specifies the operation. If it is nonzero, then given the dimensions of a tab control's display area, the dimensions of the window rectangle are obtained. If it is zero, then given the dimensions of the window rectangle, the display area of the tab control is obtained. *lParam* points to a **RECT** structure that contains the coordinates of the region to be translated (that is, either the window or the tab control's display area). On return, this structure will contain the translated coordinates.
TCM_DELETEALLITEMS	Deletes all tabs in the control. Returns nonzero if successful and zero on failure. *wParam* is 0. *lParam* is 0.
TCM_DELETEITEM	Deletes a specified tab. Returns nonzero if successful and zero on failure. *wParam* specifies the index of the tab to remove. *lParam* is 0.
TCM_GETCURSEL	Returns the index of the currently selected tab or –1 if no tab is selected. *wParam* is 0. *lParam* is 0.
TCM_GETITEM	Obtains information about the specified tab. Returns nonzero if successful and zero on failure. *wParam* specifies the index of the tab. *lParam* is a pointer to a **TC_ITEM** structure that receives the information about the item.
TCM_GETITEMCOUNT	Returns the number of tabs. *wParam* is 0. *lParam* is 0.
TCM_INSERTITEM	Creates (i.e., inserts) a new tab. Returns the index of the item being inserted or –1 on failure. *wParam* specifies the index of the tab. *lParam* is a pointer to a **TC_ITEM** structure that describes the tab.
TCM_SETCURSEL	Selects a tab. Returns the index of the previously selected tab or –1 if no tab was previously selected. *wParam* specifies the index of the tab being selected. *lParam* is 0.
TCM_SETITEM	Sets information about the specified tab. Returns nonzero if successful and zero on failure. *wParam* specifies the index of the tab. *lParam* is a pointer to a **TC_ITEM** structure that contains the information about the item.

Commonly
Used Tab
Control
Messages
Table 12-2.

your real-world applications will probably employ is **TCM_ADJUSTRECT**. This message is used to obtain the dimensions of the display area of a tab control. Remember, when you create a tab control, its window contains the tabs themselves, as well as the area in which you will display information or pop up a dialog box. The display area is the part of a tab control window that excludes the tabs. (That is, the display area is the part of the tab control window that you may use to display other items.) Since it is the display area that will contain the information associated with the tab, you will often need to know its dimensions.

Tab Notification Messages

When a tab control is accessed by the user a **WM_NOTIFY** message is generated. Tab controls can generate two selection-change notification codes: **TCN_SELCHANGE** and **TCN_SELCHANGING**. **TCN_SELCHANGING** is sent when a tab selection is about to change. **TCN_SELCHANGE** is sent after a new tab is selected.

When a **WM_NOTIFY** message is received, *lParam* will point to a **NMHDR** structure (discussed in Chapter 10). The notification code will be contained in the **code** field of the **NMHDR** structure. The handle of the tab control that generates the message is found in the **hwndFrom** field.

A Simple Tab Demonstration Program

The following short program demonstrates the tab control. It creates a tab control that has three tabs labeled Options, View, and Errors. Each time a new tab is selected, a message is displayed reporting this fact. Sample output is shown in Figure 12-2.

```
/* A simple tab control demonstration. */

#include <windows.h>
#include <commctrl.h>
#include <stdio.h>

LRESULT CALLBACK WindowFunc(HWND, UINT, WPARAM, LPARAM);

char szWinName[] = "MyWin"; /* name of window class */

HINSTANCE hInst;
HWND hwnd;
HWND hTabWnd;

char TabName[][40] = {
  "Options",
```

```
    "View",
    "Errors"
};

int WINAPI WinMain(HINSTANCE hThisInst, HINSTANCE hPrevInst,
                   LPSTR lpszArgs, int nWinMode)
{
  MSG msg;
  WNDCLASSEX wcl;

  /* Define a window class. */
  wcl.cbSize = sizeof(WNDCLASSEX);

  /* Define a window class. */
  wcl.hInstance = hThisInst; /* handle to this instance */
  wcl.lpszClassName = szWinName; /* window class name */
  wcl.lpfnWndProc = WindowFunc; /* window function */
  wcl.style = 0; /* default style */

  wcl.hIcon = LoadIcon(NULL, IDI_APPLICATION);
  wcl.hIconSm = LoadIcon(NULL, IDI_APPLICATION);

  wcl.hCursor = LoadCursor(NULL, IDC_ARROW);

  wcl.lpszMenuName = NULL; /* no menu */

  wcl.cbClsExtra = 0; /* no extra */
  wcl.cbWndExtra = 0; /* information needed */

  /* Make the window white. */
  wcl.hbrBackground = GetStockObject(WHITE_BRUSH);

  /* Register the window class. */
  if(!RegisterClassEx(&wcl)) return 0;

  /* Now that a window class has been registered, a window
     can be created. */
  hwnd = CreateWindow(
    szWinName, /* name of window class */
    "Using a Tab Control", /* title */
    WS_OVERLAPPEDWINDOW, /* window style - normal */
    CW_USEDEFAULT, /* X coordinate - let Windows decide */
    CW_USEDEFAULT, /* Y coordinate - let Windows decide */
    CW_USEDEFAULT, /* width - let Windows decide */
    CW_USEDEFAULT, /* height - let Windows decide */
    HWND_DESKTOP, /* no parent window */
    NULL, /* no override of class menu */
    hThisInst, /* handle of this instance of the program */
```

```
      NULL /* no additional arguments */
   );

   InitCommonControls();

   hInst = hThisInst; /* save the current instance handle */

   /* Display the window. */
   ShowWindow(hwnd, nWinMode);
   UpdateWindow(hwnd);

   /* Create the message loop. */
   while(GetMessage(&msg, NULL, 0, 0))
   {
     TranslateMessage(&msg); /* translate keyboard messages */
     DispatchMessage(&msg); /* return control to Windows NT */
   }
   return msg.wParam;
}

/* This function is called by Windows NT and is passed
   messages from the message queue.
*/
LRESULT CALLBACK WindowFunc(HWND hwnd, UINT message,
                            WPARAM wParam, LPARAM lParam)
{
  NMHDR *nmptr;
  int tabnumber;
  HDC hdc;
  char str[80];
  RECT WinDim;
  TC_ITEM tci;

  switch(message) {
    case WM_CREATE:
      GetClientRect(hwnd, &WinDim);  /* get size of parent window */

      /* create a tab control */
      hTabWnd = CreateWindow(
                  WC_TABCONTROL,
                  "",
                  WS_VISIBLE | WS_TABSTOP | WS_CHILD,
                  0, 0, WinDim.right, WinDim.bottom,
                  hwnd,
                  NULL,
                  hInst,
                  NULL
```

```
                    );

        tci.mask = TCIF_TEXT;
        tci.iImage = -1;

        tci.pszText = TabName[0];
        TabCtrl_InsertItem(hTabWnd, 0, &tci);

        tci.pszText = TabName[1];
        TabCtrl_InsertItem(hTabWnd, 1, &tci);

        tci.pszText = TabName[2];
        TabCtrl_InsertItem(hTabWnd, 2, &tci);
        break;
      case WM_NOTIFY: /* process a tab change */
        nmptr = (LPNMHDR) lParam;
        if(nmptr->code == TCN_SELCHANGE) {
          tabnumber = TabCtrl_GetCurSel((HWND)nmptr->hwndFrom);
          hdc = GetDC(hTabWnd);
          sprintf(str, "Changed to %s Tab.      ",
                  TabName[tabnumber]);
          SetBkColor(hdc, RGB(200, 200, 200));
          TextOut(hdc, 40, 100, str, strlen(str));
          ReleaseDC(hTabWnd, hdc);
        }
        break;
      case WM_DESTROY: /* terminate the program */
        PostQuitMessage(0);
        break;
      default:
        /* Let Windows NT process any messages not specified in
           the preceding switch statement. */
        return DefWindowProc(hwnd, message, wParam, lParam);
    }
    return 0;
}
```

In the program, just before the tab control is created, a call is made to
GetClientRect( ) to obtain the size of the main window. When the tab
control is created, it is sized to fill the entire client area of its parent window.
While this is arbitrary, it is not uncommon. After the tab control has been
constructed, its three tabs are created.

Inside **WindowFunc( )**, each time a **WM_NOTIFY** message contains the
TCN_SELCHANGE code, a message is displayed within the tab control
display area, indicating that the selection has changed to the specified tab.
The index of the newly selected tab is obtained by sending a
TCM_GETCURSEL message.

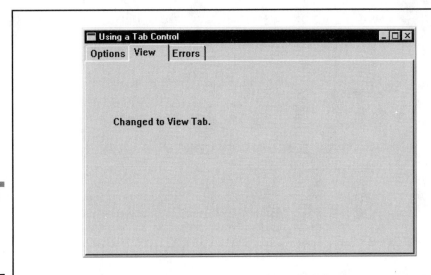

Sample output
from the first
tab control
program
Figure 12-2.

Using Tab Controls

While tab controls are quite easy to create, they are a bit tricky to use. The reason for this is that each tab will typically have associated with it a dialog box. Each time a new tab is selected, the currently displayed dialog box must be removed and the new dialog box displayed. Also, in general, you will want to fit each dialog box to the display area of the tab control. Frankly, there are many other subtle issues associated with tab controls and their associated dialog boxes that are simply beyond the scope of this book. However, in this section you will learn the general method of applying a tab control to your application. Once you understand the basics, you will be able to add other features to your tab controls on your own.

*Tab control
dialog boxes
must be
modeless.*

Since a new tab may be selected at any time, this implies that modeless (rather than modal) dialog boxes must be used. As you should recall, a modeless dialog box allows other parts of your application to be activated without deactivating the dialog box. (This differs from modal dialog boxes, which must be closed by the user before other parts of the program can be used.) Typically, when a new tab is selected, your application will close the currently displayed dialog box and then activate the next one. Because a dialog box may be closed at any time, your program must take appropriate action (such as saving its settings) before displaying the new box.

To demonstrate a tab control, the following program creates one that adds dialog boxes to the three tabs created by the preceding example. Each tab is associated with its own modeless dialog box. The first dialog box is the one created for the status bar example earlier in this chapter. The other two are simply placeholders used for the sake of illustration. Sample output from this program is shown in Figure 12-3.

```c
/* Demonstrate a tab control. */

#include <windows.h>
#include <commctrl.h>
#include <stdio.h>
#include "tab.h"

#define NUMPARTS 5

LRESULT CALLBACK WindowFunc(HWND, UINT, WPARAM, LPARAM);
BOOL CALLBACK DialogFunc1(HWND, UINT, WPARAM, LPARAM);
BOOL CALLBACK DialogFunc2(HWND, UINT, WPARAM, LPARAM);
BOOL CALLBACK DialogFunc3(HWND, UINT, WPARAM, LPARAM);
void InitStatus(HWND hwnd);

char szWinName[] = "MyWin"; /* name of window class */

HINSTANCE hInst;
HWND hwnd;
HWND hStatusWnd;
HWND hTabWnd;

int parts[NUMPARTS];

HWND hDlg = (HWND) NULL;

char TabName[][40] = {
  "Options",
  "View",
  "Errors"
};

int WINAPI WinMain(HINSTANCE hThisInst, HINSTANCE hPrevInst,
                   LPSTR lpszArgs, int nWinMode)
{
  MSG msg;
  WNDCLASSEX wcl;

  /* Define a window class. */
  wcl.cbSize = sizeof(WNDCLASSEX);

  /* Define a window class. */
  wcl.hInstance = hThisInst; /* handle to this instance */
  wcl.lpszClassName = szWinName; /* window class name */
  wcl.lpfnWndProc = WindowFunc; /* window function */
```

```
wcl.style = 0; /* default style */

wcl.hIcon = LoadIcon(NULL, IDI_APPLICATION);
wcl.hIconSm = LoadIcon(NULL, IDI_APPLICATION);

wcl.hCursor = LoadCursor(NULL, IDC_ARROW);

wcl.lpszMenuName = NULL; /* no menu */

wcl.cbClsExtra = 0; /* no extra */
wcl.cbWndExtra = 0; /* information needed */

/* Make the window white. */
wcl.hbrBackground = GetStockObject(WHITE_BRUSH);

/* Register the window class. */
if(!RegisterClassEx(&wcl)) return 0;

/* Now that a window class has been registered, a window
   can be created. */
hwnd = CreateWindow(
  szWinName, /* name of window class */
  "Using a Tab Control", /* title */
  WS_OVERLAPPEDWINDOW, /* window style - normal */
  CW_USEDEFAULT, /* X coordinate - let Windows decide */
  CW_USEDEFAULT, /* Y coordinate - let Windows decide */
  CW_USEDEFAULT, /* width - let Windows decide */
  CW_USEDEFAULT, /* height - let Windows decide */
  HWND_DESKTOP, /* no parent window */
  NULL, /* no override of class menu */
  hThisInst, /* handle of this instance of the program */
  NULL /* no additional arguments */
);

InitCommonControls();

hInst = hThisInst; /* save the current instance handle */

/* Display the window. */
ShowWindow(hwnd, nWinMode);
UpdateWindow(hwnd);

/* Create the message loop. */
while(GetMessage(&msg, NULL, 0, 0))
{
  if(!IsDialogMessage(hDlg, &msg)) {
    TranslateMessage(&msg); /* translate keyboard messages */
    DispatchMessage(&msg); /* return control to Windows NT */
```

```
      }
    }
  return msg.wParam;
}

/* This function is called by Windows NT and is passed
   messages from the message queue.
*/
LRESULT CALLBACK WindowFunc(HWND hwnd, UINT message,
                               WPARAM wParam, LPARAM lParam)
{
  NMHDR *nmptr;
  int tabnumber = 0;
  TC_ITEM tci;

  switch(message) {
    case WM_CREATE:
      hTabWnd = CreateWindow(
                  WC_TABCONTROL,
                  "",
                  WS_VISIBLE | WS_TABSTOP | WS_CHILD,
                  20, 20, 368, 220,
                  hwnd,
                  NULL,
                  hInst,
                  NULL
                );

      tci.mask = TCIF_TEXT;
      tci.iImage = -1;

      tci.pszText = TabName[0];
      TabCtrl_InsertItem(hTabWnd, 0, &tci);

      tci.pszText = TabName[1];
      TabCtrl_InsertItem(hTabWnd, 1, &tci);

      tci.pszText = TabName[2];
      TabCtrl_InsertItem(hTabWnd, 2, &tci);

      hDlg = CreateDialog(hInst, "TabDB1", hTabWnd,
                          (DLGPROC) DialogFunc1);
      break;
    case WM_NOTIFY:
      nmptr = (LPNMHDR) lParam;
      if(nmptr->code == TCN_SELCHANGE) {
        if(hDlg) DestroyWindow(hDlg);
        tabnumber = TabCtrl_GetCurSel((HWND)nmptr->hwndFrom);
```

```
                   switch(tabnumber) {
                     case 0:
                       hDlg = CreateDialog(hInst, "TabDB1",
                                   hTabWnd, (DLGPROC) DialogFunc1);
                       break;
                     case 1:
                       hDlg = CreateDialog(hInst, "TabDB2",
                                   hTabWnd, (DLGPROC) DialogFunc2);
                       break;
                     case 2:
                       hDlg = CreateDialog(hInst, "TabDB3",
                                   hTabWnd, (DLGPROC) DialogFunc3);
                       break;
                   }
                 }
                 break;
             case WM_DESTROY: /* terminate the program */
               if(hDlg) DestroyWindow(hDlg);
               PostQuitMessage(0);
               break;
             default:
               /* Let Windows NT process any messages not specified in
                  the preceding switch statement. */
               return DefWindowProc(hwnd, message, wParam, lParam);
         }
         return 0;
}


/* Options dialog function. */
BOOL CALLBACK DialogFunc1(HWND hdwnd, UINT message,
                          WPARAM wParam, LPARAM lParam)
{
  static long udpos = 0;
  static char str[80];
  static HWND hEboxWnd;
  static HWND udWnd;
  static statusCB1, statusCB2;
  static statusRB1;
  int low=0, high=10;

  switch(message) {
    case WM_INITDIALOG:
      InitStatus(hdwnd); /* initialize the status bar */

      hEboxWnd = GetDlgItem(hdwnd, ID_EB1);
      udWnd = CreateUpDownControl(
```

```
                        WS_CHILD | WS_BORDER | WS_VISIBLE |
                        UDS_SETBUDDYINT | UDS_ALIGNRIGHT,
                        10, 10, 50, 50,
                        hdwnd,
                        ID_UPDOWN,
                        hInst,
                        hEboxWnd,
                        high, low, high/2);

      /* Initialize radio buttons */
      SendDlgItemMessage(hdwnd, ID_RB2, BM_SETCHECK,
                        BST_CHECKED, 0);
      return 1;
    case WM_VSCROLL: /* process up-down control */
      if(udWnd==(HWND)lParam) {
        udpos = GetDlgItemInt(hdwnd, ID_EB1, NULL, 1);
        sprintf(str, "Power: %d", udpos);
        SendMessage(hStatusWnd, SB_SETTEXT,
                    (WPARAM) 0, (LPARAM) str);
      }
      return 1;
    case WM_COMMAND:
      switch(LOWORD(wParam)) {
        case ID_CB1: /* process Optimize checkbox */
          statusCB1 = SendDlgItemMessage(hdwnd, ID_CB1,
                        BM_GETCHECK, 0, 0);
          if(statusCB1) sprintf(str, "Optimize: Yes");
          else sprintf(str, "Optimize: No");
          SendMessage(hStatusWnd, SB_SETTEXT,
                    (WPARAM) 1, (LPARAM) str);
          return 1;
        case ID_CB2: /* process Debug checkbox */
          statusCB2 = SendDlgItemMessage(hdwnd, ID_CB2,
                        BM_GETCHECK, 0, 0);
          if(statusCB2) sprintf(str, "Debug: Yes");
          else sprintf(str, "Debug: No");
          SendMessage(hStatusWnd, SB_SETTEXT,
                    (WPARAM) 2, (LPARAM) str);
          return 1;
        case ID_CB3: /* process Win16 checkbox */
          statusCB2 = SendDlgItemMessage(hdwnd, ID_CB3,
                        BM_GETCHECK, 0, 0);
          if(statusCB2) sprintf(str, "Win16: Yes");
          else sprintf(str, "Win16: No");
          SendMessage(hStatusWnd, SB_SETTEXT,
                    (WPARAM) 3, (LPARAM) str);
          return 1;
        case ID_RB1: /* process radio buttons */
```

```
          case ID_RB2:
            statusRB1 = SendDlgItemMessage(hdwnd, ID_RB1,
                      BM_GETCHECK, 0, 0);
            if(statusRB1) sprintf(str, "Using C");
            else sprintf(str, "Using C++");
            SendMessage(hStatusWnd, SB_SETTEXT,
                      (WPARAM) 4, (LPARAM) str);
            return 1;
          case ID_RESET: /* reset options */
            SendMessage(udWnd, UDM_SETPOS, 0, (LPARAM) high /2);
            SendMessage(hStatusWnd, SB_SETTEXT, (WPARAM) 0,
                  (LPARAM) "Power: 5");
            SendDlgItemMessage(hdwnd, ID_CB1,
                      BM_SETCHECK, 0, 0);
            SendDlgItemMessage(hdwnd, ID_CB2,
                      BM_SETCHECK, 0, 0);
            SendDlgItemMessage(hdwnd, ID_CB3,
                      BM_SETCHECK, 0, 0);
            SendMessage(hStatusWnd, SB_SETTEXT, (WPARAM) 1,
                  (LPARAM) "Optimize: No");
            SendMessage(hStatusWnd, SB_SETTEXT, (WPARAM) 2,
                  (LPARAM) "Debug: No");
            SendMessage(hStatusWnd, SB_SETTEXT, (WPARAM) 3,
                  (LPARAM) "Win16: No");
            SendMessage(hStatusWnd, SB_SETTEXT, (WPARAM) 4,
                  (LPARAM) "Using C++");
            return 1;
          case IDCANCEL:
          case IDOK:
            PostQuitMessage(0);
            return 1;
      }
  }
  return 0;
}


/* Second dialog function. This is just a placeholder. */
BOOL CALLBACK DialogFunc2(HWND hdwnd, UINT message,
                          WPARAM wParam, LPARAM lParam)
{
  switch(message) {
    case WM_COMMAND:
      switch(LOWORD(wParam)) {
        case IDCANCEL:
        case IDOK:
          PostQuitMessage(0);
          return 1;
      }
```

```
  }
  return 0;
}

/* Third dialog function. This is just a placeholder. */
BOOL CALLBACK DialogFunc3(HWND hdwnd, UINT message,
                          WPARAM wParam, LPARAM lParam)
{
  switch(message) {
    case WM_COMMAND:
      switch(LOWORD(wParam)) {
        case IDCANCEL:
        case IDOK:
          PostQuitMessage(0);
          return 1;
      }
  }
  return 0;
}

/* Initialize the status bar. */
void InitStatus(HWND hwnd)
{
  RECT WinDim;
  int i;

  GetClientRect(hwnd, &WinDim);

  for(i=1; i<=NUMPARTS; i++)
    parts[i-1] = WinDim.right/NUMPARTS * i;

  /* Create a status bar */
  hStatusWnd = CreateStatusWindow(
              WS_CHILD | WS_VISIBLE,
              "Power: 5", hwnd,
              ID_STATUSWIN);


  SendMessage(hStatusWnd, SB_SETPARTS,
              (WPARAM) NUMPARTS, (LPARAM) parts);

  SendMessage(hStatusWnd, SB_SETTEXT, (WPARAM) 1,
              (LPARAM) "Optimize: No");
  SendMessage(hStatusWnd, SB_SETTEXT, (WPARAM) 2,
              (LPARAM) "Debug: No");
  SendMessage(hStatusWnd, SB_SETTEXT, (WPARAM) 3,
              (LPARAM) "Win16: No");
  SendMessage(hStatusWnd, SB_SETTEXT, (WPARAM) 4,
```

```
                          (LPARAM) "Using C++");
}
```

This program requires the following resource file:

```
#include <windows.h>
#include "tab.h"

TabDB1 DIALOG 2, 16, 180, 92
STYLE  WS_CHILD | WS_VISIBLE
{
  PUSHBUTTON "Reset", ID_RESET, 112, 40, 37, 14,
             WS_CHILD | WS_VISIBLE | WS_TABSTOP
  PUSHBUTTON "OK", IDOK, 112, 60, 37, 14,
             WS_CHILD | WS_VISIBLE | WS_TABSTOP
  EDITTEXT ID_EB1, 10, 10, 20, 12, ES_LEFT | WS_CHILD |
             WS_VISIBLE | WS_BORDER
  LTEXT "Power Factor", ID_STEXT1, 36, 12, 50, 12
  AUTOCHECKBOX "Optimize", ID_CB1, 10, 35, 48, 12
  AUTOCHECKBOX "Debug Info", ID_CB2, 10, 50, 48, 12
  AUTOCHECKBOX "Win16 Compatible", ID_CB3, 10, 65, 70, 12
  AUTORADIOBUTTON "C", ID_RB1, 112, 8, 20, 12
  AUTORADIOBUTTON "C++", ID_RB2, 112, 20, 28, 12
  LTEXT "Language", ID_STEXT2, 140, 14, 40, 12
}

TabDB2 DIALOG 2, 16, 180, 92
STYLE WS_CHILD | WS_VISIBLE
{
  PUSHBUTTON "OK", IDOK, 82, 43, 37, 14,
             WS_CHILD | WS_VISIBLE | WS_TABSTOP
  PUSHBUTTON "CANCEL", IDCANCEL, 132, 43, 37, 14,
             WS_CHILD | WS_VISIBLE | WS_TABSTOP
  LTEXT "Show contents of", ID_STEXT3, 10, 10, 60, 12
  AUTORADIOBUTTON "Registers", ID_RB3, 10, 30, 48, 12
  AUTORADIOBUTTON "Variables", ID_RB4, 10, 50, 52, 12
  AUTORADIOBUTTON "Stack", ID_RB5, 10, 70, 48, 12
}

TabDB3 DIALOG  2, 16, 180, 92
STYLE WS_CHILD | WS_VISIBLE
{
  PUSHBUTTON "OK", IDOK, 82, 43, 37, 14,
             WS_CHILD | WS_VISIBLE | WS_TABSTOP
  PUSHBUTTON "CANCEL", IDCANCEL, 132, 43, 37, 14,
             WS_CHILD | WS_VISIBLE | WS_TABSTOP
  LTEXT "Report", ID_STEXT4, 10, 10, 60, 12
  AUTOCHECKBOX "Syntax errors", ID_CB4, 10, 30, 60, 12
```

```
    AUTOCHECKBOX "Warnings", ID_CB5, 10, 50, 60, 12
    AUTOCHECKBOX "ANSI Violations", ID_CB6, 10, 70, 60, 12
}
```

The header file TAB.H is shown here:

```
#define IDM_DIALOG    100
#define IDM_EXIT      101
#define IDM_HELP      102
#define ID_UPDOWN     103
#define ID_EB1        104
#define ID_EB2        105
#define ID_CB1        106
#define ID_CB2        107
#define ID_CB3        108
#define ID_CB4        109
#define ID_CB5        110
#define ID_CB6        111
#define ID_RB1        112
#define ID_RB2        113
#define ID_RB3        114
#define ID_RB4        115
#define ID_RB5        116
#define ID_RESET      117


#define ID_STATUSWIN 200


#define ID_STEXT1      300
#define ID_STEXT2      301
#define ID_STEXT3      302
#define ID_STEXT4      303
```

The interesting portion of this program occurs inside the **WM_NOTIFY** case
of **WindowFunc( )**. It is shown here for your convenience:

```
case WM_NOTIFY:
  nmptr = (LPNMHDR) lParam;
  if(nmptr->code == TCN_SELCHANGE) {
    if(hDlg) DestroyWindow(hDlg);
    tabnumber = TabCtrl_GetCurSel((HWND)nmptr->hwndFrom);
    switch(tabnumber) {
      case 0:
        hDlg = CreateDialog(hInst, "TabDB1",
                      hTabWnd, (DLGPROC) DialogFunc1);
        break;
      case 1:
```

```
                    hDlg = CreateDialog(hInst, "TabDB2",
                              hTabWnd, (DLGPROC) DialogFunc2);
                  break;
                case 2:
                  hDlg = CreateDialog(hInst, "TabDB3",
                              hTabWnd, (DLGPROC) DialogFunc3);
                  break;
              }
            }
            break;
```

12

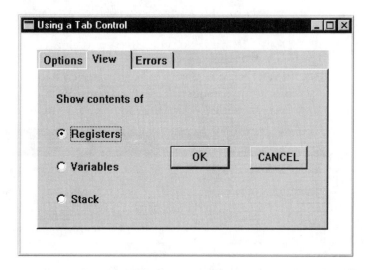

Sample output
from the
second tab
control
program

Figure 12-3.

Each time a new tab is selected, two events occur. First, the dialog box associated with the currently selected tab is removed by calling **DestroyWindow( )**. (As you should recall, to close a modeless dialog box, you must call **DestroyWindow( )** rather than **EndDialog( )**, which is used for modal dialog boxes.) Next, the current tab selection is obtained and its dialog box is created using **CreateDialog( )**. (Remember, **CreateDialog( )** creates modeless dialog boxes.) This is the general procedure you should follow with your own tab control dialog boxes.

Before moving on, you should experiment with this program. Try making changes to the dialog boxes or to the tab control. Also, tab controls may also have tooltips associated with them. As a challenge, you might want to try adding tooltips to the preceding example.

Tree-View Controls

Tree-view controls display hierarchical information in a "tree-like" manner.

Tree-view controls are used to display information using a tree structure. For example, the directory list used by Windows NT's Explorer is an example of a tree-view control. Because trees imply a hierarchy, tree-view controls should only be used to display hierarchical information. Tree-view controls are very powerful and support a large number of options. In fact, one could easily write a book about tree-view controls alone! For this reason, this section only discusses tree-view fundamentals. However, once you understand the basics, you will be able to easily incorporate the other tree-view features on your own.

Create a Tree-View Control

A tree-view control is a window that is created using either **CreateWindow( )** or **CreateWindowEx( )** and specifying the **WC_TREEVIEW** class. Typically, a tree-view control will be a child window, so the **WS_CHILD** style is needed. It is usually created using the **WS_VISIBLE** style, so that it is automatically displayed. **WS_TABSTOP** is also commonly included. Tree-view controls allow additional tree-related styles to be specified when they are created, including:

Style	Meaning
TVS_HASLINES	Lines link branches in the tree.
TVS_LINESATROOT	Lines link root to the branches.
TVS_HASBUTTONS	Expand/Collapse buttons included to the left of each branch.

Including the **TVS_HASLINES** and **TVS_LINESATROOT** styles causes lines to be drawn to each item in the tree. This gives the tree-view control its "tree-like" look. Including **TVS_HASBUTTONS** causes the standard expand/collapse buttons to be added. These buttons contain a + if the branch may be expanded at least one more level and a – if the branch is fully expanded. You may also click on these buttons to expand or collapse a branch. Typically, all three of these styles are included when a tree-view control is created. For example, the following creates a standard tree-view window.

```
hTreeWndCtrl = CreateWindow(
          WC_TREEVIEW,
          "",
          WS_VISIBLE | WS_TABSTOP | WS_CHILD |
          TVS_HASLINES | TVS_HASBUTTONS |
          TVS_LINESATROOT,
          0, 0, 100, 100,
          hwnd, /* handle of parent */
          NULL,
          hInst, /* instance handle */
          NULL
     );
```

12

When the tree-view control is first created, it is empty. You must add each item in the tree, as described in the next section.

Sending Tree-View Messages

Tree-view controls respond to several messages. Several commonly used tree-view control messages are shown in Table 12-3. You can send these messages using **SendMessage( )** or by using special macros created expressly for this purpose. Tree-view control macros corresponding to the messages in Table 12-3 are shown here. In all cases, *hTreeWnd* is the handle of the tree-view control.

BOOL TreeView_DeleteItem(HWND *hTreeWnd*, HTREEITEM *hItem*);

BOOL TreeView_Expand(HWND *hTreeWnd*, HTREEITEM *hItem*,
                     UINT *action*);

BOOL TreeView_GetItem(HWND *hTreeWnd*, TV_ITEM **lpItem*);

HTREEVIEW TreeView_InsertItem(HWND *hwnd*,
                              TV_INSERTSTRUCT **lpitem*);

BOOL TreeView_Select(HWND *hTreeWnd*, HTREEITEM *hItem*,
UINT *action*);

The only messages used by the example in this chapter are
TVM_INSERTITEM and **TVM_EXPAND**. However, your application will
probably use others.

Message	Meaning
TVM_DELETEITEM	Deletes an item from the tree list. Returns nonzero if successful and zero on failure. *wParam* is 0. *lParam* specifies the handle of the item to delete.
TVM_EXPAND	Expands or collapses the tree list one level. Returns nonzero if successful and zero on failure. *wParam* specifies the operation. It must be **TVE_COLLAPSE** (collapses tree), **TVE_COLLAPSERESET** (collapses tree and deletes child items), **TVE_EXPAND** (expands a tree), or **TVE_TOGGLE** (toggles state). **TVE_COLLAPSERESET** must be used in conjunction with **TVE_COLLAPSE**. *lParam* specifies the handle of the parent of the branch.
TVM_GETITEM	Obtains an item's attributes. Returns nonzero if successful and zero on failure. *wParam* is 0. *lParam* specifies a pointer to a **TV_ITEM** structure that receives information about the item.
TVM_INSERTITEM	Inserts an item into the tree. Returns a handle to the item being inserted or **NULL** on failure. *wParam* is 0. *lParam* specifies a pointer to a **TV_INSERTSTRUCT** that contains information about the item.
TVM_SELECTITEM	Selects a tree-view item. Returns nonzero if successful and zero on failure. *wParam* specifies the specific action. If it is **TVGN_CARET**, the item is selected. If it is **TVGN_DROPHILITE**, the item is highlighted for a drag-drop operation. If it is **TVGN_FIRSTVISIBLE**, the tree-view is scrolled so that the specified item is the first visible item. *lParam* specifies the handle of the item.

Commonly
Used
Tree-View
Control
Messages
Table 12-3.

When an item is inserted, the item's information is contained in a **TV_INSERTSTRUCT** structure, which is shown here:

```
typedef struct _TV_INSERTSTRUCT {
  HTREEITEM hParent;
  HTREEITEM hInsertAfter;
  TV_ITEM item;
} TV_INSERTSTRUCT;
```

Here, **hParent** is the handle to the parent of the item. If the item has no parent, then this field should contain **TVI_ROOT**. The value in **hInsertAfter** determines how the new item will be inserted into the tree. If it contains the handle of an item, the new item will be inserted after that item. Otherwise, **hInsertAfter** can be one of the following values:

TVI_FIRST	Insert at beginning of list
TVI_LAST	Insert at end of list
TVI_SORT	Insert in alphabetical order

12

The contents of **item** describe the item. This is a **TV_ITEM** structure, which is shown here:

```
typedef struct _TV_ITEM {
  UINT mask;
  HTREEITEM hItem;
  UINT state;
  UINT stateMask;
  LPSTR pszText;
  int cchTextMax;
  int iImage;
  int iSelectedImage;
  int cChildren;
  LPARAM lParam;
} TV_ITEM;
```

Here, the values in **mask** determine which of the other members of **TV_ITEM** contain valid data when this structure receives information from the tree-view control. The values that it may contain are shown here:

Value in Mask	Meaning
TVIF_HANDLE	**hItem** contains data.
TVIF_STATE	**state** and **stateMask** contain data.

Value in Mask	Meaning
TVIF_TEXT	**pszText** and **cchTextMax** contain data.
TVIF_IMAGE	**iImage** contains data.
TVIF_SELECTEDIMAGE	**iSelectedImage** contains data.
TVIF_CHILDREN	**cChildren** contains data.
TVIF_LPARAM	**lParam** contains data.

hItem is the handle of the item.

The **state** member contains the state of the tree-view control. Here are some common tree state values:

State	Meaning
TVIS_DROPHILITED	Item is highlighted as the target of drag/drop operation.
TVIS_EXPANDED	Branch descending from item is fully expanded. (Applies to parent items only.)
TVIS_EXPANDEDONCE	Branch descending from item is expanded one (or more) levels. (Applies to parent items only.)
TVIS_SELECTED	Item is selected.

The **stateMask** member determines which state to set or obtain. It will also be one or more of the preceding values.

When an item is being inserted into the tree, **pszText** points to the string that will be displayed in the tree. When information about an item is being obtained, **pszText** must point to an array that will receive its text. In this case, the value of **cchTextMax** specifies the size of the array pointed to by **pszText**. Otherwise, **cchTextMax** is ignored.

If there is an image list associated with the tree-view control, then **iImage** will contain the index of the image for the item when it is not selected. **iImageSelected** contains the index of the image used by the item when it is selected. (We won't be using images in the tree-view created in this chapter.)

cChildren will contain 1 if the item has child items and zero if it does not.

lParam contains application-defined data.

Tree-View Notification Messages

When a tree-view control is accessed, it generates a **WM_NOTIFY** message. There are several notification messages associated with tree-view controls. Some commonly used ones are shown here:

Notification Message	Meaning
TVN_DELETEITEM	An item has been deleted.
TVN_ITEMEXPANDING	A branch is about to expand or collapse.
TVN_ITEMEXPANDED	A branch has expanded or collapsed.
TVN_SELCHANGING	A new item is about to be selected.
TVN_SELCHANGED	A new item has been selected.

For these notification messages, when the **WM_NOTIFY** message is received, *lParam* will point to a **NM_TREEVIEW** structure. The **NM_TREEVIEW** structure is shown here:

```
typedef struct _NM_TREEVIEW {
  NMHDR hdr;
  UINT action;
  TV_ITEM itemOld;
  TV_ITEM itemNew;
  POINT ptDrag;
} NM_TREEVIEW;
```

The first field in **NM_TREEVIEW** is the standard **NMHDR** structure. The notification code will be contained in **hdr.code**. The handle of the tree control that generates the message is found in **hdr.hwndFrom** field.

The **action** field contains notification-specific information. The structures **itemOld** and **itemNew** contain information about the previously selected item (if applicable) and the newly selected item (again, if applicable). The location of the mouse at the time the message was generated is contained in **ptDrag**.

For **TVN_SELCHANGING** and **TVN_SELCHANGED**, **itemOld** describes the previously selected item and **itemNew** describes the newly selected item. For **TVN_ITEMEXPANDING** and **TVN_ITEMEXPANDED**, **itemNew** describes the item that is the parent of the branch that is expanding. For **TVN_DELETEITEM**, **itemOld** describes the item that was deleted.

12

A Tree-View Demonstration Program

The following program demonstrates a tree-view control. The program builds a simple tree and allows you to expand a branch, expand the entire tree, or collapse a branch. Each time a new tree-view item is chosen, the selection is displayed in the program's window. Sample output from the program is shown in Figure 12-4.

```
/* Demonstrate a tree-view control. */

#include <windows.h>
#include <commctrl.h>
#include <string.h>
#include "tree.h"

#define NUM 6

LRESULT CALLBACK WindowFunc(HWND, UINT, WPARAM, LPARAM);
BOOL CALLBACK DialogFunc(HWND, UINT, WPARAM, LPARAM);
void InitTree(void);
void report(HDC hdc, char *s);

char szWinName[] = "MyWin"; /* name of window class */

HINSTANCE hInst;
HWND hwnd;
HWND hTreeWndCtrl;
HTREEITEM hTreeWnd[NUM];
HWND hTreeCurrent;

int WINAPI WinMain(HINSTANCE hThisInst, HINSTANCE hPrevInst,
                   LPSTR lpszArgs, int nWinMode)
{
  MSG msg;
  WNDCLASSEX wcl;
  HANDLE hAccel;

  /* Define a window class. */
  wcl.cbSize = sizeof(WNDCLASSEX);

  /* Define a window class. */
  wcl.hInstance = hThisInst; /* handle to this instance */
  wcl.lpszClassName = szWinName; /* window class name */
  wcl.lpfnWndProc = WindowFunc; /* window function */
  wcl.style = 0; /* default style */

  wcl.hIcon = LoadIcon(NULL, IDI_APPLICATION);
  wcl.hIconSm = LoadIcon(NULL, IDI_APPLICATION);
```

```
wcl.hCursor = LoadCursor(NULL, IDC_ARROW);

wcl.lpszMenuName = "TreeViewMenu"; /* menu */

wcl.cbClsExtra = 0; /* no extra */
wcl.cbWndExtra = 0; /* information needed */

/* Make the window white. */
wcl.hbrBackground = GetStockObject(WHITE_BRUSH);

/* Register the window class. */
if(!RegisterClassEx(&wcl)) return 0;

/* Now that a window class has been registered, a window
   can be created. */
hwnd = CreateWindow(
  szWinName, /* name of window class */
  "Using a Tree-View Control", /* title */
  WS_OVERLAPPEDWINDOW, /* window style - normal */
  CW_USEDEFAULT, /* X coordinate - let Windows decide */
  CW_USEDEFAULT, /* Y coordinate - let Windows decide */
  CW_USEDEFAULT, /* width - let Windows decide */
  CW_USEDEFAULT, /* height - let Windows decide */
  HWND_DESKTOP, /* no parent window */
  NULL, /* no override of class menu */
  hThisInst, /* handle of this instance of the program */
  NULL /* no additional arguments */
);

InitCommonControls();

hInst = hThisInst; /* save the current instance handle */

/* load accelerators */
hAccel = LoadAccelerators(hThisInst, "TreeViewMenu");

/* Display the window. */
ShowWindow(hwnd, nWinMode);
UpdateWindow(hwnd);

/* Create the message loop. */
while(GetMessage(&msg, NULL, 0, 0))
{
  if(!TranslateAccelerator(hwnd, hAccel, &msg)) {
    TranslateMessage(&msg); /* translate keyboard messages */
    DispatchMessage(&msg); /* return control to Windows NT */
  }
```

```
    }
    return msg.wParam;
}

/* This function is called by Windows NT and is passed
   messages from the message queue.
*/
LRESULT CALLBACK WindowFunc(HWND hwnd, UINT message,
                           WPARAM wParam, LPARAM lParam)
{
  HDC hdc;
  static char selection[80] = "";
  NM_TREEVIEW *nmptr;
  PAINTSTRUCT paintstruct;
  int i, response;
  RECT WinDim;

  switch(message) {
    case WM_CREATE:
      /* get size of parent window */
      GetClientRect(hwnd, &WinDim);

      /* create a tree-view control */
      hTreeWndCtrl = CreateWindow(
                      WC_TREEVIEW,
                      "",
                      WS_VISIBLE | WS_TABSTOP | WS_CHILD |
                      TVS_HASLINES | TVS_HASBUTTONS |
                      TVS_LINESATROOT,
                      0, 0, 200, 200,
                      hwnd,
                      NULL,
                      hInst,
                      NULL
                    );

      InitTree();
      break;
    case WM_COMMAND:
      switch(LOWORD(wParam)) {
        case IDM_EXPAND:
          TreeView_Expand(hTreeWndCtrl, hTreeCurrent,
                    TVE_EXPAND);
          break;
        case IDM_EXPANDALL:
          for(i=0; i<NUM; i++)
            TreeView_Expand(hTreeWndCtrl, hTreeWnd[i],
                    TVE_EXPAND);
```

```
      break;
   case IDM_COLLAPSE:
     TreeView_Expand(hTreeWndCtrl, hTreeCurrent,
                     TVE_COLLAPSE);
     break;
   case IDM_EXIT:
     response = MessageBox(hwnd, "Quit the Program?",
                           "Exit", MB_YESNO);
     if(response == IDYES) PostQuitMessage(0);
     break;
   case IDM_HELP:
     MessageBox(hwnd, "Try the Tree View",
                "Help", MB_OK);
     break;
  }
  break;
case WM_NOTIFY:
 nmptr = (LPNM_TREEVIEW) lParam;
 if(nmptr->hdr.code == TVN_SELCHANGED) {
   InvalidateRect(hwnd, NULL, 1);
   if(nmptr->itemNew.hItem == hTreeWnd[0])
     strcpy(selection, "Physics.");
   else if(nmptr->itemNew.hItem == hTreeWnd[1])
     strcpy(selection, "Mechanics.");
   else if(nmptr->itemNew.hItem == hTreeWnd[2])
     strcpy(selection, "Electricity.");
   else if(nmptr->itemNew.hItem == hTreeWnd[3])
     strcpy(selection, "Momentum.");
   else if(nmptr->itemNew.hItem == hTreeWnd[4])
     strcpy(selection, "Linear Momentum.");
   else if(nmptr->itemNew.hItem == hTreeWnd[5])
     strcpy(selection, "Angular Momentum.");

   hTreeCurrent = nmptr->itemNew.hItem;
  }
  break;
case WM_PAINT:
  hdc = BeginPaint(hwnd, &paintstruct);
  report(hdc, selection);
  EndPaint(hwnd, &paintstruct);
  break;
case WM_DESTROY: /* terminate the program */
  PostQuitMessage(0);
  break;
default:
 /* Let Windows NT process any messages not specified in
    the preceding switch statement. */
```

```
      return DefWindowProc(hwnd, message, wParam, lParam);
  }
  return 0;
}

/* Report Selection */
void report(HDC hdc, char *s)
{
  char str[80];

  if(*s) {
    strcpy(str, "Selection is ");
    strcat(str, s);
  }
  else strcpy(str, "No selection has been made.");
  TextOut(hdc, 0, 200, str, strlen(str));
}

/* Initialize the tree list. */
void InitTree(void)
{
  TV_INSERTSTRUCT tvs;
  TV_ITEM tvi;

  tvs.hInsertAfter = TVI_LAST; /* make tree in order given */
  tvi.mask = TVIF_TEXT;

  tvi.pszText = "Physics";
  tvs.hParent = TVI_ROOT;
  tvs.item = tvi;
  hTreeWnd[0] = TreeView_InsertItem(hTreeWndCtrl, &tvs);
  hTreeCurrent = hTreeWnd[0];

  tvi.pszText = "Mechanics";
  tvs.hParent = hTreeWnd[0];
  tvs.item = tvi;
  hTreeWnd[1] = TreeView_InsertItem(hTreeWndCtrl, &tvs);

  tvi.pszText = "Electricity";
  tvs.item = tvi;
  tvs.hParent = hTreeWnd[0];
  hTreeWnd[2] = TreeView_InsertItem(hTreeWndCtrl, &tvs);

  tvi.pszText = "Momentum";
  tvs.item = tvi;
  tvs.hParent = hTreeWnd[1];
  hTreeWnd[3] = TreeView_InsertItem(hTreeWndCtrl, &tvs);
```

```
        tvi.pszText = "Linear";
        tvs.item = tvi;
        tvs.hParent = hTreeWnd[3];
        hTreeWnd[4] = TreeView_InsertItem(hTreeWndCtrl, &tvs);

        tvi.pszText = "Angular";
        tvs.item = tvi;
        tvs.hParent = hTreeWnd[3];
        hTreeWnd[5] = TreeView_InsertItem(hTreeWndCtrl, &tvs);
}
```

The program requires the following resource file:

```
#include <windows.h>
#include "tree.h"

TreeViewMenu MENU
{
  POPUP "&Options" {
    MENUITEM "&Expand One\tF2", IDM_EXPAND
    MENUITEM "Expand &All\tF3", IDM_EXPANDALL
    MENUITEM "&Collapse\tF4", IDM_COLLAPSE
    MENUITEM "E&xit\tF10", IDM_EXIT

  }
  MENUITEM "&Help", IDM_HELP
}

TreeViewMenu ACCELERATORS
{
  VK_F2, IDM_EXPAND, VIRTKEY
  VK_F3, IDM_EXPANDALL, VIRTKEY
  VK_F4, IDM_COLLAPSE, VIRTKEY
  VK_F10, IDM_EXIT, VIRTKEY
  VK_F1, IDM_HELP, VIRTKEY
}
```

The **tree.h** header file is shown here:

```
#define IDM_EXPAND     100
#define IDM_EXPANDALL 101
#define IDM_COLLAPSE  102
#define IDM_EXIT      103
#define IDM_HELP      104
```

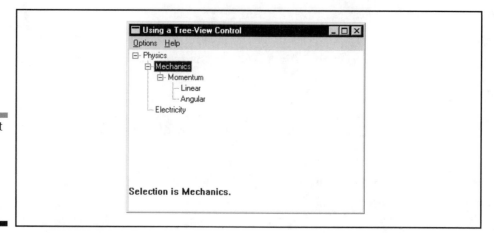

Sample output
from the
tree-view
control
program
Figure 12-4.

In the program, the function **InitTree( )** initializes the tree-view control. Notice that the handle of each item is stored in the **hTreeWnd** array. These handles are used to identify items when they are selected in the tree list. **hTreeCurrent** identifies the currently selected item. This handle is used when the user expands or collapses a branch using the menu.

Inside **WindowFunc( )**, each time a new item is selected, a **WM_NOTIFY** message is received and processed. The value of **itemNew** is checked against the list of item handles stored in the **hTreeWnd** array. When the matching handle is found, the new selection is reported.

While this example illustrates the essential aspects of tree-view controls, it just scratches the surface of their power. For example, using a tree-view, you can drag and drop an item from one tree to another. This and other features are things that you will want to explore on your own.

IN DEPTH

Editing Tree-View Labels

It is possible to create a tree-view that allows the user to modify the labels in the tree. To do so, you must include the **TVS_EDITLABELS** style when you create the tree-view control. You must also handle these two notification messages: **TVN_BEGINLABELEDIT** and **TVN_ENDLABELEDIT**. (Remember, notification messages are sent via the **WM_NOTIFY** message.) For both messages, *lParam* points to a **TV_DISPINFO** structure, shown here:

```
typedef struct _TV_DISPINFO {
  NMHDR hdr;
  TV_ITEM item;
} TV_DISPINFO;
```

When the user begins editing a label, your program will receive a **TVN_BEGIN-LABELEDIT** notification message. To allow the user to edit the label, your program must return zero. To disallow editing, return nonzero.

When the user finishes editing, your program receives a **TVN_-ENDLABELEDIT** notification message. If the editing was canceled by the user, then the **pszText** field of **item** will be null. Otherwise, it will contain the new label. If editing was canceled, your program should return zero. This causes the original label to remain. Otherwise, return nonzero to cause the new label to be used.

To experiment with editing tree-view labels, add **TVS_EDITLABELS** to the tree-view control created in the example program and then substitute the following **WM_NOTIFY** case into **WindowFunc( )**.

```
case WM_NOTIFY:
  nmptr = (LPNM_TREEVIEW) lParam;
  switch(nmptr->hdr.code) {
    case TVN_BEGINLABELEDIT:
      return 0;
    case TVN_ENDLABELEDIT:
      if(((TV_DISPINFO *) nmptr)->item.pszText)
        return 1; /* label was edited */
      else
        return 0;  /* user cancelled */
  }
  break;
```

After making these changes, you can alter the contents of a tree-view label.

12

CHAPTER 13

Property Sheets
and Wizards

This chapter describes how to create one of NT 4's most exciting controls: the *wizard*. As you probably know, a wizard is a sequenced set of dialog boxes that guide the user through a complex group of selections. The dialog boxes that constitute the wizard must be accessed in the order in which they are presented by the wizard. Wizards are used frequently in Windows NT 4. For example, when you install a new printer, the printer installation wizard is activated.

As you will soon see, wizards are built upon another common control element: the *property sheet*. A property sheet is typically used to view and set various properties associated with some item. Although they look like the tab control described in the preceding chapter, property sheets are much more powerful.

Since property sheets underpin wizards, we will begin there.

Property Sheet Basics

Property sheets allow the user to examine or alter various properties associated with some item. For example, a property sheet is typically used to set printer options or a modem configuration. From the user's perspective, a property sheet consists of one or more *pages*. Each page has a tab associated with it. A page is activated by selecting its tab. A sample property sheet is shown in Figure 13-1.

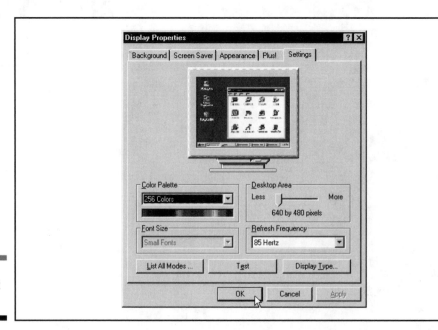

A sample
property sheet

Figure 13-1.

A property sheet provides a convenient way of managing the properties associated with some item.

From the programmer's perspective, a property sheet is a collection of one or more modeless dialog boxes. That is, each page in a property sheet is defined by a dialog box template, and interaction with the page is handled by a dialog function. Most commonly, each dialog box template is specified in your application's resource file.

All property sheets contain two buttons: OK and Cancel. Usually a third button called Apply is also included. It is also possible to include a Help button. It is important to understand that although the dialog functions associated with each page provide the mechanism by which the user sets or views the properties, only the property sheet control, itself, can accept or cancel the user's changes. Put differently, no page dialog function should include an OK or Cancel button. These two operations are provided by the property sheet control.

The dialog boxes that constitute the property sheet are enclosed within the property sheet control. The property sheet control manages interaction with and between the individual pages. As a general rule, each dialog box function responds to its own controls in the normal fashion. That is, the individual controls that make up each page are handled in the standard way by the page's dialog box function. However, each page must also respond to messages generated by the enclosing property sheet. When the property sheet needs to communicate with a page, it does so by sending it a **WM_NOTIFY** message. Each page in a property sheet must be able to respond to this message. (The details of this are discussed shortly.)

There is one very important requirement that you must follow when creating a property sheet: The modeless dialog box function associated with each page must *not* close its dialog box. That is, it must not call **DestroyWindow( )**. Instead, the enclosing property sheet control, itself, will take care of this. (If you do close one of the page dialog boxes, that dialog box will then be empty. This is a violation of Windows NT style rules, to say the least!)

13

REMEMBER: Since a property sheet is a common control, you must include the header file COMMCTRL.H in your program and link in the necessary common control library.

Creating a Property Sheet

There are four basic steps required to create a property sheet. They are:

1. Information about each page in the control must be stored in a **PROPSHEETPAGE** structure.

2. Each page must be created by calling **CreatePropertySheetPage( )**.

3. Information about the property sheet itself must be stored in a **PROPSHEETHEADER** structure.

4. The property sheet control is created and displayed by calling **PropertySheet( )**.

Let's look at each step now.

Defining a Property Sheet Page

Each page in a property sheet must be defined in a **PROPSHEETPAGE** structure. **PROPSHEETPAGE** is defined like this:

```
typedef struct _PROPSHEETPAGE {
  DWORD dwSize;
  DWORD dwFlags;
  HINSTANCE hInstance;
  union {
    LPCSTR pszTemplate;
    LPCDLGTEMPLATE pResource;
  };
  union {
    HICON hIcon;
    LPCSTR pszIcon;
  };
  LPCSTR pszTitle;
  DLGPROC pfnDlgProc;
  LPARAM lParam;
  LPFNPSPCALLBACK pfnCallback;
  UINT FAR *pcRefParent;
} PROPSHEETPAGE;
```

Here, **dwSize** must contain the size, in bytes, of the **PROPSHEETPAGE** structure.

The value of **dwFlags** determines which of the remaining members contain valid information. It must be a combination of one or more of the flags shown in Table 13-1. The flags can be combined by ORing them together.

hInstance specifies the instance handle of the application.

pszTemplate specifies the name or ID of the dialog box template associated with this page. However, if the **PSP_DLGINDIRECT** flag is included, then **pszTemplate** is ignored and the dialog box described by **pResource** is used.

Flag	Meaning
PSP_DEFAULT	Use defaults.
PSP_DLGINDIRECT	Use **pResource**, not **pszTemplate**.
PSP_HASHELP	Displays Help button.
PSP_RTLREADING	Text is displayed right-to-left. (Provides support for Hebrew or Arabic.)
PSP_USECALLBACK	Enables **pfnCallback**.
PSP_USEHICON	Enables **hIcon**.
PSP_USEICONID	Enables **pszIcon**.
PSP_USEREFPARENT	Enables reference counting.
PSP_USETITLE	Uses title specified by **pszTitle** rather than the one defined by the page's dialog box template.

The Valid Values for the **dwFlags** Member of **PROPSHEET-PAGE** Table 13-1.

If you wish to include a small icon in the tab associated with a page, then it must be specified in either the **hIcon** or the **pszIcon** member. You must also include the appropriate flag. **hIcon** specifies an icon handle. **pszIcon** specifies the name or ID of the icon as specified in a resource file.

Normally, the title of the dialog box associated with a page becomes the title of the page. This title is displayed in the tab associated with the page. However, you can specify a different title by storing a pointer to the new title in **pszTitle**. Of course, you must also include the **PSP_USETITLE** flag.

The address of the modeless dialog box function that is associated with the page must be stored in **pfnDlgProc**.

lParam is used for application-specific data.

When **pfnCallback** is enabled, it specifies a callback function that is called whenever the page is created or destroyed. This function is not needed by the examples in this chapter. However, if your application requires this function, it must have the following prototype:

```
UINT CALLBACK PropPageFunc(HWND hwnd, UINT message,
                          LPPROPSHEETPAGE lpPropSheet);
```

When called, *hwnd* will be **NULL**. The value of *message* will be either **PSPCB_CREATE** or **PSPCB_RELEASE**, which indicates whether the page is being created or destroyed, respectively. *lpPropSheet* points to the

PROPSHEETPAGE structure of the page being affected. If *message* is **PSPCB_CREATE**, then the function must return nonzero to enable page creation or zero to cancel the creation of the page. If *message* is **PSPCB_RELEASE**, the return value is not used.

pcRefParent specifies the address of a reference count variable. This member is only active if **PSP_USEREFPARENT** is specified.

Initializing Each Page

After you have loaded a **PROPSHEETPAGE** structure with the necessary information, you must create the page by calling **CreatePropertySheet-Page( )**. Its prototype is shown here:

```
HPROPSHEETPAGE CreatePropertySheetPage(
                          LPCPPROPSHEETPAGE lpPage);
```

Here, *lpPage* is a pointer to a **PROPSHEETPAGE** structure. The function returns a handle to the newly created page. You will usually want to store this handle because it is needed for some property sheet operations. The function returns **NULL** if the page cannot be created.

Initializing the PROPSHEETHEADER Structure

After you have created each page, you must initialize the **PROPSHEET-HEADER** structure associated with the property sheet. This structure is defined like this:

```
typedef struct _PROPSHEETHEADER {
  DWORD dwSize;
  DWORD dwFlags;
  HWND  hwndParent;
  HINSTANCE hInstance;
  union {
    HICON hIcon;
    LPCSTR pszIcon;
  };
  LPCSTR pszCaption;
  UINT nPages;
  union {
    UINT nStartPage;
    LPCSTR pStartPage;
  };
  union {
    LPCPROPSHEETPAGE ppsp;
    HPROPSHEETPAGE FAR *phpage;
```

```
};
    PFNPROPSHEETCALLBACK pfnCallback;
} PROPSHEETHEADER;
```

Here, **dwSize** must contain the size, in bytes, of the **PROPSHEET-HEADER** structure.

The value of **dwFlags** determines which of the remaining members contain valid information. It must be a combination of one or more of the flags shown in Table 13-2. The flags can be combined by ORing them together.

hwndParent specifies the handle of the parent window, which is usually the window that activates the property sheet.

hInstance specifies the instance handle of the application.

If you wish to include a small icon in the title bar of the property sheet, then it must be specified in either the **hIcon** or the **pszIcon** member. You must

13

Flag	Meaning
PSH_DEFAULT	Use defaults.
PSH_HASHELP	Enable Help button.
PSH_MODELESS	Creates a modeless property sheet control. By default, property sheet controls are modal.
PSH_NOAPPLYNOW	Suppresses the Apply button.
PSH_PROPSHEETPAGE	Enables the **ppsp** member and disables **phpage**.
PSH_PROPTITLE	Appends the word "Properties" to the title specified by **pszCaption**.
PSH_RTLREADING	Text is displayed right-to-left. (Provides support for Hebrew or Arabic.)
PSH_USECALLBACK	Enables **pfnCallback**.
PSH_USEHICON	Enables **hIcon**.
PSH_USEICONID	Enables **pszIcon**.
PSH_USEPSTARTPAGE	Enables **pStartPage** and disables **nStartPage**.
PSH_WIZARD	Creates a wizard.

The Valid Values for the **dwFlags** Member of **PROPSHEET-HEADER**

Table 13-2.

also include the appropriate flag. **hIcon** specifies an icon handle. **pszIcon** specifies the name or ID of the icon as specified in a resource file.

The title of the property sheet control window is pointed to by **pszCaption**.

The number of pages in the property sheet is specified by **nPages**.

The first page to be displayed when the property sheet control is activated is specified by either **nStartPage** or **pStartPage**. By default, **nStartPage** is used. **nStartPage** specifies the index of the first page. All page indexes begin at zero. If you include the flag **PSH_PSTARTPAGE**, then you must specify the name or the ID of the page in **pStartPage**.

phpage must contain a pointer to an array of property sheet page handles. These handles are created by calling **CreatePropertySheetPage( )**, described earlier. However, if you specify the **PSH_PROPSHEETPAGE** flag, then you can specify the address of an array of **PROPSHEETPAGE** structures in the **ppsp** member, instead. In this case, the handles will be created automatically and there is no need to call **CreatePropertySheetPage( )**. However, since the page handles are useful for some operations, you will usually want to create them explicitly.

When **pfnCallback** is enabled, it specifies a callback function that is called whenever the property sheet is created. Although not used by the examples in this chapter, your application may need to create such a function. If so, it must have the following prototype:

```
int CALLBACK PropSheetFunc(HWND hdwnd, UINT message,
                           LPARAM lParam);
```

When called, *hdwnd* will contain the handle of the property sheet control. The value of *message* will be either **PSCB_INITIALIZED**, which means that the property sheet is being initialized, or **PSCB_PRECREATE**, which means that the property sheet is about to be initialized. For **PSCB_INITIALIZED**, *lParam* will be zero. For **PSCB_PRECREATE**, *lParam* points to the dialog box template and *hdwnd* is **NULL**. In either case, the function must return zero.

Creating the Property Sheet Control

After the property sheet pages have been defined and the **PROPSHEETHEADER** structure has been initialized, the property sheet control can be created. This is done by calling **PropertySheet( )**, whose prototype is shown here:

```
int PropertySheet(LPCPPROPSHEETHEADER lpHeader);
```

Here, *lpHeader* is a pointer to the property sheet header structure. The function returns –1 if an error occurs or a positive value if successful. When creating a modeless property sheet control (that is, one in which you have included the **PSH_MODELESS** flag), then a handle to the property sheet is returned.

Processing Property Sheet Messages

As mentioned, a property sheet control sends messages to the page dialog box functions using the **WM_NOTIFY** message. The value of **lParam** is a pointer to a **NMHDR** structure. Recall that the **NMHDR** structure is defined like this:

```
typedef struct tagNMHDR
{
  HWND hwndFrom;
  UINT idFrom;
  UINT code;
} NMHDR;
```

13

For **WM_NOTIFY** messages associated with property sheets, **hwndFrom** is the handle of the property sheet control. **idFrom** is not used with property sheets. The value of **code** contains the *notification code*, which describes what action has taken place.

The property sheet control uses the notification messages to inform individual dialog boxes about various events. For example, notification messages are sent when a page is selected, when the user presses one of the property sheet buttons, or when the page is being deselected. The notification code specifies the precise nature of the event. Commonly used notification codes are shown in Table 13-3.

In some cases, your dialog box function must respond to a notification message by returning a value to the property sheet control. To accomplish this you will need to use the **SetWindowLong( )** function. This function sets various attributes associated with a window. The prototype for **SetWindowLong( )** is shown here:

LONG SetWindowLong(HANDLE *hwnd*, int *index*, LONG *value*);

Here, *hwnd* is the handle of the dialog box. *index* specifies the attribute to set. To return a value to a property sheet, the value of *index* will be **DWL_MSGRESULT**. The value to return is passed in *value*. Remember, your dialog box function must still return true if it processes a message and false if

Notification Code	Meaning	Expected Return Value
PSN_APPLY	Sent when user presses the Apply or OK button.	PSNRET_NOERROR (zero) to apply changes. PSNRET_INVALID_NOCHANGEPAGE to prevent changes.
PSN_HELP	Sent when user presses the Help button.	None.
PSN_KILLACTIVE	Sent when a page is losing focus or the OK button has been pressed.	Zero to allow deactivation. Nonzero to prevent deactivation.
PSN_QUERYCANCEL	Sent when user presses Cancel button.	Zero to allow cancellation. Nonzero to prevent cancellation.
PSN_RESET	Sent when user presses Cancel button.	None.
PSN_SETACTIVE	Sent when page gains focus (i.e., when activated).	Zero to allow activation. Otherwise, return index of page to activate.
PSN_WIZBACK	Sent when user presses the Back button (wizards only).	Zero to activate previous page. –1 to prevent activation of previous page.
PSN_WIZFINISH	Sent when user presses the Finish button (wizards only).	Zero to terminate wizard. Nonzero otherwise.
PSN_WIZNEXT	Sent when user presses the Next button (wizards only).	Zero to activate next page. –1 to prevent activation of next page.

Common Property Sheet Notification Codes

Table 13-3.

it does not. The return value set using **SetWindowLong( )** specifies the outcome of a **WM_NOTIFY** message only.

Sending Messages to the Property Sheet

In addition to receiving messages, your application may send messages to the property sheet control. This can be accomplished using the **SendMessage( )** function, specifying the handle of the property sheet control as the recipient of the message. All property sheet messages begin with the prefix **PSM_**. Some of the most common ones are shown in Table 13-4.

Windows NT also provides a set of macros to facilitate the sending of property sheet messages. The macros for the messages in Table 13-4 are shown here:

```
BOOL PropSheet_Apply(hPropSheet);
BOOL PropSheet_Changed(hPropSheet, hPageDialog);
BOOL PropSheet_SetCurSel(hPropSheet, hPage, Index);
VOID PropSheet_SetWizButtons(hPropSheet, Flags);
VOID PropSheet_Unchanged(hPropSheet, hPageDialog);
```

13

Message Macro	Meaning
PSM_APPLY	Sends **PSM_APPLY** message. *lParam* is zero. *wParam* is zero. Returns zero if successful and nonzero on failure.
PSM_CHANGED	Enables Apply button. *lParam* is zero. *wParam* contains the handle of page dialog box. No return value.
PSM_SETCURSEL	Changes page. *lParam* contains the handle of the new page. *wParam* contains the index of new page. Returns zero if successful and nonzero on failure.
PSM_SETWIZBUTTONS	Enables wizard buttons. (Applies only to wizards.) *lParam* must contain one or more of the following flags: **PSWIZB_BACK**, **PSWIZB_NEXT**, **PSWIZB_FINISH**, or **PSWIZB_DISABLEDFINISH**. *wParam* is zero. No return value.
PSM_UNCHANGED	Disables Apply button. *lParam* is zero. *wParam* contains the handle of page dialog box. No return value.

Common Property Sheet Messages
Table 13-4.

Your
application
should send a
PSM_CHANGED
message
whenever a
property
changes.

Here, *hPropSheet* is the handle of the property sheet control being sent the message. *hPageDialog* is the handle of the page dialog function sending the message. *Index* is the zero-based index of the next page to select. *hPage* specifies the handle of a page. *Flags* specify which wizard buttons will be enabled. Remember that the **PropSheet_SetWizButtons( )** macro applies only to wizards and is discussed in detail later in this chapter.

The **PSM_CHANGED** message is particularly important because it enables the Apply button. Your application should send this message whenever the user changes anything within a property sheet.

A Property Sheet Demonstration Program

The following program displays a property sheet that contains three pages. Although the property sheet does not actually set any real properties, it does demonstrate the necessary procedures to create and display a property sheet. Sample output is shown in Figure 13-2.

```
/* Demonstrate a Property Sheet */

#include <windows.h>
#include <stdio.h>
#include <commctrl.h>
#include "prop.h"

#define NUMSTRINGS 5
#define NUMPAGES 3

LRESULT CALLBACK WindowFunc(HWND, UINT, WPARAM, LPARAM);
BOOL CALLBACK DialogFunc1(HWND, UINT, WPARAM, LPARAM);
BOOL CALLBACK DialogFunc2(HWND, UINT, WPARAM, LPARAM);
BOOL CALLBACK DialogFunc3(HWND, UINT, WPARAM, LPARAM);

char szWinName[] = "MyWin"; /* name of window class */

HINSTANCE hInst;

HWND hDlg; /* dialog box handle */
HPROPSHEETPAGE hPs[NUMPAGES];
HWND hPropSheet;
HWND hPage[NUMPAGES];

char list[][40] = {
  "Windows NT",
  "Windows 95",
  "Windows 3.1",
```

```
        "DOS",
        "UNIX"
};

int cb1=0, cb2=0, cb3=0;
int rb1=1, rb2=0, rb3=0;
int lb1sel=0;

int WINAPI WinMain(HINSTANCE hThisInst, HINSTANCE hPrevInst,
                   LPSTR lpszArgs, int nWinMode)
{
  HWND hwnd;
  MSG msg;
  WNDCLASSEX wcl;
  HANDLE hAccel;

  wcl.cbSize = sizeof(WNDCLASSEX);

  /* Define a window class. */
  wcl.hInstance = hThisInst; /* handle to this instance */
  wcl.lpszClassName = szWinName; /* window class name */
  wcl.lpfnWndProc = WindowFunc; /* window function */
  wcl.style = 0; /* default style */

  wcl.hIcon = LoadIcon(NULL, IDI_APPLICATION);
  wcl.hIconSm = LoadIcon(NULL, IDI_APPLICATION);

  wcl.hCursor = LoadCursor(NULL, IDC_ARROW);

  /* specify name of menu resource */
  wcl.lpszMenuName = "PropSheetMenu"; /* main menu */

  wcl.cbClsExtra = 0; /* no extra */
  wcl.cbWndExtra = 0; /* information needed */

  /* Make the window white. */
  wcl.hbrBackground = GetStockObject(WHITE_BRUSH);

  /* Register the window class. */
  if(!RegisterClassEx(&wcl)) return 0;

  /* Now that a window class has been registered, a window
     can be created. */
  hwnd = CreateWindow(
    szWinName, /* name of window class */
    "Demonstrate a Property Sheet", /* title */
    WS_OVERLAPPEDWINDOW, /* standard window */
    CW_USEDEFAULT, /* X coordinate - let Windows decide */
```

```
      CW_USEDEFAULT, /* Y coordinate - let Windows decide */
      CW_USEDEFAULT, /* width - let Windows decide */
      CW_USEDEFAULT, /* height - let Windows decide */
      HWND_DESKTOP, /* no parent window */
      NULL, /* no override of class menu */
      hThisInst, /* handle of this instance of the program */
      NULL /* no additional arguments */
    );

    hInst = hThisInst; /* save the current instance handle */

    /* load accelerators */
    hAccel = LoadAccelerators(hThisInst, "PropSheetMenu");

    InitCommonControls();

    /* Display the window. */
    ShowWindow(hwnd, nWinMode);
    UpdateWindow(hwnd);

    /* Create the message loop. */
    while(GetMessage(&msg, NULL, 0, 0))
    {
      if(!TranslateAccelerator(hwnd, hAccel, &msg)) {
        TranslateMessage(&msg); /* translate keyboard messages */
        DispatchMessage(&msg); /* return control to Windows NT */
      }
    }

    return msg.wParam;
}

/* This function is called by Windows NT and is passed
   messages from the message queue.
*/
LRESULT CALLBACK WindowFunc(HWND hwnd, UINT message,
                            WPARAM wParam, LPARAM lParam)
{
  int response;
  PROPSHEETPAGE PropSheet[NUMPAGES];
  PROPSHEETHEADER PropHdr;

  switch(message) {
    case WM_COMMAND:
      switch(LOWORD(wParam)) {
        case IDM_DIALOG:
          PropSheet[0].dwSize = sizeof(PROPSHEETPAGE);
          PropSheet[0].dwFlags = PSP_DEFAULT;
```

```
PropSheet[0].hInstance = hInst;
PropSheet[0].pszTemplate = "PropSheetDB1";
PropSheet[0].pszIcon = NULL;
PropSheet[0].pfnDlgProc = (DLGPROC) DialogFunc1;
PropSheet[0].pszTitle = "";
PropSheet[0].lParam = 0;
PropSheet[0].pfnCallback = NULL;

PropSheet[1].dwSize = sizeof(PROPSHEETPAGE);
PropSheet[1].dwFlags = PSP_DEFAULT;
PropSheet[1].hInstance = hInst;
PropSheet[1].pszTemplate = "PropSheetDB2";
PropSheet[1].pszIcon = NULL;
PropSheet[1].pfnDlgProc = (DLGPROC) DialogFunc2;
PropSheet[1].pszTitle = "";
PropSheet[1].lParam = 0;
PropSheet[1].pfnCallback = NULL;

PropSheet[2].dwSize = sizeof(PROPSHEETPAGE);
PropSheet[2].dwFlags = PSP_DEFAULT;
PropSheet[2].hInstance = hInst;
PropSheet[2].pszTemplate = "PropSheetDB3";
PropSheet[2].pszIcon = NULL;
PropSheet[2].pfnDlgProc = (DLGPROC) DialogFunc3;
PropSheet[2].pszTitle = "";
PropSheet[2].lParam = 0;
PropSheet[2].pfnCallback = NULL;


hPs[0] = CreatePropertySheetPage(&PropSheet[0]);
hPs[1] = CreatePropertySheetPage(&PropSheet[1]);
hPs[2] = CreatePropertySheetPage(&PropSheet[2]);

PropHdr.dwSize = sizeof(PROPSHEETHEADER);
PropHdr.dwFlags = PSH_DEFAULT;
PropHdr.hwndParent = hwnd;
PropHdr.hInstance = hInst;
PropHdr.pszIcon = NULL;
PropHdr.pszCaption = "Sample Property Sheet";
PropHdr.nPages = NUMPAGES;
PropHdr.nStartPage = 0;
PropHdr.phpage = hPs;
PropHdr.pfnCallback = NULL;

PropertySheet(&PropHdr);
break;
case IDM_EXIT:
response = MessageBox(hwnd, "Quit the Program?",
```

```
                                     "Exit", MB_YESNO);
            if(response == IDYES) PostQuitMessage(0);
            break;
          case IDM_HELP:
            MessageBox(hwnd, "Try the Property Sheet", "Help", MB_OK);
            break;
        }
        break;
      case WM_DESTROY: /* terminate the program */
        PostQuitMessage(0);
        break;
      default:
        /* Let Windows NT process any messages not specified in
           the preceding switch statement. */
        return DefWindowProc(hwnd, message, wParam, lParam);
  }
  return 0;
}


/* The first dialog function. */
BOOL CALLBACK DialogFunc1(HWND hdwnd, UINT message,
                          WPARAM wParam, LPARAM lParam)
{
  static long index;
  int i;
  char str[80];

  switch(message) {
    case WM_NOTIFY:
      switch(((NMHDR *) lParam)->code) {
        case PSN_SETACTIVE: /* page gaining focus */
          hPropSheet = ((NMHDR *) lParam)->hwndFrom;
          SetWindowLong(hdwnd, DWL_MSGRESULT, 0);
          index = lb1sel;
          return 1;
        case PSN_KILLACTIVE: /* page losing focus */
          lb1sel = index;
          SetWindowLong(hdwnd, DWL_MSGRESULT, 0);
          return 1;
      }
      break;
    case WM_COMMAND:
      switch(LOWORD(wParam)) {
        case IDD_OPTIONS:
```

```
                    PropSheet_SetCurSel(hPropSheet, hPs[1], 1);
                    return 1;
                  case IDD_OPTIMIZE:
                    PropSheet_SetCurSel(hPropSheet, hPs[2], 2);
                    return 1;
                  case IDD_LB1: /* process a list box LBN_DBLCLK */
                    PropSheet_Changed(hPropSheet, hdwnd);
                    /* see if user made a selection */
                    if(HIWORD(wParam)==LBN_DBLCLK) {
                      index = SendDlgItemMessage(hdwnd, IDD_LB1,
                              LB_GETCURSEL, 0, 0);  /* get index */
                      sprintf(str, "%s", list[index]);

                      MessageBox(hdwnd, str, "Selection Made", MB_OK);
                    }
                    return 1;
                }
              break;
            case WM_INITDIALOG: /* initialize list box */
              for(i=0; i<NUMSTRINGS; i++)
                SendDlgItemMessage(hdwnd, IDD_LB1,
                        LB_ADDSTRING, 0, (LPARAM)list[i]);

              /* select first item */
              SendDlgItemMessage(hdwnd, IDD_LB1, LB_SETCURSEL, lb1sel, 0);

              return 1;
          }
          return 0;
        }


        /* The Second dialog function. */
        BOOL CALLBACK DialogFunc2(HWND hdwnd, UINT message,
                                  WPARAM wParam, LPARAM lParam)
        {
          switch(message) {
            case WM_NOTIFY:
              switch(((NMHDR *) lParam)->code) {
                case PSN_SETACTIVE:/* page gaining focus */
                  hPropSheet = ((NMHDR *) lParam)->hwndFrom;
                  SetWindowLong(hdwnd, DWL_MSGRESULT, 0);
                  return 1;
                case PSN_KILLACTIVE: /* page losing focus */
                  cb1 = SendDlgItemMessage(hdwnd, IDD_CB1,
```

13

```
                                   BM_GETCHECK, 0, 0);
            cb2 = SendDlgItemMessage(hdwnd, IDD_CB2,
                                   BM_GETCHECK, 0, 0);
            cb3 = SendDlgItemMessage(hdwnd, IDD_CB3,
                                   BM_GETCHECK, 0, 0);
            SetWindowLong(hdwnd, DWL_MSGRESULT, 0);
            return 1;
        }
        break;
      case WM_COMMAND:
        switch(LOWORD(wParam)) {
          case IDD_CB1:
          case IDD_CB2:
          case IDD_CB3:
            PropSheet_Changed(hPropSheet, hdwnd);
            return 1;
          case IDD_ALL:
            PropSheet_Changed(hPropSheet, hdwnd);
            SendDlgItemMessage(hdwnd, IDD_CB1, BM_SETCHECK,
                               BST_CHECKED, 0);
            SendDlgItemMessage(hdwnd, IDD_CB2, BM_SETCHECK,
                               BST_CHECKED, 0);
            SendDlgItemMessage(hdwnd, IDD_CB3, BM_SETCHECK,
                               BST_CHECKED, 0);
            return 1;
        }
        break;
      case WM_INITDIALOG: /* initialize check boxes */
        SendDlgItemMessage(hdwnd, IDD_CB1, BM_SETCHECK, cb1, 0);
        SendDlgItemMessage(hdwnd, IDD_CB2, BM_SETCHECK, cb2, 0);
        SendDlgItemMessage(hdwnd, IDD_CB3, BM_SETCHECK, cb3, 0);
        return 1;
    }
    return 0;
}

/* The Third dialog function. */
BOOL CALLBACK DialogFunc3(HWND hdwnd, UINT message,
                          WPARAM wParam, LPARAM lParam)
{
  switch(message) {
    case WM_NOTIFY:
      switch(((NMHDR *) lParam)->code) {
        case PSN_SETACTIVE: /* page gaining focus */
```

```
                    hPropSheet = ((NMHDR *) lParam)->hwndFrom;
                    SetWindowLong(hdwnd, DWL_MSGRESULT, 0);
                    return 1;
                case PSN_KILLACTIVE: /* page losing focus */
                    rb1 = SendDlgItemMessage(hdwnd, IDD_RB1,
                                    BM_GETCHECK, 0, 0);
                    rb2 = SendDlgItemMessage(hdwnd, IDD_RB2,
                                    BM_GETCHECK, 0, 0);
                    rb3 = SendDlgItemMessage(hdwnd, IDD_RB3,
                                    BM_GETCHECK, 0, 0);
                    SetWindowLong(hdwnd, DWL_MSGRESULT, 0);
                    return 1;
            }
            break;
        case WM_COMMAND:
            switch(LOWORD(wParam)) {
                case IDD_RB1:
                case IDD_RB2:
                case IDD_RB3:
                    PropSheet_Changed(hPropSheet, hdwnd);
                    return 1;
                case IDD_FASTEST:
                    PropSheet_Changed(hPropSheet, hdwnd);
                    SendDlgItemMessage(hdwnd, IDD_RB2, BM_SETCHECK, 0, 0);
                    SendDlgItemMessage(hdwnd, IDD_RB3, BM_SETCHECK, 0, 0);
                    SendDlgItemMessage(hdwnd, IDD_RB1, BM_SETCHECK, 1, 0);
                    return 1;
                case IDD_SMALLEST:
                    PropSheet_Changed(hPropSheet, hdwnd);
                    SendDlgItemMessage(hdwnd, IDD_RB1, BM_SETCHECK, 0, 0);
                    SendDlgItemMessage(hdwnd, IDD_RB2, BM_SETCHECK, 0, 0);
                    SendDlgItemMessage(hdwnd, IDD_RB3, BM_SETCHECK, 1, 0);
                    return 1;
            }
            break;
        case WM_INITDIALOG: /* initialize radio buttons */
            SendDlgItemMessage(hdwnd, IDD_RB1, BM_SETCHECK, rb1, 0);
            SendDlgItemMessage(hdwnd, IDD_RB2, BM_SETCHECK, rb2, 0);
            SendDlgItemMessage(hdwnd, IDD_RB3, BM_SETCHECK, rb3, 0);
            return 1;
    }
    return 0;
}
```

13

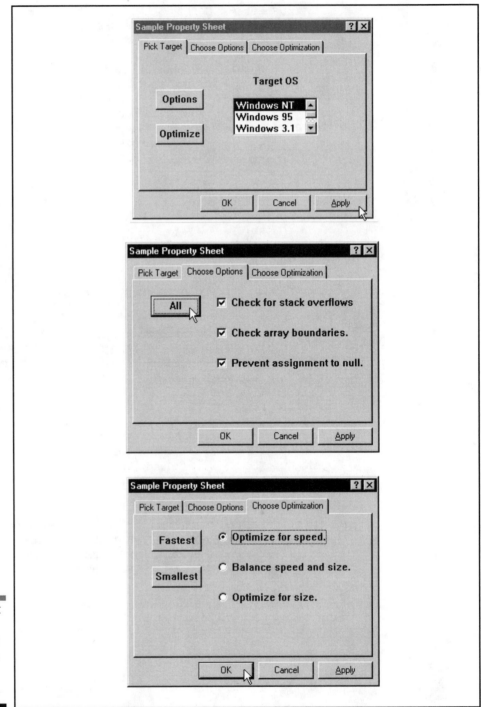

Sample output
from the
property sheet
demonstration
program
Figure 13-2.

The program requires the following resource file:

```
; Property sheet dialog boxes.
#include <windows.h>
#include <commctrl.h>
#include "prop.h"

PropSheetMenu MENU
{
  POPUP "&Property Sheet"
  {
    MENUITEM "&Activate\tF2", IDM_DIALOG
    MENUITEM "E&xit\tF10", IDM_EXIT
  }
  MENUITEM "&Help", IDM_HELP
}

PropSheetMenu ACCELERATORS
{
  VK_F2, IDM_DIALOG, VIRTKEY
  VK_F10, IDM_EXIT, VIRTKEY
  VK_F1, IDM_HELP, VIRTKEY
}

PropSheetDB1 DIALOG 10, 10, 110, 100
CAPTION "Pick Target"
{
  PUSHBUTTON "Options", IDD_OPTIONS, 11, 24, 34, 14,
             WS_CHILD | WS_VISIBLE | WS_TABSTOP
  PUSHBUTTON "Optimize", IDD_OPTIMIZE, 11, 48, 34, 14,
             WS_CHILD | WS_VISIBLE | WS_TABSTOP
  CTEXT "Target OS", 1, 66, 14, 60, 14
  LISTBOX IDD_LB1, 66, 30, 60, 33, LBS_NOTIFY |
             WS_VISIBLE | WS_BORDER | WS_VSCROLL |
             WS_TABSTOP
}

PropSheetDB2 DIALOG 10, 10, 110, 100
CAPTION "Choose Options"
{
  DEFPUSHBUTTON "All", IDD_ALL, 11, 10, 34, 14,
             WS_CHILD | WS_VISIBLE | WS_TABSTOP
  AUTOCHECKBOX "Check for stack overflows.", IDD_CB1,
             56, 10, 92, 10
  AUTOCHECKBOX "Check array boundaries.", IDD_CB2,
             56, 30, 90, 10
  AUTOCHECKBOX "Prevent assignment to null.", IDD_CB3,
             56, 50, 100, 10
```

```
}

PropSheetDB3 DIALOG 10, 10, 110, 100
CAPTION "Choose Optimization"
{
  DEFPUSHBUTTON "Fastest", IDD_FASTEST, 11, 10, 34, 14,
            WS_CHILD | WS_VISIBLE | WS_TABSTOP
  PUSHBUTTON "Smallest", IDD_SMALLEST, 11, 34, 34, 14,
            WS_CHILD | WS_VISIBLE | WS_TABSTOP
  AUTORADIOBUTTON "Optimize for speed.", IDD_RB1,
            56, 10, 90, 10
  AUTORADIOBUTTON "Balance speed and size.", IDD_RB2,
            56, 30, 90, 10
  AUTORADIOBUTTON "Optimize for size.", IDD_RB3,
            56, 50, 90, 10

}
```

The header file PROP.H is shown here:

```
#define IDM_DIALOG      100
#define IDM_EXIT        101
#define IDM_HELP        102

#define IDD_OPTIONS     201
#define IDD_OPTIMIZE    202
#define IDD_FASTEST     204
#define IDD_SMALLEST    205
#define IDD_ALL         207

#define IDD_LB1         301

#define IDD_EB1         401

#define IDD_CB1         501
#define IDD_CB2         502
#define IDD_CB3         503

#define IDD_RB1         601
#define IDD_RB2         602
#define IDD_RB3         603

#define IDD_STEXT1      700
```

In all three page dialog boxes there is one important thing to notice: Each time one is changed by the user, a **PSM_CHANGED** message is sent. For example, when the user alters the state of a check box in the Options dialog box, **PropSheet_Changed( )** is called. Once a **PSM_CHANGED** message has been sent, the Apply button will change from inactive to active. In general, you must notify the property sheet control whenever a property changes.

On the first page of the property sheet, the push buttons Options and Optimize demonstrate how pages can be selected under program control. That is, pressing Options selects the second page and pressing Optimize selects the third page. While there is no need for these push buttons in this example (since you can simply click on a page's tab to select it) these buttons illustrate the **PSM_SETCURSEL** message.

While the dialog boxes in this example are only placeholders, they illustrate the effect of using a property sheet. For example, if the user presses OK or moves to another page, then a **PSN_KILLACTIVE** message is received and any changes made by the user are saved. However, if the user presses Cancel, then any changes made to the current page are ignored. As the program is written, pressing Cancel does not undo any changes made to other pages. You might want to try adding this feature on your own. You should also try handling the **PSN_APPLY** message.

Responding to PSN_HELP

If you include the **PSP_HASHELP** flag when you create a property sheet page, then the Help button will be included in the property sheet control whenever that page is active. Pressing this button causes the **PSN_HELP** notification message to be sent. For most applications you will want to activate the Windows help system, which is described in Chapter 17, to provide on-line help relating to the property sheet control. However, the Windows help system is as sophisticated as it is complex. Fortunately, for very limited property sheets, you can respond to a **PSN_HELP** message by simply displaying a message box.

To try handling help requests, add the **PSP_HASHELP** to each property sheet page. For example, here it is added to the first page.

```
PropSheet[0].dwFlags = PSP_DEFAULT | PSP_HASHELP;
```

Next, add a handler for **PSN_HELP** to each property page dialog box function under the **WM_NOTIFY** case. For example, here is the handler for the first dialog box.

```
case PSN_HELP:
  MessageBox(hdwnd,
          "Pick Target allows you to choose\n"
          "the target operating system.",
          "Target", MB_OK);
  return 1;
```

Here is the way the Pick Target page looks with the addition of the Help button.

Creating a Wizard

A wizard is a sequenced set of property sheets.

From the programmer's point of view, a wizard is a set of sequenced property sheets. It is defined using the **PROPSHEETPAGE** and **PROPSHEETHEADER** structures defined earlier and created using the **CreatePropertySheetPage( )** and **PropertySheet( )** functions. However, to create a wizard, you must specify the **PSH_WIZARD** flag in the **dwFlags** field of the **PROPSHEETHEADER** structure. When this is done, the dialog boxes will automatically be sequenced from first to last, forming a wizard.

Enabling Wizard Buttons

Although including **PSH_WIZARD** automatically transforms your property sheet into a wizard, there are a few more steps that you will need to take in order for your wizard to perform correctly. First, you will need to enable and disable certain buttons manually. For example, on the first page, you will need to enable the Next button, but disable the Back button. On the last page, you will need to enable the Back button and the Finish button. On the pages between the first and last, the Next and Back buttons will have to be enabled. To accomplish this, either send a **PSM_SETWIZBUTTONS** message or use the **PropSheet_SetWizButtons( )** macro. As shown earlier, **PropSheet_SetWizButtons( )** has this general form:

VOID PropSheet_SetWizButtons(*hPropSheet*, *Flags*);

Here, *hPropSheet* is the handle of the property sheet control. In the *Flags* parameter, specify the button or buttons that you want to enable. Only those buttons that you specify will be enabled. The others will be disabled. The button macros are shown here:

PSWIZB_BACK
PSWIZB_NEXT
PSWIZB_FINISH
PSWIZB_DISABLEDFINISH

PSWIZB_DISABLEDFINISH creates a disabled Finish button. You can OR together two or more buttons. Therefore, to enable the Back and Finish buttons, you would use this statement:

```
PropSheet_SetWizButtons(PSWIZB_BACK | PSWIZB_FINISH);
```

13

Using a Bitmap

As you know from using Windows NT 4, most wizards specify a large bitmap on the left side of the first page. It may be specified on subsequent pages, as well. This bitmap serves to identify the wizard. While not technically required, it is highly recommended that at least the first page of any wizard that you create include such a bitmap.

Style Macros

Windows NT defines several values that help you create wizards that conform to Microsoft's style rules. These values are shown here:

Value	Meaning
WIZ_CXDLG	Width of page.
WIZ_CYDLG	Height of page.
WIZ_CXBMP	Width of bitmap.
WIZ_BODYX	X coordinate of the body of the page.
WIZ_BODYCX	Width of body, excluding the bitmap area.

These values are in terms of dialog box units.

These style macros can be used to create wizards that are the same size and shape as those used by Windows NT. They also help you position each page's controls relative to the area reserved for the bitmap. Keep in mind, however, that if a page does not require a bitmap, then you can use the entire page area. In the example that follows, the first two pages display a bitmap and the third page does not.

A Wizard Demonstration Program

The following program demonstrates a wizard. It does so by converting the previous property sheet example into a wizard. Sample output is shown in Figure 13-3.

```
/* Demonstrate a Wizard */

#include <windows.h>
#include <string.h>
#include <stdio.h>
#include <commctrl.h>
#include "prop.h"

#define NUMSTRINGS 5
#define NUMPAGES 3

#define BITMAPSIZEX 120
#define BITMAPSIZEY 226

LRESULT CALLBACK WindowFunc(HWND, UINT, WPARAM, LPARAM);
BOOL CALLBACK DialogFunc1(HWND, UINT, WPARAM, LPARAM);
BOOL CALLBACK DialogFunc2(HWND, UINT, WPARAM, LPARAM);
BOOL CALLBACK DialogFunc3(HWND, UINT, WPARAM, LPARAM);

char szWinName[] = "MyWin"; /* name of window class */

HINSTANCE hInst;

HWND hDlg; /* dialog box handle */
HPROPSHEETPAGE hPs[NUMPAGES];
HWND hPropSheet;
HWND hPage[NUMPAGES];

char list[][40] = {
   "Windows NT",
   "Windows 95",
   "Windows 3.1",
```

```
    "DOS",
    "UNIX"
};

int cb1=0, cb2=0, cb3=0;
int rb1=1, rb2=0, rb3=0;
int lb1sel=0;

HBITMAP hBit;

int WINAPI WinMain(HINSTANCE hThisInst, HINSTANCE hPrevInst,
                   LPSTR lpszArgs, int nWinMode)
{
  HWND hwnd;
  MSG msg;
  WNDCLASSEX wcl;
  HANDLE hAccel;

  wcl.cbSize = sizeof(WNDCLASSEX);

  /* Define a window class. */
  wcl.hInstance = hThisInst; /* handle to this instance */
  wcl.lpszClassName = szWinName; /* window class name */
  wcl.lpfnWndProc = WindowFunc; /* window function */
  wcl.style = 0; /* default style */

  wcl.hIcon = LoadIcon(NULL, IDI_APPLICATION);
  wcl.hIconSm = LoadIcon(NULL, IDI_APPLICATION);

  wcl.hCursor = LoadCursor(NULL, IDC_ARROW);

  /* specify name of menu resource */
  wcl.lpszMenuName = "PropSheetMenu"; /* main menu */

  wcl.cbClsExtra = 0; /* no extra */
  wcl.cbWndExtra = 0; /* information needed */

  /* Make the window white. */
  wcl.hbrBackground = GetStockObject(WHITE_BRUSH);

  /* Register the window class. */
  if(!RegisterClassEx(&wcl)) return 0;

  /* Now that a window class has been registered, a window
     can be created. */
  hwnd = CreateWindow(
    szWinName, /* name of window class */
    "Demonstrate a Wizard", /* title */
```

```
       WS_OVERLAPPEDWINDOW, /* standard window */
       CW_USEDEFAULT, /* X coordinate - let Windows decide */
       CW_USEDEFAULT, /* Y coordinate - let Windows decide */
       CW_USEDEFAULT, /* width - let Windows decide */
       CW_USEDEFAULT, /* height - let Windows decide */
       HWND_DESKTOP, /* no parent window */
       NULL, /* no override of class menu */
       hThisInst, /* handle of this instance of the program */
       NULL /* no additional arguments */
     );

     hInst = hThisInst; /* save the current instance handle */

     /* load accelerators */
     hAccel = LoadAccelerators(hThisInst, "PropSheetMenu");

     /* load bitmap */
     hBit = LoadBitmap(hThisInst, "wizbmp");

     InitCommonControls();

     /* Display the window. */
     ShowWindow(hwnd, nWinMode);
     UpdateWindow(hwnd);

     /* Create the message loop. */
     while(GetMessage(&msg, NULL, 0, 0))
     {
       if(!TranslateAccelerator(hwnd, hAccel, &msg)) {
         TranslateMessage(&msg); /* translate keyboard messages */
         DispatchMessage(&msg); /* return control to Windows NT */
       }
     }

   return msg.wParam;
}

/* This function is called by Windows NT and is passed
   messages from the message queue.
*/
LRESULT CALLBACK WindowFunc(HWND hwnd, UINT message,
                             WPARAM wParam, LPARAM lParam)
{
  int response;
  PROPSHEETPAGE PropSheet[NUMPAGES];
  PROPSHEETHEADER PropHdr;

  switch(message) {
    case WM_COMMAND:
```

```
switch(LOWORD(wParam)) {
  case IDM_DIALOG:
    PropSheet[0].dwSize = sizeof(PROPSHEETPAGE);
    PropSheet[0].dwFlags = PSP_DEFAULT;
    PropSheet[0].hInstance = hInst;
    PropSheet[0].pszTemplate = "PropSheetDB1";
    PropSheet[0].pszIcon = NULL;
    PropSheet[0].pfnDlgProc = (DLGPROC) DialogFunc1;
    PropSheet[0].pszTitle = "";
    PropSheet[0].lParam = 0;
    PropSheet[0].pfnCallback = NULL;

    PropSheet[1].dwSize = sizeof(PROPSHEETPAGE);
    PropSheet[1].dwFlags = PSP_DEFAULT;
    PropSheet[1].hInstance = hInst;
    PropSheet[1].pszTemplate = "PropSheetDB2";
    PropSheet[1].pszIcon = NULL;
    PropSheet[1].pfnDlgProc = (DLGPROC) DialogFunc2;
    PropSheet[1].pszTitle = "";
    PropSheet[1].lParam = 0;
    PropSheet[1].pfnCallback = NULL;

    PropSheet[2].dwSize = sizeof(PROPSHEETPAGE);
    PropSheet[2].dwFlags = PSP_DEFAULT;
    PropSheet[2].hInstance = hInst;
    PropSheet[2].pszTemplate = "PropSheetDB3";
    PropSheet[2].pszIcon = NULL;
    PropSheet[2].pfnDlgProc = (DLGPROC) DialogFunc3;
    PropSheet[2].pszTitle = "";
    PropSheet[2].lParam = 0;
    PropSheet[2].pfnCallback = NULL;

    hPs[0] = CreatePropertySheetPage(&PropSheet[0]);
    hPs[1] = CreatePropertySheetPage(&PropSheet[1]);
    hPs[2] = CreatePropertySheetPage(&PropSheet[2]);

    PropHdr.dwSize = sizeof(PROPSHEETHEADER);
    PropHdr.dwFlags = PSH_WIZARD; /* specify wizard */
    PropHdr.hwndParent = hwnd;
    PropHdr.hInstance = hInst;
    PropHdr.pszIcon = NULL;
    PropHdr.pszCaption = "";
    PropHdr.nPages = NUMPAGES;
    PropHdr.nStartPage = 0;
    PropHdr.phpage = hPs;
    PropHdr.pfnCallback = NULL;

    PropertySheet(&PropHdr);
    break;
```

```
      case IDM_EXIT:
        response = MessageBox(hwnd, "Quit the Program?",
                              "Exit", MB_YESNO);
        if(response == IDYES) PostQuitMessage(0);
        break;
      case IDM_HELP:
        MessageBox(hwnd, "Try the Wizard", "Help", MB_OK);
        break;
    }
    break;
  case WM_DESTROY: /* terminate the program */
    PostQuitMessage(0);
    break;
  default:
    /* Let Windows NT process any messages not specified in
       the preceding switch statement. */
    return DefWindowProc(hwnd, message, wParam, lParam);
  }
  return 0;
}

/* The first dialog function. */
BOOL CALLBACK DialogFunc1(HWND hdwnd, UINT message,
                          WPARAM wParam, LPARAM lParam)
{
  static long index;
  int i;
  char str[80];
  PAINTSTRUCT ps;
  HDC DC, memDC;

  switch(message) {
    case WM_PAINT: /* display icon */
      DC = BeginPaint(hdwnd, &ps);
      memDC = CreateCompatibleDC(DC);
      SelectObject(memDC, hBit);
      BitBlt(DC, 0, 0, BITMAPSIZEX, BITMAPSIZEY,
             memDC, 0, 0, SRCCOPY);
      EndPaint(hdwnd, &ps);
      DeleteDC(memDC);
      return 1;
    case WM_NOTIFY:
      switch(((NMHDR *) lParam)->code) {
        case PSN_SETACTIVE: /* page gaining focus */
          hPropSheet = ((NMHDR *) lParam)->hwndFrom;
          index = lb1sel;
          PropSheet_SetWizButtons(hPropSheet, PSWIZB_NEXT);
          SetWindowLong(hdwnd, DWL_MSGRESULT, 0);
          return 1;
```

```
         case PSN_KILLACTIVE: /* page losing focus */
           lb1sel = index;
           SetWindowLong(hdwnd, DWL_MSGRESULT, 0);
           return 0;
       }
       break;
     case WM_COMMAND:
       switch(LOWORD(wParam)) {
        case IDD_LB1: /* process a list box LBN_DBLCLK */
           PropSheet_Changed(hPropSheet, hdwnd);
           /* see if user made a selection */
           if(HIWORD(wParam)==LBN_DBLCLK) {
             index = SendDlgItemMessage(hdwnd, IDD_LB1,
                   LB_GETCURSEL, 0, 0);  /* get index */
             sprintf(str, "%s", list[index]);

             MessageBox(hdwnd, str, "Selection Made", MB_OK);
           }
           return 1;
       }
       break;
     case WM_INITDIALOG: /* initialize list box */
       for(i=0; i<NUMSTRINGS; i++)
         SendDlgItemMessage(hdwnd, IDD_LB1,
                   LB_ADDSTRING, 0, (LPARAM)list[i]);

       /* select first item */
       SendDlgItemMessage(hdwnd, IDD_LB1, LB_SETCURSEL, lb1sel, 0);

       return 1;
   }
   return 0;
}

/* The Second dialog function. */
BOOL CALLBACK DialogFunc2(HWND hdwnd, UINT message,
                          WPARAM wParam, LPARAM lParam)
{
  PAINTSTRUCT ps;
  HDC DC, memDC;

  switch(message) {
    case WM_PAINT: /* display icon */
      DC = BeginPaint(hdwnd, &ps);
      memDC = CreateCompatibleDC(DC);
      SelectObject(memDC, hBit);
      BitBlt(DC, 0, 0, BITMAPSIZEX, BITMAPSIZEY,
            memDC, 0, 0, SRCCOPY);
      EndPaint(hdwnd, &ps);
```

```
        DeleteDC(memDC);
        return 1;
      case WM_NOTIFY:
        switch(((NMHDR *) lParam)->code) {
          case PSN_SETACTIVE:/* page gaining focus */
            hPropSheet = ((NMHDR *) lParam)->hwndFrom;
            PropSheet_SetWizButtons(hPropSheet,
                          PSWIZB_NEXT | PSWIZB_BACK);
            SetWindowLong(hdwnd, DWL_MSGRESULT, 0);
            return 1;
          case PSN_KILLACTIVE: /* page losing focus */
            cb1 = SendDlgItemMessage(hdwnd, IDD_CB1,
                          BM_GETCHECK, 0, 0);
            cb2 = SendDlgItemMessage(hdwnd, IDD_CB2,
                          BM_GETCHECK, 0, 0);
            cb3 = SendDlgItemMessage(hdwnd, IDD_CB3,
                          BM_GETCHECK, 0, 0);
          SetWindowLong(hdwnd, DWL_MSGRESULT, 0);
          return 1;
        }
        break;
      case WM_COMMAND:
        switch(LOWORD(wParam)) {
          case IDD_CB1:
          case IDD_CB2:
          case IDD_CB3:
            PropSheet_Changed(hPropSheet, hdwnd);
            return 1;
          case IDD_ALL:
            PropSheet_Changed(hPropSheet, hdwnd);
            SendDlgItemMessage(hdwnd, IDD_CB1, BM_SETCHECK,
                          BST_CHECKED, 0);
            SendDlgItemMessage(hdwnd, IDD_CB2, BM_SETCHECK,
                          BST_CHECKED, 0);
            SendDlgItemMessage(hdwnd, IDD_CB3, BM_SETCHECK,
                          BST_CHECKED, 0);
            return 1;
        }
        break;
      case WM_INITDIALOG: /* initialize check boxes */
        SendDlgItemMessage(hdwnd, IDD_CB1, BM_SETCHECK, cb1, 0);
        SendDlgItemMessage(hdwnd, IDD_CB2, BM_SETCHECK, cb2, 0);
        SendDlgItemMessage(hdwnd, IDD_CB3, BM_SETCHECK, cb3, 0);
        return 1;
  }
  return 0;
}

/* The Third dialog function. */
```

```
BOOL CALLBACK DialogFunc3(HWND hdwnd, UINT message,
                          WPARAM wParam, LPARAM lParam)
{
  switch(message) {
    case WM_NOTIFY:
      switch(((NMHDR *) lParam)->code) {
        case PSN_SETACTIVE: /* page gaining focus */
          hPropSheet = ((NMHDR *) lParam)->hwndFrom;
          PropSheet_SetWizButtons(hPropSheet,
                        PSWIZB_FINISH | PSWIZB_BACK);
          SetWindowLong(hdwnd, DWL_MSGRESULT, 0);
          return 1;
        case PSN_WIZFINISH: /* Finish button pressed */
        case PSN_KILLACTIVE: /* page losing focus */
          rb1 = SendDlgItemMessage(hdwnd, IDD_RB1,
                        BM_GETCHECK, 0, 0);
          rb2 = SendDlgItemMessage(hdwnd, IDD_RB2,
                        BM_GETCHECK, 0, 0);
          rb3 = SendDlgItemMessage(hdwnd, IDD_RB3,
                        BM_GETCHECK, 0, 0);
          SetWindowLong(hdwnd, DWL_MSGRESULT, 0);
          return 1;
      }
      break;
    case WM_COMMAND:
      switch(LOWORD(wParam)) {
        case IDD_RB1:
        case IDD_RB2:
        case IDD_RB3:
          PropSheet_Changed(hPropSheet, hdwnd);
          return 1;
        case IDD_FASTEST:
          PropSheet_Changed(hPropSheet, hdwnd);
          SendDlgItemMessage(hdwnd, IDD_RB2, BM_SETCHECK, 0, 0);
          SendDlgItemMessage(hdwnd, IDD_RB3, BM_SETCHECK, 0, 0);
          SendDlgItemMessage(hdwnd, IDD_RB1, BM_SETCHECK, 1, 0);
          return 1;
        case IDD_SMALLEST:
          PropSheet_Changed(hPropSheet, hdwnd);
          SendDlgItemMessage(hdwnd, IDD_RB1, BM_SETCHECK, 0, 0);
          SendDlgItemMessage(hdwnd, IDD_RB2, BM_SETCHECK, 0, 0);
          SendDlgItemMessage(hdwnd, IDD_RB3, BM_SETCHECK, 1, 0);
          return 1;
      }
      break;
    case WM_INITDIALOG: /* initialize radio buttons */
      SendDlgItemMessage(hdwnd, IDD_RB1, BM_SETCHECK, rb1, 0);
      SendDlgItemMessage(hdwnd, IDD_RB2, BM_SETCHECK, rb2, 0);
      SendDlgItemMessage(hdwnd, IDD_RB3, BM_SETCHECK, rb3, 0);
```

```
        return 1;
    }
    return 0;
}
```

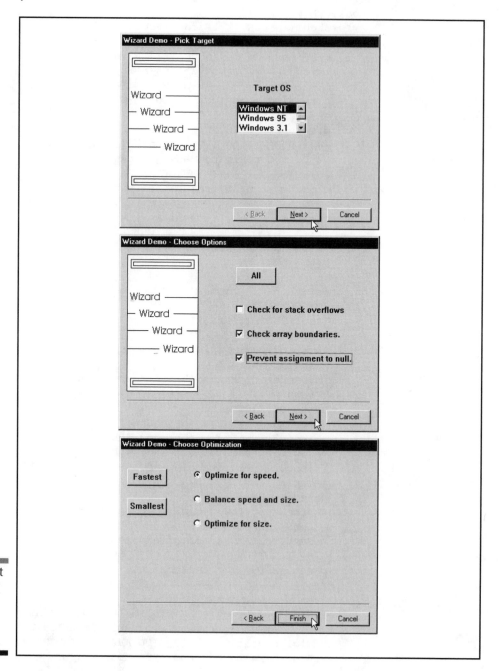

Sample output
from the
wizard
program
Figure 13-3.

This program uses the same PROP.H file as the preceding property sheet program. However, it requires this resource file:

```
; Wizard resource file.
#include <windows.h>
#include <commctrl.h>
#include "prop.h"

wizbmp BITMAP bp1.bmp

PropSheetMenu MENU
{
  POPUP "&Wizard Demo"
  {
    MENUITEM "&Start Wizard\tF2", IDM_DIALOG
    MENUITEM "E&xit\tF10", IDM_EXIT
  }
  MENUITEM "&Help", IDM_HELP
}


PropSheetMenu ACCELERATORS
{
  VK_F2, IDM_DIALOG, VIRTKEY
  VK_F10, IDM_EXIT, VIRTKEY
  VK_F1, IDM_HELP, VIRTKEY
}

PropSheetDB1 DIALOG 10, 10, WIZ_CXDLG, WIZ_CYDLG
CAPTION "Wizard Demo - Pick Target"
{
  CTEXT "Target OS", IDD_STEXT1, WIZ_BODYX, 24, 60, 14
  LISTBOX IDD_LB1, WIZ_BODYX, 40, 60, 33, LBS_NOTIFY |
              WS_VISIBLE | WS_BORDER | WS_VSCROLL |
              WS_TABSTOP
}


PropSheetDB2 DIALOG 10, 10, WIZ_CXDLG, WIZ_CYDLG
CAPTION "Wizard Demo - Choose Options"
{
  DEFPUSHBUTTON "All", IDD_ALL, WIZ_BODYX, 10, 34, 14,
                WS_CHILD | WS_VISIBLE | WS_TABSTOP
  AUTOCHECKBOX "Check for stack overflows.", IDD_CB1,
                WIZ_BODYX, 40, 92, 10
  AUTOCHECKBOX "Check array boundaries.", IDD_CB2,
                WIZ_BODYX, 60, 92, 10
  AUTOCHECKBOX "Prevent assignment to null.", IDD_CB3,
                WIZ_BODYX, 80, 100, 10
}
```

13

```
PropSheetDB3 DIALOG 10, 10, WIZ_CXDLG, WIZ_CYDLG
CAPTION "Wizard Demo - Choose Optimization"
{
  DEFPUSHBUTTON "Fastest", IDD_FASTEST, 0, 10, 34, 14,
            WS_CHILD | WS_VISIBLE | WS_TABSTOP
  PUSHBUTTON "Smallest", IDD_SMALLEST, 0, 34, 34, 14,
            WS_CHILD | WS_VISIBLE | WS_TABSTOP
  AUTORADIOBUTTON "Optimize for speed.", IDD_RB1,
                56, 10, 90, 10
  AUTORADIOBUTTON "Balance speed and size.", IDD_RB2,
                56, 30, 90, 10
  AUTORADIOBUTTON "Optimize for size.", IDD_RB3,
                56, 50, 90, 10
}
```

As you can see, very few changes are required to transform a property sheet control into a wizard. Notice, however, that you must activate the appropriate buttons each time a new page is activated. That is, your program must manually enable the Back, Next, and Finish buttons, as needed.

Since wizards are activated in a strictly linear sequence, the Options and Optimize push buttons are no longer included on the first page. Remember, it is not proper style to activate pages out of sequence when using a wizard.

One final point: Notice that the last page does not display a bitmap. In this case, the controls are not positioned relative to **WIZ_BODYX**. Instead, they are positioned relative to zero. If a page does not contain a bitmap, then you may use the entire page for your controls.

Worth the Effort

Property sheets and wizards are two of Windows NT's more sophisticated controls. Although they require a bit of work to set up, they are worth the effort because they help you handle complex input situations. In particular, wizards solve a long-standing problem in the Windows interface: how to guide a user through a complex set of options and selections that require more than one screen full of controls. Now that you know how to handle wizards, you should use one whenever a complicated input operation is required.

CHAPTER 14

Using a Header Control

447

This chapter concludes our exploration of Windows NT 4's common controls by examining the header control. A *header control* is a bar that consists of column headings. You have undoubtedly seen header controls when using Windows NT 4. For example, when using the Explorer, the detailed view of files is presented using a header control. A header control is not just a set of passive column headings. It allows the user to adjust the width of each column. It is also possible to make the header control respond to mouse clicks. As you will see, the header control is one of the more useful of the common controls because it gives you a standardized way of displaying and managing columns of information.

PORTABILITY: The header control automates a task that was previously handled manually by older programs. You will want to watch for opportunities to apply this control when porting.

Creating a Header Control

A header control is created using **CreateWindow( )** or **CreateWindowEx( )**, specifying the **WC_HEADER** window class. A header control should also include the **WS_CHILD** style. Generally, a header control is created with zero width and height. The reason for this is that the control will need to be sized to fit the client area of its parent window. It must also be sized appropriately for the currently selected font. Fortunately, the header control has a mechanism that will determine its correct dimensions after it has been created, and you do not need to handle these matters manually.

Since a header control will be resized after it is created, you can use the following call to **CreateWindow( )** to create nearly any type of header control.

```
hHeadWnd = CreateWindow(WC_HEADER, NULL,
                WS_CHILD | WS_BORDER,
                CW_USEDEFAULT, CW_USEDEFAULT,
                0, 0, hParent,
                (HMENU) ID_HEADCONTROL,
                hInst, NULL);
```

Here, **hParent** is the handle of the parent window and **hInst** is the instance handle of the application. The ID of the header control is specified by **ID_HEADCONTROL**. The dimensions of the control are irrelevant, and the control is not initially visible.

By default, the header control contains only labels and dividers. However, if you include the **HDS_BUTTONS** style when you create the control, then each heading will consist of a push button. You will see an example that makes use of this feature later in this chapter.

A header control is empty when it is first created. Each heading must be added individually. As just mentioned, the control must also be sized to fit the parent window. For these reasons, the header control should initially be invisible. It should be displayed only after it has been given headings and its size has been adjusted. Thus, you must follow these steps when creating a header control.

1. Obtain the proper dimensions for the header control and resize the control.
2. Add each heading to the control.
3. Make the header control visible.

To accomplish these steps, you will send various messages to the control, which are described next.

Sending Messages to a Header Control

A header control responds to several messages. These messages are shown in Table 14-1. You can send a header control a message using **SendMessage( )**, specifying the handle of the control as the target. However, for most of these messages Windows NT 4 defines macros that are more convenient to use. The header control message macros are shown here:

14

BOOL Header_DeleteItem(*hHeadWnd*, *index*);

BOOL Header_GetItem(*hHeadWnd*, *index*, *HdItemPtr*);

int Header_GetItemCount(*hHeadWnd*);

int Header_InsertItem(*hHeadWnd*, *index*, *HdItemPtr*);

BOOL Header_Layout(*hHeadWnd*, *LayoutPtr*);

BOOL Header_SetItem(*hHeadWnd*, *index*, *HdItemPtr*);

In all cases, *hHeadWnd* is the handle of the header control and *index* is the index of the specific heading being affected. *HdItemPtr* is a pointer to an **HD_ITEM** structure. *LayoutPtr* is a pointer to an **HD_LAYOUT** structure. Since these structures are crucial to creating and using a header control, let's examine them now.

Message	Meaning
HDM_DELETEITEM	Deletes a heading. Returns nonzero if successful and zero on failure. *wParam* specifies the index of the heading. *lParam* is zero.
HDM_GETITEM	Obtains heading information. Returns nonzero if successful and zero on failure. *wParam* specifies the index of the heading. *lParam* is a pointer to an **HD_ITEM** structure that receives the information. The value of the **mask** member of **HD_ITEM** specifies what information is obtained.
HDM_GETITEMCOUNT	Returns the number of headings or –1 on failure. *wParam* is zero. *lParam* is zero.
HDM_HITTEST	Given a point, returns index of heading that contains that point or –1 if specified point is not in a heading. *wParam* is zero. *lParam* is a pointer to an **HD_HITTESTINFO** structure that defines the point.
HDM_INSERTITEM	Inserts a heading. Returns index of item being inserted if successful and –1 on failure. *wParam* specifies the index after which the new heading is inserted. To insert the first heading, use zero for the index. To insert a heading at the end, specify an index that is greater than the number of headings currently in the header control. *lParam* is a pointer to an **HD_ITEM** structure that contains the heading being inserted.
HDM_LAYOUT	Obtains appropriate dimensions for the header control given the dimensions of its parent window's client area. Returns nonzero if successful and zero on failure. *wParam* is zero. *lParam* is a pointer to an **HD_LAYOUT** structure. Its **prc** member contains the dimensions of the parent window's client area when sent. On return, its **pwpos** member contains the suggested dimensions for the header control.

Header Control
Messages
Table 14-1.

Message	Meaning
HDM_SETITEM	Sets heading information. Returns nonzero if successful and zero on failure. *wParam* specifies the index of the heading. *lParam* is a pointer to an **HD_ITEM** structure that contains the heading's information. The value of the **mask** member of **HD_ITEM** specifies what information is set.

Header Control
Messages
(*continued*)
Table 14-1.

The HD_ITEM Structure

Each header item (i.e., heading) in a header control is defined by an **HD_ITEM** structure. This structure is shown here:

```
typedef struct _HD_ITEM
{
  UINT mask;
  int cxy;
  LPSTR pszText;
  HBITMAP hbm;
  int cchTextMax;
  int fmt;
  LPARAM lParam;
} HD_ITEM;
```

14

The value of **mask** determines which of the other members of **HD_ITEM** contain information. It can be any combination of the following values:

Value	Meaning
HDI_BITMAP	**hbm** contains the handle of a bitmap.
HDI_FORMAT	**fmt** contains format flags.
HDI_HEIGHT	**cxy** contains the height of the header.
HDI_WIDTH	**cxy** contains the width of the header.
HDI_LPARAM	**lParam** contains information.
HDI_TEXT	**pszText** and **cchTextMax** contain information.

The **cxy** member contains the width or height of the heading, depending upon whether **HDI_WIDTH** or **HDI_HEIGHT** is specified in **mask**.

pszText points to a string that acts as a column label. **cchTextMax** specifies the length of the string.

If a bitmap will be displayed in the heading, then the handle of its bitmap must be specified in **hbm**.

The value contained in **fmt** determines how the header is displayed. It consists of a combination of one justification value and one content value. The content values are **HDF_STRING** (header displays a string), **HDF_-BITMAP** (header displays a bitmap), and **HDF_OWNERDRAW** (owner draws). The justification values are **HDF_LEFT** (left justify), **HDF_CENTER** (center), **HDF_RIGHT** (right justify), and **HDF_RTLREADING** (text is displayed right to left).

The value in **lParam** is application dependent.

The HD_LAYOUT Structure

The **HD_LAYOUT** structure is used by the **HDM_LAYOUT** message to obtain appropriate dimensions for a header control given the dimensions of a bounding rectangle, which is usually the client area of the header control's parent window. **HD_LAYOUT** is defined like this:

```
typedef struct _HD_LAYOUT
{
  RECT *prc;
  WINDOWPOS *pwpos;
} HD_LAYOUT;
```

Here, **prc** is a pointer to a **RECT** structure that specifies the size of the area in which the header control will be used. These dimensions are processed by the header control, which determines what its size must be to fit within the specified region. The adjusted dimensions are returned in the **WINDOWPOS** structure pointed to by **pwpos**.

You are already familiar with the **RECT** structure. The **WINDOWPOS** structure is defined like this:

```
typedef struct tagWINDOWPOS {
  HWND hwnd;
  HWND hwndInsertAfter;
  int x;
  int y;
  int cx;
  int cy;
```

```
    UINT flags;
} WINDOWPOS;
```

Here, **hwnd** is the handle of the header control. **hwndInsertAfter** is the
handle of the previous window in the Z-order. The upper-left corner of the
window is specified by **x** and **y**. The width is contained in **cx** and the height
is contained in **cy**. The value in **flags** specifies various attributes associated
with the window. For our purposes, the **WINDOWPOS** structure is
initialized by the header control. There is no reason to alter the contents
of this structure.

Sizing the Header

To resize a header control after it has been created, you must send it an
HDM_LAYOUT message (or use the **Header_Layout( )** macro). You must
then use the dimensions and coordinates returned by this message to adjust
the size of the header control. For example, here is one way to accomplish
this:

```
RECT rect;
HD_LAYOUT layout;
WINDOWPOS winpos;

/* get size of parent window */
GetClientRect(hParent, &rect);

/* get header control layout that will fit client area */
layout.pwpos = &winpos;
layout.prc = &rect;
Header_Layout(hHeadWnd, &layout);

/* dimension header to fit current size of client area */
MoveWindow(hHeadWnd, winpos.x, winpos.y,
          winpos.cx, winpos.cy, 0);
```

First, the size of the window in which the header control must fit is obtained
by calling **GetClientRect( )**. Then, these dimensions are passed to the header
control using **Header_Layout( )**. On return, the **pwpos** member will contain
the appropriate dimensions for the header control. These dimensions are
then used in a call to **MoveWindow( )**, which resizes and positions the
header control as specified. (See the In Depth box.)

At this point the header control is still not visible. It should not be made
visible until after the actual headings have been inserted in the control.

14

Moving a Window

Sometimes you will need to change the position or the size of a window. For example, you will need to change the size of a header control to fit the dimensions of the client area of its parent window. To accomplish this, use the **MoveWindow( )** API function. Its prototype is shown here:

BOOL MoveWindow(HWND *hwnd*, int *NewX*, int *NewY*, int *NewWidth*,
            int *NewHeight*, BOOL *Repaint*);

Here, *hwnd* is the handle of the window being affected. The desired location of its upper-left corner is passed in *NewX* and *NewY*. The new width and height are specified in *NewWidth* and *NewHeight*. If *Repaint* is nonzero, the window will be repainted immediately after it has been resized. Otherwise, a repainting request will be put in the window's message queue for later processing. **MoveWindow( )** returns nonzero if successful and zero on failure.

While the **MoveWindow( )** function can change the size and location of a window, it cannot change its Z-order (that is, the order of the window in the stack of windows). If you wish to change a window's Z-order, then you will need to use **SetWindowPos( )**. It has the following prototype:

BOOL SetWindowPos(HWND *hwnd*, HWND *hWhere*, int *NewX*, int *NewY*,
            int *NewWidth*, int *NewHeight*, UINT *How*);

Here, *hwnd* is the handle of the window being affected. *hWhere* specifies where in the Z-order the window will be placed. *hWhere* can be either the handle of the window that will precede *hwnd* in the Z-order or a value that specifies an absolute location. For example, to specify the topmost window, use **HWND_TOP**. To put *hwnd* on the bottom, use **HWND_BOTTOM**. The desired location of its upper-left corner is passed in *NewX* and *NewY*. The new width and height are specified in *NewWidth* and *NewHeight*. The value of *How* determines precisely what occurs when the window is repositioned. For example, **SWP_HIDEWINDOW** hides the window and **SWP_SHOWWINDOW** makes the window visible. **SetWindowPos( )** returns nonzero if successful and zero on failure.

The coordinates that you pass in *NewX* and *NewY* have different meanings depending upon whether the window being affected is a top-level window or a child window. For child windows, the coordinates are relative to the parent window's client area. For top-level windows, the coordinates apply to the screen.

Both **MoveWindow( )** and **SetWindowPos( )** are interesting and useful functions that can help you solve a variety of problems. You might want to experiment with them a bit.

Inserting Headings into the Header Control

After the header control has been appropriately sized, you may insert headings into it. Each heading defines one column. To insert a heading, you must first load an **HD_ITEM** structure with information about the heading and then call **Header_InsertItem( )**. For example, the following fragment inserts the first column's heading into a header control.

```
HD_ITEM hditem;

hditem.mask = HDI_FORMAT | HDI_WIDTH | HDI_TEXT;
hditem.pszText = "Heading #1";
hditem.cchTextMax = strlen(hditem.pszText);
hditem.cxy = 100;
hditem.fmt = HDF_STRING | HDF_LEFT;
Header_InsertItem(hHeadWnd, 0, &hditem);
```

In this example, the header displays a string which, in this case, is "Heading #1". The string is left justified. The width of the item is specified as 100, which is arbitrary in this case.

Remember, each time you insert an item, you must specify the index of the item that the new header will follow.

Displaying the Header Control

Header controls are usually invisible when created and must be shown after they are sized and initialized.

Once you have inserted all the headings, you can finally display the header control by calling **ShowWindow( )**. For example, to display the header control whose handle is **hHeadWnd**, use the following call:

```
ShowWindow(hHeadWnd, SW_SHOW); /* display the header control */
```

Keep in mind that, at this point, you have only created the header control, which defines headings for columns of data. You have not displayed any data. This will be done by other parts of your program. However, before you

14

can use the header control, you will need to learn about the various notification messages that it can generate.

Header Notification Messages

Header controls are active rather than passive. That is, they generate messages when they are accessed by the user. For example, when the user resizes a heading, your program will be sent a message describing this event and it will need to respond appropriately. The header control generates several different messages. Which messages your program responds to is determined by how you utilize the control.

A header control sends a message to your program using the **WM_NOTIFY** message. When **WM_NOTIFY** is received, **wParam** contains the ID of the control generating the message. For most header control notification messages, **lParam** points to an **HD_NOTIFY** structure, which is defined like this:

```
typedef struct _HD_NOTIFY
{
  NMHDR hdr;
  int iItem;
  int iButton;
  HD_ITEM *pitem;
} HD_NOTIFY;
```

The **hdr** member is the standard **NMHDR** structure which we have been using. For **WM_NOTIFY** messages associated with header controls, **hdr.hwndFrom** is the handle of the header control that generated the message. **hdr.idFrom** is the header control's ID. The value of **hdr.code** contains the notification code, which describes what action has taken place. The header control notification codes are shown in Table 14-2.

The **iItem** member of **HD_NOTIFY** specifies the index of the heading that was accessed. **iButton** specifies which mouse button was pressed. For most applications this is not of interest.

The **pitem** member points to an **HD_ITEM** structure that describes the heading that was accessed. However, when an **HDN_ITEMCLICK** notification is received, **pitem** is **NULL**.

There is one exception to the preceding discussion. When an **HDN_ITEMDBLCLICK** message is received, **lParam** points directly to an **NMHDR** structure, instead of an **HD_NOTIFY** structure.

Code	Meaning
HDN_BEGINTRACK	User has started to resize a column heading. Your handler must return zero to enable tracking or nonzero to disable it.
HDN_DIVIDERDBLCLICK	User double-clicked on divider.
HDN_ENDTRACK	User has finished resizing a column heading.
HDN_ITEMCHANGED	A heading has been changed.
HDN_ITEMCHANGING	A heading is going to change. Your handler must return zero to allow a change to occur or nonzero to disallow the change.
HDN_ITEMCLICK	User clicked on a heading. Applies only to button-style headers.
HDN_ITEMDBLCLICK	User double-clicked on a heading. Applies only to button-style headers.
HDN_TRACK	User is in the process of resizing a column heading. Your handler must return zero to allow tracking to proceed or nonzero to stop tracking.

The Header Control Notification Codes **Table 14-2.**

A Simple Header Control Example

14

Now that you have seen all the pieces, a simple header control example can be assembled. The following program creates a header control that has five columns. The control is used to manage a simple mailing list that stores name and address information. The entire header control program is shown here. Sample output is shown in Figure 14-1.

```
/* A simple header control example. */

#include <windows.h>
#include <commctrl.h>
#include <string.h>
#include <stdio.h>
#include "head.h"

#define NUMCOLS 5
#define DEFWIDTH 100
#define MINWIDTH 10
#define SPACING 8
#define NUMENTRIES 7
```

```c
LRESULT CALLBACK WindowFunc(HWND, UINT, WPARAM, LPARAM);
HWND InitHeader(HWND hParent);
void InitDatabase(void);

char szWinName[] = "MyWin"; /* name of window class */

HINSTANCE hInst;
HWND hHeadWnd;

int HeaderHeight;

int columns[NUMCOLS] = {DEFWIDTH, DEFWIDTH,
                        DEFWIDTH, DEFWIDTH,
                        DEFWIDTH};

struct MailList {
  char name[40];
  char street[40];
  char city[40];
  char state[3];
  char code[11];
} data[NUMENTRIES];

int WINAPI WinMain(HINSTANCE hThisInst, HINSTANCE hPrevInst,
                   LPSTR lpszArgs, int nWinMode)
{
  MSG msg;
  WNDCLASSEX wcl;
  HANDLE hAccel;
  HWND hwnd;

  /* define a window class */
  wcl.cbSize = sizeof(WNDCLASSEX);
  wcl.hInstance = hThisInst; /* handle to this instance */
  wcl.lpszClassName = szWinName; /* window class name */
  wcl.lpfnWndProc = WindowFunc; /* window function */
  wcl.style = 0; /* default style */

  wcl.hIcon = LoadIcon(NULL, IDI_APPLICATION);
  wcl.hIconSm = LoadIcon(NULL, IDI_APPLICATION);
  wcl.hCursor = LoadCursor(NULL, IDC_ARROW);

  /* specify name of menu resource */
  wcl.lpszMenuName = "HeaderMenu"; /* main menu */

  wcl.cbClsExtra = 0; /* no extra */
  wcl.cbWndExtra = 0; /* information needed */
```

```
/* Make the window white. */
wcl.hbrBackground = GetStockObject(WHITE_BRUSH);

/* Register the window class. */
if(!RegisterClassEx(&wcl)) return 0;

/* Now that a window class has been registered, a window
   can be created. */
hwnd = CreateWindow(
  szWinName, /* name of window class */
  "Using a Header Control", /* title */
  WS_OVERLAPPEDWINDOW, /* standard window */
  CW_USEDEFAULT, /* X coordinate - let Windows decide */
  CW_USEDEFAULT, /* Y coordinate - let Windows decide */
  CW_USEDEFAULT, /* width - let Windows decide */
  CW_USEDEFAULT, /* height - let Windows decide */
  HWND_DESKTOP, /* no parent window */
  NULL, /* no override of class menu */
  hThisInst, /* handle of this instance of the program */
  NULL /* no additional arguments */
);

hInst = hThisInst; /* save the current instance handle */

/* load accelerators */
hAccel = LoadAccelerators(hThisInst, "HeaderMenu");

InitCommonControls();

/* Display the window. */
ShowWindow(hwnd, nWinMode);
UpdateWindow(hwnd);

/* Create the message loop. */
while(GetMessage(&msg, NULL, 0, 0))
{
  if(!TranslateAccelerator(hwnd, hAccel, &msg)) {
    TranslateMessage(&msg); /* translate keyboard messages */
    DispatchMessage(&msg); /* return control to Windows NT */
  }
}
return msg.wParam;
}

/* This function is called by Windows NT and is passed
   messages from the message queue.
*/
```

14

```
LRESULT CALLBACK WindowFunc(HWND hwnd, UINT message,
                             WPARAM wParam, LPARAM lParam)
{
  int response;
  RECT rect;
  HD_LAYOUT layout;
  WINDOWPOS winpos;
  HD_NOTIFY *hdnptr;
  HD_ITEM *hdiptr;
  PAINTSTRUCT ps;
  TEXTMETRIC tm;
  SIZE size;

  char str[80];
  int i, j, ColStart, chrs;
  int entry;
  int linespacing;

  HDC hdc;

  switch(message) {
    case WM_CREATE:
      hHeadWnd = InitHeader(hwnd);
      InitDatabase();
      break;
    case WM_COMMAND:
      switch(LOWORD(wParam)) {
        case IDM_EXIT:
          response = MessageBox(hwnd, "Quit the Program?",
                                "Exit", MB_YESNO);
          if(response == IDYES) PostQuitMessage(0);
          break;
        case IDM_HELP:
          MessageBox(hwnd, "Try resizing the header.",
                     "Help", MB_OK);
          break;
      }
      break;
    case WM_SIZE:
      /* Resize the header control when its parent window
         changes size. */
      GetClientRect(hwnd, &rect);
      layout.prc = &rect;
      layout.pwpos = &winpos;
      Header_Layout(hHeadWnd, &layout);

      MoveWindow(hHeadWnd, winpos.x, winpos.y,
                 winpos.cx, winpos.cy, 1);
```

```
      break;
  case WM_NOTIFY:
    if(LOWORD(wParam) == ID_HEADCONTROL) {
      hdnptr = (HD_NOTIFY *) lParam;
      hdiptr = (HD_ITEM *) hdnptr->pitem;
      switch(hdnptr->hdr.code) {
        case HDN_ENDTRACK: /* user changed column width */
          if(hdiptr->cxy < MINWIDTH) {
            hdiptr->cxy = MINWIDTH;
            columns[hdnptr->iItem] = MINWIDTH;
          }
          else
            columns[hdnptr->iItem] = hdiptr->cxy;
          InvalidateRect(hwnd, NULL, 1);
          break;
      }
    }
    break;
  case WM_PAINT:
    hdc = BeginPaint(hwnd, &ps);

    GetTextMetrics(hdc, &tm);
    linespacing = tm.tmHeight + tm.tmInternalLeading;

    for(entry = 0; entry < NUMENTRIES; entry++) {
      ColStart = 0;
      for(i=0; i<NUMCOLS; i++) {
        switch(i) {
          case 0: strcpy(str, data[entry].name);
            break;
          case 1: strcpy(str, data[entry].street);
            break;
          case 2: strcpy(str, data[entry].city);
            break;
          case 3: strcpy(str, data[entry].state);
            break;
          case 4: strcpy(str, data[entry].code);
            break;
        }

        /* add ... to truncated entries */
        GetTextExtentPoint32(hdc, str, strlen(str), &size);
        j = 2;
        while((columns[i]-SPACING) < size.cx) {
          chrs = columns[i] / tm.tmAveCharWidth;
          strcpy(&str[chrs-j], "...");
          GetTextExtentPoint32(hdc, str, strlen(str), &size);
```

```
          j++;
        }

        TextOut(hdc, ColStart+SPACING,
                HeaderHeight+(entry*linespacing),
                str, strlen(str));

        ColStart += columns[i];
      }
    }
    EndPaint(hwnd, &ps);
    break;
  case WM_DESTROY: /* terminate the program */
    PostQuitMessage(0);
    break;
  default:
    /* Let Windows NT process any messages not specified in
       the preceding switch statement. */
    return DefWindowProc(hwnd, message, wParam, lParam);
  }
  return 0;
}


/* Initialize the header control. */
HWND InitHeader(HWND hParent)
{
  HWND hHeadWnd;
  RECT rect;
  HD_LAYOUT layout;
  WINDOWPOS winpos;
  HD_ITEM hditem;

  GetClientRect(hParent, &rect);

  /* create the header control */
  hHeadWnd = CreateWindow(WC_HEADER, NULL,
                WS_CHILD | WS_BORDER,
                CW_USEDEFAULT, CW_USEDEFAULT,
                0, 0, hParent,
                (HMENU) ID_HEADCONTROL,
                hInst, NULL);

  /* get header control layout that will fit client area */
  layout.pwpos = &winpos;
  layout.prc = &rect;
  Header_Layout(hHeadWnd, &layout);

  /* dimension header to fit current size of client area */
```

```
        MoveWindow(hHeadWnd, winpos.x, winpos.y,
                   winpos.cx, winpos.cy, 0);

        HeaderHeight = winpos.cy; /* save height of header */

        /* insert items into the header */
        hditem.mask = HDI_FORMAT | HDI_WIDTH | HDI_TEXT;
        hditem.pszText = "Name";
        hditem.cchTextMax = strlen(hditem.pszText);
        hditem.cxy = DEFWIDTH;
        hditem.fmt = HDF_STRING | HDF_LEFT;
        Header_InsertItem(hHeadWnd, 0, &hditem);

        hditem.pszText = "Street";
        hditem.cchTextMax = strlen(hditem.pszText);
        Header_InsertItem(hHeadWnd, 1, &hditem);

        hditem.pszText = "City";
        hditem.cchTextMax = strlen(hditem.pszText);
        Header_InsertItem(hHeadWnd, 2, &hditem);

        hditem.pszText = "State";
        hditem.cchTextMax = strlen(hditem.pszText);
        Header_InsertItem(hHeadWnd, 3, &hditem);

        hditem.pszText = "Postal Code";
        hditem.cchTextMax = strlen(hditem.pszText);
        Header_InsertItem(hHeadWnd, 4, &hditem);

        ShowWindow(hHeadWnd, SW_SHOW); /* display the header control */

        return hHeadWnd;
    }

/* Sample data to illustrate the header control. */
void InitDatabase(void)
{
    strcpy(data[0].name, "Stan Jones");
    strcpy(data[0].street, "1101 Elm St. S.W.");
    strcpy(data[0].city, "Carlsburg");
    strcpy(data[0].state, "MT");
    strcpy(data[0].code, "59345-0089");

    strcpy(data[1].name, "Ralph Johnson");
    strcpy(data[1].street, "23978 N. Wesley Blvd.");
    strcpy(data[1].city, "Laguna Hills");
    strcpy(data[1].state, "FL");
    strcpy(data[1].code, "32465");
```

14

```
  strcpy(data[2].name, "Chris Thomas");
  strcpy(data[2].street, "1911 Robin Way");
  strcpy(data[2].city, "St. John");
  strcpy(data[2].state, "MN");
  strcpy(data[2].code, "55576");

  strcpy(data[3].name, "R. W. Ridgeway");
  strcpy(data[3].street, "P.O. Box 587");
  strcpy(data[3].city, "Goldsberry");
  strcpy(data[3].state, "MO");
  strcpy(data[3].code, "65345");

  strcpy(data[4].name, "Warren Clarence");
  strcpy(data[4].street, "3546 Newton Lane");
  strcpy(data[4].city, "Longtree");
  strcpy(data[4].state, "OH");
  strcpy(data[4].code, "43556-0234");

  strcpy(data[5].name, "William Spinoza");
  strcpy(data[5].street, "412 Monad Ave.");
  strcpy(data[5].city, "Marshall");
  strcpy(data[5].state, "SD");
  strcpy(data[5].code, "57345");

  strcpy(data[6].name, "W.S. Tempest");
  strcpy(data[6].street, "19 Water St. Apt 2A");
  strcpy(data[6].city, "Rushville");
  strcpy(data[6].state, "WI");
  strcpy(data[6].code, "53576");
}
```

The program uses the following resource file:

```
; Demonstrate a header control.
#include <windows.h>
#include "head.h"

HeaderMenu MENU
{
  POPUP "&Options"
  {
    MENUITEM "&Exit\tF2", IDM_EXIT
  }
  MENUITEM "&Help", IDM_HELP
}


HeaderMenu ACCELERATORS
{
```

```
    VK_F2, IDM_EXIT, VIRTKEY
    VK_F1, IDM_HELP, VIRTKEY
}
```

The header file HEAD.H is shown here. It contains values used by this and the subsequent example program.

```
#define IDM_EXIT        100
#define IDM_HELP        101
#define IDM_RESET       102

#define ID_HEADCONTROL  500
```

A Closer Look at the First Header Control Example

When the program receives the **WM_CREATE** message, two functions are called: **InitHeader( )** and **InitDatabase( )**. The program uses the function **InitHeader( )** to construct and initialize the header control. It is passed the handle of its parent window. It returns a handle to the header control. The header control is given an ID value of **ID_HEADCONTROL**. This value is used to identify the header control when a **WM_NOTIFY** message is received. (Remember, other types of controls can also generate **WM_NOTIFY** messages.) Most of the other elements inside the function should be clear because they implement the steps described earlier in this chapter. In this example, all columns are given the same default width, which is 100. Of course, the column widths may be adjusted by the user, dynamically.

14

Notice that the height of the header control is saved in the global variable **HeaderHeight**. Since the header control occupies space at the top of the

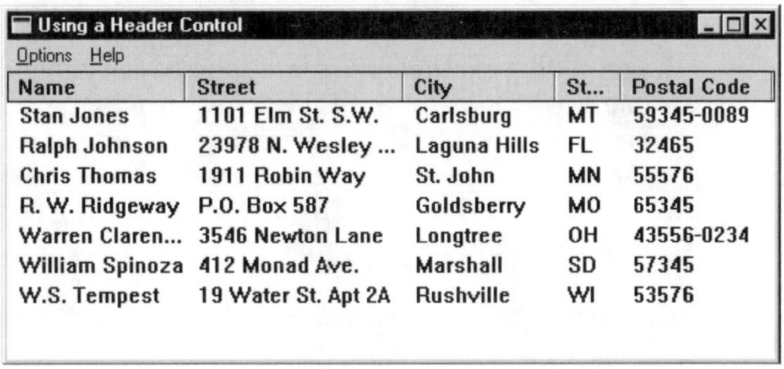

Sample output from the first header control example program

Figure 14-1.

Name	Street	City	St...	Postal Code
Stan Jones	1101 Elm St. S.W.	Carlsburg	MT	59345-0089
Ralph Johnson	23978 N. Wesley ...	Laguna Hills	FL	32465
Chris Thomas	1911 Robin Way	St. John	MN	55576
R. W. Ridgeway	P.O. Box 587	Goldsberry	MO	65345
Warren Claren...	3546 Newton Lane	Longtree	OH	43556-0234
William Spinoza	412 Monad Ave.	Marshall	SD	57345
W.S. Tempest	19 Water St. Apt 2A	Rushville	WI	53576

client area of the parent window, **HeaderHeight** is used as an offset when information is displayed in the main window.

Once the header control has been constructed, the mailing list is initialized using **InitDatabase( )**. The database is stored in an array of **MailList** structures called **data**. The **MailList** structure contains character arrays which are used to hold name and address information. The contents of the **data** array are displayed each time a **WM_PAINT** message is received. The size of each column is stored in the **columns** array.

The only header control message that the program responds to is **HDN_ENDTRACK**. This message is sent when the user has finished resizing a column header (by dragging the divider on its right side). Since the width of the column has been changed, the information displayed under the header control must be updated to reflect this change. The way this is done is by updating the value in **columns** so that it contains the new width of the header and then forcing a repaint. Notice that the user cannot reduce the size of a column to less than **MINWIDTH**. This ensures that there is always a small part of the column heading showing.

There is one thing to note inside the **WM_PAINT** handler. If the information to be displayed in a column is longer than the current width of the column, then the information is truncated and an ellipsis is added. This tells the user that more information is available than can currently be displayed.

There is one other point of interest in this program. Examine the code under the **WM_SIZE** case. As you probably know, a window receives a **WM_SIZE** message when its size is changed. The program responds to this message by altering the size of the header control so that it continues to fit its parent window. Keep in mind that this step is not technically necessary. In fact, there can be applications of a header control in which you will want its size to remain fixed. However, in this example, the header control is resized to fit the new dimensions of the window.

Enhancing the Header Control

The preceding example illustrated the basic elements necessary to create a simple header control. However, the power and utility of the header control can be expanded by taking advantage of some of its other capabilities. In this section, some of these features will be used to enhance the functionality of the header control. Specifically, the following features will be added to the preceding program:

1. Button headers are used, allowing the header to respond to mouse events.

2. When a button heading is clicked, the column will double its width.

3. When a button heading is double-clicked, the column will return to its default width.

4. When a heading is resized, the information in the column below the heading will expand or contract as the heading changes size.

Let's look at how each of these options is supported.

Creating Button Headers

It is quite easy to create button headers. Just include the header style **HDS_BUTTONS** when you create the header control. Once you have done this, each heading will become a push button that is capable of responding to mouse events. It also retains all other attributes of a standard heading. For example, you can still resize a header button by dragging its divider.

The HDS_BUTTONS style causes the column headings to become push buttons.

Responding to Mouse Events

When a button header is clicked by the mouse, it sends an **HDN_ITEMCLICK** message. When the button is double-clicked, it sends an **HDN_ITEMDBLCLICK** message. Your program can respond to these messages any way it chooses. There is no prescribed meaning to these events. The example that follows will use these messages to change the column width.

Using the HDN_TRACK Message

When the user first begins to resize a heading, the header control sends an **HDN_BEGINTRACK** message. When the user finishes resizing, the control sends **HDN_ENDTRACK**. During the resizing, the control sends a stream of **HDN_TRACK** messages. These messages can be used by your program to continually update the information displayed in the column that is being resized. Doing so allows the user to see immediately the effects of the changes being made.

An Enhanced Header Control Example

The following program incorporates the enhancements just described into the header control example. Sample output is shown in Figure 14-2.

```
/* Enhancing the header control. */

#include <windows.h>
#include <commctrl.h>
```

14

```
#include <string.h>
#include <stdio.h>
#include "head.h"

#define NUMCOLS 5
#define DEFWIDTH 100
#define MINWIDTH 10
#define MAXWIDTH 400
#define SPACING 8
#define NUMENTRIES 7

LRESULT CALLBACK WindowFunc(HWND, UINT, WPARAM, LPARAM);
HWND InitHeader(HWND hParent);
void InitDatabase(void);

char szWinName[] = "MyWin"; /* name of window class */

HINSTANCE hInst;
HWND hHeadWnd;

int HeaderHeight;

int columns[NUMCOLS] = {DEFWIDTH, DEFWIDTH,
                        DEFWIDTH, DEFWIDTH,
                        DEFWIDTH};

struct MailList {
  char name[40];
  char street[40];
  char city[40];
  char state[3];
  char code[11];
} data[NUMENTRIES];

int WINAPI WinMain(HINSTANCE hThisInst, HINSTANCE hPrevInst,
                   LPSTR lpszArgs, int nWinMode)
{
  MSG msg;
  WNDCLASSEX wcl;
  HANDLE hAccel;
  HWND hwnd;

  /* Define a window class. */
  wcl.cbSize = sizeof(WNDCLASSEX);
  wcl.hInstance = hThisInst; /* handle to this instance */
  wcl.lpszClassName = szWinName; /* window class name */
  wcl.lpfnWndProc = WindowFunc; /* window function */
  wcl.style = 0; /* default style */
```

```
wcl.hIcon = LoadIcon(NULL, IDI_APPLICATION);
wcl.hIconSm = LoadIcon(NULL, IDI_APPLICATION);
wcl.hCursor = LoadCursor(NULL, IDC_ARROW);

/* specify name of menu resource */
wcl.lpszMenuName = "HeaderMenuEnhanced"; /* main menu */

wcl.cbClsExtra = 0; /* no extra */
wcl.cbWndExtra = 0; /* information needed */

/* Make the window white. */
wcl.hbrBackground = GetStockObject(WHITE_BRUSH);

/* Register the window class. */
if(!RegisterClassEx(&wcl)) return 0;

/* Now that a window class has been registered, a window
   can be created. */
hwnd = CreateWindow(
  szWinName, /* name of window class */
  "An Enhanced Header Control", /* title */
  WS_OVERLAPPEDWINDOW, /* standard window */
  CW_USEDEFAULT, /* X coordinate - let Windows decide */
  CW_USEDEFAULT, /* Y coordinate - let Windows decide */
  CW_USEDEFAULT, /* width - let Windows decide */
  CW_USEDEFAULT, /* height - let Windows decide */
  HWND_DESKTOP, /* no parent window */
  NULL, /* no override of class menu */
  hThisInst, /* handle of this instance of the program */
  NULL /* no additional arguments */
);

hInst = hThisInst; /* save the current instance handle */

/* load accelerators */
hAccel = LoadAccelerators(hThisInst, "HeaderMenuEnhanced");

InitCommonControls();

/* Display the window. */
ShowWindow(hwnd, nWinMode);
UpdateWindow(hwnd);

/* Create the message loop. */
while(GetMessage(&msg, NULL, 0, 0))
{
  if(!TranslateAccelerator(hwnd, hAccel, &msg)) {
    TranslateMessage(&msg); /* translate keyboard messages */
```

```
        DispatchMessage(&msg); /* return control to Windows */
    }
  }
  return msg.wParam;
}


/* This function is called by Windows NT and is passed
   messages from the message queue.
*/
LRESULT CALLBACK WindowFunc(HWND hwnd, UINT message,
                            WPARAM wParam, LPARAM lParam)
{
  int response;
  RECT rect;
  HD_LAYOUT layout;
  WINDOWPOS winpos;
  HD_NOTIFY *hdnptr;
  HD_ITEM *hdiptr, hditem;
  PAINTSTRUCT ps;
  TEXTMETRIC tm;
  SIZE size;

  char str[80];
  int i, j, ColStart, chrs;
  int entry;
  int linespacing;

  HDC hdc;

  switch(message) {
    case WM_CREATE:
      hHeadWnd = InitHeader(hwnd);
      InitDatabase();
      break;
    case WM_COMMAND:
      switch(LOWORD(wParam)) {
        case IDM_RESET: /* restore default widths */
          hditem.mask = HDI_WIDTH;
          for(i=0; i<NUMCOLS; i++) {
            Header_GetItem(hHeadWnd, i, &hditem);
            hditem.cxy = DEFWIDTH;
            columns[i] = DEFWIDTH;
            Header_SetItem(hHeadWnd, i, &hditem);
          }
          InvalidateRect(hwnd, NULL, 1);
          break;
        case IDM_EXIT:
```

```
      response = MessageBox(hwnd, "Quit the Program?",
                              "Exit", MB_YESNO);
      if(response == IDYES) PostQuitMessage(0);
      break;
    case IDM_HELP:
      MessageBox(hwnd, "Try resizing the header.",
                 "Help", MB_OK);
      break;
  }
  break;
case WM_SIZE:
  /* Resize the header control when its parent window
     changes size. */
  GetClientRect(hwnd, &rect);
  layout.prc = &rect;
  layout.pwpos = &winpos;
  Header_Layout(hHeadWnd, &layout);

  MoveWindow(hHeadWnd, winpos.x, winpos.y,
          winpos.cx, winpos.cy, 1);
  break;
case WM_NOTIFY:
  if(LOWORD(wParam) == ID_HEADCONTROL) {
    hdnptr = (HD_NOTIFY *) lParam;
    hdiptr = (HD_ITEM *) hdnptr->pitem;
    switch(hdnptr->hdr.code) {
      case HDN_ENDTRACK: /* user changed column width */
        if(hdiptr->cxy < MINWIDTH) {
          hdiptr->cxy = MINWIDTH;
          columns[hdnptr->iItem] = MINWIDTH;
        }
        else
          columns[hdnptr->iItem] = hdiptr->cxy;
        InvalidateRect(hwnd, NULL, 1);
        break;
      case HDN_TRACK: /* user changing column width */
        GetClientRect(hwnd, &rect);
        if(hdiptr->cxy < MINWIDTH) {
          hdiptr->cxy = MINWIDTH;
          columns[hdnptr->iItem] = MINWIDTH;
        }
        else
          columns[hdnptr->iItem] = hdiptr->cxy;
        rect.top = HeaderHeight;
        InvalidateRect(hwnd, &rect, 1);
        break;
      case HDN_ITEMDBLCLICK: /* user double-clicked header button */
        /* return to default width */
```

```
            hditem.mask = HDI_WIDTH;
            Header_GetItem(hHeadWnd, hdnptr->iItem, &hditem);
            hditem.cxy = DEFWIDTH;
            columns[hdnptr->iItem] = DEFWIDTH;
            Header_SetItem(hHeadWnd, hdnptr->iItem, &hditem);
            InvalidateRect(hwnd, NULL, 1);
            break;
          case HDN_ITEMCLICK: /* user clicked header button */
            /* double width of button */
            hditem.mask = HDI_WIDTH;
            Header_GetItem(hHeadWnd, hdnptr->iItem, &hditem);
            hditem.cxy += hditem.cxy;
            if(hditem.cxy > MAXWIDTH) hditem.cxy = MAXWIDTH;
            columns[hdnptr->iItem] = hditem.cxy;
            Header_SetItem(hHeadWnd, hdnptr->iItem, &hditem);
            InvalidateRect(hwnd, NULL, 1);
            break;
        }
      }
      break;
    case WM_PAINT:
      hdc = BeginPaint(hwnd, &ps); /* get DC */

      GetTextMetrics(hdc, &tm);
      linespacing = tm.tmHeight + tm.tmInternalLeading;

      for(entry = 0; entry < NUMENTRIES; entry++) {
        ColStart = 0;
        for(i=0; i<NUMCOLS; i++) {
          switch(i) {
            case 0: strcpy(str, data[entry].name);
              break;
            case 1: strcpy(str, data[entry].street);
              break;
            case 2: strcpy(str, data[entry].city);
              break;
            case 3: strcpy(str, data[entry].state);
              break;
            case 4: strcpy(str, data[entry].code);
              break;
          }

          /* add ... to truncated entries */
          GetTextExtentPoint32(hdc, str, strlen(str), &size);
          j = 2;
```

```
                   while((columns[i]-SPACING) < size.cx) {
                     chrs = columns[i] / tm.tmAveCharWidth;
                     strcpy(&str[chrs-j], "...");
                     GetTextExtentPoint32(hdc, str, strlen(str), &size);
                     j++;
                   }

                 TextOut(hdc, ColStart+SPACING,
                         HeaderHeight+(entry*linespacing),
                         str, strlen(str));

                 ColStart += columns[i];
             }
         }
         EndPaint(hwnd, &ps); /* release DC */
         break;
      case WM_DESTROY: /* terminate the program */
         PostQuitMessage(0);
         break;
      default:
         /* Let Windows NT process any messages not specified in
            the preceding switch statement. */
         return DefWindowProc(hwnd, message, wParam, lParam);
    }
    return 0;
}

/* Initialize the header control. */
HWND InitHeader(HWND hParent)
{
  HWND hHeadWnd;
  RECT rect;
  HD_LAYOUT layout;
  WINDOWPOS winpos;
  HD_ITEM hditem;

  GetClientRect(hParent, &rect);

  /* create the header control */
  hHeadWnd = CreateWindow(WC_HEADER, NULL,
                WS_CHILD | WS_BORDER | HDS_BUTTONS,
                CW_USEDEFAULT, CW_USEDEFAULT,
                0, 0, hParent,
                (HMENU) ID_HEADCONTROL,
                hInst, NULL);
```

14

```
  /* get header control layout that will fit client area */
  layout.pwpos = &winpos;
  layout.prc = &rect;
  Header_Layout(hHeadWnd, &layout);
  /* dimension header to fit current size of client area */
  MoveWindow(hHeadWnd, winpos.x, winpos.y,
             winpos.cx, winpos.cy, 0);

  HeaderHeight = winpos.cy; /* save height of header */

  /* insert items into the header */
  hditem.mask = HDI_FORMAT | HDI_WIDTH | HDI_TEXT;
  hditem.pszText = "Name";
  hditem.cchTextMax = strlen(hditem.pszText);
  hditem.cxy = DEFWIDTH;
  hditem.fmt = HDF_STRING | HDF_LEFT;
  Header_InsertItem(hHeadWnd, 0, &hditem);

  hditem.pszText = "Street";
  hditem.cchTextMax = strlen(hditem.pszText);
  Header_InsertItem(hHeadWnd, 1, &hditem);

  hditem.pszText = "City";
  hditem.cchTextMax = strlen(hditem.pszText);
  Header_InsertItem(hHeadWnd, 2, &hditem);

  hditem.pszText = "State";
  hditem.cchTextMax = strlen(hditem.pszText);
  Header_InsertItem(hHeadWnd, 3, &hditem);

  hditem.pszText = "Postal Code";
  hditem.cchTextMax = strlen(hditem.pszText);
  Header_InsertItem(hHeadWnd, 4, &hditem);

  ShowWindow(hHeadWnd, SW_SHOW); /* display the header control */

  return hHeadWnd;
}

/* Sample data to illustrate the header control. */
void InitDatabase(void)
{
  strcpy(data[0].name, "Stan Jones");
  strcpy(data[0].street, "1101 Elm St. S.W.");
  strcpy(data[0].city, "Carlsburg");
```

```
        strcpy(data[0].state, "MT");
        strcpy(data[0].code, "59345-0089");

        strcpy(data[1].name, "Ralph Johnson");
        strcpy(data[1].street, "23978 N. Wesley Blvd.");
        strcpy(data[1].city, "Laguna Hills");
        strcpy(data[1].state, "FL");
        strcpy(data[1].code, "32465");

        strcpy(data[2].name, "Chris Thomas");
        strcpy(data[2].street, "1911 Robin Way");
        strcpy(data[2].city, "St. John");
        strcpy(data[2].state, "MN");
        strcpy(data[2].code, "55576");

        strcpy(data[3].name, "R. W. Ridgeway");
        strcpy(data[3].street, "P.O. Box 587");
        strcpy(data[3].city, "Goldsberry");
        strcpy(data[3].state, "MO");
        strcpy(data[3].code, "65345");

        strcpy(data[4].name, "Warren Clarence");
        strcpy(data[4].street, "3546 Newton Lane");
        strcpy(data[4].city, "Longtree");
        strcpy(data[4].state, "OH");
        strcpy(data[4].code, "43556-0234");

        strcpy(data[5].name, "William Spinoza");
        strcpy(data[5].street, "412 Monad Ave.");
        strcpy(data[5].city, "Marshall");
        strcpy(data[5].state, "SD");
        strcpy(data[5].code, "57345");

        strcpy(data[6].name, "W.S. Tempest");
        strcpy(data[6].street, "19 Water St. Apt 2A");
        strcpy(data[6].city, "Rushville");
        strcpy(data[6].state, "WI");
        strcpy(data[6].code, "53576");
}
```

14

This program uses the same HEAD.H file shown earlier. It uses the following resource file:

```
; Demonstrate an enhanced header control.
#include <windows.h>
#include "head.h"
```

```
HeaderMenuEnhanced MENU
{
  POPUP "&Options"
  {
    MENUITEM "&Reset\tF2", IDM_RESET
    MENUITEM "&Exit\tF3", IDM_EXIT
  }
  MENUITEM "&Help", IDM_HELP
}

HeaderMenuEnhanced ACCELERATORS
{
  VK_F2, IDM_RESET, VIRTKEY
  VK_F3, IDM_EXIT, VIRTKEY
  VK_F1, IDM_HELP, VIRTKEY
}
```

A Closer Look at the Enhanced Header Control Program

Most of the code in this program is similar to that found in the first header control program and will already be familiar to you. However, pay special attention to the changes. First, notice that the header control is now created with the **HDS_BUTTONS** style. This creates button headers. Next, look

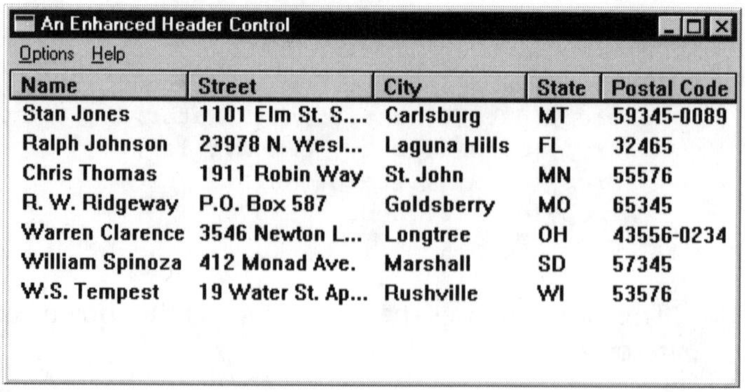

Sample output from the enhanced header control program

Figure 14-2.

Name	Street	City	State	Postal Code
Stan Jones	1101 Elm St. S....	Carlsburg	MT	59345-0089
Ralph Johnson	23978 N. Wesl...	Laguna Hills	FL	32465
Chris Thomas	1911 Robin Way	St. John	MN	55576
R. W. Ridgeway	P.O. Box 587	Goldsberry	MO	65345
Warren Clarence	3546 Newton L...	Longtree	OH	43556-0234
William Spinoza	412 Monad Ave.	Marshall	SD	57345
W.S. Tempest	19 Water St. Ap...	Rushville	WI	53576

An Enhanced Header Control — Options Help

closely at the **WM_NOTIFY** message. It is here that most of the enhancements take place. It is shown here for your convenience.

```
case WM_NOTIFY:
  if(LOWORD(wParam) == ID_HEADCONTROL) {
    hdnptr = (HD_NOTIFY *) lParam;
    hdiptr = (HD_ITEM *) hdnptr->pitem;
    switch(hdnptr->hdr.code) {
      case HDN_ENDTRACK: /* user changed column width */
        if(hdiptr->cxy < MINWIDTH) {
          hdiptr->cxy = MINWIDTH;
          columns[hdnptr->iItem] = MINWIDTH;
        }
        else
          columns[hdnptr->iItem] = hdiptr->cxy;
        InvalidateRect(hwnd, NULL, 1);
        break;
      case HDN_TRACK: /* user changing column width */
        GetClientRect(hwnd, &rect);
        if(hdiptr->cxy < MINWIDTH) {
          hdiptr->cxy = MINWIDTH;
          columns[hdnptr->iItem] = MINWIDTH;
        }
        else
          columns[hdnptr->iItem] = hdiptr->cxy;
        rect.top = HeaderHeight;
        InvalidateRect(hwnd, &rect, 1);
        break;
      case HDN_ITEMDBLCLICK: /* user double-clicked header button */
        /* return to default width */
        hditem.mask = HDI_WIDTH;
        Header_GetItem(hHeadWnd, hdnptr->iItem, &hditem);
        hditem.cxy = DEFWIDTH;
        columns[hdnptr->iItem] = DEFWIDTH;
        Header_SetItem(hHeadWnd, hdnptr->iItem, &hditem);
        InvalidateRect(hwnd, NULL, 1);
        break;
      case HDN_ITEMCLICK: /* user clicked header button */
        /* double width of button */
        hditem.mask = HDI_WIDTH;
        Header_GetItem(hHeadWnd, hdnptr->iItem, &hditem);
        hditem.cxy += hditem.cxy;
        if(hditem.cxy > MAXWIDTH) hditem.cxy = MAXWIDTH;
```

```
        columns[hdnptr->iItem] = hditem.cxy;
        Header_SetItem(hHeadWnd, hdnptr->iItem, &hditem);
        InvalidateRect(hwnd, NULL, 1);
        break;
    }
  }
  break;
```

Let's look at how each notification message is processed.

The **HDN_ENDTRACK** message is handled the same as it was in the first program.

Each time an **HDN_TRACK** message is received, the program uses the new width of the header to adjust the contents of the information displayed in the columns. It does this by updating the **columns** array with the new column width and then forcing a repaint (by calling **InvalidateRect( )**). Thus, as the user drags the divider, the information in the columns below the header control will be dynamically updated, allowing the user to see the effects of expanding or contracting a column as they are occurring. This makes it much easier for the user to set each column width appropriately because it eliminates guesswork.

When the user clicks on a header button, the **HDN_ITEMCLICK** message is sent. The program responds by doubling the width of the column. Notice that the item must be obtained using **Header_GetItem( )** and set using **Header_SetItem( )**. The reason for this is that when an **HDN_ITEMCLICK** message is received, the value of the **pitem** member of **HD_NOTIFY** is **NULL**. That is, it does not point to the item that was clicked.

When the user double-clicks on a header button, an **HDN_ITEMDBLCLICK** message is sent. The program responds by setting the width of the item to its default width. Again, notice that the item must be obtained using **Header_GetItem( )** and set using **Header_SetItem( )**. When an **HDN_ITEMDBLCLICK** message is received, **lParam** points to an **NMHDR** structure rather than an **HD_NOTIFY** structure. Thus, the item must be manually obtained and set.

There is one other enhancement in the program. When the user selects Reset from the Options menu, all columns are returned to their default widths.

Some Things to Try

It is possible to add or delete column headers dynamically. This might be useful when presenting information in various formats. For example, you could give the user the choice of what items he or she wanted to see and then adjust the header appropriately. You might want to try adding this option to the examples.

Another thing to try is giving the user the option of hiding the header control. For example, the user could use the header control to adjust the size of the columns and then remove the control from the screen. In this way, more information could be displayed.

Common Control Wrap-Up

The preceding five chapters have explored the most frequently used common controls. If you can apply these controls, you will have no trouble learning to use the remaining ones on your own. Just remember, in general, using a common control involves these basic mechanisms:

1. Creation and initialization.
2. Sending messages to the control.
3. Handling messages from the control.

As stated in the beginning of Chapter 10, the common controls give your application a sophisticated, modern look. You should take advantage of them whenever you can.

14

CHAPTER 15

Thread-Based
Multitasking

This chapter describes Windows NT's thread-based multitasking system. As mentioned at the start of this book, Windows NT supports two forms of multitasking. The first type is process-based. This is the type of multiprocessing that Windows has supported from its inception. A process is, essentially, a program that is executing. In process-based multitasking, two or more processes can execute concurrently. The second type of multitasking is thread-based. A thread is a path (or *thread*) of execution within a process. In Windows NT, every process has at least one thread, but it may have two or more. Thread-based multitasking allows two or more parts of a single program to execute concurrently. This added multitasking dimension allows extremely efficient programs to be written because you, the programmer, can define the separate threads of execution and thus manage the way that your program executes.

The inclusion of thread-based multitasking has increased the need for a special type of multitasking feature called *synchronization*, which allows the execution of threads (and processes) to be coordinated in certain well-defined ways. Windows NT has a complete subsystem devoted to synchronization, including some new features added by NT 4. Its key features are discussed in this chapter.

PORTABILITY: Windows 3.1 does not support thread-based multitasking.

Creating a Multithreaded Program

If you have never programmed for a multithreaded environment before then you are in for a pleasant surprise. Multithreaded multitasking adds a new dimension to your programming because it lets you, the programmer, more fully control how pieces of your program execute. This allows you to implement more efficient programs. For example, you could assign one thread of a program the job of sorting a file, a second thread the job of gathering information from some remote source, and another thread the task of performing user input. Because of multithreaded multitasking, each thread could execute concurrently and no CPU time would be wasted.

The thread of execution created when a program begins is called its main thread.

It is important to understand that all processes have at least one thread of execution. For the sake of discussion, this is called the *main thread*. From the main thread it is possible to create one or more other threads of execution within the same process. In general, once a new thread is created, it also begins execution. Thus, each process starts with one thread of execution and may create one or more additional threads. In this way, thread-based multitasking is supported.

Creating a Thread

To create a thread, use the API function **CreateThread( )**. Its prototype is shown here:

HANDLE CreateThread(LPSECURITY_ATTRIBUTES *lpSecAttr*,
DWORD *dwStackSize*,
LPTHREAD_START_ROUTINE *lpThreadFunc*,
LPVOID *lpParam*,
DWORD *dwFlags*,
LPDWORD *lpdwThreadID*);

Here, *lpSecAttr* is a pointer to a set of security attributes pertaining to the thread. However, if *lpSecAttr* is **NULL**, then the default security descriptor is used.

NOTE: Windows NT's security system is discussed in Chapter 21. For the purposes of this chapter, the default security descriptor is always used.

Each thread has its own stack. You can specify the size of the new thread's stack, in bytes, using the *dwStackSize* parameter. If this value is zero, then the thread will be given a stack that is the same size as the main thread of the process that creates it. In this case, the stack will be expanded, if necessary. (Specifying zero is the common approach taken to thread stack size.)

Each thread of execution begins with a call to a function, called the *thread function*, within the process. Execution of the thread continues until the thread function returns. The address of this function (i.e., the entry point to the thread) is specified in *lpThreadFunc*. All thread functions must have this prototype:

DWORD WINAPI threadfunc(LPVOID *param*);

The thread function is the entry point to a new thread of execution.

Any argument that you need to pass to the new thread is specified in **CreateThread( )**'s *lpParam*. This 32-bit value is received by the thread function in its parameter. This parameter may be used for any purpose. The function returns its exit status.

The *dwFlags* parameter determines the execution state of the thread. If it is zero, the thread begins execution immediately. If it is **CREATE_SUSPEND**, the thread is created in a suspended state, awaiting execution. (It may be started using a call to **ResumeThread( )**, discussed later.)

15

The identifier associated with a thread is returned in the double word pointed to by *lpdwThreadID*.

The function returns a handle to the thread if successful or **NULL** if a failure occurs.

Terminating a Thread

As stated, a thread of execution terminates when its entry function returns. The process may also terminate the thread manually, using either **TerminateThread( )** or **ExitThread( )**, whose prototypes are shown here:

BOOL TerminateThread(HANDLE *hThread*, DWORD *dwStatus*);

VOID ExitThread(DWORD *dwStatus*);

For **TerminateThread( )**, *hThread* is the handle of the thread to be terminated. **ExitThread( )** terminates the thread that calls **ExitThread( )**. For both functions, *dwStatus* is the termination status. **TerminateThread( )** returns nonzero if successful and zero otherwise.

Calling **ExitThread( )** is functionally equivalent to allowing a thread function to return normally. This means that the stack is properly reset. When a thread is terminated using **TerminateThread( )**, it is stopped immediately and does not perform any special cleanup activities. Also, **TerminateThread( )** may stop a thread during an important operation. For these reasons, it is usually best (and easiest) to let a thread terminate normally when its entry function returns. This is the approach used by most of the example programs in this chapter.

A Multithreaded Example

The following program creates two threads each time the Demonstrate Thread menu option is selected. Each thread iterates a **for** loop 5,000 times, displaying the number of the iteration each time it repeats. As you will see when you run the program, both threads appear to execute concurrently.

```
/* A simple multithreaded program. */

#include <windows.h>
#include <string.h>
#include <stdio.h>
#include "thread.h"

#define MAX 5000
```

```
LRESULT CALLBACK WindowFunc(HWND, UINT, WPARAM, LPARAM);
DWORD WINAPI MyThread1(LPVOID param);
DWORD WINAPI MyThread2(LPVOID param);

char szWinName[] = "MyWin"; /* name of window class */

char str[255]; /* holds output strings */

DWORD Tid1, Tid2; /* thread IDs */

int WINAPI WinMain(HINSTANCE hThisInst, HINSTANCE hPrevInst,
                   LPSTR lpszArgs, int nWinMode)
{
  HWND hwnd;
  MSG msg;
  WNDCLASSEX wcl;
  HANDLE hAccel;

  /* Define a window class. */
  wcl.cbSize = sizeof(WNDCLASSEX);
  wcl.hInstance = hThisInst; /* handle to this instance */
  wcl.lpszClassName = szWinName; /* window class name */
  wcl.lpfnWndProc = WindowFunc; /* window function */
  wcl.style = 0; /* default style */

  wcl.hIcon = LoadIcon(NULL, IDI_APPLICATION);
  wcl.hIconSm = LoadIcon(NULL, IDI_APPLICATION);

  wcl.hCursor = LoadCursor(NULL, IDC_ARROW);

/* specify name of menu resource */
  wcl.lpszMenuName = "ThreadMenu"; /* main menu */

  wcl.cbClsExtra = 0; /* no extra */
  wcl.cbWndExtra = 0; /* information needed */

  /* Make the window white. */
  wcl.hbrBackground = GetStockObject(WHITE_BRUSH);

  /* Register the window class. */
  if(!RegisterClassEx(&wcl)) return 0;

  /* Now that a window class has been registered, a window
     can be created. */
  hwnd = CreateWindow(
    szWinName, /* name of window class */
    "Demonstrate Threads", /* title */
    WS_OVERLAPPEDWINDOW, /* window style - normal */
```

15

```
    CW_USEDEFAULT, /* X coordinate - let Windows decide */
    CW_USEDEFAULT, /* Y coordinate - let Windows decide */
    CW_USEDEFAULT, /* width - let Windows decide */
    CW_USEDEFAULT, /* height - let Windows decide */
    HWND_DESKTOP, /* no parent window */
    NULL, /* no override of class menu */
    hThisInst, /* handle of this instance of the program */
    NULL /* no additional arguments */
  );

  /* load accelerators */
  hAccel = LoadAccelerators(hThisInst, "ThreadMenu");

  /* Display the window. */
  ShowWindow(hwnd, nWinMode);
  UpdateWindow(hwnd);

  /* Create the message loop. */
  while(GetMessage(&msg, NULL, 0, 0))
  {
    if(!TranslateAccelerator(hwnd, hAccel, &msg)) {
      TranslateMessage(&msg); /* translate keyboard messages */
      DispatchMessage(&msg); /* return control to Windows NT */
    }
  }
  return msg.wParam;
}

/* This function is called by Windows NT and is passed
   messages from the message queue.
*/
LRESULT CALLBACK WindowFunc(HWND hwnd, UINT message,
                            WPARAM wParam, LPARAM lParam)
{
  int response;

  switch(message) {
    case WM_COMMAND:
      switch(LOWORD(wParam)) {
        case IDM_THREAD: /* create the threads */
          CreateThread(NULL, 0,
                       (LPTHREAD_START_ROUTINE)MyThread1,
                       (LPVOID) hwnd, 0, &Tid1);
          CreateThread(NULL, 0,
                       (LPTHREAD_START_ROUTINE)MyThread2,
                       (LPVOID) hwnd, 0, &Tid2);
          break;
        case IDM_EXIT:
```

```
            response = MessageBox(hwnd, "Quit the Program?",
                                   "Exit", MB_YESNO);
            if(response == IDYES) PostQuitMessage(0);
            break;
          case IDM_HELP:
            MessageBox(hwnd,
                       "F1: Help\nF2: Demonstrate Threads",
                       "Help", MB_OK);
            break;
        }
        break;
      case WM_DESTROY: /* terminate the program */
        PostQuitMessage(0);
        break;
      default:
        /* Let Windows NT process any messages not specified in
        the preceding switch statement. */
        return DefWindowProc(hwnd, message, wParam, lParam);
    }
    return 0;
}

/* A thread of execution within the process. */
DWORD WINAPI MyThread1(LPVOID param)
{
  int i;
  HDC hdc;

  for(i=0; i<MAX; i++) {
    sprintf(str, "Thread 1: loop # %5d ", i);
    hdc = GetDC((HWND) param);
    TextOut(hdc, 1, 1, str, strlen(str));
    ReleaseDC((HWND) param, hdc);
  }
  return 0;
}

/* Another thread of execution within the process. */
DWORD WINAPI MyThread2(LPVOID param)
{
  int i;
  HDC hdc;

  for(i=0; i<MAX; i++) {
    sprintf(str, "Thread 2: loop # %5d ", i);
    hdc = GetDC((HWND) param);
    TextOut(hdc, 1, 20, str, strlen(str));
    ReleaseDC((HWND) param, hdc);
```

15

```
  }
  return 0;
}
```

This program uses the THREAD.H file shown here:

```
#define IDM_THREAD 100
#define IDM_HELP   101
#define IDM_EXIT   102
```

The program also requires this resource file:

```
#include <windows.h>
#include "thread.h"

ThreadMenu MENU
{
  POPUP "&Threads" {
    MENUITEM "Demonstrate &Threads\tF2", IDM_THREAD
    MENUITEM "E&xit\tF10", IDM_EXIT
  }
  MENUITEM "&Help", IDM_HELP
}

ThreadMenu ACCELERATORS
{
  VK_F2, IDM_THREAD, VIRTKEY
  VK_F10, IDM_EXIT, VIRTKEY
  VK_F1, IDM_HELP, VIRTKEY
}
```

Sample output from the program is shown in Figure 15-1.

A Closer Look at the Multithreaded Program

Each time the Demonstrate Threads option is chosen, the following
code executes.

```
case IDM_THREAD: /* create the threads */
  CreateThread(NULL, 0,
               (LPTHREAD_START_ROUTINE)MyThread1,
               (LPVOID) hwnd, 0, &Tid1);
  CreateThread(NULL, 0,
               (LPTHREAD_START_ROUTINE)MyThread2,
               (LPVOID) hwnd, 0, &Tid2);
  break;
```

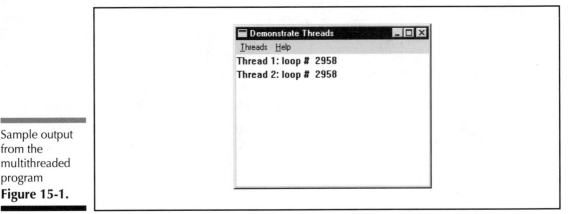

As you can see, the first call to **CreateThread( )** activates **MyThread1( )** and the second call activates **MyThread2( )**. Notice that the handle of the main window (**hwnd**) is passed as a parameter to each thread function. This handle is used by the threads to obtain a device context so that they may output information to the main window.

Once started, each thread of execution (including the main thread) runs independently. For example, while the threads are executing, you may activate the Help message box, exit the program, or even start another set of threads. If you exit the program, then any child threads will be automatically terminated.

Before continuing, you might want to experiment with this program. For example, as it now stands, each thread terminates when its associated function terminates. Try terminating a thread early, using **ExitThread( )**. Also, try starting multiple instances of each thread.

15

Alternatives to CreateThread( ) and ExitThread( )

Depending upon what C/C++ compiler you are using and what C standard library functions are employed in your program, you may need to avoid the use of **CreateThread( )** and **ExitThread( )** because they may result in small memory leaks. A *memory leak* is the loss of a small amount of memory. It is usually caused when a portion of memory allocated by a program is not released when the program terminates. For many C/C++ compilers, including Microsoft Visual C++ and Borland C++, if a multithreaded program utilizes standard C library functions and uses **CreateThread( )** and **ExitThread( )**, then small amounts of memory will be lost. (If your program does not use the C standard library, then no such losses will occur.)

A memory leak is the loss of a small amount of memory.

To eliminate this problem, you must use functions defined by the C runtime library to start and stop threads rather than those specified by the Win32 API.

In this section we will examine the alternative thread creation and termination functions provided by Microsoft and Borland. If you are using a different compiler, check your user manual to determine if you need to bypass **CreateThread( )** and **ExitThread( )** and how to do so, if necessary.

Microsoft and Borland supply the functions **_beginthread( )** and **_endthread( )**, which are used to create and terminate a thread. However, **_beginthread( )** is a generic thread function that does not provide the detailed level of control available in **CreateThread( )**. For this reason both Microsoft and Borland provide NT-enabled alternatives, which are examined next.

The Microsoft Alternatives

If you are using Microsoft Visual C++, then you will need to use **_beginthreadex( )** and **_endthreadex( )** instead of **CreateThread( )** and **ExitThread( )**. You must include the header file PROCESS.H in order to use these functions. Here is the prototype for **_beginthreadex( )**:

```
unsigned long _beginthreadex(void *secAttr, unsigned stackSize,
                             unsigned (__stdcall *threadFunc)(void *),
                             void *param, unsigned flags,
                             unsigned *threadID);
```

As you can see, the parameters to **_beginthreadex( )** parallel those to **CreateThread( )**. Furthermore, they have the same meaning as those specified by **CreateThread( )**. *secAttr* is a pointer to a set of security attributes pertaining to the thread. However, if *secAttr* is **NULL**, then the default security descriptor is used. The size of the new thread's stack, in bytes, is passed in *stackSize* parameter. If this value is zero, then the thread will be given a stack that is the same size as the main thread of the process that creates it and will be expanded, if necessary.

The address of the thread function (i.e., the entry point to the thread) is specified in *threadFunc*. For **_beginthreadex( )**, a thread function must have this prototype:

```
unsigned __stdcall threadfunc(void * param);
```

This prototype is functionally equivalent to the one for **CreateThread( )**, but uses different type names. Any argument that you need to pass to the new thread is specified in **_beginthreadex( )**'s *param* parameter.

The *flags* parameter determines the execution state of the thread. If it is zero, the thread begins execution immediately. If it is **CREATE_SUSPEND**, the thread is created in a suspended state, awaiting execution. (It may be started using a call to **ResumeThread( )**.) The identifier associated with a thread is returned in the variable pointed to by *threadID*.

The function returns a handle to the thread if successful or zero if a failure occurs.

The prototype for **_endthreadex( )** is shown here:

```
void _endthreadex(unsigned status);
```

It functions just like **ExitThread( )** by stopping the thread and returning the exit code specified in *status*.

When using **_beginthreadex( )** and **_endthreadex( )**, you must remember to link in the multithreaded library.

The Borland Alternatives

To create a thread of execution using Borland C++, you will need to use **_beginthreadNT( )**. This function requires the header file PROCESS.H. Its prototype is shown here:

```
unsigned long _beginthreadNT(void (_USERENTRY *threadFunc)(void *),
                             unsigned stackSize, void *param, void *secAttr,
                             unsigned long flags, unsigned long *threadID);
```

This function works just like **CreateThread( )** and **_beginthreadex( )** except that its parameters are ordered differently.

To terminate a thread created by **_beginthreadNT( )**, use **_endthread( )**. Unlike Microsoft, Borland does not provide a separate termination function. The prototype for **_endthread( )** is shown here:

```
void _endthread(void);
```

As you can see, it does not return an exit code.

When using this function, you must remember to link in the multi-threaded library.

15

Using the Microsoft C/C++ Thread Functions

To demonstrate the use of the C library thread functions, the preceding multithreaded program will be converted so that it uses Microsoft's

_beginthreadex( ) function. Since the meaning and order of the
parameters is the same for both **CreateThread( )** and **_beginthreadex( )**,
this is a simple matter. The three changes that need to be made are these:

1. PROCESS.H must be included in the program.
2. The prototypes of the thread functions must be changed to reflect the
   type names used by **_beginthreadex( )**.
3. The calls to **CreateThread( )** need to be replaced by calls to
   _beginthreadex( ).

You must also link your program with the multithreaded library. (To do so,
select the multithreaded library using the Project Settings property sheet.)
The following program reflects these changes.

```
/* Use Microsoft's _beginthreadex() function. */

#include <windows.h>
#include <string.h>
#include <stdio.h>
#include <process.h>
#include "thread.h"

#define MAX 5000

LRESULT CALLBACK WindowFunc(HWND, UINT, WPARAM, LPARAM);

/* use type names required by _beginthreadex() */
unsigned __stdcall MyThread1(void * param);
unsigned __stdcall MyThread2(void * param);

char szWinName[] = "MyWin"; /* name of window class */

char str[255]; /* holds output strings */

DWORD Tid1, Tid2; /* thread IDs */

int WINAPI WinMain(HINSTANCE hThisInst, HINSTANCE hPrevInst,
                   LPSTR lpszArgs, int nWinMode)
{
  HWND hwnd;
  MSG msg;
  WNDCLASSEX wcl;
  HANDLE hAccel;

  /* Define a window class. */
  wcl.cbSize = sizeof(WNDCLASSEX);
```

```
  wcl.hInstance = hThisInst; /* handle to this instance */
  wcl.lpszClassName = szWinName; /* window class name */
  wcl.lpfnWndProc = WindowFunc; /* window function */
  wcl.style = 0; /* default style */

  wcl.hIcon = LoadIcon(NULL, IDI_APPLICATION);
  wcl.hIconSm = LoadIcon(NULL, IDI_APPLICATION);

  wcl.hCursor = LoadCursor(NULL, IDC_ARROW);

  /* specify name of menu resource */
  wcl.lpszMenuName = "ThreadMenu"; /* main menu */

  wcl.cbClsExtra = 0; /* no extra */
  wcl.cbWndExtra = 0; /* information needed */

  /* Make the window white. */
  wcl.hbrBackground = GetStockObject(WHITE_BRUSH);

  /* Register the window class. */
  if(!RegisterClassEx(&wcl)) return 0;

  /* Now that a window class has been registered, a window
     can be created. */
  hwnd = CreateWindow(
    szWinName, /* name of window class */
    "Demonstrate Threads", /* title */
    WS_OVERLAPPEDWINDOW, /* window style - normal */
    CW_USEDEFAULT, /* X coordinate - let Windows decide */
    CW_USEDEFAULT, /* Y coordinate - let Windows decide */
    CW_USEDEFAULT, /* width - let Windows decide */
    CW_USEDEFAULT, /* height - let Windows decide */
    HWND_DESKTOP, /* no parent window */
    NULL, /* no override of class menu */
    hThisInst, /* handle of this instance of the program */
    NULL /* no additional arguments */
  );

  /* load accelerators */
  hAccel = LoadAccelerators(hThisInst, "ThreadMenu");

  /* Display the window. */
  ShowWindow(hwnd, nWinMode);
  UpdateWindow(hwnd);

  /* Create the message loop. */
  while(GetMessage(&msg, NULL, 0, 0))
  {
```

```
    if(!TranslateAccelerator(hwnd, hAccel, &msg)) {
      TranslateMessage(&msg); /* translate keyboard messages */
      DispatchMessage(&msg); /* return control to Windows NT */
    }
  }
  return msg.wParam;
}


/* This function is called by Windows NT and is passed
   messages from the message queue.
*/
LRESULT CALLBACK WindowFunc(HWND hwnd, UINT message,
                            WPARAM wParam, LPARAM lParam)
{
  int response;

  switch(message) {
    case WM_COMMAND:
      switch(LOWORD(wParam)) {
        case IDM_THREAD:
          /* create threads using _beginthreadex() */
          _beginthreadex(NULL, 0, MyThread1,
                         (LPVOID) hwnd, 0,
                         (unsigned *) &Tid1);
          _beginthreadex(NULL, 0, MyThread2,
                         (LPVOID) hwnd, 0,
                         (unsigned *) &Tid2);
          break;
        case IDM_EXIT:
          response = MessageBox(hwnd, "Quit the Program?",
                                "Exit", MB_YESNO);
          if(response == IDYES) PostQuitMessage(0);
          break;
        case IDM_HELP:
          MessageBox(hwnd,
                     "F1: Help\nF2: Demonstrate Threads",
                     "Help", MB_OK);
          break;
      }
      break;
    case WM_DESTROY: /* terminate the program */
      PostQuitMessage(0);
      break;
    default:
      /* Let Windows NT process any messages not specified in
      the preceding switch statement. */
      return DefWindowProc(hwnd, message, wParam, lParam);
  }
```

```
    return 0;
}

/* A thread of execution within the process. */
unsigned __stdcall MyThread1(void * param)
{
  int i;
  HDC hdc;

  for(i=0; i<MAX; i++) {
    sprintf(str, "Thread 1: loop # %5d ", i);
    hdc = GetDC((HWND) param);
    TextOut(hdc, 1, 1, str, strlen(str));
    ReleaseDC((HWND) param, hdc);
  }
  return 0;
}

/* Another thread of execution within the process. */
unsigned __stdcall MyThread2(void * param)
{
  int i;
  HDC hdc;

  for(i=0; i<MAX; i++) {
    sprintf(str, "Thread 2: loop # %5d ", i);
    hdc = GetDC((HWND) param);
    TextOut(hdc, 1, 20, str, strlen(str));
    ReleaseDC((HWND) param, hdc);
  }
  return 0;
}
```

Avoiding the C Library Functions

wsprintf( ) and lstrlen( ) are Win32 functions that can be substituted for the standard C functions sprintf( ) and strlen( ).

For many multithreaded programs, it is possible to avoid the use of the C standard library. In this case, you can use **CreateThread( )** and **ExitThread( )** without the potential for incurring memory leaks. For example, many of the programs in this book only use two C library functions: **sprintf( )** and **strlen( )**. Win32 contains substitutes for these functions called **wsprintf( )** and **lstrlen( )**, respectively. These functions contain some additional functionality that allows them to handle Unicode characters, but for the most part they work the same as their C library relatives.

Win32 also contains substitutes for several other C string handling functions, for example, **lstrcat( )**, **lstrcmp( )**, and **lstrcpy( )**. Various character functions are also provided, such as **CharUpper( )**, **CharLower( )**, **IsCharAlpha( )**, and **IsCharAlphaNumeric( )**. In general, if you are using the C standard library only for simple character handling, you can probably bypass it by using the functions built into Win32.

In the remaining examples in this chapter, threads will be created using **CreateThread( )**. The functions **wsprintf( )** and **lstrlen( )** will be substituted for **sprintf( )** and **strlen( )** to avoid the C standard library. This means that the examples that follow should be able to be compiled and correctly executed by any C/C++ compiler capable of creating Windows NT 4 programs.

Suspending and Resuming a Thread

A thread of execution may be suspended by calling **SuspendThread( )**. It may be resumed by calling **ResumeThread( )**. The prototypes for these functions are shown here:

DWORD SuspendThread(HANDLE *hThread*);

DWORD ResumeThread(HANDLE *hThread*);

For both functions, the handle to the thread is passed in *hThread*.

Each thread of execution has associated with it a *suspend count*. If this count is zero, then the thread is not suspended. If it is nonzero, the thread is in a suspended state. Each call to **SuspendThread( )** increments the suspend count. Each call to **ResumeThread( )** decrements the suspend count. A suspended thread will resume only after its suspend count has reached zero. Therefore, to resume a suspended thread implies that there must be the same number of calls to **ResumeThread( )** as there have been calls to **SuspendThread( )**.

A thread will be resumed only after its suspend count reaches zero.

Both functions return the thread's previous suspend count or –1 if an error occurs.

Thread Priorities

A thread's priority determines how much CPU time it receives.

Each thread has associated with it a priority setting. A thread's priority determines how much CPU time a thread receives. Low priority threads receive little. High priority threads receive a lot. Of course, how much CPU time a thread receives has profound impact on its execution characteristics and its interaction with other threads currently executing in the system.

A thread's priority setting is the combination of two values: the overall priority class of the process and the priority setting of the individual thread relative to that priority class. That is, a thread's actual priority is determined by combining the process priority class with the thread's individual priority level. Each priority component is examined next.

Priority Classes

You can obtain the current priority class by calling **GetPriorityClass( )** and you can set the priority class by calling **SetPriorityClass( )**. The prototypes for these functions are shown here:

DWORD GetPriorityClass(HANDLE *hApp*);

BOOL SetPriorityClass(HANDLE *hApp*, DWORD *dwPriority*);

The priority class determines the general priority category for all of the threads in a process.

Here, *hApp* is the handle of the process. **GetPriorityClass( )** returns the priority class of the application or zero on failure. For **SetPriorityClass( )**, *dwPriority* specifies the process' new priority class. The priority class values are shown here, in order of highest to lowest priority.

REALTIME_PRIORITY_CLASS
HIGH_PRIORITY_CLASS
NORMAL_PRIORITY_CLASS
IDLE_PRIORITY_CLASS

Programs are given the **NORMAL_PRIORITY_CLASS**, by default. Usually, you won't need to alter the priority class of your program. In fact, changing a process' priority class can have negative consequences on the overall performance of the computer system. For example, if you increase a program's priority class to **REALTIME_PRIORITY_CLASS** it will dominate the CPU. For the purposes of this chapter, the default priority setting of a process will be used.

Thread Priorities

A thread's priority setting determines how much CPU time it receives within its process.

For any given priority class, each individual thread's priority determines how much CPU time it receives within its process. When a thread is first created, it is given normal priority. However, you can change a thread's priority— even while it is executing.

You can obtain a thread's priority setting by calling **GetThreadPriority( )**. You can increase or decrease a thread's priority using **SetThreadPriority( )**. The prototypes for these functions are shown here:

BOOL SetThreadPriority(HANDLE *hThread*, int *Priority*);

15

int GetThreadPriority(HANDLE *hThread*);

For both functions, *hThread* is the handle of the thread. For **SetThreadPriority( )**, *Priority* is the new priority setting. For **GetThreadPriority( )**, the current priority setting is returned. The priority settings are shown here, in order of highest to lowest.

Thread Priority	Value
THREAD_PRIORITY_TIME_CRITICAL	15
THREAD_PRIORITY_HIGHEST	2
THREAD_PRIORITY_ABOVE_NORMAL	1
THREAD_PRIORITY_NORMAL	0
THREAD_PRIORITY_BELOW_NORMAL	-1
THREAD_PRIORITY_LOWEST	-2
THREAD_PRIORITY_IDLE	-15

These values are actually increments or decrements that are applied relative to the priority class of the process. Through the combination of a process' priority class and thread priority, Windows NT supports 31 different priority settings for application programs.

GetThreadPriority( ) returns **THREAD_PRIORITY_ERROR_RETURN** if an error occurs.

For the most part, if a thread has the normal priority class, you can freely experiment with changing its priority setting without fear of negatively affecting overall system performance. As you will see, the thread control panel developed in the next section allows you to alter the priority setting of threads within a process (but does not change their priority class).

Creating a Thread Control Panel

When developing multithreaded programs, it is often useful to experiment with various priority settings. It is also useful to be able to dynamically suspend and resume a thread, or even to terminate a thread. As you will see, it is quite easy, using the functions just described, to create a thread control panel that allows you to accomplish these things. Further, you can use the control panel while your multithreaded program is running. The dynamic nature of the thread control panel allows you to easily change the execution profile of a thread and observe the results.

The thread control panel developed in this section is capable of controlling two threads. For the sake of simplicity the control panel is implemented as a modal dialog box which is executed as part of the program's main thread. It relies upon global thread handles which must be defined by any program that uses the control panel.

The thread control panel is capable of performing the following actions:

♦ Setting a thread's priority

♦ Suspending a thread

♦ Resuming a thread

♦ Terminating a thread

It also displays the current priority setting of each thread.

As stated, the control panel is a modal dialog box. As you know, when a modal dialog box is activated, it usually implies that the rest of the application is suspended until the user closes the box. However, in a multithreaded program, it is possible for a modal dialog box to run in its own thread. When this is the case, the other threads in the program remain active. As mentioned, the thread control panel will be executed by the main thread of any program that uses it. Therefore, it will be executing in its own thread of execution. The advantage of this approach is that modal dialog boxes are a little easier to create than modeless ones. Also, since the dialog box may run in its own thread, there is no particular advantage, in this case, to using a modeless dialog box. As you become more familiar with multithreaded programming, you will find that it simplifies several previously difficult programming situations.

A Thread Control Panel Program

15

Here is a program that includes the thread control panel and demonstrates its use. It does so by adding the panel to the thread demonstration program shown earlier. Sample output is contained in Figure 15-2. To use the program, first begin execution of the threads (by selecting Start Threads from the Threads menu) and then activate the thread control panel. Once the control panel is active, you can experiment with different priority settings, etc.

```
/* Using a thread control panel */

#include <windows.h>
#include "panel.h"
```

```
#define MAX 50000

#define NUMPRIORITIES 5
#define OFFSET 2

LRESULT CALLBACK WindowFunc(HWND, UINT, WPARAM, LPARAM);
LRESULT CALLBACK ThreadPanel(HWND, UINT, WPARAM, LPARAM);

DWORD WINAPI MyThread1(LPVOID param);
DWORD WINAPI MyThread2(LPVOID param);

char szWinName[] = "MyWin"; /* name of window class */

char str[255]; /* holds output strings */

DWORD Tid1, Tid2; /* thread IDs */
HANDLE hThread1, hThread2; /* thread handles */

int ThPriority1, ThPriority2; /* thread priorities */
int suspend1 = 0, suspend2 = 0; /* thread states */

char priorities[NUMPRIORITIES][80] = {
  "Lowest",
  "Below Normal",
  "Normal",
  "Above Normal",
  "Highest"
};

HINSTANCE hInst;

int WINAPI WinMain(HINSTANCE hThisInst, HINSTANCE hPrevInst,
                   LPSTR lpszArgs, int nWinMode)
{
  HWND hwnd;
  MSG msg;
  WNDCLASSEX wcl;
  HANDLE hAccel;

  /* Define a window class. */
  wcl.cbSize = sizeof(WNDCLASSEX);
  wcl.hInstance = hThisInst; /* handle to this instance */
  wcl.lpszClassName = szWinName; /* window class name */
  wcl.lpfnWndProc = WindowFunc; /* window function */
  wcl.style = 0; /* default style */

  wcl.hIcon = LoadIcon(NULL, IDI_APPLICATION);
  wcl.hIconSm = LoadIcon(NULL, IDI_APPLICATION);
```

```
wcl.hCursor = LoadCursor(NULL, IDC_ARROW);

/* specify name of menu resource */
wcl.lpszMenuName = "ThreadPanelMenu"; /* main menu */

wcl.cbClsExtra = 0; /* no extra */
wcl.cbWndExtra = 0; /* information needed */

/* Make the window white. */
wcl.hbrBackground = GetStockObject(WHITE_BRUSH);

/* Register the window class. */
if(!RegisterClassEx(&wcl)) return 0;

/* Now that a window class has been registered, a window
   can be created. */
hwnd = CreateWindow(
  szWinName, /* name of window class */
  "Using a Thread Control Panel", /* title */
  WS_OVERLAPPEDWINDOW, /* standard window */
  CW_USEDEFAULT, /* X coordinate - let Windows decide */
  CW_USEDEFAULT, /* Y coordinate - let Windows decide */
  CW_USEDEFAULT, /* width - let Windows decide */
  CW_USEDEFAULT, /* height - let Windows decide */
  HWND_DESKTOP, /* no parent window */
  NULL, /* no override of class menu */
  hThisInst, /* handle of this instance of the program */
  NULL /* no additional arguments */
);

hInst = hThisInst; /* save instance handle */

/* load accelerators */
hAccel = LoadAccelerators(hThisInst, "ThreadPanelMenu");

/* Display the window. */
ShowWindow(hwnd, nWinMode);
UpdateWindow(hwnd);

/* Create the message loop. */
while(GetMessage(&msg, NULL, 0, 0))
{
  if(!TranslateAccelerator(hwnd, hAccel, &msg)) {
    TranslateMessage(&msg);
    DispatchMessage(&msg);
  }
}
return msg.wParam;
```

15

```
  }

/* This function is called by Windows NT and is passed
   messages from the message queue.
*/
LRESULT CALLBACK WindowFunc(HWND hwnd, UINT message,
                            WPARAM wParam, LPARAM lParam)
{
  int response;

  switch(message) {
    case WM_COMMAND:
      switch(LOWORD(wParam)) {
        case IDM_THREAD: /* create the threads */
          suspend1 = suspend2 = 0;
          hThread1 = CreateThread(NULL, 0,
                          (LPTHREAD_START_ROUTINE)MyThread1,
                          (LPVOID) hwnd, 0, &Tid1);
          hThread2 = CreateThread(NULL, 0,
                          (LPTHREAD_START_ROUTINE)MyThread2,
                          (LPVOID) hwnd, 0, &Tid2);
          break;
        case IDM_PANEL: /* activate control panel */
          DialogBox(hInst, "ThreadPanelDB", hwnd, (DLGPROC) ThreadPanel);
          break;
        case IDM_EXIT:
          response = MessageBox(hwnd, "Quit the Program?",
                              "Exit", MB_YESNO);
          if(response == IDYES) PostQuitMessage(0);
          break;
        case IDM_HELP:
          MessageBox(hwnd,
                    "F1: Help\nF2: Start Threads\nF3: Panel",
                    "Help", MB_OK);
          break;
      }
      break;
    case WM_DESTROY: /* terminate the program */
      PostQuitMessage(0);
      break;
    default:
      /* Let Windows NT process any messages not specified in
         the preceding switch statement. */
      return DefWindowProc(hwnd, message, wParam, lParam);
  }
  return 0;
}
```

```
/* A thread of execution within the process. */
DWORD WINAPI MyThread1(LPVOID param)
{
  int i;
  HDC hdc;

for(i=0; i<MAX; i++) {
    wsprintf(str, "Thread 1: loop # %5d ", i);
    hdc = GetDC((HWND) param);
    TextOut(hdc, 1, 1, str, lstrlen(str));
    ReleaseDC((HWND) param, hdc);
  }
  return 0;
}

/* Another thread of execution within the process. */
DWORD WINAPI MyThread2(LPVOID param)
{
  int i;
  HDC hdc;

  for(i=0; i<MAX; i++) {
    wsprintf(str, "Thread 2: loop # %5d ", i);
    hdc = GetDC((HWND) param);
    TextOut(hdc, 1, 20, str, lstrlen(str));
    ReleaseDC((HWND) param, hdc);
  }
  return 0;
}

/* Thread control panel dialog box. */
LRESULT CALLBACK ThreadPanel(HWND hdwnd, UINT message,
                             WPARAM wParam, LPARAM lParam)
{
  long i;
  HANDLE hpbRes, hpbSus;

  switch(message) {
    case WM_INITDIALOG:
      /* initialize list boxes */
      for(i=0; i<NUMPRIORITIES; i++) {
        SendDlgItemMessage(hdwnd, IDD_LB1,
            LB_ADDSTRING, 0, (LPARAM) priorities[i]);
        SendDlgItemMessage(hdwnd, IDD_LB2,
            LB_ADDSTRING, 0, (LPARAM) priorities[i]);
      }

      /* get current priority */
```

15

```
    ThPriority1 = GetThreadPriority(hThread1) + OFFSET;
    ThPriority2 = GetThreadPriority(hThread2) + OFFSET;

    /* update list box */
    SendDlgItemMessage(hdwnd, IDD_LB1, LB_SETCURSEL,
                       (WPARAM) ThPriority1, 0);
    SendDlgItemMessage(hdwnd, IDD_LB2, LB_SETCURSEL,
                       (WPARAM) ThPriority2, 0);

    /* set suspend and resume buttons for first thread */
    hpbSus = GetDlgItem(hdwnd, IDD_SUSPEND1);
    hpbRes = GetDlgItem(hdwnd, IDD_RESUME1);
    if(suspend1) {
      EnableWindow(hpbSus, 0); /* disable Suspend */
      EnableWindow(hpbRes, 1); /* enable Resume */
    }
    else {
      EnableWindow(hpbSus, 1); /* enable Suspend */
      EnableWindow(hpbRes, 0); /* disable Resume */
    }


   /* set suspend and resume buttons for second thread */
    hpbSus = GetDlgItem(hdwnd, IDD_SUSPEND2);
    hpbRes = GetDlgItem(hdwnd, IDD_RESUME2);
    if(suspend2) {
      EnableWindow(hpbSus, 0); /* disable Suspend */
      EnableWindow(hpbRes, 1); /* enable Resume */
    }
    else {
      EnableWindow(hpbSus, 1); /* enable Suspend */
      EnableWindow(hpbRes, 0); /* disable Resume */
    }

    return 1;
case WM_COMMAND:
  switch(wParam) {
    case IDD_TERMINATE1:
      TerminateThread(hThread1, 0);
      return 1;
    case IDD_TERMINATE2:
      TerminateThread(hThread2, 0);
      return 1;
    case IDD_SUSPEND1:
      SuspendThread(hThread1);
      hpbSus = GetDlgItem(hdwnd, IDD_SUSPEND1);
      hpbRes = GetDlgItem(hdwnd, IDD_RESUME1);
      EnableWindow(hpbSus, 0); /* disable Suspend */
      EnableWindow(hpbRes, 1); /* enable Resume */
```

```
                        suspend1 = 1;
                        return 1;
                      case IDD_RESUME1:
                        ResumeThread(hThread1);
                        hpbSus = GetDlgItem(hdwnd, IDD_SUSPEND1);
                        hpbRes = GetDlgItem(hdwnd, IDD_RESUME1);
                        EnableWindow(hpbSus, 1); /* enable Suspend */
                        EnableWindow(hpbRes, 0); /* disable Resume */
                        suspend1 = 0;
                        return 1;
                      case IDD_SUSPEND2:
                        SuspendThread(hThread2);
                        hpbSus = GetDlgItem(hdwnd, IDD_SUSPEND2);
                        hpbRes = GetDlgItem(hdwnd, IDD_RESUME2);
                        EnableWindow(hpbSus, 0); /* disable Suspend */
                        EnableWindow(hpbRes, 1); /* enable Resume */
                        suspend2 = 1;
                        return 1;
                      case IDD_RESUME2:
                        ResumeThread(hThread2);
                        hpbSus = GetDlgItem(hdwnd, IDD_SUSPEND2);
                        hpbRes = GetDlgItem(hdwnd, IDD_RESUME2);
                        EnableWindow(hpbSus, 1); /* enable Suspend */
                        EnableWindow(hpbRes, 0); /* disable Resume */
                        suspend2 = 0;
                        return 1;
                      case IDOK: /* actually change priorities */
                        ThPriority1 = SendDlgItemMessage(hdwnd, IDD_LB1,
                                         LB_GETCURSEL, 0, 0);
                        ThPriority2 = SendDlgItemMessage(hdwnd, IDD_LB2,
                                         LB_GETCURSEL, 0, 0);
                        SetThreadPriority(hThread1, ThPriority1-OFFSET);
                        SetThreadPriority(hThread2, ThPriority2-OFFSET);
                        return 1;
                      case IDCANCEL:
                        EndDialog(hdwnd, 0);
                        return 1;
                  }
              }
            return 0;
        }
```

15

This program requires the header file PANEL.H, shown here:

```
#define IDM_THREAD    100
#define IDM_HELP      101
#define IDM_PANEL     102
#define IDM_EXIT      103
```

```
#define IDD_LB1        200
#define IDD_LB2        201
#define IDD_TERMINATE1 202
#define IDD_TERMINATE2 203
#define IDD_SUSPEND1   204
#define IDD_SUSPEND2   205
#define IDD_RESUME1    206
#define IDD_RESUME2    207
#define IDD_TEXT1      208
#define IDD_TEXT2      209
#define IDD_TEXT3      210
```

The resource file required by the program is shown here:

```
#include <windows.h>
#include "panel.h"

ThreadPanelMenu MENU
{
  POPUP "&Threads" {
    MENUITEM "&Start Threads\tF2", IDM_THREAD
    MENUITEM "&Control Panel\tF3", IDM_PANEL
    MENUITEM "E&xit\tF10", IDM_EXIT
  }
  MENUITEM "&Help", IDM_HELP
}


ThreadPanelDB DIALOG 20, 20, 170, 140
CAPTION "Thread Control Panel"
STYLE DS_MODALFRAME | WS_POPUP | WS_CAPTION | WS_SYSMENU
{
  DEFPUSHBUTTON "Change", IDOK, 80, 105, 33, 14,
                WS_CHILD | WS_VISIBLE | WS_TABSTOP
  PUSHBUTTON "Done", IDCANCEL, 15, 120, 33, 14,
                WS_CHILD | WS_VISIBLE | WS_TABSTOP
  PUSHBUTTON "Terminate 1", IDD_TERMINATE1, 10, 10, 42, 12,
                WS_CHILD | WS_VISIBLE | WS_TABSTOP
  PUSHBUTTON "Terminate 2", IDD_TERMINATE2, 10, 60, 42, 12,
                WS_CHILD | WS_VISIBLE | WS_TABSTOP
  PUSHBUTTON "Suspend 1", IDD_SUSPEND1, 10, 25, 42, 12,
                WS_CHILD | WS_VISIBLE | WS_TABSTOP
  PUSHBUTTON "Resume 1", IDD_RESUME1, 10, 40, 42, 12,
                WS_CHILD | WS_VISIBLE | WS_TABSTOP
```

```
        PUSHBUTTON "Suspend 2", IDD_SUSPEND2, 10, 75, 42, 12,
                    WS_CHILD | WS_VISIBLE | WS_TABSTOP
        PUSHBUTTON "Resume 2", IDD_RESUME2, 10, 90, 42, 12,
                    WS_CHILD | WS_VISIBLE | WS_TABSTOP
        LISTBOX IDD_LB1, 65, 11, 63, 42, LBS_NOTIFY |
                WS_VISIBLE | WS_BORDER | WS_VSCROLL | WS_TABSTOP
        LISTBOX IDD_LB2, 65, 61, 63, 42, LBS_NOTIFY |
                WS_VISIBLE | WS_BORDER | WS_VSCROLL | WS_TABSTOP
        CTEXT "Thread 1", IDD_TEXT1, 140, 22, 24, 18
        CTEXT "Thread 2", IDD_TEXT2, 140, 73, 24, 18
        CTEXT "Thread Priority", IDD_TEXT3, 65, 0, 64, 10
}

ThreadPanelMenu ACCELERATORS
{
  VK_F2, IDM_THREAD, VIRTKEY
  VK_F3, IDM_PANEL, VIRTKEY
  VK_F10, IDM_EXIT, VIRTKEY
  VK_F1, IDM_HELP, VIRTKEY
}
```

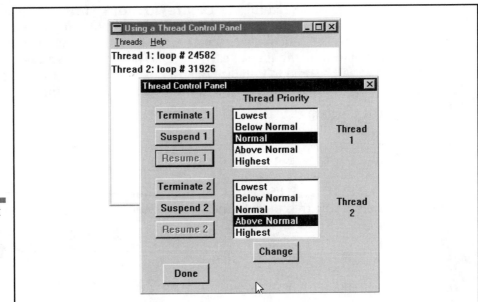

Sample output from the thread control panel sample program

Figure 15-2.

15

A Closer Look at the Thread Control Panel

Let's take a closer look at the thread control panel. To begin, notice that the program defines several global variables that are used by the control panel. They are:

```
DWORD Tid1, Tid2; /* thread IDs */
HANDLE hThread1, hThread2; /* thread handles */

int ThPriority1, ThPriority2; /* thread priorities */
int suspend1 = 0, suspend2 = 0; /* thread states */

char priorities[NUMPRIORITIES][80] = {
  "Lowest",
  "Below Normal",
  "Normal",
  "Above Normal",
  "Highest"
};
```

Here, **Tid1** and **Tid2** will hold the IDs of the two threads. **hThread1** and **hThread2** are the handles to the two threads of execution. These handles store the values returned by **CreateThread( )** when the threads are created. **ThPriority1** and **ThPriority2** hold the current priority settings of the threads. The variables **suspend1** and **suspend2** are used by the control panel to store the state of each thread. The **priorities** array holds strings that will be used to initialize the list boxes used inside the control panel dialog box. These display the priority settings of each thread.

The program also defines the following macros:

```
#define NUMPRIORITIES 5
#define OFFSET 2
```

NUMPRIORITIES defines the number of priorities a thread may have. Using the control panel, you can set a thread to one of the following priorities:

THREAD_PRIORITY_HIGHEST

THREAD_PRIORITY_ABOVE_NORMAL

THREAD_PRIORITY_NORMAL

THREAD_PRIORITY_BELOW_NORMAL

THREAD_PRIORITY LOWEST

The other two thread priority settings

THREAD_PRIORITY_TIME_CRITICAL

THREAD_PRIORITY_IDLE

are not supported because, relative to the control panel, they are of little practical value. For example, if you want to create a time-critical application, you are better off making its priority class time-critical. However, you may want to try adding these settings on your own.

OFFSET defines an offset that will be used to translate between list box indexes and thread priorities. You should recall that normal priority has the value zero. In this example, the highest priority is **THREAD_PRIORITY-_HIGHEST**, which is 2. The lowest priority is **THREAD_PRIORITY-_LOWEST**, which is –2. Since list box indexes begin at zero, the offset is used to convert between indexes and priority settings.

The thread control panel is activated by the dialog function shown here:

```
/* Thread control panel dialog box. */
LRESULT CALLBACK ThreadPanel(HWND hdwnd, UINT message,
                            WPARAM wParam, LPARAM lParam)
{
  long i;
  HANDLE hpbRes, hpbSus;

  switch(message) {
    case WM_INITDIALOG:
      /* initialize list boxes */
      for(i=0; i<NUMPRIORITIES; i++) {
        SendDlgItemMessage(hdwnd, IDD_LB1,
            LB_ADDSTRING, 0, (LPARAM) priorities[i]);
        SendDlgItemMessage(hdwnd, IDD_LB2,
            LB_ADDSTRING, 0, (LPARAM) priorities[i]);
      }

      /* get current priority */
      ThPriority1 = GetThreadPriority(hThread1) + OFFSET;
      ThPriority2 = GetThreadPriority(hThread2) + OFFSET;

      /* update list box */
      SendDlgItemMessage(hdwnd, IDD_LB1, LB_SETCURSEL,
                        (WPARAM) ThPriority1, 0);
      SendDlgItemMessage(hdwnd, IDD_LB2, LB_SETCURSEL,
                        (WPARAM) ThPriority2, 0);
```

```
    /* set suspend and resume buttons for first thread */
    hpbSus = GetDlgItem(hdwnd, IDD_SUSPEND1);
    hpbRes = GetDlgItem(hdwnd, IDD_RESUME1);
    if(suspend1) {
      EnableWindow(hpbSus, 0); /* disable Suspend */
      EnableWindow(hpbRes, 1); /* enable Resume */
    }
    else {
      EnableWindow(hpbSus, 1); /* enable Suspend */
      EnableWindow(hpbRes, 0); /* disable Resume */
    }

   /* set suspend and resume buttons for second thread */
    hpbSus = GetDlgItem(hdwnd, IDD_SUSPEND2);
    hpbRes = GetDlgItem(hdwnd, IDD_RESUME2);
    if(suspend2) {
      EnableWindow(hpbSus, 0); /* disable Suspend */
      EnableWindow(hpbRes, 1); /* enable Resume */
    }
    else {
      EnableWindow(hpbSus, 1); /* enable Suspend */
      EnableWindow(hpbRes, 0); /* disable Resume */
    }

    return 1;
  case WM_COMMAND:
    switch(wParam) {
      case IDD_TERMINATE1:
        TerminateThread(hThread1, 0);
        return 1;
      case IDD_TERMINATE2:
        TerminateThread(hThread2, 0);
        return 1;
      case IDD_SUSPEND1:
        SuspendThread(hThread1);
        hpbSus = GetDlgItem(hdwnd, IDD_SUSPEND1);
        hpbRes = GetDlgItem(hdwnd, IDD_RESUME1);
        EnableWindow(hpbSus, 0); /* disable Suspend */
        EnableWindow(hpbRes, 1); /* enable Resume */
        suspend1 = 1;
        return 1;
      case IDD_RESUME1:
        ResumeThread(hThread1);
        hpbSus = GetDlgItem(hdwnd, IDD_SUSPEND1);
        hpbRes = GetDlgItem(hdwnd, IDD_RESUME1);
        EnableWindow(hpbSus, 1); /* enable Suspend */
        EnableWindow(hpbRes, 0); /* disable Resume */
        suspend1 = 0;
```

```
                  return 1;
                case IDD_SUSPEND2:
                  SuspendThread(hThread2);
                  hpbSus = GetDlgItem(hdwnd, IDD_SUSPEND2);
                  hpbRes = GetDlgItem(hdwnd, IDD_RESUME2);
                  EnableWindow(hpbSus, 0); /* disable Suspend */
                  EnableWindow(hpbRes, 1); /* enable Resume */
                  suspend2 = 1;
                  return 1;
                case IDD_RESUME2:
                  ResumeThread(hThread2);
                  hpbSus = GetDlgItem(hdwnd, IDD_SUSPEND2);
                  hpbRes = GetDlgItem(hdwnd, IDD_RESUME2);
                  EnableWindow(hpbSus, 1); /* enable Suspend */
                  EnableWindow(hpbRes, 0); /* disable Resume */
                  suspend2 = 0;
                  return 1;
                case IDOK: /* actually change priorities */
                  ThPriority1 = SendDlgItemMessage(hdwnd, IDD_LB1,
                                   LB_GETCURSEL, 0, 0);
                  ThPriority2 = SendDlgItemMessage(hdwnd, IDD_LB2,
                                   LB_GETCURSEL, 0, 0);
                  SetThreadPriority(hThread1, ThPriority1-OFFSET);
                  SetThreadPriority(hThread2, ThPriority2-OFFSET);
                  return 1;
                case IDCANCEL:
                  EndDialog(hdwnd, 0);
                  return 1;
              }
          }
        return 0;
    }
```

15

When the control panel begins, it performs the following sequence:

1. It initializes the two list boxes used by the panel.
2. It obtains the current priority setting for each thread.
3. It highlights each thread's priority within the list boxes.
4. If a thread is suspended, then the appropriate Suspend push button is disabled. Otherwise, the corresponding Resume button is disabled.

After the dialog box has been initialized, you may change a thread's priority by first selecting the new setting in its priorities list box and then pressing the Change button. Remember, the new priority setting that you select does not become active until you press Change.

You can suspend a thread by pressing its Suspend push button. The global variables **suspend1** and **suspend2** hold the current suspend status of each thread. Zero means the thread is running. Nonzero means that the thread is suspended. To resume a suspended thread, press its Resume button. The purpose of **suspend1** and **suspend2** is to set the state of the Suspend and Resume buttons when the dialog box is initialized. Remember, for any given thread, there must be one call to **ResumeThread( )** for each call to **SuspendThread( )** in order to restart it. By disabling a thread's Suspend button after it has been suspended, you can prevent multiple calls to **SuspendThread( )**. Since the control panel can be closed and then reopened during the execution of the threads, the state of the Suspend and Resume buttons must be set whenever the panel is initialized. These variables are reset each time a new set of threads is started.

You can terminate a thread by pressing its Terminate button. Once a thread has been terminated, it cannot be resumed. Notice that the control panel uses **TerminateThread( )** to halt execution of a thread. As mentioned earlier, this function must be used with care. If you use the control panel to experiment with threads of your own, then you will want to make sure that no harmful side effects are possible.

Before moving on, you might want to experiment with the preceding program, noticing the effects of the different priority settings.

IN DEPTH

Changing the Main Thread's Priority

A thought may have occurred to you while using or reading about the thread control panel. Specifically, you may have wondered why the control panel only controls two threads—those created by the program —and not all three. As you know, all programs have at least one thread of execution, the main thread. In the example, the main thread is the third thread concurrently executing when the program is run. However, the main thread cannot be affected by the control panel. The reason for this is twofold. First, generally, you will not want to affect the priority of the main thread. It is usually better to initiate additional threads for this purpose. The second reason is that not all operations are applicable to the main thread. For example, if you suspend the execution of the main thread, your program cannot be terminated! And, since the dialog box that supports the control panel is part of the main thread, there is no way to restart it if you do suspend it. For these reasons, it is usually best to simply let the main thread execute at its default priority setting, which is **THREAD_PRIORITY_NORMAL**.

The preceding disclaimer notwithstanding, it is possible to monitor and adjust the priority setting of the main thread. To do so, you will need to acquire a handle to the thread. The easiest way to do this is to call **GetCurrentThread( )**, whose prototype is shown here:

```
HANDLE GetCurrentThread(void);
```

This function returns a psuedohandle to the current thread. The psuedohandle returned by **GetCurrentThread( )** can, however, be used any place that a normal thread handle can.

To see the effects of adjusting the priorities of the main thread, try altering the code inside the **IDM_THREAD** case of the preceding program so that **hThread2** is assigned the handle of the main thread. This change is shown here:

```
case IDM_THREAD: /* create the threads */
  hThread1 = CreateThread(NULL, 0,
                 (LPTHREAD_START_ROUTINE)MyThread1,
                 (LPVOID) hwnd, 0, &Tid1);
            CreateThread(NULL, 0,
                 (LPTHREAD_START_ROUTINE)MyThread2,
                 (LPVOID) hwnd, 0, &Tid2);

  /* assign hThread2 the handle of the main thread */
  hThread2 = GetCurrentThread();
  break;
```

After making this change, when you activate the thread control panel, Thread 2 will be the main thread. Be careful, however. If you suspend the main thread, you will not be able to terminate your program.

15

Synchronization

When using multiple threads or processes it is sometimes necessary to coordinate the activities of two or more. This process is called *synchronization*. The most common use for this is when two or more threads need access to a shared resource that may be used only by one thread at a time. For example, when one thread is writing to a file, a second thread must be prevented from doing so at the same time. The mechanism that prevents this is called *serialization*. Another reason for synchronization is when one thread is waiting for an event that is caused by another thread. In this case, there must be some means by which the first thread is held in a suspended state until the event has occurred. Then, the waiting thread must resume execution.

Before beginning, let's define the two general states that a task may be in. First, it may be *executing*. (Or, ready to execute as soon as it obtains its time slice.) Second, a task may be *blocked*, awaiting some resource or event, in which case its execution is *suspended* until the needed resource is available or the event occurs.

If you are not familiar with the need for synchronization and the serialization problem or its most common solution, the semaphore, the next section discusses it. (If this is familiar territory for you, skip ahead.)

Understanding the Synchronization Problem

Windows NT must provide special services that allow access to a shared resource to be serialized, because without help from the operating system, there is no way for one process or thread to know that it has sole access to a resource. To understand this, imagine that you are writing programs for a multitasking operating system that does not provide any synchronization support. Further, imagine that you have two multiply-executing processes, A and B, both of which, from time to time, require access to some resource R (such as a disk file) that must be accessed only by one task at a time. As a means of preventing one program from accessing R while the other is using it, you try the following solution: First, you establish a variable called **flag**, that can be accessed by both programs and initialize **flag** to 0. Next, before using each piece of code that accesses R, you wait for **flag** to be cleared, then set **flag**, access R, and finally clear **flag**. That is, before either program accesses R it executes this piece of code:

```
while(flag) ; /* wait for flag to be cleared */
flag = 1; /* set flag */

/* ... access resource R ... */

flag = 0; /* clear the flag */
```

The idea behind this code is that neither process will access R if **flag** is set. Conceptually, this approach is in the spirit of the correct solution. However, in actual fact it leaves much to be desired for one simple reason: it won't always work! Let's see why.

Using the code just given, it is possible for both processes to access R at the same time. The **while** loop is, in essence, performing repeated load and compare instructions on **flag**. In other words, it is testing **flag**'s value. When **flag** is cleared, the next line of code sets **flag**'s value. The trouble is that it is possible for these two operations to be performed in two different time slices. Between the two time slices, the value of **flag** might be accessed by a different process, thus allowing R to be used by both processes at the same time. To understand this, imagine that process A enters the **while** loop and finds that **flag** is zero, which is the green light to access R. However, before it can set **flag** to 1, its time slice expires and process B resumes execution. If B executes its **while**, it too will find that **flag** is not set and assume that it is safe to access R. However, when A resumes it will also begin accessing R. The crucial aspect of the problem is that the testing and setting of **flag** do not comprise one uninterruptable operation. Rather, as just illustrated, they can be separated by a time slice. No matter how you try, there is no way, using only application-level code, that you can absolutely guarantee that one and only one process will access R at one time.

The solution to the synchronization problem is as elegant as it is simple. The operating system (in this case Windows NT) provides a routine that in one uninterrupted operation, tests and, if possible, sets a flag. In the language of operating systems engineers, this is called a *test and set* operation. For historical reasons, the flags used to control serialization and provide synchronization between threads (and processes) are called *semaphores*. The semaphore is at the core of Windows NT synchronization system.

A semaphore synchronizes access to a resource.

Windows NT Synchronization Objects

Windows NT supports five types of synchronization objects. The first type is the classic semaphore. A semaphore can be used to allow a limited number of processes or threads access to a resource. When using a semaphore, the resource can be either completely serialized, in which case one and only one thread or process can access it at any one time, or the semaphore can be used to allow no more than a small number of processes or threads access at any one time. Semaphores are implemented using a counter that is decremented when a task is granted the semaphore and incremented when the task releases it.

The second synchronization object is the *mutex* semaphore. A mutex semaphore is used to serialize a resource so that one and only one thread or process can access it at any one time. In essence, a mutex semaphore is a special case version of a standard semaphore.

15

The third synchronization object is the *event object*. It can be used to block access to a resource until some other thread or process signals that it may be used. (That is, an event object signals that a specified event has occurred.)

The fourth synchronization object is the *waitable timer*. A waitable timer blocks a thread's execution until a specific time. Waitable timers are a new addition to Windows NT 4 and offer some exciting possibilities—especially for background tasks.

You can prevent a section of code from being used by more than one thread at a time by making it into a *critical section* using a critical section object. Once a critical section is entered by one thread, no other thread may use it until the first thread has left the critical section. (Critical sections only apply to threads within a process.)

With the exception of critical sections, the other synchronization objects can be used to serialize threads within a process, or processes themselves. In fact, semaphores are a common and simple means of handling inter-process communication.

This chapter describes how to create and use a semaphore, an event object, and a waitable timer. After you understand these synchronization objects, the mutex semaphore and the critical section will be easy for you to master on your own. Remember, at the core of all of synchronization, in one way or another, either implicitly or explicitly, is the concept of the semaphore, so we will begin there.

Using a Semaphore to Synchronize Threads

Before you can use a semaphore, you must create one using **CreateSemaphore( )**, whose prototype is shown here:

HANDLE CreateSemaphore(LPSECURITY_ATTRIBUTES *lpSecAttr*,
                             LONG *InitialCount*,
                             LONG *MaxCount*,
                             LPSTR *lpszName*);

Here, *lpSecAttr* is a pointer to the security attributes. If *lpSecAttr* is **NULL**, the default security descriptor is used.

A semaphore can allow one or more tasks access to an object. The number of tasks allowed to simultaneously access an object is determined by the value of *MaxCount*. If this value is 1, then the semaphore acts much like a mutex semaphore, allowing one and only one thread or process access to the resource at any one time.

Semaphores use a counter to keep track of how many tasks have currently been granted access. If the count is zero, then no further access can be granted until one task releases the semaphore. If the count is greater than zero, then the semaphore is said to be *signaled,* which means that another thread may be granted access. Each time a thread is granted access, the count is decremented. The initial count of the semaphore is specified in *InitialCount.* If this value is zero, then initially all objects waiting on the semaphore will be blocked until the semaphore is released elsewhere by your program. Typically, this value is set initially to 1 or more, indicating that the semaphore can be granted to at least one task. In any event, *InitialCount* must be non-negative and less than or equal to the value specified in *MaxCount.*

lpszName points to a string that becomes the name of the semaphore object. Semaphores are global objects that may be used by other processes. As such, when two processes each open a semaphore using the same name, both are referring to the same semaphore. In this way, two processes can be synchronized. The name may also be **NULL**, in which case, the semaphore is localized to one process. If *lpszName* specifies the name of an already existent semaphore, then *InitialCount* and *MaxCount* are not used.

The **CreateSemaphore( )** function returns a handle to the semaphore if successful or **NULL** on failure.

Once you have created a semaphore, you use it by calling two related functions: **WaitForSingleObject( )** and **ReleaseSemaphore( )**. The prototypes for these functions are shown here:

DWORD WaitForSingleObject(HANDLE *hObject*, DWORD *dwHowLong*);

BOOL ReleaseSemaphore(HANDLE *hSema*, LONG *Count*,
                        LPLONG *lpPrevCount*);

15

WaitForSingleObject( ) waits on a semaphore (or other type of synchronization object). It does not return until the object it is waiting on becomes available or a time-out occurs. For semaphores, *hObject* is the handle to a semaphore created earlier. The *dwHowLong* parameter specifies, in milliseconds, how long the calling routine will wait. Once that time has elapsed, a time-out error will be returned. To wait indefinitely, use the value **INFINITE**. The function returns **WAIT_OBJECT_0** when successful (that is, when access is granted). It returns **WAIT_TIMEOUT** when time-out is reached. Each time **WaitForSingleObject( )** succeeds, the counter associated with the semaphore is decremented.

ReleaseSemaphore( ) releases the semaphore and allows another thread to use it. Here, *hSema* is the handle to the semaphore. *Count* determines what value will be added to the semaphore counter. Typically, this value is 1. The *lpPrevCount* parameter points to a variable that will contain the previous semaphore count. If you don't need this count, pass **NULL** for this parameter. The function returns nonzero if successful and zero on failure.

The following program demonstrates how to use a semaphore. It reworks the first multithreaded example program so that the two threads will not execute concurrently. That is, it forces the threads to be serialized. Notice that the semaphore handle is a global variable that is created when the window is first created. This allows it to be used by all threads (including the main thread) in the program. It uses the same header and resource file as shown earlier.

```
/* A multithreaded program that uses a semaphore. */

#include <windows.h>
#include "thread.h"

#define MAX 5000

LRESULT CALLBACK WindowFunc(HWND, UINT, WPARAM, LPARAM);
DWORD WINAPI MyThread1(LPVOID param);
DWORD WINAPI MyThread2(LPVOID param);

char szWinName[] = "MyWin"; /* name of window class */

char str[255]; /* holds output strings */

DWORD Tid1, Tid2; /* thread IDs */

HANDLE hSema; /* handle to semaphore */

int WINAPI WinMain(HINSTANCE hThisInst, HINSTANCE hPrevInst,
                   LPSTR lpszArgs, int nWinMode)
{
  HWND hwnd;
  MSG msg;
  WNDCLASSEX wcl;
  HANDLE hAccel;

  /* Define a window class. */
  wcl.cbSize = sizeof(WNDCLASSEX);
  wcl.hInstance = hThisInst; /* handle to this instance */
  wcl.lpszClassName = szWinName; /* window class name */
  wcl.lpfnWndProc = WindowFunc; /* window function */
  wcl.style = 0; /* default style */
```

```
wcl.hIcon = LoadIcon(NULL, IDI_APPLICATION);
wcl.hIconSm = LoadIcon(NULL, IDI_APPLICATION);

wcl.hCursor = LoadCursor(NULL, IDC_ARROW);

/* specify name of menu resource */
wcl.lpszMenuName = "ThreadMenu"; /* main menu */

wcl.cbClsExtra = 0; /* no extra */
wcl.cbWndExtra = 0; /* information needed */

/* Make the window white. */
wcl.hbrBackground = GetStockObject(WHITE_BRUSH);

/* Register the window class. */
if(!RegisterClassEx(&wcl)) return 0;

/* Now that a window class has been registered, a window
   can be created. */
hwnd = CreateWindow(
  szWinName, /* name of window class */
  "Use a Semaphore", /* title */
  WS_OVERLAPPEDWINDOW, /* window style - normal */
  CW_USEDEFAULT, /* X coordinate - let Windows decide */
  CW_USEDEFAULT, /* Y coordinate - let Windows decide */
  CW_USEDEFAULT, /* width - let Windows decide */
  CW_USEDEFAULT, /* height - let Windows decide */
  HWND_DESKTOP, /* no parent window */
  NULL, /* no override of class menu */
  hThisInst, /* handle of this instance of the program */
  NULL /* no additional arguments */
);

/* load accelerators */
hAccel = LoadAccelerators(hThisInst, "ThreadMenu");

/* Display the window. */
ShowWindow(hwnd, nWinMode);
UpdateWindow(hwnd);

/* Create the message loop. */
while(GetMessage(&msg, NULL, 0, 0))
{
  if(!TranslateAccelerator(hwnd, hAccel, &msg)) {
    TranslateMessage(&msg); /* translate keyboard messages */
    DispatchMessage(&msg); /* return control to Windows NT */
  }
```

15

```
  }
  return msg.wParam;
}

/* This function is called by Windows NT and is passed
   messages from the message queue.
*/
LRESULT CALLBACK WindowFunc(HWND hwnd, UINT message,
                           WPARAM wParam, LPARAM lParam)
{
  int response;

  switch(message) {
    case WM_CREATE:
      hSema = CreateSemaphore(NULL, 1, 1, NULL);
      break;
    case WM_COMMAND:
      switch(LOWORD(wParam)) {
        case IDM_THREAD:
          CreateThread(NULL, 0, (LPTHREAD_START_ROUTINE)MyThread1,
                      (LPVOID) hwnd, 0, &Tid1);
          CreateThread(NULL, 0, (LPTHREAD_START_ROUTINE)MyThread2,
                      (LPVOID) hwnd, 0, &Tid2);
          break;
        case IDM_EXIT:
          response = MessageBox(hwnd, "Quit the Program?",
                               "Exit", MB_YESNO);
          if(response == IDYES) PostQuitMessage(0);
          break;
        case IDM_HELP:
          MessageBox(hwnd,
                     "F1: Help\nF2: Demonstrate Threads",
                     "Help", MB_OK);
          break;
      }
      break;
    case WM_DESTROY: /* terminate the program */
      PostQuitMessage(0);
      break;
    default:
      /* Let Windows NT process any messages not specified in
      the preceding switch statement. */
      return DefWindowProc(hwnd, message, wParam, lParam);
  }
  return 0;
}

/* A thread of execution within the process. */
```

```
DWORD WINAPI MyThread1(LPVOID param)
{
  int i;
  HDC hdc;

  /* wait for access to be granted */
  if(WaitForSingleObject(hSema, 10000)==WAIT_TIMEOUT) {
     MessageBox((HWND)param, "Time Out Thread 1",
                "Semaphore Error", MB_OK);
     return 0;
  }

  for(i=0; i<MAX; i++) {

    if(i==MAX/2) {
      /* Release at half way point.  This allows
         MyThread2 to run. */
      ReleaseSemaphore(hSema, 1, NULL);

      /* Next, once again wait for access to be granted. */
      if(WaitForSingleObject(hSema, 10000)==WAIT_TIMEOUT) {
         MessageBox((HWND)param, "Time Out Thread 1",
                    "Semaphore Error", MB_OK);
         return 0;
      }
    }

    wsprintf(str, "Thread 1: loop # %5d ", i);
    hdc = GetDC((HWND) param);
    TextOut(hdc, 1, 1, str, lstrlen(str));
    ReleaseDC((HWND) param, hdc);

  }

  ReleaseSemaphore(hSema, 1, NULL);

  return 0;
}

/* Another thread of execution within the process. */
DWORD WINAPI MyThread2(LPVOID param)
{
  int i;
  HDC hdc;

  /* wait for access to be granted */
  if(WaitForSingleObject(hSema, 10000)==WAIT_TIMEOUT) {
    MessageBox((HWND)param, "Time Out Thread 2",
```

15

```
              "Semaphore Error", MB_OK);
    return 0;
  }

  for(i=0; i<MAX; i++) {
    wsprintf(str, "Thread 2: loop # %5d ", i);
    hdc = GetDC((HWND) param);
    TextOut(hdc, 1, 20, str, lstrlen(str));
    ReleaseDC((HWND) param, hdc);
  }

  ReleaseSemaphore(hSema, 1, NULL);

  return 0;
}
```

A Closer Look at the Semaphore Program

In the program, **hSema** holds the handle to a semaphore that is used to
serialize the two threads. When execution begins, **MyThread1( )** is
activated before **MyThread2( )**. Therefore, when **MyThread1( )** is created,
it immediately acquires the semaphore and begins execution. When
MyThread2( ) is created, it cannot acquire the semaphore, so it enters a
wait state. Meanwhile, when the **for** loop inside **MyThread1( )** reaches
MAX/2, it releases the semaphore. This allows **MyThread2( )** to acquire it
and begin execution. **MyThread1( )** then enters a wait state. Finally,
MyThread2( ) finishes and releases the semaphore. This allows
MyThread1( ) to resume.

Here are some experiments to try. First, since the semaphore only allows one
thread access to it at any one time, try substituting a mutex semaphore.
Second, try allowing multiple instances of the threads to execute by
increasing the count associated with **hSema** to 2 or 3. Observe the effect.

Using an Event Object

As explained earlier, an event object is used to notify one thread or process
when an event has occurred. To create an event object, use the
CreateEvent( ) API function shown here:

HANDLE CreateEvent(LPSECURITY_ATTRIBUTES *lpSecAttr,*
                   BOOL *Manual,*
                   BOOL *Initial,*
                   LPSTR *lpszName*);

Here, *lpSecAttr* is a pointer to security attributes or **NULL**, in which case the default security descriptor is used. The value of *Manual* determines how the event object will be affected after the event has occurred. If *Manual* is nonzero, then the event object is reset only by a call to the **ResetEvent( )** function. Otherwise, the event object is reset automatically after a blocked thread is granted access. The value of *Initial* specifies the initial state of the object. If it is nonzero, the event object is set (the event is signaled). If it is zero, the event object is cleared (the event is not signaled).

lpszName points to a string that becomes the name of the event object. Event objects are global objects that may be used by other processes. As such, when two processes each open an event object using the same name, both are referring to the same object. In this way, two processes can be synchronized. The name may also be **NULL**, in which case, the object is localized to one process.

CreateEvent( ) returns a handle to the event object if successful and **NULL** otherwise.

Once an event object has been created, the thread (or process) that is waiting for the event to occur simply calls **WaitForSingleObject( )** using the handle of the event object as the first parameter. This causes execution of that thread or process to suspend until the event occurs.

To signal that an event has occurred, use the **SetEvent( )** function, shown here:

```
BOOL SetEvent(HANDLE hEventObject);
```

Here, *hEventObject* is the handle of a previously created event object. When this function is called, the first thread or process waiting for the event will return from **WaitForSingleObject( )** and begin execution.

To see how an event object operates, modify the preceding program as follows. First, declare a global handle called **hEvent**. Next, add the following line inside the **WM_CREATE** case statement:

```
hEvent = CreateEvent(NULL, FALSE, FALSE, NULL);
```

Finally, change **MyThread1( )** and **MyThread2( )** to that shown here:

```
/* First thread of execution. */
DWORD WINAPI MyThread1(LPVOID param)
{
  int i;
  HDC hdc;
```

```
   /* wait for access to be granted */
   if(WaitForSingleObject(hEvent, 10000)==WAIT_TIMEOUT) {
      MessageBox((HWND)param, "Time Out Thread 1",
               "Event Error", MB_OK);
      return 0;
   }

   for(i=0; i<MAX; i++) {
     wsprintf(str, "Thread 1: loop # %5d ", i);
     hdc = GetDC((HWND) param);
     TextOut(hdc, 1, 1, str, lstrlen(str));
     ReleaseDC((HWND) param, hdc);
   }

   return 0;
}


/* Second thread of execution. */
DWORD WINAPI MyThread2(LPVOID param)
{
   int i;
   HDC hdc;

   for(i=0; i<MAX; i++) {
     wsprintf(str, "Thread 2: loop # %5d ", i);
     hdc = GetDC((HWND) param);
     TextOut(hdc, 1, 20, str, lstrlen(str));
     ReleaseDC((HWND) param, hdc);
   }

   /* send event notification */
   SetEvent(hEvent);

   return 0;
}
```

Now, when the program executes, **MyThread1( )** is blocked until
MyThread2( ) completes and signals that it is done.

Using a Waitable Timer

The waitable timer is a Windows NT 4 innovation. Although timers are
available for all versions of Windows, they were not able to directly take part
in thread synchronization before. While it is possible to link a semaphore
with a standard timer, the waitable timer makes this process much more
convenient. Waitable timers are exciting because they will make it easier to
automate all types of background tasks.

When you create a waitable timer, you are creating a timer that will run in the background until a predetermined time is reached. A thread can wait on that timer using the **WaitForSingleObject( )** function. The thread will be blocked until the timer goes off.

Waitable timers are created using the **CreateWaitableTimer( )** function, shown here:

HANDLE CreateWaitableTimer(LPSECURITY_ATTRIBUTES *lpSecAttr*,
                      BOOL *manual*, LPCSTR *lpszName*);

Here, *lpSecAttr* points to the security descriptor to be associated with the waitable timer. If this parameter is **NULL**, then the default descriptor is used. If *manual* is nonzero, then the timer must be manually reset after each timing period. It if is zero, the timer is automatically reset. *lpszName* points to the name of the timer. To create an unnamed timer, pass **NULL** for this parameter. Named timers can be shared with other processes. Unnamed ones are local to the process in which they were created. The function returns a handle to the waitable timer if successful or **NULL** on failure.

Once a timer has been created, it is inactive. To set the timer, call **SetWaitableTimer( )**. Its prototype is shown here:

BOOL SetWaitableTimer(HANDLE *hWaitTimer*,
                  const LARGE_INTEGER *TargetTime*,
                  LONG *period*,
                  PTIMERAPCROUTINE *lpTimerFunc*,
                  LPVOID *param*,
                  BOOL *Unsuspend*);

Here, *hWaitTimer* is the handle of the timer object. *TargetTime* specifies the time at which the timer will go off. The value in *period* specifies the length of time, in milliseconds, between timer activations. If *period* is zero, then the timer only goes off once. *lpTimerFunc* points to a function that will be called when the timer goes off. This function is optional. If no such function is needed, specify **NULL** for *lpTimerFunc*. The value specified by *param* is passed to the timer function. If *Unsuspend* is nonzero, then a computer that has been operating in low-power mode will be resumed. **SetWaitable-Timer( )** returns nonzero if successful and zero on failure.

15

The function pointed to by *lpTimerFunc* must have this prototype:

```
VOID (APIENTRY *PTIMERAPCROUTINE) TimerFunc(
        LPVOID param, DWORD dwLowTime, DWORD dwHighTime);
```

Here, *param* is the value passed by **SetWaitableTimer( )**. The values in *dwLowTime* and *dwHighTime* contain the termination time in the format compatible with that contained in a **FILETIME** structure. (Time formats are described below.) Frankly, most applications of a waitable timer will not need to use a timer function.

When calling **SetWaitableTimer( )**, the target time is specified as a **LARGE_INTEGER**. This union represents time as a 64-bit integer that is compatible with the way time is represented in a **FILETIME** structure. Both are shown here:

```
typedef struct _FILETIME {
  DWORD dwLowDateTime; /* low-order 32-bits */
  DWORD dwHighDateTime; /* high-order 32-bits */
} FILETIME;

typedef union _LARGE_INTEGER {
  struct {
    DWORD LowPart;
    LONG HighPart;
  };
  LONGLONG QuadPart;
} LARGE_INTEGER;
```

A **FILETIME** structure contains the number of 100 nanosecond units that have passed since January 1, 1601.

Win32 provides functions to convert time as represented by a **FILETIME** structure from or to a more convenient form. Perhaps the easiest way to set the target time of a waitable timer is to first describe the time using a **SYSTEMTIME** structure and then convert that structure into a **FILETIME** structure (which can be assigned to a **LARGE_INTEGER**). The **SYSTEMTIME** structure is defined like this:

```
typedef struct _SYSTEMTIME {
  WORD wYear; /* year */
  WORD wMonth; /* month (1 through 12) */
  WORD wDayOfWeek; /* day of weeek (0 through 6) */
  WORD wDay; /* day of month (1 through 31) */
  WORD wHour; /* hour */
  WORD wMinute; /* minutes */
```

```
   WORD wSecond; /* seconds */
   WORD wMilliseconds; /* milliseconds */
} SYSTEMTIME;
```

Once you have initialized the fields of a **SYSTEMTIME** structure to the desired target time, you can then call **SystemTimeToFileTime( )** to convert the time into a **FILETIME** structure. The prototype for **SystemTimeToFileTime( )** is shown here:

BOOL SystemTimeToFileTime(CONST SYSTEMTIME *lpSysTime,
                                      FILETIME *lpFileTime);

The function returns nonzero if successful and zero on failure.

For most uses of a waitable timer, you will not actually have to manually set all of the fields in the **SYSTEMTIME** structure. Usually, you can obtain the current system time and then just advance the time by the desired amount. For example, if you wanted to create a timer that would go off in 1 hour, you would first obtain the current time and then increase the **wHour** field appropriately. To obtain the current system time, use **GetSystemTime( )**, shown here:

VOID GetSystemTime(SYSTEMTIME *lpSysTime);

The current time of the system is returned in the structure pointed to by *lpSysTime*. The time is specified in UTC (Coordinated Universal Time), which is essentially Greenwich Mean Time.

The following program demonstrates the use of a waitable timer. Each time you press F2, a thread of execution is created. Inside this thread, a waitable timer is created and given a target time that is ten seconds in the future. Next, the window is minimized and the thread waits on that timer. When the time interval has elapsed, the window is restored and the thread resumes execution. Notice the definition of **_WIN32_WINNT** at the top of the program. Since waitable timers are quite new, this definition may be required by some compilers to ensure that the appropriate header information is included.

15

```
/* Demonstrate a waitable timer */

/* The following is needed to ensure that waitable
   timer API functions are available. */
#define _WIN32_WINNT 0x0400

#include <windows.h>
#include "thread.h"
```

```
#define MAX 10000

LRESULT CALLBACK WindowFunc(HWND, UINT, WPARAM, LPARAM);
DWORD WINAPI MyThread1(LPVOID param);

char szWinName[] = "MyWin"; /* name of window class */

char str[255]; /* holds output strings */

DWORD Tid1; /* thread IDs */

HANDLE hWaitTimer; /* handle to semaphore */

int WINAPI WinMain(HINSTANCE hThisInst, HINSTANCE hPrevInst,
                   LPSTR lpszArgs, int nWinMode)
{
  HWND hwnd;
  MSG msg;
  WNDCLASSEX wcl;
  HANDLE hAccel;

  /* Define a window class. */
  wcl.cbSize = sizeof(WNDCLASSEX);
  wcl.hInstance = hThisInst; /* handle to this instance */
  wcl.lpszClassName = szWinName; /* window class name */
  wcl.lpfnWndProc = WindowFunc; /* window function */
  wcl.style = 0; /* default wcl */

  wcl.hIcon = LoadIcon(NULL, IDI_APPLICATION);
  wcl.hIconSm = LoadIcon(NULL, IDI_APPLICATION);

  wcl.hCursor = LoadCursor(NULL, IDC_ARROW);

  /* specify name of menu resource */
  wcl.lpszMenuName = "WaitTimerMenu"; /* main menu */

  wcl.cbClsExtra = 0; /* no extra */
  wcl.cbWndExtra = 0; /* information needed */

  /* Make the window white. */
  wcl.hbrBackground = GetStockObject(WHITE_BRUSH);

  /* Register the window class. */
  if(!RegisterClassEx(&wcl)) return 0;

/* Now that a window class has been registered, a window
   can be created. */
  hwnd = CreateWindow(
```

```
        szWinName, /* name of window class */
        "Use a Waitable Timer", /* title */
        WS_OVERLAPPEDWINDOW, /* window style - normal */
        CW_USEDEFAULT, /* X coordinate - let Windows decide */
        CW_USEDEFAULT, /* Y coordinate - let Windows decide */
        CW_USEDEFAULT, /* width - let Windows decide */
        CW_USEDEFAULT, /* height - let Windows decide */
        HWND_DESKTOP, /* no parent window */
        NULL, /* no override of class menu */
        hThisInst, /* handle of this instance of the program */
        NULL /* no additional arguments */
    );

    /* load accelerators */
    hAccel = LoadAccelerators(hThisInst, "WaitTimerMenu");

    /* Display the window. */
    ShowWindow(hwnd, nWinMode);
    UpdateWindow(hwnd);

    /* Create the message loop. */
    while(GetMessage(&msg, NULL, 0, 0))
    {
      if(!TranslateAccelerator(hwnd, hAccel, &msg)) {
        TranslateMessage(&msg); /* translate keyboard messages */
        DispatchMessage(&msg); /* return control to Windows NT */
      }
    }
    return msg.wParam;
}

/* This function is called by Windows NT and is passed
   messages from the message queue.
*/
LRESULT CALLBACK WindowFunc(HWND hwnd, UINT message,
                            WPARAM wParam, LPARAM lParam)
{
  int response;

  switch(message) {
    case WM_CREATE:
      /* create the timer */
      hWaitTimer = CreateWaitableTimer(NULL, 1, NULL);
      break;
    case WM_COMMAND:
      switch(LOWORD(wParam)) {
        case IDM_THREAD:
          CreateThread(NULL, 0, (LPTHREAD_START_ROUTINE)MyThread1,
```

```
                          (LPVOID) hwnd, 0, &Tid1);
          break;
        case IDM_EXIT:
          response = MessageBox(hwnd, "Quit the Program?",
                                "Exit", MB_YESNO);
          if(response == IDYES) PostQuitMessage(0);
          break;
        case IDM_HELP:
          MessageBox(hwnd,
                     "F1: Help\nF2: Demonstrate Timer",
                     "Help", MB_OK);
          break;
      }
      break;
    case WM_DESTROY: /* terminate the program */
      PostQuitMessage(0);
      break;
    default:
      /* Let Windows NT process any messages not specified in
      the preceding switch statement. */
      return DefWindowProc(hwnd, message, wParam, lParam);
  }
  return 0;
}

/* Demonstrate waitable timer. */
DWORD WINAPI MyThread1(LPVOID param)
{
  int i;
  HDC hdc;
  SYSTEMTIME systime;
  FILETIME filetime;
  LARGE_INTEGER li;

  /* add 10 seconds onto current system time */
  GetSystemTime(&systime);
  SystemTimeToFileTime(&systime, &filetime);
  li.LowPart = filetime.dwLowDateTime;
  li.HighPart = filetime.dwHighDateTime;
  li.QuadPart += 100000000L;

  /* set the timer */
  SetWaitableTimer(hWaitTimer, &li,
                   0, NULL, NULL, 0);

  /* minimize the window until the timer expires */
  ShowWindow((HWND) param, SW_MINIMIZE);
```

```
   /* wait for timer */
   if(WaitForSingleObject(hWaitTimer, 100000)==WAIT_TIMEOUT) {
      MessageBox((HWND)param, "Time Out Thread 1",
                 "Timer Error", MB_OK);
      return 0;
   }

   /* beep and restore window */
   MessageBeep(MB_OK);
   ShowWindow((HWND) param, SW_RESTORE);

   hdc = GetDC((HWND) param);
   for(i=0; i<MAX; i++) {
     wsprintf(str, "Thread 1: loop # %5d ", i);
     TextOut(hdc, 1, 1, str, lstrlen(str));
   }
   ReleaseDC((HWND) param, hdc);

   return 0;
}
```

This program uses the same THREAD.H header file described earlier. It uses this resource file:

```
#include <windows.h>
#include "thread.h"

WaitTimerMenu MENU
{
  POPUP "&Options" {
    MENUITEM "&Waitable Timer\tF2", IDM_THREAD
    MENUITEM "E&xit\tF10", IDM_EXIT
  }
  MENUITEM "&Help", IDM_HELP
}

WaitTimerMenu ACCELERATORS
{
  VK_F2, IDM_THREAD, VIRTKEY
  VK_F10, IDM_EXIT, VIRTKEY
  VK_F1, IDM_HELP, VIRTKEY
}
```

Uses for Waitable Timers

Waitable timers offer some interesting possibilities. For example, you could use one to create a computerized alarm clock. To do so, create a dialog box that allows the user to set the desired alarm time. Then, use that time to initialize a waitable timer. You could also use a waitable timer to help create automated backup or file transfer utilities. Although these types of tasks have always been possible by using normal timers in conjunction with other synchronization objects, the waitable timer simplifies them.

Creating a Separate Task

Although Windows NT's thread-based multitasking will have the most direct impact on how you program, it is, of course, still possible to utilize process-based multitasking where appropriate. When using process-based multitasking, instead of starting another thread within the same program, one program starts the execution of another program. In Windows NT, this is accomplished using the **CreateProcess( )** API function, whose prototype is shown here:

BOOL CreateProcess(LPCSTR *lpszName*, LPSTR *lpszComLine*,
                    LPSECURITY_ATTRIBUTES *lpProcAttr*,
                    LPSECURITY_ATTRIBUTES *lpThreadAttr*,
                    BOOL *InheritAttr*, DWORD *How*,
                    LPVOID *lpEnv*, LPSTR *lpszDir*,
                    LPSTARTUPINFO *lpStartInfo*,
                    LPPROCESS_INFORMATION *lpPInfo*);

The name of the program to execute, which may include a full path, is specified in the string pointed to by *lpszName*. Any command-line parameters required by the program are specified in the string pointed to by *lpszComLine*. However, if you specify *lpszName* as **NULL**, then the first token in the string pointed to by *lpszComLine* will be used as the program name. Thus, typically, *lpszName* is specified as **NULL** and the program name and any required parameters are specified in the string pointed to by *lpszComLine*. (If you are starting a Win16 process, then *lpszName* must be **NULL**.)

To start the execution of another program, call Create-Process( ).

The *lpProcAttr* and *lpThreadAttr* parameters are used to specify any security attributes related to the process being created. These may be specified as **NULL**, in which case the default security descriptor is used. If *InheritAttr* is nonzero handles in use by the creating process are inherited by the new process. If this parameter is zero, then handles are not inherited.

By default, the new process is run "normally". However, the *How* parameter can be used to specify certain additional attributes that affect how the new process will be created. (For example, you will use the *How* to specify a special priority for the process or to indicate that the process will be debugged.) If *How* is zero, then the new process is created as a normal process.

The *lpEnv* parameter points to a buffer that contains the new process' environmental parameters. If this parameter is **NULL**, then the new process inherits the creating process' environment.

The current drive and directory of the new process can be specified in the string pointed to by *lpszDir*. If this parameter is **NULL**, then the current drive and directory of the creating process are used.

The parameter *lpStartInfo* is a pointer to a **STARTUPINFO** structure that contains information that determines how the main window of the new process will look. **STARTUPINFO** is defined as shown here:

```
typedef struct _STARTUPINFO {
  DWORD cb; /* size of STARTUPINFO */
  LPSTR lpReserved; /* must be NULL */
  LPSTR lpDesktop; /* name of desktop */
  LPSTR lpTitle; /* title of console (consoles only) */
  DWORD dwX; /* upper left corner of */
  DWORD dwY; /* new window */
  DWORD dwXSize; /* size of new window */
  DWORD dwYSize; /* size of new window */
  DWORD dwXCountChars; /* console buffer size */
  DWORD dwYCountChars; /* console buffer size */
  DWORD dwFillAttribute; /* initial text color and background */
  DWORD dwFlags; /* determines which fields are active */
  WORD wShowWindow; /* how window is shown, SW_SHOW, etc. */
  WORD cbReserved2; /* must be 0 */
  LPBYTE lpReserved2; /* must be NULL */
  HANDLE hStdInput; /* standard handles */
  HANDLE hStdOutput;
  HANDLE hStdError;
} STARTUPINFO;
```

15

The fields **dwX**, **dwY**, **dwXSize**, **dwYSize**, **dwXCountChars**, **dwYCountChars**, **dwFillAttribute**, and **wShowWindow** are ignored unless they are enabled by including the proper value as part of the **dwFlags** field. The values for **dwFlags** are shown here:

Macro	Enables
STARTF_USESHOWWINDOW	wShowWindow
STARTF_USESIZE	dwXSize and dwYSize
STARTF_USEPOSITION	dwX and dwY

Macro	Enables
STARTF_USECOUNTCHARS	dwXCountChars and dwYCountChars
STARTF_USEFILLATTRIBUTE	dwFillAttribute
STARTF_USESTDHANDLES	hStdInput, hStdOutput, and hStdError

dwFlags may also include one or more of these values:

STARTF_FORCEONFEEDBACK	Feedback cursor is on.
STARTF_FORCEOFFFEEDBACK	Feedback cursor is off.

NOTE: The *lpTitle*, *dwXCountChars*, and *dwYCountChars* fields only apply to console applications, which will be discussed later in this book.

Generally, you will not need to use most of the fields in **STARTUPINFO** and you can allow most to be ignored. However, you must specify **cb**, which contains the size of the structure, and several other fields must be set to **NULL**.

The final parameter to **CreateProcess( )** is *lpPInfo*, which is a pointer to a structure of type **PROCESS_INFORMATION**, shown here:

```
typedef struct _PROCESS_INFORMATION {
  HANDLE hProcess; /* handle to new process */
  HANDLE hThread; /* handle to main thread */
  DWORD dwProcessId; /* ID of new process */
  DWORD dwThreadId; /* ID of new thread */
} PROCESS_INFORMATION;
```

Handles to the new process and the main thread of that process are passed back to the creating process in **hProcess** and **hThread**. The new process and thread IDs are returned in **dwProcessId** and **dwThreadId**. Your program can make use of this information or choose to ignore it.

CreateProcess( ) returns nonzero if successful and zero otherwise.

The following fragment illustrates the use of **CreateProcess( )**.

```
STARTUPINFO startinfo;
  PROCESS_INFORMATION pinfo;
  /* ... */
  startinfo.cb = sizeof(STARTUPINFO);
```

```
startinfo.lpReserved = NULL;
startinfo.lpDesktop = NULL;
startinfo.lpTitle = NULL;
startinfo.dwFlags = STARTF_USESHOWWINDOW;
startinfo.cbReserved2 = 0;
startinfo.lpReserved2 = NULL;
startinfo.wShowWindow = SW_SHOW;
CreateProcess(NULL, "test.exe",
              NULL, NULL, 0, 0,
              NULL, NULL, &startinfo, &pinfo);
```

This starts the execution of a program called TEST.EXE, which must be in the current working directory of the parent process. The program is initially visible.

Once created, the new process is largely independent from the creating process. It is possible for the parent process to terminate the child, however. To do so, use the **TerminateProcess( )** API function.

PORTABILITY: Windows 3.1 does not support **CreateProcess( )**. To start another process in Windows 3.1, the **WinExec( )** function is used. However, **WinExec( )** is obsolete and should not be used for Win32 programs. When porting older programs, be sure to replace any calls to **WinExec( )** with calls to **CreateProcess( )**.

15

CHAPTER 16

Working with Consoles

537

While the Windows graphical user interface (GUI) is excellent for most types of programs, it is cumbersome when all you need is a simple character mode program. A character mode program is one that uses mainly the ASCII character set and assumes a character-based device, such as an 80-character by 25-line display system. Thus, a character mode application is the type that is commonly written for DOS. Early versions of Windows, such as Windows 3.1, did not provide any built-in support for writing character mode programs. If you wanted one, it had to be written for DOS. Of course, this severely limited the usefulness of a character mode program in a Windows world. (The "marriage" between DOS-style programs and Windows has never been a happy one!) Fortunately, Windows NT supplies a means of creating a character mode program that is fully integrated into the Windows environment.

A character mode program uses a text-based rather than a window-based interface.

Character mode programs are supported by *consoles*, which provide the basic I/O environment necessary for their execution. Windows NT (through the Win32 library) provides several console-based API functions. By including support for consoles, Windows NT makes it easier for a character mode program to coexist with GUI programs. For example, it is now possible to write character mode programs that

A console provides I/O support for character mode programs.

♦ respond to Windows-style mouse events

♦ run in their own console session

♦ have access to the (relevant) API functions

♦ use pipes and I/O redirection

♦ allow Windows-based control over keyboard activity, if desired

While GUI programs will always be the most popular type written for Windows NT, a console is a useful alternative. Often, a program is needed that is short, requires little user interaction, and can be written quickly. For example, file utility programs often fall into this category. For these types of programs, the overhead of implementing them as full-blown GUI applications is difficult to justify. However, when these types of programs are implemented as console programs, they are easy to create and they are still fully integrated into the Windows NT environment.

This chapter describes how to write a character mode program and demonstrates several of the console-based API functions.

PORTABILITY: Consoles are not supported by Windows 3.1. They are available in Windows 95.

Understanding Character Mode

Character mode programs resemble traditional, non-windowed programs that you almost certainly have written. That is, in a character mode program no window is created. Also, there is no window function. Further, a character mode program begins with a call to **main( )**, not **WinMain( )**. In fact, generally there will not be a function called **WinMain( )** in your program. (If there is, it is simply treated as just another function with no special meaning.) For the most part, character mode programs do not use most of the Windows features discussed elsewhere in this book.

Given the preceding paragraph, you might be wondering two things. First, what general support does Windows NT give to a character mode program? Second, since a character mode program is not a Windows program in the usual sense, why not just write a DOS program instead? The answers are interrelated. First, as mentioned, a console-based, character mode program is fully integrated into the Windows NT environment. For example, mouse support is under the control of Windows NT when using a character mode program. Second, a character mode program has access to API functions, which are unavailable to a DOS program. Finally, DOS is a 16-bit environment. Windows NT uses 32 bits. For obvious reasons, most modern programs should be written for a 32-bit environment.

If you execute a character mode program from the command prompt, it will inherit that console session. However, as you will soon see, it is possible for each character mode program to allocate its own console. In fact, allocating a console is the recommended practice. A character mode program can also control several attributes of its console that are generally beyond the control of a DOS program.

All consoles maintain a cursor, which marks the place at which the next output to the console will begin. The cursor is automatically updated after each output operation. It is also possible to set the cursor location within a console to any (legal) location you desire.

Allocating a Console

A console's output buffer is called a screen buffer.

In Windows terminology, a console is the interface used by your character mode programs. It contains both input and output buffers. The output buffers are also called *screen buffers*. Each character mode program that you write will operate through a console. In Windows NT, there can be several active consoles, each running its own character mode program.

By default, a character mode program either inherits the current console or is given a console if none exists when it is run. However, a better approach is for the program to acquire its own console. The reason for this is simple: any changes to that console affect only that console and do not affect the

16

inherited console. Therefore, for the cleanest approach to implementing a character mode program, it must create its own console. To do this, use the API function **AllocConsole( )**, whose prototype is shown here:

    BOOL AllocConsole(VOID);

This function acquires a new console session for the program that calls it. The function returns nonzero if successful and zero otherwise. An allocated console is freed automatically when the program terminates.

Once a console has been allocated, it creates a window that behaves, more or less, like any other window. It includes a title, a control menu, minimize and maximize boxes, and, if needed, scroll bars.

If the character mode program is executed from within a console session, then before a new one can be allocated, the old one inherited by the program must be freed, using **FreeConsole( )**. Its prototype is shown here:

    BOOL FreeConsole(VOID);

The function returns nonzero if successful and zero otherwise.

When creating your character mode application, the best approach is to execute this sequence as the first actions taken by **main( )**.

```
FreeConsole();
AllocConsole()
```

Even if no parent console was previously in effect, no harm is done by calling **FreeConsole( )** and, in either case, a new console is allocated.

A console allocated by your program is automatically freed when your program stops running (unless the console is in use by another task, of course). Your program can also free the console explicitly by calling **FreeConsole( )**.

Giving a Title to a Console

You can give a console window a title using the **SetConsoleTitle( )** API function, shown here:

    BOOL SetConsoleTitle(LPTSTR *lpszTitle*);

Here, the string pointed to by *lpszTitle* becomes the title of the console window. The function returns nonzero if successful and zero otherwise.

Acquiring Handles to Standard Input and Output

Many of the console-based API functions require a standard handle to perform I/O. The standard handles are linked to standard input, standard output, and standard error. By default, these handles refer to the keyboard and the screen, but they may be redirected. When you write to a console, you will write to standard output. When you read from a console, you will read from standard input. Handles to console input and output are of type **HANDLE**.

To acquire a standard handle, use the **GetStdHandle( )** function, whose prototype is shown here:

HANDLE GetStdHandle(DWORD *dwStdDev*);

Here, *dwStdDev* must be one of these macros: **STD_INPUT_HANDLE**, **STD_OUTPUT_HANDLE**, or **STD_ERROR_HANDLE**, which correspond to standard input, standard output, and standard error, respectively. The function returns a handle to the device. On failure, **INVALID_HANDLE_VALUE** is returned.

Outputting Text to the Console

One way to output text to the console is to use the **WriteConsole( )** API function, whose prototype is shown here:

BOOL WriteConsole(HANDLE *hConOut*, CONST VOID **lpString*,
                  DWORD *dwLen*, LPDWORD *lpdwNumWritten*,
                  LPVOID *lpNotUsed*);

Here, *hConOut* is the handle of console output, generally obtained through a call to **GetStdHandle( )**. The string to be output is pointed to by *lpString*. The number of characters in *lpString* to output is passed in *dwLen* and the actual number of characters written is returned in the long integer pointed to by *lpdwNumWritten*. *lpNotUsed* is reserved for future use and must be **NULL**.

The string is output using the current text and background colors. The output begins at the current cursor location and the cursor location is automatically updated. The function returns nonzero if successful and zero otherwise.

It is important to understand that **WriteConsole( )** does not provide any formatting capabilities. This means that you will still need to use a function

16

like **sprintf( )** to first construct the string that you want to output if you want to use **WriteConsole( )** to write formatted data.

Inputting from the Console

To input information entered at the keyboard, use the **ReadConsole( )** function, shown here:

```
BOOL ReadConsole(HANDLE hConIn, LPVOID lpBuf,
                 DWORD dwLen, LPDWORD lpdwNumRead,
                 LPVOID lpNotUsed);
```

Here, *hConIn* is the handle linked to console input. The character array that will receive the characters typed by the user is pointed to by *lpBuf*. (This string is *not* automatically null-terminated.) The function will read up to *dwLen* characters or until ENTER is pressed. The number of characters actually read is returned in the long integer pointed to by *lpdwNumRead*. The *lpNotUsed* parameter is reserved for future use and must be **NULL**. The function returns nonzero if successful and zero otherwise.

IN DEPTH

SetConsoleMode( )

The precise operation of **ReadConsole( )** and **WriteConsole( )** is determined by the current console mode. The console mode can be set using **SetConsoleMode( )**. Its prototype is shown here:

```
BOOL SetConsoleMode(HANDLE hCon, DWORD dwNewMode);
```

Here, *hCon* is the handle of either the console's input buffer or its output buffer and *dwNewMode* specifies the new console mode. The function returns nonzero if successful and zero on failure.

The valid values for *dwNewMode* depend upon whether you are setting the mode of the input buffer or the output buffer. The values for output are **ENABLE_PROCESSED_OUTPUT** and **ENABLE_WRAP_AT_EOL_OUTPUT**. Both of these are set by default. Enabling processed output allows the console to properly handle carriage return-linefeed sequences, expand tabs, ring the bell, and process backspace characters. **ENABLE_WRAP_AT_EOL_OUTPUT** allows the console window to scroll properly and output to be wrapped in the expected fashion.

The possible values for input buffers are shown here. You can OR two or more together to obtain the desired mode.

ENABLE_ECHO_INPUT
ENABLE_LINE_INPUT
ENABLE_MOUSE_INPUT
ENABLE_PROCESSED_INPUT
ENABLE_WINDOW_INPUT

By default, all but **ENABLE_WINDOW_INPUT** are on. To receive mouse events, include **ENABLE_MOUSE_INPUT**. When **ENABLE_LINE_INPUT** is included, input obtained using **ReadConsole( )** is line-buffered. **ENABLE_ECHO_INPUT** causes characters to be echoed to the screen. It must be used in conjunction with **ENABLE_LINE_INPUT**. To allow the proper processing of carriage returns, linefeeds, and backspaces, include **ENABLE_ PROCESSED_INPUT**. It also prevents control keys from being passed to the console. To receive buffer size events, you must include **ENABLE_WINDOW_INPUT**.

You can obtain the current console mode by calling **GetConsoleMode( )**, shown here:

BOOL GetConsoleMode(HANDLE *hCon*, LPDWORD *lpdwMode*);

Here, *hCon* is the handle of either the input or output buffer. *dwMode* is a pointer to a long integer that receives the current console mode. This value will contain one or more of the previously described values. The function returns nonzero if successful and zero on failure.

Setting the Cursor Position

To position the cursor within a console window, use the **SetConsoleCursor-Position( )** function. Its prototype is shown here:

BOOL SetConsoleCursorPosition(HANDLE *hConOut*, COORD *XY*);

Here, *hConOut* is the output handle of the console and *XY* is a **COORD** structure that contains the coordinates of the desired cursor location. **COORD** is defined like this:

16

```
typedef struct _COORD {
  SHORT X;
  SHORT Y;
} COORD;
```

The function returns nonzero if successful and zero on failure.

Setting Text and Background Colors

When using a console, by default text is white and the background is black. You can change this, if you want, by using **SetConsoleTextAttribute( )**, whose prototype is shown here:

BOOL SetConsoleTextAttribute(HANDLE *hConOut*, WORD *colors*);

Here, *hConOut* is the handle linked to console output and *colors* is the value that determines the text and background colors. The value of *colors* is constructed by ORing together two or more of the following macros, which are defined in WINCON.H. (WINCON.H is automatically included when you include WINDOWS.H.)

Macro	Meaning
FOREGROUND_BLUE	Text includes blue.
FOREGROUND_RED	Text includes red.
FOREGROUND_GREEN	Text includes green.
FOREGROUND_INTENSITY	Text is shown in high intensity.
BACKGROUND_BLUE	Background includes blue.
BACKGROUND_RED	Background includes red.
BACKGROUND_GREEN	Background includes green.
BACKGROUND_INTENSITY	Background is shown in high intensity.

The actual color will be a combination of the color components that you specify. To create white, combine all three colors. For black, specify no color.

SetConsoleTextAttribute( ) returns nonzero if successful and zero on failure.

Console I/O vs. the C/C++ Standard I/O Functions

Once you have obtained a console it is permissible (indeed, completely valid) to use the C/C++ standard I/O functions and operators with it. However, using the console API functions just described does give your application more control over the console in many situations. Also, in the case of monitoring console events, only the API functions allow full integration with Windows NT. For example, mouse events are not accessible using the standard C/C++ I/O systems. They are accessible, however, by using the console API functions (as you will soon see).

For the example that follows, the standard C/C++ I/O functions are used only to illustrate their validity.

A Console Demonstration Program

Before continuing, the console functions just described are demonstrated by the following program. Its operation should be clear.

```c
/* Demonstrate Consoles */

#include <windows.h>
#include <string.h>
#include <stdio.h>

int main(void)
{
  HANDLE hStdin, hStdout;
  char str[255] = "This is an example of output to a console.";
  DWORD result;
  COORD coord;
  int x=0, y=0;

  /* free old console and start fresh with new one */
  FreeConsole();
  AllocConsole();

  /* give console window a title */
  SetConsoleTitle("Windows NT Console Demonstration");

  /* get standard handles */
  hStdin = GetStdHandle(STD_INPUT_HANDLE);
  hStdout = GetStdHandle(STD_OUTPUT_HANDLE);

  WriteConsole(hStdout, str, strlen(str), &result, NULL);
```

16

```
/* demonstrate cursor positioning */
for(x=0, y=1; y<20; y++) {
  coord.X = x;
  coord.Y = y;
  sprintf(str, "At location %d %d", x, y);
  SetConsoleCursorPosition(hStdout, coord);
  WriteConsole(hStdout, str, strlen(str), &result, NULL);
  if(y < 10) x += 5;
  else x -= 5;
}

/* change the colors */
coord.X = 0;
coord.Y = 10;
strcpy(str, "This is in red on blue background.");
SetConsoleCursorPosition(hStdout, coord);
SetConsoleTextAttribute(hStdout,
            FOREGROUND_RED | BACKGROUND_BLUE);
WriteConsole(hStdout, str, strlen(str), &result, NULL);

/* reset colors to black and white */
SetConsoleTextAttribute(hStdout,
            FOREGROUND_RED | FOREGROUND_BLUE |
            FOREGROUND_GREEN);

/* read input */
coord.X = 0;
coord.Y = 21;
strcpy(str, "Enter a string: ");
SetConsoleCursorPosition(hStdout, coord);
WriteConsole(hStdout, str, strlen(str), &result, NULL);
ReadConsole(hStdin, str, 80, &result, NULL);
str[result] = '\0'; /* null terminate */

/* display the string */
WriteConsole(hStdout, str, strlen(str), &result, NULL);

/* can use printf(), gets(), etc. */
printf("This is a test.  Enter another string: ");
gets(str);
printf("%s\n", str);
printf("Press ENTER: ");

getchar(); /* wait for keypress */

return 0;
}
```

To compile a console program you will need to use a set of compiler and linker commands different than those you have been using to compile Windows-style programs. For example, when using Microsoft Visual C++ you will need to specify Console Application when creating a workspace for your program. For Borland C++, you will need to specify the Target Model as Console when creating a new project. For other compilers, check the compiler's user manual for instructions.

Sample output from this program is shown in Figure 16-1.

Managing the Mouse

One of the main advantages of using Windows NT consoles and writing character mode Windows NT programs over simply letting DOS-style programs execute in a window is that a console gives you access to the mouse. To obtain mouse events (and other information) when using a console you must use an API console input function called **ReadConsole-Input( )**, whose prototype is shown here:

```
BOOL ReadConsoleInput(HANDLE hConIn,
                      PINPUT_RECORD lpBuf,
                      DWORD dwNum,
                      LPDWORD lpdwNumRead);
```

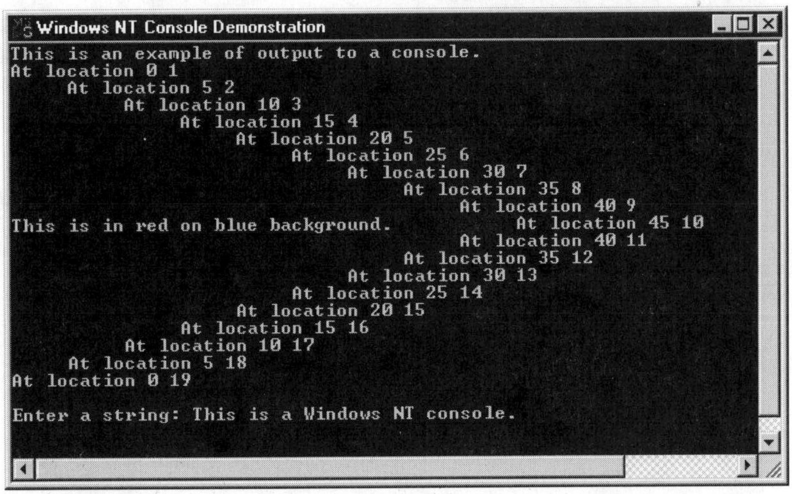

Sample output from the console demonstration program

Figure 16-1.

16

Here, *hConIn* is the handle of the console about which you want information. The parameter *lpBuf* is a pointer to a structure of type **INPUT_RECORD**, which will receive the information regarding the requested input event or events. The number of event records to input is specified in *dwNum* and the amount actually obtained by the function is returned in *lpdwNum*Read. The function returns nonzero if successful or zero otherwise.

The **ReadConsoleInput( )** function removes information about one or more input events from the console's input buffer. Each time you strike a key or use the mouse an input event is generated and the information associated with this event is stored in an **INPUT_RECORD** structure. (Certain other input events may also occur, but only the mouse and keyboard ones are of interest to us in this chapter.) The **ReadConsoleInput( )** function reads one or more of these events and makes the input event information available to your program.

Each event record is returned in a structure of type **INPUT_RECORD**, which is shown here:

```
typedef struct _INPUT_RECORD {
  WORD EventType;
  union {
    KEY_EVENT_RECORD KeyEvent;
    MOUSE_EVENT_RECORD MouseEvent;
    WINDOW_BUFFER_SIZE_RECORD WindowBufferSizeEvent;
    MENU_EVENT_RECORD MenuEvent;
    FOCUS_EVENT_RECORD FocusEvent;
  } Event;
} INPUT_RECORD;
```

The contents of **EventType** determine what type of event has occurred. It can be one of these macros:

Macro	Event
FOCUS_EVENT	Used by Windows NT.
KEY_EVENT	Key pressed.
MENU_EVENT	Used by Windows NT.
MOUSE_EVENT	Mouse event.
WINDOW_BUFFER_SIZE_EVENT	Window resized.

Only mouse and keyboard events are examined in detail here. Focus and menu events are for the internal use of Windows NT only. A buffer size event may be of interest to your program in some situations, in which case **WindowBufferSizeEvent** contains a **COORD** structure that holds the new dimensions of the screen buffer.

Each time a mouse event occurs, the **EventType** field contains **MOUSE_EVENT** and the **Event** union contains a **MOUSE_EVENT_RECORD** structure that describes the mouse event. This structure is shown here:

```
typedef struct _MOUSE_EVENT_RECORD {
  COORD dwMousePosition;
  DWORD dwButtonState;
  DWORD dwControlKeyState;
  DWORD dwEventFlags;
} MOUSE_EVENT_RECORD;
```

The **dwMousePosition** field contains the coordinates of the mouse when the event took place. Since a console is a text-based device, the coordinates are in terms of character position and row, not pixels.

For consoles, mouse coordinates are in terms of characters and rows, not pixels.

dwButtonState describes the state of the mouse buttons when the event was generated. If bit one is on, then the left mouse button is pressed. If bit two is on, then the right mouse button is pressed. If bit three is on, the middle button (if it exists) is pressed. More than one bit will be set when more than one button is pressed at the same time.

The **dwControlKeyState** field describes the state of the various control keys when the event occurred. It may contain one or more of the following macros:

SHIFT_PRESSED
RIGHT_CTRL_PRESSED
LEFT_CTRL_PRESSED
RIGHT_ALT_PRESSED
LEFT_ALT_PRESSED
ENHANCED_KEY
CAPSLOCK_ON
NUMLOCK_ON
SCROLLLOCK_ON

An enhanced key is one of those added to the standard keyboard by the IBM enhanced keyboards. For example, the extra arrow keys are enhanced keys.

16

dwEventFlags contains either **MOUSE_MOVED** (the mouse has moved) or **DOUBLE_CLICK** (a mouse button has been double-clicked).

Demonstrating the Console Mouse

The following program illustrates how to manage mouse events when using a console. Sample output is shown in Figure 16-2.

```c
/* Managing the mouse from a console. */

#include <windows.h>
#include <string.h>
#include <stdio.h>

int main(void)
{
  HANDLE hStdin, hStdout;
  char str[80] = "Press a key to stop.";
  DWORD result;
  COORD coord;
  int x=0, y=0;
  INPUT_RECORD inBuf;

  /* free old console and start fresh with new one */
  FreeConsole();
  AllocConsole();

  /* give console window a title */
  SetConsoleTitle("Mouse with Console Demonstration");

  /* get standard handles */
  hStdin = GetStdHandle(STD_INPUT_HANDLE);
  hStdout = GetStdHandle(STD_OUTPUT_HANDLE);

  WriteConsole(hStdout, str, strlen(str), &result, NULL);

  /* show mouse events until a key is pressed */
  do {
    ReadConsoleInput(hStdin, &inBuf, 1, &result);

    /* if mouse event occurs, report it */
    if(inBuf.EventType==MOUSE_EVENT) {
      sprintf(str, "Button state: %lu, X,Y: %3lu,%3lu\n",
              inBuf.Event.MouseEvent.dwButtonState,
              inBuf.Event.MouseEvent.dwMousePosition.X,
              inBuf.Event.MouseEvent.dwMousePosition.Y);
      coord.X = 0;
```

```
coord.Y = 1;
SetConsoleCursorPosition(hStdout, coord);
WriteConsole(hStdout, str, strlen(str), &result, NULL);

/* if a double click occurs, report it */
if(inBuf.Event.MouseEvent.dwEventFlags==DOUBLE_CLICK) {
  sprintf(str, "Double click\a");
  coord.X = inBuf.Event.MouseEvent.dwMousePosition.X;
  coord.Y = inBuf.Event.MouseEvent.dwMousePosition.Y;
  SetConsoleCursorPosition(hStdout, coord);
  WriteConsole(hStdout, str, strlen(str), &result, NULL);
  Sleep(600); /* wait */
  SetConsoleCursorPosition(hStdout, coord);
  strcpy(str, "              "); /* erase message */
  WriteConsole(hStdout, str, strlen(str), &result, NULL);
}

/* Leave a trail if left button is pressed while
   mouse is moved. */
if(inBuf.Event.MouseEvent.dwEventFlags==MOUSE_MOVED &&
   inBuf.Event.MouseEvent.dwButtonState==1) {
  coord.X = inBuf.Event.MouseEvent.dwMousePosition.X;
  coord.Y = inBuf.Event.MouseEvent.dwMousePosition.Y;
  SetConsoleCursorPosition(hStdout, coord);
  WriteConsole(hStdout, "*", 1, &result, NULL);
}
  }
} while(inBuf.EventType != KEY_EVENT);

return 0;
}
```

This program displays the current location of the mouse when it is within
the console window and the state of the mouse buttons, and it reports when
the mouse is double-clicked. If the mouse is moved when the left button
is pressed, a trail of asterisks will be displayed. The program continues to
execute until a key event is generated when you press a key. **Sleep( )** is
used to provide a short delay before the **Double click** message is erased
from the screen. This gives you time to read it.

16

Responding to Keyboard Events

As you know from your previous programming experience, it is quite
common for text-based programs to respond to key presses in a fashion more
subtle than simply inputting the keystroke. For example, sometimes your
program will need to know if a control key is pressed, or the state of the shift

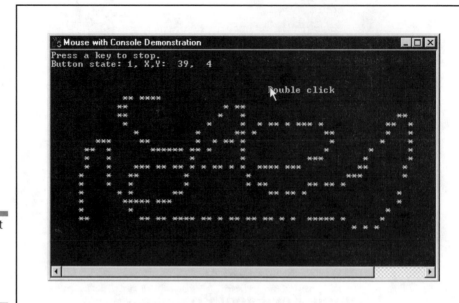

Sample output
from the
Mouse Event
program
Figure 16-2.

key. Also, some applications make use of the scan code that corresponds to
the key. Whatever the need, Windows NT gives character mode,
console-based applications access to all the information associated with a
keyboard event. Like mouse events, keyboard events are obtained by calling
ReadConsoleInput( ), described earlier.

A scan code
is a hardware-
dependent key
code that
relates to a
key's position
on the keyboard.

Each time a key is pressed a keyboard event is generated. When this event is
obtained using **ReadConsoleInput( )**, the **EventType** field of the
INPUT_RECORD structure contains the **KEY_EVENT** value. When this is
the case, then the **Event** union holds a **KEY_EVENT_RECORD** structure,
which describes the event. This structure is shown here:

```
typedef struct _KEY_EVENT_RECORD {
  BOOL bKeyDown;
  WORD wRepeatCount;
  WORD wVirtualKeyCode;
  WORD wVirtualScanCode;
  union {
    WCHAR UnicodeChar;
    CHAR AsciiChar;
  } uChar;
  DWORD dwControlKeyState;
} KEY_EVENT_RECORD;
```

If **bKeyDown** is nonzero, then a key was being pressed when the key event was generated. If it is zero, the key was being released.

The number of times a key stroke is generated when a key is held down and autorepeat takes over is returned in **wRepeatCount**. Even when a key is held down, your program may continue to receive separate events, with **wRepeatCount** containing 1. However, it is permissible for Windows NT to collapse these events into one event with the number of repeats indicated in **wRepeatCount**.

The virtual key code is returned in **wVirtualKeyCode**.

The scan (position) code of the key is returned in **wVirtualScanCode**.

The union **uChar** contains the ASCII or Unicode code of the key being pressed.

The state of the control keys (and other keys) is returned in **dwControlKeyState**. The values are the same as those described for mouse events.

A Sample Key Event Program

The following program demonstrates keyboard events. This program reports each character typed and the state of the various control keys. It continues to execute until you click the left mouse button. Sample output is shown in Figure 16-3.

```
/* Managing the keyboard from a console. */

#include <windows.h>
#include <string.h>
#include <stdio.h>

int main(void)
{
  HANDLE hStdin, hStdout;
  char str[255] = "Press the left mouse button to stop.";
  DWORD result;
  COORD coord;
  int x=0, y=0;
  int i;
  int done = 0;
  INPUT_RECORD inBuf;

  /* free old console and start fresh with new one */
  FreeConsole();
  AllocConsole();
```

16

```
/* give console window a title */
SetConsoleTitle("Keyboard Demonstration");

/* get standard handles */
hStdin = GetStdHandle(STD_INPUT_HANDLE);
hStdout = GetStdHandle(STD_OUTPUT_HANDLE);

WriteConsole(hStdout, str, strlen(str), &result, NULL);

/* Show keyboard events until left
   mouse button is pressed. */
do {
  ReadConsoleInput(hStdin, &inBuf, 1, &result);
  /* if key is pressed, report it */
  if(inBuf.EventType==KEY_EVENT) {
    sprintf(str, "Key is: %c, scan code is %d \n",
            inBuf.Event.KeyEvent.uChar,
            inBuf.Event.KeyEvent.wVirtualScanCode);

    coord.X = 0;
    coord.Y = 1;
    SetConsoleCursorPosition(hStdout, coord);
    WriteConsole(hStdout, str, strlen(str), &result, NULL);

    /* if a control, alt, etc. key is pressed, report it */
    if(inBuf.Event.KeyEvent.dwControlKeyState &&
       inBuf.Event.KeyEvent.bKeyDown) {
      coord.X = 0;
      coord.Y = 10;
      *str = '\0';
      if(inBuf.Event.KeyEvent.dwControlKeyState
         & RIGHT_ALT_PRESSED)
           strcat(str, "Right Alt key is pressed. ");
      if(inBuf.Event.KeyEvent.dwControlKeyState
         & LEFT_ALT_PRESSED)
           strcat(str, "Left Alt key is pressed. ");
      if(inBuf.Event.KeyEvent.dwControlKeyState
         & RIGHT_CTRL_PRESSED)
           strcat(str, "Right control key is pressed. ");
      if(inBuf.Event.KeyEvent.dwControlKeyState
         & LEFT_CTRL_PRESSED)
           strcat(str, "Left control key is pressed. ");
      if(inBuf.Event.KeyEvent.dwControlKeyState
         & SHIFT_PRESSED)
           strcat(str, "Shift key is pressed. ");
      if(inBuf.Event.KeyEvent.dwControlKeyState
         & NUMLOCK_ON)
```

```
            strcat(str, "Num lock key on. ");
        if(inBuf.Event.KeyEvent.dwControlKeyState
          & SCROLLLOCK_ON)
            strcat(str, "Scroll lock key is on. ");
        if(inBuf.Event.KeyEvent.dwControlKeyState
          & CAPSLOCK_ON)
            strcat(str, "Caps lock key is on. ");
        if(inBuf.Event.KeyEvent.dwControlKeyState
          & ENHANCED_KEY)
            strcat(str, "Enhanced key is pressed. ");

        SetConsoleCursorPosition(hStdout, coord);
        strcat(str, "\a");
        WriteConsole(hStdout, str, strlen(str), &result, NULL);
        SetConsoleCursorPosition(hStdout, coord);

        /* wait, then erase the message */
        Sleep(1000);
        coord.X = 0;
        coord.Y = 10;
        i = strlen(str);
        for(*str='\0'; i; i--) strcat(str, " ");
        WriteConsole(hStdout, str, strlen(str), &result, NULL);
      }
    }
    if(inBuf.EventType==MOUSE_EVENT)
      if(inBuf.Event.MouseEvent.dwButtonState==1) done = 1;

  } while(!done);

  return 0;
}
```

Using Consoles

As mentioned, console applications are especially useful for simple utility
programs that you will use yourself. Examples are file filters, test programs,
and throw-away, single-use programs. The advantage to console applications
is the ease with which they can be created. For example, consider the
following program. It displays the current local time, updated once a second.
The program runs until a key is pressed. It uses the standard ANSI C time
functions to obtain and display the local time. Sample output is shown in
Figure 16-4.

16

```
/* A simple clock program that uses a console
   application to display the current local time. */
```

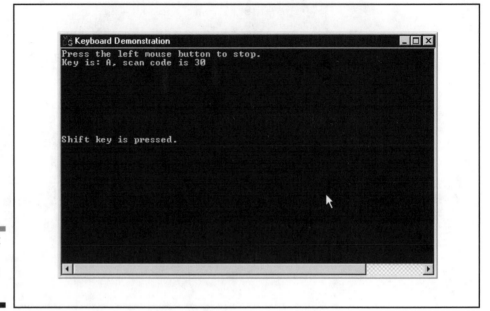

Sample output
from the key
event program
Figure 16-3.

```
#include <windows.h>
#include <string.h>
#include <stdio.h>
#include <time.h>

int main(void)
{
  HANDLE hStdin, hStdout;
  DWORD result;
  COORD coord;
  char str[80];
  INPUT_RECORD inBuf;
  time_t t;
  struct tm *localt;

  /* free old console and start fresh with new one */
  FreeConsole();
  AllocConsole();

  /* give console window a title */
  SetConsoleTitle("Current Time");
```

```
/* get standard handles */
hStdin = GetStdHandle(STD_INPUT_HANDLE);
hStdout = GetStdHandle(STD_OUTPUT_HANDLE);

coord.X = 0;
coord.Y = 0;

for(;;) {
  t = time(NULL);
  localt = localtime(&t);

  strftime(str, 79, "%I:%M:%S %p", localt);
  SetConsoleCursorPosition(hStdout, coord);
  WriteConsole(hStdout, str, strlen(str), &result, NULL);

  Sleep(1000); /* update clock once a second */

  /* if key is pressed, terminate program */
  ReadConsoleInput(hStdin, &inBuf, 1, &result);
  if(inBuf.EventType==KEY_EVENT) break;
}

  return 0;
}
```

This program is less than 40 lines long. The equivalent GUI program is much longer. While making the clock program windows-based would be better if the program is going to be used extensively, it probably isn't worth the extra time if it is a single-use program, perhaps used for some test purpose.

The point of the preceding example is not to suggest that console applications are better than GUI ones. To the contrary, the standard Windows NT interface is a substantially richer and more powerful environment. It is just that console applications give you the ability to easily create simple, character-based programs that don't have the overhead associated with a full-blown GUI application.

16

Sample output
from the
Clock program
Figure 16-4.

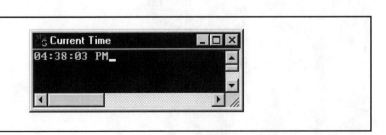

CHAPTER 17

Understanding the Help System

Windows NT 4 provides extensive support for online help. As you know from using Windows NT, nearly all applications provide the user with online instructions explaining how to use various features of the program. Most applications also provide online documentation that can be accessed via the help system. Frankly, it is not possible to write a top-notch professional Windows NT program without providing extensive online help. The programming techniques necessary to accomplish this are described here.

Two Types of Help

The Windows NT help system supports two general categories of help. The first is essentially online documentation and is sometimes called *reference help*. It is accessed via the standard Help window, such as the one shown in Figure 17-1. Using the standard Help window, you can display various help topics, search for other topics, or view the contents of a help file. Reference help is used to display detailed descriptions of various features supported by the application or to act as the online version of the program's user manual. The second category of help is *context-sensitive*. Context-sensitive help is used to display a brief description of a specific program feature within a small window. An example is shown in Figure 17-2. Both types of help are required by a professional-quality Windows NT application. As you will see, although different in style, both of these categories of help are handled in much the same way.

Reference help supports online documentation. Context-sensitive help provides information related to a specific feature.

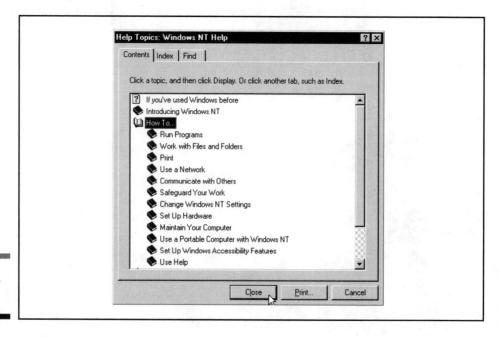

A standard Help window

Figure 17-1.

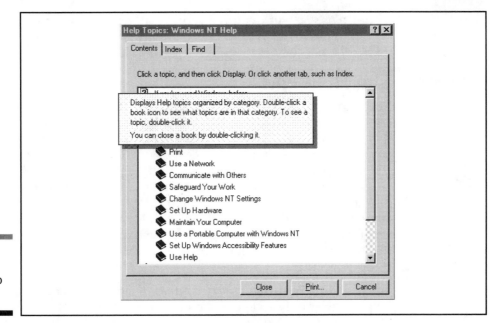

How the User Invokes Help

To properly implement the full Windows NT help system, your program
must support the four standard methods by which the user can invoke
online help. Specifically, the user may obtain help by

1. Clicking the right mouse button on an object.
2. Clicking on the **?** button and then clicking on an object.
3. Pressing F1.
4. Using a Help menu.

The first two methods are almost always used to invoke context-sensitive,
pop-up help. In most situations, F1 is also used to invoke context-sensitive
help. Occasionally, it invokes reference help. Selecting help through a menu
usually invokes reference help.

It is also permissible for a program itself to invoke help whenever it needs to
do so. For example, a program might activate the help system when the user
attempts an invalid operation.

Once the user has activated a help option, your application will respond by
calling the **WinHelp( )** API function. This function manages all help

17

requests. As you will see, it is a very versatile function. However, before examining **WinHelp( )**, you need to understand how to create a help file.

The Help File

At the core of the Windows NT help system is the *help file*. Both context-sensitive and reference help utilize one. Help files are not text files. Rather, they are specially compiled files that have the .HLP file extension. To create a help file, you must first create an RTF (Rich Text Format) file that contains all of the help topics, plus formatting, indexing, and cross-referencing information. This file will normally have the extension .RTF. It is then compiled using a help compiler. For example, the help compiler for Windows NT supplied with Microsoft's Visual C++ and Borland C++ is called HCW. The output of the help compiler is a .HLP file. Thus, relative to the help compiler, the RTF file is the source file and the .HLP file is the object file.

An RTF file contains formatting, indexing, and cross-referencing information.

The Rich Text Format language contains a large number of commands. The help compiler only accepts a subset of these commands. However, the help system also recognizes several additional, help-related commands that are not part of the general purpose RTF language. All RTF commands begin with a \. For example, \b is the RTF command for bold. It is far beyond the scope of this chapter to discuss all of them. (Indeed, an entire book is needed to fully describe the RTF language.) However, this chapter describes the most important and commonly used commands relating to help files. If you will be doing extensive work with help files, then you will need to acquire a full description of the RTF language.

In addition to the RTF file, the help compiler also uses a project file. Typically, this is a file created by the help compiler. In it are various settings and values that relate to the help file. Help project files use the .HPJ extension.

Creating a Help File

As stated, the source code for a help file must be in rich text format. This means that creating the source code for a help file is a non-trivial task. Fortunately, there are three ways that you can create a help file. First, you can use a third-party automated Help authoring package. Second, you can use a text editor that generates RTF files. Third, you can use a standard text editor and manually embed RTF commands. If you will be preparing large and complex help files, the authoring package is probably the best alternative. However, for smaller applications, either of the other two choices is adequate. Since the one option that all readers will have is the third, that is the method that will be used here.

The General Form of a Help File

All help source files have certain basic elements in common. First, the entire file must be enclosed between curly braces. That is, it must begin with a { and end with a }. Immediately following the opening curly brace must be the **\rtf** command. This command identifies the file as a rich text format file and specifies which version of the rich text format specification is being used. (We will be using version 1.) You must then define the character set used by the file. This will generally be the ANSI character set, which is specified using the **\ansi** command. You must also define the character fonts used by the file. This is done with the **\fonttbl** command. Thus, the general form of a help RTF file will look like this.

    {\rtf1\ansi \fonttbl ...

  Help File Contents

    }

Within an RTF file, additional curly braces can be used to localize the effect of various RTF commands. In this capacity, the curly braces act much like they do in a C/C++ source file: they define a block.

Some RTF Commands

Before you can create even a simple help file, you need to know a few of the most important and common RTF commands. The RTF commands used in this chapter are shown in Table 17-1. Each command is described here.

\ansi

The **\ansi** command specifies the ANSI character set. RTF files support other character sets, such as **\mac** (Macintosh character set) or **\pc** (OEM character set). However, the ANSI character set is the one that is generally used for help files.

\b

The **\b** command turns on boldface. **\b0** turns it off. However, if the **\b** command is used within a block, then only the text within that block is boldfaced and there is no need to use the **\b0** command. For example,

```
{\b this is bold} this is not
```

Here, only the text within the curly braces will be in boldface.

17

RTF Command	Meaning
\ansi	Specifies the ANSI character set.
\b	Turns on boldface.
\b0	Turns off boldface.
\f*n*	Selects the font specified by *n*.
\fs*n*	Sets font size to *n*.
\fonttbl	Defines a font table.
\footnote	Specifies keywords and index topics.
\i	Turns on italics.
\i0	Turns off italics.
\page	Indicates the end of a topic.
\par	Indicates the end of a paragraph.
\rtf*n*	Specifies which RTF specification is being used.
\tab	Moves to next tab position.
\uldb	Marks a "hot spot" link to another topic.
\v	Creates a topic link (used in conjunction with **\uldb**).

Selected
Help-Related
RTF
Commands
Table 17-1.

\fn

The **\fn** command selects a font. The font is specified by its number. The font must have been previously defined using a **\fonttbl** statement.

\fsn

The **\fsn** command sets the font size to that specified by *n*, which is specified in half-point units. For example, **\fs24** sets the font size to 12 points.

\fonttbl

Before a font can be used, it must be included in a **\fonttbl** statement. It has the following general form:

```
{\fonttbl
 {\f1\family-name font-name;}
 {\f2\family-name font-name;}
```

```
{\f3\family-name font-name;}
        .
        .
        .
{\fn\family-name font-name;}
}
```

Here, *family-name* is the name of the font family (such as **froman** or **fswiss**) and *font-name* is the name of a specific font (such as Times New Roman, Arial, or Old English) within that family. The number of the font as specified in the **\f** statement will be used to select the font. A partial list of font families and names is shown here:

Family	Fonts
\froman	Times New Roman, Palatino
\fswiss	Arial
\fmodern	Courier New, Pica
\fscript	Cursive
\fdecor	Old English

For example, the following declares font 0 to be \fswiss Arial.

```
{\fonttbl {\f0\fswiss Arial;}}
```

\footnote

The **\footnote** statement is one of the most important RTF commands when creating a help file. The reason for this is that it is used to specify topic names, context IDs, and browse sequences. The following forms of the **\footnote** command are used in this chapter.

${\footnote *string*}

K{\footnote *string*}

#{\footnote *string*}

+{\footnote *sequence-name:sequence-order*}

@(\footnote *string*)

The **$** form defines a title for a topic that is displayed in the history window of the help system. The title can include spaces. A topic title identifies the topic.

17

The **K** form specifies that *string* is a keyword or phrase and can include spaces. Keywords are displayed as index entries. If the first character of the string is a K, then it must be preceded by an extra space. The **K** form can only be used if a topic title has been specified.

The **#** defines a *context ID* that is used to create links and cross-references between topics. It is also used by your application program to access portions of the help file. In this form, *string* may not include spaces. As you will see, the context ID string is usually a macro that represents the ID value.

The **+** form defines a *browse sequence*. A browse sequence determines the linkage between topics when the browse arrows are pressed. (The browse arrows are the << and >> arrow buttons on the Help window's button bar.) In this form, the content of *sequence-name* specifies the sequence and *sequence-order* determines the position of the topic in that sequence. Browse sequences are performed in alphabetical order or numerical order based upon the values of *sequence-order*. A help file may have one or more browse sequences. To define several sequences, both the *sequence-name* and *sequence-order* specifiers in the **\footnote** command are required. If your help file has only one browse sequence, then the *sequence-name* is not required. Examples of browse sequences are contained in the example help file shown later.

To cause browse buttons to be included in the standard Help window, you must include the **Browsebuttons( )** macro in the configuration section of the project file associated with a help file that defines a browse sequence.

The **@** form of the **\footnote** command is used to embed a comment.

i

The **\i** command turns on italics. **\i0** turns it off. However, if the **\i** command is used within a block, then only the text within that block is made italic and there is no need to use the **\i0** command.

page

The **\page** command signals the end of a topic.

par

The **\par** command marks the end of a paragraph. It also causes a line to be skipped. Thus two **\par** commands in a row will skip two lines.

rtfn

The **\rtfn** command determines which RTF specification is being used. In this chapter, version 1 is used.

\tab

The **\tab** command advances one tab stop.

\uldb

To mark a *hot spot* link, specify it using the **\uldb** command. It has the following general form:

    \uldb *text*

The *text* will be shown in the standard hot spot color and font. This command is always used in conjunction with a **\v** command.

\v

The **\v** command specifies a link to another topic. It has the following general form:

    \v *context-ID*

Here, *context-ID* must be the same as specified in a **#\footnote** statement. This link is executed when the hot spot associated with the **\v** command is clicked by the user.

A Sample Help File

The following help file will be used by the example program shown later in this chapter. This file contains all the common components of a help file. Call this file HELPTEST.RTF.

```
{\rtf1\ansi
{\fonttbl{\f0\fswiss Arial;} {\f1\froman Times New Roman;}}
\fs40
\f1
@{\footnote This is a comment.  So is the following.}
@{\footnote This is a Sample Help File.}
${\footnote Contents}
Contents of Sample Help File
\f0
\fs20
\par
\par
\tab{\uldb Main Menu \v MenuMain}
\par
\tab{\uldb Main Window \v MainWindow}
\par
```

```
\tab{\uldb Main Window Push Button \v PushButtonMainWin}
\par
\tab{\uldb Push Button 1 \v PushButton1}
\par
\tab{\uldb Push Button 2 \v PushButton2}
\par
\tab{\uldb Push Button 3 \v PushButton3}
\par
\tab{\uldb List Box \v ListBox}
\par
\tab{\uldb Check Box \v CheckBox}
\par
\par
\f1
\fs30
Select a Topic.
\fs20
\f0
\page
#{\footnote MenuMain}
${\footnote Main Menu}
K{\footnote Main Menu}
{\fs24\b Main Menu}
\par
\par
The main menu allows you to display a sample
dialog box, activate the help system, display
information about this program, or terminate
the program.
\page
#{\footnote MenuMainPU}
This is the main menu for the program.
\page
#{\footnote PushButtonMainWin}
${\footnote Main Window Push Button}
K{\footnote Main Window Push Button}
{\fs24\b Main Window Push Button}
\par
\par
This is help for the main window push button.
\par
{\i This is in italics.}
\page
#{\footnote PushButtonMainWinPU}
This is the popup for the main window push button.
\page
#{\footnote PushButton1}
${\footnote Push Button 1}
```

```
K{\footnote Push Button 1}
+{\footnote Push:A}
{\fs24\b Push Button One}
\par
\par
This is help for the first push button.
\par
\par
See also {\uldb Push Button 2 \v PushButton2}
\page
#{\footnote PushButton1PU}
This is the popup for the first push button.
\page
#{\footnote PushButton2}
${\footnote Push Button 2}
K{\footnote Push Button 2}
+{\footnote Push:B}
{\fs24\b Push Button Two}
\par
\par
This is help for the second push button.
\par
\par
See Also {\uldb Push Button 3 \v PushButton3}
\page
#{\footnote PushButton2PU}
This is the popup for the second push button.
\page
#{\footnote PushButton3}
${\footnote Push Button 3}
K{\footnote Push Button 3}
+{\footnote Push:C}
{\fs24\b Push Button Three}
\par
\par
This is help for the third push button.
\par
\par
See Also {\uldb Push Button 1 \v PushButton1}
\page
#{\footnote PushButton3PU}
This is the popup for the third push button.
\page
#{\footnote MainWindow}
${\footnote Main Window}
K{\footnote Main Window}
{\fs24\b Main Window}
\par
```

17

```
\par
This is the main program window.
\page
#{\footnote MainWindowPU}
This is the main window popup help message.
\page
#{\footnote DlgPU}
${\footnote DlgPU}
This is a dialog box.
\page
#{\footnote ListBox}
${\footnote List Box}
K{\footnote List Box}
+{\footnote BOX:A}
{\fs24\b List Box}
\par
\par
This is help for the list box.
\page
#{\footnote ListBoxPU}
This is the popup for the list box.
\page
#{\footnote CheckBox}
${\footnote Check Box}
K{\footnote Check Box}
+{\footnote BOX:B}
{\fs24\b Check Box}
\par
\par
This is help for the check boxes.
\page
#{\footnote CheckBoxPU}
This is the popup for the check boxes.
\page
#{\footnote MenuDlgPU}
Activates the sample dialog box.
\page
#{\footnote MenuExitPU}
Terminates the program.
\page
#{\footnote MenuHelpPU}
Activates the Help System.
\page
#{\footnote MenuAboutPU}
Displays information about this program.
\page
}
```

In this file, the **#\footnote** commands whose IDs end in **PU** are the entry points for context-sensitive, pop-up help. The other **#\footnote** commands are used to support reference help in the standard Help window.

After you have entered this file, you must compile it using the help compiler. Call the output file HELPTEST.HLP. This file will be used by the example program. However, before you compile the file, you must define the following MAP statements within the configuration section of the project file associated with HELPTEST.RTF. As you will soon see, these values will be used to support context-sensitive, pop-up help windows.

PushButton1PU	700
PushButton2PU	701
PushButton3PU	702
ListBoxPU	703
CheckBoxPU	704
MainWindowPU	705
PushButtonMainWinPU	706
DlgPU	707
MenuDlgPU	708
MenuExitPU	709
MenuHelpPU	710
MenuAboutPU	711
MenuMainPU	712

The easiest way to define the MAP values is to include a map file in your help project. Map files use the following format to map values to identifiers.

```
identifier1       value1
identifier2       value2
identifier3       value3

        .

        .

        .

identifierN       valueN
```

17

For example, here is the map file that you can use for the sample help file:

```
PushButton1PU          700
PushButton2PU          701
PushButton3PU          702
ListBoxPU              703
CheckBoxPU             704
MainWindowPU           705
PushButtonMainWinPU    706
DlgPU                  707
MenuDlgPU              708
MenuExitPU             709
MenuHelpPU             710
MenuAboutPU            711
MenuMainPU             712
```

You must also activate the browse buttons in the standard Help window by including the **BrowseButtons( )** macro in the configuration section of your project file. Finally, if you want to give your Help window a title, you can specify one in the Options dialog box of the help compiler. If you don't specify a title, then the default title "Windows Help" will be used. The title used in the examples is "Sample Help File".

When you compile this help file, call the output file HELPTEST.HLP. This file will need to be in the same directory as the executable version of the example program shown later in this chapter.

Executing Help Using WinHelp( )

After you have created a help file and compiled it into its .HLP form, your application can access the information contained in it by invoking the **WinHelp( )** API function. Its prototype is shown here:

BOOL WinHelp(HWND *hwnd*, LPCSTR *filename*, UINT *command*,
         DWORD *extra*);

Here, *hwnd* is the handle of the invoking window. The name of the help file being activated is specified in *filename*, which may include a drive and path specifier. Precisely what action the **WinHelp( )** function takes is determined by *command*.

The valid values for *command* are shown here:

Command	Purpose
HELP_COMMAND	Executes a help macro.
HELP_CONTENTS	Obsolete, use HELP_FINDER instead.
HELP_CONTEXT	Displays a specified topic.
HELP_CONTEXTMENU	Displays context-sensitive help. This includes a "What's This?" menu.
HELP_CONTEXTPOPUP	Displays context-sensitive help.
HELP_FINDER	Displays the standard Help Topics window.
HELP_FORCEFILE	Forces correct file to be displayed.
HELP_HELPONHELP	Displays help information on Help. Requires that the WINHELP32.HLP file is available.
HELP_INDEX	Obsolete, use HELP_FINDER instead.
HELP_KEY	Displays a specific topic given its keyword.
HELP_MULTIKEY	Displays a specific topic given its alternative keyword.
HELP_PARTIALKEY	Displays a specific topic given a partial keyword.
HELP_QUIT	Closes the Help window.
HELP_SETCONTENTS	Sets the contents topic.
HELP_SETPOPUP_POS	Specifies the position of the next pop-up window displayed by the help system.
HELP_SETWINPOS	Determines the size and position of the Help window and displays it, if necessary.
HELP_TCARD	This command is ORed with other commands for training card help.
HELP_WM_HELP	Displays context-sensitive help.

Some commands require additional information. When this is the case, the additional information is passed in *extra*. The value of *extra* for each command is shown here.

17

Command	Meaning of *extra*
HELP_COMMAND	Pointer to string that contains macro.
HELP_CONTENTS	Not used. Set to zero.
HELP_CONTEXT	Context ID of topic.
HELP_CONTEXTMENU	See text.
HELP_CONTEXTPOPUP	Context ID of topic.
HELP_FINDER	Not used. Set to zero.
HELP_FORCEFILE	Not used. Set to zero.
HELP_HELPONHELP	Not used. Set to zero.
HELP_INDEX	Not used. Set to zero.
HELP_KEY	Pointer to string that contains the keyword.
HELP_MULTIKEY	Pointer to **MULTIKEYHELP** structure.
HELP_PARTIALKEY	Pointer to string containing partial keyword.
HELP_QUIT	Not used. Set to zero.
HELP_SETCONTENTS	Context ID of topic.
HELP_SETPOPUP_POS	Pointer to a **POINT** structure.
HELP_SETWINPOS	Pointer to a **HELPWININFO** structure.
HELP_WM_HELP	See text.

For the **HELP_WM_HELP** and **HELP_CONTEXTMENU** commands, the meaning of *extra* is a little more detailed than it is for the other commands. For these two commands, *extra* is a pointer to an array of **DWORD** values. These values are organized into pairs. The first value specifies the ID of a control (such as a push button, edit box, etc.) or menu item. The second value specifies the context ID of the help information linked to that control. This array must end with two zero values. These two commands are used to support context-sensitive help and to help process **WM_HELP** and **WM_CONTEXTMENU** messages, which are described next.

Responding to WM_HELP and WM_CONTEXTMENU Messages

As mentioned near the beginning of this chapter, there are two broad categories of help: reference and context-sensitive. In a correctly written

Windows NT program, the user can activate reference help (that is, activate the standard Help window) by selecting Help from a menu or, in many situations, by pressing F1. Context-sensitive help is activated either by right-clicking on a control or window, by using the **?** button, or, in some situations, by pressing F1. (The distinction between the two uses of F1 is discussed in the following section.)

Pressing F1 or using the ? button generates a WM_HELP message. Right-clicking generates a WM_CONTEXT-MENU message.

Since your program must respond differently to different types of help requests, there must be some way to tell them apart, and there is. When F1 is pressed or when the **?** button is used, a **WM_HELP** message is automatically sent to the active window. When the user right-clicks on a window or control a **WM_CONTEXTMENU** message is sent to the window that contains the control. The proper processing of these two messages is crucial to the correct implementation of online help. Both messages will be examined here.

PORTABILITY: The **WM_HELP** and **WM_CONTEXTMENU** messages are not supported by Windows 3.1 or Windows NT 3.51. Therefore, when converting older programs to Windows NT, you will want to add support for these messages.

WM_HELP

Each time your program receives a **WM_HELP** command, **lParam** will contain a pointer to a **HELPINFO** structure that describes the help request. The **HELPINFO** structure is defined like this:

```
typedef struct tagHELPINFO
{
  UINT cbSize;
  int iContextType;
  int iCtrlId;
  HANDLE hItemHandle;
  DWORD dwContextId;
  POINT MousePos;
} HELPINFO;
```

Here, **cbSize** contains the size of the **HELPINFO** structure.

iContextType specifies the type of object for which help is being requested. If it is for a menu item it will contain **HELPINFO_MENUITEM**. If it is for a window or control, it will contain **HELPINFO_WINDOW**. **iCtrlId** contains the ID of the control, window, or menu item.

17

hItemHandle specifies the handle of the control, window, or menu. **dwContextId** contains the context ID for the window or control. **MousePos** contains the current mouse position.

Most of the time, your program will respond to a **WM_HELP** message by displaying a pop-up window containing context-sensitive help. For example, to display context help about a control, your program must invoke **WinHelp( )** using the contents of **hItemHandle** as the window handle, i.e., the first parameter to **WinHelp( )**. (This will be the handle of the control.) You must specify **HELP_WM_HELP** as the command parameter and the address of the array of IDs as the extra parameter. (You will see how to do this in the example program.) Invoking **WinHelp( )** in this fashion causes it to search the array for the control ID that matches the control specified in **hItemHandle**. It then uses the corresponding context ID to obtain context-sensitive help. It displays this help in a pop-up window. It does not activate the standard Help window.

Although most often your program will respond to a **WM_HELP** message by displaying context-sensitive help, this will not always be the case. As mentioned earlier, pressing F1 may be used to invoke either reference help or context-sensitive help. Here is the distinction between the two uses: When the main window has input focus (and no child window, control, or menu is selected), then pressing F1 activates the standard Help window and displays reference help. However, pressing F1 when a control, menu, or child window is active causes context-sensitive help to be displayed. The theory behind these two uses is that when the user presses F1 from the topmost level, the user is desiring help about the entire program, not a part of it. When responding to this situation, you will invoke the full help system. However, when a control (or other child window) is active when F1 is pressed, the user is desiring help about that specific item and context-sensitive help is warranted.

Since F1 may be used to activate either reference help or context-sensitive help, you might be wondering how your program will tell the two types of requests apart. That is, pressing F1 causes **WM_HELP** to be sent no matter what type of help is being requested. The answer is quite simple: if the handle contained in **hItemHandle** is that of the main window, display reference help. Otherwise, invoke context-sensitive help as described above.

WM_CONTEXTMENU

When the user right-clicks the mouse, your program receives a **WM_CONTEXTMENU** command. **wParam** will contain the handle of the control or window being queried. If the user clicked on a control, then respond by invoking **WinHelp( )** using **wParam** as the window handle (i.e., the first parameter to **WinHelp( )**). Specify **HELP_CONTEXTMENU** as the command parameter and the address of the array of IDs as the extra parameter. You will see an example of this command in the example program.

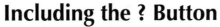

Including the ? Button

As mentioned, one way to activate context-sensitive help is through the **?** button. To include the **?** button in a window you must include the extended style **WS_EX_CONTEXTHELP**. Since this is an extended style feature, you must create the window using **CreateWindowEx( )** rather than **CreateWindow( )**. To display the **?** button in a dialog box, include the **DS_CONTEXTHELP** style.

NOTE: Current Windows style guides recommend the ? button primarily for use in dialog boxes. However, it can be used in a main window if the situation warrants.

A Help Demonstration Program

Now that you have learned about the various pieces and techniques involved in creating online help, it is time to put them to use. The following program demonstrates both reference help and context-sensitive help. It uses the help file shown earlier and illustrates various ways the file can be accessed using **WinHelp( )**. Sample output is shown in Figure 17-3.

```
/* Demonstrate the Help System */

#include <windows.h>
#include "helptest.h"

#define NUMSTRINGS 6

LRESULT CALLBACK WindowFunc(HWND, UINT, WPARAM, LPARAM);
BOOL CALLBACK DialogFunc(HWND, UINT, WPARAM, LPARAM);

char szWinName[] = "MyWin"; /* name of window class */

HINSTANCE hInst;

/* map control IDs to context IDs */
DWORD HelpArray[] = {
  IDD_PB1, IDH_PB1,
  IDD_PB2, IDH_PB2,
```

17

```
    IDD_PB3, IDH_PB3,
    ID_PB0, IDH_PB0,
    IDD_LB1, IDH_LB1,
    IDD_CB1, IDH_CB1, /* Here, both check boxes are */
    IDD_CB2, IDH_CB1, /* mapped to the same context ID. */
    0, 0
};

char lbstring[6][40] = {
  "one", "two", "three",
  "four", "five", "six"
};

int WINAPI WinMain(HINSTANCE hThisInst, HINSTANCE hPrevInst,
                   LPSTR lpszArgs, int nWinMode)
{
  HWND hwnd;
  MSG msg;
  WNDCLASSEX wcl;
  HANDLE hAccel;

  wcl.cbSize = sizeof(WNDCLASSEX);
  wcl.hInstance = hThisInst; /* handle to this instance */
  wcl.lpszClassName = szWinName; /* window class name */
  wcl.lpfnWndProc = WindowFunc; /* window function */
  wcl.style = 0; /* default style */

  wcl.hIcon = LoadIcon(NULL, IDI_APPLICATION);
  wcl.hIconSm = LoadIcon(NULL, IDI_APPLICATION);
  wcl.hCursor = LoadCursor(NULL, IDC_ARROW);

  /* specify name of menu resource */
  wcl.lpszMenuName = "HelpDemoMenu"; /* main menu */

  wcl.cbClsExtra = 0; /* no extra */
  wcl.cbWndExtra = 0; /* information needed */

  /* Make the window white. */
  wcl.hbrBackground = GetStockObject(WHITE_BRUSH);

  /* Register the window class. */
  if(!RegisterClassEx(&wcl)) return 0;

  /* Now that a window class has been registered, a window
     can be created. */
  hwnd = CreateWindowEx(
    WS_EX_CONTEXTHELP, /* display ? button */
    szWinName, /* name of window class */
```

```
      "Help System Demonstration", /* title */
      WS_SYSMENU | WS_SIZEBOX,
      CW_USEDEFAULT, /* X coordinate - let Windows decide */
      CW_USEDEFAULT, /* Y coordinate - let Windows decide */
      CW_USEDEFAULT, /* width - let Windows decide */
      CW_USEDEFAULT, /* height - let Windows decide */
      HWND_DESKTOP, /* no parent window */
      NULL, /* no override of class menu */
      hThisInst, /* handle of this instance of the program */
      NULL /* no additional arguments */
    );

    hInst = hThisInst; /* save the current instance handle */

    /* load accelerators */
    hAccel = LoadAccelerators(hThisInst, "HelpDemoMenu");

    /* Display the window. */
    ShowWindow(hwnd, nWinMode);
    UpdateWindow(hwnd);

    /* Create the message loop. */
    while(GetMessage(&msg, NULL, 0, 0))
    {
      if(!TranslateAccelerator(hwnd, hAccel, &msg)) {
        TranslateMessage(&msg); /* translate keyboard messages */
        DispatchMessage(&msg); /* return control to Windows NT */
      }
    }

    return msg.wParam;
}

/* This function is called by Windows NT and is passed
   messages from the message queue.
*/
LRESULT CALLBACK WindowFunc(HWND hwnd, UINT message,
                            WPARAM wParam, LPARAM lParam)
{
  int response;

  switch(message) {
    case WM_CREATE:
      /* define a child control window */
      CreateWindow(
        "BUTTON", /* name of control class */
        "Main Window PB", /* title */
        BS_PUSHBUTTON | WS_CHILD | WS_VISIBLE, /* push button */
```

17

```
      10, 60, 120, 30,
      hwnd, /* parent is main window */
      (HWND) ID_PB0, /* control ID */
      hInst, /* handle of this instance of the program */
      NULL /* no additional arguments */
    );
    break;
case WM_HELP: /* user pressed F1 or used ? button */
  if(((LPHELPINFO) lParam)->iContextType ==
                              HELPINFO_MENUITEM) {
    /* request for help about menu */
    switch(((LPHELPINFO) lParam)->iCtrlId) {
      case IDM_DIALOG:
        WinHelp(hwnd, "helptest.hlp", HELP_CONTEXTPOPUP,
                (DWORD) IDH_MENUDLG);
        break;
      case IDM_HELP:
        WinHelp(hwnd, "helptest.hlp", HELP_CONTEXTPOPUP,
                (DWORD) IDH_MENUHELP);
        break;
      case IDM_HELPTHIS:
        WinHelp(hwnd, "helptest.hlp", HELP_CONTEXTPOPUP,
                (DWORD) IDH_MENUABOUT);
        break;
      case IDM_EXIT:
        WinHelp(hwnd, "helptest.hlp", HELP_CONTEXTPOPUP,
                (DWORD) IDH_MENUEXIT);
        break;
      default:
        /* menu bar selected, but no option highlighted */
        WinHelp(hwnd, "helptest.hlp", HELP_CONTEXTPOPUP,
                (DWORD) IDH_MENUMAIN);
    }
  }
  else
    if(((LPHELPINFO) lParam)->hItemHandle != hwnd) {
      /* context help about a control */
      WinHelp(((LPHELPINFO) lParam)->hItemHandle,
              "helptest.hlp", HELP_WM_HELP,
              (DWORD) HelpArray);
    }
  else {
    /* standard help for main window */
    WinHelp(hwnd, "helptest.hlp", HELP_KEY,
            (DWORD) "Main Window");
  }
```

```
            break;
          case WM_CONTEXTMENU: /* user right-clicked mouse */
            if((HWND) wParam != hwnd)
              /* context help about a control */
              WinHelp((HWND) wParam, "helptest.hlp",
                      HELP_CONTEXTMENU, (DWORD) HelpArray);
            else
              /* context help about main window */
              WinHelp(hwnd, "helptest.hlp",
                      HELP_CONTEXTPOPUP, IDH_MAIN);
            break;
          case WM_COMMAND:
            switch(LOWORD(wParam)) {
              case IDM_DIALOG:
                DialogBox(hInst, "HelpDemoDB",
                          hwnd, (DLGPROC) DialogFunc);
                break;
              case IDM_HELP: /* help selected from menu */
                WinHelp(hwnd, "helptest.hlp", HELP_FINDER, 0);
                break;
              case IDM_HELPTHIS:
                MessageBox(hwnd, "Help System Sample Program V1.0",
                           "About", MB_OK);
                break;
              case IDM_EXIT:
                response = MessageBox(hwnd, "Quit the Program?",
                                      "Exit", MB_YESNO);
                if(response == IDYES) PostQuitMessage(0);
                break;
            }
            break;
          case WM_DESTROY: /* terminate the program */
            WinHelp(hwnd, "helptest.hlp", HELP_QUIT, 0);
            PostQuitMessage(0);
            break;
          default:
            /* Let Windows NT process any messages not specified in
               the preceding switch statement. */
            return DefWindowProc(hwnd, message, wParam, lParam);
      }
      return 0;
}

/* Sample dialog function. */
BOOL CALLBACK DialogFunc(HWND hdwnd, UINT message,
                         WPARAM wParam, LPARAM lParam)
```

17

```
{
  int i;

  switch(message) {
    case WM_HELP: /* use pressed F1 or used ? button */
      /* context help about a control */
      WinHelp(((LPHELPINFO) lParam)->hItemHandle,
              "helptest.hlp", HELP_WM_HELP,
              (DWORD) HelpArray);
      return 1;
    case WM_CONTEXTMENU: /* user right-clicked mouse */
      if((HWND) wParam != hdwnd)
        /* context help about a control */
        WinHelp((HWND) wParam, "helptest.hlp",
                HELP_CONTEXTMENU, (DWORD) HelpArray);
      else
        /* context help about dialog window */
        WinHelp(hdwnd, "helptest.hlp",
                HELP_CONTEXTPOPUP, IDH_DLG);
      return 1;
    case WM_COMMAND:
      switch(LOWORD(wParam)) {
        case IDCANCEL:
          WinHelp(hdwnd, "helptest.hlp", HELP_QUIT, 0);
          EndDialog(hdwnd, 0);
          return 1;
        case IDD_PB1:
          MessageBox(hdwnd, "Push Button 1",
                     "Button Press", MB_OK);
          return 1;
        case IDD_PB2:
          MessageBox(hdwnd, "Push Button 2",
                     "Button Press", MB_OK);
          return 1;
        case IDD_PB3:
          MessageBox(hdwnd, "Push Button 3",
                     "Button Press", MB_OK);
          return 1;
      }
      break;
    case WM_INITDIALOG: /* initialize list box */
      for(i=0; i<NUMSTRINGS; i++)
        SendDlgItemMessage(hdwnd, IDD_LB1,
            LB_ADDSTRING, 0, (LPARAM) lbstring[i]);
      return 1;
  }
  return 0;
}
```

The program requires the following resource file:

```
; Demonstrate the Help system.
#include <windows.h>
#include "helptest.h"

HelpDemoMenu MENU
{
  POPUP "&Dialog"
  {
    MENUITEM "&Dialog\tF2", IDM_DIALOG
    MENUITEM "E&xit\tF10", IDM_EXIT
  }
  POPUP "&Help"
  {
    MENUITEM "&Help Topics", IDM_HELP
    MENUITEM "&About", IDM_HELPTHIS
  }
}


HelpDemoMenu ACCELERATORS
{
  VK_F2, IDM_DIALOG, VIRTKEY
  VK_F10, IDM_EXIT, VIRTKEY
}

HelpDemoDB DIALOG 10, 10, 140, 110
CAPTION "Help Demonstration Dialog"
STYLE WS_POPUP | WS_SYSMENU | WS_VISIBLE | DS_CONTEXTHELP
{
  DEFPUSHBUTTON "Button 1", IDD_PB1, 11, 10, 32, 14,
            WS_CHILD | WS_VISIBLE | WS_TABSTOP
  PUSHBUTTON "Button 2", IDD_PB2, 11, 34, 32, 14,
            WS_CHILD | WS_VISIBLE | WS_TABSTOP
  PUSHBUTTON "Button 3", IDD_PB3, 11, 58, 32, 14,
            WS_CHILD | WS_VISIBLE | WS_TABSTOP
  PUSHBUTTON "Cancel", IDCANCEL, 8, 82, 38, 16,
            WS_CHILD | WS_VISIBLE | WS_TABSTOP
  AUTOCHECKBOX "Check Box 1", IDD_CB1, 66, 50, 60, 30,
            WS_CHILD | WS_VISIBLE | WS_TABSTOP
  AUTOCHECKBOX "Check Box 2", IDD_CB2, 66, 70, 60, 30,
            WS_CHILD | WS_VISIBLE | WS_TABSTOP
  LISTBOX IDD_LB1, 66, 5, 63, 33, LBS_NOTIFY |
            WS_VISIBLE | WS_BORDER | WS_VSCROLL | WS_TABSTOP
}
```

17

The header file HELPTEST.H is shown here:

```
#define IDM_DIALOG      100
#define IDM_EXIT        101
#define IDM_HELP        102
#define IDM_HELPTHIS    103

#define IDD_PB1         200
#define IDD_PB2         201
#define IDD_PB3         202
#define IDD_LB1         203
#define IDD_CB1         205
#define IDD_CB2         206

#define ID_PB0          300

#define IDH_PB1         700
#define IDH_PB2         701
#define IDH_PB3         702
#define IDH_LB1         703
#define IDH_CB1         704
#define IDH_MAIN        705
#define IDH_PB0         706
#define IDH_DLG         707
#define IDH_MENUDLG     708
#define IDH_MENUEXIT    709
#define IDH_MENUHELP    710
#define IDH_MENUABOUT   711
#define IDH_MENUMAIN    712
```

A Closer Look at the Help Demonstration Program

Most of the help program should be clear. However, a few points warrant specific attention. First, consider the declaration of **HelpArray**. This is the array that maps control IDs to context IDs. In the HELPTEST.H header file, the **IDH_** macros are given the same values that you defined in the HELPTEST.PRJ file when you created the help file. Notice that both check boxes map onto the same context ID. This is perfectly valid. If the same pop-up help message will be displayed for two or more controls, there is no reason to create duplicate messages.

Notice that the program includes the **?** button in the main window and in the dialog box. Although the **?** is mostly for use in dialog boxes, it is included in the main window for the purpose of illustration—and to make an important point. When using the **?**, it will only send messages to its own window. For example, try this experiment. Activate the dialog box and click on its **?** button. Next, move the pointer out of the dialog box. As you will see, the **?** disappears. The **?** applies only to the window in which it is defined.

Here is another point of interest: Inside the main window is a stand-alone push button. This button is, therefore, a child window of the main window. If you press F1 when this button has input focus (i.e., is selected) then you will receive pop-up help about the push button. However, if this control does not have input focus, then pressing F1 while the main window is active

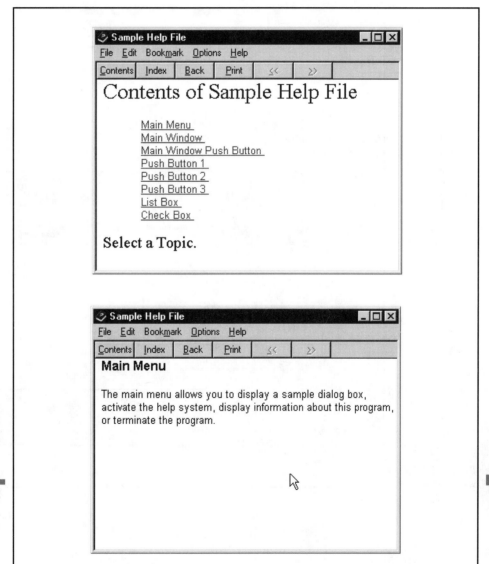

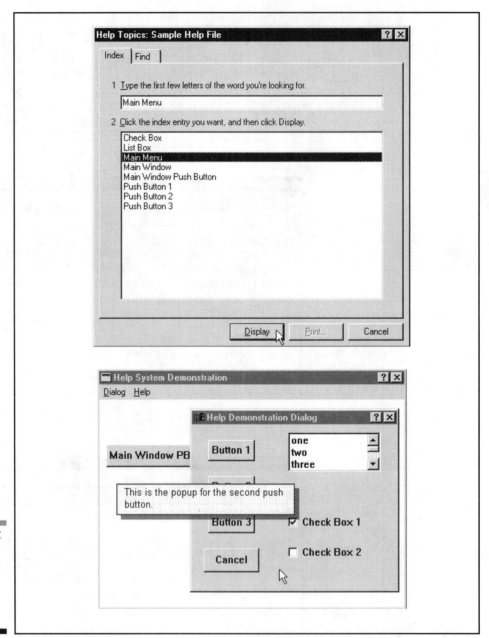

Sample output
from the help
demonstration
program
(*continued*)
Figure 17-3.

causes the main Help window to be displayed. This is in keeping with standard Windows NT style guides.

Using Secondary Windows

It is possible to use a secondary Help window. A secondary window contains a button bar, but not a menu bar. Thus it is smaller than the standard Help Topics window. A secondary Help window stays active until you close it but it allows you to continue using your application. You have almost certainly seen secondary Help windows in action.

The use of a secondary Help window is actually quite easy. First, you need to add one to your help project. To do so, simply specify its name and its type using the Windows option of the Help compiler. You will have three choices of secondary window styles:

> Procedure
> Reference
> Error Message

A Procedure window is a small window that contains the buttons Help Topics, Back, and Options. It is positioned in the upper-right corner of the screen. A Reference window also contains the Help Topics, Back, and Options buttons, but is a larger window. It is displayed with its upper-left corner near the top-left of the screen. Error Message windows are small and contain no buttons.

To use a secondary window, you must include its name when specifying the name of the help file in the call to **WinHelp( )**, using this general form.

> *filename>windowname*

For example, if a secondary window is called "HlpWin2", then the following call will use that window to display context help about the Dialog entry in the main menu in the preceding program.

```
WinHelp(hwnd, "helptest.hlp>HlpWin2", HELP_CONTEXT,
        (DWORD) IDH_MENUDLG);
```

Assuming that HlpWin2 is a Procedure window, then this will produce the Help window shown here:

17

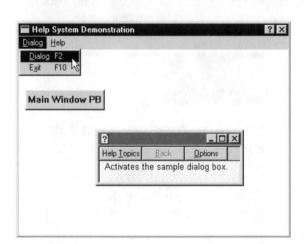

Secondary windows should be used with **HELP_CONTEXT**. Other styles override the secondary window.

Secondary windows are easy to add and they enhance the look and feel of your application. You will want to experiment with them to find which style works best for the various needs of your program.

Some Things to Try

One of the most exciting new help features is the *training card*. Training cards are used to provide "how to" instructions to the user. For example, a word processing program might use training cards to explain, step-by-step, how to format a paragraph or print a document.

As explained in the In Depth box, secondary Help windows add a whole new dimension to your help system. Try experimenting with them.

Try using the partial keyword search option **HELP_PARTIALKEY**. For example, you could display an edit box, allow users to enter the name of the item about which they wish to receive help, and then use a partial key search to display all matching topics.

One last point: There is no question that online, context-sensitive help will become an increasingly important part of any Windows NT application. It is better to build support for help into your program from the start, rather than adding it later.

CHAPTER 18

Using the Printer

589

Since Windows NT is a graphical operating system that uses bitmaps, custom character fonts, and graphics, most newcomers think printing is an arduous, complicated task. Fortunately, this is not the case. While it is true that printing is more complicated under Windows NT than say, DOS, Windows NT provides extensive built-in support for it. Indeed, most of the details are handled by the printer drivers built into Windows NT. Although there are certainly a number of things to learn, there is nothing fundamentally difficult about printing documents. Once you have mastered the essentials, you will have no trouble adding print capabilities to any of your programs.

This chapter explains how to do the following:

♦ Print text

♦ Print graphical images

♦ Scale graphical images

♦ Create and install a printing abort function

These operations are the foundation of all print jobs under Windows NT.

Before beginning, it is important to understand that when you print something, you are actually sending output to the print spooler and not directly to the printer itself. While this distinction doesn't usually have much impact on how you program, it is good to keep in mind.

Obtaining a Printer Device Context

A printer device context is required to output to a printer.

In the same way that a display device context describes and manages output to the screen, a printer device context describes and manages output to the printer. For this reason, you must obtain a printer device context before you can send output to the printer. There are two ways to obtain this device context: using **CreateDC( )** or using **PrintDlg( )**. Each is examined here.

CreateDC( )

The first way to obtain a printer device context is to use **CreateDC( )**. Its prototype is shown here:

> HDC CreateDC(LPCSTR *lpszWhat*, LPCSTR *DevName*,
> LPCSTR *NotUsed*,
> CONST DEVMODE **DevMode*);

Here, *lpszWhat* can be a pointer to either the string "DISPLAY" (to obtain a display driver) or "WINSPOOL" (to obtain a printer driver). For printing, this parameter must point to "WINSPOOL". *DevName* specifies the name of the printer as shown in the list of printers displayed by the Add Printer wizard or shown in the Printers window when you select Printers from the Control Panel. *NotUsed* must be **NULL**. *DevMode* points to a **DEVMODE** structure that contains initialization information. To use the default initialization, *DevMode* must be **NULL**. **CreateDC( )** returns a handle to the device context if successful or **NULL** on failure. After your application is through printing, delete the device context by calling **DeleteDC( )**.

PORTABILITY: In older versions of Windows, you need to specify a pointer to the name of the file that contains the printer device driver in *lpszWhat* and a pointer to the name of the printer port in *NotUsed*. This is not the case with Windows NT.

In some cases, your application will need to obtain the name of the currently selected printer. To do this, use **EnumPrinters( )** to obtain the names of available printers.

CreateDC( ) is most often used when printing does not involve interaction with the user. Although such situations are not common, they are not rare, either. For example, a system log might be printed after midnight, when no user is present. However, for most purposes (and for the examples in this chapter) you will acquire a printer DC using another of Windows NT's API functions: **PrintDlg( )**.

PrintDlg( )

PrintDlg( ) displays the standard Print common dialog box. You have certainly seen it several times while using various Windows NT applications. Its precise appearance varies, depending on what options you select, but it will look something like that shown in Figure 18-1. The advantage of using **PrintDlg( )** to obtain a device context is that it gives the user control over the printing operation. To use **PrintDlg( )**, include COMMDLG.H in your program. **PrintDlg( )** is both powerful and flexible. The following discussion describes its basic operation. However, you will want to explore this function fully if you will be working extensively with printers and printing.

PORTABILITY: **PrintDlg( )** can also activate the Print Setup common dialog box. However, Print Setup is now obsolete; it has been superseded by the new Page Setup common dialog box. See the In Depth box later in this chapter.

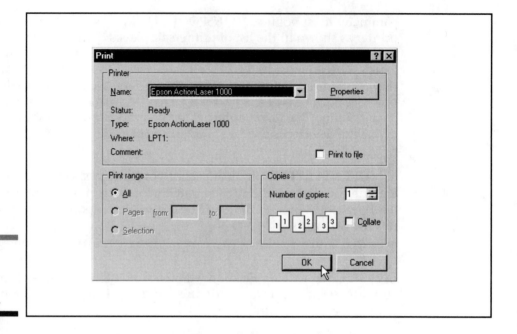

PrintDlg( ) has the following prototype:

BOOL PrintDlg(LPPRINTDLG *PrintDlg*);

It returns nonzero if the user terminates the dialog box by pressing OK. It returns zero if the user presses Cancel (or Esc) or closes the box using the system menu.

The contents of the **PRINTDLG** structure pointed to by *PrintDlg* determine how **PrintDlg( )** operates. This structure is defined like this:

```
typedef struct tagPD {
  DWORD lStructSize;
  HWND hwndOwner;
  HGLOBAL hDevMode;
  HGLOBAL hDevNames;
  HDC hDC;
  DWORD Flags;
  WORD nFromPage;
  WORD nToPage;
  WORD nMinPage;
  WORD nMaxPage;
  WORD nCopies;
  HINSTANCE hInstance;
  LPARAM lCustData;
```

```
      LPPRINTHOOKPROC lpfnPrintHook;
      LPSETUPHOOKPROC lpfnSetupHook;
      LPCSTR lpPrintTemplateName;
      LPCSTR lpSetupTemplateName;
      HGLOBAL hPrintTemplate;
      HGLOBAL hSetupTemplate;
    } PRINTDLG;
```

lStructSize contains the size of the **PRINTDLG** structure. **hwndOwner** specifies the handle of the window that calls **PrintDlg( )**.

hDevMode specifies the handle of a global **DEVMODE** structure that is used to initialize the dialog box controls prior to the call and contains the state of the controls after the call. This field may also be specified as **NULL**. In this case, **PrintDlg( )** allocates and initializes a **DEVMODE** structure and returns a handle to it in the **hDevMode** member. The **DEVMODE** structure is not used by the examples in this chapter.

hDevNames contains the handle of a global **DEVNAMES** structure. This structure specifies the name of the printer driver, the name of the printer, and the name of the port. These names are used to initialize the **PrintDlg( )** dialog box. After the call, they will contain the corresponding names entered by the user. This field may also be specified as **NULL**. In this case, **PrintDlg( )** allocates and initializes a **DEVNAMES** structure and returns a handle to it. The **DEVNAMES** structure is not used by the examples in this chapter. When both **hDevNames** and **hDevMode** are **NULL**, the default printer is used.

After the call, **hDC** will contain either the printer device context or information context depending on which value is specified in the **Flags** member. For the purposes of this chapter, **hDC** will contain a device context. (An information context simply contains information about a device context without actually creating one.)

nFromPage initializes the From edit box. On return, it will contain the starting page specified by the user. **nToPage** initializes the To edit box. On return, it will contain the ending page specified by the user.

nMinPage contains the minimum page number that can be selected in the From box. **nMaxPage** contains the maximum page number that can be selected in the To box.

nCopies initializes the Copies edit box. After the call, it will contain the number of copies to print as specified by the user. Your application must ensure that the number of copies requested by the user are actually printed.

hInstance contains the instance handle of an alternative dialog box specification if one is specified by the **lpPrintTemplateName** or **lpSetupTemplateName** members.

lCustData contains data that is passed to the optional functions pointed to by **lpfnPrintHook** or **lpfnSetupHook**.

lpfnPrintHook is a pointer to a function that preempts and processes messages intended for the Print dialog box. This element is used only if **Flags** contains the value **PD_ENABLEPRINTHOOK**. **lpfnSetupHook** is a pointer to a function that preempts and processes messages intended for the Print Setup dialog box. This element is used only if **Flags** contains the value **PD_ENABLESETUPHOOK**.

You can use a different layout (template) for the Print common dialog box. To do so, assign **lpPrintTemplateName** the address of the name of the dialog box resource that contains the new layout. **lpPrintTemplateName** is ignored unless **Flags** contains the value **PD_ENABLEPRINTTEMPLATE**.

You can use a different layout (template) for the Print Setup common dialog box. To do so, assign **lpSetupTemplateName** the address of the name of the dialog box resource that contains the new layout. **lpSetupTemplateName** is ignored unless **Flags** contains the value **PD_ENABLESETUPTEMPLATE**.

You can also use a different template for the Print common dialog box by specifying its handle in **hPrintTemplate** and specifying the **PD_ENABLEPRINTTEMPLATEHANDLE** flag. Similarly, you can use a different template for the Print Setup common dialog box by specifying its handle in **hSetupTemplate** and specifying the **PD_ENABLESETUPTEMPLATEHANDLE** flag. Otherwise, set these members to **NULL**.

REMEMBER: The Print Setup common dialog box is obsolete. Use Page Setup, instead.

The **Flags** member contains values that determine precisely how the Print dialog box will behave and which fields will be active. On return, they will indicate the user's choices. It must be any valid combination of the values shown in Table 18-1.

As mentioned, on return the **hDC** member will contain the printer's device context. Using this context, you can output to the printer using functions such as **TextOut( )** or **BitBlt( )** that operate on device contexts. After your application is through printing, delete the printer device context by calling **DeleteDC( )**.

Flag	Effect
PD_ALLPAGES	Selects the All radio button. (This is the default.) On return, this flag will be set if the All radio button is selected.
PD_COLLATE	Checks the Collate Copies check box. On return, this flag will be set if Collate Copies is checked and the selected printer driver does not support collation. In this situation, your program must perform collation manually.
PD_DISABLEPRINTTOFILE	Deactivates the Print to File check box.
PD_ENABLEPRINTHOOK	Enables the **lpfnPrintHook** member.
PD_ENABLEPRINTTEMPLATE	Uses alternative dialog box template specified by **lpPrintTemplateName.**
PD_ENABLEPRINTTEMPLATEHANDLE	Uses alternative Print dialog box template specified by **hPrintTemplate**.
PD_ENABLESETUPHOOK	Enables the **lpfnSetupHook** member.
PD_ENABLESETUPTEMPLATE	Uses alternative dialog box template specified by **lpSetupTemplateName**.
PD_ENABLESETUPTEMPLATEHANDLE	Uses alternative Setup dialog box template specified by **hSetupTemplate**.
PD_HIDEPRINTTOFILE	Suppresses the Print to File check box.
PD_NONETWORKBUTTON	Suppresses Network button.
PD_NOPAGENUMS	Deactivates the Pages radio button.
PD_NOSELECTION	Deactivates the Selection radio button.

The Values for the **Flags** Member of **PRINTDLG** Table 18-1.

Flag	Effect
PD_NOWARNING	No warning message is displayed when there is no default printer.
PD_PAGENUMS	Selects the Pages radio button. On return, this flag is set if the Pages radio button is selected.
PD_PRINTSETUP	Print Setup rather than Print dialog box is displayed. This option is obsolete. Use the Page Setup common dialog box instead.
PD_PRINTTOFILE	Checks the Print to File check box. On return, indicates that the user desires output be directed to a file.
PD_RETURNDC	Causes a device context to be returned in **hDC**.
PD_RETURNDEFAULT	On return, **hDevMode** and **hDevNames** will contain values for the default printer. No dialog box is displayed. **hDevMode** and **hDevNames** must be **NULL** when **PrintDlg( )** is called.
PD_RETURNIC	Causes an information context to be returned in **hDC**.
PD_SELECTION	Selects the Selection radio button. On return, this flag will be set if the Selection radio button is selected.
PD_SHOWHELP	Help button is displayed.
PD_USEDEVMODECOPIESAND-COLLATE PD_USEDEVMODECOPIES	Deactivates Number of Copies spin control and/or Collate check box if the printer driver does not support multiple copies or collation, respectively. If not set, the number of copies is contained in the **nCopies** member and the **PD_COLLATE** flag will be set if collation is required.

The Values for the **Flags** Member of **PRINTDLG** (*continued*)
Table 18-1.

The Printer Functions

There are several functions your program must use when printing. These functions are shown here:

    int EndDoc(HDC *hPrDC*);

    int EndPage(HDC *hPrDC*);

    int StartDoc(HDC *hPrDC*, CONST DOCINFO **Info*);

    int StartPage(HDC *hPrDC*);

In all cases, *hPrDC* is the handle of the printer device context. Also, in all cases, the functions return a nonzero, positive value if successful. On failure they return zero or less. A description of each function follows.

To start printing, you must first call **StartDoc( )**. **StartDoc( )** performs two functions. First, it starts a print job. Second, its return value is the job ID. Although the examples in this chapter do not require a print job ID, some applications will because it is needed by some print-related functions. The *Info* parameter is a structure of type **DOCINFO**, which is defined like this:

```
typedef struct _DOCINFO {
  int cbSize;
  LPCSTR lpszDocName;
  LPCSTR lpszOutput;
  LPCSTR lpszDatatype;
  DWORD fwType;
} DOCINFO;
```

Here, **cbSize** must contain the size of the **DOCINFO** structure. **lpszDocName** is a pointer to the name of the print job. **lpszOutput** is a pointer to the name of the file that will receive printed output. However, to send output to the printer device context specified by *hPrDC*, **lpszOutput** must be **NULL**. **lpszDatatype** is unused and should be **NULL**. **fwType** is also unused and should be zero.

PORTABILITY: Both **lpszDatatype** and **fwType** are used by Windows 95, but not NT 4.

To start printing a page, you must call **StartPage( )**. After each page is printed, you must call **EndPage( )**. **EndPage( )** advances the printer to a new page. Once your program is through printing, it must call **EndDoc( )**. Therefore, the following outline shows the sequence required to print a page.

```
StartDoc(dc, &info);

StartPage(dc);

  /* print a page of data here */

EndPage(dc);

EndDoc(dc);
```

PORTABILITY: For Windows 3.1, the functions performed by **StartDoc( )**, **StartPage( )**, **EndPage( )**, and **EndDoc( )** are accomplished using escape codes. These codes are sent via the **Escape( )** function. The **Escape( )** function is obsolete and you will seldom find it used in a Windows NT application. When converting older programs, you will want to replace calls to **Escape( )** with the appropriate printer function.

A Simple Printing Example

Although there are many more details that are necessary to properly add printing to a Windows NT application, the functions described in the preceding sections are sufficient to send text output to the printer. So, before we move on, let's take a look at a short example. The following program prints lines of text on the printer.

```
/* A simple printing demonstration. */

#include <windows.h>
#include <string.h>
#include <commdlg.h>
#include "print.h"

#define NUMLINES 20

LRESULT CALLBACK WindowFunc(HWND, UINT, WPARAM, LPARAM);
void PrintInit(PRINTDLG *printdlg, HWND hwnd);

char szWinName[] = "MyWin"; /* name of window class */
```

```
int X = 0, Y = 0; /* current output location */
int maxX, maxY; /* screen dimensions */

HDC memDC; /* virtual device handle */
HBITMAP hBit; /* bitmap handle */
HBRUSH hBrush; /* brush handle */

PRINTDLG printdlg;
DOCINFO docinfo;

int WINAPI WinMain(HINSTANCE hThisInst, HINSTANCE hPrevInst,
                   LPSTR lpszArgs, int nWinMode)
{
  HACCEL hAccel;
  HWND hwnd;
  MSG msg;
  WNDCLASSEX wcl;

  /* Define a window class. */
  wcl.cbSize = sizeof(WNDCLASSEX);
  wcl.hInstance = hThisInst; /* handle to this instance */
  wcl.lpszClassName = szWinName; /* window class name */
  wcl.lpfnWndProc = WindowFunc; /* window function */
  wcl.style = 0; /* default style */

  wcl.hIcon = LoadIcon(NULL, IDI_APPLICATION);
  wcl.hIconSm = LoadIcon(NULL, IDI_APPLICATION);
  wcl.hCursor = LoadCursor(NULL, IDC_ARROW);

  wcl.lpszMenuName = "PrintDemoMenu";

  wcl.cbClsExtra = 0; /* no extra */
  wcl.cbWndExtra = 0; /* information needed */

  /* Make the window white. */
  wcl.hbrBackground = GetStockObject(WHITE_BRUSH);

  /* Register the window class. */
  if(!RegisterClassEx(&wcl)) return 0;

  /* Now that a window class has been registered, a window
     can be created. */
  hwnd = CreateWindow(
    szWinName, /* name of window class */
    "Using the Printer", /* title */
    WS_OVERLAPPEDWINDOW, /* standard window */
    CW_USEDEFAULT, /* X coordinate - let Windows decide */
    CW_USEDEFAULT, /* Y coordinate - let Windows decide */
```

```
        CW_USEDEFAULT, /* width - let Windows decide */
        CW_USEDEFAULT, /* height - let Windows decide */
        HWND_DESKTOP, /* no parent window */
        NULL, /* no override of class menu */
        hThisInst, /* handle of this instance of the program */
        NULL /* no additional arguments */
      );

      /* load accelerators */
      hAccel = LoadAccelerators(hThisInst, "PrintDemoMenu");

      /* Display the window. */
      ShowWindow(hwnd, nWinMode);
      UpdateWindow(hwnd);

      /* Create the message loop. */
      while(GetMessage(&msg, NULL, 0, 0))
      {
        if(!TranslateAccelerator(hwnd, hAccel, &msg)) {
          TranslateMessage(&msg);
          DispatchMessage(&msg);
        }
      }
      return msg.wParam;
}


/* This function is called by Windows NT and is passed
   messages from the message queue.
*/
LRESULT CALLBACK WindowFunc(HWND hwnd, UINT message,
                            WPARAM wParam, LPARAM lParam)
{
  HDC hdc;
  PAINTSTRUCT ps;
  int response;
  TEXTMETRIC tm;
  char str[80];
  int i;
  int copies;

  switch(message) {
    case WM_CREATE:
      /* get screen coordinates */
      maxX = GetSystemMetrics(SM_CXSCREEN);
      maxY = GetSystemMetrics(SM_CYSCREEN);

      /* create a virtual window */
      hdc = GetDC(hwnd);
```

```
     memDC = CreateCompatibleDC(hdc);
     hBit = CreateCompatibleBitmap(hdc, maxX, maxY);
     SelectObject(memDC, hBit);
     hBrush = GetStockObject(WHITE_BRUSH);
     SelectObject(memDC, hBrush);
     PatBlt(memDC, 0, 0, maxX, maxY, PATCOPY);

     /* get text metrics */
     GetTextMetrics(hdc, &tm);

     strcpy(str, "This is displayed in the main window.");
     for(i=0; i<NUMLINES; i++) {
       TextOut(memDC, X, Y, str, strlen(str)); /* output to memory */
       TextOut(hdc, X, Y, str, strlen(str)); /* output to window */
       /* advance to next line */
       Y = Y + tm.tmHeight + tm.tmExternalLeading;
     }

     ReleaseDC(hwnd, hdc);
     break;
   case WM_COMMAND:
     switch(LOWORD(wParam)) {
       case IDM_TEXT:
         X = Y = 0;

         /* initialize PRINTDLG struct */
         PrintInit(&printdlg, hwnd);

         if(!PrintDlg(&printdlg)) break;

         docinfo.cbSize = sizeof(DOCINFO);
         docinfo.lpszDocName = "Printing text";
         docinfo.lpszOutput = NULL;
         docinfo.lpszDatatype = NULL;
         docinfo.fwType = 0;

         /* get text metrics for printer */
         GetTextMetrics(printdlg.hDC, &tm);

         strcpy(str, "This is printed on the printer.");

         StartDoc(printdlg.hDC, &docinfo);

         for(copies=0; copies < printdlg.nCopies; copies++) {
           StartPage(printdlg.hDC);

           for(i=0; i<NUMLINES; i++) {
             TextOut(printdlg.hDC, X, Y, str, strlen(str));
```

18

```
                              /* advance to next line */
                              Y = Y + tm.tmHeight + tm.tmExternalLeading;
                          }

                          EndPage(printdlg.hDC);
                      }

                      EndDoc(printdlg.hDC);
                      DeleteDC(printdlg.hDC);
                      break;
                    case IDM_EXIT:
                      response = MessageBox(hwnd, "Quit the Program?",
                                            "Exit", MB_YESNO);
                      if(response == IDYES) PostQuitMessage(0);
                      break;
                    case IDM_HELP:
                      MessageBox(hwnd, "Printing Demo", "Help", MB_OK);
                      break;
                  }
                  break;
                case WM_PAINT: /* process a repaint request */
                  hdc = BeginPaint(hwnd, &ps); /* get DC */

                  BitBlt(hdc, ps.rcPaint.left, ps.rcPaint.top,
                          ps.rcPaint.right-ps.rcPaint.left, /* width */
                          ps.rcPaint.bottom-ps.rcPaint.top, /* height */
                          memDC,
                          ps.rcPaint.left, ps.rcPaint.top,
                          SRCCOPY);

                  EndPaint(hwnd, &ps); /* release DC */
                  break;
                case WM_DESTROY: /* terminate the program */
                  DeleteDC(memDC);
                  PostQuitMessage(0);
                  break;
                default:
                  /* Let Windows NT process any messages not specified in
                     the preceding switch statement. */
                  return DefWindowProc(hwnd, message, wParam, lParam);
              }
              return 0;
            }
```

```c
/* Initialize PRINTDLG structure. */
void PrintInit(PRINTDLG *printdlg, HWND hwnd)
{
  printdlg->lStructSize = sizeof(PRINTDLG);
  printdlg->hwndOwner = hwnd;
  printdlg->hDevMode = NULL;
  printdlg->hDevNames = NULL;
  printdlg->hDC = NULL;
  printdlg->Flags = PD_RETURNDC | PD_NOSELECTION |
                    PD_NOPAGENUMS | PD_HIDEPRINTTOFILE;
  printdlg->nFromPage = 0;
  printdlg->nToPage = 0;
  printdlg->nMinPage = 0;
  printdlg->nMaxPage = 0;
  printdlg->nCopies = 1;
  printdlg->hInstance = NULL;
  printdlg->lCustData = 0;
  printdlg->lpfnPrintHook = NULL;
  printdlg->lpfnSetupHook = NULL;
  printdlg->lpPrintTemplateName = NULL;
  printdlg->lpSetupTemplateName = NULL;
  printdlg->hPrintTemplate = NULL;
  printdlg->hSetupTemplate = NULL;
}
```

The program requires the following resource file:

```
#include <windows.h>
#include "print.h"

PrintDemoMenu MENU
{
  POPUP "&Printer Demo"
  {
    MENUITEM "Print &Text\tF2", IDM_TEXT
    MENUITEM "E&xit\tF10", IDM_EXIT
  }
  MENUITEM "&Help", IDM_HELP
}

PrintDemoMenu ACCELERATORS
{
  VK_F2, IDM_TEXT, VIRTKEY
  VK_F10, IDM_EXIT, VIRTKEY
}
```

18

The header file PRINT.H is shown here. In addition to the values used by the preceding program, it includes several values that will be used by subsequent programs in this chapter.

```
#define IDM_TEXT     100
#define IDM_BITMAP   101
#define IDM_EXIT     102
#define IDM_HELP     103
#define IDM_WINDOW   104
#define IDM_ENLARGE  105

#define IDD_EB1      200
#define IDD_EB2      201
#define IDD_UD1      202
#define IDD_UD2      202

#define IDD_TEXT1    210
#define IDD_TEXT2    211
```

A Closer Look at the First Printing Program

Relative to printing, the important part of the program occurs within the **IDM_TEXT** case. It is shown here for your convenience. This code is executed whenever the user selects Print Text from the Printer Demo menu.

```
case IDM_TEXT:
  X = Y = 0;

  /* initialize PRINTDLG struct */
  PrintInit(&printdlg, hwnd);

  if(!PrintDlg(&printdlg)) break;

  docinfo.cbSize = sizeof(DOCINFO);
  docinfo.lpszDocName = "Printing text";
  docinfo.lpszOutput = NULL;
  docinfo.lpszDatatype = NULL;
  docinfo.fwType = 0;

  /* get text metrics for printer */
  GetTextMetrics(printdlg.hDC, &tm);

  strcpy(str, "This is printed on the printer.");

  StartDoc(printdlg.hDC, &docinfo);
```

```
for(copies=0; copies < printdlg.nCopies; copies++) {
  StartPage(printdlg.hDC);

  for(i=0; i<NUMLINES; i++) {
    TextOut(printdlg.hDC, X, Y, str, strlen(str));
    /* advance to next line */
    Y = Y + tm.tmHeight + tm.tmExternalLeading;
  }

  EndPage(printdlg.hDC);
}

EndDoc(printdlg.hDC);
DeleteDC(printdlg.hDC);
break;
```

Let's go through this code sequence, step by step. First, **X** and **Y**, which are used to position text both on the printer and in a window, are reset to zero. Next, a **PRINTDLG** structure is initialized by calling **PrintInit( )**. Notice that the Selection radio button and the Pages edit boxes are disabled. The Print to File check box is also hidden. These controls are not needed by the program. Next, **PrintDlg( )** is executed. Upon return, **printdlg.hDC** contains the device context of the printer selected by the user. Then, a **DOCINFO** structure is initialized. Next, a call is made to **GetTextMetrics( )** using the printer device context. Since text is going to be printed, it is necessary to obtain the text metrics as they relate to the printer in order to correctly perform carriage return/linefeed sequences. These values will not be the same as those used when text is displayed on the screen. This is an important point. The printer device context is separate and unique. It does not necessarily share any attributes in common with the window DCs used by the other parts of your program.

To start the printing process, **StartDoc( )** is called. Next, a loop is started that prints the number of copies requested by the user. This value is obtained from the **nCopies** member of **printdlg**. Since each copy will be on its own page, **StartPage( )** is called at the start of each iteration. Next, a few lines of text are sent to the printer. Notice that the device context obtained by calling **PrintDlg( )**, which is **printdlg.hDC**, is used as the target context for the **TextOut( )** function. Once you have a printer device context, it can be used like any other device context. At the end of each page, **EndPage( )** is called. When all printing is done, **EndDoc( )** is executed and the printer DC is deleted.

While this example is quite simple, it does illustrate all of the essential elements required to print a document on the printer. The remainder of this chapter shows you how to print bitmaps, add an abort box, and handle scaling. However, the fundamental approach to sending output to the printer will be the same.

Printing Bitmaps

Since Windows NT is a graphical operating system, it makes sense that you can print graphical output. And, indeed, this is the case. In fact, sending text output to the printer using **TextOut( )** as shown in the preceding example is the exception, not the rule. Most of the time, your program will need to render a printed version of a graphical bitmap. Keep in mind that this bitmap might contain text, but it will not be restricted to text. Fortunately, printing a bitmap is not, in and of itself, a difficult task. However, certain side issues need to be dealt with. First, before printing a bitmap, your program must first determine whether the selected printer is capable of displaying graphical output. (Not all printers are.) Second, in order for the printed bitmap to have the same perspective that it has on the screen, some scaling of output might need to be performed. Finally, it is not possible to select a bitmap into a printer device context. (Bitmaps can only be selected into memory DCs.) Therefore, to print a bitmap implies that you will first need to select it into a compatible DC and then copy that DC to the printer DC using a function such as **StretchBlt( )**. Let's examine each of these issues.

Determining Printer Raster Capabilities

To print a bitmap, a printer must be capable of raster operations.

Not all printers can print bitmaps. For example, some printers can only print text. In the language of Windows NT, a printer that can print a bitmap is capable of raster operations. The term *raster* originally referred to video display devices. However, it has been generalized. In its current usage, if a device has raster capabilities, then it can perform certain types of operations normally associated with a video display. In simple terms, if a printer has raster capabilities, then it can display graphical output. Today, most commonly used printers have raster capabilities. However, since there are still many printers that do not have this capability, your program must check before attempting to print a bitmap. To do this, you will use the **GetDeviceCaps( )** function. Its prototype is shown here:

   int GetDeviceCaps(HDC *hdc*, int *attribute*);

Here, *hdc* is the handle of the device context for which information is being obtained. The value of *attribute* determines precisely what device attribute is retrieved. The function returns the requested information.

There are a large number of attributes that can be returned and most are not relevant to this chapter. (However, you will want to explore **GetDeviceCaps( )** on your own. It can obtain an amazing amount of information about a device.) The attribute that we will use to see if a printer is able to display a bitmap is **RASTERCAPS**. The return value will indicate what, if any, raster capabilities the printer has. It will be one or more of these values:

Value	Meaning
RC_BANDING	Printer DC requires banding support for graphics.
RC_BITBLT	Printer DC can be target of **BitBlt( )**.
RC_BITMAP64	Printer DC can handle bitmaps larger than 64K.
RC_DI_BITMAP	Printer DC supports device independent bitmaps via the **SetDIBits( )** and **GetDIBits( )** functions.
RC_DIBTODEV	Printer DC supports **SetDIBitsToDevice( )**.
RC_FLOODFIL	Printer DC supports flood fills.
RC_PALETTE	Printer DC supports a palette.
RC_SCALING	Printer DC provides its own scaling capabilities.
RC_STRETCHBLT	Printer DC can be target of **StretchBlt( )**.
RC_STRETCHDIB	Printer DC can be target of **StretchDIBits( )**.

For the purposes of this chapter, we are interested in only two of these values: **RC_BITBLT** and **RC_STRETCHBLT**.

Maintaining Perspective

If you want the bitmap to look the same when printed as it does when displayed on the screen, then you will need to scale the image appropriately when printing it. To accomplish this, you will need to know the resolution of both the screen and the printer. For this purpose, you will once again use the **GetDeviceCaps( )** function. To obtain the number of horizontal pixels per inch, specify **LOGPIXELSX** as the attribute. To retrieve the number of vertical pixels per inch, use **LOGPIXELSY**. For example, after these calls:

```
hres = GetDeviceCaps(hdc, LOGPIXELSX);
vres = GetDeviceCaps(hdc, LOGPIXELSY);
```

In order for
a bitmap to
look the same
printed as it
does on the
screen, it must
be scaled.

hres will contain the number of pixels per inch along the X axis and **vres** will contain the number of pixels per inch along the Y axis for the device context specified by **hdc**.

Once you have found the resolution of both the video DC and the printer DC, you can compute a scaling factor. You will use this scaling factor in a call to **StretchBlt( )** to render the bitmap, in its correct perspective, on the printer.

StretchBlt( )

StretchBlt( ) copies a bitmap and is related to the **BitBlt( )** function described earlier in this book. However, **StretchBlt( )** expands or compresses the source bitmap so that it will fit and completely fill the target rectangle. Its prototype is:

BOOL StretchBlt(HDC *hDest*, int *DestX*, int *DestY*,
          int *DestWidth*, int *DestHeight*,
          HDC *hSource*, int *SourceX*, int *SourceY*,
          int *SourceWidth*, int *SourceHeight*,
          DWORD *dwRaster*);

Here, *hDest* is the handle of the target device context, and *DestX* and *DestY* are the upper-left coordinates at which point the bitmap will be drawn. The width and height of the destination bitmap are specified in *DestWidth* and *DestHeight*. The *hSource* parameter contains the handle of the source device context. The *SourceX* and *SourceY* specify the upper left coordinates in the bitmap at which point the copy operation will begin. The width and height of the source bitmap are passed in *SourceWidth* and *SourceHeight*. **StretchBlt( )** automatically expands (i.e., stretches) or contracts the source bitmap so that it will fit into the destination bitmap. This differs from the **BitBlt( )**, which performs no stretching or compressing.

StretchBlt( )
is similar to
BitBlt( ) except
that it can
expand or
compress
an image.

The value of *dwRaster* determines how the bit-by-bit contents of the bitmap will actually be copied. It uses the same values that the comparable parameter to **BitBlt( )** uses. Some of its most common values are shown here:

dwRaster Macro	Effect
DSTINVERT	Inverts the bits in the destination bitmap.
SRCAND	ANDs bitmap with current destination.
SRCCOPY	Copies bitmap as is, overwriting previous contents.
SRCERASE	ANDs bitmap with the inverted bits of destination bitmap.
SRCINVERT	XORs bitmap with current destination.
SRCPAINT	ORs bitmap with current destination.

StretchBlt( ) is important when printing bitmaps because it allows you to scale the printed version. **StretchBlt( )** shrinks or enlarges the source bitmap, as needed, so that it fits the target rectangle. By applying the scaling factors to the dimensions of the target rectangle, you can use **StretchBlt( )** to scale the printed version of the bitmap. Keep in mind, however, that if no scaling is desired, your program can use **BitBlt( )** to copy a bitmap to the printer. It is just that the printed version will not have the same perspective as the screen image. You will see examples of both in the program that follows.

Obtaining Printer-Compatible DCs

One small, but sometimes irritating, problem associated with printing bitmaps is that a bitmap can only be selected into a memory device context. Thus, you cannot select a bitmap directly into the printer DC obtained from **PrintDlg( )** or **CreateDC( )**. Instead, you will need to create a compatible memory DC, select the bitmap into that device context, and then copy it to the printer context using either **BitBlt( )** or **StretchBlt( )**.

There is one other complication. The bitmap that you want to print may not be compatible with the printer device context. When this is the case, you must also create a printer-compatible bitmap. Next, select that bitmap into the printer-compatible memory DC, copy the bitmap that you want to print into the printer-compatible bitmap, and then copy that bitmap to the printer DC. If this all seems overly complicated, it is! Nevertheless, this is the way that Windows NT is designed. However, as you will see, it is actually an easy process to implement.

A Bitmap Printing Demonstration Program

The following program adds two new features to the first printing example. One option prints a bitmap on the printer two ways: first without performing any scaling, and then with the scaling factors applied, to maintain perspective. This option allows you easily to see the difference between scaled and non-scaled output. The other option lets you print the contents of the program's main window. This is easy to do because the program uses the virtual window technology described in Chapter 7. This means that the contents of the main window are also stored in a bitmap. Thus, to print the contents of the window is simply a special case of the general procedure used to print any bitmap. Sample output is shown in Figure 18-2.

```c
/* A Bitmap Printing Demo Program. */

#include <windows.h>
#include <string.h>
#include <commdlg.h>
#include "print.h"

#define NUMLINES 25

#define BMPWIDTH 256
#define BMPHEIGHT 128

LRESULT CALLBACK WindowFunc(HWND, UINT, WPARAM, LPARAM);
void PrintInit(PRINTDLG *printdlg, HWND hwnd);

char szWinName[] = "MyWin"; /* name of window class */

int X = 0, Y = 0; /* current output location */
int maxX, maxY; /* screen dimensions */

HDC memDC, memPrDC; /* virtual device handles */
HBITMAP hBit, hBit2, hImage; /* bitmap handles */
HBRUSH hBrush; /* brush handle */

PRINTDLG printdlg;
DOCINFO docinfo;

int WINAPI WinMain(HINSTANCE hThisInst, HINSTANCE hPrevInst,
                   LPSTR lpszArgs, int nWinMode)
```

```
{
  HACCEL hAccel;
  HWND hwnd;
  MSG msg;
  WNDCLASSEX wcl;

  /* Define a window class. */
  wcl.cbSize = sizeof(WNDCLASSEX);
  wcl.hInstance = hThisInst; /* handle to this instance */
  wcl.lpszClassName = szWinName; /* window class name */
  wcl.lpfnWndProc = WindowFunc; /* window function */
  wcl.style = 0; /* default style */

  wcl.hIcon = LoadIcon(NULL, IDI_APPLICATION);
  wcl.hIconSm = LoadIcon(NULL, IDI_APPLICATION);
  wcl.hCursor = LoadCursor(NULL, IDC_ARROW);

  wcl.lpszMenuName = "PrintDemoMenu2";

  wcl.cbClsExtra = 0; /* no extra */
  wcl.cbWndExtra = 0; /* information needed */

  /* Make the window white. */
  wcl.hbrBackground = GetStockObject(WHITE_BRUSH);

  /* Register the window class. */
  if(!RegisterClassEx(&wcl)) return 0;

  /* Now that a window class has been registered, a window
     can be created. */
  hwnd = CreateWindow(
    szWinName, /* name of window class */
    "Using the Printer", /* title */
    WS_OVERLAPPEDWINDOW, /* standard window */
    CW_USEDEFAULT, /* X coordinate - let Windows decide */
    CW_USEDEFAULT, /* Y coordinate - let Windows decide */
    CW_USEDEFAULT, /* width - let Windows decide */
    CW_USEDEFAULT, /* height - let Windows decide */
    HWND_DESKTOP, /* no parent window */
    NULL, /* no override of class menu */
    hThisInst, /* handle of this instance of the program */
    NULL /* no additional arguments */
  );

  /* load accelerators */
  hAccel = LoadAccelerators(hThisInst, "PrintDemoMenu2");

  /* load the bitmap */
```

```
    hImage = LoadBitmap(hThisInst, "MyBP1"); /* load bitmap */

    /* Display the window. */
    ShowWindow(hwnd, nWinMode);
    UpdateWindow(hwnd);

    /* Create the message loop. */
    while(GetMessage(&msg, NULL, 0, 0))
    {
      if(!TranslateAccelerator(hwnd, hAccel, &msg)) {
        TranslateMessage(&msg);
        DispatchMessage(&msg);
      }
    }
    return msg.wParam;
}

/* This function is called by Windows NT and is passed
   messages from the message queue.
*/
LRESULT CALLBACK WindowFunc(HWND hwnd, UINT message,
                            WPARAM wParam, LPARAM lParam)
{
  HDC hdc;
  PAINTSTRUCT ps;
  int response;
  TEXTMETRIC tm;
  char str[250];
  int i;
  int copies;
  double VidXPPI, VidYPPI, PrXPPI, PrYPPI;
  double Xratio, Yratio;
  RECT r;

  switch(message) {
    case WM_CREATE:
      /* get screen coordinates */
      maxX = GetSystemMetrics(SM_CXSCREEN);
      maxY = GetSystemMetrics(SM_CYSCREEN);

      /* create a virtual window */
      hdc = GetDC(hwnd);
      memDC = CreateCompatibleDC(hdc);
      hBit = CreateCompatibleBitmap(hdc, maxX, maxY);
      SelectObject(memDC, hBit);
      hBrush = GetStockObject(WHITE_BRUSH);
      SelectObject(memDC, hBrush);
```

```
        PatBlt(memDC, 0, 0, maxX, maxY, PATCOPY);

      ReleaseDC(hwnd, hdc);
      break;
    case WM_COMMAND:
      switch(LOWORD(wParam)) {
        case IDM_TEXT: /* print text */
          X = Y = 0;

          /* initialize PRINTDLG struct */
          PrintInit(&printdlg, hwnd);

          if(!PrintDlg(&printdlg)) break;

          docinfo.cbSize = sizeof(DOCINFO);
          docinfo.lpszDocName = "Printing Text";
          docinfo.lpszOutput = NULL;
          docinfo.lpszDatatype = NULL;
          docinfo.fwType = 0;

          /* get text metrics for printer */
          GetTextMetrics(printdlg.hDC, &tm);

          strcpy(str, "This is printed on the printer.");

          StartDoc(printdlg.hDC, &docinfo);

          for(copies=0; copies < printdlg.nCopies; copies++) {
            StartPage(printdlg.hDC);

            for(i=0; i<NUMLINES; i++) {
              TextOut(printdlg.hDC, X, Y, str, strlen(str));
              /* advance to next line */
              Y = Y + tm.tmHeight + tm.tmExternalLeading;
            }


            EndPage(printdlg.hDC);
          }

          EndDoc(printdlg.hDC);
          DeleteDC(printdlg.hDC);
          break;
        case IDM_BITMAP: /* print a bitmap */
          /* initialize PRINTDLG struct */
          PrintInit(&printdlg, hwnd);
```

```
if(!PrintDlg(&printdlg)) break;

docinfo.cbSize = sizeof(DOCINFO);
docinfo.lpszDocName = "Printing bitmaps";
docinfo.lpszOutput = NULL;
docinfo.lpszDatatype = NULL;
docinfo.fwType = 0;

if(!(GetDeviceCaps(printdlg.hDC, RASTERCAPS)
   & (RC_BITBLT | RC_STRETCHBLT))) {
   MessageBox(hwnd, "Cannot Print Raster Images",
           "Error", MB_OK);
   break;
}

/* create a memory DC compatible with the printer */
memPrDC = CreateCompatibleDC(printdlg.hDC);
/* create a bitmap compatible with the printer DC */
hBit2 = CreateCompatibleBitmap(printdlg.hDC, maxX, maxY);
SelectObject(memPrDC, hBit2);

/* put bitmap image into memory DC */
SelectObject(memDC, hImage);

/* copy bitmap to printer-compatible DC */
BitBlt(memPrDC, 0, 0, BMPWIDTH, BMPHEIGHT,
      memDC, 0, 0, SRCCOPY);

/* obtain pixels-per-inch */
VidXPPI = GetDeviceCaps(memDC, LOGPIXELSX);
VidYPPI = GetDeviceCaps(memDC, LOGPIXELSY);
PrXPPI = GetDeviceCaps(printdlg.hDC, LOGPIXELSX);
PrYPPI = GetDeviceCaps(printdlg.hDC, LOGPIXELSY);

/* get scaling ratios */
Xratio = PrXPPI / VidXPPI;
Yratio = PrYPPI / VidYPPI;

SelectObject(memDC, hBit); /* restore virtual window */

StartDoc(printdlg.hDC, &docinfo);

for(copies=0; copies < printdlg.nCopies; copies++) {
  StartPage(printdlg.hDC);

  /* copy bitmap to printer DC, as-is */
  BitBlt(printdlg.hDC, 0, 0, BMPWIDTH, BMPHEIGHT,
```

```
                    memPrDC, 0, 0, SRCCOPY);

        /* copy bitmap while maintaining perspective */
        StretchBlt(printdlg.hDC, 0, BMPHEIGHT + 100,
                  (int) (BMPWIDTH*Xratio),
                  (int) (BMPHEIGHT*Yratio),
                  memPrDC, 0, 0,
                  BMPWIDTH, BMPHEIGHT,
                  SRCCOPY);

        EndPage(printdlg.hDC);
      }

      EndDoc(printdlg.hDC);
      DeleteDC(memPrDC);
      DeleteDC(printdlg.hDC);
      break;
    case IDM_WINDOW: /* print contents of window */
      GetClientRect(hwnd, &r);
      hdc = GetDC(hwnd);

      /* display some text in the window */
      GetTextMetrics(hdc, &tm);
      X = Y = 0;
      strcpy(str, "This is displayed in the main window.");
      for(i=0; i<NUMLINES; i++) {
        TextOut(hdc, X, Y, str, strlen(str));
        TextOut(memDC, X, Y, str, strlen(str));
        /* advance to next line */
        Y = Y + tm.tmHeight + tm.tmExternalLeading;
      }

      /* display bitmap image in the window */
      SelectObject(memDC, hImage);
      BitBlt(hdc, 100, 100, BMPWIDTH, BMPHEIGHT,
             memDC, 0, 0, SRCCOPY);

      /* save image in window for PAINT requests */
      SelectObject(memDC, hBit);
      BitBlt(memDC, 0, 0, r.right, r.bottom, hdc, 0, 0, SRCCOPY);

      /* initialize PRINTDLG struct */
      PrintInit(&printdlg, hwnd);

      if(!PrintDlg(&printdlg)) break;

      docinfo.cbSize = sizeof(DOCINFO);
```

```
docinfo.lpszDocName = "Printing Window";
docinfo.lpszOutput = NULL;
docinfo.lpszDatatype = NULL;
docinfo.fwType = 0;

/* obtain pixels-per-inch */
VidXPPI = GetDeviceCaps(memDC, LOGPIXELSX);
VidYPPI = GetDeviceCaps(memDC, LOGPIXELSY);
PrXPPI = GetDeviceCaps(printdlg.hDC, LOGPIXELSX);
PrYPPI = GetDeviceCaps(printdlg.hDC, LOGPIXELSY);

/* get scaling ratios */
Xratio = PrXPPI / VidXPPI;
Yratio = PrYPPI / VidYPPI;

if(!(GetDeviceCaps(printdlg.hDC, RASTERCAPS)
   & (RC_BITBLT | RC_STRETCHBLT))) {
   MessageBox(hwnd, "Cannot Print Raster Images",
            "Error", MB_OK);
   break;
}

/* create a memory DC compatible with the printer */
memPrDC = CreateCompatibleDC(printdlg.hDC);
/* create a bitmap compatible with the printer DC */
hBit2 = CreateCompatibleBitmap(printdlg.hDC, maxX, maxY);
SelectObject(memPrDC, hBit2);

/* copy window to printer-compatible DC */
BitBlt(memPrDC, 0, 0, maxX, maxY,
       hdc, 0, 0, SRCCOPY);

StartDoc(printdlg.hDC, &docinfo);

for(copies=0; copies < printdlg.nCopies; copies++) {
  StartPage(printdlg.hDC);

  StretchBlt(printdlg.hDC, 0, 0,
            (int) (r.right*Xratio),
            (int) (r.bottom*Yratio),
            memPrDC, 0, 0, (int) r.right, (int) r.bottom,
            SRCCOPY);

  EndPage(printdlg.hDC);
}

EndDoc(printdlg.hDC);
```

```
                    DeleteDC(printdlg.hDC);
                    DeleteDC(memPrDC);
                    ReleaseDC(hwnd, hdc);
                    break;
                case IDM_EXIT:
                    response = MessageBox(hwnd, "Quit the Program?",
                                            "Exit", MB_YESNO);
                    if(response == IDYES) PostQuitMessage(0);
                    break;

                case IDM_HELP:
                    MessageBox(hwnd, "Printing Demo", "Help", MB_OK);
                    break;
            }
            break;
        case WM_PAINT: /* process a repaint request */
            hdc = BeginPaint(hwnd, &ps); /* get DC */

            BitBlt(hdc, ps.rcPaint.left, ps.rcPaint.top,
                    ps.rcPaint.right-ps.rcPaint.left, /* width */
                    ps.rcPaint.bottom-ps.rcPaint.top, /* height */
                    memDC,
                    ps.rcPaint.left, ps.rcPaint.top,
                    SRCCOPY);

            EndPaint(hwnd, &ps); /* release DC */
            break;
        case WM_DESTROY: /* terminate the program */
            DeleteDC(memDC);
            PostQuitMessage(0);
            break;
        default:
            /* Let Windows NT process any messages not specified in
              the preceding switch statement. */
            return DefWindowProc(hwnd, message, wParam, lParam);
    }
    return 0;
}

/* Initialize PRINTDLG structure. */
void PrintInit(PRINTDLG *printdlg, HWND hwnd)
{
    printdlg->lStructSize = sizeof(PRINTDLG);
    printdlg->hwndOwner = hwnd;
    printdlg->hDevMode = NULL;
    printdlg->hDevNames = NULL;
    printdlg->hDC = NULL;
```

18

```
      printdlg->Flags = PD_RETURNDC | PD_NOSELECTION |
                        PD_NOPAGENUMS | PD_HIDEPRINTTOFILE;
      printdlg->nFromPage = 0;
      printdlg->nToPage = 0;
      printdlg->nMinPage = 0;
      printdlg->nMaxPage = 0;
      printdlg->nCopies = 1;
      printdlg->hInstance = NULL;
      printdlg->lCustData = 0;
      printdlg->lpfnPrintHook = NULL;
      printdlg->lpfnSetupHook = NULL;
      printdlg->lpPrintTemplateName = NULL;
      printdlg->lpSetupTemplateName = NULL;
      printdlg->hPrintTemplate = NULL;
      printdlg->hSetupTemplate = NULL;
    }
```

This program requires the following resource file:

```
#include <windows.h>
#include "print.h"

MyBP1 BITMAP BP.BMP

PrintDemoMenu2 MENU
{
  POPUP "&Printer Demo"
  {
    MENUITEM "Print &Text\tF2", IDM_TEXT
    MENUITEM "Print &Bitmap\tF3", IDM_BITMAP
    MENUITEM "Print &Window\tF4", IDM_WINDOW
    MENUITEM "E&xit\tF10", IDM_EXIT
  }
  MENUITEM "&Help", IDM_HELP
}


PrintDemoMenu2 ACCELERATORS
{
  VK_F2, IDM_TEXT, VIRTKEY
  VK_F3, IDM_BITMAP, VIRTKEY
  VK_F4, IDM_WINDOW, VIRTKEY
  VK_F10, IDM_EXIT, VIRTKEY
}
```

This program requires a bitmap for operation. As the program is written, the bitmap must be 256 pixels wide and 128 pixels high. However, if you change the definitions of **BMPWIDTH** and **BMPHEIGHT** you can use any size bitmap you like. The bitmap must be stored in a file called BP.BMP.

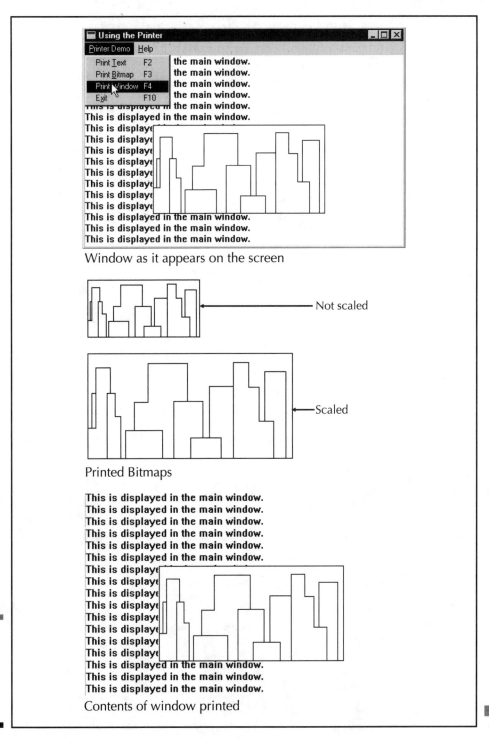

Window as it appears on the screen

Not scaled

Scaled

Printed Bitmaps

Contents of window printed

Sample
output from
the bitmap
printing
program

Figure 18-2.

A Closer Look at the Bitmap Printing Program

Let's begin by examining the **IDM_BITMAP** case. This code is executed when the user selects the Print Bitmap option. It prints the bitmap stored in BP.BMP. This code is shown here for your convenience:

```
case IDM_BITMAP: /* print a bitmap */
  /* initialize PRINTDLG struct */
  PrintInit(&printdlg, hwnd);

  if(!PrintDlg(&printdlg)) break;

  docinfo.cbSize = sizeof(DOCINFO);
  docinfo.lpszDocName = "Printing bitmaps";
  docinfo.lpszOutput = NULL;
  docinfo.lpszDatatype = NULL;
  docinfo.fwType = 0;

  if(!(GetDeviceCaps(printdlg.hDC, RASTERCAPS)
     & (RC_BITBLT | RC_STRETCHBLT))) {
    MessageBox(hwnd, "Cannot Print Raster Images",
               "Error", MB_OK);
    break;
  }

  /* create a memory DC compatible with the printer */
  memPrDC = CreateCompatibleDC(printdlg.hDC);
  /* create a bitmap compatible with the printer DC */
  hBit2 = CreateCompatibleBitmap(printdlg.hDC, maxX, maxY);
  SelectObject(memPrDC, hBit2);

  /* put bitmap image into memory DC */
  SelectObject(memDC, hImage);

  /* copy bitmap to printer-compatible DC */
  BitBlt(memPrDC, 0, 0, BMPWIDTH, BMPHEIGHT,
         memDC, 0, 0, SRCCOPY);

  /* obtain pixels-per-inch */
  VidXPPI = GetDeviceCaps(memDC, LOGPIXELSX);
  VidYPPI = GetDeviceCaps(memDC, LOGPIXELSY);
  PrXPPI = GetDeviceCaps(printdlg.hDC, LOGPIXELSX);
  PrYPPI = GetDeviceCaps(printdlg.hDC, LOGPIXELSY);

  /* get scaling ratios */
  Xratio = PrXPPI / VidXPPI;
  Yratio = PrYPPI / VidYPPI;
```

```
    SelectObject(memDC, hBit); /* restore virtual window */

    StartDoc(printdlg.hDC, &docinfo);

    for(copies=0; copies < printdlg.nCopies; copies++) {
      StartPage(printdlg.hDC);

      /* copy bitmap to printer DC, as-is */
      BitBlt(printdlg.hDC, 0, 0, BMPWIDTH, BMPHEIGHT,
             memPrDC, 0, 0, SRCCOPY);

      /* copy bitmap while maintaining perspective */
      StretchBlt(printdlg.hDC, 0, BMPHEIGHT + 100,
                 (int) (BMPWIDTH*Xratio),
                 (int) (BMPHEIGHT*Yratio),
                 memPrDC, 0, 0,
                 BMPWIDTH, BMPHEIGHT,
                 SRCCOPY);

      EndPage(printdlg.hDC);
    }

    EndDoc(printdlg.hDC);
    DeleteDC(memPrDC);
    DeleteDC(printdlg.hDC);
    break;
```

After the printer DC has been acquired and **docinfo** has been initialized, a call is made to **GetDeviceCaps( )** to determine if the printer supports the necessary raster operations. Remember, if the printer cannot print graphics, it cannot print a bitmap. Assuming that the printer can print the bitmap, a printer-compatible memory DC (**memPrDC**) and bitmap (**hBit2**) are created. The use of **maxX** and **maxY** for the dimensions of the printer-compatible bitmap is suitable for all bitmaps that are not larger than the size of the screen. (Of course, if you want to print a larger bitmap, then these dimensions would need to be larger.) Next, **hbit2** is selected into the printer-compatible memory DC.

The bitmap to be displayed (whose handle is **hImage**) is selected into the memory device context described by **memDC**. This is the same memory DC used to support the virtual window system that handles **WM_PAINT** messages. It is simply doing double-duty at this point. (A separate memory DC could have been created for this purpose, but to do so seemed unnecessarily inefficient.) Next, the bitmap is copied from **memDC** into **memPrDC**. The reason for this intermediate step is that the bitmap stored in BP.BMP is compatible with a video device context, not a printer device context. Thus, it cannot be directly selected into **memPrDC**.

The next step computes the scaling ratios. To do this, the number of pixels per inch for the screen and the printer are obtained, and a scaling factor is computed.

Finally, the bitmap can be sent to the printer. First, it is copied as is, using **BitBlt( )**. This causes the bitmap to be printed without adjusting for the perspective differences between the two devices. Next, the bitmap is printed using **StretchBlt( )** and applying the scaling factors. As you can see, the scaled bitmap closely resembles the way the bitmap looks when displayed on the screen.

The code inside the **IDM_WINDOW** is similar to that inside the **IDM_BITMAP** case just described. You should have no trouble understanding it.

Adding an Abort Function

A printing abort function allows printing to be canceled by the user.

The preceding examples sent output to the printer (actually, to the print spooler) and forgot about it. That is, as far as the program was concerned, once the output was sent to the printer its job was done. However, for real applications, things cannot be this simple. Sometimes an error occurs while printing and a print job must be stopped. Sometimes the user will change his or her mind and want to cancel a print job. To handle such situations, your program must supply a printer abort function and a modeless dialog box that allows the user to cancel a print job before it is complete. According to standard Windows style, all programs must supply such a feature. In this section, you will see how to accomplish this.

SetAbortProc( )

To install an abort function, your program must call **SetAbortProc( )**. Its prototype is shown here:

    int SetAbortProc(HDC *hPrDC*, ABORTPROC *AbortFunc*);

Here, *hPrDC* is the handle of the printer device context. *AbortFunc* is the name of the abort function that is being installed. The function returns a value that is greater than zero if successful or **SP_ERROR** on failure.

All abort functions have the following prototype:

    BOOL CALLBACK AbortFunc(HDC *hPrDC*, int *Code*);

When called, *hPrDC* will contain the handle for the printer device context. *Code* will be zero unless an error has occurred. Your application can watch this value and take appropriate action when an error is detected. The function must return nonzero to continue printing or zero to stop.

Using the Page Setup Common Dialog Box

Windows NT provides another common dialog box that helps support printing: Page Setup. It allows the user to specify the following print-related items:

♦ The size of the paper being used.

♦ The paper source (such as the paper tray).

♦ The orientation of the printed image (landscape or portrait).

♦ The left, right, top, and bottom margins

To activate the Page Setup common dialog box, call **PageSetupDlg( )**, shown here:

BOOL PageSetupDlg(LPPAGESETUPDLG *lpPSD*);

The function returns nonzero if the user presses the OK button to close the dialog box or zero if the user presses Cancel (or on error).

lpPSD points to a **PAGESETUPDLG** structure, which is defined like this:

```
typedef struct tagPSD {
  DWORD lStructSize; /* size of PAGESETUPDLG */
  HWND hwndOwner; /* handle of owner */
  HGLOBAL hDevMode; /* handle of DEVMODE structure */
  HGLOBAL hDevNames; /* handle of DEVNAMES structure */
  DWORD Flags; /* various initialization flags */
  POINT ptPaperSize; /* size of paper */
  RECT rtMinMargin; /* minimum acceptable margins */
  RECT rtMargin; /* margins */
  HINSTANCE hInstance; /* handle for lpPageSetupTemplateName */
  LPARAM lCustData; /* data for lpfnPageSetupHook */
  LPPAGESETUPHOOK lpfnPageSetupHook; /* alternative hook function */
  LPPAGEPAINTHOOK lpfnPagePaintHook; /* alternative paint function */
  LPCSTR lpPageSetupTemplateName; /* alternative template name */
  HGLOBAL hPageSetupTemplate; /* alternative template handle */
} PAGESETUPDLG;
```

Many of the fields in **PAGESETUPDLG** are the same as those used by **PRINTDLG**. However, notice these: **ptPaperSize**, **rtMinMargin**, and **rtMargin**. On return, **ptPaperSize** will contain the size of the paper selected by the user in either thousandths of an inch or hundredths of millimeters. **rtMinMarg** specifies the minimum margin sizes that the user may select. **rtMargin** specifies the initial margins and on return will contain the margins selected by the user.

The following fragment displays the default Page Setup dialog box:

```
PAGESETUPDLG psd;
/* ... */
psd.lStructSize = sizeof(PAGESETUPDLG);
psd.hwndOwner = hwnd;
psd.hDevMode = psd.hDevNames = NULL;
psd.Flags = 0;
PageSetupDlg(&psd);
```

This displays the dialog box shown here.

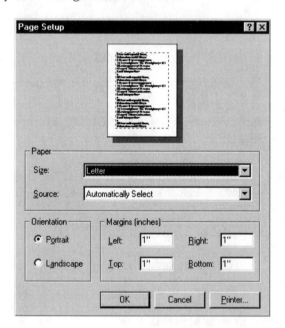

You might want to experiment with the Page Setup dialog box. It supports a number of useful options.

Inside the abort function, you must implement a message loop. However, instead of using **GetMessage( )** to retrieve messages, you must use **PeekMessage( )** with the **PM_REMOVE** option, instead. The reason for this is that **GetMessage( )** waits for a message if one is not already in the message queue. **PeekMessage( )** does not. Thus, a skeletal abort function looks like this:

```
/* Printer abort function. */
BOOL CALLBACK AbortFunc(HDC hdc, int err)
{
  MSG message;

  /* if code is less than zero, handle the error */

  while(PeekMessage(&message, NULL, 0, 0, PM_REMOVE)) {
    if(!IsDialogMessage(hDlg, &message)) {
      TranslateMessage(&message);
      DispatchMessage(&message);
    }
  }

  return printOK; /* printOK is a global variable */
}
```

*PeekMessage( )
is similar to
GetMessage( )
except that it
does not wait
for a message
to be queued.*

The handle of the modeless dialog box that is used to cancel the print job must be stored in **hDlg**. The global variable **printOK** must be initially set to nonzero. However, if the user cancels the print job, this variable will be set to zero. This action is accomplished by a modeless dialog box, which is described next.

The Cancel Printing Dialog Box

After the abort function has been installed, your program must activate a modeless dialog box that allows the user to cancel the print job. Although this dialog box can provide additional features and controls, it must contain at least one button, called Cancel, that cancels the print job. When the user presses Cancel, the dialog box sets a global variable to zero. This global variable must be the same one returned by the abort function described in the preceding section.

A Complete Printing Example

The following program adds an abort function to the preceding program. It also adds one other element: an enlarging option. Using this option, you can set scale factors for the X and Y dimensions. By default, these factors are 1 and thus no enlargement takes place. However, they can be set anywhere between 1 and 10. Using these factors, you can print a bitmap up to ten

times as large as its original size. You can also enlarge only one dimension.
Sample output from the program is shown in Figure 18-3.

```c
/* Using an Abort Function and Enlargement. */

#include <windows.h>
#include <string.h>
#include <commdlg.h>
#include <commctrl.h>
#include "print.h"

#define NUMLINES 25
#define SCALEMAX 10

#define BMPWIDTH 256
#define BMPHEIGHT 128

LRESULT CALLBACK WindowFunc(HWND, UINT, WPARAM, LPARAM);
BOOL CALLBACK EnlargeDialog(HWND, UINT, WPARAM, LPARAM);
void PrintInit(PRINTDLG *printdlg, HWND hwnd);

BOOL CALLBACK AbortFunc(HDC hdc, int err);
LRESULT CALLBACK KillPrint(HWND, UINT, WPARAM, LPARAM);

char szWinName[] = "MyWin"; /* name of window class */

int X = 0, Y = 0; /* current output location */
int maxX, maxY; /* screen dimensions */

HDC memDC, memPrDC; /* store the virtual device handle */
HBITMAP hBit, hBit2, hImage; /* bitmap handles */
HBRUSH hBrush; /* store the brush handle */

PRINTDLG printdlg;
DOCINFO docinfo;

HINSTANCE hInst;

int Xenlarge = 1, Yenlarge = 1;

int printOK = 1;

HWND hDlg = NULL;

int WINAPI WinMain(HINSTANCE hThisInst, HINSTANCE hPrevInst,
                   LPSTR lpszArgs, int nWinMode)
{
  HACCEL hAccel;
```

```
HWND hwnd;
MSG msg;
WNDCLASSEX wcl;

/* Define a window class. */
wcl.cbSize = sizeof(WNDCLASSEX);
wcl.hInstance = hThisInst; /* handle to this instance */
wcl.lpszClassName = szWinName; /* window class name */
wcl.lpfnWndProc = WindowFunc; /* window function */
wcl.style = 0; /* default style */

wcl.hIcon = LoadIcon(NULL, IDI_APPLICATION);
wcl.hIconSm = LoadIcon(NULL, IDI_APPLICATION);
wcl.hCursor = LoadCursor(NULL, IDC_ARROW);

wcl.lpszMenuName = "PrintDemoMenu3";

wcl.cbClsExtra = 0; /* no extra */
wcl.cbWndExtra = 0; /* information needed */

/* Make the window white. */
wcl.hbrBackground = GetStockObject(WHITE_BRUSH);

/* Register the window class. */
if(!RegisterClassEx(&wcl)) return 0;

/* Now that a window class has been registered, a window
   can be created. */
hwnd = CreateWindow(
  szWinName, /* name of window class */
  "Using the Printer", /* title */
  WS_OVERLAPPEDWINDOW, /* standard window style */
  CW_USEDEFAULT, /* X coordinate - let Windows decide */
  CW_USEDEFAULT, /* Y coordinate - let Windows decide */
  CW_USEDEFAULT, /* width - let Windows decide */
  CW_USEDEFAULT, /* height - let Windows decide */
  HWND_DESKTOP, /* no parent window */
  NULL, /* no override of class menu */
  hThisInst, /* handle of this instance of the program */
  NULL /* no additional arguments */
);

hInst = hThisInst;

/* load accelerators */
hAccel = LoadAccelerators(hThisInst, "PrintDemoMenu3");

/* load the bitmap */
```

```
    hImage = LoadBitmap(hThisInst, "MyBP1"); /* load bitmap */

    InitCommonControls();

    /* Display the window. */
    ShowWindow(hwnd, nWinMode);
    UpdateWindow(hwnd);

    /* Create the message loop. */
    while(GetMessage(&msg, NULL, 0, 0))
    {
      if(!TranslateAccelerator(hwnd, hAccel, &msg)) {
        TranslateMessage(&msg);
        DispatchMessage(&msg);
      }
    }
    return msg.wParam;
}

/* This function is called by Windows NT and is passed
   messages from the message queue.
*/
LRESULT CALLBACK WindowFunc(HWND hwnd, UINT message,
                            WPARAM wParam, LPARAM lParam)
{
  HDC hdc;
  PAINTSTRUCT ps;
  int response;
  TEXTMETRIC tm;
  char str[250];
  int i;
  int copies;
  double VidXPPI, VidYPPI, PrXPPI, PrYPPI;
  double Xratio, Yratio;
  RECT r;

  switch(message) {
    case WM_CREATE:
      /* get screen coordinates */
      maxX = GetSystemMetrics(SM_CXSCREEN);
      maxY = GetSystemMetrics(SM_CYSCREEN);

      /* create a virtual window */
      hdc = GetDC(hwnd);
      memDC = CreateCompatibleDC(hdc);
      hBit = CreateCompatibleBitmap(hdc, maxX, maxY);
      SelectObject(memDC, hBit);
      hBrush = GetStockObject(WHITE_BRUSH);
```

```
      SelectObject(memDC, hBrush);
      PatBlt(memDC, 0, 0, maxX, maxY, PATCOPY);

      ReleaseDC(hwnd, hdc);
      break;
    case WM_COMMAND:
      switch(LOWORD(wParam)) {
        case IDM_ENLARGE:
          DialogBox(hInst, "EnlargeDB", hwnd, (DLGPROC) EnlargeDialog);
          break;
        case IDM_TEXT: /* print text */
          X = Y = 0;

          /* initialize PRINTDLG struct */
          PrintInit(&printdlg, hwnd);

          if(!PrintDlg(&printdlg)) break;

          docinfo.cbSize = sizeof(DOCINFO);
          docinfo.lpszDocName = "Printing Text";
          docinfo.lpszOutput = NULL;
          docinfo.lpszDatatype = NULL;
          docinfo.fwType = 0;

          StartDoc(printdlg.hDC, &docinfo);

          strcpy(str, "This is printed on the printer.");

          /* get text metrics for printer */
          GetTextMetrics(printdlg.hDC, &tm);

          printOK = 1;
          SetAbortProc(printdlg.hDC, (ABORTPROC) AbortFunc);
          hDlg = CreateDialog(hInst, "PrCancel", hwnd,
                              (DLGPROC) KillPrint);

          for(copies=0; copies < printdlg.nCopies; copies++) {
            StartPage(printdlg.hDC);

            for(i=0; i<NUMLINES; i++) {
              TextOut(printdlg.hDC, X, Y, str, strlen(str));
              /* advance to next line */
              Y = Y + tm.tmHeight + tm.tmExternalLeading;
            }

            EndPage(printdlg.hDC);
          }
```

18

```
    if(printOK) {
      DestroyWindow(hDlg);
      EndDoc(printdlg.hDC);
    }

    DeleteDC(printdlg.hDC);
    break;
  case IDM_BITMAP: /* print a bitmap */
    /* initialize PRINTDLG struct */
    PrintInit(&printdlg, hwnd);

    if(!PrintDlg(&printdlg)) break;

    docinfo.cbSize = sizeof(DOCINFO);
    docinfo.lpszDocName = "Printing bitmaps";
    docinfo.lpszOutput = NULL;
    docinfo.lpszDatatype = NULL;
    docinfo.fwType = 0;

    if(!(GetDeviceCaps(printdlg.hDC, RASTERCAPS)
       & (RC_BITBLT | RC_STRETCHBLT))) {
      MessageBox(hwnd, "Cannot Print Raster Images",
                 "Error", MB_OK);
      break;
    }

    /* create a memory DC compatible with the printer */
    memPrDC = CreateCompatibleDC(printdlg.hDC);
    /* create a bitmap compatible with the printer DC */
    hBit2 = CreateCompatibleBitmap(printdlg.hDC, maxX, maxY);
    SelectObject(memPrDC, hBit2);

    /* put bitmap image into memory DC */
    SelectObject(memDC, hImage);

    /* copy bitmap to printer-compatible DC */
    BitBlt(memPrDC, 0, 0, BMPWIDTH, BMPHEIGHT,
           memDC, 0, 0, SRCCOPY);

    /* obtain pixels-per-inch */
    VidXPPI = GetDeviceCaps(memDC, LOGPIXELSX);
    VidYPPI = GetDeviceCaps(memDC, LOGPIXELSY);
    PrXPPI = GetDeviceCaps(printdlg.hDC, LOGPIXELSX);
    PrYPPI = GetDeviceCaps(printdlg.hDC, LOGPIXELSY);

    /* get scaling ratios */
    Xratio = PrXPPI / VidXPPI;
```

```
Yratio = PrYPPI / VidYPPI;

SelectObject(memDC, hBit); /* restore virtual window */

StartDoc(printdlg.hDC, &docinfo);

printOK = 1;
SetAbortProc(printdlg.hDC, (ABORTPROC) AbortFunc);
hDlg = CreateDialog(hInst, "PrCancel", hwnd,
                    (DLGPROC) KillPrint);

for(copies=0; copies < printdlg.nCopies; copies++) {
  StartPage(printdlg.hDC);

  /* copy bitmap to printer DC using enlargement
     factors but no perspective scaling */
  StretchBlt(printdlg.hDC, 0, 0,
             BMPWIDTH * Xenlarge,
             BMPHEIGHT * Yenlarge,
             memPrDC, 0, 0, BMPWIDTH, BMPHEIGHT,
             SRCCOPY);

  /* enlarge bitmap while maintaining perspective */
  StretchBlt(printdlg.hDC, 0, BMPHEIGHT+100*Yenlarge,
             (int) (BMPWIDTH*Xratio*Xenlarge),
             (int) (BMPHEIGHT*Yratio*Yenlarge),
             memPrDC, 0, 0,
             BMPWIDTH, BMPHEIGHT,
             SRCCOPY);

  EndPage(printdlg.hDC);
}

if(printOK) DestroyWindow(hDlg);

EndDoc(printdlg.hDC);
DeleteDC(printdlg.hDC);
DeleteDC(memPrDC);
break;
case IDM_WINDOW: /* print contents of window */
GetClientRect(hwnd, &r);
hdc = GetDC(hwnd);

/* display some text in the window */
GetTextMetrics(hdc, &tm);
X = Y = 0;
strcpy(str, "This is displayed in the main window.");
```

```
for(i=0; i<NUMLINES; i++) {
  TextOut(hdc, X, Y, str, strlen(str));
  TextOut(memDC, X, Y, str, strlen(str));
  /* advance to next line */
  Y = Y + tm.tmHeight + tm.tmExternalLeading;
}

/* display bitmap image in the window */
SelectObject(memDC, hImage);
BitBlt(hdc, 100, 100, 256, 128,
       memDC, 0, 0, SRCCOPY);

/* save image in window for PAINT requests */
SelectObject(memDC, hBit);
BitBlt(memDC, 0, 0, r.right, r.bottom, hdc, 0, 0,
       SRCCOPY);

/* initialize PRINTDLG struct */
PrintInit(&printdlg, hwnd);

if(!PrintDlg(&printdlg)) break;

docinfo.cbSize = sizeof(DOCINFO);
docinfo.lpszDocName = "Printing Window";
docinfo.lpszOutput = NULL;
docinfo.lpszDatatype = NULL;
docinfo.fwType = 0;

/* obtain pixels-per-inch */
VidXPPI = GetDeviceCaps(memDC, LOGPIXELSX);
VidYPPI = GetDeviceCaps(memDC, LOGPIXELSY);
PrXPPI = GetDeviceCaps(printdlg.hDC, LOGPIXELSX);
PrYPPI = GetDeviceCaps(printdlg.hDC, LOGPIXELSY);

/* get scaling ratios */
Xratio = PrXPPI / VidXPPI;
Yratio = PrYPPI / VidYPPI;

if(!(GetDeviceCaps(printdlg.hDC, RASTERCAPS)
   & (RC_BITBLT | RC_STRETCHBLT)))
{
  MessageBox(hwnd, "Cannot Print Raster Images",
             "Error", MB_OK);
  break;
}

/* create a memory DC compatible with the printer */
memPrDC = CreateCompatibleDC(printdlg.hDC);
```

```
                     /* create a bitmap compatible with the printer DC */
                     hBit2 = CreateCompatibleBitmap(printdlg.hDC, maxX, maxY);
                     SelectObject(memPrDC, hBit2);

                     /* copy window to printer-compatible DC */
                     BitBlt(memPrDC, 0, 0, maxX, maxY,
                            hdc, 0, 0, SRCCOPY);

                     StartDoc(printdlg.hDC, &docinfo);

                     printOK = 1;
                     SetAbortProc(printdlg.hDC, (ABORTPROC) AbortFunc);
                     hDlg = CreateDialog(hInst, "PrCancel", hwnd,
                                         (DLGPROC) KillPrint);

                     for(copies=0; copies < printdlg.nCopies; copies++) {
                       StartPage(printdlg.hDC);

                       StretchBlt(printdlg.hDC, 0, 0,
                                  (int) (r.right*Xratio) * Xenlarge,
                                  (int) (r.bottom*Yratio) * Yenlarge,
                                  memPrDC, 0, 0,
                                  (int) r.right, (int) r.bottom,
                                  SRCCOPY);

                       EndPage(printdlg.hDC);
                     }

                     if(printOK) DestroyWindow(hDlg);

                     EndDoc(printdlg.hDC);
                     DeleteDC(printdlg.hDC);
                     DeleteDC(memPrDC);
                     ReleaseDC(hwnd, hdc);
                     break;
                   case IDM_EXIT:
                     response = MessageBox(hwnd, "Quit the Program?",
                                           "Exit", MB_YESNO);
                     if(response == IDYES) PostQuitMessage(0);
                     break;
                   case IDM_HELP:
                     MessageBox(hwnd, "Printing Demo", "Help", MB_OK);
                     break;
                 }
                 break;
               case WM_PAINT: /* process a repaint request */
                 hdc = BeginPaint(hwnd, &ps); /* get DC */
```

18

```
      BitBlt(hdc, ps.rcPaint.left, ps.rcPaint.top,
             ps.rcPaint.right-ps.rcPaint.left, /* width */
             ps.rcPaint.bottom-ps.rcPaint.top, /* height */
             memDC,
             ps.rcPaint.left, ps.rcPaint.top,
             SRCCOPY);

      EndPaint(hwnd, &ps); /* release DC */
      break;
    case WM_DESTROY: /* terminate the program */
      DeleteDC(memDC);
      PostQuitMessage(0);
      break;
    default:
      /* Let Windows NT process any messages not specified in
         the preceding switch statement. */
      return DefWindowProc(hwnd, message, wParam, lParam);
  }
  return 0;
}

/* Initialize PRINTDLG structure. */
void PrintInit(PRINTDLG *printdlg, HWND hwnd)
{
  printdlg->lStructSize = sizeof(PRINTDLG);
  printdlg->hwndOwner = hwnd;
  printdlg->hDevMode = NULL;
  printdlg->hDevNames = NULL;
  printdlg->hDC = NULL;
  printdlg->Flags = PD_RETURNDC | PD_NOSELECTION |
                    PD_NOPAGENUMS | PD_HIDEPRINTTOFILE;
  printdlg->nFromPage = 0;
  printdlg->nToPage = 0;
  printdlg->nMinPage = 0;
  printdlg->nMaxPage = 0;
  printdlg->nCopies = 1;
  printdlg->hInstance = NULL;
  printdlg->lCustData = 0;
  printdlg->lpfnPrintHook = NULL;
  printdlg->lpfnSetupHook = NULL;
  printdlg->lpPrintTemplateName = NULL;
  printdlg->lpSetupTemplateName = NULL;
  printdlg->hPrintTemplate = NULL;
  printdlg->hSetupTemplate = NULL;
}

/* Enlargement factor dialog function */
```

```
BOOL CALLBACK EnlargeDialog(HWND hdwnd, UINT message,
                            WPARAM wParam, LPARAM lParam)
{
  static int tempX=1, tempY=1;

  static long temp;
  static HWND hEboxWnd1, hEboxWnd2;
  static HWND udWnd1, udWnd2;
  int low=1, high=SCALEMAX;


  switch(message) {
    case WM_INITDIALOG:
      hEboxWnd1 = GetDlgItem(hdwnd, IDD_EB1);
      hEboxWnd2 = GetDlgItem(hdwnd, IDD_EB2);
      udWnd1 = CreateUpDownControl(
                   WS_CHILD | WS_BORDER | WS_VISIBLE |
                   UDS_SETBUDDYINT | UDS_ALIGNRIGHT,
                   10, 10, 50, 50,
                   hdwnd,
                   IDD_UD1,
                   hInst,
                   hEboxWnd1,
                   SCALEMAX, 1, Xenlarge);

      udWnd2 = CreateUpDownControl(
                   WS_CHILD | WS_BORDER | WS_VISIBLE |
                   UDS_SETBUDDYINT | UDS_ALIGNRIGHT,
                   10, 10, 50, 50,
                   hdwnd,
                   IDD_UD2,
                   hInst,
                   hEboxWnd2,
                   SCALEMAX, 1, Yenlarge);

      tempX = Xenlarge;
      tempY = Yenlarge;
      return 1;
    case WM_VSCROLL: /* process up-down control */
      if(udWnd1==(HWND)lParam)
        tempX = GetDlgItemInt(hdwnd, IDD_EB1, NULL, 1);
      else if(udWnd2==(HWND)lParam)
        tempY = GetDlgItemInt(hdwnd, IDD_EB2, NULL, 1);
      return 1;
    case WM_COMMAND:
      switch(LOWORD(wParam)) {
```

```
          case IDOK:
            Xenlarge = tempX;
            Yenlarge = tempY;
          case IDCANCEL:
            EndDialog(hdwnd, 0);
            return 1;
        }
      break;
  }
  return 0;
}


/* Printer abort function. */
BOOL CALLBACK AbortFunc(HDC hdc, int err)
{
  MSG message;

  while(PeekMessage(&message, NULL, 0, 0, PM_REMOVE)) {
    if(!IsDialogMessage(hDlg, &message)) {
      TranslateMessage(&message);
      DispatchMessage(&message);
    }
  }

  return printOK;
}

/* Let user kill print process. */
LRESULT CALLBACK KillPrint(HWND hdwnd, UINT message,
                            WPARAM wParam, LPARAM lParam)
{
  switch(message) {
    case WM_COMMAND:
      switch(LOWORD(wParam)) {
        case IDCANCEL:
          printOK = 0;
          DestroyWindow(hDlg);
          hDlg = NULL;
          return 1;
        }
      break;
  }
  return 0;
}
```

The resource file for the program is shown here:

```
#include <windows.h>
#include "print.h"

MyBP1 BITMAP BP.BMP

PrintDemoMenu3 MENU
{
  POPUP "&Printer Demo"
  {
    MENUITEM "&Enlarge\tF2",  IDM_ENLARGE
    MENUITEM "Print &Text\tF3",  IDM_TEXT
    MENUITEM "Print &Bitmap\tF4",  IDM_BITMAP
    MENUITEM "Print &Window\tF5",  IDM_WINDOW
    MENUITEM "E&xit\tF10",  IDM_EXIT
  }
  MENUITEM "&Help",  IDM_HELP
}

PrintDemoMenu3 ACCELERATORS
{
  VK_F2,  IDM_ENLARGE,  VIRTKEY
  VK_F3,  IDM_TEXT,  VIRTKEY
  VK_F4,  IDM_BITMAP,  VIRTKEY
  VK_F5,  IDM_WINDOW,  VIRTKEY
  VK_F10,  IDM_EXIT,  VIRTKEY
}

EnlargeDB DIALOG 10, 10, 97, 77
CAPTION "Enlarge Printer Output"
STYLE WS_POPUP | WS_SYSMENU | WS_VISIBLE
{
  PUSHBUTTON "OK", IDOK, 10, 50, 30, 14,
            WS_CHILD | WS_VISIBLE | WS_TABSTOP
  PUSHBUTTON "Cancel", IDCANCEL, 55, 50, 30, 14,
            WS_CHILD | WS_VISIBLE | WS_TABSTOP
  LTEXT "X Scale Factor", IDD_TEXT1,  15, 1, 25, 20
  LTEXT "Y Scale Factor", IDD_TEXT2,  60, 1, 25, 20
  EDITTEXT IDD_EB1, 15, 20, 20, 12, ES_LEFT | WS_CHILD |
          WS_VISIBLE | WS_BORDER
  EDITTEXT IDD_EB2, 60, 20, 20, 12, ES_LEFT | WS_CHILD |
          WS_VISIBLE | WS_BORDER
}
```

```
PrCancel DIALOG 10, 10, 100, 40
CAPTION "Printing"
STYLE WS_CAPTION | WS_POPUP | WS_SYSMENU | WS_VISIBLE
{
  PUSHBUTTON "Cancel", IDCANCEL, 35, 12, 30, 14,
             WS_CHILD | WS_VISIBLE | WS_TABSTOP

}
```

Some Things to Try

When it comes to printing, there is virtually no end to things you can experiment with. Here are some ideas: Try printing color images. If your printer only supports black and white, experiment with different color translations and shades of gray. Another interesting challenge is to print sideways on the page. This is useful for wide print-outs. Finally, the examples in this chapter did not implement any form of collation. You should try to implement this on your own.

Sample output from the final printing demonstration program

Figure 18-3.

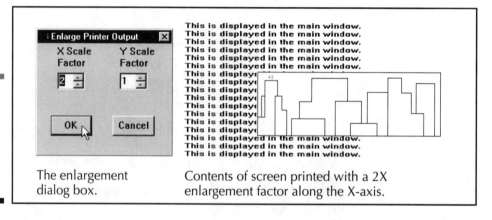

The enlargement dialog box.

Contents of screen printed with a 2X enlargement factor along the X-axis.

CHAPTER 19

Using the System Registry and Creating Screen Savers

This chapter discusses two topics that at first may seem unrelated: screen savers and the system registry. However, as you will see, the ability to understand and use the registry is necessary for the creation of all but the most simple screen savers. The reason for this is that a typical screen saver needs to store configuration information about itself. The screen saver uses this information to configure itself each time it pops up. Under Windows NT, the proper place to store such information is in the system registry. In fact, screen savers are one of the few smaller applications that make use of the registry. For this reason they serve as excellent practical examples of registry utilization.

Although screen savers are some of the simpler Windows NT applications that you will write, they are also some of the most interesting from the programmer's point of view. They are also the one type of application that virtually all programmers want to write. Indeed, it is rare to find a programmer who has not thought about creating his or her own screen saver. While screen savers were initially invented to prevent phosphor burn on idle screens, they have taken on a life of their own. Today most screen savers provide either an entertaining message, an interesting graphics display, a company logo, or a humorous animated sequence. As you will see, creating your own screen saver is one of the easier Windows NT programming tasks.

The system registry is a much more mundane topic. It is also one of the more important Windows NT programming issues. As you probably know, the registry is designed to take the place of .INI initialization files. It stores information about the state and configuration of your computer and of its software. Most programmers are initially intimidated by the registry, but it is really quite straightforward.

This chapter develops two simple screen savers. The first is non-configurable and does not use the registry. Its purpose is to introduce the basic elements common to all screen savers. The second screen saver can be configured and stores its configuration information in the registry. Keep in mind that neither screen saver generates interesting, engaging, or exciting output. They simply illustrate the mechanics involved in creating a screen saver. However, you can use these examples as starting points from which you can develop your own screen saver ideas.

PORTABILITY: If you have written a screen saver for Windows 3.1 or used the registry under Windows 3.1, you already have a basic understanding of these two items. However, both are somewhat different under Windows NT. Specifically, screen savers are a little easier to implement and the registry supports some new API functions.

Screen Saver Fundamentals

A screen saver is actually one of the easiest Windows NT applications to develop. One of the reasons for this is that it does not create a main window. Instead, it uses the desktop (that is, the entire screen) as its window. It also does not contain a **WinMain( )** function or need to create a message loop. In fact, a screen saver requires only three functions, two of which may be empty placeholders.

19

When you create a screen saver, your program must include the header file SCRNSAVE.H and you must include SCRNSAVE.LIB when linking. The screen saver library provides the necessary support for screen savers. This is why your screen saver code need only contain three functions. The rest of the details are handled by the screen saver library.

When creating screen savers, you must include SCRNSAVE.H and link in SCRNSAVE.LIB.

The Screen Saver Functions

The three functions that every screen saver must provide are shown here:

Function	Purpose
ScreenSaverProc( )	This is the screen saver's window procedure. It is passed messages and must respond appropriately.
ScreenSaverConfigureDialog( )	This is the dialog function for the screen saver's configuration dialog box. It can be empty if no configuration is supported.
RegisterDialogClasses( )	This function is used to register custom class types. It will be empty if no custom classes are used.

Although the names of these functions are defined by Windows NT, you must supply the functions themselves in the source code to your screen saver. (That is, they are not provided by Win32.) Let's take a closer look at these three functions, now.

ScreenSaverProc( ) is a window procedure. Its prototype is shown here:

LRESULT WINAPI ScreenSaverProc(HWND *hwnd*, UINT *message*,
WPARAM *wParam*, LPARAM *lParam*);

It is passed messages in the same way as other window procedures. There is one important difference, however. If the function does not process a message, it must call **DefScreenSaverProc( )** rather than **DefWindow-Proc( )**. Also, the window handle passed to **ScreenSaverProc( )** in *hwnd* is the handle for the entire screen. That is, it is the handle of the desktop. Your screen saver will make use of this fact.

ScreenSaverConfigureDialog( ) is the dialog box function that handles the screen saver's configuration dialog box. It has the following prototype:

```
BOOL WINAPI ScreenSaverConfigureDialog(HWND hdwnd,
                                       UINT message,
                                       WPARAM wParam,
                                       LPARAM lParam);
```

If your screen saver does not require configuration, then the only thing this function must do is return zero. If the screen saver supports a configuration dialog box, then it must be defined in the screen saver's resource file and given the ID value of **DLG_SCRNSAVECONFIGURE**. This value is defined in SCRNSAVE.H as 2003.

RegisterDialogClasses( ) is used to register custom window classes, such as custom controls. It has this prototype:

```
BOOL WINAPI RegisterDialogClasses(HINSTANCE hInst);
```

If your screen saver does not use a custom window class, simply return nonzero.

As mentioned, **ScreenSaverProc( )** will call **DefScreenSaverProc( )** if it does not process a message. The prototype for **DefScreenSaverProc( )** is shown here:

```
LRESULT WINAPI DefScreenSaverProc(HWND hwnd, UINT message,
                                  WPARAM wParam, LPARAM lParam);
```

Two Screen Saver Resources

All screen savers must define two special resources: an icon and a string. The icon, whose ID must be **ID_APP**, is used to identify the screen saver. The string resource, whose identifier must be **IDS_DESCRIPTION**, contains a description of the screen saver. It will be displayed by the Control Panel (under Display Properties) in a list box that describes the available screen savers. This string must be no more than 24 characters long. **ID_APP** and **IDS_DESCRIPTION** are defined in SCRNSAVE.H.

String resources are defined in a resource file using the **STRINGTABLE** statement. It has this general form:

```
STRINGTABLE
{
  ID1  "string"
  ID2  "string"
      .
      .
      .
  IDn  "string"
}
```

Here, *ID* is the identifier associated with the string. Your program can refer to a string resource by its ID value. A program can load a string resource by calling **LoadString( )**. However, for the purposes of a screen saver, the **IDS_DESCRIPTION** string is not used by the screen saver itself. Rather, it simply provides a description of the screen saver inside the Control Panel.

PORTABILITY: Screen savers written for Windows 3.1 or Windows 95 may not have defined the **IDS_DESCRIPTION** string. Be sure to check this when porting.

Other Programming Considerations

SCRNSAVE.H defines several global variables. The one of interest to us in this chapter is **hMainInstance**. This will contain the instance handle of the screen saver. This handle will be needed if your screen saver creates a window, for example. Other global variables are defined within SCRNSAVE.H, which may be useful to your screen saver. You will want to examine the contents of this header file.

A screen saver is driven by a timer.

All screen savers are driven by a timer. Each time the timer goes off, the screen saver receives a **WM_TIMER** message and updates the screen display. Your screen saver must start the timer when it is first activated and destroy the timer when it is destroyed. (Timers were described in Chapter 6.)

After you have compiled the screen saver, you must rename it so that it has the .SCR extension rather than .EXE. Next, copy the renamed screen saver into the proper directory. For most users, the directory that holds screen savers will be WINNT\SYSTEM32. (The easiest way to determine which directory to use is to see which one holds the screen savers currently installed on your system.) Once you have renamed and copied the screen saver to the proper directory, you can select your new screen saver using the control panel.

Creating a Minimal Screen Saver

We will begin by creating a bare bones screen saver. It simply displays a
text-based message that moves about the screen. It cannot be configured and
does not use the **ScreenSaverConfigureDialog( )** function. It does,
however, illustrate the basic elements of a screen saver. Here is the complete
listing for the minimal screen saver:

```c
/* A miminal screen saver. */
#include <windows.h>
#include <scrnsave.h>

/* This is the message displayed on the screen. */
char str[80] = "NT 4 Screen Saver #1";

/* This is timer delay. */
int delay = 200;

/* Screen Saver Function */
LRESULT WINAPI ScreenSaverProc(HWND hwnd, UINT message,
                               WPARAM wParam, LPARAM lParam)
{
  static HDC hdc;
  static unsigned int timer;
  static RECT scrdim;
  static SIZE size;
  static int X = 0, Y = 0;
  static HBRUSH hBlkBrush;
  static TEXTMETRIC tm;

  switch(message) {
    case WM_CREATE:
      timer = SetTimer(hwnd, 1, delay, NULL);
      hBlkBrush = GetStockObject(BLACK_BRUSH);
      break;
    case WM_ERASEBKGND:
      hdc = GetDC(hwnd);

      /* get coordinates of screen */
      GetClientRect(hwnd, &scrdim);

      /* erase the screen */
      SelectObject(hdc, hBlkBrush);
      PatBlt(hdc, 0, 0, scrdim.right, scrdim.bottom, PATCOPY);
```

```
        /* get and save height and length of string */
        GetTextMetrics(hdc, &tm);
        GetTextExtentPoint32(hdc, str, strlen(str), &size);

        ReleaseDC(hwnd, hdc);
        break;
      case WM_TIMER:
        hdc = GetDC(hwnd);

        /* erase previous output */
        SelectObject(hdc, hBlkBrush);
        PatBlt(hdc, X, Y, X + size.cx, Y + size.cy, PATCOPY);

        /* move string to new location */
        X += 10; Y += 10;
        if(X > scrdim.right) X = 0;
        if(Y > scrdim.bottom) Y = 0;

        /* output string */
        SetBkColor(hdc, RGB(0, 0, 0));
        SetTextColor(hdc, RGB(0, 255, 255));
        TextOut(hdc, X, Y, str, strlen(str));

        ReleaseDC(hwnd, hdc);
        break;
      case WM_DESTROY:
        KillTimer(hwnd, timer);
        break;
      default:
        return DefScreenSaverProc(hwnd, message, wParam, lParam);
  }

  return 0;
}

/* Placeholder Dialog Box Function */
BOOL WINAPI ScreenSaverConfigureDialog(HWND hdwnd, UINT message,
                                WPARAM wParam, LPARAM lParam)
{
  return 0;
}

/* No classes to register. */
BOOL WINAPI RegisterDialogClasses(HINSTANCE hInst)
{
  return 1;
}
```

The screen saver requires the following resource file:

```
#include <windows.h>
#include <scrnsave.h>

ID_APP ICON SCRICON.ICO

STRINGTABLE
{
  IDS_DESCRIPTION "My Screen Saver #1"
}
```

As this resource file implies, you will need to create an icon for your screen saver. Save it in a file called SCRICON.ICO.

A Closer Look at the First Screen Saver

Each time the screen saver is activated, it receives two messages. The first is **WM_CREATE**. Your screen saver must use this message to perform any initializations it requires, as well as to start the timer. In this example, the timer has a period of 200 milliseconds. Thus, it will interrupt the screen saver 5 times a second. In this example, the black brush is also obtained when the screen saver is created.

The next message received by your screen saver is **WM_ERASEBKGND**. When this message is received, your screen saver must clear the entire screen. There are, of course, several ways to do this. The method employed by the example is to obtain the coordinates of the screen, select the black brush, and then use **PatBlt( )** to fill the specified region with black (i.e., nothing). Remember, *hwnd* contains the handle of the desktop, so the call to **GetClientRect( )** returns the dimensions of the entire screen.

Since the message displayed by the screen saver does not change, its dimensions are also obtained and stored when **WM_ERASEBKGND** is received.

Each time the timer goes off, **WM_TIMER** is sent to the screen saver. In response, the screen saver first erases the message from its current location, advances the location counters, and then redisplays the message.

When the user presses a key or moves the mouse, the screen saver receives a **WM_DESTROY** message. When this occurs, the screen saver must cancel the timer and perform any other shut-down tasks.

Since this screen saver has no user-configurable data or custom control classes, the functions **ScreenSaverConfigureDialog( )** and **RegisterDialogClasses( )** are simply placeholders.

Problems with the First Screen Saver

While the preceding screen saver shows the basics, it is inadequate for actual use. First, the message displayed on the screen cannot be changed. Second, the delay period is fixed. Both of these items are subject to personal taste and should be configurable by the user. Fortunately, it is easy to add this capability to the screen saver. However, doing so raises one interesting problem: where is the configuration data going to be stored? To allow the screen saver to be configured requires that the delay time and the message be stored on disk somewhere. When the screen saver executes, it must be able to retrieve these settings. While it is certainly possible, in this simple case, to store the information in a normal data file, a better solution exists. Therefore, before developing a configurable screen saver, a short discussion of one of Windows NT's most important features is required.

Understanding the System Registry

As pointed out by the preceding section, when a program contains configurable options, there must be some way to store these options. In the early days of computing, each program would create its own special data file that contained its configuration settings. Such files often used file extensions such as .CFG or .DAT. (In fact, you can still find examples of these types of files, although they are becoming increasingly rare.) While such an individualized approach was adequate for operating systems such as DOS, it was not appropriate for multitasking systems, such as Windows. For example, it was possible for two or more programs to use the same name for their configuration files, causing confusion. To solve this problem, early versions of Windows created the .INI file extension, which was reserved for program initialization files. Windows also defined its own initialization file, called WIN.INI. Applications were free to use this file to hold their own configuration information or to create their own, private .INI files.

The system registry stores configuration information.

While .INI files helped bring order to configuration files, they were not a perfect solution. One reason for this is that it was still possible for two different applications to use the same name for their .INI files. Also, when a computer had several applications loaded onto it, there were often a very large number of .INI files. Further, in some cases it was beneficial for one program to know if another program was also installed on the system. Using .INI files, this was not always an easy thing to determine. To finally solve the configuration file problem, Microsoft abandoned .INI files, and invented an entirely new approach called the *system registry*, or just *registry* for short. While the registry was partially supported by Windows 3.1, it was enhanced for Windows NT (and Windows 95). It is important to understand that

Windows NT still supports the older .INI files. However, for new applications, you must use the registry to hold configuration information.

For various reasons, the registry has the reputation of being difficult to use and understand. However, this reputation is not deserved. Indeed, the truth is quite the contrary. As you will see, using the registry is straightforward. Once you have mastered only a few new API functions, you will have no trouble using it.

PORTABILITY: The registry was largely ignored under Windows 3.1 and most Windows 3.1 programs do not use it. However, under Windows NT, all new applications are expected to use the registry. You should make this change when porting older programs.

The Registry Structure

The registry is a special, hierarchical database maintained by Windows NT that stores information related to three entities: the user, the machine, and the installed software. For the most part, it stores configuration settings relating to these items. The information stored in the registry is in its binary form. For this reason, there are only two ways by which you may alter or examine the contents of the registry: by using REGEDIT or REGEDT32, the standard registry editors, or by using the registry management API functions. You cannot, for example, edit the registry using a text editor.

A registry key is a node in the registry tree.

The registry is a set of keys structured as a tree. A *key* is, for practical purposes, a node in the tree. The name of a key is essentially the name of a node. A key may be empty, have subkeys, or contain values. Typically, these values consist of configuration information for a program. Thus, to use the registry, your program will create a key and store its configuration information under that key. When it needs this information, it will look up the key and then read the information. If the user changes the configuration settings, then your program will simply write those new values to the registry. Using the registry really is just this easy.

The Built-In Keys

The registry contains five built-in keys. Each key forms the root node for its own subtree of keys. The names of the built-in keys are shown here.

Key	Purpose
HKEY_CLASSES_ROOT	Holds information used for OLE. Also defines associations between file extensions and applications.
HKEY_CURRENT_CONFIG	Changes to the hardware configuration defined under **HKEY_LOCAL_MACHINE**. This key is new to NT 4 and provides compatibility with Windows 95. The same information also appears under HKEY_LOCAL_MACHINE\System\Current-ControlSet\HardwareProfiles\Current.
HKEY_CURRENT_USER	Holds information related to the currently logged in user. This is where user-related, application program configuration information is usually stored.
HKEY_LOCAL_MACHINE	Holds information about the system, including the hardware configuration, device drivers, installed software, and start-up data. These settings apply no matter which user is logged on.
HKEY_USERS	Holds the preferences for each user of the machine.

These five keys are always open and may be used by your application. However, generally an application will only use two of these keys: **HKEY_LOCAL_MACHINE**, which is used to store any system-wide configuration options relating to the machine, and **HKEY_CURRENT_USER**, which is used to store configuration options relating to the user.

Typically, an installation program will create a key under **HKEY_LOCAL_MACHINE** that contains the name and version number of an application package, plus the name of the company that created the application. Other application-related data may also be stored under **HKEY_LOCAL_MACHINE**. Under **HKEY_CURRENT_USER**, a program will store configuration options selected by the user. Default user configuration information may also be written under this key when the program is installed. Typically, the application will use this information when it begins execution. The configuration data for the screen saver will be stored under this key.

Since the screen saver in this chapter is a simple, example program, it doesn't require any special installation. Thus, we won't be using **HKEY_LOCAL_MACHINE**. However, the techniques used to read and write data to and from the registry using this key are the same as for the **HKEY_CURRENT_USER**.

There are several standard subkeys which will normally be found in the registry. For example, under **HKEY_CURRENT_USER**, some of the standard subkeys are **Software**, **Control Panel**, and **Environment**. When you add the configuration settings for a new program to the registry, you will typically do so under the **Software** subkey of **HKEY_CUR-RENT_USER**. However, since screen savers contain configuration information that can be changed by the Control Panel, they usually store their information under the **Control Panel** key. Although the standard subkeys will exist on all computers running Windows NT, they are not automatically open.

Since the registry is a set of hierarchical trees, you will need to specify a full path to the key that you want. Key paths are similar in concept to directory paths. Each key is separated from the one preceding it using a backslash (\) character. For example, if you access a key called **Screensaver** under the **Control Panel** subkey of **HKEY_CURRENT_USER**, the key path will look like this:

    HKEY_CURRENT_USER\Control Panel\Screensaver

A key may also include a period.

Recall that in C/C++, the backslash character signals the start of an escape sequence when used in a string. Therefore, when specifying a string in a C/C++ program that contains a backslash, you must use two backslashes for each backslash character you need. For example, to specify the preceding path as a C/C++ string, use the following:

    "HKEY_CURRENT_USER\\Control Panel\\Screensaver"

If you forget to use the two backslashes, your registry functions will not work properly.

In Windows NT terminology, a *hive* is a key hierarchy that descends directly from either **HKEY_LOCAL_MACHINE** or **HKEY_USERS**. Some registry operations work on hives. For example, you can save or load a hive.

Registry Values

The registry allows several different types of data to be stored as values under a key. When you store or retrieve data, you must specify its name and its type. Table 19-1 shows the types of data supported by the registry. You will always add a value to the registry under a key that you have defined. There is no concept of simply adding a value to the registry by itself.

Creating and Opening a Key

All registry operations take place relative to an open key. The five predefined keys described earlier are always open. Therefore, you will use one of the predefined keys as the starting point when opening any other key. To open an existing key, use **RegOpenKeyEx( )**. Its prototype is shown here:

```
LONG RegOpenKeyEx(HKEY hKey, LPCSTR SubKey,
                  DWORD NotUsed, REGSAM Access,
                  PHKEY Result);
```

Data Type	Meaning
REG_BINARY	Generic type used to specify any binary data.
REG_DWORD	Long, unsigned integer.
REG_DWORD_LITTLE_ENDIAN	Long, unsigned integer stored with least significant byte first. This is called little-endian format.
REG_DWORD_BIG_ENDIAN	Long, unsigned integer stored with most significant byte first. This is called big-endian format.
REG_EXPAND_SZ	A string that contains unexpanded environmental variables.
REG_LINK	A Unicode symbolic link.
REG_MULTI_SZ	An array of strings. The last two strings must be null.
REG_NONE	Undefined type.
REG_RESOURCE_LIST	A resource list for a device driver.
REG_SZ	Normal, null-terminated string.

The Data Types Supported by the Registry

Table 19-1.

Here, *hKey* is the handle of an already open key, which may be one of the predefined keys. The key being opened must be a subkey of *hKey*. The name of the subkey is pointed to by *SubKey*. *NotUsed* is reserved and must be zero. *Access* determines the access privileges for the subkey handle. This value can be any combination of the values shown in Table 19-2. *Result* is a pointer to a variable that, on return, contains the handle of the subkey.

The function returns **ERROR_SUCCESS** if successful. On failure, an error code is returned. The function fails if the specified key does not exist.

Although you can use **RegOpenKeyEx( )** to open a registry key, you will probably find that more often you will use another registry function called **RegCreateKeyEx( )**. This function serves a dual purpose: it will open an existing key or, if the specified key does not exist, it will create it. Its prototype is shown here:

```
LONG RegCreateKeyEx(HKEY hKey, LPCSTR SubKey,
                    DWORD NotUsed, LPSTR Class,
                    DWORD How, REGSAM Access,
                    LPSECURITY_ATTRIBUTES SecAttr,
                    PHKEY Result, LPDWORD WhatHappened);
```

Access Value	Purpose
KEY_ALL_ACCESS	Allows all accesses.
KEY_CREATE_LINK	Allows the creation of a symbolic link.
KEY_CREATE_SUB_KEY	Allows the creation of subkeys.
KEY_ENUMERATE_SUB_KEYS	Allows the enumeration of subkeys.
KEY_EXECUTE	Allows read access.
KEY_NOTIFY	Allows change notification.
KEY_QUERY_VALUE	Allows read access to subkey data.
KEY_READ	Allows all read accesses. Same as **KEY_ENUMERATE_SUB_KEYS	KEY_NOTIFY	KEY_QUERY_VALUE**.
KEY_SET_VALUE	Allows write access to subkey data.
KEY_WRITE	Allows all write accesses. Same as **KEY_CREATE_SUB_KEY	KEY_SET_VALUE**.

Key Access
Privilege
Values
Table 19-2.

Here, *hKey* is the handle of an open key. *SubKey* is a pointer to the name of the key to open or create. *NotUsed* is reserved and must be zero. *Class* is a pointer to the class or object type for the key. This value is only used for keys being created and can be a string of your own choosing.

The value of *How* can be one of the following:

    REG_OPTION_VOLATILE

    REG_OPTION_NON_VOLATILE

    REG_OPTION_BACKUP_RESTORE

If you specify **REG_OPTION_VOLATILE**, then the key is volatile and will not be stored on disk. Thus its value will be lost when the computer is turned off. Specifying **REG_OPTION_NON_VOLATILE** creates a non-volatile key, which is stored on disk. This is the default. If you specify **REG_OPTION_BACKUP_RESTORE**, then the key is opened with the necessary access rights to allow it to be backed up or restored. In this case, the value in *Access* is not used.

Access determines the access privileges of the key. It may be any valid combination of the values shown in Table 19-2**.**

SecAttr is a pointer to a **SECURITY_ATTRIBUTES** structure that defines the security descriptor for the key. If this value is **NULL**, then the default descriptor is used.

On return, the variable pointed to by *Result* will contain the handle of the key that has just been created or opened. *WhatHappened* is a pointer to a variable that, on return, describes which action took place. It will either be **REG_CREATED_NEW_KEY**, if a new key was created, or **REG_OPENED_EXISTING_KEY,** if an already existing key was opened.

RegCreateKeyEx( ) can create several keys at the same time. For example, if *SubKey* contains the string "\\CoName\\AppName", then the keys **CoName** and **AppName** are created if they do not already exist.

PORTABILITY: Windows 3.1 does not support any of the registry functions that end in **Ex**. For example, it does not support **RegCreateKeyEx( )**. Instead, older applications use **RegCreateKey( )**. When converting older applications, you will want to watch for opportunities to convert older functions into their Windows NT, **Ex** form.

Storing Values

Once you have obtained an open key, you can store values under it. To do this, use **RegSetValueEx( )**. Its prototype is shown here:

LONG RegSetValueEx(HKEY *hKey*, LPCSTR *Name*,
                DWORD *NotUsed*, DWORD *DataType*,
                CONST LPBYTE *lpValue*, DWORD *SizeOfValue*);

hKey is the handle of an open key that has been opened with **KEY_SET_VALUE** access rights. *Name* is a pointer to the name of the value. If this name does not already exist, it is added to the key. *NotUsed* is currently reserved and must be set to zero.

DataType specifies the type of data that is being stored. It must be one of the values specified in Table 19-1. *lpValue* is a pointer to the data being stored. *SizeOfValue* specifies the size of this data (in bytes). For string data, the null-terminator must also be counted.

For example, the following call to **RegSetValueEx( )** stores the string "This is a test" in the value **StringTest**.

```
strcpy(str, "This is a test");
RegSetValueEx(hRegKey, "StringTest", 0, REG_SZ,
              (LPBYTE) str, strlen(str)+1);
```

As mentioned, notice that the null terminator must be counted as part of the size of a string. This is why 1 is added to the value of **strlen( )**.

RegSetValueEx( ) returns **ERROR_SUCCESS** if successful. On failure, it returns an error code.

Retrieving Values

Once you have stored a value in the registry, it can be retrieved at any time by your program (or by any other program). To do so, use the **RegQueryValueEx( )** function, shown here:

LONG RegQueryValueEx(HKEY *hKey*, LPSTR *Name*,
                LPDWORD *NotUsed*, LPDWORD *DataType*,
                LPBYTE *Value*, LPDWORD *SizeOfData*);

hKey is the handle of an open key, which must have been opened with **KEY_QUERY_VALUE** access privileges. *Name* is a pointer to the name of the value desired. This value must already exist under the specified key. *NotUsed* is currently reserved and must be set to **NULL**.

DataType is a pointer that, on return, contains the type of the value being retrieved. This will be one of the values shown in Table 19-1. *Value* is a pointer to a buffer that, on return, contains the data associated with the specified value. *SizeOfData* is a pointer to a variable that contains the size of the buffer in bytes. On return, *SizeOfData* will point to the number of bytes stored in the buffer.

For example, the following call to **RegQueryValueEx( )** retrieves the string associated with the value **StringTest**.

```
char str[80];
long size = 80;
RegQueryValueEx(hRegKey, "StringTest", NULL, REG_SZ,
                (LPBYTE) str, &size);
```

RegQueryValueEx( ) returns **ERROR_SUCCESS** if successful. On failure, it returns an error code.

Closing a Key

To close a key, use **RegCloseKey( )**, shown here:

LONG RegCloseKey(HKEY *hKey*);

Here, *hKey* is the handle of the key being closed. The function returns **ERROR_SUCCESS** if successful. On failure, an error code is returned.

IN DEPTH

Some Additional Registry Functions

Although the registry functions described in this chapter are the only ones needed by the configurable screen saver, there are several other registry-related functions that you will want to explore on your own. Here are some of the other, commonly used functions:.

Function	Purpose
RegDeleteKey( )	Deletes a key.
RegDeleteValue( )	Deletes a value.
RegEnumKeyEx( )	Enumerates the subkeys of a given key.

Function	Purpose
RegEnumValue( )	Enumerates the values associated with a given key.
RegLoadKey( )	Loads a key subtree (i.e., a hive) from a file.
RegQueryInfoKey( )	Obtains detailed information about a key.
RegSaveKey( )	Saves an entire subtree (i.e., a hive), beginning at the specified key, to a file. Values are also saved.

One good way to learn more about the registry is to write a program that enumerates and displays all of the keys and values it contains. When experimenting with the registry remember one caution: do not change its values. Doing so may stop your computer from working.

Using the Registry Editors

Your program interacts with the registry using the registry API functions. However, if you want to examine (or even alter) the contents of the registry, you may do so using REGEDIT or REGEDT32. Both display the registry, including all keys and values. You can add, delete, and modify both keys and values. Normally, you will not want to manually change the registry. If you do so incorrectly, your computer might stop working! However, using a registry editor to view the structure and contents of the registry is completely safe and it will give you a concrete understanding of the registry's organization.

Creating a Configurable Screen Saver

To transform the simple screen saver shown at the start of this chapter into a configurable one, three additions must be made: First, a configuration dialog box must be defined in the screen saver's resource file. Second, the **ScreenSaverConfigureDialog( )** function must be filled in. Third, the configuration settings must be stored in the registry and retrieved each time the screen saver executes. Here is the complete program that contains these enhancements:

> **NOTE:** The following program uses a spin control, which is one of Windows NT's common controls. For this reason, you will need to include COMCTL32.LIB when linking.

```c
/* A Configurable Screen Saver */
#include <windows.h>
#include <scrnsave.h>
#include <commctrl.h>
#include <string.h>
#include "scr.h"

#define DELAYMAX 999
#define MSGSIZE 80

/* This is the screen saver's message. */
char str[MSGSIZE+1] = "NT 4 Screen Saver #2";

/* This is timer delay. */
long delay;

unsigned long datatype, datasize;
unsigned long result;

/* This is a registry key. */
HKEY hRegKey;

/* Screen Saver Function */
LRESULT WINAPI ScreenSaverProc(HWND hwnd, UINT message,
                               WPARAM wParam, LPARAM lParam)
{
  static HDC hdc;
  static unsigned int timer;
  static RECT scrdim;
  static SIZE size;
  static int X = 0, Y = 0;
  static HBRUSH hBlkBrush;
  static TEXTMETRIC tm;
```

```
switch(message) {
  case WM_CREATE:
    /* open screen saver key or create, if necessary */
    RegCreateKeyEx(HKEY_CURRENT_USER,
       "Control Panel\\Screen Saver.MyScrSaver",
       0, "Screen Saver", 0, KEY_ALL_ACCESS,
       NULL, &hRegKey, &result);

    /* if key was created */
    if(result==REG_CREATED_NEW_KEY) {
      /* set its initial value */
      delay = 100;
      RegSetValueEx(hRegKey, "delay", 0,
         REG_DWORD, (LPBYTE) &delay, sizeof(DWORD));
      RegSetValueEx(hRegKey, "message", 0,
         REG_SZ, (LPBYTE) str, strlen(str)+1);
    }
    else { /* key was already in registry */
      /* get delay value */
      datasize = sizeof(DWORD);
      RegQueryValueEx(hRegKey, "delay", NULL,
         &datatype, (LPBYTE) &delay, &datasize);

      /* get message */
      datasize = MSGSIZE;
      RegQueryValueEx(hRegKey, "message", NULL,
         &datatype, (LPBYTE) str, &datasize);
    }

    RegCloseKey(hRegKey);

    timer = SetTimer(hwnd, 1, delay, NULL);
    hBlkBrush = GetStockObject(BLACK_BRUSH);
    break;
  case WM_ERASEBKGND:
    hdc = GetDC(hwnd);

    /* Get coordinates of screen */
    GetClientRect(hwnd, &scrdim);

    /* erase the screen */
    SelectObject(hdc, hBlkBrush);
    PatBlt(hdc, 0, 0, scrdim.right, scrdim.bottom, PATCOPY);

    /* get and save height and length of string */
    GetTextMetrics(hdc, &tm);
    GetTextExtentPoint32(hdc, str, strlen(str), &size);
```

```
                    ReleaseDC(hwnd, hdc);
                    break;
                case WM_TIMER:
                    hdc = GetDC(hwnd);

                    /* erase previous output */
                    SelectObject(hdc, hBlkBrush);
                    PatBlt(hdc, X, Y, X + size.cx, Y + size.cy, PATCOPY);

                    /* move string to new location */
                    X += 10; Y += 10;
                    if(X > scrdim.right) X = 0;
                    if(Y > scrdim.bottom) Y = 0;

                    /* output string */
                    SetBkColor(hdc, RGB(0, 0, 0));
                    SetTextColor(hdc, RGB(0, 255, 255));
                    TextOut(hdc, X, Y, str, strlen(str));

                    ReleaseDC(hwnd, hdc);
                    break;
                case WM_DESTROY:
                    KillTimer(hwnd, timer);
                    break;
                default:
                    return DefScreenSaverProc(hwnd, message, wParam, lParam);
            }

        return 0;
    }

    /* Configuration Dialog Box Function */
    BOOL WINAPI ScreenSaverConfigureDialog(HWND hdwnd, UINT message,
                        WPARAM wParam, LPARAM lParam)
    {
        static HWND hEboxWnd;
        static HWND udWnd;

        switch(message) {
            case WM_INITDIALOG:
                /* open screen saver key or create, if necessary */
                RegCreateKeyEx(HKEY_CURRENT_USER,
                    "Control Panel\\Screen Saver.MyScrSaver",
                    0, "Screen Saver", 0, KEY_ALL_ACCESS,
                    NULL, &hRegKey, &result);

                /* if key was created */
                if(result==REG_CREATED_NEW_KEY) {
```

```
        /* set its initial value */
        delay = 100;
        RegSetValueEx(hRegKey, "delay", 0,
           REG_DWORD, (LPBYTE) &delay, sizeof(DWORD));
        RegSetValueEx(hRegKey, "message", 0,
           REG_SZ, (LPBYTE) str, strlen(str)+1);
      }
      else { /* key was already in registry */
        /* get delay value */
        datasize = sizeof(DWORD);
        RegQueryValueEx(hRegKey, "delay", NULL,
           &datatype, (LPBYTE) &delay, &datasize);

        /* get message */
        datasize = MSGSIZE;
        RegQueryValueEx(hRegKey, "message", NULL,
           &datatype, (LPBYTE) str, &datasize);
      }

      /* create delay spin control */
      hEboxWnd = GetDlgItem(hdwnd, IDD_EB1);
      udWnd = CreateUpDownControl(
                  WS_CHILD | WS_BORDER | WS_VISIBLE |
                  UDS_SETBUDDYINT | UDS_ALIGNRIGHT,
                  20, 10, 50, 50,
                  hdwnd,
                  IDD_UPDOWN,
                  hMainInstance,
                  hEboxWnd,
                  DELAYMAX, 1, delay);

      /* initialize edit box with current message */
      SetDlgItemText(hdwnd, IDD_EB2, str);

      return 1;
    case WM_COMMAND:
      switch(LOWORD(wParam)) {
        case IDOK:
          /* set delay value */
          delay = GetDlgItemInt(hdwnd, IDD_EB1, NULL, 1);

          /* get message string */
          GetDlgItemText(hdwnd, IDD_EB2, str, MSGSIZE);

          /* update registry */
          RegSetValueEx(hRegKey, "delay", 0,
            REG_DWORD, (LPBYTE) &delay, sizeof(DWORD));
```

```
              RegSetValueEx(hRegKey, "message", 0,
                REG_SZ, (LPBYTE) str, strlen(str)+1);

              /* fall through to next case ... */
          case IDCANCEL:
            RegCloseKey(hRegKey);
            EndDialog(hdwnd, 0);
            return 1;
          }
      break;
  }
  return 0;
}

/* No classes to register. */
BOOL WINAPI RegisterDialogClasses(HINSTANCE hInst)
{
  return 1;
}
```

The resource file required by the program is shown here:

```
; Dialog box for screen saver.
#include <windows.h>
#include <scrnsave.h>
#include "scr.h"

ID_APP ICON SCRICON.ICO

STRINGTABLE
{
  IDS_DESCRIPTION "My Screen Saver #2"
}

DLG_SCRNSAVECONFIGURE DIALOGEX 18, 18, 110, 60
CAPTION "Set Screen Saver Options"
STYLE DS_MODALFRAME | WS_POPUP | WS_VISIBLE | WS_CAPTION |
      WS_SYSMENU
{
  PUSHBUTTON "OK", IDOK, 20, 40, 30, 14,
            WS_CHILD | WS_VISIBLE | WS_TABSTOP
  PUSHBUTTON "Cancel", IDCANCEL, 60, 40, 30, 14,
            WS_CHILD | WS_VISIBLE | WS_TABSTOP
  EDITTEXT IDD_EB1, 5, 5, 24, 12, ES_LEFT | WS_CHILD |
            WS_VISIBLE | WS_BORDER
  EDITTEXT IDD_EB2, 5, 20, 65, 12, ES_LEFT | WS_CHILD |
            WS_VISIBLE | WS_BORDER | ES_AUTOHSCROLL |
```

```
          WS_TABSTOP
  LTEXT "Delay in milliseconds", IDD_TEXT1, 35, 7, 100, 12
  LTEXT "Message", IDD_TEXT2, 76, 22, 30, 12
}
```

The header file SCR.H is shown here:

```
#define IDD_EB1      200
#define IDD_EB2      201

#define IDD_UPDOWN   202

#define IDD_TEXT1    203
#define IDD_TEXT2    204
```

A Closer Look at the Configurable Screen Saver

Let's begin by examining the **ScreenSaverConfigureDialog( )** function.
This dialog function allows two items to be configured: the delay period
and the message that is displayed. It is shown here for your convenience.
When this dialog function is executed, it produces the dialog box shown in
Figure 19-1.

```
/* Configuration Dialog Box Function */
BOOL WINAPI ScreenSaverConfigureDialog(HWND hdwnd, UINT message,
                  WPARAM wParam, LPARAM lParam)
{
  static HWND hEboxWnd;
  static HWND udWnd;

  switch(message) {
    case WM_INITDIALOG:
      /* open screen saver key or create, if necessary */
      RegCreateKeyEx(HKEY_CURRENT_USER,
          "Control Panel\\Screen Saver.MyScrSaver",
          0, "Screen Saver", 0, KEY_ALL_ACCESS,
          NULL, &hRegKey, &result);

      /* if key was created */
      if(result==REG_CREATED_NEW_KEY) {
        /* set its initial value */
        delay = 100;
        RegSetValueEx(hRegKey, "delay", 0,
            REG_DWORD, (LPBYTE) &delay, sizeof(DWORD));
        RegSetValueEx(hRegKey, "message", 0,
            REG_SZ, (LPBYTE) str, strlen(str)+1);
      }
```

```
              else { /* key was already in registry */
                /* get delay value */
                datasize = sizeof(DWORD);
                RegQueryValueEx(hRegKey, "delay", NULL,
                    &datatype, (LPBYTE) &delay, &datasize);

                /* get message */
                datasize = MSGSIZE;
                RegQueryValueEx(hRegKey, "message", NULL,
                    &datatype, (LPBYTE) str, &datasize);
              }

              /* create delay spin control */
              hEboxWnd = GetDlgItem(hdwnd, IDD_EB1);
              udWnd = CreateUpDownControl(
                          WS_CHILD | WS_BORDER | WS_VISIBLE |
                          UDS_SETBUDDYINT | UDS_ALIGNRIGHT,
                          20, 10, 50, 50,
                          hdwnd,
                          IDD_UPDOWN,
                          hMainInstance,
                          hEboxWnd,
                          DELAYMAX, 1, delay);

              /* initialize edit box with current message */
              SetDlgItemText(hdwnd, IDD_EB2, str);

              return 1;
          case WM_COMMAND:
            switch(LOWORD(wParam)) {
              case IDOK:
                /* set delay value */
                delay = GetDlgItemInt(hdwnd, IDD_EB1, NULL, 1);

                /* get message string */
                GetDlgItemText(hdwnd, IDD_EB2, str, MSGSIZE);

                /* update registry */
                RegSetValueEx(hRegKey, "delay", 0,
                  REG_DWORD, (LPBYTE) &delay, sizeof(DWORD));
                RegSetValueEx(hRegKey, "message", 0,
                    REG_SZ, (LPBYTE) str, strlen(str)+1);

                /* fall through to next case ... */
              case IDCANCEL:
                RegCloseKey(hRegKey);
                EndDialog(hdwnd, 0);
                return 1;
```

```
        }
      break;
    }
  return 0;
}
```

When the dialog box is first executed, it receives the standard **WM_INITDIALOG** message. When this happens, the dialog box either opens or creates the registry key **Screen Saver.MyScrSaver**, which is a subkey of **Control Panel**, which, in turn, is a subkey under the built-in key **HKEY_CURRENT_USER**. That is, the key path being opened (or created) is

HKEY_CURRENT_USER\Control Panel\Screen Saver.MyScrSaver

As mentioned, since screen saver configuration data can be modified by the Control Panel, it is usually stored under the **Control Panel** key. If the specified key does not already exist in the registry (as it won't when you first run the screen saver), then **RegCreateKeyEx( )** creates it for you. If it does already exist, then the key path is opened. The registry path created by the program (as displayed by REGEDIT) is shown in Figure 19-2. Notice that the configurable screen savers supplied with Windows NT are also shown.

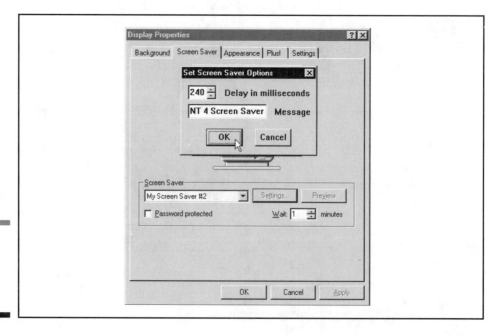

The screen saver configuration dialog box

Figure 19-1.

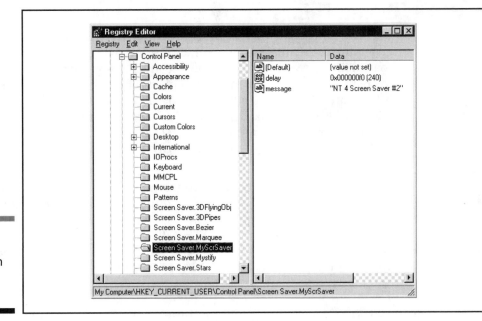

After **RegCreateKeyEx( )** returns, the contents of **result** are examined to determine whether the key was created or opened. If the key was created, then the registry is given initial, default values for the delay period and the message. Otherwise, those values are read from the registry.

Once the initialization information has been obtained, the dialog box creates a spin control, which is used to set the delay period, and an edit box, which is used to set the message. The box also contains two push buttons. If the user selects Cancel, then any changes made by the user are ignored. If the user presses OK, then the contents of the spin control and edit box are used to update the registry.

Now, look at the code inside the **WM_CREATE** statement of **ScreenSaverProc( )**. This code performs exactly the same registry sequence as the dialog box. Of course, instead of being used to allow the user to view and/or modify the configuration, **ScreenSaverProc( )** uses the registry information to control the execution of the screen saver. One other point: since it is possible that the user will execute the screen saver without ever having activated the configuration dialog box, the code inside **WM_CREATE** must also be able to create the screen saver keys and set the values. That is, you cannot simply assume that the key **Control Panel\Screen Saver.MyScrSaver** and the values **delay** and **message** are already in the registry.

Some Things to Try

The first thing that you will probably want to try is having the screen saver generate a more interesting graphics display. The purpose of this chapter was to explain the system registry and the mechanics of screen savers. It was not to create an exciting screen saver—this is left to you! One easy starting point is to create a full-screen bitmap and use it as a backdrop. Of course, you must alter the backdrop, too. Otherwise the screen saver won't actually "save" the screen. If you have a scanner, then a simple, yet effective way to create a custom screen saver is to display a digitized photo.

Because the configurable screen saver is an example program, no entries under **HKEY_LOCAL_MACHINE** relating to the program were made in the registry. Normally, entries are made under this key by installation programs when you install large applications. For fun, you might want to write your own installation program which installs the screen saver and its icon, adding an entry under **HKEY_LOCAL_MACHINE** in the process. To add an application under **HKEY_LOCAL_MACHINE**, use a key path similar to the one shown here:

HKEY_LOCAL_MACHINE\Software\YourName\AppName\Version

There is one other registry key that you might find interesting: **HKEY_PERFORMANCE_DATA**. This key is different from the other built-in keys for two reasons: First, even though you will use the registry functions to access it, it is not stored in the registry. Second, accessing this key allows you to obtain performance data about the software in your system. This key will be valuable if you are optimizing your applications.

CHAPTER 20

Supercharging Menus

We will now return to one of the most fundamental elements of a Windows program: the menu. In Chapter 4 you learned menu basics. Here, you will learn how to supercharge them!

Even though the topic of menus may seem rather tame, this is only a surface impression. The menuing subsystem supports a substantial number of sophisticated and advanced features. Menus are also a feature on which the new Windows NT 4 user interface has placed added emphasis. In this chapter we will explore two general categories of enhanced menus: dynamic and free-floating, pop-up menus. Both of these give you extended control over the contents of your application's menus and the way such menus can be used.

Dynamic Menus

A dynamic menu responds to changing conditions at run time.

Although most simple Windows NT applications statically define their menus in resource files, more sophisticated applications frequently need to add or delete menu items dynamically, during run time, in response to changing program conditions. For example, a word processor may define different options in its File menu, depending on the type of file being edited. A compiler may include one set of debugging options for C code and another for C++ programs. Menus that change in response to conditions that occur at run time are called *dynamic menus*. The advantage of dynamic menus is that they present the user with a list of options that are appropriate to the current state of the program.

Windows NT includes several menu management API functions that allow you to manipulate the contents of menus during the execution of your program. The functions used in this chapter are **InsertMenuItem( )**, **EnableMenuItem( )**, **DeleteMenu( )**, **GetMenu( )**, and **GetSubMenu( )**. Before developing an example, these (and other) functions are described.

Adding an Item to a Menu

To add an item to a menu at run time, use **InsertMenuItem( )**, shown here:

```
BOOL InsertMenuItem(HMENU hMenu, UINT Where,
                    BOOL How, LPMENUITEMINFO MenuInfo);
```

InsertMenuItem( ) adds an item to the menu whose handle is specified by *hMenu*. The new menu item is inserted into the menu immediately before the item specified by *Where*. The precise meaning of *Where* is determined by the value of *How*. If *How* is nonzero, then *Where* must contain the index at which point the new item is inserted. (Indexing begins at zero.) If *How* is zero, then *Where* must contain the menu ID of an existing item at which point the new item is inserted. The menu item being added is defined by the **MENUITEMINFO** structure pointed to by *MenuInfo*. **MENUITEMINFO** is defined like this:

```
typedef struct tagMENUITEMINFO
{
  UINT cbSize;
  UINT fMask;
  UINT fType;
  UINT fState;
  UINT wID;
  HMENU hSubMenu;
  HBITMAP hbmpChecked;
  HBITMAP hbmpUnchecked;
  DWORD dwItemData;
  LPSTR dwTypeData;
  UINT cch;
} MENUITEMINFO;
```

Here, **cbSize** must contain the size of the **MENUITEMINFO** structure.

The value of **fMask** determines which of the other members of **MENUITEMINFO** contain valid information when setting menu information. That is, it determines which of the other members are active. (It is also used to specify which members will be loaded when menu information is retrieved.) It must be a combination of one or more of these values:

fMask Value	Activates
MIIM_CHECKMARKS	**hbmpChecked** and **hbmpUnchecked**
MIIM_DATA	**dwItemData**
MIIM_ID	**wID**
MIIM_STATE	**fState**
MIIM_SUBMENU	**hSubMenu**
MIIM_TYPE	**fType** and **dwTypeData**

The type of the menu item is determined by **fType**. It can be any valid combination of the following values:

fType Value	Meaning
MFT_BITMAP	The low-order word of **dwTypeData** specifies a bitmap handle. The menu item is displayed as a bitmap.
MFT_MENUBARBREAK	For menu bar, causes the item to be put on a new line. For pop-up menus, causes the item to be put in a different column. In this case, the item is separated using a bar.
MFT_MENUBREAK	Same as **MFT_MENUBARBREAK** except that no separator bar is used.
MF_OWNDERDRAW	Owner drawn item.
MFT_RADIOCHECK	Radio button check mark style is used when the item is selected rather than the normal menu check mark. **hbmpChecked** must be NULL.
MFT_RIGHTJUSTIFY	For menu bars only. Right justifies the item. Subsequent items are also right justified.
MFT_SEPARATOR	Places a horizontal dividing line between menu items. The values in **dwTypeData** and **cch** are ignored. This type cannot be used for menu bar items.
MFT_STRING	**dwTypeData** is a pointer to a string that describes the menu item.

The state of the menu item is determined by **fState**. It can be any valid combination of the following values:

fState Value	Meaning
MFS_CHECKED	Item is checked.
MFS_DEFAULT	Item is the default selection.
MFS_DISABLED	Item is disabled.
MFS_ENABLED	Item is enabled. Items are enabled by default.
MFS_GRAYED	Item is disabled and grayed.
MFS_HILITE	Item is highlighted.
MFS_UNCHECKED	Item is unchecked.
MFS_UNHILITE	Item is unhighlighted. Items are unhighlighted by default.

The ID value associated with the menu item is specified in **wID**.

If the item being inserted is a pop-up submenu, then its handle must be in **hSubMenu**. Otherwise, this value must be **NULL**.

You can specify bitmaps that will be used to indicate a menu item's checked and unchecked state in **hbmpChecked** and **hbmpUnchecked**. To use the default check mark, specify **NULL** for both of these members.

The value of **dwItemData** is application-dependent. If unused, set this value to zero.

The menu item itself is specified in **dwTypeData**. It will be either a pointer to a string or the handle of a bitmap, depending upon the value of **fType**.

When a menu item is being retrieved, **cch** will contain the length of the string if **fType** is **MFT_STRING**. The value of **cch** is ignored when the menu item is being set.

InsertMenuItem( ) returns nonzero if successful and zero on failure.

PORTABILITY: **InsertMenuItem( )** is not supported by Windows 3.1. Instead, menu items were dynamically inserted into a menu using **AppendMenu( )** or **InsertMenu( )**. While these functions are still supported by Windows NT, the use of **InsertMenuItem( )** is recommended.

Deleting a Menu Item

To remove a menu item, use the **DeleteMenu( )** function, shown here.

BOOL DeleteMenu(HMENU *hMenu*, UINT *ItemID*, UINT *How*);

Here, *hMenu* specifies the handle of the menu to be affected. The item to be removed is specified in *ItemID*. The value of *How* determines how *ItemID* is interpreted. If *How* is **MF_BYPOSITION,** then the value in *ItemID* must be the index of the item to be deleted. This index is the position of the item within the menu, with the first menu item being zero. If *How* is **MF_BYCOMMAND,** then *ItemID* is the ID associated with the menu item. **DeleteMenu( )** returns nonzero if successful and zero on failure.

If the menu item deleted is a pop-up submenu, then that pop-up menu is also destroyed. There is no need to call **DestroyMenu( )**. (**DestroyMenu( )** is described in Chapter 4.)

Obtaining a Handle to a Menu

As you have just seen, to add or delete a menu item requires a handle to the menu. To obtain the handle of the main menu, use **GetMenu( )**, shown here:

HMENU GetMenu(HWND *hwnd*);

GetMenu( ) returns the handle of the menu associated with the window specified by *hwnd*. It returns **NULL** on failure.

Given a handle to a window's main menu, you can easily obtain the handles of the pop-up submenus contained in the main menu by using **GetSubMenu( )**. Its prototype is shown here:

HMENU GetSubMenu(HMENU *hMenu*, int *ItemPos*);

Here, *hMenu* is the handle of the parent menu and *ItemPos* is the position of the desired pop-up menu within the parent window. (The first position is zero.) The function returns the handle of the specified pop-up menu or **NULL** on failure.

Obtaining the Size of a Menu

Frequently, when working with menus dynamically, you will need to know how many items are in a menu. To obtain the number of menu items, use **GetMenuItemCount( )**, shown here:

int GetMenuItemCount(HMENU *hMenu*);

Here, *hMenu* is the handle of the menu in question. The function returns –1 on failure.

Enabling and Disabling a Menu Item

Sometimes a menu item will only apply to certain situations and not to others. In such cases, you may wish to temporarily disable an item, enabling it later. To accomplish this, use the **EnableMenuItem( )** function, shown here:

BOOL EnableMenuItem(HMENU *hMenu*, UINT *ItemID*, UINT *How*);

The handle of the menu is passed in *hMenu*. The item to be enabled or disabled is specified in *ItemID*. The value of *How* determines two things. First, it specifies how *ItemID* is interpreted. If *How* contains **MF_BYPOSITION**, then the value in *ItemID* must be the index of the item to be deleted. This index is the position of the item within the menu, with the first menu item being zero. If *How* contains **MF_BYCOMMAND**, then *ItemID* is the ID associated with the menu item. The value in *How* also determines whether the item will be enabled or disabled, based on which of the following values are present.

MF_DISABLED	Disables the new menu item.
MF_ENABLED	Enables the new menu item.
MF_GRAYED	Disables the menu item and turns it gray.

To construct the desired value of *How,* OR together the appropriate values.

EnableMenuItem( ) returns the previous state of the item or –1 on failure.

Moving Up to NT 4: GetMenuItemInfo( ) and SetMenuItemInfo( )

Sometimes you will want to obtain detailed information about or make detailed adjustments to a menu. The easiest way to do this is to use two of Windows NT 4's new menu management functions, **GetMenuItemInfo( )** and **SetMenuItemInfo( )**, whose prototypes are shown here:

```
BOOL GetMenuItemInfo(HMENU hMenu, UINT ItemID,
              BOOL How, LPMENUITEMINFO MenuInfo);
BOOL SetMenuItemInfo(HMENU hMenu, UINT ItemID,
              BOOL How, LPMENUITEMINFO MenuInfo);
```

These functions get and set all of the information associated with a menu item. The menu containing the item is specified by *hMenu*. The menu item is specified by *ItemID*. The precise meaning of *ItemID* is determined by the value of *How*. If *How* is nonzero, then *ItemID* must contain the index of the item. If *How* is zero, then *ItemID* must contain the menu ID of the item. For **GetMenuItemInfo( )**, the **MENUITEMINFO** structure pointed to by *MenuInfo* will receive the current information about the item. For **SetMenuItemInfo( )**, the contents of the structure pointed to by *MenuInfo* will be used to set the menu item's information.

Both functions return nonzero if successful and zero on failure.

As you can guess, you could use **SetMenuItemInfo( )** to perform relatively simple menu management functions, such as enabling or disabling a menu item. However, using **SetMenuItemInfo( )** and **GetMenuItemInfo( )** for these types of operations is inefficient. They should be reserved for more complex or subtle menu manipulations.

Dynamically Adding Menu Items

Now that the basic menu management functions have been discussed, it is time to see them in action. Let's begin by dynamically inserting and deleting an item. To do this, we will use a simple program that draws various GDI objects in the main window. The program contains two menus. The first menu is called Options. The second menu is called Draw. The Options menu lets the user select various options relating to the program. The Draw menu lets the user select which object will be drawn. The following program demonstrates dynamic menu management by adding an item to or deleting an item from its Options menu. Pay special attention to the **IDM_ADDITEM** and **IDM_DELITEM** cases inside **WindowFunc( )**. This is the code that adds or deletes a menu item. Sample output is shown in Figure 20-1.

```
/* Dynamically managing menus. */

#include <windows.h>
#include <string.h>
#include <stdio.h>
#include "menu.h"

LRESULT CALLBACK WindowFunc(HWND, UINT, WPARAM, LPARAM);

char szWinName[] = "MyWin"; /* name of window class */

int WINAPI WinMain(HINSTANCE hThisInst, HINSTANCE hPrevInst,
                   LPSTR lpszArgs, int nWinMode)
{
  HWND hwnd;
  MSG msg;
  WNDCLASSEX wcl;
  HACCEL hAccel;
```

```
/* Define a window class. */
wcl.cbSize = sizeof(WNDCLASSEX);
wcl.hInstance = hThisInst; /* handle to this instance */
wcl.lpszClassName = szWinName; /* window class name */
wcl.lpfnWndProc = WindowFunc; /* window function */
wcl.style = 0; /* default style */

wcl.hIcon = LoadIcon(NULL, IDI_APPLICATION);
wcl.hIconSm = LoadIcon(NULL, IDI_APPLICATION);
wcl.hCursor = LoadCursor(NULL, IDC_ARROW);

/* specify name of menu resource */
wcl.lpszMenuName = "DynMenu"; /* main menu */

wcl.cbClsExtra = 0; /* no extra */
wcl.cbWndExtra = 0; /* information needed */

/* Make the window white. */
wcl.hbrBackground = GetStockObject(WHITE_BRUSH);

/* Register the window class. */
if(!RegisterClassEx(&wcl)) return 0;

/* Now that a window class has been registered, a window
   can be created. */
hwnd = CreateWindow(
  szWinName, /* name of window class */
  "Using Dynamic Menus", /* title */
  WS_OVERLAPPEDWINDOW, /* standard window */
  CW_USEDEFAULT, /* X coordinate - let Windows decide */
  CW_USEDEFAULT, /* Y coordinate - let Windows decide */
  CW_USEDEFAULT, /* width - let Windows decide */
  CW_USEDEFAULT, /* height - let Windows decide */
  HWND_DESKTOP, /* no parent window */
  NULL, /* no override of class menu */
  hThisInst, /* handle of this instance of the program */
  NULL /* no additional arguments */
);

/* load the keyboard accelerators */
hAccel = LoadAccelerators(hThisInst, "DynMenu");

/* Display the window. */
ShowWindow(hwnd, nWinMode);
UpdateWindow(hwnd);

/* Create the message loop. */
```

```
    while(GetMessage(&msg, NULL, 0, 0))
    {
      if(!TranslateAccelerator(hwnd, hAccel, &msg)) {
        TranslateMessage(&msg); /* translate keyboard messages */
        DispatchMessage(&msg); /* return control to Windows NT */
      }
    }
    return msg.wParam;
}

/* This function is called by Windows NT and is passed
   messages from the message queue.
*/
LRESULT CALLBACK WindowFunc(HWND hwnd, UINT message,
                             WPARAM wParam, LPARAM lParam)
{
  HDC hdc;
  RECT rect;
  HMENU hmenu, hsubmenu;
  int response;
  int count;
  MENUITEMINFO miInfo;

  switch(message) {
    case WM_COMMAND:
      switch(LOWORD(wParam)) {
        case IDM_ADDITEM: /* dynamically add menu item */
          /* get handle of main menu */
          hmenu = GetMenu(hwnd);

          /* get handle of 1st popup menu */
          hsubmenu = GetSubMenu(hmenu, 0);

          /* get number of items in the popup */
          count = GetMenuItemCount(hsubmenu);

          /* append a separator */
          miInfo.cbSize = sizeof(MENUITEMINFO);
          miInfo.fMask = MIIM_TYPE;
          miInfo.fType = MFT_SEPARATOR;
          miInfo.fState = 0;
          miInfo.wID = 0;
          miInfo.hSubMenu = NULL;
          miInfo.hbmpChecked = NULL;
          miInfo.hbmpUnchecked = NULL;
          miInfo.dwItemData = 0;
          miInfo.dwTypeData = 0;
          InsertMenuItem(hsubmenu, count, 1, &miInfo);
```

```
                    /* append new menu item */
                    miInfo.fMask = MIIM_TYPE | MIIM_ID;
                    miInfo.fType = MFT_STRING;
                    miInfo.wID = IDM_NEW;
                    miInfo.dwTypeData = "E&rase (This is New Item)";
                    InsertMenuItem(hsubmenu, count+1, 1, &miInfo);

                    /* deactivate the Add Item option */
                    EnableMenuItem(hsubmenu, IDM_ADDITEM,
                                MF_BYCOMMAND | MF_GRAYED);

                    /* activate the Delete Item option */
                    EnableMenuItem(hsubmenu, IDM_DELITEM,
                                MF_BYCOMMAND | MF_ENABLED);
                    break;
                case IDM_DELITEM: /* dynamically delete menu item */
                    /* get handle of main menu */
                    hmenu = GetMenu(hwnd);

                    /* get handle of 1st popup menu */
                    hsubmenu = GetSubMenu(hmenu, 0);

                    /* delete the new item and the separator */
                    count = GetMenuItemCount(hsubmenu);
                    DeleteMenu(hsubmenu, count-1, MF_BYPOSITION | MF_GRAYED);
                    DeleteMenu(hsubmenu, count-2, MF_BYPOSITION | MF_GRAYED);

                    /* reactivate the Add Item option */
                    EnableMenuItem(hsubmenu, IDM_ADDITEM,
                                MF_BYCOMMAND | MF_ENABLED);

                    /* deactivate the Delete Item option */
                    EnableMenuItem(hsubmenu, IDM_DELITEM,
                                MF_BYCOMMAND | MF_GRAYED);
                    break;
                case IDM_EXIT:
                    response = MessageBox(hwnd, "Quit the Program?",
                                    "Exit", MB_YESNO);
                    if(response == IDYES) PostQuitMessage(0);
                    break;
                case IDM_NEW: /* erase window */
                    hdc = GetDC(hwnd);
                    GetClientRect(hwnd, &rect);
                    SelectObject(hdc, GetStockObject(WHITE_BRUSH));
```

```
          PatBlt(hdc, 0, 0, rect.right, rect.bottom, PATCOPY);
          ReleaseDC(hwnd, hdc);
          break;
        case IDM_LINES:
          hdc = GetDC(hwnd);
          MoveToEx(hdc, 10, 10, NULL);
          LineTo(hdc, 100, 100);
          LineTo(hdc, 100, 50);
          LineTo(hdc, 50, 180);
          ReleaseDC(hwnd, hdc);
          break;
        case IDM_ELLIPSES:
          hdc = GetDC(hwnd);
          Ellipse(hdc, 100, 100, 300, 200);
          Ellipse(hdc, 200, 100, 300, 200);
          ReleaseDC(hwnd, hdc);
          break;
        case IDM_RECTANGLES:
          hdc = GetDC(hwnd);
          Rectangle(hdc, 100, 100, 24, 260);
          Rectangle(hdc, 110, 120, 124, 170);
          ReleaseDC(hwnd, hdc);
          break;
        case IDM_HELP:
          MessageBox(hwnd, "Try Adding a Menu Item",
                     "Help", MB_OK);
          break;
      }
      break;
    case WM_DESTROY: /* terminate the program */
      PostQuitMessage(0);
      break;
    default:
      /* Let Windows NT process any messages not specified in
         the preceding switch statement. */
      return DefWindowProc(hwnd, message, wParam, lParam);
  }
  return 0;
}
```

The resource file required by the program is shown here:

```
; Dynamic Menus
#include <windows.h>
```

```
#include "menu.h"

DynMenu MENU
{
  POPUP "&Options"
  {
    MENUITEM "&Add Item\tF2", IDM_ADDITEM
    MENUITEM "&Delete Item\tF3", IDM_DELITEM, GRAYED
    MENUITEM "E&xit\tF10", IDM_EXIT
  }
  POPUP "&Draw"
  {
    MENUITEM "&Lines\tF4", IDM_LINES
    MENUITEM "&Ellipses\tF5", IDM_ELLIPSES
    MENUITEM "&Rectangles\tF6", IDM_RECTANGLES
  }
  MENUITEM "&Help", IDM_HELP
}

; Define menu accelerators
DynMenu ACCELERATORS
{
  VK_F2, IDM_ADDITEM, VIRTKEY
  VK_F3, IDM_DELITEM, VIRTKEY
  VK_F10, IDM_EXIT, VIRTKEY
  VK_F4, IDM_LINES, VIRTKEY
  VK_F5, IDM_ELLIPSES, VIRTKEY
  VK_F6, IDM_RECTANGLES, VIRTKEY
  VK_F1, IDM_HELP, VIRTKEY
}
```

The MENU.H header file is shown here. It also includes a few values that are used by later programs in this chapter.

```
#define IDM_EXIT          100
#define IDM_LINES         101
#define IDM_ELLIPSES      102
#define IDM_RECTANGLES    103
#define IDM_HELP          104

#define IDM_ADDITEM       200
#define IDM_DELITEM       201

#define IDM_NEW           300
#define IDM_NEW2          301
#define IDM_NEW3          302
```

A Closer Look at the First Dynamic Menu Program

Most of this program is straightforward and easy to understand. When the program begins, the Options menu initially contains only three selections: Add Item, Delete Item, and Exit. Initially, Delete Item is grayed and, therefore, may not be selected. To add the Erase option, select Add Item. After the Erase item has been dynamically added to the menu, the Delete Item option is activated and the Add Item option is grayed. When Delete Item is selected, Erase is removed from the menu, Add Item is reactivated, and Delete Item is once again grayed. This procedure prevents the new menu item from being added or deleted more than once.

Look closely at the code under **IDM_ADDITEM**. Notice how the handle to the Options pop-up menu is obtained. First, you must retrieve the handle of its outer menu, which in this case is the program's main menu, using **GetMenu( )**. Next, you must use **GetSubMenu( )** to obtain the handle of its first pop-up menu, which is Options. Next, the program obtains a count of the number of items in the menu. This step is technically unnecessary since, in this simple example, we already know this value. However, this step is included for the sake of illustration because, in a real-world program, you may not always know how many items a menu contains. Next, the program adds a separator and then the Erase menu item.

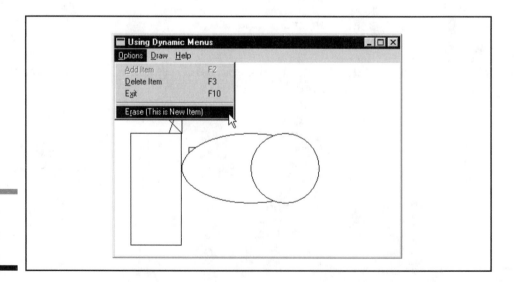

Adding
menu items
dynamically

Figure 20-1.

Creating Dynamic Pop-Up Menus

To create a
pop-up menu,
use Create-
PopupMenu( ).

In addition to adding new items to an existing menu, you can dynamically create an entire pop-up menu. (That is, you can create a pop-up menu at run time.) Once you have created the menu, it can then be added to an existing menu. To dynamically create a pop-up menu, you first use the API function **CreatePopupMenu( )**, shown here:

HMENU CreatePopupMenu(void);

This function creates an empty menu and returns a handle to it. After you have created a menu, you add items to it using **InsertMenuItem( )**. Once the menu is fully constructed, you can add it to an existing menu, also using **InsertMenuItem( )**.

20

Menus created using **CreatePopupMenu( )** must be destroyed. If the menu is attached to a window, then it will be destroyed automatically. A menu is also automatically destroyed when it is removed from a parent menu by a call to **DeleteMenu( )**. Dynamic menus can be destroyed explicitly by calling **DestroyMenu( )**.

The following program is an enhanced version of the preceding program. It dynamically creates a pop-up menu that contains three items: Erase, Black Pen, and Red Pen. Selecting Erase erases the window. Choosing Black Pen selects the black pen (which is the default pen). Choosing Red Pen selects the red pen. After a pen has been selected, it is used to draw the shapes available in the Draw menu. Pay close attention to the way that the pop-up menu is constructed and attached to the Options menu.

```
/* Adding a popup menu. */

#include <windows.h>
#include <string.h>
#include <stdio.h>
#include "menu.h"

LRESULT CALLBACK WindowFunc(HWND, UINT, WPARAM, LPARAM);

char szWinName[] = "MyWin"; /* name of window class */

int WINAPI WinMain(HINSTANCE hThisInst, HINSTANCE hPrevInst,
                   LPSTR lpszArgs, int nWinMode)
{
  HWND hwnd;
  MSG msg;
```

```
WNDCLASSEX wcl;
HACCEL hAccel;

/* Define a window class. */
wcl.cbSize = sizeof(WNDCLASSEX);
wcl.hInstance = hThisInst; /* handle to this instance */
wcl.lpszClassName = szWinName; /* window class name */
wcl.lpfnWndProc = WindowFunc; /* window function */
wcl.style = 0; /* default style */

wcl.hIcon = LoadIcon(NULL, IDI_APPLICATION);
wcl.hIconSm = LoadIcon(NULL, IDI_APPLICATION);
wcl.hCursor = LoadCursor(NULL, IDC_ARROW);

/* specify name of menu resource */
wcl.lpszMenuName = "DynPopUpMenu"; /* main menu */

wcl.cbClsExtra = 0; /* no extra */
wcl.cbWndExtra = 0; /* information needed */

/* Make the window white. */
wcl.hbrBackground = GetStockObject(WHITE_BRUSH);

/* Register the window class. */
if(!RegisterClassEx(&wcl)) return 0;

/* Now that a window class has been registered, a window
   can be created. */
hwnd = CreateWindow(
  szWinName, /* name of window class */
  "Adding a Popup Menu", /* title */
  WS_OVERLAPPEDWINDOW, /* standard window */
  CW_USEDEFAULT, /* X coordinate - let Windows decide */
  CW_USEDEFAULT, /* Y coordinate - let Windows decide */
  CW_USEDEFAULT, /* width - let Windows decide */
  CW_USEDEFAULT, /* height - let Windows decide */
  HWND_DESKTOP, /* no parent window */
  NULL, /* no override of class menu */
  hThisInst, /* handle of this instance of the program */
  NULL /* no additional arguments */
);

/* load the keyboard accelerators */
hAccel = LoadAccelerators(hThisInst, "DynPopUpMenu");

/* Display the window. */
ShowWindow(hwnd, nWinMode);
UpdateWindow(hwnd);
```

```
    /* Create the message loop. */
    while(GetMessage(&msg, NULL, 0, 0))
    {
      if(!TranslateAccelerator(hwnd, hAccel, &msg)) {
        TranslateMessage(&msg); /* translate keyboard messages */
        DispatchMessage(&msg); /* return control to Windows NT */
      }
    }
    return msg.wParam;
}

/* This function is called by Windows NT and is passed
   messages from the message queue.
*/
LRESULT CALLBACK WindowFunc(HWND hwnd, UINT message,
                                WPARAM wParam, LPARAM lParam)
{
  HDC hdc;
  HMENU hmenu, hsubmenu;
  RECT rect;
  static HMENU hpopup;
  int response;
  int count;
  MENUITEMINFO miInfo;
  static HPEN hCurrentPen, hRedPen;

  switch(message) {
    case WM_CREATE:
      /* create red pen */
      hRedPen = CreatePen(PS_SOLID, 1, RGB(255, 0, 0));
      /* get black pen */
      hCurrentPen = GetStockObject(BLACK_PEN);
      break;
    case WM_COMMAND:
      switch(LOWORD(wParam)) {
        case IDM_ADDITEM: /* dynamically add popup menu */
          /* get handle of main menu */
          hmenu = GetMenu(hwnd);

          /* get handle of 1st popup menu */
          hsubmenu = GetSubMenu(hmenu, 0);

          /* get number of items in the menu */
          count = GetMenuItemCount(hsubmenu);

          /* create new popup menu */
          hpopup = CreatePopupMenu();
```

```
/* add items to dynamic popup menu */
miInfo.cbSize = sizeof(MENUITEMINFO);
miInfo.fMask = MIIM_TYPE | MIIM_ID;
miInfo.fType = MFT_STRING;
miInfo.wID = IDM_NEW;
miInfo.hSubMenu = NULL;
miInfo.hbmpChecked = NULL;
miInfo.hbmpUnchecked = NULL;
miInfo.dwItemData = 0;
miInfo.dwTypeData = "&Erase";
InsertMenuItem(hpopup, 0, 1, &miInfo);

miInfo.dwTypeData = "&Black Pen";
miInfo.wID = IDM_NEW2;
InsertMenuItem(hpopup, 1, 1, &miInfo);

miInfo.dwTypeData = "&Red Pen";
miInfo.wID = IDM_NEW3;
InsertMenuItem(hpopup, 2, 1, &miInfo);

/* append a separator */
miInfo.cbSize = sizeof(MENUITEMINFO);
miInfo.fMask = MIIM_TYPE;
miInfo.fType = MFT_SEPARATOR;
miInfo.fState = 0;
miInfo.wID = 0;
miInfo.hSubMenu = NULL;
miInfo.hbmpChecked = NULL;
miInfo.hbmpUnchecked = NULL;
miInfo.dwItemData = 0;
InsertMenuItem(hsubmenu, count, 1, &miInfo);

/* append popup menu to main menu */
miInfo.fMask = MIIM_TYPE | MIIM_SUBMENU;
miInfo.fType = MFT_STRING;
miInfo.hSubMenu = hpopup;
miInfo.dwTypeData = "&This is New Popup";
InsertMenuItem(hsubmenu, count+1, 1, &miInfo);

/* deactivate the Add Popup option */
EnableMenuItem(hsubmenu, IDM_ADDITEM,
               MF_BYCOMMAND | MF_GRAYED);

/* activate the Delete Popup option */
EnableMenuItem(hsubmenu, IDM_DELITEM,
               MF_BYCOMMAND | MF_ENABLED);
break;
```

```
case IDM_DELITEM: /* dynamically delete popup menu */
  /* get handle of main menu */
  hmenu = GetMenu(hwnd);

  /* get handle of 1st popup menu */
  hsubmenu = GetSubMenu(hmenu, 0);

  /* delete the new popup menu and the separator */
  count = GetMenuItemCount(hsubmenu);
  DeleteMenu(hsubmenu, count-1, MF_BYPOSITION | MF_GRAYED);
  DeleteMenu(hsubmenu, count-2, MF_BYPOSITION | MF_GRAYED);

  /* reactivate the Add Popup option */
  EnableMenuItem(hsubmenu, IDM_ADDITEM,
                 MF_BYCOMMAND | MF_ENABLED);


  /* deactivate the Delete Popup option */
  EnableMenuItem(hsubmenu, IDM_DELITEM,
                 MF_BYCOMMAND | MF_GRAYED);
  break;
case IDM_EXIT:
  response = MessageBox(hwnd, "Quit the Program?",
                        "Exit", MB_YESNO);
  if(response == IDYES) PostQuitMessage(0);
  break;
case IDM_NEW: /* erase */
  hdc = GetDC(hwnd);
  GetClientRect(hwnd, &rect);
  SelectObject(hdc, GetStockObject(WHITE_BRUSH));
  PatBlt(hdc, 0, 0, rect.right, rect.bottom, PATCOPY);
  ReleaseDC(hwnd, hdc);
  break;
case IDM_NEW2: /* select black pen */
  hCurrentPen = GetStockObject(BLACK_PEN);
  break;
case IDM_NEW3: /* select red pen */
  hCurrentPen = hRedPen;
  break;
case IDM_LINES:
  hdc = GetDC(hwnd);
  SelectObject(hdc, hCurrentPen);
  MoveToEx(hdc, 10, 10, NULL);
  LineTo(hdc, 100, 100);
  LineTo(hdc, 100, 50);
  LineTo(hdc, 50, 180);
  ReleaseDC(hwnd, hdc);
```

```
          break;
        case IDM_ELLIPSES:
          hdc = GetDC(hwnd);
          SelectObject(hdc, hCurrentPen);
          Ellipse(hdc, 100, 100, 300, 200);
          Ellipse(hdc, 200, 100, 300, 200);
          ReleaseDC(hwnd, hdc);
          break;
        case IDM_RECTANGLES:
          hdc = GetDC(hwnd);
          SelectObject(hdc, hCurrentPen);
          Rectangle(hdc, 100, 100, 24, 260);
          Rectangle(hdc, 110, 120, 124, 170);
          ReleaseDC(hwnd, hdc);
          break;
        case IDM_HELP:
          MessageBox(hwnd, "Try Adding a Menu", "Help", MB_OK);
          break;
      }
      break;
    case WM_DESTROY: /* terminate the program */
      PostQuitMessage(0);
      break;
    default:
      /* Let Windows NT process any messages not specified in
         the preceding switch statement. */
      return DefWindowProc(hwnd, message, wParam, lParam);
  }
  return 0;
}
```

$eol

The header file MENU.H is the same as was used before. However, this program uses the following resource file:

```
; Dynamic Popup Menus
#include <windows.h>
#include "menu.h"

DynPopUpMenu MENU
{
  POPUP "&Options"
  {
    MENUITEM "&Add Popup\tF2", IDM_ADDITEM
    MENUITEM "&Delete Popup\tF3", IDM_DELITEM, GRAYED
    MENUITEM "E&xit\tF10", IDM_EXIT
```

```
    }
    POPUP "&Draw"
    {
      MENUITEM "&Lines\tF4", IDM_LINES
      MENUITEM "&Ellipses\tF5", IDM_ELLIPSES
      MENUITEM "&Rectangles\tF6", IDM_RECTANGLES
    }
    MENUITEM "&Help", IDM_HELP
}

; Define menu accelerators
DynPopUpMenu ACCELERATORS
{
  VK_F2, IDM_ADDITEM, VIRTKEY
  VK_F3, IDM_DELITEM, VIRTKEY
  VK_F10, IDM_EXIT, VIRTKEY
  VK_F4, IDM_LINES, VIRTKEY
  VK_F5, IDM_ELLIPSES, VIRTKEY
  VK_F6, IDM_RECTANGLES, VIRTKEY
  VK_F1, IDM_HELP, VIRTKEY
}
```

Sample output from this program is shown in Figure 20-2.

Most of the program is straightforward. However, notice one important point: The **MIIM_SUBMENU** flag must be set and the handle of the pop-up menu must be in **hSubMenu** when a pop-up menu is inserted into a menu.

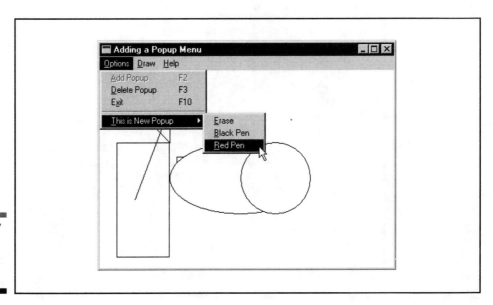

A dynamically created pop-up menu

Figure 20-2.

IN DEPTH

Changing the Menu Bar

Menu items may be added to the menu bar itself, in exactly the same way they are added to any other menu. There is only one additional action your program must take: it must redraw the menu bar in order for the changes to be displayed. To accomplish this, call **DrawMenuBar( )**, shown here:

    BOOL DrawMenuBar(HWND *hwnd*);

Here, *hwnd* specifies the handle of the window whose menu bar will be redrawn. The function returns nonzero if successful and zero on failure.

To try modifying the contents of the menu bar, change the **IDM_ADDITEM** handler in the pop-up menu program so that it looks like this:

```
/* dynamically add a popup menu to menu bar*/
case IDM_ADDITEM:
  /* get handle of menu bar */
  hmenu = GetMenu(hwnd);

  /* get number of items in the menu bar */
  count = GetMenuItemCount(hmenu);

  /* create new popup menu */
  hpopup = CreatePopupMenu();
  /* add items to dynamic popup menu */
  miInfo.cbSize = sizeof(MENUITEMINFO);
  miInfo.fMask = MIIM_TYPE | MIIM_ID;
  miInfo.fType = MFT_STRING;
  miInfo.wID = IDM_NEW;
  miInfo.hSubMenu = NULL;
  miInfo.hbmpChecked = NULL;
  miInfo.hbmpUnchecked = NULL;
  miInfo.dwItemData = 0;
  miInfo.dwTypeData = "&Erase";
  InsertMenuItem(hpopup, 0, 1, &miInfo);

  miInfo.dwTypeData = "&Black Pen";
  miInfo.wID = IDM_NEW2;
  InsertMenuItem(hpopup, 1, 1, &miInfo);

  miInfo.dwTypeData = "&Red Pen";
```

```
miInfo.wID = IDM_NEW3;
InsertMenuItem(hpopup, 2, 1, &miInfo);

/* append popup menu to menu bar */
miInfo.fMask = MIIM_TYPE | MIIM_SUBMENU;
miInfo.fType = MFT_STRING;
miInfo.hSubMenu = hpopup;
miInfo.dwTypeData = "&New Popup";
InsertMenuItem(hmenu, count+1, 1, &miInfo);

/* get handle of 1st popup menu */
hsubmenu = GetSubMenu(hmenu, 0);
/* deactivate the Add Popup option */
EnableMenuItem(hsubmenu, IDM_ADDITEM, MF_BYCOMMAND |
               MF_GRAYED);
/* activate the Delete Popup option */
EnableMenuItem(hsubmenu, IDM_DELITEM, MF_BYCOMMAND |
               MF_ENABLED);

/* redraw the menu bar */
DrawMenuBar(hwnd);
break;
```

After making these changes, the pop-up menu will be added to the menu bar instead of the first drop-down menu. You should also make similar changes to the **IDM_DELITEM** handler so that it deletes the selection from the menu bar. Here is what the menu bar looks like after adding the new item:

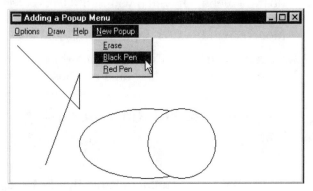

If you want to make extensive changes to the contents of the menu bar, you might want to use **SetMenu( )** instead of making the changes individually. **SetMenu( )** replaces the entire main menu of a window with another. It has this prototype:

BOOL SetMenu(HWND *hwnd*, HMENU *hmenu*);

Here, *hwnd* is the handle of the window being affected and *hmenu* is the handle of the new menu. The old menu should be destroyed by calling **DestroyMenu( )**. If you know that your application will need to use two or more different main menus, you could construct them in advance and then use **SetMenu( )** to swap them in, when needed. This approach will usually be more efficient than making many changes to the menu bar by hand.

Finally, if you want to dynamically create a main menu (i.e., a menu bar), use the **CreateMenu( )** function. Its prototype is shown here:

HMENU CreateMenu(void);

It returns a handle to an empty menu which your program must then fill in using the same approach as that used for dynamic pop-up menus.

Using Floating Menus

Floating menus are not attached to the menu bar.

Although stand-alone, or *floating,* menus have been available to Windows programmers for quite some time, they have taken on a new importance in Windows NT 4. They have also gained some new features and abilities. Further, interest in floating menus has increased because they are now part and parcel of the new Windows NT 4 user interface. For example, when you click the right mouse button on nearly any interface item, you will activate a floating menu. Or, when you right-click on the desktop, you will see a menu that allows you to perform various functions relating to the desktop. No modern Windows NT application should be without these types of menus.

Floating menus are also called *context menus* and *shortcut menus*. This book will use the term floating menu because it is the most descriptive.

Activating a Floating Menu

A floating menu is activated using **TrackPopupMenuEx( )**. Its prototype is shown here:

BOOL TrackPopupMenuEx(HMENU *hMenu*, UINT *Flags*, int *X*, int *Y*,
                    HWND *hwnd*, LPTPMPARMS *OffLimits*);

Here, *hMenu* is the handle of the menu that will be activated.

Various options are specified in *Flags*. This parameter may be any valid (i.e., non-mutually exclusive) combination of the values shown in Table 20-1.

Flags Value	Meaning
TPM_BOTTOMALIGN	Floating menu pops up with bottom edge at *Y*.
TPM_CENTERALIGN	Floating menu pops up centered left-to-right relative to *X*.
TPM_HORIZONAL	If the menu cannot be fully displayed at the location specified by *X* and *Y*, the horizontal alignment of the menu is given priority.
TPM_LEFTALIGN	Floating menu pops up with left side at *X*. (This is the default.).
TPM_LEFTBUTTON	Left mouse button operates the menu. (This is the default.)
TPM_NONOTIFY	Menu does not send notification messages.
TPM_RETURNCMD	The ID of the item selected is returned.
TPM_RIGHTALIGN	Floating menu pops up with right side at *X*.
TPM_RIGHTBUTTON	Right mouse button operates the menu.
TPM_TOPALGIN	Floating menu pops up with top edge at *Y*. (This is the default.)
TPM_VCENTERALIGN	Floating menu pops up centered top-to-bottom relative to *Y*.
TPM_VERTICAL	If the menu cannot be fully displayed at the location specified by *X* and *Y*, the vertical alignment of the menu is given priority.

20

The Values for the *Flags* Parameter of **TrackPopup-MenuEx( )** **Table 20-1.**

You may specify zero for *Flags*. Doing so causes the default configuration to be used.

The location *on the screen* at which to display the menu is specified in *X* and *Y*. Therefore, these coordinates are in terms of screen units, not window or dialog units. To convert between screen and window units, use either the **ClientToScreen( )** or the **ScreenToClient( )** function. In its default configuration, **TrackPopupMenuEx( )** displays the menu with its upper left corner at the location specified by *X* and *Y*. However, you can use the *Flags* parameter to alter this placement.

The handle of the window that invokes **TrackPopupMenuEx( )** must be passed in *hwnd*.

You may specify a portion of the screen that is off limits to the floating menu. To do so, specify the extent of that region in the **TPMPARAMS** structure pointed to by *OffLimts*. **TPMPARAMS** is defined like this:

```
typedef struct tagTPMPARAMS
{
  UINT cbSize;
  RECT rcExclude;
} TPMPARAMS;
```

Here, **cbSize** must contain the size of the **TPMPARAMS** structure. **rcExclude** contains the coordinates of the excluded region. The coordinates specified in **rcExclude** must be in terms of screen units. *OffLimts* may be **NULL** if no part of the screen is being excluded.

TrackPopupMenuEx( ) returns nonzero if successful and zero on failure. However, if **TPM_RETURNCMD** is specified in *Flags*, then the ID of the menu item selected is returned. Zero is returned if no item is chosen.

PORTABILITY: In Windows 3.1, floating menus were activated using **TrackPopupMenu( )**. This function is still supported by Windows NT. However, the new function **TrackPopupMenuEx( )** is recommended because it gives you more control.

Demonstrating Floating Menus

The following program modifies the previous program by making the Draw menu into a floating, pop-up menu. Thus, it is no longer part of the menu bar. Instead, it is activated by pressing the right mouse button. When this occurs, the floating menu is displayed at the location of the mouse pointer when the button was pressed. Sample output is shown in Figure 20-3.

```
/* Floating Menus */

#include <windows.h>
#include <string.h>
#include <stdio.h>
#include "menu.h"

LRESULT CALLBACK WindowFunc(HWND, UINT, WPARAM, LPARAM);

char szWinName[] = "MyWin"; /* name of window class */

HINSTANCE hInst;
```

```
int WINAPI WinMain(HINSTANCE hThisInst, HINSTANCE hPrevInst,
                   LPSTR lpszArgs, int nWinMode)
{
  HWND hwnd;
  MSG msg;
  WNDCLASSEX wcl;
  HACCEL hAccel;

  /* Define a window class. */
  wcl.cbSize = sizeof(WNDCLASSEX);
  wcl.hInstance = hThisInst; /* handle to this instance */
  wcl.lpszClassName = szWinName; /* window class name */
  wcl.lpfnWndProc = WindowFunc; /* window function */
  wcl.style = 0; /* default style */

  wcl.hIcon = LoadIcon(NULL, IDI_APPLICATION);
  wcl.hIconSm = LoadIcon(NULL, IDI_APPLICATION);
  wcl.hCursor = LoadCursor(NULL, IDC_ARROW);

  /* specify name of menu resource */
  wcl.lpszMenuName = "FloatMenu"; /* main menu */

  wcl.cbClsExtra = 0; /* no extra */
  wcl.cbWndExtra = 0; /* information needed */

  /* Make the window white. */
  wcl.hbrBackground = GetStockObject(WHITE_BRUSH);

  /* Register the window class. */
  if(!RegisterClassEx(&wcl)) return 0;

  /* Now that a window class has been registered, a window
     can be created. */
  hwnd = CreateWindow(
    szWinName, /* name of window class */
    "Using a Floating Popup Menu", /* title */
    WS_OVERLAPPEDWINDOW, /* standard window */
    CW_USEDEFAULT, /* X coordinate - let Windows decide */
    CW_USEDEFAULT, /* Y coordinate - let Windows decide */
    CW_USEDEFAULT, /* width - let Windows decide */
    CW_USEDEFAULT, /* height - let Windows decide */
    HWND_DESKTOP, /* no parent window */
    NULL, /* no override of class menu */
    hThisInst, /* handle of this instance of the program */
    NULL /* no additional arguments */
  );
```

```
/* load the keyboard accelerators */
hAccel = LoadAccelerators(hThisInst, "FloatMenu");

hInst = hThisInst; /* save instance handle */

/* Display the window. */
ShowWindow(hwnd, nWinMode);
UpdateWindow(hwnd);

/* Create the message loop. */
while(GetMessage(&msg, NULL, 0, 0))
{
  if(!TranslateAccelerator(hwnd, hAccel, &msg)) {
    TranslateMessage(&msg); /* translate keyboard messages */
    DispatchMessage(&msg); /* return control to Windows */
  }
}
return msg.wParam;
}

/* This function is called by Windows NT and is passed
   messages from the message queue.
*/
LRESULT CALLBACK WindowFunc(HWND hwnd, UINT message,
                            WPARAM wParam, LPARAM lParam)
{
  HDC hdc;
  HMENU hmenu, hsubmenu;
  RECT rect;
  static HMENU hpopup;
  int response;
  int count;
  MENUITEMINFO miInfo;
  POINT pt;
  static HPEN hCurrentPen, hRedPen;

  switch(message) {
    case WM_CREATE:
      /* create red pen */
      hRedPen = CreatePen(PS_SOLID, 1, RGB(255, 0, 0));
      /* get black pen */
      hCurrentPen = GetStockObject(BLACK_PEN);
      break;
    case WM_COMMAND:
      switch(LOWORD(wParam)) {
        case IDM_ADDITEM: /* dynamically add popup menu */
          /* get handle of main menu */
          hmenu = GetMenu(hwnd);
```

```
/* get handle of 1st popup menu */
hsubmenu = GetSubMenu(hmenu, 0);

/* get number of items in the menu */
count = GetMenuItemCount(hsubmenu);

/* create new popup menu */
hpopup = CreatePopupMenu();

/* add items to dynamic popup menu */
miInfo.cbSize = sizeof(MENUITEMINFO);
miInfo.fMask = MIIM_TYPE | MIIM_ID;
miInfo.fType = MFT_STRING;
miInfo.wID = IDM_NEW;
miInfo.hSubMenu = NULL;
miInfo.hbmpChecked = NULL;
miInfo.hbmpUnchecked = NULL;
miInfo.dwItemData = 0;
miInfo.dwTypeData = "&Erase";
InsertMenuItem(hpopup, 0, 1, &miInfo);

miInfo.dwTypeData = "&Black Pen";
miInfo.wID = IDM_NEW2;
InsertMenuItem(hpopup, 1, 1, &miInfo);

miInfo.dwTypeData = "&Red Pen";
miInfo.wID = IDM_NEW3;
InsertMenuItem(hpopup, 2, 1, &miInfo);

/* append a separator */
miInfo.cbSize = sizeof(MENUITEMINFO);
miInfo.fMask = MIIM_TYPE;
miInfo.fType = MFT_SEPARATOR;
miInfo.fState = 0;
miInfo.wID = 0;
miInfo.hSubMenu = NULL;
miInfo.hbmpChecked = NULL;
miInfo.hbmpUnchecked = NULL;
miInfo.dwItemData = 0;
InsertMenuItem(hsubmenu, count, 1, &miInfo);

/* append popup menu to main menu */
miInfo.fMask = MIIM_TYPE | MIIM_SUBMENU;
miInfo.fType = MFT_STRING;
miInfo.hSubMenu = hpopup;
miInfo.dwTypeData = "&This is New Popup";
InsertMenuItem(hsubmenu, count+1, 1, &miInfo);
```

```
    /* deactivate the Add Popup option */
    EnableMenuItem(hsubmenu, IDM_ADDITEM,
                   MF_BYCOMMAND | MF_GRAYED);

    /* activate the Delete Popup option */
    EnableMenuItem(hsubmenu, IDM_DELITEM,
                   MF_BYCOMMAND | MF_ENABLED);
    break;
case IDM_DELITEM: /* dynamically delete popup menu */
    /* get handle of main menu */
    hmenu = GetMenu(hwnd);

    /* get handle of 1st popup menu */
    hsubmenu = GetSubMenu(hmenu, 0);

    /* delete the new popup menu and the separator */
    count = GetMenuItemCount(hsubmenu);
    DeleteMenu(hsubmenu, count-1, MF_BYPOSITION | MF_GRAYED);
    DeleteMenu(hsubmenu, count-2, MF_BYPOSITION | MF_GRAYED);

    /* reactivate the Add Popup option */
    EnableMenuItem(hsubmenu, IDM_ADDITEM,
                   MF_BYCOMMAND | MF_ENABLED);

    /* deactivate the Delete Popup option */
    EnableMenuItem(hsubmenu, IDM_DELITEM,
                   MF_BYCOMMAND | MF_GRAYED);
    break;
case IDM_EXIT:
    response = MessageBox(hwnd, "Quit the Program?",
                          "Exit", MB_YESNO);
    if(response == IDYES) PostQuitMessage(0);
    break;
case IDM_NEW: /* erase */
    hdc = GetDC(hwnd);
    GetClientRect(hwnd, &rect);
    SelectObject(hdc, GetStockObject(WHITE_BRUSH));
    PatBlt(hdc, 0, 0, rect.right, rect.bottom, PATCOPY);
    ReleaseDC(hwnd, hdc);
    break;
case IDM_NEW2: /* select black pen */
    hCurrentPen = GetStockObject(BLACK_PEN);
    break;
```

```
        case IDM_NEW3: /* select red pen */
          hCurrentPen = hRedPen;
          break;
        case IDM_LINES:
          hdc = GetDC(hwnd);
          SelectObject(hdc, hCurrentPen);
          MoveToEx(hdc, 10, 10, NULL);
          LineTo(hdc, 100, 100);
          LineTo(hdc, 100, 50);
          LineTo(hdc, 50, 180);
          ReleaseDC(hwnd, hdc);
          break;
        case IDM_ELLIPSES:
          hdc = GetDC(hwnd);
          SelectObject(hdc, hCurrentPen);
          Ellipse(hdc, 100, 100, 300, 200);
          Ellipse(hdc, 200, 100, 300, 200);
          ReleaseDC(hwnd, hdc);
          break;
        case IDM_RECTANGLES:
          hdc = GetDC(hwnd);
          SelectObject(hdc, hCurrentPen);
          Rectangle(hdc, 100, 100, 24, 260);
          Rectangle(hdc, 110, 120, 124, 170);
          ReleaseDC(hwnd, hdc);
          break;
        case IDM_HELP:
          MessageBox(hwnd, "Try Pressing Right Mouse Button",
                     "Help", MB_OK);
          break;
      }
    break;
  case WM_RBUTTONDOWN: /* popup floating menu */

    /* convert window coordinates to screen coordinates */
    pt.x = LOWORD(lParam);
    pt.y = HIWORD(lParam);
    ClientToScreen(hwnd, &pt);


    /* get handle of draw menu */
    hmenu = LoadMenu(hInst, "Draw");

    /* get 1st popup menu */
    hsubmenu = GetSubMenu(hmenu, 0);
```

```
              /* activate floating popup menu */
              TrackPopupMenuEx(hsubmenu, 0, pt.x, pt.y,
                                hwnd, NULL);
              DestroyMenu(hmenu);
              break;
          case WM_DESTROY: /* terminate the program */
              PostQuitMessage(0);
              break;
          default:
              /* Let Windows NT process any messages not specified in
                 the preceding switch statement. */
              return DefWindowProc(hwnd, message, wParam, lParam);
      }
    return 0;
}
```

The program uses the same MENU.H file shown as previous programs. It requires this resource file:

```
; Floating Menus
#include <windows.h>
#include "menu.h"

FloatMenu MENU
{
  POPUP "&Options"
  {
    MENUITEM "&Add Popup\tF2", IDM_ADDITEM
    MENUITEM "&Delete Popup\tF3", IDM_DELITEM, GRAYED
    MENUITEM "E&xit\tF10", IDM_EXIT
  }
  MENUITEM "&Help", IDM_HELP
}

; This menu will popup
Draw MENU
{
  POPUP "&Draw" {
    MENUITEM "&Lines\tF4", IDM_LINES
    MENUITEM "&Ellipses\tF5", IDM_ELLIPSES
```

```
      MENUITEM "&Rectangles\tF6", IDM_RECTANGLES
  }
}

; Define menu accelerators
FloatMenu ACCELERATORS
{
  VK_F2, IDM_ADDITEM, VIRTKEY
  VK_F3, IDM_DELITEM, VIRTKEY
  VK_F10, IDM_EXIT, VIRTKEY
  VK_F4, IDM_LINES, VIRTKEY
  VK_F5, IDM_ELLIPSES, VIRTKEY
  VK_F6, IDM_RECTANGLES, VIRTKEY
  VK_F1, IDM_HELP, VIRTKEY
}
```

20

Notice that in this version, the Draw menu is not part of the main, menu-bar menu. Instead, it is a stand-alone menu. Thus, it will not be displayed until it is invoked.

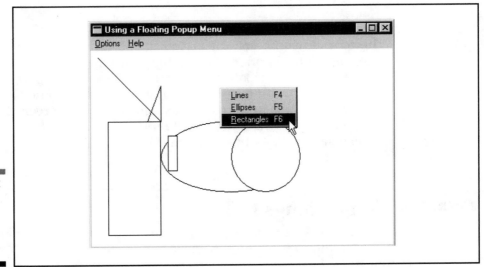

Sample output from the floating menu program

Figure 20-3.

A Closer Look at the Floating Menu Program

Most of the program is unchanged from its previous version. However, notice the code under **WM_RIGHTBUTTON**. It is used to activate the Draw menu. It is shown here for your convenience:

```
case WM_RBUTTONDOWN: /* popup floating menu */

  /* convert window coordinates to screen coordinates */
  pt.x = LOWORD(lParam);
  pt.y = HIWORD(lParam);
  ClientToScreen(hwnd, &pt);

  /* get handle of draw menu */
  hmenu = LoadMenu(hInst, "Draw");

  /* get 1st popup menu */
  hsubmenu = GetSubMenu(hmenu, 0);

  /* activate floating popup menu */
  TrackPopupMenuEx(hsubmenu, 0, pt.x, pt.y,
                   hwnd, NULL);
  DestroyMenu(hmenu);
  break;
```

This code causes the Draw menu to pop up with its upper left corner positioned at the location of the mouse when the right button is pressed. However, since the coordinates specified in **TrackPopupMenuEx( )** are in terms of screen units, the program must convert the mouse's location (which is in window units) into screen units using **ClientToScreen( )**. Next, the menu must be loaded, using **LoadMenu( )**, and its first (and only) pop-up menu obtained. After these steps have been taken, the menu can be displayed.

Some Things to Try

Here is an easy experiment to try: In the first example program in this chapter, the Erase option was added to or removed from the Options menu manually, by the user. This approach was used only for the sake of illustration. It is possible to add or remove the Erase option automatically, under program control. For example, when the window is empty (as it is when the program begins), do not display the Erase option. As soon as the user draws something in the window, activate Erase. Once the user has erased the window, deactivate the Erase option. Automating the inclusion of the Erase option in this way reflects the way that dynamic menus are used in real applications.

You might want to see the effects of using the **MFT_RADIOCHECK** style when inserting a menu item.

You will also want to try the various options available to the **TrackPopup-MenuEx( )** function. Specifically, try defining an excluded region. Also, try having the menu aligned differently.

Finally, try integrating free-floating context menus with the Help system. For ideas about how this might be done, observe how commercial programs handle this situation.

20

CHAPTER 21

DLLs, Security, and OLE

703

We have come a long way from Chapter 1. If you have worked through the preceding 20 chapters, then you are well on your way to becoming an accomplished Windows NT 4 programmer. But there are three more topics with which you need to be familiar. The first is how to create and use your own dynamic link libraries (DLLs). The second is the NT security system. The third is OLE. Frankly, any of these topics could easily fill a book of its own. (In fact, a complete discussion of OLE requires more than one volume!) For obvious reasons, it is not possible to deal with these topics in great detail here. However, a general understanding is important and an overview of each is presented.

Creating DLLs

As you know, the Win32 API library is stored as a dynamic link library. This means that when your application program uses an API function, the code for that function is not actually added to your program's object file. Instead, loading instructions are supplied. Only when your program is loaded for execution are the dynamically linked APIs added. It is possible for you to create your own dynamic link libraries that work in the same way. As you will see, the process is easier than you might expect.

Dynamic Linking vs. Static Linking

Static linking takes place at compile time. Dynamic linking occurs at run time.

Before beginning, let's review the difference between static linking and dynamic linking. As just explained, dynamic linking occurs at run time. The code for dynamically linked functions does not appear in your program's .EXE file. By contrast, static linking occurs at compile time. The code for statically linked functions is physically added to your program's .EXE file. Functions that will be statically linked are usually stored in either .OBJ or .LIB files. For example, when you write a large program consisting of several separate compilation units (files), the linker will combine the .OBJ files for each module when it creates the .EXE file. In this case, the .EXE file will contain all of the code found in the .OBJ files.

When you use dynamic linking, the code for the functions that will be dynamically linked will be stored in a .DLL file that is separate from the rest of your program. As you will see, your program will link in a small amount of code that contains the loading instructions for the DLL functions, but the functions themselves will not be included.

Why Create a DLL?

You might be wondering why you would want to create your own dynamic link library. Frankly, for small programs there are no advantages. It is easier to link all of the functions used by your program at compile time. However, for large software systems involving several components that share a custom function library, the advantages can be enormous. For example,

1. Placing functions in a DLL reduces the size of each component because the functions are not duplicated in each program when stored on disk. Although disk space is currently plentiful and cheap, it is still wrong to waste it.
2. Using DLLs makes upgrading easier. When a function stored in a normal library is changed, each module using that function must be recompiled. When using dynamic linking, only the DLL file must be recompiled. All applications using that DLL will automatically use the new version of the function the next time they are executed.
3. Using DLLs can make it easier to fix code "in the field." For example, if you have a misbehaving, mission-critical program, it is far easier to download a repaired dynamic link library than it is to download the entire application. This is quite important for programs used in remote environments, such as spacecraft, unmanned monitoring posts, and the like.

Of course, nothing is without its costs. The downside to using your own DLLs is that your program is now in two (or more) pieces. This makes the management of that program harder and does open up some failure paths. For example, if the dynamic link library is out of synch with the application, trouble is sure to follow. That said, when building large software systems, the benefits of dynamic linking exceed its drawbacks.

DLL Basics

Functions defined in a DLL must be exported.

Functions in DLLs must be imported by applications that use them.

Before looking at an example DLL, there are a few rules that apply to building and using them with which you need to be familiar. First, any function contained in a DLL that will be called by code outside the DLL must be *exported*. Second, to use a function contained in a DLL, you must *import* it. When using C/C++, export is accomplished using the **dllexport** keyword and import is done with **dllimport**. **dllexport** and **dllimport** are extended keywords supported by both Microsoft Visual C++ and Borland C++.

21

PORTABILITY: In Windows 3.1, functions exported from DLLs had to be specified in the EXPORTS section of the .DEF file associated with the DLL. Although this is still allowed, **dllexport** provides a more convenient alternative.

The **dllexport** and **dllimport** keywords cannot be used by themselves. Instead, they need to be preceded by another extended keyword: _ _**declspec**. Its general form is shown here:

_ _declspec(*specifier*)

where *specifier* is a storage class specifier. For DLLs, *specifier* will be either **dllexport** or **dllimport**. For example, to export a function called **MyFunc( )**, you would use a line like this:

```
__declspec(dllexport) void MyFunc(int a)
```

To simplify the syntax of declaring imported and exported functions, most programmers create a macro name that can be substituted for the rather long _ _**declspec** specification. For example:

```
#define DllExport __declspec (dllexport)
```

Now, **MyFunc( )** can be exported using this simpler statement:

```
DllExport void MyFunc(int a)
```

If your DLL is compiled as a C++ program and you also want C programs to be able to use it, then you will need to add the "C" linkage specification, as shown here,

```
#define DllExport extern "C" __declspec (dllexport)
```

If your DLL will be used by both C and C++ programs, specify C linkage for its functions.

This prevents the standard C++ name mangling (also called name decoration) from taking place. Name mangling is the process by which the name of a function is modified to include type-related information. This process is used to distinguish between different forms of overloaded functions, between member functions of different classes, functions in different name spaces, etc. We will include the C linkage specification for the examples in this book to avoid any possible troubles in this regard. (If you are compiling C programs, then do not add **extern "C"** since it isn't needed and it will not be accepted by the compiler.)

At the time of this writing, the use of **dllimport** is technically not necessary for functions. It is recommended because it allows more efficient code to be generated. **dllimport** is necessary when importing data, however.

When compiling a DLL, you must tell the compiler that a DLL is being created. The easiest way to do this is to simply specify that you are creating a DLL when creating a new project. If you are unsure about what compiler options to set, refer to your compiler's user manual.

After you have compiled a DLL, two files will be present. One will contain the DLL functions and will use the .DLL extension. The other will contain loading information for the functions and will use the .LIB extension. You must link the .LIB file into any program that will be using your DLL.

The .DLL file must be in a directory where it will be found when your application is loaded. Windows NT searches for DLLs in the following sequence: It first searches the directory that held the application. Next, it looks in the current working directory. Then it examines the standard DLL directory, which for Windows NT is WINNT\SYSTEM32. Next, it searches the Windows directory. Finally, it searches any directories specified in the PATH variable. It is strongly suggested that when you are experimenting with DLLs, you keep them in the same directory as the application and not in any of the standard directories. This way, you avoid any chance of accidentally overwriting a DLL that is used by your system's software.

If a program requires a DLL that cannot be found, the program will not be executed and a message box will be displayed on the screen.

A Simple DLL

Let's begin by creating a very simple dynamic link library. Here is the source code for a DLL that contains only one function: **ShowMouseLoc( )**. This function displays the location of the mouse when a button-press message is received. Recall that mouse button-press messages contain, in **lParam**, the coordinates of the mouse at the time at which the message was generated. To show the location of the mouse, pass this value to **ShowMouseLoc( )** along with the desired device context. The function displays the coordinates. As you can see, **ShowMouseLoc( )** is declared as an exported function.

```
/* A simple DLL. */
#include <windows.h>
#include <string.h>

#define DllExport extern "C" __declspec (dllexport)

/* This function displays the coordinates of the mouse
```

```
        at the point at which a mouse button was pressed.

     hdc:    Specifies the device context in which to
             output the coordinates.
     lParam: Specifies the value of lParam when the
             button was pressed.
*/
DllExport void ShowMouseLoc(HDC hdc, LPARAM lParam)
{
  char str[80];

  wsprintf(str, "Button is down at %d, %d",
           LOWORD(lParam), HIWORD(lParam));
  TextOut(hdc, LOWORD(lParam), HIWORD(lParam),
          str, strlen(str));
}
```

To follow along, enter this file now, calling it MYDLL.CPP. Next, create a DLL project. To do this using Visual C++, select Dynamic-link Library in the New Project Workspace dialog box. For Borland C++, select Dynamic Library in the Target Type list box when creating the project. Next, compile the library. This will result in these two files being created: MYDLL.DLL and MYDLL.LIB. As explained, the .DLL file will contain the dynamic link library itself. The .LIB file contains loading information that must be linked with any application that uses the library.

Creating a Header File

As it must for any other library function that your program uses, your program must include the prototypes to functions contained in a DLL. This is why you must include WINDOWS.H in all Windows NT 4 programs, for example. The easiest way to include prototypes for the functions in your DLL is to create a companion header file. For example, the header file for MYDLL is shown here. To follow along with the example, call this file MYDLL.H.

```
#define DllImport extern "C" __declspec (dllimport)

DllImport void ShowMouseLoc(HDC hdc, LPARAM lParm);
```

Using the DLL

Once your dynamic link library has been compiled and put in the proper directory, and a header file for it has been created, it is ready for use. Here is a simple program that uses MYDLL.DLL. It simply displays the location of the mouse whenever the left or right mouse button is pressed. Sample output is shown in Figure 21-1. When you compile this program, you must be sure to include MYDLL.LIB in your link list. When you run the program, **ShowMouseLoc( )** will be automatically loaded from MYDLL.DLL when your program is executed.

```c
/* Use ShowMouseLoc() from DLL */

#include <windows.h>
#include <string.h>
#include "mydll.h"

LRESULT CALLBACK WindowFunc(HWND, UINT, WPARAM, LPARAM);

char szWinName[] = "MyWin"; /* name of window class */

int WINAPI WinMain(HINSTANCE hThisInst, HINSTANCE hPrevInst,
                   LPSTR lpszArgs, int nWinMode)
{
  HWND hwnd;
  MSG msg;
  WNDCLASSEX wcl;

  /* Define a window class. */
  wcl.cbSize = sizeof(WNDCLASSEX);

  wcl.hInstance = hThisInst; /* handle to this instance */
  wcl.lpszClassName = szWinName; /* window class name */
  wcl.lpfnWndProc = WindowFunc; /* window function */
  wcl.style = 0; /* default style */

  wcl.hIcon = LoadIcon(NULL, IDI_APPLICATION);
  wcl.hIconSm = LoadIcon(NULL, IDI_APPLICATION);
  wcl.hCursor = LoadCursor(NULL, IDC_ARROW);

  wcl.lpszMenuName = NULL; /* no main menu */
  wcl.cbClsExtra = 0; /* no extra */
  wcl.cbWndExtra = 0; /* information needed */

  /* Make the window white. */
  wcl.hbrBackground = GetStockObject(WHITE_BRUSH);

  /* Register the window class. */
  if(!RegisterClassEx(&wcl)) return 0;

  /* Now that a window class has been registered, a window
     can be created. */
  hwnd = CreateWindow(
```

21

```
      szWinName, /* name of window class */
      "Demonstrate a DLL", /* title */
      WS_OVERLAPPEDWINDOW, /* window style - normal */
      CW_USEDEFAULT, /* X coordinate - let Windows decide */
      CW_USEDEFAULT, /* Y coordinate - let Windows decide */
      CW_USEDEFAULT, /* width - let Windows decide */
      CW_USEDEFAULT, /* height - let Windows decide */
      HWND_DESKTOP, /* no parent window */
      NULL, /* no override of class menu */
      hThisInst, /* handle of this instance of the program */
      NULL /* no additional arguments */
    );

    /* Display the window. */
    ShowWindow(hwnd, nWinMode);
    UpdateWindow(hwnd);

    /* Create the message loop. */
    while(GetMessage(&msg, NULL, 0, 0))
    {
      TranslateMessage(&msg); /* translate keyboard messages */
      DispatchMessage(&msg); /* return control to Windows NT */
    }
    return msg.wParam;
}

/* This function is called by Windows NT and is passed
   messages from the message queue.
*/
LRESULT CALLBACK WindowFunc(HWND hwnd, UINT message,
                            WPARAM wParam, LPARAM lParam)
{
  HDC hdc;

  switch(message) {
    case WM_RBUTTONDOWN: /* process right button */
      hdc = GetDC(hwnd); /* get DC */
      ShowMouseLoc(hdc, lParam); /* call DLL function */
      ReleaseDC(hwnd, hdc); /* Release DC */
      break;
    case WM_LBUTTONDOWN: /* process left button */
      hdc = GetDC(hwnd); /* get DC */
      ShowMouseLoc(hdc, lParam); /* call DLL function */
      ReleaseDC(hwnd, hdc); /* Release DC */
      break;
    case WM_DESTROY: /* terminate the program */
```

```
          PostQuitMessage(0);
          break;
      default:
        /* Let Windows NT process any messages not specified in
            the preceding switch statement. */
        return DefWindowProc(hwnd, message, wParam, lParam);
  }
  return 0;
}
```

Using DllMain( )

DllMain( ) provides initialization and termination for a DLL.

Some DLLs will require special startup or shutdown code. To allow for this, all DLLs have a function that is called when the DLL is being initialized or terminated, called **DllMain( )**. This function is defined by you, in your dynamic link library source file. However, if you don't define this function, then a default version is automatically provided by the compiler. This is why we did not need one for the preceding DLL. Of course, all but the most simple DLLs will provide their own.

21

DllMain( ) has the following prototype:

BOOL WINAPI DllMain(HANDLE *hInstance*, ULONG *What*,
LPVOID *NotUsed*);

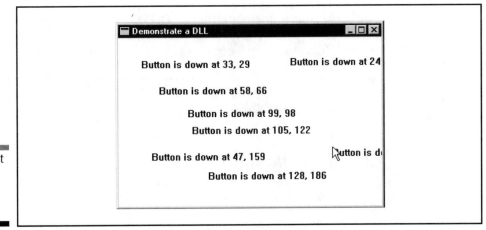

Sample output from the first DLL program
Figure 21-1.

When this function is called by Windows NT, *hInstance* is the instance handle of the DLL, *What* specifies what action is occurring, and *NotUsed* is reserved. The function must return nonzero if successful and zero on failure.

The value in *What* will be one of the following:

Value	Meaning
DLL_PROCESS_ATTACH	Process is beginning use of DLL.
DLL_PROCESS_DETACH	Process is releasing DLL.
DLL_THREAD_ATTACH	Process has created a new thread.
DLL_THREAD_DETACH	Process has destroyed a thread.

When *What* contains **DLL_PROCESS_ATTACH**, it means that a process has loaded the DLL. (In technical terms, it means that the library has been mapped into the process' address space.) If **DllMain( )** returns zero in response to this action, the process attempting to attach to the DLL is terminated. For each process that uses the DLL, **DllMain( )** will only be called once with **DLL_PROCESS_ATTACH**.

When *What* contains **DLL_PROCESS_DETACH**, the process no longer needs the DLL. This typically occurs when the process itself terminates. It also occurs when a DLL is being explicitly released.

When a process that has already attached a DLL creates a new thread, then **DllMain( )** will be called with **DLL_THREAD_ATTACH**. When a thread is destroyed, **DllMain( )** is called with **DLL_THREAD_DETACH**. Multiple thread attach and detach messages can be generated by a single process.

In general, your implementation of **DllMain( )** must take appropriate action, based on the contents of *What*, whenever it is called. Of course, such appropriate action may be to do nothing other than return nonzero.

PORTABILITY: DLLs created for Windows 3.1 do not use **DllMain( )**. They use **LibMain( )**, instead.

Adding a DllMain( ) to MYDLL

To see exactly how and when **DllMain( )** is called, add **DllMain( )** to MYDLL.CPP, as shown here:

```
#include <windows.h>
#include <string.h>
```

```
#define DllExport extern "C" __declspec (dllexport)

/* This function is called during initialization and
   termination. */
BOOL WINAPI DllMain(HANDLE hInstance, ULONG what,
                    LPVOID Notused)
{
  switch(what) {
    case DLL_PROCESS_ATTACH:
      MessageBox(HWND_DESKTOP, "Process attaching DLL.",
                 "DLL Action", MB_OK);
      break;
    case DLL_PROCESS_DETACH:
      MessageBox(HWND_DESKTOP, "Process detaching DLL.",
                 "DLL Action", MB_OK);
      break;
    case DLL_THREAD_ATTACH:
      MessageBox(HWND_DESKTOP, "Thread attaching DLL.",
                 "DLL Action", MB_OK);
      break;
    case DLL_THREAD_DETACH:
      MessageBox(HWND_DESKTOP, "Thread detaching DLL.",
                 "DLL Action", MB_OK);
      break;
  }
  return 1;
}

/* This function displays the coordinates of the mouse
   at the point at which a mouse button was pressed.

   hdc:    Specifies the device context in which to
           output the coordinates.
   lParam: Specifies the value of lParam when the
           button was pressed.
*/
DllExport void ShowMouseLoc(HDC hdc, LPARAM lParam)
{
  char str[80];

  wsprintf(str, "Button is down at %d, %d",
           LOWORD(lParam), HIWORD(lParam));
  TextOut(hdc, LOWORD(lParam), HIWORD(lParam),
          str, strlen(str));
}
```

As you can see, each time **DllMain( )** is called, a message box is displayed that explains why. Notice that **MessageBox( )** uses **HWND_DESKTOP** for its first parameter. This allows the message box to be displayed independently of any application, because **HWND_DESKTOP** refers to the screen.

One other point: **DllMain( )** is not exported from MYDLL because it is not called by application programs. It is called by Windows NT only.

Demonstrating DllMain( )

The following program demonstrates **DllMain( )**. As before, it uses the **ShowMouseLoc( )** function to display the location of the mouse when its left or right button is pressed. However, it also creates another thread of execution each time you press a key on the keyboard. When you run this program, pay close attention to when and why **DllMain( )** is called. Sample output is shown in Figure 21-2. Also, remember to link this program with MYDLL.LIB.

```c
/* Demonstrate DLL initialization. */

#include <windows.h>
#include <string.h>
#include <stdio.h>
#include "mydll.h"

#define MAX 10000

LRESULT CALLBACK WindowFunc(HWND, UINT, WPARAM, LPARAM);

DWORD WINAPI MyThread(LPVOID param);

char szWinName[] = "MyWin"; /* name of window class */

char str[255] = ""; /* holds output string */

DWORD Tid1; /* thread ID */

int WINAPI WinMain(HINSTANCE hThisInst, HINSTANCE hPrevInst,
                   LPSTR lpszArgs, int nWinMode)
{
  HWND hwnd;
  MSG msg;
  WNDCLASSEX wcl;

  /* Define a window class. */
  wcl.cbSize = sizeof(WNDCLASSEX);

  wcl.hInstance = hThisInst; /* handle to this instance */
```

```
    wcl.lpszClassName = szWinName; /* window class name */
    wcl.lpfnWndProc = WindowFunc; /* window function */
    wcl.style = 0; /* default style */

    wcl.hIcon = LoadIcon(NULL, IDI_APPLICATION);
    wcl.hIconSm = LoadIcon(NULL, IDI_APPLICATION);
    wcl.hCursor = LoadCursor(NULL, IDC_ARROW);

    wcl.lpszMenuName = NULL; /* no main menu */
    wcl.cbClsExtra = 0; /* no extra */
    wcl.cbWndExtra = 0; /* information needed */

    /* Make the window white. */
    wcl.hbrBackground = GetStockObject(WHITE_BRUSH);

    /* Register the window class. */
    if(!RegisterClassEx(&wcl)) return 0;

    /* Now that a window class has been registered, a window
       can be created. */
    hwnd = CreateWindow(
      szWinName, /* name of window class */
      "Using DllMain", /* title */
      WS_OVERLAPPEDWINDOW, /* window style - normal */
      CW_USEDEFAULT, /* X coordinate - let Windows decide */
      CW_USEDEFAULT, /* Y coordinate - let Windows decide */
      CW_USEDEFAULT, /* width - let Windows decide */
      CW_USEDEFAULT, /* height - let Windows decide */
      HWND_DESKTOP, /* no parent window */
      NULL, /* no override of class menu */
      hThisInst, /* handle of this instance of the program */
      NULL /* no additional arguments */
    );

    /* Display the window. */
    ShowWindow(hwnd, nWinMode);
    UpdateWindow(hwnd);

    /* Create the message loop. */
    while(GetMessage(&msg, NULL, 0, 0))
    {
      TranslateMessage(&msg); /* translate keyboard messages */
      DispatchMessage(&msg); /* return control to Windows NT */
    }
    return msg.wParam;
}

/* This function is called by Windows NT and is passed
```

```
   messages from the message queue.
*/
LRESULT CALLBACK WindowFunc(HWND hwnd, UINT message,
                              WPARAM wParam, LPARAM lParam)
{
  HDC hdc;
  PAINTSTRUCT ps;

  switch(message) {
    case WM_RBUTTONDOWN: /* process right button */
      hdc = GetDC(hwnd); /* get DC */
      ShowMouseLoc(hdc, lParam); /* call DLL function */
      ReleaseDC(hwnd, hdc); /* Release DC */
      break;
    case WM_LBUTTONDOWN: /* process left button */
      hdc = GetDC(hwnd); /* get DC */
      ShowMouseLoc(hdc, lParam); /* call DLL function */
      ReleaseDC(hwnd, hdc); /* Release DC */
      break;
    case WM_CHAR: /* start a thread when a key is pressed */
      CreateThread(NULL, 0,
                   (LPTHREAD_START_ROUTINE)MyThread,
                   (LPVOID) hwnd, 0, &Tid1);
      break;
    case WM_PAINT:
      hdc = BeginPaint(hwnd, &ps);
      strcpy(str, "Press a key to start a thread.");
      TextOut(hdc, 1, 1, str, strlen(str));
      EndPaint(hwnd, &ps);
      break;
    case WM_DESTROY: /* terminate the program */
      PostQuitMessage(0);
      break;
    default:
      /* Let Windows NT process any messages not specified in
         the preceding switch statement. */
      return DefWindowProc(hwnd, message, wParam, lParam);
  }
  return 0;
}

/* Another thread of execution. */
DWORD WINAPI MyThread(LPVOID param)
{
  int i;
```

```
    HDC hdc;

    for(i=0; i<MAX; i++) {
      sprintf(str, "In thread: loop # %5d ", i);
      hdc = GetDC((HWND) param);
      TextOut(hdc, 1, 20, str, strlen(str));
      ReleaseDC((HWND) param, hdc);
    }
    return 0;
}
```

When you run this program, you will see the "Process attaching DLL" message box when the program begins. When you press a key, a new thread is started. This causes a "Thread attaching DLL" message box to be displayed. When the thread ends, the "Thread detaching DLL" message box is shown. When you terminate the program, the last thing you will see is the "Process detaching DLL" message box. You might want to experiment with this program a little, making sure you understand when and why **DllMain( )** is called.

Although you may not have an immediate need for one, custom DLLs offer valuable advantages in many situations. As you have seen, they are easy to create. You should have no reluctance toward using one when the time comes.

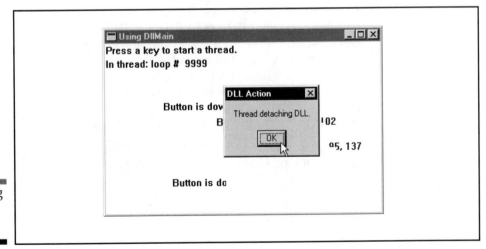

Demonstrating
DllMain( )
Figure 21-2.

Run-Time Dynamic Linking

Most often, when you use functions defined in a DLL, your program calls those functions by name in its source code. This is the way all of the API functions have been called by the sample programs in this book and it is the way that **ShowMouseLoc( )** was called. When this is the case, the DLL that contains the functions is loaded when the application is loaded. This is called *load-time dynamic linking*. However, it is possible to load dynamic link libraries at run time.

If your application does not make explicit calls to one or more functions stored in a DLL, then that library will, for obvious reasons, not be loaded when your program begins execution. However, it is still possible to call functions contained in that DLL. To do so, your program must manually load the DLL and then obtain pointers to the functions that it wishes to use. This process is called *run-time dynamic linking*.

At the core of run-time dynamic linking are these three functions:

HMODULE LoadLibrary(LPCSTR *DllName*);

BOOL FreeLibrary(HMODULE *hMod*);

FARPROC GetProcAddress(HMODULE *hMod*, LPCSTR *FuncName*);

LoadLibrary( ) loads the DLL specified by *DllName* and returns a handle to it. **FreeLibrary( )** frees the DLL when it is no longer needed. **GetProcAddress( )** returns a pointer to the function named by *FuncName* that is contained in the DLL specified by *hMod*. Using this pointer, you can then call the desired function. Be careful, though. The name of the function must match exactly the name specified within the DLL. C++ name mangling may distort function names. You might want to avoid this by using the C linkage specification.

To try run-time dynamic linking, make these changes to the second sample DLL program. First, define this global handle:

```
HMODULE hlib;
```

Next, add this sequence to **WinMain( )**, just before the message loop begins:

```
hlib = LoadLibrary("MYDLL.DLL");
if(!hlib) MessageBox(hwnd, "Cannot Load Library",
                     "Error", MB_OK);
```

Then, inside **WindowFunc( )**, define this function pointer:

```
void (*f)(HDC, LPARAM);
```

Finally, change the mouse handlers as shown here:

```
case WM_RBUTTONDOWN: /* process right button */
  hdc = GetDC(hwnd); /* get DC */

  /* get pointer to ShowMouseLoc */
  f = (void (*)(HDC, LPARAM)) GetProcAddress(hlib,
      "ShowMouseLoc");

  /* call ShowMouseLoc */
  (*f)(hdc, lParam);

  ReleaseDC(hwnd, hdc); /* Release DC */
  break;
case WM_LBUTTONDOWN: /* process left button */
  hdc = GetDC(hwnd); /* get DC */

  /* get pointer to ShowMouseLoc */
  f = (void (*)(HDC, LPARAM)) GetProcAddress(hlib,
      "ShowMouseLoc");

  /* call ShowMouseLoc */
  (*f)(hdc, lParam);

  ReleaseDC(hwnd, hdc); /* Release DC */
  break;
```

You will also want to add a call to **FreeLibrary( )** when a **WM_DESTROY** message is received. After making these changes, the program will load the library dynamically and call **ShowMouseLoc( )** through a pointer, rather than directly.

While you will normally use load-time dynamic linking, run-time linking does offer increased flexibility. For example, your application could take advantage of a DLL function if the DLL exists on the current machine. If it doesn't, the program could select an alternative.

21

Security

As mentioned in Chapter 1, Windows NT contains built-in security support that complies with the DOD's C2 security level. The security subsystem performs several functions. Its two primary duties are to control access to the computer and to control access to various objects. The first function is handled by the Windows NT log-in facility. The second is managed by controlling access privileges. The types of objects that can be secured include files (NTFS only), pipes, processes, threads, registry keys, printers, desktops, and synchronization objects (such as semaphores). In addition to these functions, Windows NT's security system also provides for audit trails of security events, memory protection, and operating system tamper protection.

Support for NT's security system is built into the Win32 API library. Fortunately, such support is nearly transparent and adds little (if any) overhead to an application. Applications that do not make special use of the security system are virtually unaffected by its existence. For example, several of the API functions used in the preceding chapters have required a security descriptor. In these cases, we were able to simply pass **NULL** for this parameter, which caused the default descriptor to be used. In reality, many NT programmers will never need to make explicit use of the security features, but it is still important to understand their general operation.

Defining Terms

The first step to mastering NT's security system is understanding the meaning of several terms. A *security descriptor* determines who has access to an object and how that object may be accessed. It is represented by a **SECURITY_DESCRIPTOR** structure. Your program does not deal directly with the members of this structure. Instead, it uses various API functions to interrogate or adjust its contents. A security descriptor contains information about the owner and its group. It also contains a discretionary access-control list and a system access-control list.

A security descriptor governs access to an object.

Owners and groups are represented by *SIDs* (security IDs). A SID is a unique number that encodes various bits of security information.

A SID is a user's security ID.

An *access-control list*, or ACL, is a list that determines who has access to an object. An ACL consists of *access-control entries*, or ACEs. An ACE specifies a user or group along with its access rights relative to the object. ACLs are also used to provide audit trails of access attempts.

An access control list contains access control entries.

There are two varieties of ACLs: discretionary and system. A *discretionary access-control list*, or DACL, is used to specify who has access to the object and precisely what type of access that user or group has. Thus, an object's DACL determines the access rights of other users or groups relative to the object. If an object does not have a DACL, then all access rights are granted to all users. The owner of the object controls the contents of the DACL. A *system ACL*, or SACL, determines what type of access events will be logged in the audit trail. The system administrator controls the contents of the SACL.

An access
token
describes a
user's security
attributes.

An *access token* identifies a user and describes the user's security attributes. Among other things, it contains the user's SID, privileges, and a default DACL.

Each process has a set of privileges defined for it. Privileges are represented as **LUID**s, which are 64-bit integers. LUID stands for Locally Unique IDentifier. Examples of privileges are the ability to set the system time and the right to shut down the system. In some cases, privileges can be adjusted to allow a process to perform special tasks.

How Security Works

In general, here is how the Windows NT security subsystem controls access to an object: Each securable object has associated with it a security descriptor that defines who owns the object, and how and by whom it can be accessed. When a user logs on, he or she is given an access token that identifies that user. It also identifies any groups to which the user may belong. Each program executed by the user will have a copy of the access token. When a process attempts to access a controlled object, the user's access token is compared against the object's DACL. If an ACE in the list matches the access token, then access is granted. Otherwise, it is denied. Thus, in order for a user to access an object, the user must be allowed access to that object and have the proper privileges for the type of access desired. This is the way users and their privileges are linked with processes.

21

The log-on process itself is managed by the *security account manager* (SAM). As you know, logging on requires a user name and a password. Thus, the password provides the basic security for the entire NT system.

Some Security-Related API Functions

The various elements of Windows NT security are manipulated through a large number of API functions. Here are some common ones:

Function	Purpose
AdjustTokenPrivileges( )	Enables or disables existing privileges.
GetAce( )	Gets a pointer to an access control entry.
GetFileSecurity( )	Gets a file's security setting.
GetSecurityDescriptorDacl( )	Gets a pointer to a security descriptor's DACL.
GetSecurityDescriptorSacl( )	Gets a pointer to a security descriptor's SACL.
GetSecurityInfo( )	Gets a copy of security descriptor given a handle to an object.

Function	Purpose
InitializeSecurityDescriptor( )	Initializes a security descriptor.
LogonUser( )	Logs on a user.
SetFileSecurity( )	Sets a file's security.
SetSecurityDescriptorDacl( )	Adds a DACL to a security descriptor.
SetSecurityDescriptorSacl( )	Adds an SACL to a security descriptor.

Experimenting with Security

The NT security system is not difficult to use. It is large, however, and this makes it feel more complicated than it really is. A good way to start learning about security is to write a program that sets the system time using the **SetSystemTime( )** API function. The system time is a global resource that requires the proper privileges to set. When you are logged in as an Administrator, then you already have the necessary rights to set the time. However, if you log in as a User, by default you will not have this right. Experiment with ways that you can grant any user the right to set the time.

If you are using the NT File System, then try controlling access to a file. Here is another area you may want to explore. Security applies to network environments, too. For example, remote printers can be secured. However, before experimenting with network security, make sure that you won't accidentally lock out users!

A Jump Start to OLE

OLE is one of the most exciting disciplines in Windows programming. It is playing an increasingly important role in nearly all major applications and is finding its way into even smaller software products. Unfortunately, the OLE subsystem is both large and complex. To fully describe it requires a complete book. As such, a detailed discussion is beyond the scope of this chapter. This section is designed only to provide you with a "jump start" to OLE programming.

NOTE: To master OLE programming you will need to invest substantial time and effort. You will also need to have available to you a set of OLE reference guides. One you should definitely read is *Inside OLE, 2nd Ed.*, by Kraig Brockschmidt (Redmond, WA, Microsoft Press, 1995).

What is OLE ?

OLE stands for Object Linking and Embedding.

OLE stands for Object Linking and Embedding. In the broadest sense, OLE is a form of interprocess communication. Specifically, it allows one application to link or embed information created by another application. When this is done, a *compound document* is created. A compound document is also referred to as an *OLE document*.

It is important to understand that OLE has gone through a rather extensive evolution since it was first introduced. OLE version 1.0 was devised in 1991, but it was seldom used. However, with the advent of OLE version 2, the capabilities and applicability of OLE took a quantum jump. For this reason, the number of OLE-compatible applications has increased substantially.

The most important thing that you need to understand about OLE 2 is that it is more than just an improved version of OLE 1. While OLE version 1 was designed specifically to support the linking and embedding of objects, OLE 2 is designed to support the creation of extensible applications. While part of the extensibility of an application is linking and embedding, OLE 2 goes far beyond these two operations.

Since OLE 2 has completely supplanted OLE 1, the rest of this chapter will simply use the term OLE.

What are Linking and Embedding?

When an object is linked, only a reference to the object is included in a compound document.

Since linking and embedding are at the core of OLE, it is important that you understand what these two terms mean. A compound document may include two types of objects: *linked* and *embedded*. When an object is linked, the compound document contains a reference (i.e., *link*) to the object, but the object itself is not actually stored in the document. When an object is embedded, the actual object itself becomes part of the compound document. Each method has advantages and disadvantages.

When an object is embedded, the object itself is included in the compound document.

The main advantage to object linking is that the linked object may be changed by another application and these changes will automatically be reflected in your compound document. Put differently, a linked object always ensures that your document will contain the latest version of the object. A secondary advantage is that the size of the compound document will be smaller than it would be if the object were embedded because only a link to the object (not the object itself) is contained in the document. The principal disadvantage to object linking is that the object is not fixed in your compound document. For example, if you inadvertently change a linked object, it will also be changed within any document to which it is linked. Also, a compound document that contains linked objects is not complete by itself.

The advantage to embedded objects is that they are contained within the compound document. Thus, if your document contains only embedded objects, it can be copied to another computer and still contain all of its information. The disadvantage of embedded objects is that the size of the compound document will be larger because it actually contains the object.

The Component Object Model

OLE is based on the *component object model* (COM). This model defines the way the OLE-compatible applications interact with each other. Specifically, it defines (among other things) interfaces, memory management, interprocess communication, and dynamic loading of a required object. However, the single most important thing that you need to understand about OLE (and its most fundamental design attribute) is that it uses standard interfaces. It is through these interfaces that one application communicates with another.

In the component object model there are two types of applications: *containers* and *servers*. In the simplest sense, a container is an application that requires data and a server is an application that supplies data. A container is often a compound document. Another term for container is *client*. The way a container and server communicate is through the interfaces defined by OLE.

OLE Interfaces

The nature and contents of each interface are defined by the component object model. An application that desires OLE compatibility simply implements one or more of these interfaces. Here are some of the interfaces. There are, of course, many more.

Interface Name	Purpose
IUnknown	Gateway to all other interfaces.
IMalloc	Memory allocation.
IOleContainer	Provides support of OLE containers.
IDataObject	Supports data transfer and change notifications.
IViewObject	Manages views.
IDispatch	Supports OLE automation.
IDropSource	Implemented by sources of drag/drop items.
IDropTarget	Implemented by targets of drag/drop items.

An OLE interface is implemented as a table of function pointers. These pointers point to the functions that comprise the interface. To expose an interface, a server returns a pointer to that interface's table. When a client seeks communication with a server, it obtains a pointer to the server's interface table. The client may then call the functions provided by the server through the pointers in the function table. The client has no knowledge of or access to the details of the implementation of the function it calls. It only knows that it is accessing standard functions through a standard interface.

While there are several interfaces defined by OLE, most OLE-based programs will not implement them all. But the one interface they will all have is called **IUnknown**. Using the **QueryInterface( )** function defined by **IUnknown**, one application can find out what interfaces are available in another.

The fundamental value in interfaces is that one OLE-compliant application can take advantage of functionality provided by another OLE-based program. If you think about this for a moment, the implications are enormous.

21

OLE Automation

Another aspect of OLE is called OLE automation. Using OLE automation, it is possible for one application to access, control, and manipulate another application's objects. OLE automation is designed to allow the creation of sophisticated system-wide tools that have access to the functionality of the various applications contained within the system.

OLE Controls

Another OLE entity is the OLE control. An OLE control is essentially a super-charged dialog box that is OLE-compliant. OLE controls use OLE automation and represent some of the most exciting uses of OLE to date. In fact, one of the newest programming topics is ActiveX, which is, essentially, a special type of OLE control.

Is OLE the Future of Windows?

Although OLE was initially designed only to support object linking and embedding, its role has been dramatically expanded. The COM interface model defined by OLE has applications far beyond linking and embedding. Also, OLE automation opens the way to an entirely new class of application programs, and OLE controls are already widely used. Most importantly, the concepts in OLE present an alternative, object-oriented way to view the entire Windows environment. Although nothing is certain in the rapidly changing computer field, it is safe to say at this point that OLE will be an important part of Windows programming well into the future.

What Next?

Windows NT is one of the largest and most complex software systems ever created. There is much more to Windows NT than can be described in any single book. Topics such as networking, data compression, data exchange, and animation come to mind. Furthermore, large subsystems, such as OLE, have exploded the amount of information that a Windows programmer needs to know. And the Web revolution continues to expand the Windows environment. But don't worry. Whatever your Windows NT programming future holds, you now have the foundation upon which to pursue it.

Index

N

O

U

V

W

X

Z

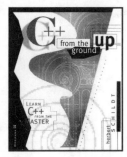

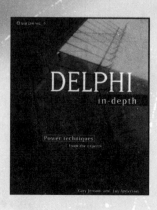

FUTURE CLASSICS FROM

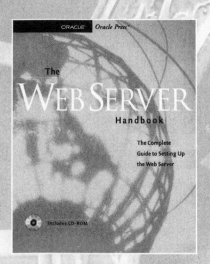

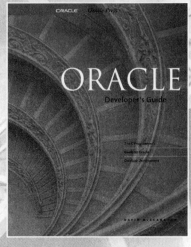

THE WEB SERVER HANDBOOK

by Cynthia Chin-Lee and Comet

Learn how to set up and maintain a dynamic and effective Web site with this comprehensive guide that focuses on Oracle's new Web solutions.

ISBN: 0-07-882215-7
Price: $39.95 U.S.A.
Includes One CD-ROM

ORACLE MEDIA OBJECTS HANDBOOK

by Dan Shafer

The power, flexibility, and ease of Oracle Media Objects (the cross-platform multimedia authoring tools) are within your reach with this definitive handbook.

ISBN: 0-07-882214-9
Price: $39.95 U.S.A.
Includes One CD-ROM

ORACLE DEVELOPER'S GUIDE

by David McClanahan

Loaded with code for common tasks, developers will find all the information they need to create applications and build a fast, powerful, and secure Oracle database.

ISBN: 0-07-882087-1
Price: $34.95 U.S.A.

ORACLE: THE COMPLETE REFERENCE
Third Edition

by George Koch and Kevin Loney

ISBN: 0-07-882097-9
Price: $34.95 U.S.A.

ORACLE DBA HANDBOOK

by Kevin Loney

ISBN: 0-07-881182-1
Price: $34.95 U.S.A.

ORACLE: A BEGINNER'S GUIDE

by Michael Abbey and Michael J. Corey

ISBN: 0-07-882122-3
Price: $29.95 U.S.A.

TUNING ORACLE

by Michael J. Corey, Michael Abbey, and Daniel J. Dechichio, Jr.

ISBN: 0-07-881181-3
Price: $29.95 U.S.A.

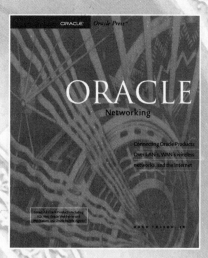

ORDER BOOKS DIRECTLY FROM OSBORNE/McGRAW-HILL

For a complete catalog of Osborne's books, call 510-549-6600 or write to us at 2600 Tenth Street, Berkeley, CA 94710

☎ **Call Toll-Free,** *24 hours a day, 7 days a week, in the U.S.A.*
U.S.A.: 1-800-262-4729   *Canada:* **1-800-565-5758**

✉ **Mail** *in the U.S.A. to:*   *Canada*
McGraw-Hill, Inc.   *McGraw-Hill Ryerson*
Customer Service Dept.   *Customer Service*
P.O. Box 182607   *300 Water Street*
Columbus, OH 43218-2607   *Whitby, Ontario L1N 9B6*

📠 **Fax** *in the U.S.A. to:*   *Canada*
1-614-759-3644   **1-800-463-5885**
                                                    Canada
                                                    orders@mcgrawhill.ca

SHIP TO:

Name _____

Company _____

Address _____

City / State / Zip _____

Daytime Telephone *(We'll contact you if there's a question about your order.)*

ISBN #	BOOK TITLE	Quantity	Price	Total
0-07-88				
0-07-88				
0-07-88				
0-07-88				
0-07-88				
0-07088				
0-07-88				
0-07-88				
0-07-88				
0-07-88				
0-07-88				
0-07-88				
0-07-88				
0-07-88				

Shipping & Handling Charge from Chart Below		
Subtotal		
Please Add Applicable State & Local Sales Tax		
TOTAL		

Shipping & Handling Charges

Order Amount	U.S.	Outside U.S.
$15.00 - $24.99	$4.00	$6.00
$25.00 - $49.99	$5.00	$7.00
$50.00 - $74.99	$6.00	$8.00
$75.00 - and up	$7.00	$9.00
$100.00 - and up	$8.00	$10.00

Occasionally we allow other selected companies to use our mailing list. If you would prefer that we not include you in these extra mailings, please check here: ☐

METHOD OF PAYMENT

☐ Check or money order enclosed (payable to Osborne/McGraw-Hill)

☐ AMERICAN EXPRESS   ☐ DISCOVER   ☐ MasterCard   ☐ VISA

Account No. ☐☐☐☐☐☐☐☐☐☐☐☐☐☐☐☐

Expiration Date _____

Signature _____

In a hurry? Call with your order anytime, day or night, or visit your local bookstore.

Thank you for your order   Code BC640SL